Social Psychology in the 80's

4th Edition

Social Psychology in the 80s

4th Edition

Kay Deaux   *Purdue University*

Lawrence S. Wrightsman   *University of Kansas*

In collaboration with Carol K. Sigelman and Eric Sundstrom

Brooks/Cole Publishing Company   *Monterey, California*

Brooks/Cole Publishing Company
A Division of Wadsworth, Inc.

Printed in the United States of America

10   9   8   7   6   5

Library of Congress Cataloging in Publication Data

Deaux, Kay.
    Social psychology in the 80s.

    Third ed. by Lawrence S. Wrightsman, Kay Deaux, in
collaboration with Carol K. Sigelman, Mark Snyder, and
Eric Sundstrom.
    Bibliography: p.
    Includes indexes.
    1. Social psychology.   I. Wrightsman, Lawrence
Samuel.   II. Title.   III. Title: Social psychology in
the eighties.
HM251.D358   1983   302   83-7379
ISBN 0-534-02926-4

Subject Editor: Claire Verduin
Production Coordinator: Fiorella Ljunggren
Manuscript Editor: Rephah Berg
Permissions Editor: Carline Haga
Interior and Cover Design: Victoria A. Van Deventer
Cover Photo: Bonnie Hawthorne
Art Coordinator: Judith Macdonald
Interior Illustrations: Nigel Holmes and Art by Ayxa
Photo Editor: Jude K. Blamer
Photo Research: Craven Designs Studios, Inc., and Roberta Guerette, Omni-Photo Communications, Inc.
Typesetting: Graphic Typesetting Service, Los Angeles, California
Cover Printer: Lehigh Press Lithographers, Pennsauken, New Jersey
Printer and Binder: R.R. Donnelley & Sons Company, Crawfordsville, Indiana

(Credits continue on p. 565)

To Jim and Lois

Preface

Social psychology is in a dynamic phase of development. In the 1970s, many critics were predicting its demise, pointing to a variety of ways in which the field had failed to live up to its promise. When we wrote the third edition of this book in 1981, pessimism about the field had receded and signs of growth were evident. Now, only three years later, those small signs seem to us to have become large banners. It is a testament to the renewed vitality of the field that there is so much new to report in the space of a relatively few years. Social psychologists are vigorously pushing new frontiers, while at the same time renewing their commitment to the early pioneers of the field who advocated a science that would take place in both laboratory and field, testing basic theory and investigating applied problems.

This revision highlights many of these new thrusts. The persistent concern of social psychologists with individual cognitions has intensified with new work on the self and with the exploration of basic processes of social cognition. Chapter 3 presents a considerably expanded treatment of the self as a central concept in social psychology, and Chapter 4 discusses much of the new work in social cognition, moving beyond the more limited emphasis on attribution theory in the third edition. Renewed interest in group processes, long forecast by a small number of investigators, is recognized with a broadening of the chapter on group behavior (Chapter 14) and the inclusion of an entirely new chapter on intergroup relations (Chapter 16). Increasing activity in applied arenas is reflected in Chapter 18, in which a section on psychology and the law has been added to previous sections on behavioral medicine and energy conservation. Finally, as social psychology continues to expand its geographical boundaries, more attention is being paid to crosscultural issues and to research done in other countries and with other populations. This work, too, is covered more fully in this edition, both in Chapter 13 and throughout the text.

As social psychologists have expanded their horizons, they have also defined their center more clearly. In Chapter 1, we take account of this sharper focus by emphasizing only three theories that appear to be guiding most current research: role theory, various forms of reinforcement theory, and cognitive models of behavior. Psychoanalytic theory and field theory are now interpreted in a historical context, which also provides the framework for a discussion of the milestones that mark the development of our field.

Many other changes have been made in this edition, reflecting new developments in the field as well as the suggestions and comments we have received from colleagues and students who have used previous editions of the book. Coverage of attitudes has been reduced to two chapters, although with little sacrifice of the content previously covered in three chapters. Consideration of group and individual differences has been combined in a single chapter, and the presentation of moral development has been eliminated.

The number of new studies and topics included in this edition is truly large, as suggested by the fact that over 500 references have been added. To cite just a few of these additions, we point to the coverage of research on loneliness in Chapter 6, work on pornography and aggression toward women in Chapter 7, processes of group socialization and social impact in Chapter 14, and new developments in behavioral medicine and psychology and the law in Chapter 18.

The content of social psychology can be organized in many ways. *Social Psychology in the 80s* moves from theories and methods through individual and group processes to more applied topics—an organization that we find very satisfactory. At the same time, however, each chapter stands as an independent unit, and instructors who have used previous editions report using the chapters in a variety of orders with success. Improved cross-referencing of topics and a detailed subject index will aid those who choose to cover the chapters in a different order.

We believe that the most important benefit of a textbook is that it facilitates the learning process, and, with each new edition of this book, we have tried to make that process more effective. As in previous editions, each chapter opens with a chapter outline and closes with a summary. Important terms in each chapter are boldfaced when they first appear and are defined in the Glossary, which follows Chapter 18. A list of glossary terms, without definitions, also appears at the end of each chapter. A number of new visual elements have been incorporated in this edition to aid in learning. Photo essays are used to illustrate some of the important concepts and processes; questions have been added to graphs to extend students' understanding of the results; and graphic art prepared by Nigel Holmes highlights other important concepts.

A study guide and an instructor's manual accompany this text. The instructor's manual provides multiple-choice and discussion questions for each text chapter, as well as extensive suggestions for further reading, classroom discussion, demonstration, and individual-involvement exercises. The study guide includes the following for each chapter: a chapter preview; a list of basic terms, concepts, and theories; a set of completion items; and sample multiple-choice and short-answer questions. Prepared by Karla McPherson, this workbook gives students the opportunity to identify and evaluate their understanding of material presented in the text.

In all of this, we have tried to offer a dynamic and engaging introduction to the field of social psychology. Throughout all previous editions, instructors and students have helped us achieve our goal. We hope that you, the instructors and students using this edition, will benefit from past contributions and will make your own contributions to future developments in this textbook and in the field.

Kay Deaux

Lawrence S. Wrightsman

Acknowledgments

■ For this edition

As this textbook moves into its fourth edition, we look back with gratitude to the many people who have contributed to its previous editions. Professors, students, editors, and production people at Brooks/Cole have all had an impact on the shape and contents of this book. Although the list is too long to repeat here, we have not forgotten the contributions that these people made.

For this edition, as for the earlier ones, we have received help and advice from many sources. As we began to develop plans for this revision, we benefited from the comments of many students, too numerous to mention, who had taken the time to write to us with their opinions about the second edition. As our plans for the fourth edition became clearer, we asked a number of colleagues to comment on the previous edition and to evaluate our proposed changes for the present revision. For their helpful reviews, we thank the following people: Robert Arkin, University of Missouri; Steve Baumgardner, University of Wisconsin; Jayne Grackenbach, University of Northern Iowa; Robert Lowman, Kansas State University ; Richard Moreland, University of Pittsburgh; Dean Pruitt, State University of New York at Buffalo; Stanley Sadava, Brock University; Steve Slane, Cleveland State University; and Russell Veitch, Bowling Green State University.

With these recommendations in hand, we proceeded to revise the text, often substantially. Individual chapters were reviewed for us by the following people: Elizabeth Rice Allgeier, Bowling Green State University; Robert Arkin, University of Missouri; Andrew Baum, U.S. University–School of Medicine; Sharon Brehm, University of Kansas; Russell Clark, Florida State University; James Jones, American Psychological Association and University of Delaware; Marianne LaFrance, Boston University; Richard Moreland, University of Pittsburgh; Linda Putnam, Purdue University; Harry Reis, University of Rochester; Brendan Gail Rule, University of Alberta; Eliot Smith, Purdue University; Russell Veitch, Bowling Green State University; Dan Wegner, Trinity University; and Sharon Wolf, Purdue University.

The Brooks/Cole "family" has continued to be a source of enthusiasm and efficiency to us. Often it seems as if the entire company were contributing to the realization of this book, and, indeed, it would not be inappropriate to list the full B/C staff in this acknowledgment section. Special attention, however, must be focused on the smaller set of people who devoted enormous effort to this project. As editor, Claire Verduin continued to show her special blend of praise and concern, ably assisted by Pat Carnahan. As the book moved into production, Fiorella Ljunggren took charge, surmounting seemingly impossible deadlines with enthusiasm and dedication. The copyediting of Rephah Berg was exceptional, pinpointing distortion of form as well as confusion of content. Permissions were handled flawlessly by Carline Haga. The art department at B/C, headed by Stanley Rice, devoted many hours, days, and weeks to this revision. We are grateful to all of them, especially Vicki Van Deventer, Judy Macdonald, and Jude Blamer. Without the herculean efforts of all these people, this revision would not be.

Brief Contents

Contents

4. Social Knowledge: Impressions & Explanations of People   80

5. Interpersonal Communication   106

6. Affiliation, Attraction, & Love   136

Social Psychology in the 80s

4th Edition

1

Theories as Explanations of Social Behavior

The purpose of psychology is to give us a completely different idea of the things we know best.

■ PAUL VALÉRY

Truth emerges more easily from error than from confusion.

■ FRANCIS BACON

The phases of the moon. Possession by spirits. Fate. The right opportunity. Good chemistry between people. What do these terms have in common? All have been offered at one time or another to explain some aspect of human behavior. Human beings have always tried to explain their own behavior. Philosophers have perhaps the longest record of speculation on human nature; both Aristotle and Plato, for example, combined political theory with thoughts about the nature of human beings. Other disciplines have joined the quest during the past centuries. Social psychology, though a relative newcomer to this inquiry, has provided a great many insights during the past several decades. With roots both in philosophy and in empirical science, social psychology has set as its goal the understanding, explanation, and prediction of human social behavior—certainly a broad and rich field of study.

Just what kind of behavior would be of interest to a social psychologist? Gordon Allport (1968) suggested that "social psychologists regard their discipline as an attempt to understand how the *thought*, *feeling*, and *behavior* of individuals are influenced by the *actual*, *imagined* or *implied* presence of others" (p. 3). In this useful definition, the term *implied presence* refers to the fact that people often act with an awareness that they belong to particular cultural, occupational, or social groups. Furthermore, even when we are alone, our behavior may be influenced by our awareness that we are performing a role in a complex social structure, thus reflecting the implied presence of others. If we fail at our job, if our physical appearance changes, or if we get arrested, our reactions are affected by an awareness of others and our relationships to them.

The ramifications of Allport's definition are thought-provoking. Just how far does the concern of social psychology extend? Clearly within the domain of social psychology is the behavior of a young man sitting on a crowded bus as a frail old woman stands wearily in the aisle beside him. Does he offer her his seat? Or does he pretend to be engrossed in a book or in the passing scenery? Does he feel any concern about what she thinks of him? About what others are thinking? When a young woman enters a doctor's office for an eye examination, her actions also may be affected by the presence of others. The ophthalmologist asks her to look at the eye chart, trying first one lens and then another. The young woman's task is a straightforward one of determining and reporting which lens gives a clearer image, but she may be thinking "Am I giving the right answer? What if I really can't tell the difference? Does the doctor know if I'm making a mistake?" Such questions reflect her concern about the impression she is making; certainly they demonstrate that many responses in such a situation are social behavior.

Not all activities carried out by humans are social behaviors. For example, if you pick an apricot off a tree, eat it, immediately get sick, and thereafter avoid eating apricots (at least those straight off the tree), your reactions occur whether other people are present or not and probably do not reflect an awareness of others. Reflex actions, such as removing your hand from a hot stove, are nonsocial; the immediate physical response is the same regardless of the presence or the awareness of others. However, your oral response to touching a hot stove may well be colored by the presence of others. Certain internal responses—glandular, digestive, excretory—are generally considered to be beyond the realm of social psychology. However, nausea, constipation, or other physical responses may result from feelings associated with the actions or presence of other people. Even the time of dying may be a response to social considerations. David Phillips (1970, 1972) has suggested that Jews "postpone" the date of dying until after significant events, such as Yom Kippur, the Day of Atonement. In Jewish populations in both New York City and Budapest, he found a "death dip"—a significant decrease in death rates—during the months prior to Yom Kippur.

Thus, a great deal of any person's behavior—perhaps more than you first realized—is social.

■ I. A history of social psychology

To understand modern-day social psychology, we should look, if only briefly, at the roots of this science. Since its beginning, generally dated as 1897

PHOTO 1-1. *Social behavior can occur everywhere, including a crowded subway.*

(see Box 1-1), social psychology has evolved in both its theories and its methods. New theoretical developments have come to the forefront, and earlier views of the nature of human behavior have been rejected. Not all social psychologists today share a single theoretical perspective: in a later section of this chapter, we will consider three different viewpoints that seek to explain human behavior. By considering the history of the field first, we can better understand how these three primary perspectives evolved, and we can see where progress has been made.

Norman Triplett's study of the effects of competition on an individual's behavior, performed in a laboratory at Indiana University in the late 1800s, is generally considered to be the first social-psychological experiment. (This experiment will be described more fully in Chapter 2.) Not too many years later, two textbooks bearing the title *Social*

Psychology appeared—one written by Edward Ross, a sociologist, and the other by William McDougall, a psychologist. Despite Triplett's early example, social psychology was not very experimental in its early years. Descriptions and speculations were more prominent than scientific tests, and the territory of social psychology was not very clearly defined.

During the early part of the 20th century, psychological thought about human behavior was dominated by two trends: Freudian theory, on the one hand, and behaviorism (made prominent by John B. Watson), on the other. Between the experimental concerns of behaviorism, focusing on learning and the role of external stimuli, and the more internally directed speculations of psychoanalytic theory, social psychology began to define its domain. Both of these reigning viewpoints had an effect on social psychology. Psychoanalytic the-

BOX 1-1. Milestones in social psychology

1897   Triplett conducts the first social-psychological experiment.

1908   Edward Ross and William McDougall each publish a textbook titled *Social Psychology.*

1921   The *Journal of Abnormal Psychology* becomes the *Journal of Abnormal and Social Psychology.*

1924   Floyd Allport publishes an influential text on social psychology.

1934   George Herbert Mead writes *Mind, Self, and Society*, stressing the interaction between self and others.

1935   The first *Handbook of Social Psychology* is published, edited by Carl Murchison.

1936   Muzafir Sherif explains the process of conformity in *The Psychology of Social Norms.*

1939   John Dollard and his associates present the frustration-aggression theory.

1941   Neal Miller and John Dollard present *Social Learning and Imitation*, a theory that extends behavioristic principles to the realm of social behavior.

1945   Kurt Lewin founds the Research Center for Group Dynamics.

1954   The first edition of the modern *Handbook of Social Psychology*, edited by Gardner Lindzey, is published.

1957   Leon Festinger publishes *A Theory of Cognitive Dissonance*, presenting a model that stresses the need for consistency between cognition and behavior.

1958   Fritz Heider lays the groundwork for attribution theory with the publication of *The Psychology of Interpersonal Behavior.*

1959   John Thibaut and Harold Kelley publish *The Social Psychology of Groups*, a foundation for social-exchange theory.

1960   The *Journal of Abnormal and Social Psychology* splits into two separate publications, a *Journal of Abnormal Psychology* and a *Journal of Personality and Social Psychology.* ∎

---

ory, for example, raised a concern with the process of **socialization**[1] and the limits of rationality (see Box 1-2). Behaviorism stressed the importance of experimental methods and the influence of environmental factors on behavior. Yet, neither of these perspectives was sufficient to describe the more complex interactions that take place among adult human beings.

In the 1930s, social psychology became more articulate about the distinctly social aspects of human behavior. Although the first social-psychology handbook, published in 1935, still showed

some uncertainty about the boundaries of social psychology (including discussions of insect populations and domesticated animals, as well as the "black man," the "yellow man," and the "red man"), a number of pioneers were beginning to define the territory of the emerging discipline. In 1934 the sociologist George Herbert Mead laid the groundwork for symbolic interactionism, a theory that deals with the importance of interactions between oneself and other people. Muzafer Sherif in 1936 published a book titled *The Psychology of Social Norms*, in which the process of conformity to group norms was first demonstrated scientifically. Kurt Lewin began to formulate his principles of field theory, pointing to the importance of both the person and the environment in explaining human

---

[1]Terms printed in **boldface** type are listed in the "Glossary Terms" section at the end of each chapter and are defined in the Glossary, which follows Chapter 18.

BOX 1-2. Psychoanalytic theory

Sigmund Freud (1856–1939)

Psychoanalytic theory, which was developed by Sigmund Freud and his followers, is essentially a theory of personality that developed as part of an approach to psychotherapy. In conceptualizing the structure of personality, Freud posited three sets of forces—called the **ego,** the **id,** and the **superego**—that are constantly in conflict over the control of behavior. According to Freud, when the ego has control over the two other sets of forces in the personality, the person has made a rational adjustment to his or her environment. Even though unconscious id forces such as aggressive and sexual urges will continue to seek discharge, these will be released in healthful, socially acceptable ways if the ego is in control. Dreams and slips of the tongue, for example, are means by which such unconscious urges express themselves. The ego uses a number of devices, called **defense mechanisms,** that deny reality and operate at an unconscious level. By using these defense mechanisms, the ego can reduce tensions that might otherwise erupt from the id and the superego.

Some elements of psychoanalytic theory can be found in social-psychological models. For example, discussions of aggressive behavior (see Chapter 8) sometimes invoke psychoanalytic concepts of instinct and defense mechanisms. A more general influence derives from the emphasis of psychoanalytic theory on socialization—the process of acquiring behaviors that are considered appropriate by society. For example, how does a child learn to be a responsible, moral person? According to Freud, the superego develops as a result of early socialization processes. The substance of the superego is distilled from the teachings and admonitions of parents, teachers, other authorities, and peers. Eventually these messages become internalized as *conscience.* This development has been offered as one explanation of altruistic behavior (see Chapter 9).

For the modern social psychologist, psychoanalytic concepts rarely contribute to theory. However, the emphasis of psychoanalysis on internal process and conflicts between the individual and society still underlies the way we think about human behavior. ■

behavior. In 1939 John Dollard and his associates produced the frustration-aggression theory, an explanation of human aggression that, though invoking many concepts of psychoanalytic theory, also brought the experimental method to bear.

These developments in social psychology were accelerated by the events of World War II. Many people began to realize the great importance of understanding more about human behavior. How could a Hitler rise to power; how could warfare be prevented? At a more practical level, the war effort directed the efforts of many general psychologists to more specifically social problems. How could attitudes of the troops be changed, for example, to achieve high morale? How could families be persuaded to eat unusual foods like sweetbreads in order to save the beef for the fighting forces?

Many other historical factors have contributed to the climate that allowed social psychology to

PHOTO 1-2. *During World War II, persuasion attempts were numerous, and social psychologists began to develop theories about attitude change.*

flourish; within the past 50 years, these various forces have produced the field that we now know as social psychology. Most scholars would consider Kurt Lewin to be the founder of modern social psychology. Lewin defined a field that was both broad and more clearly delineated than previous definitions of the field had been. In formulating **field theory,** Lewin proposed that human behavior is a function of both the person and the environment (see Box 1-3). Both, he said, must be considered if we are to understand human behavior. Lewin also stressed the importance of both theory and application for a full understanding. His concept of *action research* (to be discussed more extensively in Chapter 18) called for a constant interchange between laboratory and field and between theoretical formulations and practical problems.

From these beginnings, modern social psychology has developed. Interest in problems such as conformity, aggression, and the interaction of society and self has continued. Many new questions about human behavior have been raised—the nature of interpersonal attraction, the process of communication, the patterns of group interaction, and the resolution of intergroup conflict. These and many other areas of current research will be discussed in the chapters that follow. True to the spirit of Lewin, we will consider practical applications as well as theoretical models.

Three theoretical models dominate current social psychology: a reinforcement orientation, a role orientation, and a cognitive orientation. Before discussing these theoretical models in more detail, however, we should give some thought to just what theories are and why we have them.

■ II. Theories in social psychology

Anyone who offers an explanation of why a social relationship exists or how it functions is, at one level, reflecting a theory of social behavior. In this

BOX 1-3. Kurt Lewin's field theory

*Kurt Lewin
(1890–1947)*

The fundamental contribution of field theory, as developed by Kurt Lewin (1951), is the proposition that human behavior is a function of both the person and the environment; expressed in symbolic terms, $B = f(P,E)$. Thus, a person's behavior is related both to characteristics within the person (heredity, abilities, personality, state of health, and so on) *and* to the social situation in which the person presently exists (for example, the presence of others or the extent to which the person's goals may be blocked). Although this proposition may seem obvious to us now, its statement in the early development of social psychology marked a clear shift from the individual emphasis of psychoanalytic theory, on the one hand, and the external emphasis of behaviorism, on the other hand.

In defining his view of social psychology, Lewin stressed several properties of field theory. All actions, he suggested, are influenced by the field in which they take place. Thus, analysis must be based on the situation as a whole and must consider the dynamic interchange between parts of the system. The more current term *general systems theory* is based on a similar assumption.

The most basic construct in field theory is the **life space,** the total subjective environment that each of us experiences (Lewin, 1938). All psychological events—including thinking, acting, and dreaming—are a function of the life space, "which consists of the person and the environment viewed as one constellation of interdependent factors" (Deutsch, 1968, p. 417).

Another major emphasis of field theory is the *here and now.* To Lewin, psychological events must be explained by the properties of the life space that exist in the present. According to field theorists, if a 29-year-old man is unmarried, shy, and self-deprecatory in his relationships with others, the fact that an auto accident permanently disfigured his face at age 12 is not sufficient explanation for his later behavior. The young man's present reluctance to date is only a function of contemporary properties of the field—properties that may, however, include his present feelings about his appearance or his present memories of humiliating comments about his face. The past can influence present behavior only indirectly, in the form of representations or alterations of past events carried into the present.

The specific theoretical constructs that Lewin introduced are not used much in current social-psychological theorizing, but the general orientation that he espoused is very much in evidence. The belief that social-psychological phenomena can be studied experimentally, that psychological events must be studied in relation to one another, that both the individual and the group are important—these ideas are a part of the Lewinian legacy and continue to influence both theory and research. ∎

sense, we are all theorists forming explanations for the events that occur around us, although our theories may be vague, idiosyncratic, and not verifiable.

Within science, the term *theory* is used more specifically, and theories are considered essential to the scientific enterprise. Generally speaking, we can consider a theory to be a set of conventions created as a way of representing reality (Hall & Lindzey, 1978). A more formal definition of *theory* is "a set of interrelated hypotheses or propositions concerning a phenomenon or set of phenomena" (Shaw & Costanzo, 1982, p. 4).

Every theory makes a rather arbitrary set of

assumptions about the nature of the behavior it seeks to describe and explain. It also contains a set of empirical definitions and **constructs.** Theories developed by different groups of scientists vary in their assumptions, constructs, and emphases; yet, all theories serve common purposes. One of these purposes is to organize and explicate the relation between diverse bits of knowledge about social phenomena (Hendrick & Jones, 1972). We all have a tremendous accumulation of knowledge about human behavior. Some of this knowledge is based on personal experience; some is based on recent public events; and some is based on what we glean from books, movies, or the accounts of friends. Similarly, the scientists of human social behavior have an extensive set of observations and empirical data, and theory provides a convenient way of organizing them (Shaw & Costanzo, 1982). In short, a theory integrates known empirical findings within a logically con-

sistent and reasonably simple framework (Hall & Lindzey, 1978).

Another vital function of any theory in social psychology is to indicate gaps in knowledge, so that further research can lead to a more comprehensive understanding of social phenomena. Theory guides future investigations; it provides a source of **hypotheses** to test predictions about the world. Theory may also anticipate kinds of events that we can expect to occur, even if the particular conditions have not yet been encountered (Shaw & Costanzo, 1982). For example, in the physical sciences, theoretically derived hypotheses that were made decades ago by Albert Einstein about the relation between space and time have been tested only recently, since the advent of supersonic travel.

Data generated by a theory may not always support the original theoretical framework—the research may, in fact, show that the theory itself has to be revised or even ultimately rejected. A

theory is simply a model of behavior, and as such it may have a limited life span. Without the use of some theory, however, the task of understanding the variety of social behavior would be tremendously difficult.

Which theory should be used? Every social scientist must consider—and finally answer—this important question. No one theory adequately accounts for all social phenomena, just as no single theory in the physical sciences can account for all observations. At present, social psychology uses several basic theoretical approaches. Sometimes more than one of these approaches may be useful in explaining the same event, perhaps with varying degrees of success or perhaps with equal accuracy. In other cases, theories may be applicable to totally different domains of behavior and therefore cannot be compared.

Judging the ultimate validity or "goodness" of any theory is difficult and often requires the accumulation of considerable data. Shaw and Costanzo (1982) have suggested three necessary characteristics of a good theory: (1) the propositions of a theory must be logically consistent among themselves, (2) the theory must agree with known facts and with future observations, and (3) the theory must be able to be tested in order to determine its usefulness. Other desirable characteristics of a theory noted by Shaw and Costanzo include simplicity, ease of relating to real-world observations, and usefulness in generating further research.

In this chapter we shall describe three broad theories of social psychology: role theory, reinforcement theory, and cognitive theory. Each of these theories has a different orientation, set of assumptions, and set of constructs, and each can be evaluated in terms of the criteria specified above. Within each of these general theoretical approaches, it is also possible to develop more limited models (sometimes called "minitheories") that attempt to explain a much narrower range of human behavior. Many of these more limited theories will be discussed here and in subsequent chapters.

Our purpose at this point, then, is to show how the theoretical approach that an investigator adopts will lead that investigator to ask certain kinds of questions about the behavior he or she is research-

ing. Depending on the basic assumptions of the theory that investigators are using, they will focus on the individual or on the environment, on past learning or on present circumstances, on limited behaviors or on global events.

To show how theory can influence the kinds of questions that are asked and, in turn, the kinds of answers that are obtained, we will focus on one particular kind of social interaction—a case of young lovers. Shakespeare immortalized the cause of young love in his tale of Romeo and Juliet. More recently, the tale was updated in the Broadway musical and the film *West Side Story*, in which Tony and Maria tried to find love despite the gang warfare between the Sharks and the Jets.

Let's update that story to the 1980s and consider a modern-day Tony and Maria who have fallen in love. Tony is from a wealthy family, raised in luxury and expected to take over the family business. Maria is from a less prosperous home, eager to improve her station in life through her own efforts but quite in love with Tony. Despite parental opposition from both families (Tony's family wants him to marry a wealthy woman, Maria's family wants her to marry a Catholic), the two wed.

Time passes, and family opposition diminishes. Tony and Maria have their share of conflicts, but they develop a good marriage and begin to raise a family. Tony does indeed assume control of the family business, and Maria devotes herself to the care of the children. As the children grow older, however, Maria begins to think more of her earlier ambitions to develop other skills, and she soon establishes her own business—a telephone-answering service. Eventually she expands to business services and finally to running a tax-accounting firm.

Throughout the course of their marriage, Tony and Maria have alternating periods of calm and conflict. So do most couples. Such a history has almost a mundane quality about it; yet, its very familiarity makes it a prime candidate for social-psychological inquiry. Why do people fall in love? How do their relationships change over time? Why do some marriages succeed while others fail?

The answers to these questions depend in part on one's assumptions about human nature. For social psychologists, assumptions are often embedded in a theoretical network. In discussing the three basic theoretical orientations of social psychology, we will first consider the basic concepts of each theory and then show how these principles have contributed to various areas of social investigation. Then we will return to the case of Tony and Maria, considering what kinds of questions an investigator might ask if he or she were operating out of that particular theoretical model.

■ III. Role theory

A. Basic assumptions and concepts

Role theory has its origin in the theatrical conception of roles as parts that actors play in a dramatic presentation (Shaw & Costanzo, 1982). Although this idea of roles can be dated back to classical times, more recent use of the concept is found in the sociology literature. As we noted earlier, George Herbert Mead discussed the idea of self in relation to the interactions one has with other people. Since Mead, social scientists from a variety of disciplines—anthropology, sociology, and psychology—have found the concept of role useful.

Although we are using the term *role theory*, it is not in fact a single theory. Rather, it is a loosely linked network of hypotheses and a set of rather broad constructs (Shaw & Costanzo, 1982). Generally, role theory does not consider individual determinants of behavior. Rarely, for example, does it consider such concepts as personality, attitudes, and motivation. Instead, behavior is explained mainly by reference to the roles, role expectations and demands, role skills, and reference groups operating on the participants in a social interaction. Further, in contrast to the more psychological theories that we will discuss later, role theory gives more attention to larger social networks and organizations.

What is a **role**? Following the lead of Shaw and Costanzo, we can define a role as "the functions a person performs when occupying a particular [position] within a particular social context" (1982, p. 296). For one look at the concept of roles, consider Figure 1-1. To gain additional understanding of the concept of role, let's look at a student named Gloria McWilliams.

As a student, Gloria McWilliams performs certain behaviors—she attends classes, prepares assignments, makes an application for graduation, and so on. When interacting with Gloria in her role as a student, other people assume that she will act in certain ways. Their assumptions about her behavior are called **role expectations.** For example, professors expect their students to attend class with some regularity and to show some concern about grades. Some instructors may expect a certain amount of deference from their students, whereas others may not. (Similarly, students may have role expectations for their professors, expecting them to be on time for class, to be dynamic lecturers, to be experts on the topic, and to be understanding when an exam is missed, as just a few examples.) **Norms** are more generalized expectations about behavior that are learned in the course of socialization (Biddle & Thomas, 1966). We may, for example, hold general norms about the appropriate interactions between women and men, or between authority figures and their subordinates, that have developed from experience with more specific role relationships.

Role conflict results when a person holds several positions that have incompatible demands (*interrole conflict*) or when a single role has expectations that are incompatible (*intrarole conflict*). Of course, we all fill a number of different roles every day. For example, while studying for an important final exam, Gloria McWilliams may receive a call from the local kindergarten teacher reporting that her son is ill and must be taken home from school. At the same time, her husband may come home and announce that his boss is coming over for dinner. In this example, the roles of student, mother, and wife cannot be satisfied at the same time, and interrole conflict is produced. In contrast, Gloria would experience *intrarole* conflict if she had to choose between studying for a history exam and typing a psychology term paper that was due the same day.

FIGURE 1-1. One person can play many roles.

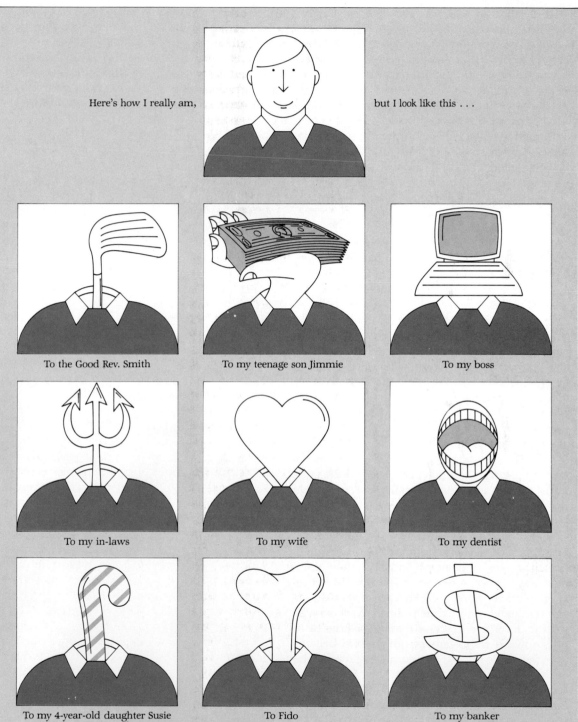

To say that people "perform a series of roles" does not mean that people are pretending; nor does it mean that they necessarily are being deceitful or deceptive. To a significant extent, we behave in ways that are in agreement with the settings we are in and the positions we hold. It is true that there is some latitude in what behaviors are considered acceptable in a particular setting; even an occasional sleeper may be tolerated in some large classes if he or she does not snore too loudly! But the role defines the limits of what is appropriate in the setting.

B. Contributions to social psychology

The concept of role has been used often in social psychology: terms such as *role model*, *role playing*, and *role taking* appear frequently in the literature. Use of this concept allows us to understand why people's behavior may change when their position in a social system is altered.

A vivid demonstration of the effect of roles is seen in Lieberman's (1965) study of the attitudes of factory workers. In an initial testing phase, Lieberman assessed the attitudes of virtually every worker in a Midwestern home-appliance factory toward union and management policies. About a year later, he went back to the same factory and again assessed workers' attitudes—this time selecting two specific groups of workers. Members of the first group had been promoted to the position of foreman in the intervening year, a position that should ally them more closely to the position of management. A second group of workers had been elected stewards, a union position. Did the attitudes of these workers change as a function of their new roles in the organization? In both cases, the answer is yes, when the responses were compared with those of a control group of workers who remained in the same position. Workers who became foremen expressed more positive attitudes toward management officers and became more favorable toward the incentive system, a policy that paid workers according to what they produced. In contrast, workers who had been elected union stewards became more positive in their attitudes toward union officers and favored the seniority

policy over ability criteria. In each case, attitudes shifted according to the new role the worker occupied.

Eighteen months later, the researchers returned to the factory again. By this time, some of the foremen had been returned to nonsupervisory jobs, and some of the stewards had also returned to

PHOTO 1-3. An example of interrole conflict: A working mother brings her baby to the office.

their original positions. Once again, shifts in attitudes were detected. The former foremen once again became less positive toward management, and the former stewards became somewhat less strongly in favor of union officers. Thus, this study serves as a striking illustration of the influence of roles on our attitudes and beliefs.

In recent years the general ideas of role theory have been evident in the increasing concern with concepts of the self. The concept of self is not a new one for social psychologists. In 1922 Charles Cooley discussed the self-concept as a "looking-glass self," presenting the idea that the self is defined on the basis of our interactions with others. Recently, however, a great deal more attention has been given to the development of the self-concept and the ways in which people monitor their selves in social interaction. In Chapter 3 we will discuss many of these newer theories. Models of *self-awareness* point to conditions when we become most aware of ourselves. The concept of *self-monitoring* focuses on the tendency of some people to monitor the way they are perceived by others, often choosing particular behaviors in response to the social context. At a more general level, theories of *self-presentation* and impression management show how many actions may be chosen for their usefulness in achieving particular goals. In other words, we may select a certain role depending on what we want and what the situation allows.

The insights of role theory provide a basis for understanding aspects of the communication process (see Chapter 5). Role theory can also help us understand the positions of leaders and subordinates in an organization (see Chapter 15), where behavior may be influenced by a person's position in the organizational structure. In each of these topics, we will see the influence of role theory on the formulation of research questions.

C. Applications to case example

A role theorist interested in the development of a relationship would—to use a sports analogy—look at the positions rather than at particular players. Hence, the interesting aspects of Tony and Maria's relationship would be the roles that they played at particular points in time. A role theorist would consider the transition of Tony and Maria from son and daughter to husband and wife. What behaviors would Tony adopt because he was a husband, then an executive at his family's business, and later a father? How would Maria's behavior be affected by the conflict between roles of mother, wife, and businessperson?

Some of the more current self theories that derive from role theory would direct our attention to the self-concepts of Tony and Maria. How would Tony view himself as he shifted from wealthy son to novice husband? How would Maria view herself as she shifted from middle class to upper class, from daughter to wife, and from income beneficiary to income producer? The answer to each of these questions would be sought in the current status of Tony and Maria. Past history would be less important than the roles they were currently playing. For the role theorist, then, the marital relationship would be viewed as a set of positions, role expectations, and role enactments. Tony and Maria would simply be one example of a more general structural model.

■ IV. Reinforcement theory

A. Basic assumptions and concepts

A second approach to social behavior relies on the psychological principles of reinforcement and learning. As we noted earlier in this chapter, experimental psychologists in the early part of the century were strongly influenced by the behavioristic principles of John Watson. Later psychologists such as Clark Hull, Kenneth Spence, and B. F. Skinner elaborated the process by which learning takes place. The central focus of **reinforcement theory** is an analysis of the relation between stimuli and responses. A **stimulus** is an external or internal event that brings about an alteration in a person's behavior (Kimble, 1961). This alteration in behavior is called a **response.** If a response leads to a favorable outcome for the person, a state of **reinforcement** then exists; that is, the person has been rewarded for his or her response. As the sociologist George Homans has written, in applying reinforcement theory to social behavior, "If a man takes an action that is followed by a reward, the probability that he will repeat the action increases" (1970, p. 321). In contrast, actions that are not rewarded tend to be discarded, and actions that are punished may be actively avoided.

Early reinforcement theorists, including Pavlov, extended their power of explanation by developing the concepts of generalization and discrimination. **Stimulus generalization** is a "process whereby a novel stimulus evokes a response which had been previously learned to a separate but similar stimulus" (Shaw & Costanzo, 1982, p. 33). In other words, if you have been reinforced for being nice to your Aunt Julia, reinforcement theory would predict that you might be nice to your Uncle Pete as well, even if you had not been reinforced for that behavior in the past. This principle allows reinforcement theorists to explain a wider range of behaviors than they could if each single behavior had to be reinforced separately. The flip side of generalization is **stimulus discrimination,** a process of learning to make distinctions among stimuli. Thus, through experience we may learn that Uncle Pete is pleasant but Uncle Al is a bit gruff. Being able to make such distinctions allows us to develop more complex ways of responding to our social environment.

Basic reinforcement theorists (sometimes called S-R theorists, for *stimulus-response*) see complex behaviors as chains of simpler S-R associations. For example, the verbal behavior used in giving a complicated answer to the highway patrol officer's question "Why were you speeding?" would be analyzed as a chain of specific responses, or verbal associations. Similarly, a student's pursuit of a college degree could be represented as a chain of specific S-R connections.

The basic ideas of reinforcement theory have continued to influence social psychologists, but the concepts have moved considerably beyond the simple S-R model. One major development has been the greater reliance on cognitive principles, considering the functioning person as an intermediary step between the stimulus and the response. Such a model is sometimes called an S-O-R model, where *O* refers to the human organism. We will look at two types of reinforcement theory that are prominent in social psy-

chology: social-learning theory and social-exchange theory.

Social-learning theory.   In 1941 Neal Miller and John Dollard laid the foundations for modern social-learning theory by proposing that imitation could be explained by basic principles of stimulus, reward, and reinforcement. Their basic assumptions were (1) that imitation, like most human

PHOTO 1-4. A boy tries to match the behavior of his father.

behavior, is learned and (2) that social behavior and social learning can be understood through the use of general learning principles. Miller and Dollard gave imitation a central place in explaining how the child learns to behave socially and, specifically, in how the child learns to talk—which is, after all, a social act. Furthermore, they proposed that imitation was important in maintaining discipline and conformity to the norms of a society. Suppose, for example, that both a young boy and his older brother wait for their father to arrive home from work. It is the father's custom to bring each son a piece of candy. The older brother starts running toward the garage because he hears a car pull up in the driveway. The younger child imitates his brother's response and discovers that he is rewarded for it. In other situations, the younger son continues to emulate his brother's behavior: he reacts to frustration by screaming; he combs his hair the same way; he begins using the same four-letter words.[2] Imitation has become rewarding, and the imitative response is generalized to many situations.

More recently, Albert Bandura has developed a broader view of **social-learning theory.** According to this theory, social learning can occur through direct response consequences or, more frequently, through the observation of the behavior of others. The behavior of another person (termed a *model*) may serve as a source of information. The observer may then use this information to perform the same behavior, even if no reinforcement is present. In fact, Bandura and his colleagues would argue that reinforcement has its major influence in whether or not a behavior is performed—but not in whether it is initially learned. Such learning can have embarrassing outcomes; as Kaufmann (1973) notes, a 5-year-old boy may hear certain obscenities but give no evidence of having learned them until he bursts out swearing in front of his teacher and class.

As we suggested, this modern version of social-learning theory assumes that a number of cognitive processes accompany learning. The photo essay on p. 19 illustrates some of the hypothesized steps in the sequence of observational learning. First,

the observer must pay attention to the model, a state that is influenced both by characteristics of the model (is the model someone you like, is that person's behavior relevant to your own concerns?) and by characteristics of the observer (is the observer alert, aware of what's going on?). At the retention stage, cognitive processes come into play strongly; Bandura suggests that the individual may code the observed event, organize it in terms of past experience, and symbolically rehearse the behavior. Motor reproduction, the third stage in the photo essay, depends in part on the person's ability to actually perform the observed behavior. I may carefully observe Martina Navratilova play tennis, for example, and rehearse in my mind how she serves; yet, when I get out on the court, I may be quite incapable of duplicating her behavior. Finally, the presence of reinforcements—either from others or from oneself—will determine whether the learned behavior will actually be performed.

As we can see, social-learning theory allows for much more complicated forms of learning than the early reinforcement models did. Perhaps even more complex are the ideas of social-exchange theory, which also has its roots in earlier reinforcement models.

Social-exchange theory.   The other theory that relies on principles of reinforcement to predict human behavior is **social exchange theory,** which also incorporates some basic economic principles. According to this theory, interactions between people depend on the rewards and costs involved—people will seek out those relationships that promise greater rewards than costs and will avoid those relationships in which costs are greater than rewards.

George Homans (1958, 1974), who presented one of the first models of social exchange, assumes that people are basically hedonistic—in other words, they seek to maximize pleasure and minimize pain. In interacting with one another, people make exchanges to achieve pleasure. Such exchanges can vary both in quantity and in type. One can exchange both material and nonmaterial goods; approval and prestige, for example, are nonmaterial goods. Homans believes that those

[2]This story is adapted from Miller and Dollard (1941).

who give to others create pressure in others to reciprocate, in order to create an equitable exchange relationship.

The work of John Thibaut and Harold Kelley (Kelley & Thibaut, 1978; Thibaut & Kelley, 1959) presents a more complex version of social-exchange theory. Whereas Homans relied on basic principles derived from animal learning experiments to define rewards, Thibaut and Kelley conceptualize rewards and costs in distinctly human terms (Shaw & Costanzo, 1982). Thibaut and Kelley base their theory on the process of interaction—a situation that occurs when two persons act and react to each other and when the actions of one person can have an effect on the other.

To analyze the possible outcomes of an interaction, Thibaut and Kelley presented the outcome matrix (see Figure 1-2). In principle, we could identify all possible actions of Person A in a relationship and all possible actions of Person B. For each possible combination of actions, a particular outcome could be defined. Let's consider a simple example to see how the outcome matrix is used. Ann and Lisa, who are roommates, are trying to decide how to spend a Saturday. Ann observes that their apartment is a mess and suggests that they clean it together. Lisa had planned to go cycling for the day and suggests that Ann join her. In this simple example, we will assume that those are the only two options available for each—cleaning and cycling. For Lisa, cycling is more rewarding; for Ann, cleaning is more rewarding. If these two women were not interacting, there would be no question about which choice would be made— Lisa would grab her bike and Ann would grab her broom. Yet, because they are related, we would have to consider the outcomes of this choice. For Lisa, guilt might be a cost of the choice to cycle as she realized that Ann was doing more than her fair share of the work. In turn, Ann would find

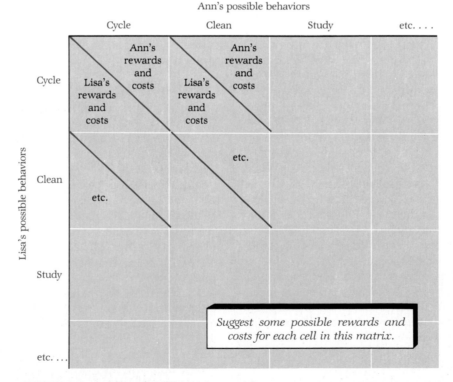

FIGURE 1-2. Social-exchange outcome matrix.

A. *As she prepares to leave for an appointment, Heather's mother puts the final touches on her makeup.*

B. *Watching her mother closely, Heather demonstrates the first step in the sequence of observational learning.*

C. *Handling a tube of mascara requires certain motor skills that Heather, at a younger age, would not have possessed.*

Observational Learning

How do we learn all the things we know? Sometimes, as either children or adults, we must be carefully taught—how to do multiplication tables, how to drive a car, or how to manage a good serve in tennis. But much of our learning is acquired less formally, through the process of observing other people doing things that we would like to do.

Adults often serve as models for their children's behavior, either intentionally or unintentionally. In the sequence of observational learning shown here, a mother is completing her makeup, perhaps unaware that she is serving as a teacher in her child's learning. Wanting to look like "Mommy," Heather watches closely and then tries to duplicate the behavior. Although the final result may be a bit sloppy the first few times—as anyone who has been around young children will recognize—the elements of the behavior have been established, and practice will refine the skills.

D. *Although her skills may still be a bit shaky, Heather shows that she has learned the new behavior.*

the situation more negative because of possible resentment toward Lisa's pleasure-seeking. In exchange relationships, therefore, the participants must calculate rewards and costs for each possible combination of actions, determining which outcome will be most beneficial for both.

Although this example is a simple one, the application of Thibaut and Kelley's social-exchange model is very broad. Processes of cooperation, competition, marital relationships, power relationships, bargaining, and negotiation have all been studied using their basic principles.

B. Contributions to social psychology

The applications of reinforcement principles to social psychology have been extensive. In their simplest forms, the principles have been used to explain some aspects of interpersonal attraction (see Chapter 6). For example, Donn Byrne (1971) has proposed that we like people who are similar to us on a variety of dimensions because such similarity is reinforcing. Robert Zajonc (1965) has used basic learning models to show why the presence of an audience will sometimes facilitate performance and sometimes impair it (see Chapter 14). Many of our basic attitudes may be learned through a process of learning and reinforcement. We like objects and people that provide rewards, and we dislike those that provide pain or displeasure (see Chapter 10).

As noted before, social-exchange theory can be applied to a wide range of phenomena, from marital interaction to international negotiation. In all these applications, however, the principles of reinforcement are considerably more complex than their origins in animal learning theory. The ability of humans to think and to form symbols requires a rather cognitive model of reinforcement.

C. Applications to case example

Approaching the marital relationship, the classic reinforcement theorist would look for reinforcement patterns. Why did Maria decide to marry Tony? Money? Prestige? Emotional warmth? Later decisions in the lives of Tony and Maria would also be interpreted in terms of potential reinforcers.

Thus, the reinforcement theorist interested in marital relationships would try to define the patterns of stimulus, response, and reinforcement that lead to interpersonal attraction.

More recent models of reinforcement, such as social-learning theory and social-exchange theory, would direct our attention to a broader range of questions. Social-exchange theory, in particular, would be well suited to the exploration of marital relationships. For the social-exchange theorist, a major concern would be the rewards and costs that the relationship offers each partner. Maria's decision to develop her own business, for example, might be viewed in terms of increased rewards and decreased costs for such an action. Her choice, however, would have to be interpreted in conjunction with Tony's behaviors. The ultimate resolution of their marriage would be viewed as a negotiation of rewards and costs accompanying each choice—and the comparison level for other possible outcomes. Whereas classic reinforcement theory, as well as the more contemporary social-learning theory, would lead us to look at the behavior of Tony and Maria separately, social-exchange theory would require us to consider the choices of both partners as part of the exchange relationship. This difference—in this case between theories that both have their roots in reinforcement principles—again shows us how important theories can be in shaping the questions we ask.

■ V. Cognitive theory

A. Basic assumptions and concepts

In the history of psychology, there have been numerous reactions against the behavioristic, or reinforcement, orientation. Whereas some investigators have shunned mentalistic concepts, others have seen such concepts as the only route to a true understanding of human behavior. *Gestalt theorists,* led by Koffka and Köhler in the 1930s, stressed perception and thought. They described the insight that makes problem solving possible, and they made the basic assumption that "the whole is greater than the sum of its parts." In doing so, they moved away from an analysis of observable stimuli and responses and toward the inference of internal cognitive processes.

The **phenomenological approach** also represents a reaction against behavioristic principles. According to this viewpoint, we can understand a person's behavior only by knowing how that person perceives the world. Previous stimuli and responses are influential only if they are represented in a person's consciousness. Kurt Lewin's field theory (see Box 1-3), emphasizing the notion of life space, is related to the phenomenological approach. For Lewin, however, aspects of the life space did not have to be represented in consciousness to be influential (Jones, in press).

Gestalt theory, the phenomenological approach, and Lewin's field theory all provide a background for current cognitive theories of social psychology. The current theories, however, have moved considerably beyond their predecessors in their more explicit consideration of cognitive mechanisms and cognitive structure. To understand some basic terms, we can consider a **cognition** as knowledge that is acquired through experience (Shaw & Costanzo, 1982). Cognitions are, in turn, organized into some form of **cognitive structure,** a set of principles and processes believed to organize our cognitive experience. In the most recent work in cognitive psychology, computer analogies are often used to describe cognitive structure.

What assumptions does the cognitive theorist make about human behavior? Generally, cognitive theorists are not concerned with concepts such as reinforcement and learning. Although the cognitive theorist may use terms such as *stimulus* and *response*, their meaning is much more complex than as used by reinforcement theorists. For cognitive theorists, a stimulus involves a complex pattern of organization rather than a simple external object—an idea that reflects the earlier thinking of Gestalt theorists. Cognitive theorists are most interested in concepts such as knowing, meaning, and understanding (Shaw & Costanzo, 1982). Thus, their interest is primarily in internal processes—processes that must be inferred rather than directly observed. Unlike the phenomenologists, cognitive theorists do not restrict their concern to those cognitions of which the person is consciously aware.

B. Contributions to social psychology

It has been said that social psychology has been cognitive for a very long time (Zajonc, quoted in Jones, in press). Indeed, it is easy to find examples of cognitive theorizing throughout the history of social psychology, from the early interest in attitudes, through the work of Muzafer Sherif on the influence of frame of reference in our perception of neutral stimuli, and including Kurt Lewin's emphasis on life space. Yet, although the threads can be easily seen in earlier work, the fabric of a cognitive social psychology is more recent.

Many of the social-psychological studies discussed in subsequent chapters rely on some form of cognitive theory. In Chapter 4, for example, we will see how our impressions of other people are formed and how we explain the events that occur around us. In forming initial impressions and in storing memories for later use, we are evidencing cognitions. Many theories of attitude change are also based on cognitive principles (see Chapter 11). Cognitive-consistency theories, for example, assume that we want our various attitudes, or our attitudes and our behaviors, to be consistent with one another. When they are not consistent, we often make changes. For example, suppose that you are an admirer of football heroes and opposed to the use of drugs. How do you reconcile your beliefs when you read about drug use among professional football players? This contradiction might cause some shift in your attitudes, either toward football players ("They're not so great after all") or toward drug use ("Maybe the dangers have been exaggerated")—changes which might not be directly observable but which can be inferred if we rely on cognitive theory.

C. Applications to case example

Cognitive theory would focus our attention on the knowledge that Tony and Maria have and on the meaning of various experiences to them. As in basic learning theory, the emphasis would be primarily on one individual. However, unlike basic learning theory, cognitive theories would lead us to consider the ways in which Maria regarded Tony and vice versa. A cognitive psychologist interested in this relationship might, for example, consider how one partner in a marriage explains the behavior of the other. In arguments, are attributions made to the other person or to circumstances? What schemata are present (see Chapters 3 and 4) that affect a person's interpretation of events? What beliefs does each partner hold about the activities of a mother, a husband, or a business owner? Which of Maria's activities does Tony remember, and which does he forget? Why are some remembered and some forgotten? In general, the cognitive psychologist would pay less attention to the actual events in a relationship and would look more closely at each partner's views of those events.

■ VI. A comparison of theories

Each of the three major theories that we have discussed makes a set of specific assumptions about human behavior, defining certain variables as important and others as incidental. Each theory, in turn, points an investigator in certain directions, suggesting some questions to ask and ignoring others. Having considered the central features of each theory separately, let's now compare them directly. Table 1-1 summarizes the results of these comparisons across five dimensions: the unit of analysis, historical or contemporary emphasis, internal or external emphasis, individual or social-structural emphasis, and assumptions about human nature.

Units of analysis. Each of the three theories that we have examined points to one concept as its centerpiece. For role theory, this concept is roles, formed as people interact with one another in a larger social system. For reinforcement theory, social behavior is explained by looking at specific stimulus-response-reinforcement connections. Although the more contemporary reinforcement theories, such as social exchange and social learning, consider rather complex units, their focus is still on discrete behaviors. For cognitive theory, the basic unit is cognitions or, more generally, cognitive structure.

Historical versus contemporary emphasis. The three theories diverge somewhat in the extent to which they emphasize historical versus contemporary causes for behavior. Role theory places the greatest weight on the present. (Lewin's field theory, presented in Box 1-3, was also very contemporary in its emphasis.) Both reinforcement theories and cognitive theories give more attention to historical antecedents of present behavior. Neither, however, has as historical an emphasis as psychoanalytic theory, which was briefly described in Box 1-2. In that case, nearly all behavior was explained by events that occurred when a person was very young. Reinforcement and cognitive theories, in contrast, both assume that behavior can and does change with new reinforcements or with new experience.

Internal versus external events. A third dimension on which theories differ is the emphasis they place on internal and on external events. Role theory tends to stress external roles and situations (although, as we shall see in Chapter 3, the current emphasis on the self-concept allows a great deal of consideration of internal events as well). Classic reinforcement theory is concerned only with external events, uninterested in and even antagonistic to the notion of "mentalistic" concepts. However, more contemporary versions of reinforcement theory, such as social-learning and social-exchange theories, give more attention to internal thoughts, expectancies, and mediating cognitions. Cognitive theories are very internal in their focus, stressing internal cognitive structures almost exclusively.

Individual versus social structure. Although reinforcement theory and cognitive theory differ in the extent to which they consider external events, they are alike in their emphasis on the individual as opposed to the social structure. Reinforcement theories give more attention to individual learning histories and, in the case of social-learning and social-exchange theories, to individual differences in cognitive abilities and in interaction goals. Cognitive theory also puts more emphasis on the individual than on the social structure, reflecting a continuing interest of psychologists in the individual rather than in the group level of analysis. In contrast, role theory virtually ignores individual differences; it looks instead at the common features of roles, role conflicts, and role expectations as the determinants of behavior.

Assumptions about human nature. Both classical reinforcement theory and role theory assume that human nature lacks an essence; rather, people act in response to stimuli (reinforcement theory) or in response to the expectations of the role they are fulfilling (role theory). In both cases, however, recent modifications of the theory have inserted the person more directly into the theory, acknowledging an organism (an *O* between the stimulus and response) in the case of reinforcement theory and giving greater attention to the self-concept in the case of role theory. Cognitive theory, in contrast, rests its case on the human being as a cognitive being—thinking, interpreting, and finding meaning in events. At the same time, cognitive theory has been accused of giving too little attention to other aspects of human behavior, such as emotion and action, and allowing the analogy of the computer to direct attention away from these other basic aspects of human nature.

Another way to compare these three theories is to consider how well they fit the criteria proposed by Shaw and Costanzo (1982), discussed earlier in this chapter. How well does each of these theories meet the standards of logical consistency, agreement with data, and testability? In fact, each theory comes out rather well. Each of our three theories is logically consistent, and each can be subject to various tests. At the same time, each theory may have some difficulty in explaining certain kinds of data and results. Each of these theories restricts itself to certain areas of social behavior and often has little to say about others.

Will one of these theories come to dominate social psychology in the future? Right now, such a prospect seems unlikely. None of these theories seems in danger of "going under," becoming of historical interest rather than remaining a viable way to look

TABLE 1-1. A comparison of three theories in social psychology

	Role theory	*Reinforcement theory*	*Cognitive theory*
Central concept, or unit of analysis	Roles	Stimulus-response units	Cognitions
Causes of behavior (historical or contemporary)	Contemporary ("You are what role you hold now")	Both—past reinforcement history and present reinforcement contingencies are both important	Both—memories and cognitive structure influence behavior, as do current events
Emphasis on internal process or external events	Emphasis on roles and situations	Emphasis on external stimuli	Emphasis on internal processes
Emphasis on individual or social structure	Social structure	Individual learning	Individual cognitions
Assumptions about human nature	People act in response to the expectations for the roles they hold	People's behaviors are determined by patterns of reinforcement	People are cognitive beings, who form cognitive structures and act on the basis of their cognitions

at the world. In each of the three theoretical orientations, considerable development has taken place in recent years. Often these elaborations involve "borrowing" assumptions from another theory, as has been true of the frequent use of cognitive concepts in both reinforcement and role theories. From this cross-fertilization, a single, more comprehensive theory may evolve.

For now, however, we have several theories to help us understand human social behavior. Each theory points us in a slightly different direction.

As Runkel and McGrath have observed, "A theory is a guide to tell you where to look for what you want to observe" (1972, p. 23). Thus, depending on what theoretical orientation we adopt, we may observe different aspects of human behavior. Yet, by being aware of the assumptions we are making—as a theory forces us to do—we are better prepared to find the truth. As Francis Bacon observed, "Truth emerges more easily from error than from confusion."

VII. SUMMARY

Social psychology is the field of study concerned with interpersonal behavior. It includes in its domain not only actual interpersonal behavior but also any behavior in which the presence of others is imagined or anticipated. Hence, very little human behavior lies outside the realm of social psychology.

Although the first social-psychological experiment was conducted in 1897, major developments in the field have been concentrated in the last 50 years. Reacting against behaviorism, on the one hand, and psychoanalytic theory, on the other, social psychology has developed a unique approach to understanding human behavior. Kurt Lewin is generally considered the father of this modern development.

Theories are sets of hypotheses formulated to explain phenomena. The three theoretical approaches that dominate current social psychology are: role theory, reinforcement theory, and cognitive theory.

Role theory seeks to explain social behavior through an analysis of roles, role obligations, role expectations, and role conflicts. A role is a socially defined pattern of behavior that accompanies a particular position within a social context. In recent years, concepts from role theory have been used to explain a variety of phenomena related to the self and the self-concept.

Reinforcement theory first limited its concern to stimuli, responses, and reinforcements, concentrating only on events external to the person. More recent uses of reinforcement theory within social psychology include social-learning theory and social-exchange theory, both of which include numerous cognitive concepts in their models. In addition, social-exchange theory has shifted the focus from the individual to the interacting dyad, considering the rewards and costs for both partners in an interaction.

Cognitive theory finds some roots in early work by both Gestalt and phenomenological theorists. It has developed much more elaborate concepts of cognitive structure, however, often borrowing models from the field of computer technology.

Theories can be compared on a number of dimensions, including their unit of analysis, emphasis on historical or contemporary situations, focus on internal or external events, emphasis on individuals or social structures, and basic assumptions about human nature. All theories serve as a guide to the investigator seeking explanations for human behavior.

GLOSSARY TERMS

cognition	life space	social-exchange theory
cognitive structure	norms	socialization
construct	phenomenological approach	social-learning theory
defense mechanisms	reinforcement	stimulus
ego	reinforcement theory	stimulus discrimination
field theory	response	stimulus generalization
hypothesis	role	superego
id	role expectations	

Methods of Studying Social Behavior

Research is the invasion of the unknown.
■ DeWITT STETTON, JR.

The whole of science is nothing more than a refinement of everyday thinking.
■ ALBERT EINSTEIN

Theories give us ways to look at the world. They provide a general framework for our understanding, and they also tell us what specific events to look for. As we saw in Chapter 1, a social-learning theorist may look for models that influence a person's behavior, whereas the investigator with a Freudian bent may turn to early childhood experiences to find the causes of adult behavior. Put another way, it has been said that "we are prone to see what lies behind our eyes rather than what appears before them" (Beveridge, 1964, p. 99).

"Behind our eyes," however, encompasses a lot of territory, and it is from this territory that experimental hypotheses emerge. Social psychologists, like other scientists, begin their pursuit of knowledge with an idea and then proceed to test that idea to determine its validity. All the research that will be discussed in this book began with an idea— sometimes a formally derived hypothesis, sometimes an intuitive leap, and sometimes just an accident. How ideas develop will be the first topic of this chapter; how ideas are translated into scientific study will be our focus in the rest of the chapter.

■ I. Formulating hypotheses

Perhaps the best way to describe the development of an idea is to describe what is historically considered the first social-psychological experiment. Norman Triplett, who was a psychologist at Indiana University in the late 19th century, was also a bicycle enthusiast. In studying the records of the Racing Board of the League of American Wheelmen, Triplett observed that cyclists' times were faster when the cyclists were racing against each other rather than simply racing against a clock. On the basis of this observation, Triplett proposed a theory of dynamogenesis (which is an origin of current theories of social facilitation, to be discussed in Chapter 14). Basically, his model suggested that the presence of other people acts as a stimulant to the performer.

If such a model were true, Triplett reasoned, it would hold for activities other than bicycle racing.

To test his hypothesis, Triplett returned to his psychology laboratory with 40 children and a set of fishing reels. He asked some children to wind the reels by themselves, while others wound reels in competition with another child. Triplett's hypothesis was confirmed: children in competition performed faster than children alone (Triplett, 1897). Thus, Triplett began with a simple observation, outside of his laboratory pursuits, and translated that thought into a psychological experiment that dealt with one of the core issues of social psychology: how the actions of others can influence the individual.

There are, of course, many ways to test any given idea; the diversity of these methods will be the concern of this chapter. First, however, we need to consider where ideas come from. It has been said that "most of the knowledge and much of the genius of the research worker lie behind [the] selection of what is worth observing" (Beveridge, 1964, p. 103). But how are selections made?

Curiosity and observation must be the starting points (Silverman, 1977). For the social psychologist, this curiosity will concern human behavior; observation will focus on people and their interactions. Research ideas may develop from a general interest in some topic, such as persuasion or group processes or love. In other instances, a specific event may be perplexing, and, like Sherlock Holmes, the social psychologist will try to unravel the mystery and arrive at a solution. In still other cases, an investigator may be involved in one project and, like the fabled princes of Serendip, accidentally discover some other significant information about human behavior, quite removed from the original research focus. In each case, however, curiosity and observation are at the root of the investigation.

McGuire (1973) has suggested some specific ways in which testable hypotheses about human behavior may be derived (see Table 2-1 on p. 30). Some of these approaches are based on a considerable body of past research; the investigator builds on past theory and data to develop increasingly complex hypotheses. Other approaches begin from more direct observation of people's behavior, as the investigator tries to define the basic psychological processes that may underlie the observed events. One example of the latter approach is to analyze the practitioner's rule of thumb (see No. 6 in Table 2-1).

Consider the style of the door-to-door encyclopedia representative. You yourself may have been on the receiving end of such house calls, in which the seller begins the pitch with a simple request. Having granted the sales representative five minutes of your time, you may have found yourself two hours later still listening to a talk on the virtues of the books. Such an experience, though annoying at the time, could nonetheless be the source of an experimental hypothesis if you were a social psychologist. In fact, research on this very issue has been conducted, and the results are referred to, not inappropriately, as the "foot-in-the-door" effect. Social psychologists have learned that a large request is more likely to be granted if it is preceded by the granting of a small request than if no request precedes it (Freedman & Fraser,

1966). This particular issue of compliance will be discussed at greater length in Chapter 12. For the present, however, it serves to illustrate how mundane the sources of some experimental ideas can be.

Other hypotheses may be developed from much more sophisticated theoretical networks or from a large body of previous research. Some of the sources that McGuire suggests deal with these more developed bases of hypothesis generation. The hypothetico-deductive method, for example, is perhaps best represented by Clark Hull's learning theory, in which numerous postulates were formulated. These postulates allowed the prediction of specific relationships, such as the relationship between level of hunger and speed of learning a response.

All the approaches that McGuire suggests have been used by social psychologists to develop hypotheses. Once a hypothesis is formulated, the investigator must then devise some means of test-

PHOTO 2-1. *From bicycle racing to research: The inspiration for Norman Triplett.*

TABLE 2-1. Some approaches to hypothesis generation

1. Intensive case study
   Example: Most psychoanalytic theory began with the extended analysis of individual patients. In treating a hysterical patient named Dora, for instance, Freud developed some of his theories about unconscious sexual impulses.

2. Accounting for a paradoxical incident
   Example: A cult of Illinois citizens in the mid-1950s fervently predicted the end of the world. Yet, when the designated day arrived and the world did not end, the enthusiasm of the believers for their cause did not wane (Festinger, Riecken, & Schachter, 1956). This incident led to a hypothesis about the effects of commitment on subsequent behavior.

3. Use of analogy
   Example: Borrowing from the medical principles of immunization as a means of resisting disease, McGuire (1964) developed research showing how familiarity with attitudinal issues could increase later resistance to persuasion.

4. Hypothetico-deductive method
   Example: In this more formal method, the investigator combines a number of principles from previous research and, through logical deductive methods, arrives at a set of predictions. Hullian learning theory exemplifies this approach.

5. Functional or adaptive approach
   Example: The investigator considers a particular pattern of events and then generates the principles that must be operating in order for the event to occur. Horner (1972) did this when she suggested that a "fear of success" keeps many people who have high achievement needs from actually meeting their goals.

6. Analyzing the practitioner's rule of thumb
   Example: Television commercials and magazine advertisements frequently show a celebrity praising a product, which suggests that advertisers believe that status sells products. This observation could lead to a series of hypotheses about the effects of the communicator's status on attitude and behavior change.

7. Trying to account for conflicting results
   Example: Many people believe, and research often shows, that our first impressions of a person have the most lasting effect. Yet, other research indicates that the most recent information carries the greatest weight. Research hypotheses can be developed to predict when "primacy" will be important and when "recency" will be important (see Chapter 4).

8. Accounting for exceptions to general findings
   Example: Most research shows that a performance by a woman will be rated less favorably than an equivalent performance by a man. Yet, on a few occasions, this devaluation will not occur (Taynor & Deaux, 1973). These exceptions to the rule provide an intriguing source of hypotheses.

9. Reducing observed complex relationships to simpler component relationships
   Example: The complex process of attitude change can be broken down into separate stages, as the investigator might form hypotheses about the initial reception of the message, the cognitive processing of the arguments, or the long-term retention of change (see Chapter 11).

ing that hypothesis. And although the hypothesis-generation phase of research is in many ways the most exciting aspect of the research process, the latter stages are no less critical. Nor are they simple or automatic, as Box 2-1 illustrates.

■ II. Testing hypotheses

There is no one right way to test a hypothesis. Social psychologists have developed a warehouse of methods, many of which may be appropriate

BOX 2-1. If at first you don't succeed . . .

Research reports in professional journals often make the research process sound easy. Apparently the investigators came up with a good hypothesis, tested it, obtained interesting results, and then quickly published their findings in the journal. In truth, the course of research is not so smooth.

Alan Gross and Anthony Doob (1976) provide an interesting account of their attempts to test the frustration-aggression hypothesis in a natural setting. Though inexperienced, they decided to move outside the laboratory to see whether experiencing frustration leads people to become more aggressive. After considerable thought, they decided that traffic jams were a good source of frustration, and although they did not think it reasonable to cause a series of major traffic jams, it seemed possible to arrange for a single driver to stall a car at a traffic light. The honking that occurs on such occasions could be used as a likely measure of aggression—but what factors might affect that aggression? Various bumper stickers on the stalled car were one possibility;

the number of people in the car was another. Finally Gross and Doob decided on the status of the car, suggesting that people would be less likely to honk at a high-status car than at a low-status car. For graduate students, finding a low-status car was no problem; however, obtaining a high-status car posed more of a problem. A rented Chrysler proved to be the solution.

After a few more practical problems were encountered and solved, the field experiment was conducted. Data were collected and analyzed, and the statistical analyses showed that the data supported the initial hypothesis: people were less likely to honk at the driver of a stalled high-status car. So far, so good. But when the report was written up and submitted to a journal, the editor of that journal found the study uninteresting. The editor of a second journal concurred. Fortunately, however, this story has a happy ending. On their third try, Doob and Gross had a positive response, and the study of horn honking now occupies a place in the social-psychology literature (Doob & Gross, 1968). ■

for any single question. In fact, every method has strengths and weaknesses, and the ultimate strategy of the scientist should be to test a single hypothesis through a diversity of methods, thereby increasing one's confidence in the validity of the hypothesis. Before delving into the characteristics of each method, however, let us consider how a single hypothesis might be tested in a variety of settings: the laboratory, the field, and across cultures.

A. The hypothesis

The behavior of the individual in a group is one of the central issues of social psychology. Although the effects of a group are numerous, let us for the moment consider only one aspect: **deindividuation.** This term, suggested by Festinger, Pepitone, and Newcomb (1952), refers to a state of relative

anonymity, in which the group member does not feel singled out or identifiable. In the late 19th century, LeBon (1896) observed crowd behavior and postulated a similar notion to explain why persons in a mob lose their sense of responsibility. From these general observations, then, it is possible to develop a specific hypothesis concerning the effects of anonymity on subsequent behavior. Let us focus on the following hypothesis: Greater degrees of anonymity will result in a greater frequency of antisocial behavior.

Formulating such a hypothesis represents the first stage of the research process. The next step is to develop a means of testing the validity of that hypothesis. As noted before, there are many ways that a single hypothesis can be tested. To demonstrate the truth of this assertion, we will consider three different studies in three different settings, each of which was designed to test the relationship between anonymity and antisocial behavior.

B. A laboratory investigation

In a psychology laboratory at New York University, Zimbardo (1970) conducted a study in which four students were asked to share the responsibility for giving another student a set of electric shocks. The guise for giving those shocks was that the experimenter was interested in people's reactions to the pain of another person; in fact, however, the experimenter was interested in the level of aggressive behavior (as measured by the duration of electric shocks given) as a function of anonymity. (We will discuss the issue of deception later in this chapter.) To vary the conditions of anonymity, Zimbardo had half of his subjects dressed in hoods. These students never gave their names, and they performed the experiment in the dark. (Photo 2-2 pictures several of the deindividuated students.) The other half of the subjects in this experiment had their individuality emphasized: they were greeted by name, were given large name tags, and got to know one another on a first-name basis. Both groups of subjects were free to give as much or as little shock to the other student as they wished.

In this laboratory setting, the deindividuation hypothesis was confirmed: subjects in the anonymity condition gave more shock to the other students than did subjects in the individuated condition. Although the laboratory has been the set-

PHOTO 2-2. *Subjects in the deindividuated condition in Zimbardo's laboratory experiment.*

ting most frequently used by social psychologists to test their hypotheses, it is certainly not the only setting available. Let us consider two other settings that were used to test the same hypothesis.

C. A field investigation

The social psychologist who moves outside the laboratory to test a hypothesis is basically concerned with increasing the natural quality of the situation: naturalness of the behavior, the setting, and the treatment (Tunnell, 1977). Often the investigator's role in such a study is simply to observe what occurs, with little or no intervention. To test the hypothesis concerning deindividuation, one might therefore look for natural settings that would differ in the degree of anonymity they provided. For example, in a large urban center, we might expect anonymity to be much more pervasive than in a small university town where people are more likely to be acquainted. Thus, greater antisocial behavior could be predicted, on the basis of our hypothesis, in the large city than in the small town.

To test the deindividuation hypothesis in these circumstances, Zimbardo and Fraser bought a used car and left it on a busy street adjoining the Bronx campus of New York University. At the same time, a similar car was left on a street near the Stanford University campus in Palo Alto, California. Within 26 hours the car in New York was stripped of battery, radiator, air cleaner, radio antenna, windshield wipers, side chrome, all four hubcaps, a set of jumper cables, a can of car wax, a gas can, and the one tire worth taking. Meanwhile, in Palo Alto, the second car remained unharmed. In fact, one day when it rained, a passerby lowered the hood so the motor would not get waterlogged!

Although automobile-parts thieves and hooded students are obviously quite different, from the point of testing a hypothesis the conclusion remains the same: greater anonymity leads to a greater frequency of antisocial behavior.

D. A cross-cultural investigation

What is true in industrialized countries may not be true in other parts of the world. Consequently, experimenters who want to determine the universality of their hypotheses may often look to other societies for a means of testing their ideas. One source for such tests is the Human Relations Area File (HRAF), a collection of information assembled by ethnographers on more than 200 cultures throughout the world.

Watson (1973) used the material available in this file to test the anonymity/antisocial-behavior hypothesis in yet another context. He assumed that the extensive use of masks and of face and body paint by warriors serves as a guarantee of anonymity. Consequently, he hypothesized that societies in which use of paint and disguise was extensive would have a tradition of more aggressive and ferocious warfare than societies in which disguise was less frequent. To test the hypothesis, Watson simply categorized societies described in the HRAF on two dimensions: intensity of warfare (as indicated by reports of such practices as torture, sacrifice of prisoners, headhunting, and fighting to the death in all battles) and the presence or absence of paints and disguise as a prelude to battle. Once again, the hypothesis concerning anonymity and aggression was supported: those societies that engaged in more aggressive forms of warfare were also more likely to don heavy disguises than were the more peaceful cultures (see Table 2-2).

In Watson's study, it is more difficult to determine the direction of cause and effect than it is, for example, in the laboratory experiment. The **correlational method** (the study of the interrelationship between two sets of events) may tell us

that two factors are associated, but we don't generally know which factor causes which. It could be, as hypothesized, that anonymity leads to aggression. However, it is also possible that aggressive people are more likely to seek anonymity. Or, as a third possibility, perhaps some other factor, such as climate, leads both to aggression and to a desire for anonymity. In contrast, the experimenter in the laboratory first manipulated anonymity and then measured aggression, so that we are quite certain which factor came first and hence is the cause.

E. Choice of a method

The three examples above show that there are many ways and places to test a single hypothesis. Given such abundance, how does the investigator decide on one way to test a hypothesis? There are many reasons for any particular choice, including convenience, a particular investigator's preference, and the history of past research in the area. Whatever the choice, the investigator must carefully consider the strengths and weaknesses of each method as they may affect the outcome. Let us now look more carefully at each of the methods.

■ III. Major methods of social-psychological research

Social psychologists have developed an extensive repertoire of methods to help them answer questions about human behavior. We will discuss seven of these methods: laboratory experiments, field experiments, quasi-experimental research, field studies, archival research, simulation and role playing, and surveys and interviews. In each case, we will consider both the advantages and disadvantages of the method.

A. The laboratory experiment

Zimbardo's study of the effect of anonymity on students' willingness to shock another student is one example of a laboratory experiment. As another example, consider the following study by Deaux and Emswiller (1974). College students reported to a laboratory at Purdue University, where they

TABLE 2-2. Relationship between changes in physical appearance before battle and extremity of aggression in warfare among 23 linguistically and geographically independent cultures

	Deindividuation	
Aggression	Changed appearance	Unchanged appearance
High	12	1
Low	3	7

NOTE: $N = 23$; $\chi^2 = 7.12$, $df = 1$, $p < .01$.

were told that they would be asked to explain and evaluate the performance of another student. This other student was supposedly being asked to identify blurred pictures and to verbally name each item. The subjects, who were seated individually in booths, heard the student's answers over a set of headphones. Subjects had a sheet with the correct answers in front of them. When the other student (either a male or a female) had successfully completed the test, each subject was asked to evaluate the performance on a questionnaire provided by the experimenters.

In this study, as in other laboratory experiments, the researcher's aim is to test the effects of one or more independent variables on one or more dependent variables. **Independent variables** in an experiment are those factors that are controlled or arranged by the experimenter and may often be considered the cause of a behavior. **Dependent variables** are those behaviors of the subject that are observed or recorded by the experimenter.

In Deaux and Emswiller's experiment, there were two independent variables: the sex of the student who had performed the visual discrimination task and the sex linkage of the task itself. In some cases, the objects of the task discrimination were female-linked objects, such as whisks, colanders, and pincushions. In other cases, the list of objects included traditionally male-identified things, such as Phillips screwdrivers, lug wrenches, and tire rods. The dependent variable in Deaux and Emswiller's experiment consisted of the subjects' answers to a series of questions about the student's performance. Of particular interest were responses to one question that asked how much luck versus skill was responsible for the observed student's performance.

The results of this study showed that when a male did well on a masculine task, subjects were apt to conclude that his performance was largely the result of skill. When a woman did well on the same task, subjects rated her as lucky. On the feminine task, there was no difference in the reasons given for the successful performance of males and females. Thus, the investigators were able to conclude that evaluations of performance (the dependent variable) vary as a function of the sex of the performer and the type of task (the independent variables).

Characteristic of the laboratory experiment is the investigator's ability to control the independent and dependent variables. Indeed, this aspect of control is one of the most important features of the laboratory experiment. In the above example, the experimenters were able to manipulate systematically the performance that subjects observed: the sequence of responses that the student had made, the number of correct and incorrect answers, and the specific items on the test were all determined by the experimenters. Through this control, numerous extraneous variables could be eliminated. For example, many judgments are influenced by the attractiveness of the person being judged. However, Deaux and Emswiller were not interested in this variable, and they were able to eliminate it by allowing the subjects to hear only voices and not actually see the person they were judging. Similarly, in controlling the dependent variable, the experimenters were able to phrase the evaluation questions exactly as they wished, enabling them to focus precisely on certain kinds of judgments.

In addition to control, the laboratory experiment offers another important advantage: the ability to assign subjects randomly to conditions. In order for investigators to draw conclusions about cause and effect, they must be sure that the pattern of results was not due to some systematic difference in the groups being compared. By randomly assigning subjects to listen to either a male or a female and to evaluate either a masculine or a feminine task, the experimenters can control for the possibility that some people are more familiar with one or the other task. On the average, this procedure of **randomization** ensures an equality of subject characteristics across the various experimental conditions. Such a principle has been important in the development of other sciences and is important to the development of social-psychological knowledge as well.

One other characteristic of the laboratory experiment should be mentioned—the **manipulation check.** Although experimenters are able to control the independent variable, it is still important for them to be sure that the subjects in the experiment perceive the manipulation as it is intended. For example, in Deaux and Emswiller's study, the experimenters wanted to be sure that subjects did perceive the objects in the perception task as masculine and feminine. To find out, they included in their set of dependent measures a question that asked subjects how masculine or feminine they perceived the task to be. Statistically significant differences in the subjects' responses to this question as a function of the task condition gave the experimenters confidence that their results were due to the variables that they manipulated.

Advantages. The major advantages of the laboratory experiment have been summarized above. Principal among these is the ability of the experimenter to control the independent variables and to randomly assign subjects to conditions. These two capabilities provide some basis for drawing conclusions about cause and effect. Furthermore, the laboratory allows the investigator to "sort out" factors—to simplify the more complex events of the natural world by breaking them down into their component parts.

Other advantages of the laboratory experiment are somewhat more mundane, convenience being one of the major ones. Most psychological laboratories are located on university campuses, where there is an abundant supply of students to serve as subjects and where the experimenter has easy access to facilities. Procedures at many universities make a "subject pool" readily available, and hence the investigator is spared the difficulty of recruiting subjects individually.

Disadvantages. Although the laboratory experiment has many advantages, it has some substantial disadvantages as well. In recent years, these disadvantages have become the topic of considerable debate. Three issues of concern have been the possible irrelevance of the laboratory setting, the reactions of subjects to the laboratory setting, and the possible influence of experimenters on their results. (Questions of deception and ethics, though primarily focused on certain laboratory experiments, are not exclusive to this method and will be discussed in more general terms in a later section of this chapter.)

The issue of irrelevance concerns the artificiality of the laboratory setting and the fact that many of the situations created in the laboratory bear little direct relation to the situations a person encounters in real life. Aronson and Carlsmith (1968) have argued persuasively for the distinction between **experimental realism** and **mundane realism**. They contend that, in the laboratory, one can devise situations that have impact and that

PHOTO 2-3. *Experimental realism and mundane realism.* Experimental realism *refers to the amount of impact in the situation—that is, the extent to which the subject is involved and paying attention to the situation.* Mundane realism *refers to the similarity of the situation to "real world" events. In the aggression study pictured on the left, mundane realism is low (people rarely encounter shock machines in the "real world"), but the experimental realism is high. The photograph on the right could depict a field study of television-viewing habits. Mundane realism is high, but the impact of the situation on the children appears low.*

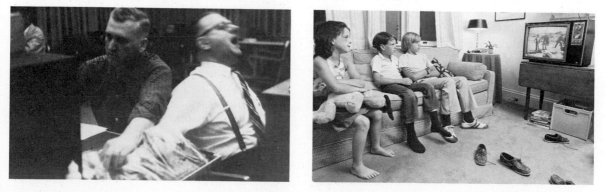

evoke valid psychological processes (experimental realism), even if the situation itself does not look like the real world (mundane realism). Yet, despite the persuasiveness of Aronson and Carlsmith's arguments, it remains true that many laboratory tasks seem suspiciously artificial and that their **external validity** has not been demonstrated. *External validity* refers to the "generalizability" of research findings to other populations, treatment variables, and measurement variables (Campbell & Stanley, 1966). Although this criterion must be applied to all social-psychological studies, it is in the case of laboratory experiments that its applicability has been questioned most vigorously. Thus, although college students' evaluations of the performance of another student on an object-perception task *may* parallel the judgments of a supervisor rating male and female employees in an organization, we cannot be absolutely certain that the situations are similar.

A second criticism of the laboratory experiment focuses on the reactions of subjects to the laboratory setting. These reactions may involve **demand characteristics** and **evaluation apprehension.** The first term refers to the fact that the experimental setting may evoke certain demands—that is, expectations on the part of subjects to act as they think the experimenter would wish (Orne, 1969). For example, if you were in a psychology experiment in which somebody asked you to indicate your attitude toward nuclear disarmament, then asked you to listen to a speech in which nuclear disarmament was advocated, and then once again asked for your attitude, you might well suspect that the experiment was concerned with attitude change. A subject in this situation who wanted to please the experimenter or do the "right thing" might well indicate a change of attitude on paper, without really believing it. Such a response would represent an influence of the demand characteristics of the situation but not necessarily the influence of the experimenter's intended variable.

Evaluation apprehension refers to the concerns that a subject has about being observed and judged while in the laboratory setting. Some people are afraid to be studied—perhaps the psychologist will discover that they're "crazy" or "stupid." Because

subjects come to a laboratory experiment knowing that the investigator is interested in some aspect of their behavior, they may try to present themselves in a favorable light. (This specific problem concerning the laboratory setting is related to the more general issue of impression management, which will be discussed in Chapter 3.) Again, the issue is the veridicality of subjects' behavior; that is, are the subjects acting as they normally would in such a situation, or are they modifying their behavior *because of* the laboratory setting?

An interesting experiment by Sigall, Aronson, and Van Hoose (1970) examined the problem of evaluation apprehension. In this experiment, subjects were faced with the choice between cooperating with the experimenter, which meant conveying negative information about themseves, or negating the experimenter's demands and looking good. Most subjects chose to look good. Their choice points out the importance of self-presentation strategies and also suggests limitations of the experimenter's power to influence behaviors that do not match the subjects' own aspirations.

A final criticism of the laboratory experiment concerns **experimenter expectancies** (Rosenthal, 1966). It has been shown in a variety of situations that an experimenter, knowing the hypothesis of the study, can unwittingly influence the results of the study. For example, in tests involving rats running down an alley, Rosenthal and his colleagues found that experimenters who believed their rats were the faster group obtained results that supported their belief—even though their rats were in fact no more predisposed to speed than the other group of rats. With human interaction, the influence of expectation is even more likely. Through vocal inflection or subtle facial movements, an experimenter may unconsciously influence the subject's behavior and thus bias the results. In this instance, we are questioning the **internal validity** of the experiment (Campbell & Stanley, 1966): are the results due to the independent variables that were manipulated or to some other uncontrolled element in the situation?

Generally, social psychologists can avoid these potential threats. For example, instructions can be tape-recorded in advance to ensure that they are exactly the same for all subjects. Other techniques include the use of a "blind" experimenter, who is not informed of the experimental hypothesis and is therefore unlikely to exert a systematic bias on the results.

In summary, the laboratory experiment offers the most precise control of variables and the greatest ability to isolate those factors that are believed to be important, uncontaminated by extraneous variables and competing events. At the same time, however, the artificiality of the laboratory setting can create another set of problems that reduce the correspondence between laboratory-obtained findings and real-life behavior.

B. The field experiment

"Hello, would you like to try a free sample of pizza?" You might encounter a demonstrator making this request at your local supermarket and think nothing of it. Yet, for some shoppers at a Kansas City store, this overture meant that they were subjects in a social-psychological field experiment. Investigators Smith, Gier, and Willis (1982) wanted to find out whether a brief interpersonal touch would increase compliance of shoppers with a request to sample a new food product. Half the times that demonstrators made their request, they lightly touched the shopper on the upper arm; on the other 50% of the occasions, no touch accompanied the request. In all other respects the message of the demonstrator was the same. Touch did indeed have an effect. When touched, 79% of the shoppers sampled the product and 37% bought it. In contrast, only 51% of the shoppers who were not touched agreed to try the product, and fewer than 20% made a purchase.

This study is a typical example of the field experiment. As in the laboratory experiment, the experimenter in the field has control of the independent variables and the random assignment of subjects to conditions. In the supermarket study, the independent variable controlled by the experimenter was the presence or absence of a touch. The subjects in the experiment (in this case the shoppers in the supermarket) were randomly assigned to their conditions by alternating touch and no-touch approaches every half hour.

PHOTO 2-4. *Like pizza, free samples of gum could be part of a field experiment.*

Advantages. The advantages of the field experiment are probably obvious. By focusing on behavior in a natural setting, the experimenter can be much more confident of the external validity of his or her findings. Furthermore, because subjects are generally unaware of their status as subjects, the problems of reactivity and the subjects' desire to be seen in a positive light are eliminated. In addition, because control over the independent variable and principles of randomization are maintained, the field experiment allows the same possibilities for conclusions about cause and effect as the laboratory experiment does.

Disadvantages. Although the field experiment may seem to be an ideal combination of the strict rules of experimentation with the realism of natural behavior settings, it too has some disadvantages. These potential problems concern the nature of the independent variable, the nature of the dependent variable, the ethics of the experiment, and the practical difficulties involved.

Because the experimenter is working in a complex natural setting where many events may be occurring simultaneously, the independent variable in the study must be fairly obvious. For example, suppose you wanted to see whether people would help a person who dropped some packages. If the packages were dropped in the middle of a crowded rock concert, the behavior would probably go unnoticed by the majority of people in the audience. Thus, the investigator conducting a field experiment must be sure that the independent variable is sufficiently strong to make an impact on potential subjects. Otherwise, a failure to respond will be difficult to interpret.

The dependent variable in a field experiment must also be selected carefully. The experimenters must be able to readily observe and reliably judge the dependent-variable behavior. In the supermarket experiment, for example, it was very easy for the experimenters to record whether a person tried the sample product and whether the product was purchased. In contrast, if the experimenters had been interested in more subtle facial reactions that might indicate approval of the product, their task would have been much more difficult. Because of these difficulties, the dependent variables in field experiments tend to be rather large-scale behaviors, frequently scored in a present-or-absent fashion. (We will discuss the statistical limits of such measures later in this chapter.)

An additional problem in field experimentation concerns ethics. Is it reasonable for a social psychologist to involve individuals in an experiment without their knowledge or permission? This question has been discussed extensively (Carlsmith, Ellsworth, & Aronson, 1976; Kelman, 1968; McGuire, 1967; Selltiz, Wrightsman, & Cook, 1976). Although there is no simple answer, most social scientists would agree that field experiments are reasonable if the independent variables are normal occurrences in a person's daily life and if the setting is a public one. The less the experimenter's intervention inconveniences the subjects or involves them emotionally, the less serious the ethics question becomes. For example, an experiment in which someone drops packages on the street raises fewer ethical questions than one in which people are accosted by a stranger who is apparently having an epileptic fit. The latter situation would probably be ruled out by most investigators, whereas the former would be ethically acceptable. On each occasion, however, the investigator must carefully consider the harm or inconvenience that an experimental intervention could cause.

Finally, the field experiment often poses practical problems. In contrast to the laboratory scientist, the investigator in the field has no control over the majority of events in the environment; unexpected events may reduce or destroy the effectiveness of the manipulation. Stores can close for lack of business, other product demonstrators may claim the best location, or store personnel may change their policies toward research on the premises. A field experimenter must study the setting carefully before the research begins and must be aware of as many contingencies as possible. Often the experimenter must also get permission from store owners or from the local police force beforehand to ensure that the events to be staged will not be misinterpreted and will not violate local laws.

In summary, the field experiment has many advantages, combining control and randomization principles with a realistic setting. At the same time, because the field experimenter cannot control the environment, the precision and the complexity of laboratory experiments cannot be attained.

C. Quasi-experimental research

What influence does television have on our behavior? Does watching television, as many have claimed, lead to an increase in crime and violence? Hennigan and her colleagues (Hennigan, Del Rosario, Heath, Cook, Wharton, & Calder, 1982) used a type of quasi-experimental research to answer these questions. FBI crime statistics on murder, assault, larceny, auto theft, and burglary served as the dependent variable in this research. To assess the amount of television viewing in selected cities and states, these investigators took advantage of a naturally occurring sequence in the introduction of television to the United States. In the 1950s, the Federal Communications Commission (FCC) regulated access to television, putting a freeze on new licenses. Some cities received television before the freeze; other communities had to wait several years until the freeze was lifted.

If television does increase crime, then we should see an increase in those cities where television was present and no substantial change in crime rates where television was absent. In turn, when the freeze was lifted, the latter group of cities should have shown a similar increase in crime rates. Looking at the crime rates in a large number of cities and states both before and after television was introduced, Hennigan and her colleagues found no evidence for an increase in violent crimes. For crimes of larceny (theft), however, television did have an impact. As Figure 2-1 shows, states that had television before the freeze had a noticeable increase in thefts during the years after 1951, when television became available there. Similarly, in states that received television after the freeze was lifted in 1956, crimes of larceny rose sharply after the freeze.

This study is an example of quasi-experimental research. In quasi-experimental research, the investigator does not have full experimental control over the independent variables—in this case, the FCC decisions—but does have a choice about how, when, and for whom the dependent variable is measured. Generally, such experiments involve behavior in a natural setting and focus on the effect of intervention in a system of ongoing behavior. Often the intervention results from a policy decision by a government agency, as we saw here. In other cases, the intervention may be a natural disaster, such as a flood, earthquake, or tornado. Power blackouts in New York City and other urban cen-

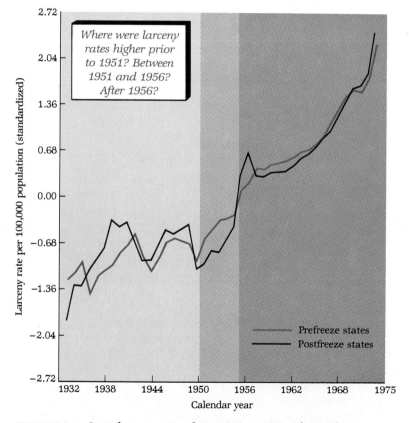

FIGURE 2-1. State larceny rates from 1933 to 1974. The prefreeze states show a sharp increase in larceny dating from 1951, when they first had access to television. The postfreeze states, which received television later, also show a rise in larceny but not until after 1956, when television came to their areas.

ters, for example, could serve as the independent variable in a study of reactions to stressful events, as could the eruption of Mt. St. Helens. The experimenter would have no control over the independent variable, but he or she could carefully select a set of dependent variables to measure the effects of stress.

Of course, the investigator still has to explain why this particular cause-and-effect relationship occurred. Hennigan and her colleagues considered a number of possible reasons for the increase in theft following the introduction of television. Because the effect was mainly on burglary and not on other, more violent crimes, they suggest that the programs may have emphasized an upper-class life-style and shown a lot of consumer goods. For the viewer who could not afford that kind of luxury, resentment may have led to crime.

Advantages. One unique advantage of quasi-experimental research conducted in a natural setting is that it allows us to study very strong variables that cannot be manipulated or controlled by an experimenter. In the wake of a tornado, for example, the investigator can study reactions to highly distressing events, much more consequential than anything that could be done in the laboratory. Often, too, quasi-experimental research deals with policy decisions that have consequences for very large numbers of people—in the study of television and crime, residents of 68 cities. The broad impact of such decisions gives considerable external validity to the research findings in a manner rarely matched in the more limited laboratory or field experiment.

Disadvantages. Because the investigator has no control over the independent variable in quasi-experimental research, it is always possible that other uncontrolled variables are affecting the dependent-variable behavior. Random assignment of subjects to conditions can rarely be assumed in the quasi-experimental design, either. However, there are a number of statistical procedures by which investigators can increase their confidence in the validity of the proposed cause-and-effect relationship (see Campbell & Stanley, 1966; Cook & Campbell, 1979).

When a natural disaster is the independent variable, the investigator faces the additional problem of preparation. Natural disasters usually arrive with little or no warning, thus giving the investigator little time to design a study and to prepare appropriate measuring instruments. Often such research must be done "on the run." Furthermore, the arbitrariness of events in the quasi-experimental world does not allow the experimenter to vary factors according to any theoretical model. Intensity of a stressful event, for example, might be important in predicting how people respond to stress. Nonetheless, it is clearly impossible for the experimenter to control such a variable, and he or she must accept whatever levels occur naturally.

In summary, quasi-experimental research offers some clear advantages to investigators in terms of the impact and complexity of situations that can be studied; in addition, it allows investigators to study some situations that cannot be studied in any other manner. At the same time, experimenters have less control in this situation than in the true experiment, and they must interpret results more cautiously.

D. The field study

A 12′ × 57′ steel cylinder, placed 205 feet below the surface of the Pacific Ocean, provided the site for an exotic field study by Radloff and Helmreich (1968). This cylinder, capable of sleeping ten persons, was named SEALAB II and was designed by the U.S. Navy to study human capabilities for living and working under water (see Figure 2-2). Radloff and Helmreich were interested in the effects of psychological stress on human behavior, and they obtained the permission of the navy officials to observe the aquanauts in their undersea world.

The conditions in SEALAB II were undoubtedly stressful. In addition to the potential physical dangers from a ruptured wall or broken porthole, the living conditions themselves were unpleasant. The inside of the capsule was extremely confined and crowded, and there was little privacy. To make matters worse, the habitat rested unevenly on the ocean floor at a 6° angle, causing drawers to slide open or shut and objects to slide off tables. In

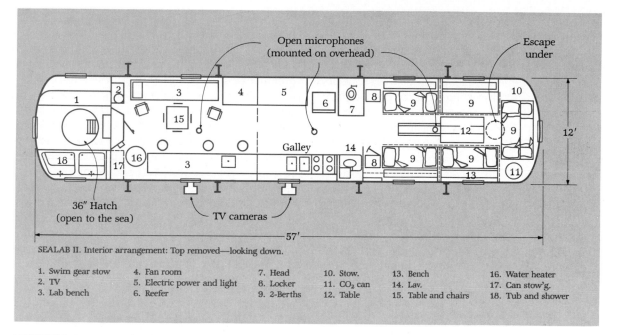

SEALAB II. Interior arrangement: Top removed—looking down.

1. Swim gear stow	4. Fan room	7. Head	10. Stow.	13. Bench	16. Water heater
2. TV	5. Electric power and light	8. Locker	11. CO_2 can	14. Lav.	17. Can stow'g.
3. Lab bench	6. Reefer	9. 2-Berths	12. Table	15. Table and chairs	18. Tub and shower

FIGURE 2-2. Diagram of SEALAB II.

addition, the aquanauts were expected to make a series of diving expeditions outside the capsule, where they were subjected to the typical hazards of deep-sea diving at 200 feet.

In their intensive study of this small group of men, Radloff and Helmreich collected hundreds of pieces of information. Some of this information consisted of objective behavioral measures—for example, number of excursions made outside the capsule, number of telephone calls made to the surface, and types of activities conducted within SEALAB. Other dependent measures were collected by questionnaire, measuring various personality characteristics and moods before and after dives. Still other information comprised demographic facts such as birth order, marital status, age, and years of diving experience.

From these measures, the investigators were able to gain a wealth of information about the behavior of groups of men in a stressful situation and the factors that may predict successful or unsuccessful adjustment. For example, they found that men born in small towns adjusted better to the SEALAB

environment than men raised in urban areas. At a group level, the investigators observed an increase in camaraderie as the test period wore on.

Not all field studies are conducted in such exotic locales. Barker and Schoggen (1973), for example, focused their study on the residents of a small Midwestern town, population 830, and compared behaviors observed there to those seen in a similarly small English village. A major goal of this research was to make a complete classification of each town's behavior settings, defined as public places or occasions that evoke their own typical pattern of behavior. Newcomb (1961) conducted his year-long field study of students at Bennington College in Vermont, focusing on the change in values and attitudes of students from the beginning of the year to the end.

Most field studies are characterized by their in-depth consideration of a limited group of people. The investigator in this setting plays a more reactive role than in the field experiment. Rather than manipulating some aspect of the environment and observing the changes that occur, the investigator in the field study records as much information as possible about the situation without altering it in any substantial way. Most often, people in the environment are aware of the investigator's presence and the general purpose of the investigation. Many times the investigator is a **participant observer**—that is, someone actively engaged in the activities of the group while at the same time maintaining records of the group members' behaviors.

Observation is the key element of the field-study method. Because "people watching" is a fairly common activity for most of us, it is often hard to appreciate how difficult systematic scientific observation can be. First, one must become very familiar with the environment and aware of the kinds of behaviors that are most likely to occur. Next, one must decide which types of behavior are to be recorded. For example, should one focus on easily recorded behaviors, such as (in the case of the SEALAB study) telephone calls made from the underwater laboratory or excursions taken outside the laboratory? Or is one interested in charting the locations used and the number of people in each location? Or is the interest in smaller units of behavior, such as facial expressions and vocal pitch? The choice of one or more of these categories depends on the questions that the investigator has posed. Although field-study investigators do not purposely manipulate conditions, they are no less likely than any other experimenters to have a specific set of questions formulated in advance of the actual study. Without such questions, field observation becomes mired in a hopeless array of competing events.

Once categories of behavior are selected for observation, the investigator must devise specific methods of recording the desired information. Finally, the observer must conduct a series of preliminary investigations to determine the **reliability** of the measures. In other words, it must be demonstrated that a series of different observers watching the same event and using the same methods will code the behavior in the same way. Without such reliability, a coding system merely reflects one observer's biases and cannot be used as a basis for a scientific statement.

Advantages.   The major advantage of the field study is its realism. The focus of the study is on events as they normally occur in a real-life setting. Furthermore, because most field studies take place over an extended period, they provide information about the sequence and development of behaviors that cannot be gained in the one-shot observation typical of field and laboratory experiments. Additionally, the duration of the field study generally allows collection of several types of dependent measures. For example, in the study of aquanauts, the measures included observations, questionnaires, and demographic information. Such a variety of measures, when they are directed at the assessment of a limited number of concepts, gives us greater confidence in the conclusions than if any one of the measures were taken alone.

Disadvantages.   Although well-conducted field studies furnish a wealth of data, the lack of control in such settings can be a problem. Because there is no controlled independent variable, it is difficult to form conclusions about cause and effect. Although there are some statistical techniques available to assist in making causal conclusions, the process is more difficult than in the controlled experimental design.

A second potential problem in the field study is the subjects' awareness of the investigator's observations. When subjects are aware of being observed, their behavior may be reactive—that is, influenced by the process of observation. Most experienced observers believe, however, that in a long-term field study the subjects become indifferent to the observer's presence, although the problem remains a serious one in briefer studies.

In summary, the field study allows the investigator to study intensively a series of events in a real-life setting. Although field studies are not always the best means of testing particular experimental hypotheses, they may serve as a rich source of information that can provide the basis for more stringent experimental tests.

E. Archival research

A political rally begins as the speaker steps up to the podium. As the speaker launches into his remarks, the crowd continues to grow. Does the size of the crowd bear any relation to the amount of influence that the speaker exerts on individual listeners? Of course, as the number of people at the rally increases, we expect the absolute number of people who are influenced to increase. But will the proportion of allies be any greater?

Newton and Mann (1980) tested this hypothesis in the context of religious crusade meetings, using an archival research method. These Australian investigators obtained records from the Billy Graham Evangelistic Association on four crusades that took place in Australia in 1978 and 1979. From these records, they extracted two kinds of information: the number of people who attended each meeting and the number who stepped forward at the end of the sermon to make a religious commitment. Figure 2-3 shows the relationship between crowd size and proportion of "inquirers." As predicted, crowd size was related to commitment—the larger the crowd, the greater the proportion of those who came forward—although the relationship held true only for rallies held on weekdays.

Archival research refers to the analysis of any existing records that have been produced or maintained by persons or organizations other than the experimenter. In other words, the original reason for collecting the records was not a social-psychological experiment. Records of a private organization, such as the Graham association, are one example. Other sources of material include newspaper reports, government records, books and magazines, folk stories, personal letters, and speeches by public figures. The study of the use of war paint and societal aggression discussed earlier in the chapter provides another example of archival research. In this case, the material in the Human Relations Area File was originally compiled by social scientists (generally anthropologists) but not for the purpose of testing the hypothesis of deindividuation and aggression.

Advantages. Archival research has a number of advantages. First of all, it allows the investigator to test hypotheses over a wider range of time and societies than would otherwise be possible. Many records date back for centuries, a period of time that cannot be examined using the other methods we have discussed. Demonstrating the validity of a hypothesis in a number of cultures and historical periods, instead of being restricted to a single group in the present time and place, gives us considerable confidence in the validity of that hypothesis as a test of human behavior in general.

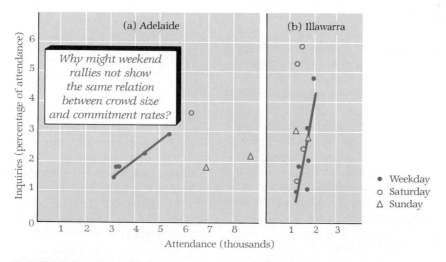

FIGURE 2-3. Relationship between crowd size and percentage of people who made religious "inquiries" after the meeting. The larger the crowd, the greater the proportion of people who made commitments.

A second advantage of the archival method is that it uses **unobtrusive measures**—measures that did not cause reactivity in the participants at the time they were collected (Webb, Campbell, Schwartz, & Sechrest, 1966). Because the information used in archival research was originally collected for some other purpose, there is little or no chance that demand characteristics or evaluation apprehension will be problems for the present investigator.

Disadvantages. Although experimenters doing archival research did not collect the data personally and thus are spared some problems in terms of reactivity, they may encounter difficulties in terms of data availability. Frequently an investigator will not be able to locate the kind of data needed to test a hypothesis. Not being able to design the dependent measures, the investigator is left at the mercy of those who collected the data. Sometimes, of course, creativity and ingenuity will help the investigator to locate the kinds of data needed; in other cases, however, missing or inaccurate records will prevent an adequate experimental test. Even if the material is available, it is sometimes difficult to categorize it in the way necessary to answer the research question. Careful methods of content analysis must be developed for material that is nonquantitative, much as categories are developed for observational research (see p. 42). Such procedures are time-consuming, although the development of computer programs has provided a welcome assist in some instances.

In summary, archival research offers the investigator tremendous opportunities for examining data from a wide range of times and places. Although relying on data that were collected for another purpose may cause problems for the investigator, the appeal of archival research, particularly when used in conjunction with other research methods, is strong.

F. Simulation and role playing

One of the most dramatic studies in social psychology is the prison-**simulation** experiment (see Photo 2-5) conducted at Stanford University by Phillip Zimbardo and his colleagues (Haney, Banks, & Zimbardo, 1973). The simulation began with wailing police sirens as nine young men were picked up at their homes, spread-eagled and frisked, handcuffed, taken to the police station and booked, and finally driven blindfolded to a "prison" in the basement of the Stanford psychology building. There, three other young men dressed as guards supervised the "prisoners'" activities in a small area of the building that had been outfitted with typical prison cells, a small "yard," and even a solitary-confinement "hole."

The subjects in this research project were college students who had answered a newspaper ad for volunteers to take part in a psychological study of prison life. Before acceptance, all applicants were screened, and those selected were judged to be the most stable, most mature, and least antisocial students. All the students agreed to serve in either the guard or the prisoner role and were randomly assigned to one of the two roles by the experimenter.

At the Stanford University "prison," conditions were made as realistic as possible. Prisoners were referred to only by number; their meals were bland and their toilet visits were supervised; they were assigned to work shifts and were lined up three times a day for a count. The guards were allowed to set up most of their own rules for running the prison; however, the use of punishment or physical aggression was prohibited. The project was scheduled to run for two weeks.

During this time, the experimenters maintained constant observation of the situation, using both audio- and videotape equipment, and they administered a series of questionnaire measures as well. However, the intended two-week simulation study had to be abruptly terminated at the end of six days.

Within that six-day period, the behavior of the college men had degenerated rapidly. Guards increasingly enjoyed their power; for example, they issued arbitrary commands to do pushups and refused requests to go to the toilet. Prisoners lapsed into depression and helplessness and began to develop both physical and emotional distress symptoms. It was clear to the experimenters that although the reality of a prison had undoubtedly

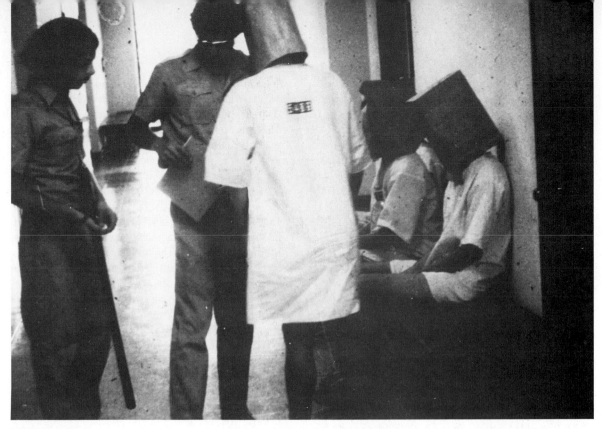

PHOTO 2-5. *"Prisoners" and "guards" in the Stanford prison experiment.*

been created, the situation was too dangerous. After terminating the experiment, the researchers held several sessions with the participants to deal with their emotional reactions to the experience, and they maintained contact with each student for a year after the study to ensure that the negative effects of the prison simulation did not persist.

Not all simulation studies are so dramatic. Subjects may simply be brought to a bare room, given the description of an experimental setting, and asked to act as if they were in the real situation. In this case, the participant in the simulation is being asked to play the role of a subject, rather than a more dramatic role, such as a prisoner or a guard. Somewhere between these two extremes are studies that simulate international decision making, in which subjects are given a large playing board and asked to make political and economic decisions for imaginary countries (Streufert, Castore, & Kliger, 1967). In still another form of simulation, computer programs are developed to model some aspect of behavior, and hundreds or thousands of hypothetical subjects (or computer runs) may be used to test a hypothesis.

Although the range of simulation studies is considerable, the aim of each is to imitate some aspect of a real-world situation in order to gain more understanding of people's psychological processes.

Advantages. The success of a simulation or role-play study depends strongly on the degree of involvement that the experimental setting can engender (Geller, 1978). If the subjects get deeply involved in the setting, then the simulation may well approximate the real-life conditions that it intends to match. Furthermore, because participants are fully informed of the purposes of the study in advance, they basically take on the role of co-investigators, a role that is both ethically and humanistically more satisfying in many respects than the more typical experimental subject role, in which the subject is unaware of many of the experimenter's intentions (Kelman, 1968). An additional advantage of the simulation is that it

may allow the investigator to study in the laboratory phenomena and situations that are difficult
to study in the real world. For example, it is difficult for social scientists to gain access to prisons
or to negotiations between warring countries;
however, the investigator can simulate them in the
laboratory or on the computer with the additional
advantages of experimental control of variables
and random assignment of subjects.

Disadvantages.   In spite of their advantages,
simulation and role playing are two of the most
controversial methods in the social-psychological
repertoire (Cooper, 1976; Forward, Canter, &
Kirsch, 1976; Hendrick, 1977; Miller, 1972). Critics
of the method claim that when one asks subjects
to act as if they were in a certain role, the subjects
will do only what they think they *might* do, not
necessarily what they *would* do in the real situation (Aronson & Carlsmith, 1968; Carlsmith et al.,
1976).

In addition, the problems of experimental
demands and evaluation apprehension, discussed
earlier in relation to laboratory experiments, are
even more serious when the subject is fully informed
of the purposes of the study. Proponents of role
playing, however, argue that, to some degree, the
participant in an experiment is always playing a
role, whether it is the general role of subject or a
more specific role defined by the investigator.
Computer simulations avoid these particular criticisms, but questions can be raised about their
correspondence to actual behavior.

This controversy is difficult to resolve and will
probably continue for several years. Some of the
issues in the controversy can be resolved empirically, by social psychologists conducting experiments directed at the methodological practices
themselves. Other aspects of the argument may
be more philosophical and, like the theories of
Chapter 1, may reflect overriding views of human
nature.

G. Surveys and interviews

An assessment of the quality of life in the United
States was the objective of a large-scale interview
study conducted by Campbell, Converse, and Rogers (1976). Using a carefully selected sample of
2164 persons, 18 years or older and representing
all segments of the population and all regions of
the country, these investigators conducted lengthy
interviews to determine how satisfied people were
with their life in general and with particular areas
such as job, marriage, and health. The initial results
of the study showed that most people were reasonably happy with their lives. However, a closer
analysis showed that subjective feelings of satisfaction are very clearly related to objective characteristics of the life situation. For example, degree
of marital satisfaction is related to educational
level, as illustrated in Figure 2-4. People with less
education are more likely to report that they are
completely satisfied with their marriage than those
with more education. It is also worth noting that
the differences between men and women in
reported marital satisfaction are greatest at the
two extremes of educational level.

This study of the perceived quality of life is an
example of an **interview** study, in which a
researcher questions people according to a predetermined schedule and records their answers.
Similar to this is the **questionnaire survey,** in
which respondents read the questions themselves
and provide written answers (Jacoby, in preparation). Although many other methods in social
psychology make use of questionnaires as part of
their procedures, survey and interview methods
rely *solely* on this type of information. In both
cases, the investigator defines an area for research
and designs a set of questions that will elicit the
beliefs, attitudes, and self-reported experiences of
the respondent in relation to the research topic.

Designing a good questionnaire is not as easy as
it might appear. Considerations that enter into the
design include the wording of questions, the pro-
vision of sufficient responses, and the format of
the questionnaire itself (Jacoby, in preparation).
For example, the wording of a question may sys-

FIGURE 2-4. Relationship of marital satisfaction to
educational level.

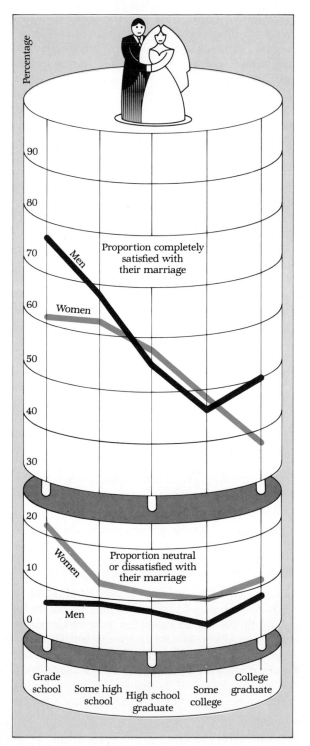

Percentage

Proportion completely satisfied with their marriage

Men

Women

Women

Men

Proportion neutral or dissatisfied with their marriage

90

80

70

60

50

40

30

20

10

0

Grade school   Some high school   High school graduate   Some college   College graduate

tematically bias the answers. Politicians often use this tactic to their advantage. For example, a question that begins "I agree that Candidate X . . ." is more likely to receive a positive response than a question that begins with "Does Candidate X . . ." Considerable pretesting is necessary to ensure that the questions are objective, unbiased, understandable to the average respondent, and specific enough to elicit the desired information.

When the interviewer administers the questionnaire, additional precautions are necessary. Experimenter bias, discussed earlier in relation to laboratory experiments, can be a problem in the interview method if the interviewer consciously or unconsciously encourages some responses and discourages or seems uninterested in others. Hence, interviewers must be carefully trained to standardize their delivery of questions. In addition, the interviewer must be able to develop rapport, so that the respondent will be willing to answer questions straightforwardly and honestly.

In both questionnaire surveys and interviews, the investigator must be concerned with *sampling procedures.* If the researcher wants to generalize to a larger population—for example, the entire population of the United States and Canada—it is not necessary to contact every member of that population. A sample or a subset of perhaps 2000 people can be chosen that will, if selected properly, be an accurate reflection of the total population. Improper sample selection, however, is almost certain to produce inaccurate results. For example, many televised news programs feature a roving reporter who asks passing pedestrians their opinion on some topical issue. Such samplings are undoubtedly not systematic and probably tell us very little about the general population.

Advantages.   A major advantage of both survey questionnaires and interviews is that they can be very straightforward and specific. Rather than devising a situation to elicit desired behavior or finding a natural situation in which to observe that behavior, constructors of questionnaires directly question people about the topic under investigation. In some cases, this is the only approach to desired information. For example, if

PHOTO 2-6. *Survey and interview methods rely solely on the information provided by the respondents' answers.*

you were interested in the events of a person's childhood, directly asking the person about those events might be the only way to find out.

Interview and survey-questionnaire research methods also have their own particular advantages and disadvantages, which tend to balance out. For instance, survey questionnaires are easier and more economical to use than interview procedures. In addition, they provide greater anonymity for the respondent, which is important for sensitive or personal issues. Face-to-face interviews, however, allow the interviewer to gather additional information from observation. Furthermore, the interviewer can clarify questions that may be confusing to the respondent and can also be sure which person in the household is answering the questions.

Disadvantages. Perhaps the major difficulty with self-report data, whether from interviews or surveys, is the issue of accuracy. When asked about childhood events, for example, a respondent may or may not recall what actually happened. Even for more recent events, either unintentional or deliberate bias may occur. Surveys of sexual behavior are frequently questioned on these grounds: critics suggest that people may be less than honest in describing their own sexual practices. Other topics may lead to embellishments by the respondent, who attempts to appear favorably. (This process is another form of evaluation apprehension, discussed earlier in relation to the experimental method.)

Survey questionnaires and interviews have opposite sets of weaknesses. The survey questionnaire gives the investigator less control over the situation and cannot assure the conditions under which the questionnaire is being administered, who is answering it, and whether the respondent fully understands the questions. For its part, the interview is more costly, more time-consuming, and more susceptible to examiner bias.

In summary, questionnaire and interview methods allow the investigator to ask directly about the issues of concern. Particularly with questionnaires, very large-scale studies are possible, thus allowing greater generalizability of the results. Both methods, however, rely on the accuracy and honesty of the respondent and depend on self-reports of behavior rather than observations of the behavior itself.

■ IV. Some issues in research

Social psychologists have a variety of research methods at their disposal. From this wealth of possibilities, how does the investigator decide on one particular method? Further, once the investigator has formulated a question or hypothesis and selected a research method, what other issues must he or she consider? In this section, we will deal with some of the major concerns that face the experimenter as an idea becomes translated into a research project.

A. Selection of method and setting

As we have seen, each method has its own set of advantages and disadvantages. In the abstract, there is no best method. In a particular case, however, there may be a method that is most appropriate to use, and this decision returns us to a consideration of hypothesis formulation.

In the initial stages of research, questions may be only vaguely defined. An investigator may be interested in something concrete, such as communes, the jury system, or a particular religious group. Such topics would probably guide the investigator to the natural setting—that is, to a field study—or to the use of a survey or interview method. In other cases, the investigator's questions may involve something more abstract—for example, why people like each other, what causes aggression, or how we attribute intentionality to others' behavior. Here the possibilities for study are much more numerous. To illustrate this distinction, reconsider the case of Triplett, who did the first study in social psychology. Had he been interested in the behavior of cyclists, his likely choices would have been to observe or to ask questions of the cyclists themselves or perhaps to dig into the archival records of past races. His concern was not, however, the concrete topic of cyclists but, rather, the more abstract concept of competition and the effect of the presence of others on performance. With this concept in mind, he was free to retreat to his laboratory and use children instead of cyclists and fishing reels instead of racing bikes.

Ellsworth (1977), in discussing the selection of a research method, notes that there are some basic concerns that the investigator always has. "In brief, one wants an instance that is capable of disconfirming the hypothesis, that allows for fairly precise specification of both independent and dependent variables, that is free of serious confounds, and that is informative, allowing the investigator to collect supplementary data that will be helpful in understanding the results" (p. 606).

The possibility of disconfirming the hypothesis is important. Although scientists, like most people, enjoy finding out that they are right, it is crucial that their experiments be not simply a demonstration of what was known all along but, rather, a true questioning process. As the eminent biologist Albert Szent-Györgyi once stated, "Research means going out into the unknown with the hope of finding something new to bring home. If you know in advance what you are going to do or even find there, then it is not research at all: then it is only a kind of honorable occupation" (1971).

Sometimes an investigator will begin in the laboratory, testing a theory under highly controlled conditions, and then move out to the field to see whether the same principles hold. On other occasions, a reverse strategy is used, as when relationships observed in a field study are then taken back to the laboratory for testing with the hope of more precisely defining cause-and-effect relationships. Such a back-and-forth strategy was, in fact, one of the dictums of Kurt Lewin, often considered the forefather of modern social psychology.

The advantages of such a strategy should be evident after our discussion of the various research methods. Because each method has its own particular set of weaknesses, it is impossible to rely on any single one for a full understanding of a phenomenon. Thus, the question is not which method is best but which set of methods will be best. As Webb and his colleagues note, "If a proposition can survive the onslaught of a series of imperfect measures, with all their irrelevant error, confidence should be placed in it" (Webb et al., 1966, p. 3). This principle of *triangulation*—of focusing on a single concept from a variety of vantage points—represents a key strategy in the conduct of social-psychological research.

B. Units of analysis

An investigator's decisions do not end with the definition of a question and the choice of a research method. The next decisions to be made concern the types of data that will be collected and the procedures to be used for analyzing those data. Depending on the way a hypothesis is framed, an investigator may be interested in the *frequency*, the *rate*, or the *level* of a particular behavior. For example, we might ask how often married couples engage in physical aggression or what percentage of people are willing to help a person who has fallen down in a subway. These are questions about frequency of occurrence. On other occasions, the concern may be with the rate of a behavior, as measured in units of behavior per person or per segment of time. For example, we might want to know how many contacts a kindergarten teacher has with pupils each day. Still other questions might focus on the specific level of a behavior, as when one measures the degree of attraction between two persons or the level of shock a subject administers in an aggression experiment.

A second and related issue concerns how to analyze the data we collect. Although this is not the place for an elaborate discussion of statistics, a few basics should be mentioned that will aid in understanding the research to be discussed in later chapters. In general, we can talk about four types of questions that may be asked when analyzing data: they involve central tendency, variability, association, and measures of difference.

In the case of *central tendency*, we are asking what the average response for a group of people is. For example, what is the average income of a college graduate, or what is the average attitude of Canadians on the issue of independence for Quebec?

Variability refers to the dispersion of responses (Thorngate, 1974). For example, rather than knowing the average opinion of Canadians about independence for Quebec, it might be more informative to know the degree to which these opinions vary. Are most Canadians generally favorable toward the separatist movement, or do the opinions vary widely from strong opposition to strong support?

A third question that the investigator may ask involves the *association* between two variables. In the study of religious crusades, for example, the analysis dealt with the correlation between two types of data—size of crowd and number of conversions.

Finally, an investigator may be concerned with the *differences* among two or more groups. "Are men more satisfied with marriage than women?" is an example of this type of question. Another example would be a study that asked whether high-status or low-status speakers were more effective in changing listeners' attitudes.

In each of the last two examples, we are concerned only with one factor: sex in the first example and prestige of the communicator in the second example. Often, however, social psychologists are interested in looking at the effects of two or more independent variables simultaneously. For example, earlier in the chapter we discussed an experiment by Deaux and Emswiller (1974) in which subjects were asked to evaluate the performance of either a male or a female who successfully completed either a masculine or a feminine task. This study is an example of a 2×2 factorial experiment: one factor was the sex of the stimulus person (either male or female), and the other factor was the sex linkage of the task (also with two levels, masculine and feminine).[1] One reason for combining two or more factors in a single experiment is to more closely approximate the real world, where many factors may operate simultaneously. Often the results of such experiments give us more information than we would have if we studied only one variable at a time. These results are frequently found in the form of **interaction,** as shown in Figure 2-5. *Interaction* is a statistical term referring to the fact that the effect of one variable depends on the level or state of the other variable. Thus, in the example in Figure 2-5, the evaluations that subjects made about male and female students' performances depended on the type of task. On the masculine task, judgments about the male and female students were very different, whereas on the feminine task, the judgments were almost identical. In such a case, information about the **main effect**—the effect that either one of the variables has by itself, not considering the other factor—is much less informative than the combined information represented by the interaction.

C. Ethics of research

Beyond the technical issues already discussed, there is another set of concerns that an investi-

---

[1]Actually, the Deaux and Emswiller experiment had a third factor, the sex of the subject, thus making it a $2 \times 2 \times 2$ factorial design. This factor did not affect the results, however; male and female subjects made the same judgments.

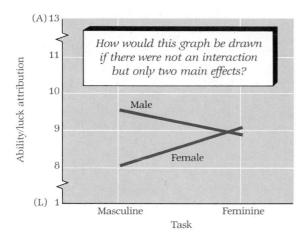

FIGURE 2-5. A two-way interaction: Ability/luck attributions as a function of sex of task and performer.

gator must consider before conducting an experiment—the ethical aspects. In recent years, social psychologists have become increasingly aware of the ethical questions involved in research. In part, pressures for such consideration have originated in the federal and state governments. The U.S. Department of Health and Human Services has issued a set of guidelines, for example, that all recipients of grants and contracts must follow. Within the profession, there has been considerable concern as well, evidenced in numerous books and articles (for example, Carlsmith et al., 1976; Cook, 1976; Kelman, 1968; Schlenker & Forsyth, 1977) and by a set of guidelines developed by the American Psychological Association (1973). In fact, some research has shown that social psychologists are far more stringent in their ethical evaluation of research practices than other academicians, law professors, and the students who frequently participate in such research (Rugg, 1975; Schwartz & Gottlieb, 1981).

The ethical issues in research are numerous and complex, and they cannot be fully resolved in this chapter. There are, however, a number of important points we should consider briefly.

One concern is the level of pain or stress that a subject experiences. This question is more prominent in the medical and biological sciences because experimentation with new drugs or surgical procedures can have irreversible effects. For social psychologists, the concern is generally with psychological rather than physical harm. For example, an investigator interested in the effects of negative personal evaluation on subsequent interaction may purposely expose a subject to uncomplimentary information. Such information can cause considerable stress. Other experimental situations may give the subject an opportunity to shock another person, sometimes with coercion from the experimenter to increase the level of shock (Milgram, 1963). In such cases, even if no shock is actually being delivered, subjects may get very upset as they try to comply with the experimenter's demands.

An experimenter should always try to minimize the amount of stress that a subject experiences. At the same time, it is difficult to argue that stressful events should never be studied (West & Gunn, 1978). Although it is certainly more pleasant to focus one's research attention on positive forms of human behavior, humans do display a reasonable amount of undesirable behavior as well. The social psychologist, in seeking to understand the full range of human behavior, is obligated to consider both positive and negative aspects of human interaction.

One solution is use of *informed consent.* Insofar as possible, the experimenter should inform subjects in advance about the requirements of the experiment and obtain their consent to participate. Thus, if a subject is to be exposed to electrical shock, it is the experimenter's obligation to inform the subject of that fact in advance. Although informed consent is an important principle for any area of study, it is much more important in those studies in which the potential for stress or pain is high.

Informed-consent procedures are relatively easy to institute in the laboratory experiment, in which the investigator has a great deal of control over the total situation. But what of the field experiment? As discussed earlier, field experiments are generally carried out without the knowledge of the participants. For that reason, the investigator must plan field experiments carefully. *Invasion of privacy* is an important consideration. If a subject has been fully informed of procedures and has given consent, the experimenter will probably not be intruding unfairly. In a situation such as the field experiment, however, in which informed consent is not the rule, the investigator must be particularly concerned about unreasonable intrusion. Although it is difficult to formulate specific criteria for an acceptable field experiment, we saw in our earlier discussion of such experiments that their similarity to a normal situation is a working rule of thumb.

In the field study, in which the experimenter does not tamper with the environment, some of the ethical concerns are resolved. Even in this setting, however, investigators must consider carefully the potential for invading the privacy of individuals.

Another ethical concern of experimenters relates to the practice of deceiving subjects, either by withholding certain information or by purposely misleading them. Such procedures are fairly common in social-psychological research (Gross & Fleming, 1982). Scientifically, there is some justification for such procedures. The problems of demand characteristics and evaluation apprehension, discussed earlier, lead many investigators to develop elaborate scenarios so that the subject will

PHOTO 2-7. Some research studies are done in the laboratory; others, by observing people in their natural environment.

be unaware of the true purpose of the experiment. However, although deception can occasionally be justified, it is undoubtedly true that the technique has been abused. To counter this practice, many social psychologists have argued strongly for role playing as an alternative approach to research, although, as we have seen, that method is not without its own set of problems.

When informed consent is required, deceptive experiments are less likely. If deception is part of the procedure, it is critical that the experimenter undertake a thorough debriefing with all participants as soon as the experiment is completed. **Debriefing,** a term borrowed from the space program and the military, refers to the process whereby an experimenter reveals the complete procedure to the subject. An investigator should be certain that subjects are not permanently harmed by their experience and that they leave the laboratory feeling no worse than they did on entering.

A final ethical concern of the social psychologist concerns the confidentiality of the data that are obtained and the anonymity of the participants. Protecting subjects' confidentiality should be done routinely by investigators, and the subjects should be informed that confidentiality is preserved.

Few questions of ethics are easily resolved, and often the investigator must carefully weigh the question of scientific value against the rights of the subject. Ultimately, investigators must decide for themselves whether or not to conduct an experiment, although numerous checks exist in the form of colleague and review-committee sanctions. Each time a study is begun, the investigator must consider all the available options and determine the best way to answer the research question, keeping a multitude of complex factors in balance.

In conclusion, the process of "invading the unknown" is complex but exciting. The investigator must make numerous decisions along the way, and each one will contribute to the ultimate success or failure of the project. Not all questions are easily answered; their solutions may take dozens of studies and years of effort by many investigators. The results of many such efforts will be the topic of the remainder of this book.

V. SUMMARY

Research is an exacting and exciting endeavor. The process of research is a lengthy one, beginning with an idea and moving through decisions on how to test the idea, completion of the actual research, and, finally, analysis and interpretation of the data. Each of these stages is important to the final product, which is the answer to some question about human behavior.

Sources for experimental hypotheses are numerous, ranging from casual observation to complex hypothetico-deductive systems. Once a question is formulated, there are many ways to attempt to answer it. Any question can be answered using several methods.

At least seven specific methods are available to the social-psychology researcher: laboratory experiments, field experiments, quasi-experimental research, field studies, archival research, simulations and role playing, and surveys and interviews. Each of these methods has certain advantages and disadvantages.

The selection of any one research method depends in part on the question being asked. In the long run, however, it is important for the investigator to test each question with a variety of methods, thereby canceling out the disadvantages of each single method and gaining more confidence in the validity of the research results. Further, different types of statistical analysis techniques are required to test different hypotheses.

Finally, investigators must give careful thought to ethical issues. Social-psychology research involves people, and the rights of these participants in the research process must be recognized and protected at all times.

GLOSSARY TERMS

archival research	experimenter expectancies	mundane realism
correlational method	external validity	participant observer
debriefing	independent variables	questionnaire survey
deindividuation	interaction	randomization
demand characteristics	internal validity	reliability
dependent variables	interview	simulation
evaluation apprehension	main effect	unobtrusive measure
experimental realism	manipulation check	

The Self

Show me the sensible person who likes himself or herself! I know myself too well to like what I see. I know but too well that I'm not what I'd like to be.
■ GOLDA MEIR

The image of myself which I try to create in my own mind that I may love myself is very different from the image which I try to create in the minds of others in order that they may love me.
■ W. H. AUDEN

Portions of this chapter are based on material prepared by Mark Snyder for earlier editions of this book.

"Begin at the beginning," the King of Hearts told the White Rabbit in *Alice in Wonderland*. And so we begin our understanding of social behavior with the self, a starting point for most of the more complex interactions discussed later.

The concept of the self is one of the oldest and most enduring ideas in psychology, dating from the first definitions of the field itself. Yet, it is an idea not limited to psychology. Early philosophers advised us to "know thyself," and poets have told us "To thine own self be true"; more recent scribes have written hundreds of books dealing with ways to self-knowledge. Further reflecting this interest, the *Oxford English Dictionary* lists over 100 words that focus on the self, from *self-abasement* to *self-wisdom*.

How often do you think about aspects of yourself? When you decided to go to college, did you wonder whether you had the ability or the drive to succeed? When you go out with someone, do you worry whether your date will find you charming, interesting, and fun to be with? When you're alone in your room at night, do you ever introspect, weighing the good points and bad points of your self? For most of us, all these moments are common occurrences.

The self is clearly important—but is it a topic for social psychology? Yes, as we shall see, it is, for the self is a *social* construction, formed on the basis of our interaction with others. Not only is the self defined in the process of such interactions, but it can affect a wide range of social behaviors. How we judge other people, how we communicate with them, whether we choose to be leaders or followers, when we are willing to help a person in need—each of these behaviors can be influenced by our view of ourselves.

Later chapters will deal with some of these consequences of self-reference. In this chapter, to begin at the beginning, we will look at the basic idea of a self. First we will consider how the self is defined, looking at some of the components of the more general notion of self. Then we will describe some of the situations that make people more aware of themselves, and we will consider some forms of self-analysis—the ways that people evaluate their own abilities and explain their actions. Finally, we will look at the self in social interaction, describing the ways in which people choose to present themselves to other people.

■ I. Nature of the self

In trying to describe the self, we will not have to review all 100 of the dictionary terms. Instead, we will limit ourselves to a few terms that psychologists have found to be most useful in describing the self: *self-concept, self-schema,* and *self-esteem.* First, however, it is important to consider some of the theoretical viewpoints dealing with what and why the self is.

A. Theories of the self

Philosopher and psychologist William James was one of the most articulate theorists of the self, and his writings still influence current thought. For James, the sense of self—or that which a person regards as "me"—was defined in the broadest possible terms. The self, according to James, includes body and mind, clothes and house, spouse and children, ancestors and friends, reputation and possessions (James, 1890). Experiences that involve any one of these elements, he believed, affect one's sense of well-being and self-worth. Nearly 100 years later, most contemporary psychologists would agree that the self is defined in terms of many features and that almost any experience we have may have implications for our self-concepts.

James also believed that the experience of selfhood is very much a social experience—that is, our personal identities are critically dependent on our relationships with other people. In fact, it was James who first sensitized us to the identity-threatening consequences that would occur if relationships with people were eliminated:

If no one turned around when we entered, answered when we spoke, or minded what we did, but if every person we met "cut us dead," and acted as if we were nonexisting things, a kind of rage and impotent despair would ere long well up in us, from which the cruelest bodily tortures would be a relief; for these would make us feel that, however bad might be our plight, we had not sunk to such a depth as to be unworthy of attention at all [1890, Vol. 1, pp. 293–294].

James's ideas have continued to influence theorists of the self. Many other theorists have also discussed the self, such as Charles Cooley (1902/1922), George Herbert Mead (1934), and Harry Stack Sullivan (1953). Although these theorists emphasize different aspects of self-development, they all agree on the social construction of the self. We have a sense of self because of our interactions with other people, and those interactions become internalized as part of what we think about ourselves. These thoughts that we have about ourselves—the **self-concept**—serve to define our identity, and in turn they influence the way that we react to later events and circumstances.

B. Components of the self-concept

Because so many elements can be part of the self-concept, many investigators have tried to define a few limited categories. William James, for example, divided the elements of the "me" into three categories: the material me, the social me, and the spiritual me. Included in the material me are one's body, clothing, family, house, and all other material possessions. The central component of the social me is the recognition we receive from friends and acquaintances—in particular, the favorable regard experienced in relationships with other people. Characteristics of the spiritual me are our inner experiences, abilities, sensibilities, values, and ideals, which are the most enduring parts of our sense of selfhood.

Yet, not every aspect of the self may be equally important to all people. One person may focus on the material me, another person on the social me. To chart the features of a particular person's identity, psychologists have developed the "Who Am I" technique. With this method, people are asked to provide answers to the question "Who am I?" (for details, see Bugental & Zelen, 1950; Gordon, 1968; Kuhn & McPartland, 1954). Their answers to this question constitute the **spontaneous self-concept**—the self-description that a person gives without any guidelines from an experimenter as

to what dimensions might be important. In using this method, it is assumed that people will mention the things that are most salient or central to them. Among college students, the most common responses deal with age, gender, student status, interpersonal style (for example, shy or friendly), personality characteristics (for example, moody or optimistic), and body image (Gordon, 1968).

The prominence of certain features in the spontaneous self-concept can be influenced by the environment. McGuire and his colleagues have shown that the self-concept will often reflect features of identity that make people distinct from those around them (McGuire & McGuire, 1981). For example, in one investigation, fourth-grade children were asked to tell the investigators about themselves. As the results displayed in Figure 3-1 show, children were much more likely to mention their gender spontaneously when they came from households in which that gender was in the minority. For example, being female was a particularly important feature of the spontaneous self-concepts of girls who came from families with males in the majority. In contrast, if a girl came from a family that had a larger portion of females, she was much less likely to mention that she was a girl when asked for a self-description.

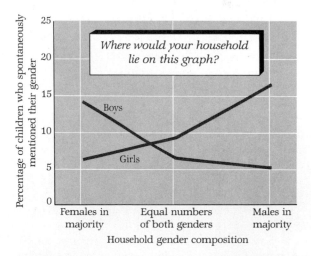

FIGURE 3-1. Prominence of gender in the spontaneous self-concept in relation to gender composition of respondents' households.

The spontaneous self-concept can also be influenced by immediate circumstances. For example, McGuire has found that children who are taller or shorter than average are more likely to mention their height than are children of average height; children who are older or younger than most of their classmates are more likely to mention age (McGuire & Padawer-Singer, 1976). At a broader cultural level, the self-concept can also be affected by social and political circumstances, as Box 3-1 shows. Thus, we define ourselves, at least in part, in terms of our differences from other people, a definition process that clearly illustrates the importance of social factors to the self-concept.

C. Self-schemata

Concepts of the self are not simply surface descriptions that we use when someone asks us who we are. Beyond that, beliefs about the self may affect the way we see the world and the way we retain information about experiences and events. Cognitive psychologists have developed the notion of a **schema**—a cognitive structure that aids in the processing of information. As we will see in Chapter 4, such cognitive structures can influence our interpretations of other people and events. The concept of schema can also be applied to the self (**self-schema**). As defined by Markus, self-schemata are "cognitive generalizations about the self, derived from past experience, that organize and

BOX 3-1. Self-concepts of Israeli children

Both Arab and Jewish children live in Israel, but their circumstances are quite different. The Jewish children are part of the predominant religious group, while Arab children are part of a more marginal group in that society. Hence, even though their nationality is the same, we might expect these two groups of children to have somewhat different self-concepts. John Hofman and his colleagues considered this question, assessing the self-concept of 740 Jewish adolescents and 750 Arab adolescents in Jewish and Arab schools in Israel (Hofman, Beit-Hallahmi, & Hertz-Lazarowitz, 1982).

In some respects, these two groups were similar, reflecting common concerns that adolescents of all groups and countries have. In other respects, however, they differed. The most prominent elements of self-concept among the Jewish children were self-praise, life satisfaction, and world outlook. Among the Arab children, factors such as self-criticism, religion, and peer relationships stood out. In general, the Arab children had a less favorable self-concept, perhaps reflecting their more marginal status within Israeli society. ■

PHOTO 3-1. *Traveling alone often allows time for self-reflection.*

guide the processing of self-related information contained in the individual's social experiences" (1977, p. 64).

As we have already seen, people may have very different self-concepts. In the same way, people's self-schemata may differ. For example, some people think of themselves as very independent, others as rather dependent; for still other people, the dimension of independence/dependence is irrelevant to their self-concept. To understand how these different self-schemata can affect the organization of information, Markus (1977) selected three groups of people who defined themselves differently in terms of independence: some rated themselves as extremely independent, some as extremely dependent, and others more neutrally, suggesting that neither end of this dimension was particularly central to their self-concept. Markus then asked each of these groups of subjects to participate in a series of tasks that included making judgments about the self and providing descriptions of behavioral events that related to independence or dependence. Her results showed how the self-schema can affect the processing of information. Subjects who described themselves as independent, for example, showed much faster agreement when provided a list of adjectives that related to independence. They were also able to think of more specific incidents of their own independent behavior than either of the other groups was—but they were less able to think of occasions when they had been dependent. Subjects who had described themselves as dependent showed just the opposite pattern, responding well when dealing with dependency but taking more time with independence and providing fewer examples of it. The aschematics—people who did not clearly define themselves in terms of either independence or dependence—showed no differences in information processing between the two kinds of tasks.

Independence is just one dimension that has been used to illustrate the operation of the self-schema. In fact, almost any personality trait is probably central to the schemata of some people and irrelevant for others. Honesty may be the organizing principle for some people, while masculinity or femininity may be a central concept for other people (Markus, Crane, Bernstein, & Siladi, 1982). Self-schemata may also operate in more general terms. For example, Kuiper and MacDonald (1982) compared normal subjects with mildly depressed subjects, using a task similar to Markus's. Normal subjects recalled significantly more positive information about themselves than negative information. In contrast, depressives recalled equal amounts of the two kinds of self-descriptive information and generally took more time to make all judgments.

Nor are self-schemata limited to verbal material. Part of our self-concept also involves visual images—for example, what we look like (or how we would like to look). Investigators have found that people are more likely to remember photographs of themselves that most closely resemble their physical self-image than to remember pictures that are more discrepant from that self-image, even though all the photos were taken at the same time (Yarmey & Johnson, 1982). For example, if you think of yourself as a serious person, you might be more likely to remember a picture that portrayed you without a smile, rather than one that showed you laughing merrily at the camera. Thus, in a variety of ways, our visions of ourselves affect our visions of the world.

D. Self-esteem

The self-concept, as we have described it so far, is rather neutral: the components of the self may vary, but they are not necessarily good or bad. Yet, a number of psychologists have suggested that any judgment we make involves some evaluation of good or bad (Rychlak, 1973, 1975; Zajonc, 1980), and this evaluation process can apply to the self as well. As Pearl Bailey once stated, "There's a period of life when we swallow a knowledge of ourselves and it becomes either good or sour inside."

This evaluation of oneself in either positive or negative ways is termed **self-esteem.** Psychologists have developed a number of measures to assess self-esteem (for example, Coopersmith, 1967). In general, these measures assume that a person's self-esteem is relatively stable. In other words, it is believed that some people tend to feel good about themselves most of the time, while others rate themselves more negatively a good part of the time.

Although self-esteem shows a certain degree of stability, it can be temporarily affected by particular events. For example, failing to get a promotion or losing a job would probably cause a person to become more negative in his or her self-evaluations. In contrast, falling in love or being elected president of an organization would probably increase self-esteem. Not only can such events cause a shift in general self-evaluation, but they may affect a person's memory for past events as well. Natale and Hantas (1982) hypnotized subjects and then read them a series of either positive or negative self-referent statements, thereby creating moods of either elation or depression. Subjects were then asked to recall personal memories, either happy, sad, or ordinary. Mood affected memory: depressed subjects recalled fewer happy memories and more sad ones. All subjects, however, recalled more pleasant than unpleasant memories, suggesting that people may have a general tendency to remember positive experiences. Similar results have been reported by other investigators, underlining the importance of mood both to present thoughts and to past recall (Bower, 1981; Isen, Shalker, Clark, & Karp, 1978; Snyder & White, 1982).

Our satisfaction with life in general appears to be closely tied to our own feelings of self-worth. Specific role relationships may also affect feelings of personal adequacy. In an interesting comparison of psychological well-being of U.S. adults in 1957 and 1976, Bryant and Veroff (1982) found that the relative importance of certain role relationships appears to be changing. For example, in 1957 marital happiness played a more important part in overall satisfaction for both men and women than in 1976. However, satisfaction with the role of parent contributed more to the overall happiness of both sexes in 1976. For men, dissatisfactions with their job became less central to their happiness in the 1970s. One possible reason for this shift is the greater uncertainty about employment in the later period. Perhaps, as conditions become worse for a great many people, individual job problems are less diagnostic of one's own personal worth. It is also worth noting that this investigation of well-being showed many fewer sex differences in 1976 than in 1957, suggesting that changes in attitudes during the two intervening decades may have made the male and female outlooks more similar.

■ II. Becoming aware of the self

Although the self is always with us, one's awareness and concern with self-concepts may vary from time to time. For example, if you are in the habit of walking immediately to the television set after you get up in the morning, switching on the national news, and then walking into the kitchen for coffee, you probably do not engage in much self-reflection when you do this for the 50th day in a row. Langer (1978a) has called such behaviors "mindless," suggesting that the self is not engaged in sequences of behavior that are overlearned. In other situations, as in the deindividuation studies discussed in Chapter 2, particular circumstances may minimize attention to the self, creating a sense of anonymity. In contrast, if you walk into a party filled with people you have never met, all of whom turn to stare at you as you enter, you will probably engage in considerable self-reflection, wondering how you look and what your next move should be. In this second example, we see how important the environment can be to our awareness of our selves.

A. A theory of self-perception

Daryl Bem (1967, 1972) has proposed a **self-perception theory,** suggesting that we become aware of ourselves simply by watching what we do. As Bem has described this process, "Individuals come to 'know' their own attitudes, emotions, and other internal states partially by inferring them from observations of their own overt behavior and/ or the circumstances in which this behavior occurs" (1972, p. 5). In other words, he suggests that people don't have a great deal of "inside information" about who they are or why they do things. Rather, much as an outside observer would do, people look at what they are doing and infer a reason for that behavior.

Bem's theory, which relies greatly on the behavioristic principles of B. F. Skinner, assumes that we are generally aware of *reinforcement contingencies* that affect our behavior. For example, suppose you find yourself doing two hours of weight-reducing exercises every day. Why might you be doing this, and what does it say about you? Perhaps, in stopping to think about it, you realize that you have been sweating vigorously ever since your favorite date said that he or she liked only thin and well-conditioned people. In that case, you might conclude that the extrinsic reinforcement from your favorite date was the main cause of your behavior. But what if your date didn't care a bit about your physical condition? Without this external motivator, you—as well as a neutral observer—might conclude that exercise reflected an internal value or attitude that you had—perhaps a belief in the importance of fitness. Thus, observing your own behavior would lead to inferences about the self. Bem would not claim that all aspects of the self are defined in terms of this "after the fact" observation process, but he claims that the process does operate whenever internal cues are weak or ambiguous.

Can we also learn about ourselves from being aware of what we don't do? For example, if I see myself jogging every morning, I may well conclude that jogging reflects something about my self-definition. But what if I don't jog—does that say something as well? Earlier research in the psychology of problem solving suggested that people are less adept at using negative instances of an event than at using positive instances when trying to find a solution, even if both instances logically provide the same amount of information. The same tendency seems to be true in the self-perception process, as people are more likely to infer characteristics about themselves on the basis of what they did do than on the basis of what they did not do (Fazio, Sherman, & Herr, 1982). Thus, if I am a regular jogger, I may well see myself as energetic and athletic. However, if I do not jog or engage in other sports, I am less likely to label myself unathletic or lazy, even though the characterization may be equally true.

B. Self-perception of emotions

Whereas Bem dealt more generally with images of the self, Schachter and his colleagues have looked more specifically at one particular aspect, that of emotional experience (Schachter, 1964; Schachter & Singer, 1962). Again, however, they point to the importance of environmental cues as a guide to self-definition. According to Schachter, the experience of emotion depends on two factors: a state of physiological arousal and an appropriate cognitive label for that arousal.

To test their ideas, Schachter and Singer (1962) conducted an ingenious experiment, using a drug (epinephrine) that causes an increased state of arousal—flushed face, increased heart rate, and occasional trembling. All subjects in this experiment were told that the experimenter was studying the effects of certain drugs on visual abilities. Some subjects who were given epinephrine were told correctly what the effects of the drug would be. Others were misinformed: the experimenter suggested that the drug would cause such sensations as numbness in the feet. A third group was given the same shot of epinephrine but was provided no information about the expected side effects. Finally, a fourth group of subjects was given a placebo that contained no epinephrine at all and was given no explanation.

After receiving either a drug or a placebo, each subject was taken to a waiting room where one other person was waiting for the vision tests to begin. This person was not simply another subject, however. He was a confederate of the experimenter, instructed to engage in a variety of euphoric

PHOTO 3-2. *Awareness of one's own behavior may lead to inferences about the self: "I jog, therefore I must be concerned about my health."*

and occasionally silly activities while waiting with the true subject. Hula hoops, paper airplanes, and imaginary basketball games were all part of his act, intended to make an emotional label of euphoria or happiness available to the subject.

To summarize the experiment so far, each of the four groups of subjects is in a somewhat different condition. Subjects in three of the groups are experiencing a state of arousal, due to the epinephrine, but only one of these three groups has been told to expect this arousal state. All four of the groups have been in the presence of a humorous confederate, who might make them feel rather euphoric as well. Now let us think back to Schachter's original hypothesis. Emotional experience depends on having both a state of physiological arousal and an appropriate label for that arousal. For the subjects who were told the correct side effects of epinephrine, an explanation for their arousal was easy to find. They felt aroused because of the drug. For the subjects who got epinephrine but either received no warning about its effects or were given misleading information, what explanation was available? The cause of their arousal wasn't the drug, so it must be something else. And as Figure 3-2 shows, this "something else" was identified as a euphoric mood, influenced by the antics of their partner. In other words, when these subjects could not explain their arousal internally, they looked to an external cue to label their arousal.

For subjects in the placebo condition, who had no physiological arousal to explain, self-reported euphoria was also less.

These predictions are not limited to happy emotions. Using similar procedures, but instructing the confederate to act in a hostile manner, Schachter and Singer (1962) also showed how the emotional experience of anger could be influenced in the same way. Subjects who had an explanation for their arousal reported less anger than subjects who did not.

Can our emotions really be manipulated so easily? Perhaps not as easily as Schachter and Singer suggested. Later research has qualified these earlier findings, pointing out that although environmental cues certainly do aid in the interpretation of arousal, it is not so certain that one state of arousal will be automatically misinterpreted in favor of environmental explanations (Marshall & Zimbardo, 1979; Rule & Nesdale, 1983).

C. States of self-awareness

Although drugs and strangely behaving confederates may indeed cause introspection, we could also ask how often people think about themselves in the course of daily events, when experimenters are not present to construct unusual circumstances. Do people think about themselves more often than they think about their families, for example, or their jobs or their favorite TV shows? To answer

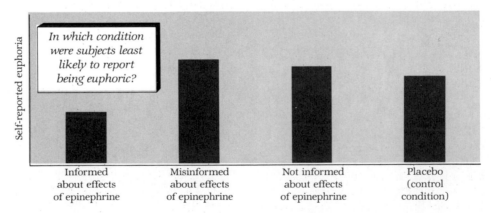

FIGURE 3-2. Amount of euphoria reported by subjects in the four conditions of Schachter and Singer's experiment.

these questions, two investigators recently asked 107 persons, ranging in age from 19 to 63 and in occupations from clerical worker to manager, to record their thoughts at selected times each day for one week (Csikszentmihalyi & Figurski, 1982). Subjects did not know when they would be asked to reflect on their thoughts. Rather, they responded whenever they heard a beep from the electronic paging device that they had been asked to carry with them. Approximately 45 times during the course of the week, each person recorded his or her thoughts and feelings, constituting more than 4700 observations in total.

As Figure 3-3 shows, the self was not at the top of the list. More often, people reported thinking about their work or about chores and home or reported having no thoughts at all. However, thoughts about the self were more common than thoughts about food, about television and radio, or about the research project itself. The investigators also asked their subjects to describe how they felt at the moment—how happy they felt, how active and alert they felt, and whether they would rather be doing something else at that time. Responses made to these questions when thinking about the self suggested that self-reflection is not necessarily a pleasant state. When thinking about themselves, compared with the times when they were thinking about other topics, subjects reported being less happy, being less active, and wishing they were doing something other than thinking about themselves. These patterns were true only when subjects were engaged in some voluntary activity, however, not when they were doing something because they were obliged to.

Wicklund and his associates have proposed a theory of self-awareness in order to describe when people will focus attention on themselves and what happens when they do (Wicklund, 1975; Duval & Wicklund, 1972; Wicklund & Frey, 1980). Wicklund defines self-awareness—sometimes called **objective self-awareness**—as "focused attention directed toward just one facet of the self" (Wicklund & Frey, 1980, p. 36). There are many ways in which this self-awareness can arise. In laboratory experiments, investigators have used a variety of techniques, including placing a mirror

in front of the subject, playing back a tape recording of the subject's own voice, and confronting the subject with a camera. Self-awareness can also be induced by placing a person in an unfamiliar and unstructured situation, similar to the party situation we described earlier.

What happens when a person is in a state of self-awareness? According to Wicklund, a person will engage in a process of self-evaluation, considering how his or her behavior matches with some internal rule or standard. If there is a discrepancy between these two things—as there often is—then the person will experience some negative feelings and frequently will try to avoid further self-reflection. For example, in one experiment, subjects who had experienced a discrepancy between their own

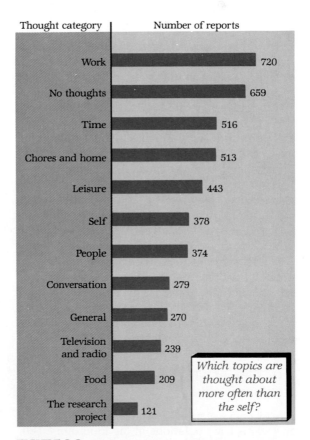

FIGURE 3-3. Most common categories of thought reported by Csikszentmihalyi and Figurski's subjects.

performance and an ideal standard left the exper- imental laboratory more quickly than subjects who either had not engaged in self-focusing or had not experienced a discrepancy between their perfor- mance and the standard (Duval & Wicklund, 1972).

Self-awareness can also lead to changes in behavior, often in a positive direction. Thus, if a person experiences self-awareness while making a decision about how to act, the behavior may well reflect the person's concern with meeting some internal standard. As one example, subjects in an experiment by Duval, Duval, and Neely (1979) watched a videotape about venereal disease epi- demics either immediately before or after a period of self-focused attention. When asked whether they would be willing to assist in a prevention program to help stop an epidemic, both groups of subjects were likely to volunteer their services—much more than were subjects who had seen the videotape but had not been focused on themselves. Thus, self- awareness may be aversive, but it may also be a guide for behavior that reflects the internalized norms and values of a society.

Although research has often focused on aware- ness of one particular aspect of self at one partic- ular point in time, shifts in self-focused attention are much more fluid. In fact, some recent inves- tigators have suggested that self-attention can best be represented as a continual adjustment process. In this model (presented by Carver & Scheier, 1981, 1982), comparisons between behavior and inter- nal standards constitute a series of feedback loops, paralleling the *cybernetic* models of control devel- oped in communication. Faced with one situation and with a focus on one internal standard, the person will make adjustments until the particular discrepancy is eliminated. Given another set of cues and/or focus on a different aspect of the self, the feedback process will begin anew.

D. Individual differences in self-awareness

As we have seen, self-awareness can be induced by various manipulations in the laboratory. Self- focused attention can also take place without these techniques, however, and some people are more

likely than others to engage in this process. To measure these natural tendencies, Fenigstein, Scheier, and Buss (1975) developed what they termed a "Self-Consciousness Scale." **Self-con- sciousness** is defined as a disposition to focus attention inward on the self and can be further analyzed in terms of two kinds of self-conscious- ness—public and private. *Private self-conscious- ness* involves a focus on more personal aspects of the self, such as bodily sensations, beliefs, moods, and feelings. *Public self-consciousness* relates to a more outward concern, involving an awareness of how one is seen as a social object by others (Scheier & Carver, 1981). Table 3-1 shows examples of questions that tap each of these dimensions.

People who differ in level of self-consciousness have been found to differ in a variety of behaviors. For example, people who score high on measures of *private* self-consciousness are more aware of their internal feelings, more rapid in making self- descriptive statements, and more likely to take action to reduce discrepancies between their cur- rent situation and their internal standards (Carver, 1979; Mueller, 1982). They are also more aware of changes in their internal bodily states (Scheier, Carver, & Gibbons, 1979). Because of this latter tendency, it has been suggested that people high in private self-consciousness are apt to remain healthier because they can recognize stresses to their bodies and take action before such stresses are damaging (Mullen & Suls, 1982). Again we see that the process of focusing on the self, although

---

TABLE 3-1. Sample items assessing private and public self-consciousness

Private self-consciousness
1. I'm always trying to figure myself out.
2. I reflect about myself a lot.
3. I'm generally attentive to my inner feelings.

Public self-consciousness
1. I'm concerned about what other people think of me.
2. I'm self-conscious about the way I look.
3. I'm concerned about my style of doing things.

it may arouse negative feelings, can have positive consequences.

■ III. Analyzing the self

As we have seen, there are many occasions that can cause a person to focus attention on the self. On such occasions, people may become more introspective, analyzing "how I'm doing" and "what I'm doing." Often they turn to other people for the answers to these questions. Some people, of course, may avoid such questions. Snyder and his colleagues, for example, found that clinical inpatients (diagnosed as neurotic, psychotic, and schizophrenic) were less inclined to want feedback about themselves than were students and faculty members at the University of Kansas (Snyder, Ingram, Handelsman, Wells, & Huwieler, 1982). Among the clinical patients, however, desire for feedback varied substantially, and the authors suggest that seeking out feedback may be a positive step for the clinical patient to take.

Although we cannot be certain that seeking feedback is adaptive for all people on all occasions, we do know that people often engage in such searches. There are a number of ways that people can analyze their abilities and actions. Direct questions are not the only method, but most tactics involve some reliance on other people.

A. Evaluating abilities

Some judgments about ourselves are easy to make. For example, there is relatively little room for error in deciding whether one's hair is red or black or how old—or tall—one is. These objective judgments are quite easy to make, and there is generally very little disagreement between a person's self-description and an outside observer's description of that same person.

In other areas, judgments cannot be made with as much certainty because there are no objective standards on which a person can rely. For example, when people are asked to judge how much ability they have in a particular area, agreement between these people and other observers of their performance is typically quite low (Mabe & West, 1982). There are a number of possible reasons for these discrepancies. People may not present an accurate evaluation of themselves, for example—they may choose to look good rather than be accurate (see Section IV of this chapter). Another possible explanation is that people simply don't have much experience in evaluating themselves in some areas: you may know that you can fix a meal, but you haven't done enough cooking to say whether you are a particularly good or bad cook.

One way for a person to find out more about his or her abilities is to become more involved in the area of concern. Research has shown that we are more likely to seek out tasks in which we are uncertain of our abilities than those in which we have a rather good understanding of our ability (Trope & Ben-Yair, 1982). For example, if Mack is uncertain about his ability to solve crossword puzzles, he might do one every day for a week and find out just how well he could perform. With more experience with a task, we are in a better position to evaluate our ability, and we may no longer feel it necessary to seek out that kind of task. After a week of doing crossword puzzles, Mack may be quite certain that he has no talent or liking for those black and white boxes. His attempts at self-evaluation on that particular dimension may cease. In fact, Meyer and Starke (1982) have found that people who believe they have low ability on a task will avoid situations that would provide additional feedback. At the same time, people who have high ability may sometimes continue to seek opportunities for evaluation, perhaps still seeking to learn just how good they are.

As we have indicated, some characteristics, such as hair color or eye color, can be evaluated with little or no reference to other people. Similarly, with crossword puzzles, it is easy to know whether you have completed the puzzle or not. Many skills, aptitudes, and values, however, can be evaluated only by comparing oneself with other people. Festinger (1954) developed **social-comparison theory** to explain this process. The theory states that, in the absence of a physical or objective standard of correctness, we will seek other people as a means of evaluating ourselves. Whether it is our attitudes toward Iranians or a new dress style or the latest rock group, we are often motivated to evaluate our own beliefs and abilities by comparing them with social reality (Latané, 1966; Radloff, 1961; Singer & Shockley, 1965; Suls & Miller, 1977).

Self-evaluation through social comparison is more fruitful when we choose to make our comparisons with people who are generally similar to us (Castore & DeNinno, 1977; Goethals & Darley, 1977). Similarity, in this case, is gauged on the basis of characteristics related to the task in question (Goethals & Darley, 1977; Wheeler, Koestner, & Driver, 1982). For example, if Anita is trying to evaluate her tennis game, she probably will not choose to compare herself with tournament champion Martina Navratilova, nor is she likely to choose a 6-year-old who has just picked up a racquet. Rather, she will probably compare herself to someone just slightly better than she is, reflecting what Festinger (1954) termed a *unidirectional drive upward*. By choosing this comparison other, Anita is choosing to compare with a standard that she might be able to match in the future. Later, if her tennis game improves, her standard of comparison will probably rise as well.

In the area of opinions, it is not as easy to conceptualize upward or downward comparisons, but similarity of the comparison other is still important. For example, in comparing opinions on the fairness of a new student fee policy, most students would probably initially choose to compare their opinions with those of another student rather than with those of a university administrator. Sex of the

comparison other has been found to be an important dimension of comparison. For example, when subjects in an experiment were allowed to choose one person with whom they would like to compare their performance, both males and females generally showed a stronger preference for someone of the same sex (Suls, Gaes, & Gastorf, 1979; Suls, Gastorf, & Lawhon, 1978; Zanna, Goethals, & Hill, 1975).

B. Causal attributions

Our curiosity about ourselves often goes beyond deciding how we feel, what we believe, or how well we did in comparison with other people. Many times we want to figure out *why* we acted in a particular way or why a certain outcome occurred. This process of inferring the explanations or causes of events has been termed **causal attribution.** (As we shall see in Chapter 4, causal attributions are made for the behavior of other people as well.)

Fritz Heider, whose work (1944, 1958) serves as the mainspring for much of the work on attribution processes, suggested that we all act as "naive psychologists," trying to discover cause-and-effect relations in the events that occur around us. These attempts to make sense of our world are the central focus of attribution theory.

More specifically, we can state three basic assumptions about the attribution process (Jones, Kanouse, Kelley, Nisbett, Valins, & Weiner, 1972). First, it is assumed that people attempt to assign causes for events. These explanations are not necessarily accurate; we may be wrong in our interpretation of an event, but the explanation can still satisfy our need to understand. (See Box 3-2 for a debate related to this issue.) Second, the assignment of causes for events is systematic. In other words, social psychologists believe that there are definite patterns in the explanations that we use. Finally, and perhaps most important, the explanations that we derive have consequences for our feelings and behaviors. Depending on how someone interprets an event, that person may decide that he or she is a successful person, an unfortunate soul, or simply a pawn of the fates, and his or her future actions may reflect those beliefs.

PHOTO 3-3. *A game of squash with a friend provides an opportunity for direct social comparison.*

BOX 3-2. Telling more than we can know?

Theories of causal attribution clearly assume that people are thinking, cognitive beings. But is it really possible for us to know why we act in certain ways? Nisbett and Wilson (1977) have suggested it is not. According to these authors, people have little direct access to higher-order cognitive processes: we may be unaware of stimuli that affect our responses, we may be unaware of our responses themselves, and we may be unaware of the connection between the two. As an example of their argument, Nisbett and Wilson describe an experiment in which the subject's task was to grasp two ropes that were hanging from the ceiling too far apart to allow a person to grab one and then walk over to the other. For some people, one of the ropes was set swinging slightly. People in this group were able to solve the problem easily, holding onto one rope and waiting until the other swung into reach. Yet, when asked how they had solved the problem, these same people did not mention having noticed the swinging rope, thus apparently unaware of an important influence on their thinking and behavior.

If people are unaware of such influences, how do they answer when asked why they did something? Nisbett and Wilson suggest that people may rely on general implicit theories of behavior (see Chapter 4) or on other people's opinions about cause and effect. Is this a problem for attribution and other theories that rely on self-reports? Perhaps not so much as Nisbett and Wilson would claim. A number of investigators have pointed out that self-reports can have validity in many, though not all, circumstances (for example, Ericcson & Simon, 1980; Smith & Miller, 1978). Also, if a person believes that a particular cause is responsible for his or her behavior, that belief may continue to affect behavior—even if the belief is not accurate. ■

Any event can have a variety of possible causes. To create some order in this abundance, Heider (1958) suggested that causes can be classified into two basic types: *dispositional* (or personal) and *situational* (or environmental). In the cartoon on p. 68, for example, Lois has come up with a variety of situational causes for her first gray hair. Each of these claimed causes is external to her—some person or event in the environment. Alternatively, it would be possible for Lois to assign a dispositional cause to the event (for example, the fact that she is growing older).

"Growing old" is an attribution that would require some change in the self-concept—a change that many people find aversive. People often avoid making such attributions, preferring to "accentuate the positive and denunciate the negative," at least when it comes to themselves. This tendency to accept greater personal responsibility for positive outcomes than for negative outcomes has been termed the **self-serving attribution bias.** And a pervasive bias it is. Zuckerman (1979), analyzing several dozen studies that looked at people's explanations of their own performance, found a systematic tendency for people to claim that success on a task is due, for example, to their ability or the amount of effort they exerted—qualities that are associated with the people themselves. In contrast, when people fail, they are much more likely to seek situational causes, looking outside themselves for an explanation. The self-serving bias is also in evidence when people estimate the effect that they have on other people's outcomes. A professor, for example, is more likely to claim responsibility when his or her students do well than when they do poorly (Arkin, Cooper, & Kolditz, 1980).

Although the self-serving bias is pervasive, it can be modified. For example, what if you knew that the explanations you gave for your performance were going to be subject to public scrutiny? Weary and her colleagues asked this question in a recent experiment (Weary, Harvey, Schwieger, Olson, Perloff, & Pritchard, 1982). Subjects were asked to act as a therapist for a person suffering from a fear of class examinations and to evaluate their performance as a therapist when the session was completed. Half the subjects were asked to

Attributions of causality.

sign the self-evaluation questionnaire to assure their identifiability, and the experimenter watched as they filled out the questionnaire (the public-attribution condition). The other subjects were guaranteed anonymity in their self-evaluations, and the experimenter was not present (private-attribution condition). The self-serving attributional bias was much more evident in the private-attribution condition. Presumably, the public subjects were concerned about their ability to defend their judgments to others and became more humble as a result. The self-serving attribution bias may also be reduced if you already have a reason to feel good about yourself. In contrast, if something has happened to make you feel generally bad about yourself, then you will probably be more likely to claim responsibility for success or avoid responsibility for failure in a subsequent situation (McCarrey, Edwards, & Rozario, 1982).

The self-serving bias is an example of a *motivational* influence on the attribution process. Our explanations are affected by our wishes to appear to ourselves and others in a certain way. There are also *informational* influences on the explanations we give for our own behavior (Miller & Ross, 1975). The result may again be a certain form of bias (when compared against the judgments that neutral observers might make), but this bias is due to the type of information we have available, not to any intentions to look good (Monson & Snyder, 1977). For example, suppose a representative of the Salvation Army approached you on the street and asked for a donation. Suppose further that

you refused, having just given a donation to another member of that organization an hour earlier. Now a bystander who observed only the second contact might conclude that you were rather stingy, or at least not generous toward the Salvation Army. In contrast, your own image of your self might quite deservedly be that you are a generous person. This difference in the available information that people have when making attributions illustrates the kind of cognitive biases that can occur. Often, an observer has little information about the historical determinants—what has happened before—and hence will focus totally on the here and now. In contrast, each of us has a great deal of information about our own past behaviors, and we take these into account when explaining our actions.

Thus, the process of self-analysis and self-understanding is a complex one, influenced by what we know, what we want to believe, and what kinds of people we choose as points of comparison.

■ IV. Presenting the self

We often talk as if there were a single self, stable and defined, even though occasionally influenced by motivations and circumstances. Yet, many social psychologists believe it is more appropriate to think in terms of multiple selves, different views of the self that may be displayed in different situations

PHOTO 3-4. Mimes' rendition of the multiplicity of the self.

(for example, Gergen, 1971, 1981). Once again, we find that William James has anticipated more recent statements (although his reference to males only is more dated):

> A man has as many social selves as there are individuals who recognize him and carry an image of him in their mind. . . . But as the individuals who carry the images form naturally into classes, we may practically say that he has as many different social selves as there are distinct groups of persons about whose opinions he cares. He generally shows a different side of himself to each of these different groups. Many a youth who is demure enough before his parents and teachers swears and swaggers like a pirate among his "tough" young friends. We do not show ourselves to our children as to our club companions, to our masters and employers as to our intimate friends [1890, Vol. 1, p. 294].

This view that there are multiple selves suggests that people may choose to present different aspects of themselves on different occasions. Schlenker (1980, p. 6) has defined **impression management** as "the conscious or unconscious attempt to control images that are projected in real or imagined social interactions." When these images deal with some aspect of the self, we call the process **self-presentation** (Schlenker, 1980). Before we look more closely at some of the specific techniques of impression management, let's consider the theoretical background on which ideas of self-presentation are based.

A. Theories of self-presentation

Theorists of the tradition known as *symbolic interactionism*, notably C. H. Cooley (1902/1922) and G. H. Mead (1934), have stressed that participants in social interactions try to "take the role of the other" and see themselves as others see them. This process both allows them to know how they appear to others and permits them to guide their social behavior so that it has the desired effect. Thus, by taking the role of the other, a politician can choose the right clothes and speech patterns to please rural constituents and then effectively change each of these to court the favor of party bosses.

Erving Goffman has drawn analogies to the world of theater in formulating his theory of the *presentation of self in everyday life* (Goffman, 1959, 1967). Goffman has described social interaction as a theatrical performance in which each individual acts out a "line"—a set of carefully chosen verbal and nonverbal acts that express one's self. One major feature of a person's line, termed the "face," is defined as the positive social value gained from one's interaction. For Goffman, one of the fundamental rules of social interaction is mutual commitment. By this he means that each participant will work to keep all members of the interaction "in face" through their self-presentation. To do so, each person has a repertoire of face-saving devices, an awareness of the interpretation that others place on his or her acts, a desire to sustain each member's face, and the willingness to use his or her repertoire of impression-managing techniques.

Maintaining face is not the goal of social interaction. Rather, maintaining face is a necessary background for social interaction to continue. Incidents that threaten the face of a participant also threaten the survival of the relationship. Consequently, when events challenge the face of a participant, corrective processes called *face-work* are initiated to avert any embarrassment that might interfere with the conduct of the relationship. Thus, we conspicuously overlook or help others apologize for the social blunders and potentially embarrassing *faux pas* that they commit. In short, for Goffman, social interaction requires its participants to be able to regulate their self-presentation so that it will be perceived and evaluated appropriately by others.

In a related approach, C. N. Alexander has also suggested that self-presentation is a fundamental facet of social interaction (Alexander & Knight, 1971; Alexander & Lauderdale, 1977; Alexander & Sagatun, 1973). According to the **situated-identities theory,** for each social setting there is a pattern of social behavior that conveys an identity particularly appropriate to that setting. This behavioral pattern is called a *situated identity.* Alexander claims that people strive to create the most favorable situated identities for themselves in their social encounters. For example, a college professor might aim for a highly academic identity when presenting a paper at a professional meeting, a somewhat more relaxed identity during lectures, and a casual and informal situated identity at a social gathering of friends. Clearly, the concept of a situated identity is similar to that of a role (see Chapter 1). But a situated identity is tied much more to a specific situational context than a role is. Moreover, roles focus on behaviors that are expected or appropriate; situated identities deal more with the image one chooses to project in a particular social interaction.

Each of these three theories of self-presentation agrees that other people are always forming impressions of us and using these impressions to guide their interactions with us (Chapter 5 will explore this point in more detail). Further, each theory points to a variety of tactics that individuals may use to manage and control the image they present to others. There are a number of reasons that self-presentation occurs so often (Schlenker, 1980). One reason is to gain social approval, finding it pleasant to be liked by others. Although social approval can be an end in itself, it may also serve as a means to other goals (Arkin, 1980). If you make a favorable impression on another person, you may also find yourself the recipient of money, power, or friendship—goals that, for many, are more important than immediate social approval. Impression management may also allow a sense of control in a situation, in that a person may be able to structure the outcome, at least partly, depending on which aspect of self is presented. This combination of reasons serves as powerful motivation for the use of self-presentation tactics.

B. Choosing a public image

Just as there are many reasons for engaging in self-presentation, there are a variety of images one can choose. The choice of an image, of course, depends on just what one wants other people to think. Sometimes our aim is to look good; at other times, we may be concerned with avoiding looking bad. For example, just before taking an exam, you may hear another student complain how little sleep

A. *Getting breakfast is a family project. For Carolyn, her roles as mother and wife predominate in this setting.*

B. *The roles of mother and wife may be forgotten as Carolyn conducts an important committee meeting at the office.*

C. *Talking with her boss, Carolyn assumes a slightly different role—more careful and less expansive.*

How many roles does a person play in the course of a day? One? Two? Six? Most of us play more than one, as different situations and different relationships call for different aspects of our selves. In the photographs shown here, a career woman named Carolyn plays several roles—as a wife, a mother, a junior executive, a subordinate, and a lover. Although some characteristics may remain constant throughout all these situations, other aspects may change. With her boss, Carolyn may be more guarded, for example, than when she is in charge of her own meeting. With her family, she may be more informal than when she is at work. Changes such as these, both subtle and obvious, are parts of our multiple selves.

D. *Back home again, roles still fluctuate—from a client's phone call to a daughter's request to a husband's arms.*

he had the previous night—the phone kept ringing, two cats were fighting in the alley, the people upstairs had the stereo on too loud. In fact, this student may be setting up excuses in advance, preparing reasons for a possible failing performance on the exam. The strategies by which people manufacture protective excuses for any possible future failures are called **self-handicapping strategies** (Berglas & Jones, 1978; Jones & Berglas, 1978).

In an empirical demonstration of self-handicapping strategies in action, Berglas and Jones (1978) asked two groups of college students to work on a problem-solving task. One group received problems that could be solved, while the other group had to work on problems that had no solutions. Before proceeding to a second problem-solving session, subjects were given a choice of two drugs that were ostensibly of interest to the experimenter. One of these drugs was supposed to enhance performance; the other was described as impairing performance. Subjects who had previously worked on solvable problems generally chose the drug that would improve their performance. The other group of subjects, whose experience probably led them to believe that they might not do well on the next task either, showed a strong preference for the interfering drug. By handicapping themselves through the use of a drug, they would have a convenient excuse if they did poorly on the second task. In the language of attribution theory, they had prepared a situational explanation for their possible failure and thus would be able to avoid negative dispositional explanations. (For another example of self-handicapping strategies, see Box 3-3.)

More generally, Jones and Berglas (1978) suggest that people may be particularly likely to use self-handicapping strategies when they are concerned with maintaining an image of self-competence, an image established on the basis of some past success but an image that the person may not be confident of continuing. In the entertainment world, for example, the film director who had a smash success on his or her last film may run into constant problems in making the next film—problems that may in part be caused by the director's trying to set up excuses in case that film is not a hit. And if the second film is a smash hit as well, in spite of the problems, then so much the better for the director's self-image!

Sometimes our desire for a favorable self-presentation will lead us to associate with people who themselves have a record of success. For example, have you ever told people that you are from the same town as some television personality, that you went to school with a well-known politician, or that you are distantly related to some prominent historic figure? These attempts at *basking in reflected glory* can be particularly evident on college campuses where there are winning athletic teams. On the Monday morning after a victory, students often wear clothing that identifies them as student-body members and talk excitedly about how "we" won the big game. In contrast, defeat on Saturday much less frequently brings out the school sweatshirts and colors, and students are more apt to talk about how "they" lost the game. In their studies of this phenomenon, Cialdini, Borden, Thorne, Walker, and Freeman (1976) have not only documented the tendency to publicly advertise one's association with winners but also provided evidence that basking in reflected glory is a self-presentation strategy designed to enhance the esteem that others have for us.

A more particular image that people may choose to present to others concerns their sex roles. For example, think of the man who is always projecting a "macho" image or the woman who spends hours each day applying makeup. Although past discussions of gender have tended to assume that differences between males and females are stable, reflecting either biological differences or early socialization experiences (see Chapter 13), it has become quite clear that some aspects of male and female behavior reflect self-presentation strategies (Deaux, 1977). Thus, a woman may choose to act more or less feminine in a situation, or a man to act more or less masculine, depending on the image that the person wishes to present.

Consider an experiment by von Baeyer, Sherk, and Zanna (1981). Female job applicants were scheduled to be interviewed by male interviewers, described either as valuing the traditional female stereotype of emotionality and deference or as being

BOX 3-3. Self-handicapping in the swimming pool

Do athletes engage in self-handicapping strategies? Would a top tennis player slack off in practice before a big tournament? Would a star receiver stay out too late before the big football game? Neither of these behaviors would be recommended for accomplishing a great performance—yet, some players may deliberately handicap themselves in this manner, attempting to protect their self-esteem in the event of loss.

Frederick Rhodewalt and his students observed the performance of 27 members of the Princeton men's swimming team to learn more about self-handicapping strategies (Rhodewalt, Saltzman, & Wittmer, 1982). Using a scale that has been developed to assess people's general tendencies to handicap themselves, the investigators divided the swimmers into two groups—high self-handicappers and low self-handicappers. During the season, records of attendance at practice were kept during each week prior to a meet. In addition, the swimming coaches were asked to evaluate the practice performance of each swimmer during each of the weeks.

We would expect that swimmers who had strong tendencies to handicap themselves would practice less before a meet than those low in such tendencies. By cutting back on practice, the high self-handicapper would have an excuse for poor performance. Such differences should be particularly strong when the upcoming meet is an important one, because self-esteem would be more at stake. The results of the Rhodewalt study are shown below. Although high and low self-handicappers did not differ in practice before unimportant meets, there were differences—both in actual attendance and in the coach's ratings—before important meets.

Presumably, collegiate swimmers are not alone in these tendencies. In fact, Rhodewalt and his colleagues have found similar results for professional golfers, and we could guess that the self-handicapping net spreads to other sports as well. ■

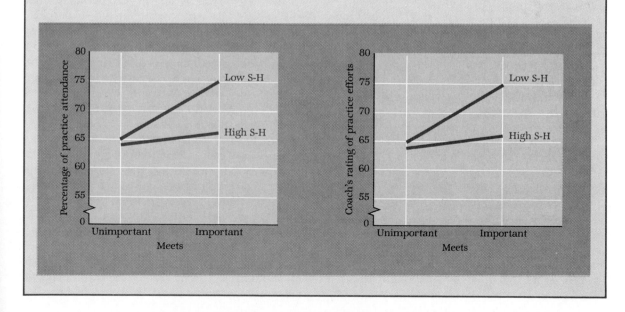

in favor of more independent, career-oriented women. When the women arrived for their scheduled interviews, the experimenters made careful observations of what they wore and recorded their answers to the interviewer's questions. The values that the women expected of the interviewer clearly affected the self-presentation strategies they chose. Women who expected a traditional interviewer looked more "feminine," not only in their overall appearance and demeanor but also in their use of makeup and choice of accessories. During the interviews, these women also gave more traditional responses to questions about marriage and children. In contrast, women who expected an interviewer who valued career-oriented women were less apt to fulfill the traditional female stereotype in their behavior and appearance.

This tailoring of sex-role images is not limited to women. Similar studies have found that men will also alter their presentation to fit the presumed values of another person (for example, Jellison, Jackson-White, Bruder, & Martyna, 1975). Although not all the relevant studies have been done, we would also expect that other basic characteristics could also be subject to self-presentational concerns. A Black person, for example, might choose to speak and dress differently when appearing before a predominantly Black and a predominantly White group. Similarly, a White could make the same kinds of changes in an attempt to create a positive impression on one or the other group. In these and many other cases, concerns with self-presentation may cause marked shifts in behaviors as a person moves from one audience to another.

C. Self-presentation tactics

In addition to the more general images that people sometimes seek to project, there are a variety of specific tactics that people may use in presenting themselves to others. Jones and Pittman (1982) have identified five major tactics of self-presentation, which differ according to the particular attribute the person is trying to gain. These five tactics are ingratiation, intimidation, self-promotion, exemplification, and supplication. Let us look at each of these tactics in more detail.

1. *Ingratiation.* Perhaps the most common of presentation techniques, ingratiation is defined as "a class of strategic behaviors illicitly designed to influence a particular other person concerning the attractiveness of one's personal qualities" (Jones & Wortman, 1973, p. 2). In other words, the main goal of the ingratiator is to be seen as likable.

There are a number of ways this can be accomplished. One common tactic is to give compliments to another person. Such flattery should not be given indiscriminately, however, as successful ingratiation requires a certain amount of credibility and sincerity. Another ingratiation tactic is to conform to the other person's opinions and behaviors. As one character states in Molière's play *The Miser,* "I find the best way to win people's favor is to pretend to agree with them, to fall in with their precepts, encourage their foibles, and applaud whatever they do." This viewpoint assumes, correctly, that we tend to like people whose beliefs, attitudes, and behaviors are similar to our own (see Chapter 6). Such a tactic will not work, however, if the target suspects ingratiation (Kauffman & Steiner, 1968).

2. *Intimidation.* In contrast to the goal of affection sought by the person who uses ingratiation, the person using intimidation as a strategy seeks to arouse fear. By creating the image of a dangerous person, the intimidator seeks to control an interaction by the exercise of power. Jones and Pittman (1982) offer the example of a sidewalk robber, who attempts to create fear in the victim and thereby gain money or jewelry. One can also think of cases in which parents would present this image to a child or professors to a student. Threats are obviously not very pleasant, and they may cause the other person to try to escape the situation. For this reason, Jones and Pittman suggest that intimidation may be used most often in relationships that are in some respects non-voluntary, in which escape is not easily accomplished.

3. *Self-promotion.* If a person's goal is to be seen as competent, either on some general ability, such as intelligence, or on some more specific skill, such as playing the banjo, self-promotion is the tactic most often used. Sometimes a self-promoter will acknowledge minor flaws in order to be more

credible in claiming skills in areas that are important (Jones, Gergen, & Jones, 1963). Similarly, the self-promoter may acknowledge weaknesses, if they are already known to the target person, and then go on to emphasize positive traits that the person was not aware of (Baumeister & Jones, 1978). A danger in the use of self-promotion is the possible mismatch between self-promoted claims of competence and reality. For example, if I claim that I am a great racquetball player, I had better either be good or avoid getting on the court with the person toward whom I used this tactic.

4. *Exemplification.* "You go on home. I'll stay here at the office and work four more hours to finish this project, even though I may have to miss my daughter's birthday party." This is an example of the tactic of exemplification, designed to elicit perceptions of integrity and moral worthiness—and often to arouse guilt in the target person as well. The exemplifier may be a martyr or the leader of a revolutionary cause or simply a person who likes to appear as a sufferer. In each case, however, the goal is to influence the impressions that others form and, in turn, their behaviors toward either the person or the cause.

5. *Supplication.* In this fifth tactic of self-presentation, a person advertises his or her weakness and dependence on another person. Unlike the exemplifier, who is seeking respect, the supplicant is seeking sympathy. Jones and Pittman suggest that this is often the tactic of last resort, used when a person is unable to use any of the other strategies. Although it may not be the preferred tactic, we can think of many occasions when people may use this technique. For example, a man may claim to be "all thumbs" and thus unable to sew a button on his shirt; or a woman may say she's afraid of electricity, thus avoiding the repair of a broken lamp. A student may claim ignorance of typing skills, hoping that a generous roommate will offer to type a term paper. In each case, the person is presenting an image of helplessness, hoping to elicit a sense of obligation from the target.

A person may use all five self-presentation tactics on different occasions. Hence, although some people may "specialize" in one or another tactic,

it is quite likely that each of us has used each tactic on more than one occasion. Further, it is possible to use elements of more than one strategy on the same occasion. For example, a person might want to be both liked and respected by another person and could engage in both ingratiation and self-promotion within the same conversation—an "I'm OK, you're OK" approach. Whatever choice or combination, the person's aim is to create the desired impression on someone else, thereby increasing the chances of obtaining the desired response. This model thus reflects the social-exchange theories discussed in Chapter 1.

D. Individual differences in self-presentation

The message of theory and research on self-presentation is clear: people strive to influence the images that others form of them during social interaction. Although probably everyone engages in such actions from time to time, there are important differences in the extent to which people can and do control their self-presentations. Some people engage in impression management more often and with greater skill than others. For example, professional actors are trained to manipulate the images that they project to the audience. Successful politicians, too, have long practiced the art of wearing the right face for the right constituency (see Box 3-4).

Outside these professional realms, people also differ in the extent to which they can and do exercise control over their verbal and nonverbal self-presentation. These differences are captured by the psychological construct of **self-monitoring** (Snyder, 1979). High self-monitoring persons are particularly sensitive to the expressions and the self-presentations of others in social situations, and they use these as cues in monitoring their own self-presentation for purposes of impression management. High self-monitoring persons are identified by their high scores on the Self-Monitoring Scale (Snyder, 1974). For example, the high self-monitoring person endorses such statements as these:

1. In different situations and with different people, I often act like very different persons.

BOX 3-4. Presidential rhetoric: Self-presentation in action

Campaign promises made by candidates as they run for election often seem to be forgotten when they take office. One possible explanation for these apparent shifts in position is that new information leads to a real change in opinion. According to this *cognitive adjustment* interpretation, the officeholder may be exposed to arguments that did not surface during the campaign and may be forced to alter his or her view of the proper course. A second, more cynical explanation is that politicians never intend to fulfill their campaign promises. Rather, the claims they present on the campaign trail may simply represent a self-presentation strategy, designed to elicit a favorable impression—and votes—from their audiences.

To test these competing hypotheses, Tetlock (1981) compared preelection and post-election statements by 20th-century U.S. presidents. Preelection statements were made during the five months before the election; postelection statements were gathered from three points in time—one month after taking office, during the second year of office, and during the third year. Tetlock reasoned that if cognitive adjustment were the major reason for shifts in policy, then changes should be gradual as the official acquired increasing amounts of information. In contrast, the self-presentation hypothesis would predict more rapid changes in policy statements, already evident during the first month in office. To assess these possible changes, he evaluated the com-

plexity of statements that presidents made, ranging from simple, limited-dimensional statements at one end of the scale to more complex, multidimensional statements at the other end.

Tetlock's results give strong support to the self-presentation interpretation. Presidential policy statements became significantly more complex immediately after a president took office and did not change much over the three-year period. The suddenness of this shift and the level pattern after election are not consistent with a more general accumulation of information leading to cognitive adjustment. The trends were very similar for all the presidents during the 20th century, with only one exception. Statements by Herbert Hoover became simpler after he took office than before.

But what if an elected official planned to run for reelection? Under these conditions, the self-presentation hypothesis predicts, statements would once again be simplified as the election drew near. And that is exactly what Tetlock found. Including only presidents who decided to run for reelection after their first term, he compared statements made in their next-to-last year in office with statements made in the last year prior to the election. Significant drops in complexity of statements were found, as these candidates prepared once again to present themselves to the voters. ■

2. I am not always the person I appear to be.
3. I may deceive people by being friendly when I really dislike them.

According to their peers, high self-monitoring persons are good at learning what is socially appropriate in new situations, have good control of their emotional expressions, and can effectively use these abilities to create the impressions they

want. In fact, they are such polished actors that they can effectively adopt the mannerisms of a reserved, withdrawn, and introverted person and then do an abrupt about-face and portray themselves, equally convincingly, as friendly, outgoing, and extroverted (Lippa, 1976, 1978a). In self-presentation situations, high self-monitoring persons are quite likely to seek out and consult social-comparison information about appropriate patterns of self-presentation. They invest considerable effort in attempting to "read" and understand others (Berscheid, Graziano, Monson, & Dermer, 1976; Jones & Baumeister, 1976).

You may detect similarities between the concept of self-monitoring and that of public self-consciousness, as discussed earlier. In fact, the two concepts are related, though only moderately so (Scheier & Carver, 1980). The person high in self-consciousness may be aware of the impression that he or she is making but will not necessarily act on that information. In contrast, high self-monitors use this information to guide their self-presentation so as to gain approval or power in an interaction. In other words, a high degree of self-consciousness may be necessary for self-monitoring behavior, but it is not sufficient for impression management to occur.

Let's consider an experiment by Snyder and Monson (1975) to see how self-monitors operate. In this study, group-discussion conditions sensitized individuals to different peer reference groups that could provide cues to the social appropriateness of one's self-presentation. High self-monitoring persons were keenly attentive to these differences, as shown in Figure 3-4. They were conforming when conformity was the most appropriate interpersonal orientation and nonconforming when reference-group norms favored autonomy in the face of social pressure. Low self-monitoring persons were virtually unaffected by the differences in social setting. Presumably, their self-presentations were accurate reflections of their own personal attitudes and dispositions. In a similar study, Danheiser and Graziano (1982) found that high self-monitoring subjects were more likely to be cooperative when they expected future interaction with a partner than when they did not, while low self-monitors did not vary their behavior in response to these future prospects.

The utility of this skill in the work world was recently shown by Caldwell and O'Reilly (1982). Some positions in organizations have been called "boundary spanning" positions. People who hold these positions are responsible for filtering and transmitting information across organizational boundaries and must be able to adapt to a variety

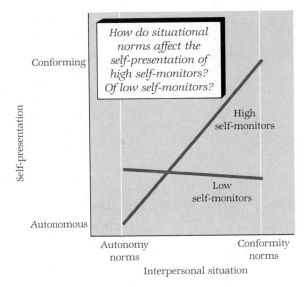

FIGURE 3-4. Autonomy and conformity in self-presentations of high self-monitoring and low self-monitoring persons when faced with group norms calling for autonomy or conformity.

of pressures and competing opinions. Caldwell and O'Reilly reasoned that persons scoring high in self-monitoring should be more successful in these positions because they have the ability to perceive cues and modify their behavior accordingly. They measured the self-monitoring tendencies of 93 field representatives whose jobs required boundary spanning and assessed their job performance. High self-monitors did indeed do better in these jobs, and the differences were particularly important during the early stages of employment. These results are important, for they suggest that self-monitoring is not just a skill to be sought by those who wish to deceive but can be an adaptive skill in environments that contain a complex mixture of people and policies.

E. Self-presentation and human nature

Self-presentation appears to be a basic fact of social life. In a variety of ways, people influence the images of their "selves" that they project to other people. Where is the "real" self in all this? As suggested earlier in the chapter, it may be more useful to think of multiple selves than a single self.

I may present different faces to my best friend, to the university president, and to my mother. Each of these faces may be one aspect of my true self. As Jones and Pittman (1982) have observed, self-presentation tactics are most often a matter of selecting certain characteristics and omitting others, rather than deliberate deception.

Is impression management good or bad? Clearly, it can be either. Erving Goffman has pointed out both the potentials and the pitfalls:

> Too little perceptiveness, too little *savoir faire* [that is, too little impression management], too little pride and considerateness, and the person ceases to be someone who can be trusted to take a hint about himself or give a hint that will save others embar-

rassment. Such a person comes to be a real threat to society; there is nothing much that can be done with him. . . . Too much *savoir faire* or too much considerateness, and he becomes someone who is too socialized, who leaves the others with the feeling that they do not know how they really stand with him, nor what they should do to make an effective long term adjustment [Goffman, 1955, p. 227].

The same tactic of self-presentation can be applied to creating an honest image or a deceptive one, to influencing others for altruistic purposes or for exploitative ones. We may or may not approve of a particular goal that self-presentation serves, but certainly the presentation of self is an integral part of everyday social interaction.

V. SUMMARY

Since the time of William James, psychologists have recognized the importance of the concept of self and the ways in which the self is defined by social interaction. The *self-concept* has many components, and self-descriptions may be affected by the prominence of certain features in the environment.

Self-schemata are cognitive generalizations about the self that influence how we organize and remember events and experiences. People vary in what dimensions are central to their self-schemata. *Self-esteem* refers to one's positive or negative evaluation of one's self.

Self-perception theory says that we become aware of ourselves by watching what we do, much as outside observers would form judgments of us on the basis of what they saw. In the area of emotions, we may interpret the same physiological state of arousal differently, depending on the cues available in our environment.

We do not spend all our time thinking about ourselves. Some conditions, however, can create a state of *objective self-awareness*, at which time we will focus attention specifically on some aspect of the self and compare ourselves with some

internal standard. People who are high in *self-consciousness* are more likely to engage in this process than people who are low in self-consciousness.

To evaluate our abilities, we often engage in *social-comparison* processes, looking to other people as a way of gauging our own performance. Social comparison is more likely with people who are similar on relevant dimensions. We also often try to explain why we have engaged in certain behaviors or why we succeeded or failed at something. These explanations are termed *causal attributions*. Causal attributions can be classified as dispositional (referring to the person) or situational (referring to some factor outside the person). Often, our explanations show a self-serving bias: we accept more personal responsibility for positive outcomes than for negative outcomes.

People often engage in *self-presentation* strategies to influence the impression they make on other people. Theories of self-presentation include symbolic interactionism, Goffman's discussion of the presentation of self, and the theory of situated identities.

Self-handicapping strategies are techniques used to provide protective excuses for a possible future failure. Specific tactics of self-presentation include ingratiation, intimidation, self-promotion, exemplification, and supplication. Some people, termed high *self-monitors*, are particularly sensitive to the impressions they make on other people.

GLOSSARY TERMS

causal attribution
impression management
objective self-awareness
schema
self-concept
self-consciousness

self-esteem
self-handicapping strategies
self-monitoring
self-perception theory
self-presentation
self-schema

self-serving attribution bias
situated-identities
   theory
social-comparison theory
spontaneous self-concept

4

Social Knowledge: Impressions & Explanations of People

To know one's self is wisdom, but to know one's neighbor is genius.

■ MINNA ANTRIM

The cause is hidden, but the result is well known.

■ OVID

I. **Forming impressions of people**
   A. Accuracy of impressions
   B. Features of impression formation

II. **Organizing impressions: Categories and principles**
   A. Implicit personality theory
   B. Schemata and prototypes
   C. Stereotypes
   D. Belief in a just world

III. **Explaining behavior: Attributions of causality**
   A. Covariation and causal schemata
   B. Correspondent inference
   C. Causes for success and failure
   D. Biases in the attribution process

IV. **The process of social cognition**
   A. Encoding: Getting the information in
   B. Storage and retrieval: Getting the information out

V. **Summary**

Knowing ourselves is one form of understanding. Yet, although social psychologists may begin with consideration of the self, as we have done in Chapter 3, they do not stop there. Social psychology is about people and their interactions, and to understand these interactions, we need to understand how people view one another. Perhaps, as Minna Antrim suggests, truly knowing another person requires genius. If that is true, then most of us spend a great deal of time aspiring to genius status, as we constantly try to understand and interpret the behavior of the people around us.

Why do we do this? For most people, it is important to know and understand the behavior of others because these other people can affect our own lives. Predicting whether an approaching stranger is going to be a harmless beggar or a dangerous mugger may enable one to avoid bruises and thefts. Seeking out new people at a party may lead to love or rejection. Other people play such an influential part in our lives that understanding and predicting their behavior is of critical importance.

Social psychologists have devoted much effort to understanding the process of acquiring social knowledge. As an example of how varied the issues of social cognition can be, consider the following situation. You are sitting in a chair reading a book, and you happen to glance out the window toward the house next door. Suddenly you see a man run out the front door, jump into a car in the driveway, and speed away. Perhaps the first question is: Do you recognize the man? If you don't, perhaps he was a burglar, completing a heist of your neighbor's jewel collection. Would you recognize the man if the police asked you to view a lineup? This is a basic question of the accuracy of our perception. Typically, however, we do more than simply recall objective characteristics—we often add meaning to these events as well. What if the man were White rather than Black, tall rather than short, fat rather than thin? Would you form any general impressions of his character on the basis of these physical characteristics? Social psychologists try to understand how we form impressions of other people and how different kinds of information affect these initial judgments.

Now let's make this scenario slightly different. Suppose you recognize the man as the brother of your best friend. In this case, the likely question would not be who he was or what his personality was like but *why* he was running out the door so fast. At this point, you would probably engage in a process of causal attribution, attempting to infer causes or explanations for the event you had just witnessed. This is a second level of social inference.

There is still another level of questioning that can be applied to this situation, though one that is more likely to be of interest to the psychologist than to the person casually glancing out a window. This level concerns the basic processes of social cognition—how we encode information, how we store it, and how we later retrieve it from memory. These questions, though somewhat more abstract, are fundamental to the issues of social knowledge and will be covered in this chapter as well. Through all these levels, we can see that the person is an *active perceiver*. Information about other people does not just imprint on our brain. Rather, we actively make interpretations and draw inferences, using a variety of assumptions and rules—rules which we may or may not be aware of but which influence our views nonetheless.

■ I. Forming impressions of people

First impressions are important, we are often told. When you meet someone for the first time, what do you notice? Eye color? Skin color? Whether the person seems friendly or shy? In trying to decide what another person is like, we use a variety of cues to form an impression of that person.

A. Accuracy of impressions

Twenty-five years ago, the study of social perception focused mainly on the issue of accuracy of impressions. Despite a great deal of research, the overall result was frustration, resulting, in part, from methodological dead ends. Traits, after all, are not concrete entities that can be weighed and measured; rather, they are psychological constructs. Therefore, to determine whether a judgment is accurate, we must first have a reliable way of assessing the presence or absence of a given trait in the person being judged. The obstacles to such assessment, however, have proved insurmountable so far.

Even when an observer is asked to make judgments about objective events, accuracy is elusive. In jury trials, eyewitness testimony is often used as evidence against the defendant (Loftus, 1979). Research by social psychologists, however, suggests that such reports may often be in error. For example, in one study using the natural medium of television, viewers of a news broadcast witnessed a street mugging in New York and then saw a police lineup of six persons that included the mugger. Only 14% of the viewers who called the station in response to a request by the announcer correctly identified the mugger. Audience members at a legal conference who watched the same film did only slightly better: just under 20% made the correct identification (Buckhout, 1980).

Another investigation of eyewitness accuracy (Brigham, Maass, Snyder, & Spaulding, 1982) allowed the witnesses direct contact with the "suspects." In this experiment, one Black and one White man entered a convenience store separately, and each had direct contact with the clerk, making a purchase and asking for directions as well. About two hours later, two men entered the store, identified themselves as law interns, and showed the clerk two sets of pictures that included photographs of both men who had been in the store earlier. The overall rate of correct identification by the clerks was 34.2%, hardly impressive testimony to the accuracy of impressions.

B. Features of impression formation

Accuracy is indeed an elusive quality. Yet, the impression that we form of another person is real to us, whether or not it is accurate. For example, if I conclude that a person is nasty, I will probably avoid future meetings with that person if at all possible and may never know whether my impression was accurate. For this reason, there has been considerable interest in studying the features that affect one's impressions of other people. We will consider three aspects of this process: central traits,

the issue of adding versus averaging information, and the primacy or recency of information.

Central traits.   When we form an impression of another person, some pieces of information carry greater weight than others and are able to modify the whole picture. Asch (1946) called such influential characteristics **central traits.** Asch showed that the *warm/cold* dimension was a central one that could strongly affect the organization of people's impressions. For example, when the adjective *cold* was included in a list of seven stimulus words purportedly describing a person, only about 10% of the subjects believed that the person in question would also be generous or humorous. However, when *warm* replaced *cold*, about 90% of the subjects described the person as generous, and more than 75% described the person as humorous. By contrast, when the words *polite* and *blunt* were substituted for *warm* and *cold*, the resulting impressions were not much different from each other. Asch therefore concluded that politeness/bluntness was not a central trait.

These apparently minor differences in description can have pronounced effects. Extending Asch's work, Kelley (1950) introduced a guest lecturer to several university classes. Some of the students were told in advance that this lecturer was, among other characteristics, a rather warm person; others, that he was rather cool. The lecturer then gave the identical talk to each group. The impressions that class members reported after the lecture were quite different, however, and were consistent with the initial description of him as warm or cold. Furthermore, class members who had been led to expect a warm person interacted more with the lecturer in discussion.

More recent research has shown that the role of central traits is not quite as simple as Asch originally thought. Studies by Wishner (1960) and others show that the centrality of any particular trait depends, first, on the other information that is presented about a person and, second, on the judgments that the subject is asked to make. In other words, the specific effects of "warm" and "cold" may be weak if other information is redundant in meaning with those traits. Similarly, "warm" and "cold" may not be particularly influential if one is asked to make a judgment about athletic prowess. Yet, despite these limitations, we still can say that central traits often influence broader judgments.

Adding versus averaging methods. Often, when we ask what someone is like, we are given a list of personality traits that presumably describe the person. For example, you might be told by a friend that your blind date for Friday night is "open-minded, clever, and modest, but kind of quiet." How do you integrate these pieces of information? Social psychologists have developed two basic models to explain how this kind of information is combined: the *additive model* and the *averaging model* (Brewer, 1968; Rosnow & Arms, 1968). To illustrate how these models work, let us consider your hypothetical blind date. Would your impression of the person differ if you had been told only that the date was open-minded and clever?

Both the additive and the averaging models begin by assuming that traits can be scaled in their likability: some traits convey very favorable information about a person, while others indicate negative information. (An example of the rank ordering of some common traits, derived from a longer list developed by Anderson, 1968b, is shown in Table 4-1.)

The *averaging model* claims that we use the mean value of the traits provided to form our impression of a person (Anderson, 1965, 1974). The averaging model predicts that you would have a more favorable impression of your blind date if you were given only the description "open-minded and clever," because both these traits are very desirable and thus have high values, or scores near the top of the ranked list in Table 4-1. Inclusion of the traits "modest" and "quiet" would reduce the average, as they are less attractive traits and have low values, or scores near the bottom of the ranked list.

TABLE 4-1. The likableness of personality-trait words

What is the "best" thing you can say about someone's personality? What is the "worst"? Norman H. Anderson and his associates have obtained likableness ratings for 555 words that are used as personality-trait descriptions; that is, subjects rated each word on a seven-point scale ranging from "least favorable or desirable" to "most favorable or desirable." The average rating given each word by the 100 college students forms the value for that word. In the list below, only the relative rankings are given; in using these words in research, numerical values are assigned to each trait. Such a listing is tremendously useful in research on impression formation, for it gives us an empirical indication of the value of different traits. Of course, these likableness ratings are colored by the particular group of raters; some other group might rate *polite* as more or less favorable than this group (which made it 53rd in a list of 555 terms). And the likableness of traits can change over time; *logical* may not be as highly valued as it once was (in this group it is 94th).

Such a listing is interesting in what it reveals about our preferences. *Sincere* is rated most favorably of all 555 terms, while *liar* and *phony* are the very least desirable. These say something about our values. Interestingly, the very middle term in the list (278th in ranking) is *ordinary*. The entire list cannot be reprinted here, but some extremes and highlights are included.

Rank	Term	Rank	Term	Rank	Term
1	sincere	80	ethical	531	loud-mouthed
2	honest	100	tolerant	540	greedy
3	understanding	150	modest	546	deceitful
4	loyal	200	soft-spoken	547	dishonorable
5	truthful	251	quiet	548	malicious
6	trustworthy	278	ordinary	549	obnoxious
7	intelligent	305	critical	550	untruthful
8	dependable	355	unhappy	551	dishonest
9	open-minded	405	unintelligent	552	cruel
10	thoughtful	465	disobedient	553	mean
20	kind-hearted	500	prejudiced	554	phony
30	trustful	520	ill-mannered	555	liar
40	clever				

The *additive* (or *summation*) model, in contrast, predicts that one's judgment is based on the sum of the trait values, rather than on the average (Anderson, 1962). According to this model of information integration, adding the values of the traits "modest" and "quiet" to the values for "clever" and "open-minded" would increase the favorability of the overall evaluation. Table 4-2 shows more precisely how these two models work.

Which model is correct? The majority of the evidence is more strongly supportive of the averaging model. To further complicate the issue, however, it appears that a simple average is not the best solution. Some traits are more important than others in influencing our impressions. To account for these variations, Anderson (1968a) has proposed a weighted-averaging model, which predicts impressions on the basis of an average of scores that have each been weighted according to their importance. This more complicated version of the averaging model appears to best account for our integration of information about people.

Primacy and recency effects.   Most of us probably exert extra effort to look nice and be charming when meeting someone for the first time, as on a job interview or on our first meeting with

PHOTO 4-1. *In a job interview the first impression is especially important because the applicant has few or no opportunities to provide additional information.*

new in-laws. In doing this, we are assuming that another person's first impression of us may be influential. What evidence is there for the power of first impressions? Put another way, which information is more influential—the first information in another person's perception of us (**primacy effect**) or the latest information (**recency effect**)?

To study the effects of first impressions, Luchins (1957a, 1957b) wrote two short paragraphs describing some of the day's activities of a boy named Jim. In one paragraph, Jim walked to school with friends, basked in the sun on the way, talked

---

TABLE 4-2. Adding versus averaging in the integration of impressions

When given a list of traits that describe another person, how do we integrate the information given by these traits? The adding model and the averaging model agree that we, in effect, assign a value to each trait. But the models differ in regard to how these values are integrated.

Consider the data below, bearing in mind that we have assigned relative likableness values to each trait.

Let us say that we are given the following traits for two men:

Gary		Steve	
Understanding	(+3)	Understanding	(+3)
Poised	(+2)	Sharp-witted	(+2)
Confident	(+1)	Congenial	(+2)
		Resourceful	(+2)
		Loud-mouthed	(−3)

The additive model would sum the values for each person, giving each a score of +6. Thus, the additive model would predict that our overall impressions of the two men would be equally favorable. However, the averaging model would get a mean value for the traits for each, giving Gary a +2 and Steve a +1⅕. The averaging model would predict that our overall evaluation of Gary would be better than that of Steve.

with acquaintances in a store, and greeted a girl whom he had recently met. In the other paragraph, Jim's activities were similar, but his style was different: he walked home from school alone, stayed on the shady side of the street, waited quietly for service in a store, and did not greet the girl whom he had recently met. The first paragraph (E) made subjects think of Jim as an extrovert; the second paragraph (I) made him seem an introvert.

Luchins then combined the two paragraphs in either the E–I order or the I–E order. After reading the two paragraphs, subjects were asked to rate Jim on a personality-trait checklist. The results of this and several other studies showed evidence of a primacy effect. In other words, subjects rated Jim as more extroverted when the E paragraph came first and more introverted when the I paragraph was first, even though each narrative contained identical information. Thus, first impressions are apparently very important in determining our final impressions of other people.

Under certain conditions, however, these results can be altered and a recency effect occurs instead. For example, if some additional activity intervenes between the two parts of the description, the more recent information will have a stronger effect (Luchins, 1957b, 1958; Mayo & Crockett, 1964; Rosenkrantz & Crockett, 1965). For example, if you met Joan at a party last month and formed a slightly negative impression but then encountered her again this week and reacted positively, your impression is more likely to be positive than negative. However, if one is explicitly instructed to combine all known information about a person, the recency effect may be eliminated (Leach, 1974).

■ II. Organizing impressions: Categories and principles

In coming to know other people, we do not respond simply to their external characteristics or to the traits by which they are described. Rather, we approach the world with certain assumptions about people, based on our experience. At a general level, we may have overriding **philosophies of human nature**—expectancies that people will possess certain qualities and will behave in certain ways (see Box 4-1). At a more specific level, we may have particular ways of categorizing people and events. Stereotypes, for example, have long been recognized as one way in which we organize our thoughts about certain groups of people. More recently, social psychologists have begun to use such words as *prototype* and *schema* to describe other categories of impressions. In this section, we will consider some of these categories and principles that affect our interpretation of the people and events around us.

A. Implicit personality theory

Through development and experience, each of us develops his or her own **implicit personality theory**—a set of unstated assumptions about what traits are associated with one another. Such theories are considered implicit because they are rarely stated in formal terms; nonetheless, they often dominate our judgments of other people (Cronbach, 1955; Schneider, 1973; Schneider, Hastorf, & Ellsworth, 1979; Wegner & Vallacher, 1977).

For example, Rosenberg and Sedlak (1972) have found that college students, in describing the people they know, use the terms *intelligent, friendly, self-centered, ambitious,* and *lazy* with the greatest frequency. Use of these terms is not random, however. People described as intelligent are also likely to be described as friendly and are rarely described as self-centered. Thus, many people apparently hold an implicit personality theory that says intelligence and friendliness go together, whereas intelligence and self-centeredness do not. Such theories may be true or may be false as judged against the actual occurrence of such characteristics in real life. In fact, one of the features that distinguish implicit personality theories from more formal psychological theories is their lesser likelihood of being tested and found incorrect. Because we may not even be aware that we make an association between, for example, intelligence and friendliness, we may be much less likely to notice exceptions to the rule.

The use of such implicit theories reflects our

BOX 4-1. Philosophies of human nature

An analysis of writings by philosophers, theologians, and social scientists has generated the proposition that our beliefs about human nature have six basic dimensions (Wrightsman, 1964). These dimensions are believed to define a basic framework, or template, by which we judge the actions and characteristics of others. The first four dimensions listed below can be combined to show a generally positive or negative view of the world; the fifth and sixth dimensions are concerned with multiplexity, or beliefs about the extent of individual differences in human nature.

1. Trustworthiness versus untrustworthiness. On the one hand, we may generally believe that people are trustworthy, moral, and responsible, echoing the beliefs of psychotherapist Carl Rogers that such attributes as "positive, forward-moving, constructive, realistic, trustworthy" are "inherent in [the] species" (1957, p. 200). On the other hand, we may endorse Freud's more pessimistic view that "with a few exceptions, human nature is basically worthless" (E. L. Freud, 1960, p. 79). Of course, many people's beliefs lie between these extremes. During the 1960s, college students tended to be quite optimistic about people; more recent generations have become more pessimistic in their beliefs about the basic trustworthiness of people (Baker & Wrightsman, 1974; Hochreich & Rotter, 1970).

2. Strength of will and rationality versus lack of willpower and rationality. Many people believe that human beings can control their outcomes and that they understand themselves. This viewpoint is reflected in proponents of the self-help movement, ranging from Mary Baker Eddy to Dale Carnegie to Werner Erhard. In contrast, others adopt the view that people are basically irrational and lack self-determination.

3. Altruism versus selfishness. Do you believe that people are basically altruistic, unselfish, and sincerely interested in others? Or are you more likely to think that people are generally selfish and that they are interested only in themselves and are unconcerned with the fate of others?

4. Independence versus conformity to group pressures. One perspective would say that people are generally independent and able to maintain their beliefs in the face of group pressures to the contrary. A more pessimistic view would say that people readily give in to the pressures of other individuals, groups, and society at large. (Stanley Milgram's research on obedience, discussed in Chapter 12, provides some support for the latter belief.)

5. Variability versus similarity. Some people believe that people are quite different from one another in personality and interests and that people can easily change. Others believe that people are similar and can change very little. In personality theory, the *idiographic* approach represents a belief in the uniqueness of each individual (Allport, 1961, 1962), while the *nomothetic* approach classifies people in large groups or categories when attempting to explain behavior.

6. Complexity versus simplicity. One way of viewing people is to believe that they are basically complicated and hard to understand. Alternatively, we may take the position that people are rather simple and quite easy to understand. Probably many psychologists would endorse the viewpoint that people are rather complex.

Beliefs about human nature can vary widely from one individual to another and from one group of people to another. What are your philosophies of human nature? ■

need to simplify and integrate information, enabling us to deal more easily with the complexities of human interaction. Given a limited amount of information, we can fill in the details and make a person more understandable in terms of our own experience. These theories may then persist, even in the face of contradictory evidence, because we have developed a rationale for the theory that we formed (Anderson, Lepper, & Ross, 1980).

Each of us probably has his or her own implicit personality theory, which could be assessed through conversations and letters or from free descriptions elicited by experimenters. In an interesting use of the archival method, Rosenberg and Jones (1972) showed that it is possible to assess the implicit personality theories of historical figures, in this case the writer Theodore Dreiser. Analyzing *A Gallery of Women* (1929), a collection of sketches about 15 women, these investigators tabulated all the traits used by Dreiser in describing women; Table 4-3 summarizes the 99 most frequently occurring traits. By statistical analysis, Rosenberg and Jones reduced these traits to three basic dimensions: hard/soft, male/female, and conforms/does not conform. Hardness was closely related to maleness in Dreiser's implicit theory but not identical with it; in contrast, sex and conformity were believed to

be quite independent characteristics. It is interesting to consider this pattern of Dreiser's in conjunction with current stereotypes about men and women (to be discussed in more detail in Chapter 10). Dreiser was clearly concerned with the outward physical characteristics of women, as evidenced by the relative frequencies of traits listed in Table 4-3. Although such descriptions might suggest a rather superficial view of women, he did not associate women with conformity, thus deviating from at least one aspect of the commonly held stereotype.

Another approach to understanding people's implicit personality theories is represented in the work of psychologist George Kelly. In developing a cognitive theory of human behavior, Kelly was concerned with the links between our perceptions and our behavior. A crucial mediating link in this chain is our interpretation of the events and stimuli in our world. As Kelly asserts:

> [People] look at [their] world through transparent patterns or templates which [they] create and then attempt to fit over the realities of which the world is composed. . . . Let us give the name constructs to these patterns that are tried on for size. They are ways of construing the world [1955, Vol. 1, pp. 8–9].

TABLE 4-3. The 99 most frequently occurring trait categories in *A Gallery of Women*, by Theodore Dreiser

Trait category	Frequency	Trait category	Frequency
Young	100	Colorful, graceful, intelligent, poor, reads, religious, studies, tall	15
Beautiful	67	Fool, good-looking, literary, pagan	14
Attractive	44	Aspirant, determined, good, had means, sad, society person, not strong, tasteful	13
Charming, dreamer	41		
Poetic	39	Ambitious, careful, defiant, different, erratic, genial, happy, lonely, man, varietistic	12
Interesting, worker	32		
Artistic	29	Clever, genius, indifferent, Irish, manager, nice, old, pale, quiet, restless, serious, shrewd, sincere, successful, suffering, sympathetic, thin, understanding	11
Gay	26		
Practical, romantic, writer	25		
Conventional, girl	24		
Free, strong	23		
Woman	22	American, communist, crazy, critical, emotional, enthusiastic, fearful, fighter, forceful, great, handsome, hard, lovely, had money, painter, physically alluring, playful, repressed, reserved, skilled, sophisticated	10
Unhappy	20		
Intellectual, radical, sensitive, sensual	19		
Kind, cold	18		
Vigorous	17		
Able, drinker, generous, troubled	16		

Construct is a key term for Kelly. A construct is a way of interpreting the world and a guide to behavior. Kelly's fundamental assumption is that we are all scientists. Just as a scientist tries to understand and predict events, each human being tries in the same way to choose constructs that will make the world understandable and predictable. According to Kelly's theory, people do not strive for reinforcement or seek to avoid anxiety; instead, they try to *validate their own construct systems.* Furthermore, Kelly has discarded the notion of an objective, absolute truth in favor of a phenomenological approach—that is, conditions have meaning only as they are construed by the individual.

According to Kelly, every construct we use (such as "cheap" or "likable") gives us a basis for classifying the similarities and differences between people, objects, and events. Each person has developed only a limited number of constructs, often arranged in order from more to less important. One person's constructs are never completely identical with another person's, although they may be similar. To the extent that their construct systems are similar, Kelly believes, people's behavior will be similar as well.

B. Schemata and prototypes

Discussions of implicit personality theories and construct systems emphasize certain dimensions that are used in judging other people. More recently, social psychologists have begun to use such terms as *schemata, scripts,* and *prototypes* to describe how we interpret the world around us. Actually, the concept of a schema is not a new idea. In 1932 the psychologist Sir Frederick Bartlett introduced the term *schema* as a way of representing the memory process. In doing so, he was arguing against the associationist (or S-R) school of thought that prevailed, suggesting that some form of meaning structure needed to be hypothesized in order to account for alterations in memory between stimulus presentation and recall. In other words, people do not simply respond to what they see; rather, they interpret it on the basis of previous experience—experience that is represented in memory as a schema.

As we saw in Chapter 3, a *self-schema* is defined as a generalization about the self, based on experience, that we use in interpreting events related to the self. Just as we have schemata about the self, we may also have schemata about other people. In fact, these schemata may be quite similar, emphasizing similar dimensions (Fong & Markus, 1982). We can define this more general form of **schema** as follows: an organized configuration of knowledge, derived from past experience, that we use to interpret our experience. Obviously, this is a very general definition. Yet, despite a certain vagueness in the concept, which often makes it difficult to pin down, many investigators believe that it is a useful concept in explaining how we form impressions and react to other people's behavior (Hastie, 1981; Taylor & Crocker, 1981). We can think of many forms of schemata—those based on verbal material, those based on visual material, those dealing with individual persons, and those dealing with social groups (Hastie, 1981). In each case, the schema provides a basis for evaluating experience, affects what we remember or don't remember about an experience, and influences what we will do in the future.

Cantor and Mischel (1979) have used the term **prototype** to refer to a particular type of schema. According to these authors, a prototype is an abstract representation of the attributes associated with a personality type; it is stored in memory and used to organize information about an individual. We may think of a prototype as a specific instance of a more general schema (Fiske & Taylor, 1983). For example, you may have a prototype of the extroverted person that brings to mind particular habits, traits, and mannerisms. Prototypes can also operate at different levels of categorization. Thus, under the general idea of extroversion, you may think of a "comic joker" or a "public relations" type. At an even more specific level, you may think of different types of comic jokers—a circus clown, a popular comedian, or the practical joker in the local fraternity. One of the tasks of cognitive social psychologists is to determine which of these levels is most important in person perception: Which level is the one that people naturally use to categorize others? Research has shown that people will use the level that provides the greatest differentiation between concepts while providing the most meaningful, or "richest," definition within concepts.

C. Stereotypes

A **stereotype** can be thought of as one particular type of schema—a schema about members of an identifiable group (Hamilton, 1979, 1981). Thus, when I see a person with red hair, I may activate my "red-haired person" schema, reacting to that person on the basis of more general beliefs and experiences I have regarding this category of person.

Thinking of stereotypes in this way represents somewhat of a shift for social psychologists (Ashmore & Del Boca, 1981). It was the journalist Walter Lippmann (1922) who first introduced the term *stereotype* to the social science literature, describing stereotypes as "pictures in our heads." In many respects, this idea of a picture or template is similar to the more recent notion of schema. Yet, whereas the word *schema* is not pejorative, Lippmann viewed stereotypes in more negative terms, seeing them as a way for people to protect their relative standing in society. For example, if White people are dominant, they may use negative stereotypes of Blacks to rationalize their position. Psychoanalytic theorizing reinforced this idea of stereotypes as a defense mechanism, emphasizing stereotypes as a product of unconscious needs and defensive drives. In the 1950s, work by Adorno and his colleagues on the "authoritarian personality" firmly placed stereotypes in the category of bad things to have.

Although stereotypes certainly may contain negatively valued characteristics, most psychologists today would not consider them automatically bad things to have. Rather, they are simply one example of the kind of categories we form in order to make our world more orderly and predictable. Like other categories, they may be resistant to change and therefore persist over time. Asking *why* such persistence occurs has led investigators to explore a variety of the ways we may bias our perceptions.

One reason for the persistence of stereotypes is

that we often "fill in" information that may not be there. Given a stereotype about red-haired people, for example, I may assume that red-haired Rhonda is fiery and temperamental. Even if I do not see her act in that manner, I may remember her as such, allowing my stereotype to persist.

Another interesting question concerns our stereotypes of groups in which we are a member, compared with our stereotypes of "out-groups." Generally, our views of the characteristics of our own group are more complex (Linville, 1982; Park & Rothbart, 1982). For example, when members of a sorority were asked to describe members of their own sorority and members of another sorority, they saw much greater similarity among members of the other sorority. In other words, they were more willing to judge members of the other sorority using a common stereotypic category, while seeing greater diversity among the members of their own group. (See Box 4-2 for another example.) Are members of an out-group also judged more negatively? Not necessarily. Although they may be (see Brewer, 1979a), we may also judge out-groups more positively on some occasions. In general, the difference between judgments of in-groups and out-groups appears to be one of extremity: groups that are defined in simpler terms tend to be rated more extremely, in either a positive or a negative direction.

In discussing person prototypes, we suggested that there are various levels of categorization—for example, an extroverted person, a comic, and a TV comedian. Stereotypes operate in the same way. Thus, a person may have a stereotype of men in general, stereotypes of macho men, athletic men, and scholarly men, and even more detailed stereotypes of baseball players, football players, and tennis players. Differences between views of in-groups and out-groups may reflect these different levels of categorization (Park & Rothbart, 1982). In judging members of a group that we do not know very well, we may see them all mainly as members of "Group X," with a common set of attributes. In contrast, when we view our own group members, whom we know much better, we may use a finer level of categorization to distinguish among the different types of group members.

BOX 4-2. Social stereotypes in Iran

Are people from the United States seen as emissaries of the "Great Devil" in postrevolutionary Iran? The media presentations in Iran, as reported by the press, would suggest that Iranians' stereotypes of Westerners are quite negative. To explore these current stereotypes, Beattie, Agahi, and Spencer (1982) asked Iranian men in three occupational groups—university lecturers, taxi drivers, and skilled industrial workers—to ascribe traits to Americans, the English, Arabs, and Iranians. The date of the study was October and November 1980, near the climax of the hostage crisis.

Their results may be somewhat surprising. Men in all three occupational groups rated the Americans in favorable terms; "progressive" was the trait most likely to be ascribed to Americans. English people were viewed somewhat less positively, and there was greater divergence among the occupational groups in defining a stereotype. Stereotypes of the Arabs were uniformly unfavorable, including such characteristics as "dirty" and "lazy."

In viewing themselves, these Iranian respondents showed the least consensus, consistent with other findings on judgments of in-group members. Perhaps not surprising, considering their contact with Western values, university lecturers held the least favorable stereotypes of Iranians.

In general, stereotypes were more extreme among groups that had the least education and the least personal contact with members of the group they were judging. Overall, the results call into question the effectiveness of media in shaping stereotypes, given the strong anti-American feeling that was being transmitted at the time. ■

Another kind of cognitive bias that can affect the formation and persistence of stereotypes is the **illusory correlation,** an overestimation of the strength of a relationship between two variables (Chapman & Chapman, 1969). In an illusory correlation, the variables may not be related at all, or the relationship may be much weaker than believed. One explanation for this kind of bias relates to the frequency of the events that we try to explain (Hamilton, 1981). For example, if two types of information both occur infrequently, we will tend to make an association between them even if no real association exists (see Figure 4-1). In a demonstration of this bias, subjects were given a set of descriptive statements about a variety of people. Two-thirds of these people were identified as being members of Group A, while the remaining third were identified as members of Group B. In addition to their group identification, each person was also described by a single behavior, either a desirable behavior (for example, "John visited a sick friend in the hospital") or an undesirable behavior (for example, "John always talks about himself and his problems"). Among both Group A and Group B members, approximately two-thirds of the individuals were described by positive behaviors and approximately one-third by negative behaviors. Thus, in this experiment two kinds of information were given to subjects: group membership and type of behavior. When asked to make judgments about the typical member of each group, subjects showed evidence of the illusory correlation. They judged members of Group B to be less likable than members of Group A, suggesting a perceived link between frequencies. The smaller number of Group B members was associated with the smaller number of undesirable behaviors, even though the proportions of undesirable behaviors were identical for the two groups.

Categorizing information on the basis of group membership may be more economical—it is easier to talk about 1 group than about 20 individuals—but it obviously has its problems. For example, the presence of a few deviant individuals in a group may color our perception of the group as a whole (Rothbart, Fulero, Jensen, Howard, & Birrell, 1978). Similarly, if we are asked to recall the

FIGURE 4-1. The illusory correlation. In the diagram, two types of people are represented: square heads and round heads. Some of the square heads and some of the round heads are smiling, and some of each group are frowning. According to the research on the illusory correlation, if you were shown each of these faces separately and then later asked which type of person would be more likely to frown, you would tend to say "round heads," because people tend to make associations between infrequent events—in this case, round heads and frowns.

details of a group discussion, we tend to remember what members of certain groups said (for example, what "some woman" said) but often forget which particular individual was responsible for the remark (Taylor, Fiske, Etcoff, & Ruderman, 1978).

Thus, many of our stereotypes are based on cognitive "errors." These "errors" are most likely to occur when we do not have extensive contact with the group in question and when we do not have any additional information about the individual members of the group. Because undesirable behaviors are also believed to be less common than desirable behaviors (Kanouse & Hanson, 1972; Lay, Burron, & Jackson, 1973), these two sets of infrequent and unfamiliar events (contact with a group we infrequently encounter and an undesirable behavior) may be linked in our mind, creating stereotypes that we use in the future.

However, stereotypes are not totally the product of "errors" in cognitive processing. Motivational factors such as those suggested by Walter Lippmann must still be considered important. Yet, the recent cognitive analysis has allowed us to see more clearly how stereotypes relate to other kinds of social inference.

D. Belief in a just world

Implicit personality theories, schemata, and stereotypes are all ways that we organize information and form categories to interpret the character of persons we encounter. Another way of viewing the world is to look at the events that happen to people and to find principles to explain those outcomes. Social psychologist Melvin Lerner has suggested that many people have a **belief in a just world**—a belief that "there is an appropriate fit between what people do and what happens to them" (Lerner, 1966, p. 3). For Lerner, the belief in a just world is not only a cognitive principle; it develops out of a motivational context as well. Lerner suggests that we develop a sense of our own deservingness and that, in turn, we realize that in order to believe in our deservingness, we need to believe that others also get what they deserve in the world.

But what happens if events appear to be unjust? Lerner suggests that such events threaten our belief in a just world and that, accordingly, we will try to correct the situation in some way (Lerner, 1975, 1977; Lerner, Miller, & Holmes, 1976). On some occasions we may rectify the situation by compensating the victim of injustice—by giving aid to refugees, for example. Other times we may try to punish the harmdoer (if we can find one). Yet, in other instances when we do not seem to be able to reestablish justice, we may convince ourselves that no injustice has occurred.

By blaming the victim, we can maintain our belief that people get what they deserve (Ryan, 1971). Martin Symonds (1975), a psychiatrist, has interviewed hundreds of victims of rapes, assaults, and kidnapings and finds that many of these victims receive, instead of sympathy, inquisitions and censure from their friends and family. When a person has been mugged, for example, a frequent response of friends, family, and the police is to interrogate the person relentlessly about *why* he or she got into such an unfortunate situation. "Why were you walking in that neighborhood alone?" "Why didn't you scream?" "Why were you carrying so much money?" Such reactions reflect our pervasive need to find rational causes for apparently senseless events. In the case of rape, observers tend to attribute responsibility to the victim. This tendency is most pronounced when other explanations for the event are not apparent. For example, a victim who is described as unacquainted with her assailant is seen as more responsible for a rape than when she is acquainted with him (Smith, Keating, Hester, & Mitchell, 1976). In general, men are more likely to attribute responsibility to the female victim than women are (Feild, 1978; Selby, Calhoun, & Brock, 1977). The same type of rationale has been used by some people to account for the assassination of public figures (see Photo 4-2).

Derogation of the victim does not always occur, however. Indeed, it is particularly unlikely when someone else's suffering threatens our own feelings of deservingness and justice. For example, Sorrentino and Boutilier (1974) found that observers who are told to expect a similar fate to that of the victim are less likely to malign the victim. Subjects in their experiment observed a female undergraduate receive a series of electrical shocks as a "learner" in a teaching-effectiveness project. Some of the subjects were told that they would also serve as "learners" later; others were told that they would not. Anticipation of a similar fate led to a significant reduction in the assignment of negative characteristics to the learner. Such a pattern is, of course, consistent with the sex differences in attribution of responsibility for rape, where we can assume that women are more likely to anticipate a similar fate than men are.

PHOTO 4-2. *Martin Luther King, victim of assassination. In April 1968, right after Dr. King's murder, a representative sample of 1337 American adults were asked: "When you heard the news [of the assassination], which of these things was your strongest reaction: (1) anger, (2) sadness, (3) shame, (4) fear, (5) he brought it on himself?" About one-third (426) of the respondents chose the response "brought it on himself" (Rokeach, 1970). For these respondents, Lerner's "just world" hypothesis applies: since Dr. King was killed, he must have deserved to be killed.*

At a more general level, Lerner (1977) has suggested that the individual's first concern is his or her own deservingness and the ability to believe in a world where justice prevails. Often this belief leads a person to simply ignore evidence of injustice. Thus, we may skip those articles in the newspaper that deal with suffering in other countries, and we may avoid neighborhoods in our own town where evidence of poverty is prominent. Yet, many of those same occasions may lead us to offer direct assistance—perhaps because they represent only a minimal threat to our own state of justice and deservingness. Not being personally threatened, we may feel free to offer assistance and to correct the unjust consequences of others (Miller, 1977). In contrast, when the threat to our own state of deservingness is apparent, we seem to be much more likely to choose other strategies, such as blaming the victims and seeing them as a direct cause of their own misfortunes, thereby sparing ourselves the fear that a similar fate may befall us.

■ III. Explaining behavior: Attributions of causality

In maintaining a belief in a just world by derogating the victim, we are engaging in a form of **causal attribution**—the process of inferring the explanations of causes for events. As we saw in Chapter 3, people often try to account for their own outcomes, looking either to themselves or to someone or something in the environment as a cause of any particular event. In the same way, we also try to explain the behavior of other people. For example, if you were watching two politicians debate on television, and Candidate Jones suddenly lashed out in a personal attack on Candidate Smith, how would you interpret the behavior? Would you infer something about Jones's personality? Or would you decide that Smith must have done something to provoke the attack? Or would you conclude that there was something particular about the setting or the circumstances that caused this event to happen?

As we saw in Chapter 3, one basic way of categorizing causal attributions is to follow the lead of Fritz Heider, separating them into *dispositional* (or personal) and *situational* (or environmental) causes. Later theorists have extended this basic idea, exploring the more complicated ways in which our attributions of causality are formed. Let us now look more closely at some of the recent developments—specifically, at the principles of covariation and causal schemata, the process of correspondent inference, and the attribution of causes for success and failure. Each of these developments can be identified closely with a particular social psychologist, although many investigators have contributed research to each model.

A. Covariation and causal schemata

Harold Kelley assumes that we try to explain events in much the same way as a scientist would: armed with a series of observations of people's behavior, we try to figure out what cause might be responsible for a particular action. According to the principle of *covariation*, "an effect is attributed to the one of its possible causes with which, over time, it varies" (Kelley, 1967, p. 108). In other words, Kelley believes that we look for a systematic pattern of relationships and infer cause and effect from that pattern. This model obviously assumes that we have more than one opportunity to observe a particular person, and it assumes that we have observed other people in similar situations as well.

Building on Heider's general distinction between dispositional and situational causes, Kelley has pointed to three general types of explanation that may be used when trying to interpret someone's behavior: an attribution to the *actor*, or the person who is engaging in the behavior in question; an attribution to the *entity*, or the target person with whom the actor is behaving; and an attribution to the *circumstances*, or the particular setting in which the behavior occurs (Kelley, 1967). Thus, if Susan runs away from Joe at a restaurant, we might attribute the event to something about Susan ("She is a basically hysterical person"), to something about Joe ("He is an insulting boor"), or to the particular circumstances ("The restaurant's vichyssoise had mold in it, and it made Susan sick").

Each of these explanations is reasonable; the trick is to decide on one as *the* explanation. Kelley suggests that, to do this, we use three basic kinds of information: consensus, consistency, and distinctiveness. *Consensus* information is the knowledge we have about the behavior of other actors in the same situation. For example, if everyone in the restaurant jumped up and ran out, we would say the behavior had high consensus. In contrast, if Susan ran out alone, her behavior would have low consensus. The second source of information, *consistency*, is our knowledge about the actor's

behavior on other occasions. Does Susan habitually run out of restaurants and out of movies and concerts as well, or is this the only time that she has created such a scene? Finally, one can use distinctiveness as a source of information. *Distinctiveness* is concerned with the variation in behavior among different entities, or targets. Does Susan run away only from Joe, or has she also run away from Rita, Peter, and Lila on other occasions?

Kelley suggests that if we have information about each of these three factors, our causal explanations will be quite predictable. These predictable explanations, which have been confirmed by subsequent research (Major, 1980; McArthur, 1972; Orvis, Cunningham, & Kelley, 1975), are outlined in Table 4-4. Depending on the particular combination of information we have about the people involved, we will explain the event by attributing it to the actor, to the entity, or to the circumstances. When the pattern of information is less clear than that outlined in Table 4-4, we may use some combination of these three factors to explain the event (Major, 1980; McArthur, 1972).

Although the covariation model has a kind of precise elegance, it is clearly an idealized model. Often we do not have available the kinds of information the model requires: we may not have observed a person on previous occasions, or we may not know how other people have behaved in the same situation. What do we do in such cases if we want to explain behavior? Kelley (1972) suggests that we rely on causal schemata. According to Kelley, a **causal schema** is "a conception of the manner in which two or more causal factors interact in relation to a particular kind of effect" (1972, p. 152). From our observations of people, we develop certain beliefs about causes and effects. These beliefs, or schemata, are then used to explain a particular person's behavior. In other words, Kelley is suggesting that we rely on some general beliefs, rather than needing all possible information about one person in one situation, when we attempt to explain a particular behavior.

There are, of course, many possible kinds of causal schemata, but let us consider just two of the more general ones. For some events, we may use a *multiple sufficient-cause model*. In this case,

---

TABLE 4-4. Kelley's model of attribution: Why did Professor Martinez criticize Paul?

Attributions are made to the actor when:
Consensus is low
Consistency is high
Distinctiveness is low
Example: No other professors criticize Paul (low consensus); Professor Martinez criticized Paul last year, last month, and twice last week (high consistency); and Professor Martinez criticized every other student in the class as well (low distinctiveness). Conclusion: The behavior is attributed to Professor Martinez—for example, "Professor Martinez is a mean professor."

Attributions are made to the entity when:
Consensus is high
Consistency is high
Distinctiveness is high
Example: Every other professor criticizes Paul (high consensus); Professor Martinez criticized Paul last year, last month, and twice last week (high consistency); and Professor Martinez was friendly to all the other members of the class (high distinctiveness). Conclusion: The behavior is attributed to Paul—for example, "Paul is stupid and lazy."

Attributions are made to the circumstances when:
Consistency is low
Example: Professor Martinez has never criticized Paul before (low consistency). Conclusion: The behavior is attributed to a particular set of circumstances and not to either Paul or Professor Martinez—for example, "Paul said something today that Professor Martinez misinterpreted."

---

we decide that any number of factors may be responsible for a particular event. For example, if we saw a father give his son an affectionate hug, we could decide either that the father was generally a warm person or that the son had just done something special. Either of these explanations is possible; the one we select will depend on the information we have available. If we knew that the son had done nothing special, we would decide that the father was an affectionate person; if we knew that the father was generally inhibited about showing affection, we would conclude that the son had done something unusual to deserve the hug. The point here is that either attribution would be sufficient to explain the event.

In other cases, we use a *multiple necessary-cause model.* In this model at least two causes are necessary to explain the event. Often we use the multiple necessary-cause model to explain fairly extreme events. For example, Howard suddenly starts fighting with Tom. Did Tom do something to provoke Howard, or is Howard the kind of person who is likely to start a fight? In such a case, most people would conclude that both statements

were true: Tom provoked Howard, and Howard is the kind of guy who starts fights. It takes two people to start an argument, so the saying goes; or, in other terms, it takes two causes to explain an effect.

In summary, causal schemata are a kind of shorthand. If we have unlimited information, the covariation model may represent our inference processes accurately. But in many situations we try to explain events without having all the information, and in such cases we will rely on a causal schema to make sense of the behavior we observe.

B. Correspondent inference

In our attempts to explain the events that occur around us, we do, as suggested by the covariation and causal-schema models, make a general distinction between dispositional and situational causes. Beyond this general process, however, we also make some very specific attributions about the personal characteristics of the actor. Edward Jones and his colleagues (Jones & Davis, 1965; Jones & McGillis, 1976) have focused on the ways we make these dispositional attributions—that is, on the way we observe an event and infer the intentions and characteristics of the actor.

If you are watching someone act in a certain situation, you are probably aware not only of the behavior itself but also of some of the consequences of that behavior. For example, if you see John give Maria a bouquet of flowers at the office, you may also observe that Maria is very pleased by the gift. Perhaps, you may infer, John's intention was simply to make Maria happy. However, if you happen to know that Maria is the vice-president's personal secretary and that John is trying to get a promotion, you may begin to suspect that the intended consequences of John's actions were not simply to please Maria. This illustrates one of the factors that Jones and his colleagues believe are most important in our inference process: the consequences of an action. Jones suggests that, in observing a person's behavior, we consider not only the effects of that behavior itself but also the possible effects of alternative behaviors that the person might have engaged in. For example, if you knew that John had two tickets for a hit play but did not ask Maria to go with him, you might suspect that making Maria happy was less important to John than being seen as a friendly person around the office. In this analysis, the impression John makes in the office would be a *noncommon effect*—that is, a consequence that could be achieved only by giving the flowers to Maria at work—whereas the effect of making Maria happy could have been achieved in at least two ways. Jones and his colleagues believe that the fewer the noncommon effects, the more likely those effects are to be influential in our attribution of characteristics to the actor. Research has supported this prediction (Newtson, 1974).

Jones also suggests that our tendency to infer dispositional causes for another person's behavior is influenced by what we initially expect the actor to do (Jones & McGillis, 1976). If the actor does something quite divergent from what we expect, we are much more likely to wonder why the event happened and to seek an explanation in the personality of the actor. If we are familiar with the setting in which this unexpected event occurs, person attributions are apt to be particularly strong (Lalljee, Watson, & White, 1982). For example, observing someone begin to recite Hamlet's soliloquy in your own room is much more likely to invoke a person attribution than the same behavior would be if observed at a party in an unfamiliar locale (unless you are an actor, accustomed to dramatic monologues recited in your room).

There are two basic kinds of expectancies that we form. The first, *category-based expectancies*, are assumptions we make based on the individual's membership in a particular group or category. Stereotypes, discussed earlier, are one form of such category-based expectancies. For example, if we assume that most men are not gentle, then we would probably take particular note of a man who was playing gently with children and would tend to attribute his behavior to something special about his personality. A second form of expectancies is *target-based*. These expectancies are based on information we have about the particular individual in other situations. For example, having seen

PHOTO 4-3. *Informed that this man is a professor, you might expect certain behaviors from him, depending on your stereotype of professors—reading esoteric books, for example, or neglecting his personal appearance. In contrast, if you were told that he was a homeless bum, you would probably take more notice of his reading behavior because it would be unexpected.*

Lionel behave gently with many children on many occasions, we would probably expect Lionel to be gentle, no matter what our general expectations of men were.

You may notice that these two kinds of expectancies are very similar to the concepts of consensus and consistency that were discussed earlier. Both category-based expectancies and consensus refer to information we have about a group of people, which we may use in inferring the causes for a particular person's behavior. Similarly, target-based expectancies and consistency both rely on our information about the particular actor.

Although the attribution models of Kelley and Jones are similar in some respects, Jones pays much more attention to the specific dispositional attributions that are made. To use his terms, the concern is with the *correspondence* between a behavior and a dispositional attribution. If John performs a friendly act, do we infer that John is a friendly person? As we have seen, in making this inference we look to the consequences of the action—that is, to the number of noncommon effects and to the expectedness of the effects. When both these factors are low, we are likely to infer that the person intended the behavior, and in turn we will infer that the intention was a result of a particular personality disposition—in this case, friendliness. Under other conditions, such as when the behavior is expected and the noncommon effects are numerous, there may be low correspondence; we will not infer a particular personality disposition in order to explain the behavior. Thus, the Jones model takes us one step further in explaining behavior, from pointing generally to something about the person to labeling the specific traits that are believed to be responsible.

C. Causes for success and failure

Bernard Weiner has developed a model of attribution that refers to a much more specific area of behavior than do the models of Kelley and Jones. Weiner's model deals with the explanations we arrive at for the success and failure of people on particular tasks (Frieze, 1976; Weiner, 1974; Weiner, Frieze, Kukla, Reed, Rest, & Rosenbaum, 1972). Why did Linda get promoted so quickly? Why did

David flunk the calculus exam? These are the kinds of questions that Weiner's model attempts to answer.

Like Kelley's and Jones's models, Weiner's basic model rests on the foundations established by Fritz Heider. Like Kelley, Weiner believes that one of the dimensions of our judgments is a comparison between dispositional and situational causes, which he refers to as the *internal/external* dimension. In addition, he posits a second dimension, called *temporary/stable*. Weiner suggests that these two dimensions are independent of each other and that, therefore, we can describe causal explanations by means of a two-by-two table (see Figure 4-2).[1]

In each of the categories, there are a variety of possible causes that we can use to explain someone's performance (including our own). The two dimensions are important to keep in mind, however, because they have different consequences. The temporary/stable dimension is assumed to be most important to us in forming expectancies, or predictions of how someone will do in the future (Valle & Frieze, 1976). For example, if we believe that Linda's excellent job performance was due to her ability or to the ease of the assignment, we would expect her to do well again if she were given the same assignment. If we decide that the reason for her success was something temporary, such as a fleeting good mood or pure chance, we would be unlikely to be confident of her future success. In trying to explain failure, the same principles hold true. Failure that is attributed to stable factors is likely to yield predictions of future failure, whereas failure that is attributed to more temporary causes allows the possibility of future improvement.

The second dimension of causal attribution in Weiner's model—internal versus external explanation—is believed to relate primarily to the rewards or punishments that follow a performance. We are more likely to reward people if we believe that their success was of their own mak-

---

[1]More recently, Weiner has suggested that there is a third important dimension—intentionality—that cross-cuts the two other dimensions. However, because less work has dealt with this dimension, we shall limit our discussion to the internality and stability factors.

	Temporary/stable dimension	
	Temporary	Stable
Internal	Effort, mood, fatigue	Ability, intelligence, physical characteristics
External	Luck, chance, opportunity	Task difficulty, environmental barriers

Internal/external dimension

> *How are you likely to explain success or failure? In which cell would your explanations belong?*

FIGURE 4-2. Weiner's model of causal attribution, showing typical attributions that represent each category.

ing—due, for example, to their ability or their hard work—than if we think that chance or some other external factor was responsible. Punishment is also more likely when failure is attributed internally, rather than externally. If David failed his exam because he didn't try hard enough, we are likely to be much more critical of him than we would be if we thought his failure was the consequence of an unreasonably hard test.

Our choice among these possible causes can be affected by a variety of factors. Initial expectancies may be important, for example, in deciding between a stable cause and a more temporary cause. If we expected someone to do well, then we will probably attribute that person's success to ability or skill. In contrast, if we expected the person to fail, then we are more apt to attribute the person's success to some more temporary cause. Category-based expectancies for members of a particular group may affect attributions as well. For example, people are more likely to attribute a woman's success to temporary factors while explaining similar success by a male as due to ability (Deaux, 1976). Similarly, Whites are more likely to see ability as responsible for the success of a White than of a Black (Yarkin, Town, & Wallston, 1982); both Blacks and Whites are more likely

to attribute failure to a lack of ability in the out-group than in their own group (Whitehead, Smith, & Eichhorn, 1982).

Such biases in evaluation are important in their own right. They become even more important when we realize that attributions are not "the end of the line"; instead, the explanations that we form may influence other kinds of behavior. Heilman and Guzzo (1978) have provided a vivid demonstration of some of these consequences. In a simulated organizational setting, business students were asked to assume the role of an employer and to make raise and promotion decisions for a set of hypothetical employees. The information provided about the employees stressed one of four causes for their recent successful job performance: high ability, considerable effort, a relatively easy assignment, or pure chance. The behavior of the role-playing supervisors strongly supported the validity of Weiner's two dimensions. Supervisors recommended raises only to those employees whose performance had been explained by either ability or effort; in other words, rewards were given for internally caused success but were not given when external factors were believed to be responsible. Promotion was reserved for those employees who were said to be high in ability. Presumably, subjects believed that future performance could be ensured only if high ability (an internal *and* stable characteristic) was present but not necessarily if exceptional effort (a more temporary characteristic) had been shown.

Weiner's model of attribution is more limited than the others we have considered, focusing strictly on explanations for successful and unsuccessful performances in an achievement context. Furthermore, recent research has indicated that our reactions to events and our explanations of them may be more complicated than the simple fourfold table suggests (for example, Smith & Kluegel, 1982). Nevertheless, Weiner's model is an important approach because, more than the others, it points to some of the consequences that attribution patterns may have for other behaviors.

D. Biases in the attribution process

When explaining the performance of members of an in-group or out-group, we may choose different reasons for success and failure. This is just one example of how attributions may be biased. Although attribution models originally tended to view the perceiver as a fairly rational creature who observed behavior, weighed evidence, and assigned plausible causes, researchers soon discovered that such rationality is not always the rule. Instead, we now know that there are many ways in which explanations can be biased. Some of these biases have a motivational base, as we seek to put our own or our friends' behavior in a favorable light. Other biases reflect limitations in our cognitive processing. Both kinds, motivational and cognitive, are important in that they provide revealing information about how we view the world (see Fiske & Taylor, 1983).

Overestimating dispositional causes. One of the most basic tendencies of the observer—so basic that it has been called the **fundamental attribution error**—is to overemphasize the actor as a cause of events (Ross, 1977). Like a personality theorist, we tend to see something in the actor as the cause of an event, neglecting situational factors as possible influences.

As an example of this bias, imagine yourself watching a quiz show in which a woman is asked to make up questions and a man is asked to answer them. The questioner, drawing on her own area of expertise, poses a difficult set of questions, and the respondent is only moderately successful in providing answers. When asked to judge the general intellectual ability of each contestant, whom would you rate more favorably? If you are like the subjects in an experiment by Ross, Amabile, and Steinmetz (1977), you would probably rate the questioner as more intelligent than the respondent. Yet, in this judgment, you would be neglecting an important situational factor—specifically, the control and choice assigned to the questioner, which allowed her to select particular areas and avoid others. Had the roles in the situation been reversed, so that the woman became the respondent and the man became the questioner, the man probably would have displayed similar finesse, and your judgments of intelligence would have been reversed.

You may have experienced this same phenom-

enon in playing a game of trivia with a friend. In tapping your own area of expertise, you feel quite intelligent as your friend fails to answer several questions in a row. Yet, when your friend takes over the questioning, he or she appears to be the intelligent one. Ross and his colleagues point out how this particular error can be pervasive in our judgments of the powerful and the powerless: we may overestimate the capability of those in power, forgetting to consider the role requirements that give the powerful an advantage over the powerless.

Why do we make this error? One reason, say Jellison and Green (1981), is that we have a norm for internality in this society. We believe that people should be responsible for their own outcomes, and we value internally caused outcomes while disparaging externally caused ones. Another reason is that the actor in a situation is often more prominent than the other aspects of the environment. We tend to focus directly on the actor in many situations, ignoring background factors and social context, and then we place undue reliance on that which we have observed most closely.

Is this tendency to place more emphasis on dispositional factors really an error? Social psychologists do not agree on this point (Harvey, Town, & Yarkin, 1981; Reeder, 1982). As noted earlier in this chapter, accuracy is an elusive quality. Just as it is difficult to determine exactly what traits a person has, so it is difficult to say what the "true" cause of an event is. A tendency to attribute to dispositional factors is certainly pervasive, but to what degree that is "wrong" is uncertain. However, in cases in which situational constraints are severe, it is clear that dispositional causes cannot have much effect, despite our tendency to see them as important.

Actors and observers. This general tendency to overestimate dispositional factors often stops short of our own behavior. Jones and Nisbett (1972) have suggested that although we are likely to attribute the behavior of other people to their personality traits, we are prone to believe that our own behavior is situationally determined. Thus, if asked why your friend Ira likes Denise, you are likely to respond by listing Ira's personality characteristics. Yet, if asked why *you* like Denise, you will probably describe more of Denise's traits than your own (Nisbett, Caputo, Legant, & Marecek, 1973).

Perceptual salience is one explanation for this effect as well. If you are the actor, you are more likely to focus on the events around you, whereas observing another person generally places the focus on the person. Another explanation for the actor-observer effect stresses differences in the information available to actors and observers (Monson & Snyder, 1977). Often, the observer has little information about the historical determinants— what has happened before—and consequently will focus totally on the here and now. In watching an actor give in to a social-influence attempt, for example, the observer may conclude that the person is weak-willed and easily persuaded. In contrast, the actor has a great deal of information about his own past behavior. Knowing that past social-influence attempts generally have been unsuccessful, the actor may attribute his present behavior to the persuasiveness of the speaker. Such differences between actors and observers are often particularly apparent in laboratory experiments, where situational forces generally are quite strong.

There are factors that can alter the actor-observer difference. For example, if you are asked to empathize with the person you are observing, you will be less likely to use dispositional explanations and more likely to find situational ones (Brehm & Aderman, 1977). Switching from the role of the actor to the role of observer of oneself also leads to a decrease in situational attributions (Storms, 1973). In other words, our ways of making causal attributions are not always the same: different perspectives and different kinds of information can bias our explanations in one direction or another.

Underusing consensus information. Many attribution models assume that we explain an individual's behavior by using information about what other people have done. Yet, this consensus information often seems to be far less important than information about the individual (Major, 1980; McArthur, 1972). At times we may completely ignore consensus information. For example, Nis-

bett and Borgida (1975) gave subjects information about how people in general had behaved in previous studies of altruism and obedience. The information that virtually no one had been willing in the past to help in a particular experiment had no effect on the subjects' predictions of a target person's behavior when asked to participate in the same experiment. The subjects confidently predicted that the target person would help in the experiment. In other words, consensus information was ignored, which is a behavior pattern consistent with the general disregard of base-rate information described by Kahneman and Tversky (1973).

General consensus information may not be weighed heavily because it is not considered particularly trustworthy (Fiske & Taylor, 1983). Who are these people? Are they similar to me? Would they act in the same way that people I know and like would act? As an extreme example, consider how important the behaviors of people in Afghanistan would be in deciding whether a neighbor's behavior was reasonable. Probably you would decide that those behaviors were not terribly relevant. Only when the sample-based consensus is relevant will consensus exert a strong effect (Kassin, 1979), and even then the influence will be diminished if the person has clear ideas about what is to be expected.

PHOTO 4-4. *Information about the shopping behavior of these Mexican women—even if such information indicated unanimous agreement—probably wouldn't influence your predictions about a suburban U.S. shopper's purchases in a local supermarket.*

Relationship to the actor. Another source of attributional bias occurs when we are asked to make judgments about people who have some relationship to us. Jones and Davis (1965) have pointed to two factors that increase our tendencies to make dispositional attributions: hedonic relevance and personalism. **Hedonic relevance** refers to the extent to which a person's actions are rewarding or costly to the observer. To the extent that Anna's behavior has a direct effect on you, you are more likely to attribute causality to Anna than you would be if her actions did not affect you. **Personalism** is a closely related concept that refers to the perceived intentionality of a person's actions, or the degree to which a perceiver believes that another's behavior is directed at him or her. If you believe that Anna intended to affect you by her behavior, your attributions about Anna will be made more strongly (Potter, 1973). Not only the kind of attributions made but the very act of making attributions is affected by our perceived relationship with the actor (Leone, Graziano, & Case, 1978).

Even the expectation of interacting with someone can lead us to make more dispositional attributions to that person (Monson, Keel, Stephens, & Genung, 1982). In part, this bias may reflect our need to predict and control our environment. By focusing on the person, we may think ourselves better prepared than if we had attributed the event to chance or to some circumstance.

Temporal effects in attribution. Explanations are not always offered at the moment an event occurs. Sometimes we think back to a past event and infer the causes for it. At other times, in the course of recollection, we may reinterpret an event from the perspective of the present. Do these changes in perspective affect the pattern of attributions? Miller and Porter (1980) suggest that attributions may become more situational with the passage of time. One reason may be that figure (the actor) and ground (the situation) become more similar as we look back. Another reason may be that our need for predictability and control is not as strong when we reflect on past history as it is when we interact in the present.

Either of these reasons could account for a decrease in dispositional attributions and an increase in situational ones.

■ IV. The process of social cognition

Attributions concern the "what" of social knowledge—what kinds of explanations we use for what kinds of events. To fully understand the use of social knowledge, however, we need to ask questions at another level as well: *why* and *how* do we think about people and events in the way we do? In this case, our concern is with the process of social cognition. Social psychologists have become increasingly interested in these kinds of process issues in recent years. In doing so, they have established important links with the field of cognitive psychology, and models from the two fields have begun to converge.

To approach some of these process issues, let us consider the concept of schema once again. A schema, as we have seen, is a way of organizing information. Its influence can be quite broad, affecting not only how we interpret the world but also what we remember about events that have occurred. Figure 4-3 diagrams how schemata are thought to work. At the "input" end of the process, events are interpreted in terms of existing schemata. If no appropriate schemata exist, new ones may be formed to account for the person or the event. Once events are stored in long-term memory according to the schemata, they will then influence what we recall at a future date. As an example, assume that you see a greasy-haired man standing in front of the jewelry counter at your local department store. Do you have a schema or a stereotype of greasy-haired men? If not, you may watch the man closely and make some inferences about what such men are like. Perhaps you already have a schema for greasy-haired men—perhaps you think they tend to be disreputable and not to be trusted. In that case, you may interpret this particular man's behavior in terms of your schema, possibly even making inferences about the probability that he intends to steal a gold watch. Some time later, when thinking about this particular incident, you may even think that you saw him steal the watch, depending on what aspects of the event and what inferences you stored in your memory. Thus, schemata may affect both the encoding and the retrieval of information. Let us look more closely at these two aspects of the social cognition process.

A. Encoding: Getting the information in

Encoding consists in taking in external stimuli and creating internal representations of them (Fiske & Taylor, 1983). The correspondence between these two things is not necessarily one-to-one. Instead, as we form internal representations, we may omit details, change features, and even make up elements that were not present in the original event. The greasy-haired man, for example, may have already been wearing a gold watch that we did not notice; perhaps his clothes were clean, rather than dirty as we now recall; and did he really have a scar across his forehead? What we store depends on the attention that we pay to the event itself. At least two aspects of an event seem to affect our attention and, in turn, affect the schemata that

we select to use; they are salience and vividness.

Salience refers to the distinctiveness of a stimulus relative to the context (Fiske & Taylor, 1983). For example, a 6′8″ basketball player is salient in a roomful of midgets but would not be particularly noticeable on a basketball court. A woman would be salient at an otherwise all-male meeting of a corporate board of directors but would not be readily distinguished at a women's luncheon. Salient stimuli attract our attention by virtue of being different in some way from the surroundings. Salient events are those that are unexpected—those that are generally not predictable on the basis of our prior knowledge (Fiske & Taylor, 1983).

Vividness refers to the intensity or emotional interest of the stimulus itself (Fiske & Taylor, 1983). For example, a live concert is more vivid than a recording, no matter where it takes place, and a Technicolor movie is probably more vivid than a black-and-white film.

Both salience and vividness may affect the attention we give to an event and the kind of information we store in our memory. The effects of

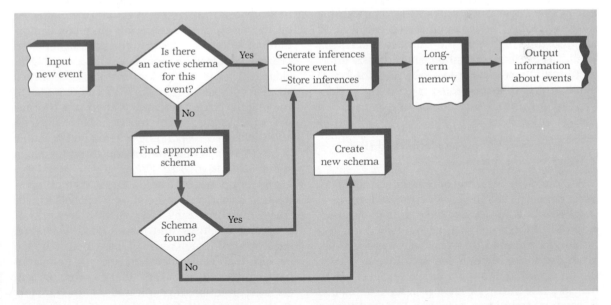

FIGURE 4-3. Flow chart representing the ways in which schemata operate in the social cognition process. Stimuli and events occur at the left end of the diagram (the input), and recall is represented at the right end (the output). In between, inferences are made and stored in memory.

salience are much more established, however. If a person or an event is salient, we are more likely to pay attention to it, we are more likely to see it as causally responsible, we evaluate it more extremely, and we recall it more readily (Fiske & Taylor, 1983). The effects of vividness are more elusive (Taylor & Thompson, 1982). Although it makes sense to think that vivid stimuli would be encoded more rapidly and remembered better, the evidence for the specific effects of vividness is mixed. One possibility is that vividness is important only for some people, perhaps people who have a natural tendency to use vivid visual imagery when they observe events (Swann & Miller, 1982).

When we already have schemata in our memory for certain classes of events, our encoding of new information will be affected by these schemata. Both congruent and incongruent information may be encoded more readily than irrelevant information (Hastie, 1981). Information that is consistent with a schema may be quickly stored with the existing schema. Inconsistent information, in contrast, may take longer to code but may also attract attention because of its relation to the schema. For example, seeing a professor buying philosophy books might fit easily into an existing schema; seeing the same professor excelling in weightlifting might take more time to process but would also attract attention. In contrast, information that is irrelevant to a schema—for example, learning that the professor grew up in Kansas—might attract little attention and cause no change in the schema.

B. Storage and retrieval: Getting the information out

Although it is easy to conceptualize the difference between encoding processes and retrieval processes, it is somewhat more difficult to measure the difference. When giving eyewitness testimony, for example, if you cannot remember what a burglar looked like, is that a failure to encode the information or an inability to retrieve it from memory? Cognitive psychologists have developed a variety of techniques to tease out these different processes. For example, if you watch a film of a couple having dinner and are told in advance that the woman is a librarian, you will presumably encode information about her in terms of your schema (or, at a more specific level, your stereotype) of librarians, and you may recall information in terms of that same schema. However, what if you learn that she is a librarian only after you have seen the film? Under these conditions, your initial encoding could not have been affected by the schema, but your recall could have. Both processes will affect the degree to which you remember schema-consistent and schema-inconsistent information. However, schemata appear to exert more influence on encoding than on retrieval (Cohen, 1981).

Recall can also be affected by a process called *priming*. The **priming effect** refers to the fact that a schema is more likely to be used if it has been activated recently. In one study that showed this memory effect, people first read a list of traits that emphasized either positive traits such as adventurousness or more negative characteristics such as recklessness. Shortly after seeing these traits, in what they believed to be an unrelated task, they read a story about a man named Donald who favored activities such as skydiving and demolition derbies. Evaluations of Donald were affected by the prior, and presumably unrelated, information. When an "adventurous" schema had been primed, people were more favorable toward Donald than when a "reckless" schema had been primed (Higgins, Rholes, & Jones, 1977). Another way of viewing the priming effect is to think of a "storage bin" of schemata. If a memory has been called up recently, the corresponding schema will probably be at the top of the bin, ready to be used if a suitable situation arises (Wyer & Srull, 1981).

Memory is not an easy concept. Current investigators have developed elaborate models to represent memory, using ideas such as networks of propositions, links and nodes, and activation sequences. Although many of these models are too detailed for our consideration here, it is important to recognize the crucial role that memory plays in our interpretation of people and events. Our view of the present is influenced by our recall of the past, and that recall, as we have seen, can be shaped and distorted by a variety of events.

V. SUMMARY

Knowing what other people are like and why they behave the way they do is important for us to predict and understand our world. Accuracy is a difficult quality to establish, as demonstrated both by early investigators and by recent research on eyewitness testimony. Yet, there are many principles we use reliably in our judgment of other people.

Three aspects of the impression-formation process are the importance of *central traits*, the prominent use of an averaging model (as opposed to an additive model), and *primacy* and *recency* effects.

Often we approach situations with more general beliefs, as reflected in our *philosophies of human nature*. More individualized conceptions of human behavior are termed *implicit personality theories*, describing our beliefs about how certain traits go together. More recently, investigators have begun to use the terms *schemata* and *prototypes* to describe more specific organized knowledge structures.

Stereotypes can be viewed as one particular type of schema about a recognizable group. Stereotypes of out-groups are generally more extreme and more homogeneous than stereotypes of in-groups. Formation of stereotypes may reflect an *illusory correlation* between two actually unrelated characteristics. At a more general level, a *belief in a just world* may affect the way we interpret and respond to events.

Attribution theories deal specifically with the causes we assign to events. In general, actions may be given either a dispositional attribution or a situational attribution. Harold Kelley, Edward Jones, and Bernard Weiner each have developed models of the attribution process, deriving from the early work of Fritz Heider. Each of these models deals with the relation between the available information and the inferences we draw in trying to explain the cause of an event.

As in the simpler impression-formation process, biases in causal attribution are frequent. For example, we tend to overestimate the influence of dispositional factors (the *fundamental attribution error*). Actors and observers often emphasize different causes for events, in part because of differences in the information available to them. Consensus information may be ignored. Events that have personal relevance are often judged differently than events that are not personally relevant.

At a more general level, psychologists have begun to explore the actual process of social cognition. At the input end of the chain, events are encoded according to certain principles. *Salience* of the stimulus is an important factor in this initial encoding process; *vividness* may also be a factor in some cases. At the output end of the chain, storage and retrieval are central concerns.

GLOSSARY TERMS

belief in a just world	illusory correlation	prototype
causal attribution	implicit personality theory	recency effect
causal schema	personalism	salience
central traits	philosophies of human nature	schema
fundamental attribution error	primacy effect	stereotype
hedonic relevance	priming effect	vividness

5

Interpersonal Communication

Language exists only when it is listened to as well as spoken. The hearer is an indispensable partner.

■ JOHN DEWEY

Those of us who keep our eyes open can read volumes into what we see going on around us.

■ E. T. HALL

In Chapter 3 we saw that the self is not defined in a vacuum but is the product of social experiences. And in Chapter 4 we explored the ways in which a person comes to know other people. Now we are going to put those two pieces together, by looking at the process of communication itself. How does one person express emotions and convey information to another person? And how does the other person receive those messages and then choose a way to respond? Such interactions are at the heart of social psychology.

Communication processes are basic to the study of most of the material in the remainder of this book. Expressions of friendship, affection, and love depend on the ability of people to communicate their feelings; so do expressions of anger, mistrust, and hatred. Relationships begin to falter as people claim they can't communicate anymore; international negotiations are beset with "communication breakdowns." Communication often seems like the most important concept in the understanding of human behavior. Yet just what does the word mean, and how is the communication process conceptualized?

■ I. The meaning of communication

It has often been said that one can't *not* communicate. In other words, although a particular interaction may be filled with tension and stress, and verbal communication may actually cease, the communication process continues. Signs and messages continue to be transmitted between one person and the other, even if the goals of the interaction may have changed. This chapter focuses on the ways messages can be communicated; but first let's consider some basic definitions of the communication process itself.

The term *communication* is widely used and has been applied to situations ranging from information processing within the individual to large-scale sociocultural systems, mass communication and influence, and communication networks. We will focus primarily on a phenomenon somewhere between these extremes: interpersonal communication—that is, the interactions that take place

between two persons. Such interactions are characterized by the close proximity of the interactants, the maximal number of communication channels that are available, and the immediacy of the feedback (Miller, 1978).

Communication theorists have developed many models in an attempt to represent the communication process. For example, an early and influential model by Shannon and Weaver (1949) conceptualized the communication process as shown in Figure 5-1. According to this model, there are five necessary components of the communication process: source, transmitter, channel, receiver, and destination. In addition, Shannon and Weaver introduced the concept of *noise*, defined as any disturbance that interferes with transmission. Later this model was revised to include a concept of *feedback*, which attempted to deal with the fact that the receiver may not always receive the same message that the transmitter has sent.

Two other terms are helpful in understanding the communication process: *encoding* and *decoding*. *Encoding* refers to the way a message is transmitted by the source. For example, if I want to express anger, I may choose particular words and may show particular facial expressions to convey my anger. In some cases, this expression may be rather subtle: rather than simply saying "I'm mad at you," I may encode my message in less direct ways, such as a twist of the mouth. Will you know I am angry? This is the point at which decoding enters the picture. *Decoding* refers to the process of interpreting a message. Perhaps you will accurately decode my message and conclude that I am angry. Perhaps, however, my message is too subtle, and your interpretation will not pick up the clues that I intended to send. Both in sending and in receiving, the communication process can be altered.

Shannon and Weaver's model has had a tremendous influence on the study of communication, particularly in the field of computer science. However, more recent communication theorists have had some problems with the model. Perhaps the most basic difficulty lies in the one-way assumptions of the model, as illustrated by the arrows in Figure 5-1. Can communication be accurately

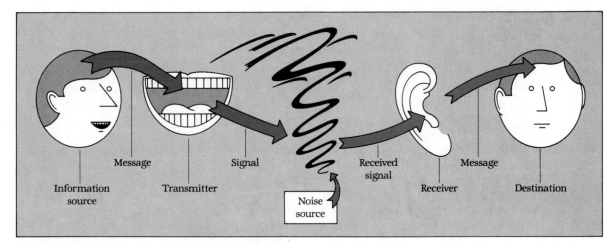

FIGURE 5-1. Shannon and Weaver's model.

described as a one-way street? Recent theorists don't think so. For example, if Joan is talking with Elena, Joan is indeed transmitting a message verbally and may be sending a number of nonverbal messages as well. Yet, at the same time that Elena is interpreting those messages, trying to understand what Joan is saying and meaning, Elena herself will be communicating as well. By her posture, her facial expression, and her general attentiveness, she will be sending messages to Joan at the same time as she is receiving them.

Recent work in communication theory, developing beyond the Shannon and Weaver model, has stressed at least four aspects of the communication process. First, communication is assumed to be a *shared social system*—a system in which two or more persons are involved, both with their own expectations and intentions (Scott, 1977). Second, communication is an *ongoing dynamic system*. From this viewpoint, studying sequences of behavior is more important than studying isolated stimulus-and-response connections. Each action can, in fact, be seen simultaneously as a cause and as an effect (Fisher, 1978). Third, most recent communication theorists believe that verbal and nonverbal communications are part of the same system. Although it is sometimes useful to isolate single communication channels for analysis (for example, speech, eye behavior, or physical distancing), it is impor-

tant to remember that they naturally occur together and may parallel or contradict one another in important ways (Miller, 1978). Finally, many recent investigators have pointed out the importance of the *relational* component of communication. Rather than focusing exclusively on the content of communication, these investigators also examine how the exchange of messages may define a relationship, particularly in terms of the balance of power that exists between the two participants (Miller & Rogers, 1976; Parks, 1977; Rogers & Farace, 1975). In other words, the focus is not only on *what* is being said but on *how* it is being said.

Although recent models of the communication process seem more realistic than the earlier models, they have made the study of communication much more complicated. Instead of looking at isolated segments in an interchange or taking simple summary measures of the frequency of various behaviors, recent investigators have begun to conduct painstaking analyses of ongoing patterns of interaction, frequently breaking the analyses down into very fine-grained segments (Duncan & Fiske, 1977). An example of the relational analysis of conversation is shown in Box 5-1. By approaching the coding of communication in this manner, investigators are able to look more closely at the *meaning* of an interchange—at how the participants are complementing or contradicting each other

BOX 5-1. Relational analysis

Relational analysts believe that each individual message can be described by one of three control dimensions (Rogers & Farace, 1975). A "one-up" message represents an attempt to gain control in an exchange; a "one-down" message indicates that one is yielding control by either seeking or accepting the control of the other person; and a "one-across" message represents a movement toward neutralizing the control in the interaction. To see how these dimensions work, consider the following conversation between a husband and wife. The arrow after each statement indicates whether the statement is coded as one-up (↑), one-down (↓), or one-across (→).

Wife: We don't do anything together any more. ↑
Husband: What do you mean? ↓
Wife: Well, as a family we don't do very much. ↑
Husband: Oh, I don't know. →
Wife: Don't you feel I do the major portion of the disciplining of the children? ↓
Husband: The time we're together you don't. ↑
Wife: Well, just for the record, I have to disagree. ↑
Husband: Well, just for the record, you're wrong. ↑
Wife: Well, then, we completely disagree. ↑

and how they may be establishing stable patterns or fighting for control. This analytical approach to communication is surely more complicated than just examining *what* is being said.

Because communication involves so many elements, it is no wonder that so-called communication breakdowns and communication gaps occur so often. It is also not surprising that the study of communication is important to our understanding of human behavior and fundamental to social psychology. Having considered some of the basic issues in the conceptualization of communication, let us now turn to a consideration of the channels through which communication takes place—

remembering, however, that none of the channels is ever used alone.

■ II. Channels of communication

When the word *communication* is mentioned, many people think automatically of language. Speech has, after all, often been designated as a unique ability that distinguishes humans from other primates. Yet, many other channels of communication serve us in exchanging messages with others and can be just as important. Among these are facial expressions, eye contact, physical touch, body gestures, and even the distance that we put between ourselves and others. However, because speech is perhaps the most obvious of the communication channels, we shall begin there.

A. Language and paralanguage

"When I use a word, it means just what I choose it to mean, neither more nor less," said Humpty-Dumpty in Lewis Carroll's classic *Through the Looking-Glass*. Such confidence in the encoding of one's message is admirable but perhaps not realistic. Although the choice of words and the combination of these words into sentences represent our most controlled form of communication, the levels of meaning involved in such choices are numerous.

Linguists have developed a number of models to represent the language process. The elements in these models are numerous, and we can deal only briefly with their components. At the most basic level are *phonemes*—that is, sequences of elementary sounds in any language, such as a "p" sound or a "th" sound. At a slightly higher level are *morphemes*, the minimal meaningful forms in the language (Brown, 1965); in somewhat oversimplified terms, morphemes are the basic word forms in a language. *Dog*, *chase*, and *cat* are examples of morphemes. At a higher level, the linguist deals with grammar, which combines a set of rules for the construction of words (morphological rules) and a set of rules for the construction of sentences (syntactic rules).

Although these concepts are basic to linguistic analysis, our own concern really lies at the level of *semantic analysis*—what is the meaning transmitted through our verbal language? To begin with, meaning depends in part on the cultural context. In other words, when speaking with people, we tend to assume we share a set of meanings—that is, we believe that the meaning we invest in words or sentences will be perceived in the same way by the listener. Such assumptions do not always hold true, however. For example, people from different cultures are more likely to misunderstand one another than people from the same culture, even though they all speak the same language.

Even within a single culture, however, a variety of meanings may be implied in very similar sentence structures. One recent approach to analyzing the various meanings is *grammatical case analysis*, the examination of the underlying features of various grammatical forms. Such analysis has shown, for example, that men and women tend to use different language structures in their speech. College men are more apt to use sentence cases that are neutral, are objective, and describe the initiator of an action, whereas college women more frequently use cases referring to the experience and style of an action (Barron, 1971; Cashell, 1978). For instance, men might be more likely to talk about actions, such as "He hit the ball" or "She kicked the stone." Women, in contrast, are more likely to describe feelings, such as "He hates the professor" or "She feels sad."

At a simpler level, it is evident that we can convey an entire range of moods and emotions through our choice of words. The parent who tells a child "You make me furious" is obviously conveying a different message from one who says "You make me very happy." Thus a one- or two-word change in a sentence can entirely change its meaning. Another example of the importance of our choice of words is the recent development of *assertiveness training*, which stresses the choice of language that people use to achieve their goals. Assertiveness training differentiates among assertive, aggressive, and submissive forms of communication, all of which may be aimed at accomplishing the same goal (see Box 5-2). Although nonverbal forms of communication may also differ, the primary emphasis of assertiveness training has been on the verbal language chosen to express one's point.

PHOTO 5-1. *The translation of words doesn't always capture the meaning.*

Not all verbal communication is expressed in words and sentences; communication can also be made through vocal sounds and modifications that are not considered language but nonetheless convey meaning. These sounds are called **paralanguage.** The study of paralanguage deals with *how* something is said, not *what* is said (Knapp, 1978). Examples of paralanguage include speech modifiers such as pitch, rhythm, intensity, and pauses, as well as vocalizations such as laughing, crying, yawning, groaning, sneezing, and snoring (Trager, 1958). Each of these paralanguage forms can convey meaning in a communication. For example, the person who yawns while you are talking sends a very clear message of boredom; less obviously, perhaps, the person who speeds up his or her speech while talking to you may be conveying either anxiety or excitement.

Recently, glowing claims have been made that objective analysis of voice patterns can detect whether someone is telling the truth. Proponents of the spectrographic analysis of vocal stress patterns have argued for this method as a reliable lie detector. Although such claims appear to be overstated, it is true that we can transmit a considerable amount of information through paralinguistic cues. For example, a low voice pitch tends to convey pleasantness, boredom, or sadness, whereas a high pitch conveys anger, fear, surprise, or general activity. Moderate variations in pitch may communicate anger, boredom, or disgust, whereas more extreme voice variations indicate

BOX 5-2. The assertive response

In many interactions, we disagree with the statements or actions of another person. How do we respond? Recently, many advocates of assertiveness training have suggested that there are three possible responses to most situations: a passive response, an aggressive response, or an assertive response. The passive response is to do nothing—to inhibit one's own feelings for fear of offending the other person. An aggressive response, in contrast, directly attacks the other person. With the third possibility, the assertive response, a person can make his or her feelings known without attacking the other person.

As an example, pretend that you have spent several hours preparing an elaborate birthday dinner for a friend, and then the friend shows up an hour late, at which point the roast is burnt and the salad is soggy. What would you say? The passive response might be to say nothing—perhaps pouting as you ate or not engaging in conversation but refusing to deal with the problem directly. An aggressive response is easy to picture: pots and pans could go sailing across the room, and angry verbal attacks on your onetime friend could accompany them. A third strategy of response would be assertive: to state that you are annoyed but without verbally attacking your friend. These three different strategies would probably produce quite different results, and they illustrate the importance of both language and paralanguage in interaction. ■

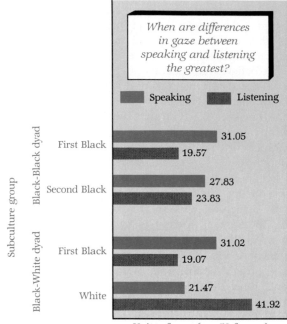

FIGURE 5-2. Mean other-directed gaze in film frames per 50 frame units. The bar graph shows the results of a study by Marianne LaFrance and Clara Mayo (1976). When two Blacks were talking to each other, they both looked at each other more while they were talking rather than while they were listening. In contrast, when a Black and a White were paired with each other, the White person gazed at the other person much more while listening (about 80% of the time), whereas the Black person looked at his or her partner primarily while talking. As a result, while the White was talking and the Black was listening, little eye contact occurred.

pleasantness, happiness, and surprise (Knapp, 1978; LaFrance & Mayo, 1978).

Paralinguistic cues also play an important role in managing communication. The rules of turn taking in a conversation, for example, are highly dependent on vocal cues, in many instances even more than on the actual content of the communication (Duncan & Fiske, 1977; Wiemann & Knapp, 1975). For instance, if you want to keep talking even though you sense that the other person wants to take a turn, you may increase the volume and rate of your speech and decrease the frequency and duration of pauses (Knapp, 1978; Rochester, 1973). At the same time, the other person may persist in an attempt to gain entrance by using vocal "buffers" (like "Ah . . ." or "Er . . .") or by increasing the rapidity of responses, as if to say "Hurry up so I can talk."

Even though we know that words sometimes fail, it may seem as if the tremendous variety of linguistic and paralinguistic forms of communi-

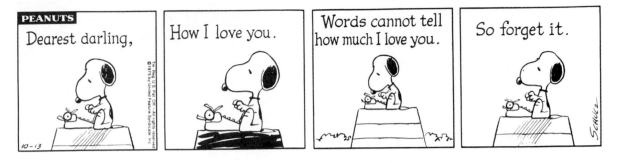

cation should be sufficient to communicate virtually any thought or feeling. Yet, beyond these verbal forms of communication, there is a wealth of nonverbal communication modes that sometimes support, sometimes contradict, and sometimes go beyond the verbal message.

B. Eye contact

"Drink to Me Only with Thine Eyes," "the eyes of a woman in love," "seeing eye to eye" are all examples of expressions and song titles in our culture that testify to the importance of eyes as communicators. The pervasiveness of optic symbols in myth and religion also exemplifies the importance we assign to this mode of communication. Indeed, we perhaps depend more on the eye behavior of other people than on any other nonverbal communication form, although, as we shall see later, this dependence sometimes causes problems.

Investigators of the phenomena of *gaze* (looking directly at the face of another person) and *mutual gaze* (two persons looking directly at each other)[1] have shown that they serve four major functions: regulating the flow of conversation, monitoring feedback, expressing emotions, and communicating the nature of the interpersonal relationship (Argyle, Ingham, Alkema, & McCallin, 1973; Kendon, 1967; Knapp, 1978).

Regulating conversation. Gaze serves an important role in initiating communication and in maintaining it once a conversation has begun. For example, if your professor is looking around the classroom for someone to supply the correct answer, you are likely to avoid eye contact if you failed to read the material the night before; however, you will probably return the professor's gaze if you know the correct answer and can discuss it. Similarly, you will probably ignore a gaze from a stranger at a bar if you don't want to be bothered, but you might return the look if you were interested in establishing a new relationship.

Observing unacquainted college students meet in a laboratory setting, Cary (1978) found that mutual gaze predicted the beginning of conversations. If students looked at each other at their first encounter, they were likely to engage in conversation. If they looked at each other again, as one student entered the room where the other one was sitting, conversation was even more likely.

Once a conversation has begun, gaze continues to play an important role. Consider these figures from a study by Argyle and Ingham (1972). During a typical two-person conversation, gaze occurs approximately 61% of the time, and mutual gaze accounts for 31% of the total interaction time. The average length of an individual gaze is about three seconds, whereas the average duration of mutual gaze is slightly more than one second. White adult speakers tend to gaze at the other person more often when they are listening (75% of the time) and less often when they are speaking (41%). Among Blacks, however, this pattern reverses, although the overall amount of gaze remains the same (LaFrance & Mayo, 1976; see Figure 5-2).

Ethnic differences in typical patterns of gaze can create substantial problems in communication. For example, LaFrance and Mayo observed

[1]The terms *gaze* and *mutual gaze* are often used interchangeably with *eye contact* in general usage. However, many investigators prefer the former terms because actual eye contact is difficult to measure in the laboratory: looking in the general direction of someone's face cannot be distinguished from direct eye-to-eye contact (von Cranach & Ellgring, 1973).

PHOTO 5-2. *Consider the functions that gaze may be serving in this interaction. Even when a person's vision is impaired, other nonverbal channels that accompany gaze can help convey the intended message.*

that when Blacks and Whites converse, they often misinterpret the signals for taking turns in the conversation. "When the White listener . . . encountered a pause with sustained gaze from a Black speaker, the White was cued to speak, and both found themselves talking at once. In the obverse situation, by directing his gaze at the Black listener, the White speaker often did not succeed in yielding the floor and had to resort to direct verbal questioning" (LaFrance & Mayo, 1976, p. 551). Such differences can certainly create discomfort in a conversation, and they may cause errors in judgment about the other person's intentions and motives as well.

Monitoring feedback. Gaze also serves the function of conveying feedback to the speaker; it is interpreted as a sign of attention, interest, or attraction. In fact, people trying to convey a feeling of interest often deliberately gaze directly at the speaker. Persons with strong needs for approval engage in a higher proportion of direct gazing than do those less inclined to seek approval (Lefebvre, 1975). However, observers apparently are not obliv-

ious to such behavior (Lefebvre, 1975); although they rate a high-gazer as warmer and friendlier, they are also likely to believe that the person is ingratiating in an attempt to be better liked (see Chapter 3).

Although the motives for gaze may sometimes be suspect, in general we respond positively to eye contact. In fact, even the belief that the other person has gazed at us often seems to engender liking. In a demonstration of this effect, Kleinke and his colleagues (Kleinke, Bustos, Meeker, & Staneski, 1973) asked male and female subjects to engage in a ten-minute conversation. At the end of the period, the subjects were told that their partner had gazed at them far more or far less than the average number of times, independent of the actual direct-gaze frequency. When told the gaze frequency was less than normal, subjects rated their partners as less attentive. Interestingly, the report of supposedly above-average rates of gazing produced different effects on men and women. When women thought their male partner had looked at them more than might be expected, their attraction to him did not increase. For males, the effect was the opposite: they were more attracted to the woman when they believed she had gazed at them more than the average number of times.

Expressing emotions.   The eyes also convey emotion. Although we will discuss this in greater detail later when we consider facial expressions, it is worth noting at this point that the eyes are one of three major areas of the face that convey emotion (the other two being the brows and forehead and the lower face and mouth). People are often described as smiling with their eyes, as having an icy stare, or as having a glint in their eyes that indicates an emotional state. Paul Ekman and his colleagues have done extensive work in charting exactly what movements of the eyes and face indicate which emotions (Ekman, 1972; Ekman & Friesen, 1975). As just one example, the emotion of anger is generally conveyed by drawing the brows together, tensing the lower and upper eyelids, and staring hard with the eyes. Our dependence on the eyes as a sign of emotion is easily illustrated by the discomfort we feel when conversing with people in opaque sunglasses, when "I can't tell what they're thinking" is a frequent complaint.

Defining relationships.   The fourth function of gaze, and perhaps the most relevant for social psychology, is the communication of the nature of interpersonal relationships. Like and dislike are clearly conveyed by the use of direct gaze; so are status relationships of dominance and submission.

We tend to look more at people we like than at people we dislike (Efran & Broughton, 1966; Exline & Winters, 1965). This gaze pattern has been observed in the laboratory with people who have interacted only briefly. It has also been observed with dating couples, whose interactions are obviously much more extensive. Couples who score higher on a measure of romantic love (see Chapter 6) spend more time looking at each other than those who report being less involved in a relationship (Rubin, 1970).

In addition to conveying positive feelings, extended gaze may also indicate the intensity of a relationship. Kimble and Forte (1978) asked women

to communicate either a positive or a negative message to a male assistant. When the women were asked to act as if they were strongly involved in the message, they looked at the assistant more than when they were instructed to appear less certain about the message. This effect of intensity was true for both positive and negative messages. In fact, it was slightly stronger for the negative messages.

Another example of how gaze conveys intensity in a negative as well as a positive sense is supplied by Ellsworth and Carlsmith (1968). They arranged for an interviewer to evaluate college students either positively or negatively in the context of a laboratory experiment. If the interviewer engaged in a lot of eye contact with the student while making complimentary remarks, then the student rated the interviewer quite positively. In contrast, if the interviewer gazed at the student frequently while giving him or her a negative evaluation, then the student rated the interviewer lower than in a similar situation without eye contact. An even more dramatic demonstration of how prolonged direct gazing can convey intensity was shown by an experiment at traffic intersections. When drivers were stopped at an intersection, a stare from a person standing on the corner caused the drivers to depart much more rapidly than when no one was staring at them (Ellsworth, Carlsmith, & Henson, 1972).

Gaze is also an important indicator of status differences in a relationship. Exline and his colleagues have explored the gaze patterns of high- and low-status people interacting with each other (Exline, 1971; Exline, Ellyson, & Long, 1975). In some of their studies, status differences were manipulated by the experimenter; in other studies, the investigators looked at real-life status relationships, such as that between an ROTC officer and a lower-status cadet. In all cases, the low-status person gazed at a partner more than the high-status person did.

Although higher-status people generally gaze at a partner less often, there is a specific pattern in the gaze behavior of the high-status person. *Visual dominance behavior*, characteristic of people in high-status positions, involves a greater tendency to look at the other person when speaking than when listening. The effectiveness of this visual dominance pattern was demonstrated convincingly in a field study of ROTC officers at their training camp. Those leaders who showed a visual dominance pattern were given the highest leadership ratings, whereas those officers who engaged in a lower ratio of direct gaze while speaking to direct gaze while listening were rated less favorably on leadership abilities. From this study it is, of course, difficult to know whether individuals who engage in visual dominance behavior are more likely to be selected as leaders or whether occupying a leadership position encourages the development of visual dominance behavior. Nevertheless, the effectiveness of such behavior in communicating power and status is clear.

Henley (1977) has suggested that the status differences described above may help to explain the pervasive sex differences in eye behavior. In general, women engage in much more eye contact than men do (Duncan, 1969), consistent with the finding that the lower-status person looks directly at others more often than a higher-status person (in this case, the male). Women are also less likely to engage in staring and are more apt to avert the gaze of the other (Henley, 1977).

Overall, it is evident that eye contact or gaze provides substantial amounts of information in the communication process. The eyes are not the only channel, however; other nonverbal channels also convey important information.

C. Facial expressions

The study of facial expressions has a long scientific history, dating from the classic work of Charles Darwin *The Expression of the Emotions in Man and Animals* (Darwin, 1872). Darwin believed that there are evolutionary connections between animal and human facial expression and that certain facial expressions may serve to communicate the same message across species.

Investigators since Darwin have continued to be interested in the ways that facial expressions convey emotions. Most investigators have focused their attention on six primary emotions: surprise, fear, anger, disgust, happiness, and sadness. An exten-

sive research program by Paul Ekman and his colleagues has provided an exact description of the facial expressions involved in each of these emotional states (Ekman, 1972; Ekman & Friesen, 1975; Ekman, Friesen, & Ellsworth, 1972). For example, in depicting surprise, a person will typically raise the eyebrows and drop the jaw; there will be horizontal wrinkles across the forehead; the upper eyelid will be raised while the lower lid is drawn down, and the white of the eye will show above the iris and often below as well. Ekman terms this the **facial affect program**: the connection between an emotional experience and a particular pattern of facial-muscle activity. Other investigators also have shown, using a technique called *facial electromyography,* that subtle muscular activity in the face differentiates among various emotional states (Schwartz, Fair, Salt, Mandel, & Klerman, 1976).

In support of the universality of emotional expression postulated by Darwin, Ekman and others have also shown that members of very different cultural groups show a consistency in labeling emotional expressions. Thus, samples of people from Europe, South America, and preliterate societies in New Guinea all were able to correctly identify most of the primary emotions from photographs of faces of North Americans (Ekman et al., 1972; Izard, 1969).

However, the fact that an emotion can be recognized by respondents from different cultures does not mean that the same emotion will always be displayed in similar circumstances. In some societies, for example, it is not considered appropriate to display emotional reactions in actual communication, even though such emotions might be experienced. Similarly, even within our own society, certain situations may call for restraint in the expression of an emotion. As an example, consider what your reaction would be to the sight and smell of the overflowing and odorous garbage can in a neighbor's kitchen. Although you might experience disgust, it is also quite likely that you would mask your emotional expression when talking with your neighbor. These qualifications of emotional expression, which Ekman terms **display rules,** can result from personal habits, situational pressures, or cultural norms.

The recognition of display rules brings us closer

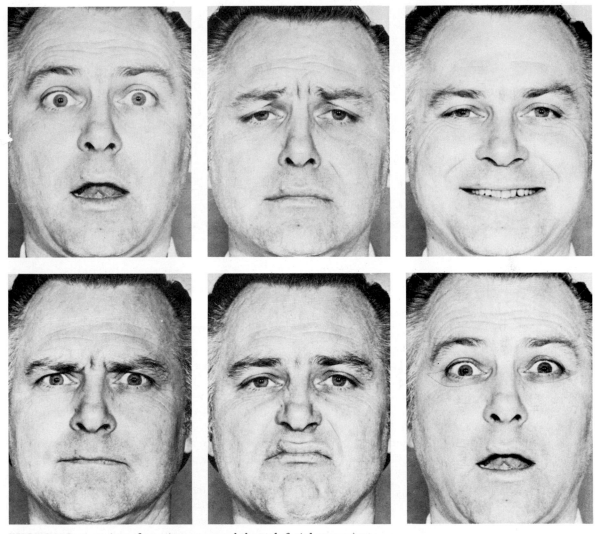

PHOTO 5-3. *A variety of emotions conveyed through facial expressions.*

to the central issue of this chapter—namely, communication. Although the abstract expression of emotions is of interest in its own right, it is the ways in which we transmit these emotions to the other person that affect the communication process. This distinction between the expression of emotion and the communication of emotion is an important one. As an example of this distinction, consider a study by Kraut and Johnston (1979) on smiling behavior. Exploring a wide range of natural settings, including bowling alleys, hockey games, and public walkways, these investigators observed the frequency of smiling and attempted to relate these occasions to simultaneously occurring events. Their results showed that people were most likely to smile when talking to other people; in contrast, when people experienced positive emotional events alone, they were far less likely to smile. Figure 5-3 shows the results of two of these studies, which dealt with reactions to scores at a bowling alley and discussions of weather conditions in a public walkway.

The results of the study by Kraut and Johnston suggest that a major function of the smile is to

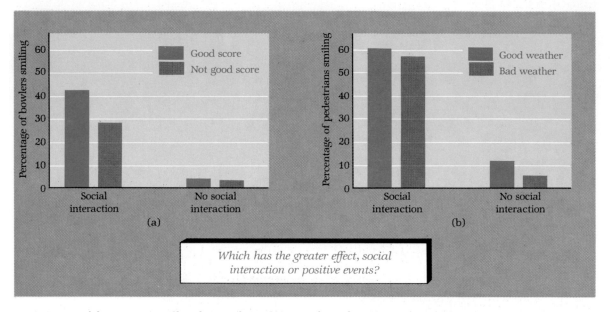

FIGURE 5-3. (a) Percentage of bowlers smiling after a good or other score, when the bowlers were facing the pins or facing their teammates; (b) social interaction, the weather, and percentage of pedestrians smiling.

communicate happiness to other persons. In other words, facial expressions such as a smile may be less an automatic response to a particular stimulus than a conscious choice to affect the communicated message. This idea, of course, allows for the possibility that a smile may be used to mask some other emotion that is being experienced, and, as we shall later, such masking attempts are common.

D. Body movements and gestures

Other parts of the body get involved in the communication process as well. Movements of the head, hands, legs, feet, and torso can all serve to communicate messages. To impose some order on the multitude of possible body movements, Birdwhistell (1970) proposed a model called **kinesics,** which is intended to parallel the previously mentioned model for verbal communication called "linguistics." Continuing the linguistics/kinesics analogy, Birdwhistell proposed the terms *kinemes* and *kinemorphs* to represent basic units of body movement (these terms are similar in meaning to *phonemes* and *morphemes,* discussed earlier). On

the basis of extensive observations, mostly in the United States, Birdwhistell proposed that there are approximately 50 to 60 basic kinemes—that is, classes of body movements that form the core of nonverbal body language. For example, he suggests that there are four basic kinemes of the nose area: a wrinkled nose, compressed nostrils, both nostrils flared, and a single nostril flared. Continuing the parallel to linguistics, Birdwhistell suggests that kinemes, like phonemes, rarely occur in isolation. Instead, several basic units may occur simultaneously, constituting a kinemorph. Although Birdwhistell's approach to classifying body movements is ambitious, it is not without criticism. In particular, the usefulness of the kinesics/linguistics analogy has been questioned (Dittman, 1971). A major point of argument is whether kinesics is a separate language in itself or whether kinemes depend in large part on their verbal context. Nonetheless, whether the analogy holds or not, Birdwhistell's work has been important in categorizing the wide variety of body movements that are displayed.

Nonverbal behaviors that are directly linked with

spoken language have been termed **illustrators** (Ekman & Friesen, 1972). For example, if you are asked to direct someone to the library, it is likely that you will gesture as well as use verbal explanations. Other research has shown how speech and movement behavior are tightly bound together; if a person is unable to use one channel (gestures, for example, when talking on the telephone), the other channel may be used more extensively (Graham & Heywood, 1975).

Not all body gestures accompany verbal language, however. On some occasions, a gesture may substitute for a spoken phrase. Such gestures, termed **emblems,** are nonverbal acts that are clearly understood by the majority of the members of a culture (Johnson, Ekman, & Friesen, 1975). For example, the wave of a hand in greeting is widely recognized in our society. Less friendly gestures may be equally well recognized. Other emblems may be shared by smaller groups, such

as the two-fingered horns sign of Texas football fans. As you might suspect, the meaning conveyed by the same emblem across cultures can differ dramatically. A similar gesture may convey two quite different meanings, and the same meaning may be translated into different gestures. Because emblems typically replace rather than accompany other forms of communication, these disparities in meaning can cause much confusion among members of different cultures.

So far we have discussed body language as an accompaniment to or a substitute for particular verbal utterances. In addition to this function, body movements and gestures can also indicate the nature of the relationship between two persons in a conversation. For example, status differences in a relationship are often communicated by body position (see Photo 5-4). The higher-status person in a relationship will generally look more relaxed: arms and legs in asymmetrical positions and a

PHOTO 5-4. *Body position and status. Can you make an estimate of the relative status of these two men by looking at their body positions? What other cues would you use to judge status differences?*

backward lean to the body. In contrast, the lower-status person is more likely to maintain a fairly rigid position, with body upright, feet together and flat on the floor, and arms close to the body (Mehrabian, 1969b, 1972; Scheflen, 1972). Once again, these status differences in nonverbal behavior frequently parallel observed sex differences in body language (Henley, 1977): men are far more apt to adopt an open stance, whereas women more frequently show the closed positions typical of a lower-status person.

Attraction can also be conveyed through body movements and gestures. People who like each other are more likely to lean forward with their bodies, to have a direct body orientation toward the other person, and to show a more relaxed body position (Mehrabian, 1969a, 1972). These signs are clearly interpreted and, in turn, may create feelings of liking or disliking for the other person (Clore, Wiggins, & Itkin, 1975).

E. Touch

Perhaps one of the most basic means of communication is touch. Long before a child has developed language skills and has learned body illustrators and emblems, he or she communicates through tactile contact. The parent and child, for example, depend on touch for much of their early communication.

Touch takes different forms in different kinds of relationships (Heslin & Patterson, 1982). For example, at a professional or functional level, we may be touched by a barber, a dentist, or a tennis pro without giving it much thought. Social-polite touch is more personal but not intimate, illustrated by routine handshakes when people first meet. Other forms of touch may involve more intimate interactions, as in friendship, love, or sexual involvement.

As with other nonverbal behaviors, interpretations of particular forms of touch may differ according to the situation and the people involved. Nguyen, Heslin, and Nguyen (1975), for example, have found that men and women perceive some kinds of touching quite differently. Women make a distinction between forms of touching that indicate warmth and friendship and those that indi-

PHOTO 5-5. *Touch is a major channel of communication between this father and his young child.*

cate sexual desire; for men, in contrast, these two forms of touching are interchangeable in meaning.

Sex differences in response to touch have also been observed when touch occurs in a simple functional context. For example, in an experimental study in the Purdue University library, students who checked out books were briefly touched or not touched on the hand by the library clerk (Fisher, Rytting, & Heslin, 1976). The female students who were touched briefly responded positively: they liked the clerk and even the library more than those who had not been touched. Among males, however, similar increases in liking did not occur. An even more striking demonstration of sex differences in reaction to touch is provided by Whitcher and Fisher (1979). Male and female patients in an Eastern U.S. university hospital were either touched or not touched during a preoperative teaching interaction with the nurse. The touches themselves were relatively brief and professional—a brief touch on the patient's hand and an approximately one-minute contact on the patient's arm. The dependent measures in this study included both questionnaire responses and physiological measures taken immediately after surgery. The results showed striking evidence for the positive effects of touch on women. Female patients who had been touched reported less fear and anxiety on the questionnaire measures and showed lower blood pressure readings after surgery. For the male patients, in contrast, the brief touch by the nurse produced negative effects; these men showed less positive reactions than a no-touch control group and had increased blood pressure readings.

How a person reacts to touch depends on several factors. Major (1981) has suggested that when the status of the two persons is approximately equal, or when status is ambiguous, men and women will show the different reactions just described—positive reactions for women and negative reactions for men. However, when the toucher is clearly higher in status than the recipient, both men and women will react positively to the touch.

Touch can in itself convey information about status. As observers, we are more apt to attribute characteristics of dominance and high status to the person who initiates a touch, while assigning qualities of submissiveness and low status to the person who receives the touch (Major & Heslin, 1978). There is some evidence that these attributions mirror reality, in that touch may be more frequently initiated by older persons toward younger and by higher-socioeconomic-status persons toward lower-status persons (Major, 1981).

Once again, we find that male/female differences in touching show parallels with the status patterns of touch behavior (Henley, 1977). From infancy on, females are touched more than males, and men are more likely to initiate touch with women than women are with men (Major, 1981).

F. Interpersonal distance

The forms of communication that we have discussed so far have all involved some part of the body as a way of transmitting messages. At this point we shall turn to something more abstract—the distance between bodies as a mode of communication. Anthropologist Edward Hall (1959,

1963, 1966) is probably the individual most responsible for pointing out how the *interpersonal distance* established between two or more persons can communicate a variety of messages. On the basis of extensive observations, primarily within the United States, Hall has proposed a categorization of *distance zones* to describe the patterns typically found in different types of interactions. The four major zones are termed *intimate, personal, social,* and *public. Intimate zones* range in distance from actual physical contact to about 18 inches (approximately .5 meter). In the intimate zone "the presence of the other person is unmistakable . . . because of the greatly stepped-up sensory inputs. Sight (often distorted), olfaction, heat from the other person's body, sound, smell, and the feel of the breath all combine to signal unmistakable involvement with another body" (Hall, 1966, p. 116). This zone generally indicates a high level of intimacy between the participants, although there are exceptions, as when strangers are crowded together in an elevator. In the latter instance, the distance is uncomfortable because it conflicts with the feelings that the occupants may have for the total strangers against whom they are crushed.

The *personal distance zone* extends from 1½ to 4 feet (about .5 to 1.25 meters) and typifies the distance that we usually maintain between ourselves and friends (at the closer end) and ourselves and acquaintances in everyday conversations, for example (at the farther end).

Greater distances, ranging from 4 to 12 feet (1.25 to 3.5 meters), represent the *social distance zone* and are typically used for business interactions or very casual social interactions. For example, your interactions with a clerk at the grocery store probably fall into this category, as do typical professor/student interactions.

Finally, Hall describes a *public distance zone* where interpersonal distance ranges from 12 to 25 feet (about 3.5 to 7.5 meters). Interactions at these distances are typically quite formal, such as a public address or an interaction with a judge or celebrity.

As indicated by Hall's categorization, greater liking is usually communicated by smaller interpersonal distance. For example, the optimal distance between friends is less than the distance between two interacting strangers (Sundstrom & Altman, 1976). Similarly, both college students and junior high school students have been observed to sit closer to people they like (Aiello & Cooper, 1972; Byrne, Ervin, & Lamberth, 1970). On the reverse side of the coin, people will report being uncomfortable when the distance between them and others is greater than usual during a conversation (DeRisi & Aiello, 1978).

Because intimacy and interpersonal distance are so closely related, we often use distance to send messages to other people. For example, if you want to communicate liking for another person, you will probably decrease the interpersonal distance. If you're not fond of a person, you will probably choose instead to "keep your distance." In a demonstration of this behavior, Rosenfeld (1965) asked female students to talk with another student (actually a confederate of the experimenter) with the goal either of appearing friendly or of avoiding the appearance of friendliness. Approval-seeking women placed their chairs an average of 4.75 feet from the confederate; students seeking to avoid affiliation placed their chairs an average of 7.34 feet away.

Interpersonal distance can convey status messages as well as affiliative messages. In general, peers stand closer together than do people of unequal status (Mehrabian, 1969b). For example, Lott and Sommer (1967) observed seating patterns of students of different academic rank and found that seniors sat closer to other seniors than to either first-year students or professors. In a field study, Dean, Willis, and Hewitt (1975) observed conversations between military personnel. Navy men maintained a greater distance when they initiated a conversation with a superior than when they initiated a conversation with a peer, and this difference grew larger as the difference in rank increased. For the superiors, however, such differences did not exist, indicating the freedom of the higher-status person to define the boundaries of the conversation.

Once again, we find that a nonverbal form of communication can convey a variety of messages. Because of the many possibilities involved in all forms of communication, it is necessary to maintain a broad perspective when interpreting communicative behavior. In addition to considering the mode of communication, we must also examine the setting and the overall pattern of communicated messages.

■ III. Combining the channels

As this chapter has shown, communication is a multichanneled phenomenon. In only the most unusual cases do we rely on just one form of communication; most often messages are transmitted back and forth through a variety of verbal and nonverbal modes. But just how do these channels combine? And are the various channels always used at the same time? Let's see how the various pieces of the communication puzzle fit together.

A. Basic dimensions of communication

Although the ways we communicate with other people may seem to have endless variety, investigators have discovered that there are three major dimensions of communicative behavior. Osgood, Suci, and Tannenbaum (1957), dealing mainly with verbal material, defined these three dimensions as general *evaluation, social control,* and *activity.* Early investigators of facial movements and the expression of emotion also defined three dimensions: pleasantness/unpleasantness, sleep/tension, and attention/rejection (Schlosberg, 1954). More recently, Mehrabian (1969a) analyzed a variety of nonverbal behaviors and, through a statistical technique known as factor analysis, described three similar factors. As shown in Table 5-1 (p. 124), Mehrabian relates evaluation or liking to a series of immediacy cues, social control or status to relaxation cues, and responsiveness to activity cues.

Thus, according to Mehrabian, when you are attracted to someone, you are most likely to communicate this feeling through a variety of immediacy cues—by touching, by decreasing the distance between yourself and the other person, by leaning forward, and by maintaining eye contact. Dislike would be communicated in just the opposite way—by refraining from physical contact,

A. *The intimate zone: for close friends and lovers.*

A CLOSER LOOK:
Interpersonal Distance

"The closer you get, the further I fall . . ." As the words to a popular Alabama song testify, distance is an important form of interpersonal communication. It is a message that we can read in the actions of other people and one that we can use ourselves to communicate both liking and status. Closer distances convey liking and more equal status; farther distances suggest less friendly relationships and greater differences in status.

When people are psychologically close, they often position themselves physically close as well—typically less than half a yard, as shown in Photo A. More casual relationships, exemplified by two colleagues conversing by the water fountain, call for greater distance. In more formal settings, such as the interchange between two businessmen in Photo C, interpersonal distance tends to be even greater, ranging from 4 to 12 feet. A public situation, often involving limited interaction between strangers, may call for large distances between participants, often extending to the outer limit at which interpersonal communication can take place.

B. *The personal zone: for casual friends and acquaintances.*

C. *The social zone: for business transactions and impersonal contact.*

D. *The public zone: for public events and formal occasions.*

TABLE 5-1. Nonverbal cues of liking, status, and activity

Immediacy cues (indicate like or dislike for the other person)
    Touching (as in holding hands or touching shoulders)
    Distance (physical distance separating the two persons)
    Forward lean
    Eye contact
    Orientation (facing directly or angled away from the other person)

Relaxation cues (indicate status differences between two persons)
    Arm-position asymmetry (for example, hands clasped or arms folded symmetrically)
    Sideways lean
    Leg-position asymmetry (both feet flat on the floor or legs crossed)
    Hand relaxation
    Neck relaxation
    Reclining angle

Activity cues (indicate responsiveness to the other person)
    Movements
      Trunk-swivel movements
      Rocking movements
      Head-nodding movements
      Gesticulation
      Self-manipulation
      Leg movements
      Foot movements
    Facial expressions
      Facial pleasantness
      Facial activity
    Verbalization
      Communication length
      Speech rate
      Halting quality of speech
      Speech-error rate
      Speech volume
      Intonation

mainly by activity cues, including amount of facial activity and rate of speech.

Thus far we have assumed, to paraphrase Gertrude Stein, that a channel is a channel is a channel. In other words, we have acted as if all the channels of communication were equally important. But is that assumption true? What if communication cues are not consistent with one another? Which ones do we rely on the most?

Mehrabian and his colleagues (Mehrabian & Weiner, 1967; Mehrabian & Ferris, 1967) conducted a set of experiments in which vocal, facial, and verbal cues were combined in inconsistent fashion. For example, positive words might be spoken in negative tones, or positive facial expressions might accompany a negative message. On the basis of these experiments, the investigators derived the following formula:

$$\text{Perceived attitude} = .07 \text{ (verbal)} + .38 \text{ (vocal)} + .55 \text{ (facial)}$$

This formula suggests that people use facial cues the most to interpret communications and verbal cues the least.

Although the exact numbers in the above formula may vary from one situation to another, other investigators have also found that visual cues have far more influence than auditory cues on the interpretation of communication. In a series of experiments, Rosenthal and his colleagues paired various combinations of auditory and visual messages and examined their effects in the communication of dominance and liking (DePaulo, Rosenthal, Eisenstat, Rogers, & Finkelstein, 1978). Once again, visual cues proved to be more influential than vocal cues. In this study, subjects' preference for visual information was most noticeable when facial expressions were paired with auditory cues; body gestures did not exert as strong an effect as facial cues. These investigators also found that visual cues are more significant when people are interpreting liking messages and less so when the messages concern status or dominance. Finally, women showed a greater reliance on visual messages than men did.

increasing the interpersonal distance, leaning away, and avoiding eye contact. In a similar manner, status relationships can be communicated by a combination of relaxation cues. In general, Mehrabian proposes that the greater the communicator's status relative to the addressee, the more the communicator will be relaxed (Mehrabian, 1969a). Finally, Mehrabian suggests that the responsiveness of one person to the other is communicated

There are instances, however, when the visual message may be discarded in favor of the spoken message. Consider a series of studies by Daphne Bugental and her colleagues (Bugental, Kaswan, & Love, 1970; Bugental, Love, & Gianetto, 1971). These investigators asked children to interpret situations in which either a woman or a man was conveying one message with the face while expressing a contradictory verbal message. In judging women, the children tended to believe a negative verbal message and ignore an accompanying smile. With men, in contrast, the children relied more on the facial expression than on the verbal message. Why would the children's reactions to men and women be different? To explore this question, Bugental and her colleagues observed the behavior of fathers and mothers with their children. They found that mothers tended to be less consistent in combining channels of communication—they were just as likely to smile when saying negative things as when saying positive things. Fathers were more consistent, smiling when they said positive things and not smiling when they said negative things. As a result, children may learn to disregard the facial channel of their mothers' communication, because it is a less reliable indicator of meaning, and pay more attention to their fathers' facial messages.

Like parent/child interactions, marital relationships involve a great deal of nonverbal communication. In fact, the ability of partners to interpret each other's messages may say a great deal about the state of the relationship (see Box 5-3).

B. Equilibrium model of intimacy

To further understand how the channels of communication combine, many investigators have focused on the development of intimacy. We have seen that there are a variety of cues that indicate the level of intimacy in a relationship, such as the amount of eye contact and the distance between the participants. To explain how these various cues combine to produce the desired level of intimacy in a social encounter, Argyle and Dean (1965) have proposed an *equilibrium model.* According to these authors, every interpersonal encounter engenders both approach and avoidance pressures; a person

may seek warmth, love, or security, but, at the same time, he or she may also fear rejection and seek to avoid certain contacts with the other person. Depending on the situation, an appropriate balance, or state of equilibrium, will be established through regulation of the nonverbal channels of communication. If this equilibrium is disturbed, as, for example, by one person's press for more intimacy than the other person wants, Argyle and Dean suggest that the latter person will alter some of the nonverbal channels to restore the equilibrium. For instance, during a casual conversation with an acquaintance, the other person sits much closer to you than seems appropriate. Such an imbalance would probably lead you to alter your own nonverbal communication—either by increasing the distance between the two of you or perhaps by avoiding eye contact, orienting your body away from the person, or making facial signs that indicate discomfort. Thus, the basic assumption of the model is that loss of equilibrium in one channel of communication can be compensated for by alterations in other channels—in other words, the model proposes a set of compensatory functions.

To test this model, investigators have manipulated one of the communication channels and looked at the effects of these manipulations on another channel. For example, investigators may vary the distance between persons and then assess the amount of eye contact or gaze between participants. Considerable support for the equilibrium model has been found using this method (Cappella, 1981; Heslin & Patterson, 1982). For example, it was found that as people interact at closer distances, amount of eye contact tends to decrease (Argyle & Dean, 1965; Russo, 1975). In similar fashion, body orientation becomes less direct as interpersonal distance decreases (Aiello & Jones, 1971; Patterson, Mullens, & Romano, 1971; Pellegrini & Empey, 1970). Still other research has shown that as an interviewer's questions become increasingly personal, the interviewee will initiate less eye contact with the interviewer (Carr & Dabbs, 1974; Schulz & Barefoot, 1974).

Not all research supports the equilibrium model, however. For example, males and females often react differently to disturbances of equilibrium in

BOX 5-3. Failures of marital communication

When marriages fail, the partners often claim that there has been a failure of communication. Such statements reflect the fact that in marriage, one of the most intense and intimate of human relationships, communication is a central process. On the one hand, this intimacy can make possible very rich and complex communications between partners. On the other hand, the intensity of the relationship may increase the potential for misunderstanding.

Patricia Noller (1980, 1981) has investigated the ways in which married couples communicate, looking at both the encoding and decoding abilities of the partners. To study encoding abilities, she presented one partner with a description of a situation and a hypothetical reaction to that situation. For example, the wife might be told to imagine that she was sitting alone with her husband on a winter evening and felt cold. She would be asked also to assume that she was wondering whether her husband was cold as well and to ask him "I'm cold; aren't you?"

After one partner—the wife, in this example—had made a statement, it was the other partner's task to decode the statement. Noller provided this second partner with three possible interpretations of the message and asked him to select one, on the basis of his understanding of his wife's statement. Possible interpretations of "I'm cold" might be the intended message (wondering whether the partner is cold as well), a request for physical affection, or an accusation that the partner showed a lack of consideration in keeping the house too cold.

How did couples do on this task? Couples who scored high on a measure of marital adjustment communicated significantly better than couples who scored low on this measure, testifying to the association between effective communication and marital happiness. In general, women were better at sending messages than men were. This superiority was especially evident for positive messages, which men encoded surprisingly poorly.

Why were the men, particularly men in less satisfactory marriages, not effective in this communication task? Perhaps they simply lacked communication skills in general. Another explanation would focus on the marital relationship itself, suggesting that these men would show communication deficits only when interacting with their wives. To answer this question, Noller (1981) asked the same subjects to decode messages sent by strangers. In this case, the men had few problems. Thus, the ability to decode messages is not just a general trait but can be sharply influenced by particular features of a relationship. Husbands and wives may indeed experience failures of communication, but such failures are more apt to be a consequence than a cause of the problem. ■

a relationship (Aiello, 1972, 1977a, 1977b). Although the model generally holds true for men—in that they increase their gaze behavior as the distance between them and another person increases—women show a different pattern. When the distance between participants is greater than six to eight feet, women no longer increase their gaze behavior, as shown in Figure 5-4. This figure also shows that women engage in more eye contact at short distances than men do, suggesting that the sexes have different equilibrium points for intimacy in relationships.

Thus, although Argyle and Dean's equilibrium model is helpful in explaining how nonverbal communication cues establish intimacy levels in a relationship, it must be modified to allow for individual differences in the point of equilibrium. Cultural differences may also affect the way in which equilibrium is established, as described in Box 5-4.

BOX 5-4. Bilingualism and nonverbal behavior

Many people have observed that people from different cultures show different nonverbal behaviors. But what of the person who is bilingual? In a fascinating demonstration of the close connection between verbal and nonverbal channels of communication, Grujic and Libby (1978) studied French Canadian bilinguals who were equally proficient in French and English. In their study, Grujic and Libby varied both the spoken language in a 30-minute conversation and the ethnic identification of the partner. Thus, in some cases, the subject would speak French to a person identified as English; in other cases, the subject would speak English to a person identified as English; and so on. The results showed that the ethnic identification of the partner didn't matter, but the language of the conversation

did. When French was spoken, subjects sat closer to their partner at the beginning of the conversation, moved closer during the course of the conversation, gestured more, and interacted longer.

In terms of the compensation principle, this study suggests that different ways of establishing intimacy are used in English and in French. When speaking English, subjects maintained intimacy by looking at the partner more but smiling less. When speaking French, just the reverse occurred: there was more smiling but less gaze. Thus, in both cases, some intimacy was established—but the language of the conversation had strong effects on the nonverbal channels that were used. ■

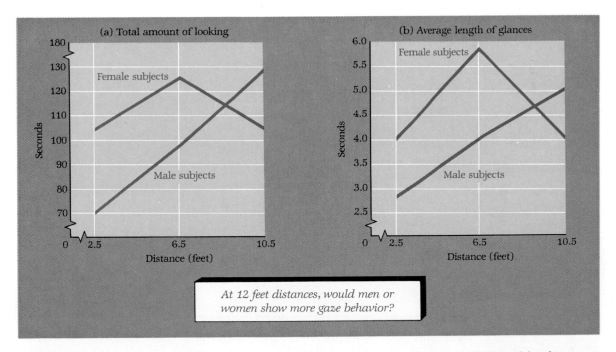

At 12 feet distances, would men or women show more gaze behavior?

FIGURE 5-4. Sex differences in gaze and distance. As measured either by total amount of looking (a) or by average length of glances (b), men and women show different gaze patterns as a function of distance.

A further problem for the model is the fact that compensation may not be the only response to a change in equilibrium (Breed, 1972). Surely there are occasions when an increase by one person in the level of intimacy is reciprocated rather than avoided. For example, when you are with someone you like in a romantic setting, won't you be more apt to respond positively to increases in intimacy rather than to try to reduce the intimacy level? The following model takes this possibility into account.

C. Arousal model of intimacy

Patterson (1976) has proposed a model of intimacy behavior that allows for either reciprocal or compensatory reactions to a change in the equilibrium level (see Figure 5-5). Basically, his model relies on the concept of *arousal*. Patterson suggests that small changes in the intimacy level will probably not be noticed, and hence no behavior changes will occur. At some threshold point, however, a sufficient change in the intimacy level of the interaction will be noticed, and, consequently,

some behavioral adjustment will be necessary.

What adjustment will be made, however, depends on how the person labels the state of arousal. Following a model developed by Schachter (see Chapter 3), Patterson assumes that a given state of arousal can be labeled either positive or negative, depending on the circumstances. For example, in the romantic setting suggested earlier, physical contact or intensified gazes initiated by your lover would probably be a positive experience and would lead you to reciprocate the behavior. In contrast, the same behavioral display by a stranger on a park bench would most likely be labeled negatively and would in turn lead to compensatory adjustments on your part—turning your body away, avoiding the gaze, or getting up and leaving. The arousal model of intimacy incorporates the equilibrium principles proposed by Argyle and Dean (1965) but adds another dimension as well. By this model, we can predict that the same type of change in the behavior of one person may lead to two quite different reactions in the other person, depending on a variety of situational factors.

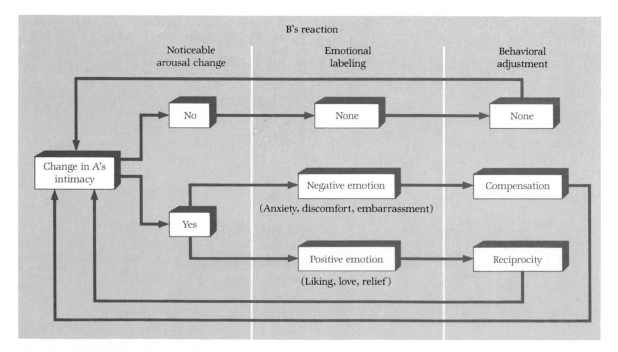

FIGURE 5-5. Arousal model of interpersonal intimacy.

Yet, even this model does not account for all the complexities in the communication process. As we noted in the beginning of this chapter, communication is a two-way street. Analyzing the reactions and interpretations of only one person in an interchange is simply not sufficient. Recognizing this limitation, Patterson (1982) has recently proposed a much more complex model of nonverbal exchange, based on the sequence of responses between two participants. This model considers how much involvement each person wants and how the actual level of involvement matches each set of expectations. Although it is too early to evaluate the success of this new model, we can appreciate its attempt to consider more realistic communication patterns.

■ IV. Some special cases of communication

We spend a great deal of our time communicating with other people. Although it is impossible to consider all the situations in which interpersonal communication takes place, let's look at a few specific cases of the communication process.

A. Initial encounters

When we meet someone for the first time, the initial encounter is often accompanied by some uncertainty. Not knowing the other person, we can't predict how he or she will behave; we are also unfamiliar with the style of speech, the nonverbal behaviors, and the beliefs, attitudes, and values of the stranger. Communication theorists have suggested that one of the functions of communication in initial encounters is to reduce this level of uncertainty (Berger & Calabrese, 1975). As an interaction develops, this uncertainty may decrease, and our communication patterns may change as well. For example, Lalljee and Cook (1973) studied in detail the first nine minutes of conversation between previously unacquainted college students and found that speech patterns shifted considerably in the course of that short interchange. In the earliest stages of the interaction, speech rate was considerably less than in later stages. Moreover, in the

initial stages of the interaction, students were more likely to fill pauses in the conversation with "ers," "ahs," and "ums," reflecting the uncertainty of the encounter. Nonverbal behaviors also may increase in frequency as communication progresses (Berger & Calabrese, 1975).

Questions are important in the process of communication. Through questions and answers, we develop a process of turn taking, making interaction easier (Knapp, 1978; LaFrance & Mayo, 1978). When participants in a conversation are not allowed to use questions, considerable disruption can occur (Kent, Davis, & Shapiro, 1978). The length of each participant's turn tends to increase, because the main mechanism for turning over the floor is absent. A ban on questions disrupts nonverbal behavior as well, as interactants in this situation gaze less at each other than do people who are conversing in more normal circumstances. In addition, such conversations are much less structured, and when people are asked to reconstruct the dialogues from these conversations, given only a list of the individual sentences out of order, they find it difficult.

The sex of the participants in initial encounters affects the nature of the developing communication. Two women, for example, show much more immediacy in their initial encounters than do two men: they orient their bodies more directly toward each other, and they talk more, gesture more, and gaze more at each other (Ickes, 1981). When men and women interact, the situation becomes somewhat more complex. Nonverbal expressions of stereotypical masculinity and femininity (Lippa, 1978b) become an additional component of the situation. Somewhat surprisingly, it appears that the male and female who are most traditionally sex-typed (a male who is highly masculine in his personality characteristics and a female who is highly feminine) have the most difficulty in initial encounters (Ickes & Barnes, 1978; Ickes, 1981). Compared with male/female dyads who are less traditionally sex-typed, these couples talk less, gesture less, and look at each other less frequently. They also smile and laugh less often than do less sex-typed couples during the course of an informal five-minute encounter. Not surprisingly, these cou-

PHOTO 5-6. Communication in initial encounters.

ples report being less attracted to each other at the end of the brief encounter. These dramatic differences in communication patterns in a short five-minute interchange illustrate the variety that exists in initial encounters.

B. Self-disclosure

Initial encounters are characterized by uncertainty, as people try to learn more about each other. A quite different form of communication takes place when people know each other very well and feel comfortable in expressing very personal feelings and beliefs. **Self-disclosure,** or self-revelation, refers to the revealing of personal information about oneself.

Not all information about oneself is equally likely to be revealed in the process of self-disclosure. Jourard (1971), for example, has found that people are more likely to reveal information about attitudes and opinions than about their personalities and their bodies. Sex differences are also apparent in self-disclosure. Women report more self-disclosure than men (Jourard, 1971), and they tend to talk about different things. In studying communication between pairs of best friends, Davidson and Duberman (1982) found that although women and men were equally likely to talk about topical issues, such as politics, current events, work, or movies, the sexes differed in their discussion of relational and personal topics. Women were more likely to talk specifically about their relationship with their friend and were also more likely to talk about personal aspects of their lives. These same women also reported much more reliance on nonverbal cues in communicating with their best friends.

Although men and women may differ in the content of their communication, both show evidence of reciprocity in self-disclosure. In other words, if one person increases the intimacy of the disclosures, the other person is likely to respond with a similar increase in intimacy (Cozby, 1973; Davis & Skinner, 1974; Worthy, Gary, & Kahn, 1969).

In longer-term relationships, however, strict reciprocity is no longer the rule in communication (Altman, 1973; Derlega, Wilson, & Chaikin, 1976; Morton, 1978). Although the overall intimacy level of such exchanges tends to be higher than in new relationships, there does not seem to be a one-for-one exchange of intimate information in any single conversation. Over the course of many conversations, however, these more intimate relationships probably also evidence a balance in level of self-disclosure. In other words, the specific rules of communication may change considerably as we move from the initial encounter to more stable relationships (which are discussed in more detail in Chapter 6).

C. Deceptive communication

In discussing self-disclosure, we often assume that people convey honest information about themselves. Yet, there is no doubt that people sometimes lie. Political scandals, criminal proceedings, and extramarital affairs are often the occasion for determined attempts to tell another person something other than the truth.

It is often believed that such deceptive communications are easily detected. In 1905, for example, Sigmund Freud suggested that "he that has eyes to see and ears to hear may convince himself that no mortal can keep a secret. If his lips are silent, he chatters with his fingertips; betrayal oozes out of him at every pore" (Freud, 1905/1959). More recently, trial lawyer Louis Nizer has pointed to cues that are associated with witnesses' attempts to deceive jurors (Nizer, 1973). Included among these cues are a tendency to look at the ceiling, a self-conscious covering of the mouth before answering questions, and a crossing of the legs. Are these beliefs in the detectability of deception justified? Do liars regularly expose themselves through the various communication channels? To answer these questions, first, we must determine whether there are reliable verbal and nonverbal messages that are sent when a person is lying, and, second, we must find out whether an observer can reliably interpret those cues.

Research directed at the first part of our answer has revealed a wide variety of communicative cues that accompany deception. In other words, although the liar may be controlling the content of the message, many of the other communication channels appear to "leak" information. For example, people who are being deceptive use speech differently: they make factual statements less often, they are prone to make vague, sweeping statements, and they frequently leave gaps in their conversation, apparently in an attempt to avoid saying something that would give them away (Knapp, Hart, & Dennis, 1974). The voice alters as well, in that liars are apt to have a higher pitch than truthtellers (Ekman, Friesen, & Scherer, 1976). An increase in manipulative gestures also accompanies lying in many instances: the deceiver is more apt to touch the face with the hand, for example, echoing the observations of Louis Nizer (Ekman & Friesen, 1974), or to play with glasses or some other external object (Knapp et al., 1974). Facial expression, in contrast, seems to be a less reliable indicator of deception. Some people smile while they are lying, whereas others maintain a placid expression (McClintock & Hunt, 1975; Mehrabian, 1971). Perhaps the latter situation is due to the fact that we have much more control over our facial expressions: we are aware of what emotion is being expressed in our face, but we are less aware of what the other parts of our body are saying.

Although liars send a large variety of nonverbal clues to their deceit, observers apparently do not use all of this information. People given both vocal and facial cues, for example, are no better at detecting deception than people who only hear the deceptive message (Zuckerman, DePaulo, & Rosenthal, 1981). This lack of difference suggests that people rely heavily on vocal cues in distinguishing truth from falsehood, a suggestion supported in recent research (DePaulo, Lassiter, & Stone, 1982; Zuckerman, Amidon, Bishop, & Pomerantz, 1982).

In overrelying on the auditory message, we may be missing important information being conveyed through other channels. In fact, most research suggests that people are not very good at detecting deception in others. Communication, as we have stressed, takes place through a variety of channels, and accurate decoding requires attending to all of those channels.

■ V. Communication and social interaction

As we noted at the beginning of this chapter, our study of communication is an attempt to put two pieces together—the self and the other person. Throughout this chapter, we have seen how communication depends on both partners in an interchange. Expressions of intimacy, for example, involve an adjustment by each person contingent on the other person's actions. Self-disclosure tends to be reciprocal, with partners matching each other's self-revelations. As yet, however, we have not given sufficient attention to what these partners bring to an interaction.

Many times—perhaps most of the time—we begin communication with some prior expectations. In an initial encounter, for example, we may form expectations on the basis of a person's physical appearance or style of dress. Our implicit personality theories, discussed in Chapter 4, may lead us to assume that the presence of some characteristics implies the possession of others. With people we know well, these expectations can be based on a wealth of past experience. How do these expectations affect the communication process?

Often, our expectations are confirmed in the process of interaction. Such confirmation is not surprising, of course, if the expectations are based on a long history of interchange. The wife of 20 years may know from experience, for example, that her husband will get angry when she tells him to get a haircut or that he will smile when she talks about their daughter's progress in school. More interesting, perhaps, is evidence that our expectations can affect even an initial encounter and can shape that encounter accordingly. This process is known as the **self-fulfilling prophecy**—the fact that a perceiver's beliefs about a target person may elicit behavior from the target person that will confirm the expectancy.

As analyzed by Darley and Fazio (1980), expectancy confirmation involves a sequence of events (see Figure 5-6). Initially, one person (the perceiver) has some expectancy about another person (the target). In communicating with the target, the perceiver may then act according to that expectancy—being friendly, for example, if the target is thought to be a nice person, or acting aggressively if the target is believed to be hostile. In turn, the target person may respond in a way that is consistent with the perceiver's beliefs—and may even come to believe that those behaviors are characteristic of the self (recall our discussion of self-construction in Chapter 3).

There is considerable evidence for the self-fulfilling prophecy. Snyder and Swann (1978), for example, told subjects in a competitive game that their partner was either hostile or nonhostile. A belief that the target was hostile led perceivers to act more competitively toward the target, and the target, in turn, responded with greater hostility than when the perceiver's initial expectations were for nonhostility. In another study demonstrating the power of initial expectations, male students engaged in a ten-minute telephone conversation with a female student whom they believed to be either physically attractive or unattractive (Snyder, Tanke, & Berscheid, 1977). Analysis of the conversations showed that males who believed they were interacting with an attractive female were friendlier, more outgoing, and generally more sociable. Thus, the beliefs of the perceiver were enacted in the communication process. And, as the self-fulfilling prophecy would suggest, the target women provided behavioral confirmation. In actuality, these women did not differ in physical attractiveness, and they did not know what impression the men had been given. Nonetheless, women who conversed with men who believed they were highly attractive were rated as more sociable, poised, and humorous by objective observers.

The sequence of expectancy confirmation does not necessarily stop when a particular conversation ends. If people treat me as competent, for example, and I act competently in response, I may begin to see myself as a competent person. This self-conception of competence may cause me to act more confidently in the future, taking the

FIGURE 5-6. The expectancy confirmation sequence.

sequence one step further. These consequences have been demonstrated in the laboratory. Subjects who confirmed expectations of being either introverted or extroverted continued to show these behaviors, impressing a neutral observer as either introverted or extroverted, depending on the preceding sequence (Fazio, Effrein, & Falender, 1981).

Communication processes such as these form the core of social interaction. Our views of ourselves and of others are constantly being communicated and interpreted, defining the present and laying the groundwork for the future.

VI. SUMMARY

The communication process underlies most aspects of human social behavior. Although the forms of communication are varied, it has been truthfully said that we can't *not* communicate. Early models of the communication process described a one-way flow from a transmitter to a receiver. More recent models stress that communication (1) is a shared social system, (2) is an ongoing and dynamic process, (3) combines both verbal and nonverbal channels, and (4) contains relational as well as content messages.

There are many channels through which we can communicate. Among these are language and paralanguage, eye contact and gaze, facial expressions, body movements and gestures, touch, and interpersonal distance. Through each of these channels we can communicate emotions, liking and disliking, and indications of dominant or submissive status.

Language is the most obvious form of communication. *Paralanguage*, which refers to other types of meaningful vocalization, can also convey meaning ranging from excitement to boredom.

Eye contact or gaze serves at least four functions in a communicative interaction: (1) regulating the flow of conversation, (2) monitoring feedback, (3) expressing emotions, and (4) communicating the nature of the relationship. Both sex and ethnic differences have been observed in the use of gaze as a means of communication.

Facial expressions can convey a variety of emotions, and these basic emotional expressions can be identified by people in very different cultures throughout the world. However, although the *facial affect program* (the connection between an emotional experience and a particular pattern of facial-muscle activity) may be constant across cultures, there are tremendous variations in the *display rules* that regulate whether an emotion will be expressed. Many facial expressions, such as the smile, may be less the automatic expression of an emotion than a chosen way to communicate an emotion.

Body movements and gestures have been classified in a system called *kinesics* that attempts to parallel linguistic models. Some body movements (called *illustrators*) are directly linked with spoken language; others (called *emblems*) substitute for a spoken phrase.

Touch is a part of many interactions, varying from the functional to the sexual. Like many other forms of nonverbal communication, touch is used and reacted to quite differently by women and men.

The distance between two persons also communicates a variety of messages. Four zones have been identified that are typical of different types of interactions: (1) intimate zones, (2) personal distance zones, (3) social distance zones, and (4) public distance zones.

In most communication situations, the various channels of communication are combined, although not each channel has equal impact. Three major dimensions of communication have been identified (liking, status, and responsiveness), each of which is indicated by a variety of nonverbal cues. With particular regard to the liking dimension, two models of intimacy have been proposed. The *equilibrium model* proposes a balance between approach and avoidance pressures in an interaction and suggests that pressures for intimacy in one channel will result in compensatory moves away from intimacy in other channels. The *arousal model* suggests that responses to changes in the intimacy level of an interaction will depend on how that situation is defined: sometimes increases in intimacy will be reciprocated, and other times they will be avoided.

In initial encounters, particular patterns of speech and nonverbal behaviors have been observed. The characteristics of an initial encounter vary greatly, depending on the sex and personality of the participants, as well as on the expectations they have about each other. *Self-disclosure* between persons in an interaction often tends to show reciprocity.

When people are being deceptive, a variety of verbal and nonverbal cues are displayed that differ from the normal state. Evidence suggests that we overrely on auditory cues, often failing to use other channels to detect deception.

Our beliefs about people not only affect the way we communicate with them but also affect the way they interact with us, often creating a *self-fulfilling prophecy*.

GLOSSARY TERMS

display rules	illustrators	self-disclosure
emblems	kinesics	self-fulfilling prophecy
facial affect program	paralanguage	

6

Affiliation, Attraction, & Love

Nobody loves me, well do I know,
Don't all the cold world tell me so?
■ HATTIE STARR

Love is much nicer to be in than an
automobile accident, a tight girdle, a
higher tax bracket, or a holding pattern
over Philadelphia.
■ JUDITH VIORST

Those of us who need people "are the luckiest people in the world," a popular song tells us. But don't we all need people? For many of us, at least, friends and lovers are among the most important aspects of life, and the process of developing relationships is one of our most challenging goals. When we look at ourselves, when we look at other people, and when we develop channels of communication, we are beginning to move toward relationships with other people. The kinds of relationships we form are numerous. Some people are only casual acquaintances; others become spouses or lovers. Some relationships last; others end in boredom or distress. And sometimes we may be lonely, wanting relationships we do not have. These many forms of interpersonal involvement are the concern of this chapter.

■ I. Alone or together?

A. Isolation and loneliness

Suppose you were offered $50 a day to remain in a room by yourself. You are free to leave whenever you want. The room has no windows but is equipped with a lamp, a bed, a chair, a table, and bathroom facilities. Food is brought at mealtime and left outside your door, but you see no one. You are allowed no companions, no telephone, no books, magazines, or newspapers, and no radio or television. If you were to volunteer for such a project, how long could you remain?

In an effort to understand people's needs to affiliate with other people, Schachter (1959) placed five male students in a setting similar to the one described. All the participants were volunteers. One of them was able to remain in the room for only 20 minutes before he had an uncontrollable desire to leave. Three volunteers remained in their rooms for two days. Afterward, one of these students said that he had become quite uneasy and would not want to do it again, but the other two seemed rather unaffected by their isolation. The fifth volunteer remained in isolation for eight days. On his release the student admitted that he was growing uneasy and nervous, but no serious effects from the isolation were observed.

These five students differed in their reactions to isolation—in this case, isolation in a strange room arranged by an experimenter. In other circumstances, people also have varying reactions to isolation. Some people, as Suedfeld (1982) notes, seek out isolation, finding it exhilarating, stimulating, or conducive to religious experience. The explorer, the artist, or the mystic may all seek out extensive amounts of time to be alone. Yet, for other people, being isolated from other people can be deeply disturbing.

All of us spend some time alone. In a study in which college students were asked to keep track of their activities over a three-day period, Deaux (1978) found that students spent about 25% of their waking hours alone. For some students, these hours alone may have been enjoyable; for others, being alone may have been a painful experience.

Being alone is not the same as being lonely. Aloneness is an objective state, easily assessed by any observer. Loneliness is a subjective experience and depends on our interpretations of events. Many definitions of loneliness have been offered (Peplau & Perlman, 1982). Although these vary in subtle ways, most of them touch on three particular elements. First, as we have indicated, loneliness is a subjective experience and cannot be measured by simply observing whether someone is alone or with other people. Second, loneliness generally results from some deficiencies in a person's social relationships. Third, loneliness is unpleasant. As Holden Caulfield despaired in Salinger's *Catcher in the Rye*, "I was crying and all. I don't know why, but I was. I guess it was because I was feeling so damn depressed and lonesome" (Salinger, 1953, p. 138). Although a feeling of loneliness may not always lead to such anguish, it is, by definition, always an unpleasant experience.

Rubenstein and Shaver (1982) asked people to describe in detail the feelings they experienced when they were lonely. Four general factors emerged from these descriptions: desperation, in the sense of being panicked and helpless; depression; impatient boredom; and self-deprecation. Although each of these factors taps a slightly different emotion, all of them reflect the unhappiness inherent in being lonely.

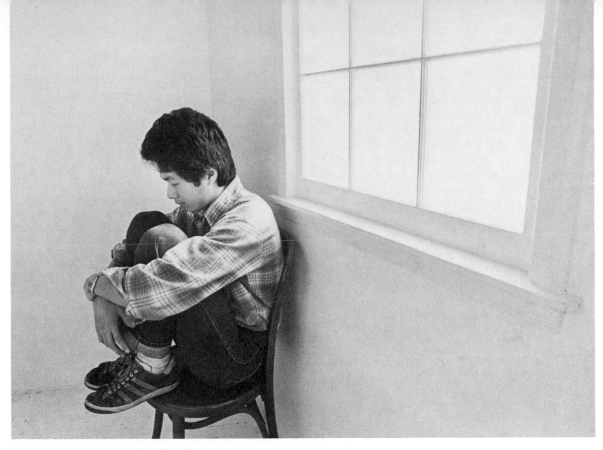

PHOTO 6-1. *The anguish of loneliness.*

Why do people get lonely? Weiss (1973) has suggested that there are two general types of loneliness: emotional isolation, in which the person does not have an attachment to one particular person, and social isolation, in which the person does not have a network of friends or relatives. These two types of loneliness do not always go together. For example, a student may live in a dormitory, eating, studying, and having bull sessions with friends, and yet feel emotionally isolated without an intimate relationship with one special person.

Either of these conditions may lead to an experience of loneliness, as Rubenstein and Shaver (1982) found. People who had no spouse or lover and people who had no close friends were both apt to report feelings of loneliness. In addition, there were other reasons given for being lonely. Simply being alone was one cause (although, as we have seen, not everyone reacts to isolation in this way). Other causes of loneliness were forced isolation, such as you might experience if you were confined to a hospital bed for a long time, and dislocation, as happens to many people when they move to a new town, begin a new job, or enter college.

Just as people differ in the reasons they give for being lonely, so they differ in their reactions to that state. For some people, particularly those who are severely lonely, a sad passivity is most likely. Crying, sleeping, drinking, taking tranquilizers, and just watching television aimlessly are typical responses. Other responses to loneliness may be more active and probably more helpful. Rubenstein and Shaver (1982) found three other common reactions to loneliness: some people engage in activities, despite their solitude, such as working on a hobby, studying, exercising, or going to a movie; others (particularly those with high incomes) go on shopping sprees; still others attempt social contact, calling someone on the telephone or visiting a friend.

Some types of people are more prone to loneliness than others; some types of situations are more likely to cause feelings of loneliness than others. An important distinction to be made here is the difference between *trait loneliness* and *state loneliness* (Shaver, 1982). Trait loneliness is a stable pattern of feeling lonely, which often changes little with the situation. In general, people who are low in self-esteem, generally viewing themselves in negative terms, are more likely to report being lonely (Jones, Freemon, & Goswick, 1981; Peplau, Miceli, & Morasch, 1982). People who report having meaningful interactions with other people are less likely to experience loneliness; conversely, lonely people report a lack of intimate self-disclosure with close friends (Solano, Batten, & Parish, 1982). Interestingly, the sheer amount of time spent interacting with females, but not males, also seems to be associated with loneliness: in a study by Wheeler, Reis, and Nezlek (in press), the more time college students spent with women, the less lonely they said they were.

State loneliness is a more temporary experience, often caused by some dramatic change in one's life. Students, for example, often experience state loneliness when they enter college, leaving behind the familiarity of home and high school and entering a new and often bewildering environment. This loneliness often goes away as new social networks are established (Shaver, 1982).

Coping with loneliness depends in large measure on the attributions that the person makes for his or her unhappiness. Students who blame their own deficiencies for their loneliness are more likely to remain unhappy. In contrast, the person who sees loneliness as only a temporary state is less likely to remain unhappy and may be more apt to take corrective actions. One of the best counters to loneliness appears to be the establishment of meaningful relationships with friends. It is the presence of friends, rather than relatives or romantic partners, that most clearly distinguishes between the lonely college student and the contented college student (Cutrona, 1982).

We often think that age is related to loneliness and that old people are probably the most unhappy of all. However, research shows that this common assumption is not true, as illustrated in Figure 6-1. In fact, reported loneliness seems to decrease as people get older, perhaps because older people have developed a more stable network of relationships.

B. Reasons for affiliation

As we have seen, contacts with other people are often an antidote for loneliness. But what are the reasons for affiliation? What do we gain from social interaction that we cannot experience alone?

There are several reasons that we may wish to affiliate with people or become a member of a group. For example, **social-exchange theory** would suggest that people affiliate as a means to an end (for more on this theory, see Section II-B). In this case, the individual has goals that can be met only by affiliating with others. For example, Irv, a tennis buff, needs to have at least one other companion who plays tennis; he may even join a tennis club in order to achieve his goals.

Reinforcement theory suggests that other people represent rewards in and of themselves. According to this viewpoint, needs such as those for approval and for development of an identity can be met only by other people. Although it is sometimes difficult to distinguish these two theories, the basic distinction has to do with means versus ends. Of course, the same person or group of persons may serve both goals: companionship in and

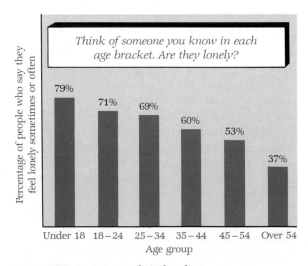

FIGURE 6-1. Age trends in loneliness.

PHOTO 6-2. *Stable networks of friendships may forestall loneliness among older people.*

of itself may be important, along with the achievement of some goal such as a tennis match.

Another implicit value of affiliation is the opportunity for self-evaluation. As we saw in Chapter 3, social comparison provides a way for people to evaluate their own skills and beliefs.

Still another purpose that affiliation serves is the reduction of anxiety. We saw earlier that the initial reaction to isolation may be a state of extreme anxiety. If so, Stanley Schachter reasoned, perhaps the reverse is true as well: anxiety may lead to a desire for affiliation. In his initial study, Schachter (1959) told female introductory-psychology students at the University of Minnesota that they would receive a series of electrical shocks. Subjects in the "high anxiety" condition were told that the shocks would be painful but that there would be no permanent damage. In contrast, subjects in the "low anxiety" condition were led to expect virtually painless shocks that would feel, at worst, like a tickle. After receiving this description, the students were told that there would be a ten-minute delay while the equipment was set up. Each subject was allowed to choose whether she would wait by herself or with some of the other subjects in the same experiment. After the subjects had made this choice, the experiment was terminated. Schachter's concern was only with the choices that subjects would make, and no shocks were administered.

As Schachter predicted, the level of induced anxiety influenced the waiting preferences. Of the 32 subjects in the high-anxiety condition, 20 wanted to wait with other subjects; only 10 of the 30 subjects in the low-anxiety condition chose to wait with others. The adage "Misery loves company" was confirmed.

What is it about being with others that makes affiliation so desirable for highly anxious subjects? There are at least two possible explanations. First, the presence of others may serve as a distraction, allowing the subject to temporarily forget about the impending shocks. Alternatively, people in this situation may be unsure of their reactions and seek out other people as a means of social comparison. If the first explanation is true, then any other person would be desirable. But if social comparison is critical, then it would be important to seek out people who were in a similar situation.

To test out these two explanations, Schachter (1959) conducted a second experiment. This time all subjects were told that they would receive painful shocks; hence all subjects were in a high-anxiety condition. Each subject was given the choice of waiting alone or with others, but the characteristics of the others were varied. Some subjects were given the choice of waiting alone or waiting with other female students who were taking part in the same experiment. Other subjects could wait either alone or with female students who were not participating in the experiment but instead were waiting to see their faculty advisers.

The results of the study were clear. Subjects who had the opportunity to wait with others in the same experiment showed a clear preference for doing so. In contrast, subjects who could wait with students not involved in the experiment showed a unanimous preference for waiting alone. These findings suggest that distraction is apparently *not* an explanation of the link between anxiety and affiliation. Further, instead of concluding that misery loves company, Schachter suggests it is more appropriate to say that "misery loves miserable company."

There is a third explanation for Schachter's results that does not require the company to be miserable—only to be in the same situation. Faced with an unfamiliar situation, people may seek cognitive clarity—in other words, they may want to know more about the situation. Babies, for example, often turn to their mothers when unexpected or novel events occur. In the same manner, college students faced with electrical shock may seek the company of others in order to appraise the situation (Shaver & Klinnert, 1982). This need to understand the situation may be as strong as or stronger than the need to assess one's own reactions.

Although the evidence quite clearly supports the relation between anxiety and the desire for affiliation, it is much less certain that such affiliation actually does *reduce* anxiety. Evidence has been presented on both sides of the argument (Buck & Parke, 1972; Epley, 1974; MacDonald, 1970; Wrightsman, 1960, 1975). Yet, whether or not affiliation is an effective anxiety reducer, the fact that people choose to affiliate when they are anxious remains important for our understanding of affiliative behavior.

C. Affiliation patterns in everyday life

In laboratory experiments such as those just described, it is possible to determine some of the reasons that people might choose to affiliate with other people. Yet, although such laboratory experiments are a very good way to verify cause-and-effect relationships, they tell us little about people's natural patterns of affiliation in everyday life. How often do people choose to spend time with other people rather than to be by themselves? What kinds of people are selected for affiliation and interaction?

To answer these questions, investigators have begun in their own backyards—on the college campuses where they are located. Latané and Bidwell (1977), for example, simply observed people in a variety of locations on the Ohio State and University of North Carolina campuses, recording whether each person they observed was alone or in the presence of other people. Overall, about 60% of the people they saw were with at least one other person. Interestingly, women were much more likely to be with other people than men were, suggesting that, at least in public places, women may affiliate more than men.

Pursuing this general strategy, Deaux (1978) asked students at Purdue University to keep records of their interactions over a three-day period, recording at each 15-minute interval of their waking hours whether they were alone or with other people. The advantage of this strategy over the simple observation method is that data could be collected for a single person over a longer period, and private as well as public affiliation patterns could be tapped. However, the possible disadvantage of this method is that the investigator had to rely on self-report data, whose shortcomings were discussed in Chapter 2.

In general, men and women did not differ in their overall patterns of affiliation. The only exception was in the case of same-sex groups: men reported 20% of their time in such groups, whereas women reported only 14%. This particular difference supports the arguments of anthropologist Lionel Tiger (1969), who has suggested that males are more likely to bond together as a result of hereditary links to earlier animal behavior.

One other interesting sex difference emerged when a closer look was taken at the kinds of activities in which the students were engaged. Focusing on those periods when students reported talking, which we might consider to be most indicative of affiliation, Deaux (1978) found that women spent more time engaged in conversation than men; furthermore, women were more likely to talk with a person of the same sex than men were.

Looking more closely at social interaction patterns, Wheeler and Nezlek (1977) asked first-year college students to keep track of all interactions that they had during two-week periods in both the fall and the spring semesters. By limiting the interactions to those that lasted ten minutes or more, the investigators hoped to focus on situations in which affiliation was actually occurring, as opposed

PHOTO 6-3. *Social interaction can reduce the initial stress of a new environment.*

to more casual exchanges such as getting a homework assignment or checking a book out of the library. By these criteria, there is evidence of much greater same-sex affiliation. Fifty-six percent of the first-year students' interactions were with a person of the same sex. During the first semester, the women students spent significantly more time engaged in some kind of interaction than the men; but by the second semester this difference had disappeared. As one explanation of this difference, Wheeler and Nezlek suggest that women may be more likely to look to social interaction as a way to deal with the initial stress of adjusting to college.

These same investigators have shown that social interaction is related to physical and psychological well-being. Particularly for women, satisfying social interaction was associated with fewer reported health problems (Reis, Wheeler, Kernis, Spiegel, & Nezlek, 1982).

Outside the boundaries of the college campus, much less research has been done. In one of the few studies to consider a broader range of people, Booth (1972) interviewed 800 adults in Nebraska. He found that although men and women reported having a similar number of close friends, women seemed to have closer and more frequent contact with their friends and relatives than men did. It is risky, of course, to conclude anything about basic gender differences, because the occupational statuses of the men and women in this sample were very different. Most of the men were employed outside the home, whereas the majority of the women were homemakers and may therefore have had more time to develop and maintain friendships of a close and personal nature.

These studies begin to provide us with a picture of human social interaction. It is interesting to note how often we choose to be with someone of the same sex. Although opposite-sex interactions frequently draw more attention, affiliation with someone of the same sex is an obviously important aspect of many people's social life.

■ II. Attraction

So far we have considered why people choose to affiliate, and we have looked at some of the general patterns of social interaction. Yet, given these general needs for affiliation, how do people choose which people they want to be with? Why are they friendly with or attracted to some people, while they reject or dislike others? In this section we move from the general nature of affiliation to the specific reaction of attraction.

A. Antecedents of interpersonal attraction

What characteristics of people make them attractive? Considerable research has been conducted on interpersonal attraction, perhaps reflecting the importance that many of us place on being liked. On the basis of this research, we can say that the odds are in favor of our liking a person if that person—

1. has similar beliefs, values, and personality characteristics;
2. satisfies our needs;
3. is physically attractive;
4. is competent;
5. is pleasant or agreeable;
6. reciprocates our liking; and
7. is in geographical proximity to us.

Let's consider each of these factors in turn.

Similarity of beliefs, values, and personality. We like people whose attitudes and values appear to agree with ours, and we dislike those who seem to disagree with us (Byrne, 1971; Griffitt, 1974; M. F. Kaplan, 1972). If their personalities are like ours, the attraction is even stronger. Most of the early studies that demonstrated this relationship were done in the laboratory, using verbal descriptions of hypothetical persons, and the findings were consistent and sometimes even surprising. For example, researchers found that Whites preferred associating with Blacks who had attitudes like their own, rather than with Whites who had opposing attitudes (Byrne & Wong, 1962; Moss & Andrasik, 1973; Rokeach, 1968; Stein, Hardyck, & Smith, 1965). However, the value of these find-

ings was challenged because of their artificial nature; that is, the other person was described only on paper, and the subject was explicitly made aware of the degree of similarity or dissimilarity in attitudes, thus creating the possibility of strong demand characteristics (Levinger, 1972; Wright & Crawford, 1971).

Field studies provide a broader view of this relationship. In an early field study, Newcomb (1961) gave male college students free housing if they agreed to fill out seemingly endless questionnaires about their attitudes and their liking for their housemates. The results of this massive study showed generally that men whose attitudes were similar at the beginning of the semester came to like each other more by the end of the testing period. More recently Kandel (1978) conducted an extensive questionnaire study with over 1800 male and female adolescents ages 13–18. By comparing the attitudes and values of each student with those of his or her best friend, she was able to show strong support for the similarity relationship. Some areas of similarity were more important than others, however. Best friends were most apt to be similar with respect to certain demographic variables such as grade, sex, race, and age. Friends also tended to have similar attitudes toward drug use; in contrast, friends did not always share attitudes toward parents and teachers.

Looking at a broader range of characteristics, Hill and Stull (1981) questioned college roommates representing both sexes, all years, and a variety of religious and ethnic backgrounds. Among female roommates, similarity in values was very important. Value similarity was very high among pairs who had chosen to be roommates, and it was also influential in predicting which assigned roommates decided to stay together. Once again, we find differences between women and men—sharing values with others was less important for men. Thus, there is increasing evidence that women and men may define and experience friendship differently.

People who are dissimilar are not always disliked, however. In fact, on some occasions we may even *prefer* the dissimilar person. For example, if a person is stigmatized (Novak & Lerner, 1968) or is of lower status (Karuza & Brickman, 1978), we may prefer that person to be dissimilar to us in attitudes, perhaps because too much similarity to a less desirable person is threatening to our self-image. Furthermore, even our initial tendency to dislike those who are dissimilar to us can be modified, and often quite easily. Simply having the opportunity to predict a person's attitudes (Aderman, Bryant, & Donelsmith, 1978) or being allowed to discuss areas of disagreement (Brink, 1977) will substantially increase our liking for the initially dissimilar person.

Complementarity of need systems. There are also times when opposites attract. According to the theory of need **complementarity,** people choose relationships in which their basic needs can be mutually gratified (Winch, Ktsanes, & Ktsanes, 1954). Sometimes the result of this choice is a pairing of apparent opposites, as when a very dominant person is attracted to a very submissive partner. Other times the opposition may be more apparent than real, as when women with traditional views of their own roles prefer men with traditionally masculine attributes (Seyfried & Hendrick, 1973). In this case, both partners may believe in traditional sex roles, but the specific characteristics they favor in themselves and their partners may be opposite. In general, the complementarity principle seems reasonable, and there is some evidence that it operates in long-term relationships (Kerckhoff & Davis, 1962). Other investigators (Levinger, Senn, & Jorgensen, 1970) have been less encouraging, however, and we must conclude that the complementarity principle probably operates only on a few dimensions and in a limited number of situations.

Perhaps one reason for the ambiguous findings in this area is that investigators have failed to consider the total picture of needs in a relationship. Needs may exist in various domains, and the resources that one person brings to the relationship may be exchanged for some virtue in another area (Foa, 1971). In an intriguing demonstration of this more complex pattern of needs, Harrison and Saeed (1977) examined 800 advertisements in the lonely-hearts column of a widely circulated weekly tabloid. By analyzing both what people offered (such as "good-looking woman of high moral standards who will offer good company") and what they sought ("seeks wealthy older man with good intentions"), these investigators discovered some interesting aspects of the exchange relationship in male/female pairs. For example, women were more likely to offer physical attractiveness, and men were more likely to seek it. In similar fashion, men were more likely to offer financial security and women to request it. Supporting the similarity principle, good-looking advertisers of both sexes sought a good-looking partner. Further, some evidence of the more complex exchanges that may occur was shown by the self-described attractive women who sought financially well-to-do men (see also Box 6-1).

BLOOM COUNTY by Berke Breathed

BOX 6-1. Courtship in the personal column

Do heterosexual and homosexual persons look for the same qualities in a prospective partner? Deaux and Hanna (in press) considered this question by analyzing the same material that Harrison and Saeed (1977) used—namely, personal advertisements in newspapers. These investigators gathered 800 such ads, representing equal numbers of heterosexual females, homosexual females, heterosexual males, and homosexual males. Each ad was coded in terms of what the person requested and what was offered.

Heterosexuals and homosexuals did differ in some respects. In general, heterosexuals sought a broader range of characteristics, more often mentioning attractiveness, personality, hobbies, financial status, and religion than the homosexual advertisers. In contrast, homosexuals were more likely to seek particular sexual habits and characteristics.

In many respects, gender was more influential than sexual orientation. Men, whether homosexual or heterosexual, were more likely to seek physical attractiveness and to describe themselves in physical terms. Women were more likely to mention psychological characteristics, when describing both what they offered and what they sought.

Looking just at the heterosexual advertisers, we find results similar to those of Harrison and Saeed (1977). Heterosexual women were most likely to offer physical attractiveness and to seek financial security, while heterosexual men offered financial status and security and provided objective physical descriptors.

Homosexual advertisers showed some interesting differences. For homosexual women, physical characteristics were much less important than for heterosexual women, and greater emphasis was placed on hobbies, interests, and sincerity in the prospective relationship. Although physical appearance was downplayed by the homosexual women, it was emphasized by the homosexual men. Among this latter group, physical characteristics were mentioned most often, and personality factors appeared much less important than they were for the heterosexual male. Sexuality was also a more central issue for the male homosexuals than for any other group.

As we can see, interpersonal attraction is not a simple process. Both gender and sexual preference influence one's choices. What is highly important to one person may be merely incidental to another. ■

Thus, both similarity and complementarity may play some role in attraction. To date, however, the evidence for similarity is much stronger and much more broadly based as well, applying to both same-sex and opposite-sex friendships in both laboratory and field settings. Complementarity, in contrast, has been found primarily in romantic heterosexual pairings, and we don't know how important it is either in same-sex friendships or in homosexual romantic pairs.

Physical attractiveness. Aristotle wrote that "beauty is a greater recommendation than any let-

ter of introduction," and things have not changed much in the last 2300 years. Physical appearance remains a critical determinant of success in our society (Berscheid & Walster, 1974), and the vast amounts of money spent on cosmetics, plastic surgery, diet foods, and contemporary fashions attest to the degree of concern that we invest in our appearance.

Such investments seem to pay off, because there is an implicit assumption in our society that "what is beautiful is good" (Dion, Berscheid, & Walster, 1972). As one example, Dion (1972) showed college women some photographs of children who had allegedly misbehaved. Some of the children were physically attractive, and others were not. Particularly when the misbehavior was severe, the beautiful children were given the benefit of the doubt. Respondents tended to disregard the misbehavior of the attractive children, whereas less beautiful children who committed the same acts were called maladjusted and deviant. Even children themselves are aware of these differences. Dion (1977) has found that children as young as 3 years will prefer pretty children to less attractive peers.

In fact, it is difficult to overestimate the effect that another person's physical appearance has on our initial impressions. Studies have shown that the highly attractive person is more likely to be recommended for hiring after a job interview (Dipboye, Arvey, & Terpstra, 1977; Dipboye, Fromkin, & Wiback, 1975), to have his or her written work evaluated favorably (Landy & Sigall, 1974), and to be seen as an effective psychological counselor (Cash, Begley, McCown, & Weise, 1975) and is less likely to be judged maladjusted or disturbed (Cash, Kehr, Polyson, & Freeman, 1977). Such studies powerfully demonstrate the extent to which we rely on physical appearance in making our judgments of others. Even a characteristic such as height, over which the person has no control, may be the basis for greater or less liking, as shown in Photo 6-4.

One reason we are beckoned by the physically attractive lies in our hope that their attractiveness will "rub off" on us. Many years ago sociologist W. W. Waller (1937) observed that we gain a great deal of prestige by being seen with an attractive

person of the other sex. This "rating and dating" complex has been verified in more recent research. For example, Sigall and Landy (1973) found that a male makes the most favorable impression on observers when he is accompanied by a good-looking female companion. He is viewed most negatively when his female companion is physically unattractive. Such "rub-off" effects may be one-sided, however. Although men gain in likability when their female partner is highly attractive, women do not necessarily receive equal benefits. Bar-Tal and Saxe (1976) showed subjects slides of presumably married couples, in which both the husband and the wife varied in their physical attractiveness. The unattractive male who was paired with an attractive wife was judged to have the highest income, the greatest professional success, and the highest intelligence. In contrast, the unattractive woman paired with an attractive husband gained no advantage by the pairing—she was judged solely on her own level of attractiveness.

Although women may not gain from having an attractive partner, physical attractiveness is not unimportant for the male himself. In fact, Harry Reis and his colleagues have found that the more attractive a man is, the more social interaction he has with women—and the less he has with other men. For women, somewhat surprisingly, amount of social interaction is unrelated to physical attractiveness. For both sexes, however, high attractiveness is associated with the *quality* of social interactions: highly attractive people report more satisfaction and more pleasurable interactions (Reis, Nezlek, & Wheeler, 1980; Reis, Wheeler, Spiegel, Kernis, Nezlek, & Perri, in press).

PHOTO 6-4. The higher the better? It is widely believed that taller people are viewed more positively than shorter people. For example, Michael Korda, in his popular book Power: How to Get It, How to Use It!, *states that "height means something to people, and it's not wise to forget it" (1975, p. 51). In support of this contention, Feldman (1971) has reported that short men receive lower starting salaries and are less likely to be hired than are tall men and that in U.S. presidential elections the taller candidate nearly always wins (Jimmy Carter was an exception in 1976). Laboratory experiments have shown that, when a man is described as being high in status, subjects judge him to be taller than when the man is described as being low in status (Wilson, 1968). Whether these findings are also true of women is not known.*

But why is there this sex difference, somewhat contrary to popular wisdom? At least part of the answer lies in the relationship between physical attractiveness and feelings of social competence. In males, these two characteristics are related, and attractive males are likely to be more assertive and less fearful of women. Among women, the association is just the opposite: attractive women are less assertive and are less likely to initiate contacts with men.

Physical appearance is clearly important for both men and women, although the effects are not always the same. There is yet another way that physical attractiveness plays a role: the similarity in attractiveness between two partners is important. Research has supported the **matching hypothesis**—that people tend to relate to people who approximately equal them in evaluated beauty (Murstein, 1972; Murstein & Christy, 1976; Price & Vandenberg, 1979). Such is the case not only for opposite-sex relationships but for same-sex friends as well (Cash & Derlega, 1978). Thus, in the abstract we may prefer the most attractive person (Walster, Aronson, Abrahams, & Rottman, 1966), but in more reality-based settings we choose someone who is close to our own level of attractiveness. Apparently, in making such choices, we combine information about the person's attractiveness with our own probability judgment of being accepted (Shanteau & Nagy, 1979)—and, with such a strategy, matching often results.

Competence. We like people who are intelligent, able, and competent more than we do those who are not. Although physical attractiveness is a more readily apparent piece of information, intelligence may be ultimately more important. Thus, when Solomon and Saxe (1977) provided people clear information about a woman's physical appearance and her intelligence, intelligence was a much more important determinant of attraction toward that person. In addition, the perception that someone is intelligent can generalize to other characteristics as well. Reversing the "beautiful is good" pattern, Gross and Crofton (1977) demonstrated that what is good is beautiful: people described by a positive set of characteristics, including intelligence, were judged as more physically attractive than those described in less glowing terms.

Although the generality of our attraction to intelligent and competent people has been well established, there are some important exceptions. For example, men judging women in the abstract readily report preferring a competent woman to an incompetent woman (Deaux, 1972; Spence & Helmreich, 1972). However, if faced with a situation in which they will actually interact with that woman, men no longer show a preference for competence (Hagen & Kahn, 1975). Such findings suggest that many characteristics may not be guarantees of attraction; rather, they depend on the sex of the person and perhaps other characteristics as well.

Pleasant or agreeable characteristics. Not surprisingly, we like people who are nice or who do nice things. As discussed in Chapter 4, personality characteristics vary in their likability, and we will be more attracted to someone who has various positive traits than to someone who demonstrates more negative habits (Kaplan & Anderson, 1973). Beyond evaluating the characteristics of another person in and of themselves, however, we are also concerned with the interpersonal implications of these traits (Clore & Kerber, 1978). In other words, when evaluating another person's characteristics, we give some consideration to what those traits or behaviors mean for us. For example, "considerate" not only is a favorable description of another person but also implies that we ourselves will receive some positive outcomes from interacting with that person. At the more negative pole, we tend to be least attracted to persons who can be described in terms that not only suggest negative aspects of their personality but imply negative consequences for us as well (such as "unappreciative" or "dishonest").

Reciprocal liking. We are attracted to people who like us. Heider's balance theory, to be considered in Chapter 11, predicts, for example, that if Susan likes herself and Bonnie likes Susan, a cognitively balanced state will result in which Susan likes Bonnie in return. In other words, liking and disliking are often reciprocal. Backman and Secord (1959) found that if members of a discussion group were told that other group members liked them very much, they were most likely to choose those same members when asked to form smaller groups later in the experimental session. The opposite is also true: we tend to dislike those people who have indicated negative feelings toward us. Finally, our tendency toward balance can be taken even one step further. Aronson and Cope (1968) have demonstrated the truth of the maxim "My enemy's enemy is my friend." Two persons who share in their dislike for a third person will tend to be more attracted to each other than those who do not share this common bond.

Propinquity. All else being equal, we tend to like people who live close to us better than those who are at some distance. This factor of **propin-**

quity has even been put to music, as in the song from *Finian's Rainbow* that says "When I'm not near the one I love, I love the one I'm near." More recently, Stephen Stills has advised us to love the one we're with. At a more scientific level, Festinger, Schachter, and Back (1950) found that residents of an apartment complex were more apt to like and interact with those who lived on the same floor of the building than with people who lived on other floors or in other buildings. Members of Air Force bomber crews develop closer relationships with coworkers who are stationed near them than with coworkers stationed a few yards away (Kipnis, 1957). And students in a classroom where alphabetical seating is required are more likely to report friendships with people whose names begin with the same letter than with those whose names are at some distance away in the class roll (Byrne, 1961).

Why is propinquity a factor in attraction? In part, the effect may be due to simple familiarity (see Photo 6-5). There is a mass of evidence for the **mere exposure effect**; that is, repeated exposure to the same stimulus leads to greater attraction toward that object (Harrison, 1969; Matlin, 1970; Saegert, Swap, & Zajonc, 1973; Zajonc, 1968). We are more likely to see people who live close to us than those who live far away, and just that frequency of contact may increase our liking for them.

In addition, simple social interaction will increase our liking for people (Werner & Latané, 1976; Insko & Wilson, 1977). In fact, even the anticipation of interaction seems to increase our liking for another person (Darley & Berscheid, 1967), particularly when the person is either initially disliked or ambivalently valued. As Tyler and Sears (1977) suggest, we may even come to like obnoxious people when we know that we must live with them.

B. Theoretical explanations of interpersonal attraction

We have seen how a variety of antecedent conditions contribute to interpersonal attraction. Now let's explore some of the possible explanations for these relationships, using theories as a way of helping to understand and organize the multiple findings. The basic models that we will consider are the *reinforcement/affect theory, social-exchange theory,* and *equity theory.*

Reinforcement/affect theory. Perhaps the most basic explanation of interpersonal attraction relies on the concept of reinforcement—that we like people who reward us and dislike people who punish us. As formulated by Byrne and Clore (1970), interpersonal attraction can be conceptualized as a basic learning process. This model assumes that most stimuli can be classified as rewards or punishment, and it assumes that rewarding stimuli elicit positive feelings, or affect, whereas punishing stimuli elicit negative feelings, or affect. Our evaluations of people or objects are, in turn, based on the degree of positive or negative affect we experience, and neutral stimuli that are associated with the affect will gain the capacity to produce similar feelings. Lott and Lott (1974) have proposed a similar model.

To look at this theory in more concrete terms, let's consider some of the factors we discussed previously. Somebody doing nice things for us, for example, would undoubtedly be a positive, rewarding experience. Byrne and Clore (1970) would suggest that the reward value of this experience would create positive affect and, in turn, would lead us to positively evaluate (or like) the person associated with that reward. To take it one step further, they would also predict that other people and objects associated with that situation (for example, the place where the interaction occurred or other people present at the time) would also tend to be liked more because of the conditioning process. Byrne and his colleagues (Byrne, 1971) have marshaled an impressive array of support for this apparently simple principle.

Social-exchange theory. The general assumption that reinforcement is an important basis of interpersonal attraction is not challenged by social-exchange theory. However, unlike the simple reinforcement theory just discussed, social-exchange theory is much more explicit about considering *both* parties involved in the relationship. Attraction does, after all, involve two persons, and

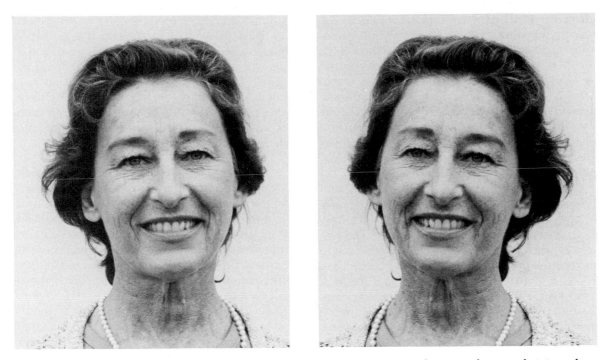

PHOTO 6-5. *The effects of "mere exposure." Can you see any difference between these two photographs? In a clever test of the mere exposure hypothesis, Mita, Dermer, and Knight (1977) asked subjects to indicate their preference for one of two pictures of themselves. In fact, the two photographs were identical, but in one case the image was simply reversed in printing. Friends of the subjects were also asked to indicate their preferences. The subjects themselves showed a strong preference for the mirror image—in other words, for the picture that looked like the image they saw of themselves daily in the mirror. Friends of the subjects, in contrast, preferred the true image—the face as they saw it in their interactions with the subject.*

it seems reasonable to assume that we should consider how the two persons interact, rather than focus only on the characteristics of the other person while ignoring the perceiver.

As we saw in Chapter 1, social-exchange theory conceptualizes interactions in terms of costs and rewards (Kelley & Thibaut, 1978; Thibaut & Kelley, 1959). A person in a relationship presumably weighs the rewards, or gains, against the costs; to the extent that the gains outweigh the costs, the attraction to and positive feelings for the other person will be stronger. For example, in a particular relationship, you may feel you are gaining companionship, romance, and excitement and are losing only a small measure of independence. In that case you would probably feel quite good about the relationship.

Yet, there are other factors to consider as well. Social-exchange theory suggests that people may compare the gains in a relationship against some baseline that they have come to expect. This *comparison level* is based on past experiences, and any present relationship will be judged as satisfactory only if it exceeds the comparison level. This comparison level can change over time; for example, as you grow older, you may demand more from a relationship than you did when you were a teenager. The comparison level may also be specific to situations. For example, the calculations of *outcome value* (rewards minus costs) may be quite different when deciding on a dentist than when deciding on a lover.

One other factor enters into the calculations of social-exchange theory—the *comparison level for alternatives.* Imagine that you have been in a relationship for some time, a relationship that is generally good and exceeds your comparison level. Then you meet an exciting stranger, who promises far more rewards and fewer costs. What would you do? In all likelihood, there would be some instability as you decided whether to go for the more attractive option. In contrast, if your current relationship offered few rewards and considerable costs, there might be little hesitation in choosing the exciting stranger.

This example underlines how important subjective evaluations are in the social-exchange process. Rewards and costs are not objective standards that can be measured with a ruler. Rather, they depend on individual beliefs, on attributions about ourselves and others, and they are subject to constant change (Kelley, 1979). As a result, it may be difficult to assess exact outcomes in a complex interaction. Still, the general idea that we do consider such factors in the course of a relationship is very convincing.

Equity theory. With **equity theory** we take one step further in considering both parties in a relationship. According to equity theory, we consider not only our own costs and rewards in a relationship but also the costs and rewards for the other person (Hatfield & Traupmann, 1981; Walster, Walster, & Berscheid, 1978). Ideally, there will be a balance between these two ratios. This theory suggests that we have some notion of what we deserve from a relationship, and this notion is based in part on what the other partner in the relationship is getting. The person who feels that the relationship is out of balance will become distressed and will try to restore the balance, either by actually altering the inputs and outcomes or by psychologically altering his or her perception of the gains and costs that both partners are experiencing.

One of the interesting predictions of equity theory is that we become dissatisfied whenever the relationship is out of balance—whether we are overbenefited or underbenefited compared with our partner. Thus, if the rewards I experience in a relationship are great and the costs are small, I will not necessarily be satisfied. If my partner's outcomes are either much greater or much less than mine, I will feel some distress. These predictions have been verified in studies of husbands and wives: the greatest happiness and satisfaction were reported by those who felt the relationship was equitable, although those who believed they were overbenefiting were less unhappy than those who felt they were underbenefiting (Traupmann, Petersen, Utne, & Hatfield, 1981).

Each of these three theories points to important aspects of the attraction process. At the most basic level, reinforcement theory tells us a great deal about the factors that will influence our attraction to another person. Most of the antecedents to attraction that we discussed earlier can, in fact, be handled by a simple reinforcement model. Yet, when we consider a more active interaction between two persons, additional factors are needed to explain interpersonal attraction. Both social-exchange theory and equity theory take us in that direction, considering both partners as necessary components of the explanation. With this in mind, let's move beyond the simple cataloguing of factors that affect attraction and consider some of the deeper relationships that people have.

■ III. Romance and love

Perhaps the ultimate in affiliation and attraction is love. Philosophers and songwriters, novelists and poets have for centuries debated the meaning of love; yet, until quite recently, social psychologists have avoided the subject. Berscheid and Walster (1978) suggest three reasons for this neglect. First, "love and marriage were regarded as belonging to the field of romance, not of science" (Burgess & Wallin, 1953, p. 11). Thus, although simpler forms of attraction might be studied by the social scientist, it was believed that real love was too mysterious and too intangible for scientific study. Even when the possibility of the study of love was acknowledged, however, the subject was often considered taboo. Like sexual behavior, love was considered to be a topic off limits to researchers, representing an unreasonable intrusion into personal and intimate matters. For example, in the 1920s, a professor was fired from the University of Minnesota because he approved a questionnaire on attitudes toward sex (which included such "unreasonable" questions as "Have you ever blown into the ear of a person of the opposite sex in order to arouse their passion?"). A third and perhaps more practical reason for the lack of study of love is simply that it is difficult. Without claiming it impossible, many investigators nonetheless have found it hard to approach this complex topic. Certainly, the laboratory tradition of social psychology in which subjects participate in brief, one-time sessions does not lend itself easily to the study of love. Love can't be manipulated in the laboratory, and the causes and consequences of love are not easily isolated in a single brief session. Despite these barriers, social psychologists have recently begun to study love in earnest. (For more discussion, see Duck & Gilmour, 1981a, 1981b, 1981c; Duck, in press.)

A. Conceptions of love

Whereas attraction can be defined simply as "a tendency or predisposition to evaluate a person or symbol of that person in a positive or negative way" (Berscheid & Walster, 1978), definitions of love have generally been more complex. Walster and Walster (1978) suggest that there are two kinds of love: *passionate* (or romantic) *love* and *companionate love.* They offer the following description of passionate love: "A state of intense absorption in another. Sometimes 'lovers' are those who long for their partners and for complete fulfillment. Sometimes 'lovers' are those who are ecstatic at finally having attained their partners' love, and, momentarily, complete fulfillment. A state of intense physiological arousal" (p. 9).

In contrast to this more intense state of feeling, Walster and Walster suggest that there is a second, and perhaps more familiar, form of love. *Companionate love* is defined as the affection we feel for those with whom our lives are deeply inter-

PHOTO 6-6. *Companionate love may last for decades, while passionate love often has a short duration.*

twined. In contrast to the sometimes momentary state of romantic love, companionate love reflects longer-term relationships and may be a later stage in a romantic relationship.

Basic to conceptions of love is the idea of caring. In a love relationship, behavior is often motivated by concerns for the partner's interests rather than one's own. In contrast, primary concern with one's own needs seems to be more characteristic of casual attraction than of more intense love relationships (Steck, Levitan, McLane, & Kelley, 1982).

It should be noted that the sex of the lovers is not an implicit part of these definitions. Although social psychologists have tended to focus on the heterosexual relationship, love relationships between persons of the same sex may also be considered in this framework.

B. Measurement of romantic love

Describing love is far easier than measuring it. One could, of course, simply ask people whether they were in love. However, to know what this feeling means to the people involved, more specific questions need to be asked. Social psychologist Zick Rubin (1970, 1973) has taken some of the initial steps in this measurement process by devising a Love Scale to measure degrees of romantic involvement. Some of the statements from this scale are shown in Figure 6-2, along with a few items from a Liking Scale that he developed at the same time.

Love-Scale Items

1. If I could never be with _____, I would feel miserable.
2. I would forgive _____ for practically anything.
3. I feel that I can confide in _____ about virtually everything.

Liking-Scale Items

1. I think that _____ is unusually well adjusted.
2. Most people would react very favorably to _____ after a brief acquaintance.
3. _____ is the sort of person who I myself would like to be.

FIGURE 6-2. Examples of Rubin's love and liking scales. Scores on individual items can range from 1 to 9, with 9 always indicating the positive end of the continuum. There are nine items on each scale.

These scales were presented to 158 couples at the University of Michigan who were dating but not engaged. They were asked to complete both the Love Scale and the Liking Scale with respect to their dating partner and then with respect to a close friend of the same sex. The average scores for the men and women in Rubin's study are shown in Figure 6-3, which shows that the love scores of men and women for their respective dating partners were almost identical. However, women *liked* their dating partners significantly more than they were liked in return. This difference is due to the fact that women rated their partners higher on task-oriented dimensions such as intelligence and leadership potential, perhaps consistent with certain stereotypes about men and women (see Chapter 10). Men and women reported liking their same-sex friends equally, but women indicated greater love toward their same-sex friends than men did. This deeper involvement in same-sex associations for women is consistent with some research about affiliation patterns that we discussed earlier.

Rubin's work shows that there is a conceptual distinction between liking and romantic love. Other findings that suggest that these two measures are different include the finding that the two partners' love scores were more closely related to each other than their liking scores were. In addition, Rubin found that the higher the partners' love scores, the more likely they were to expect that they would marry; liking scores, in contrast, were less strongly related to this prediction.

C. Stimulants to romantic love

The romantic ideal suggests that we meet someone, immediately become smitten, and fall deeply in love with the person, who then completely fulfills our ideal (Averill & Boothroyd, 1977). However, this image of two persons in love and unaffected by circumstances may be oversimplified. A number of studies have suggested that situational factors may strongly affect the degree to which we report being in love.

Parental interference is one such factor. If two young persons are in love, what effect will the attitude of their parents have on the development of their relationship? Some research suggests that

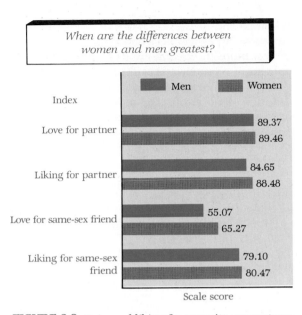

FIGURE 6-3. Love and liking for opposite-sex partners and same-sex partners.

parental disapproval will only strengthen the romantic ties of a young couple. Driscoll, Davis, and Lipetz (1972) conducted a test of this so-called *Romeo and Juliet effect.* They asked 91 married couples (married, on the average, for four years) and 49 dating couples (who had dated for an average of eight months) to respond to a variety of questionnaire measures. Included were measures of assessed parental interference, romantic love, and conjugal love (the latter similar to our earlier definition of companionate love). Not too surprisingly, parental interference and romantic love were not strongly related for those couples who were already married. However, for the unmarried couples, greater parental interference was associated with stronger romantic love. Conjugal love was less strongly related to parental interference. From these data, it cannot be said with certainty that heightened parental interference intensified the relationship, but Driscoll and his colleagues repeated the measures six to ten months later to determine changes in both interference and reported love. Here they found even stronger evidence for the Romeo and Juliet effect. Reports of

increasing parental interference were accompanied by greater feelings of romantic love, and less parental interference appeared to diminish the reports of love. Thus, the Montagues and the Capulets, in Shakespeare's play of young romance, may have set a pattern for future generations of parents; and, as was true for Romeo and Juliet, the parental interference produced the opposite effect from what the parents intended.

Some writers have suggested that even negative emotional experiences may be associated with feelings of passion. In what is probably the first study conducted on a wobbly suspension bridge over a canyon, Dutton and Aron (1974) had a female interviewer ask males who were crossing the bridge to fill out a brief questionnaire and to compose a story based on one of the pictures from the Thematic Apperception Test (TAT). After the men had completed this task, while standing 230 feet above the rocks, the female experimenter gave each man her telephone number, saying that if he was interested, she could explain the experiment to him at a later time. As a comparison group, Dutton and Aron arranged for other young men to have a similar encounter but this time on a much more solid bridge only 10 feet above a shallow stream. Apparently fear did increase attraction: men on the high bridge were more likely to call the interviewer later and showed more sexual imagery in their TAT stories. Nine of the 18 subjects in the high-fear condition called the experimenter later, whereas only 2 of the 16 in the low-fear condition did. Thus, an unrelated frightening event does seem to be related to increased sexual attraction.

Such evidence of unrelated arousal being linked to attraction has led Walster and her colleagues (Berscheid & Walster, 1978; Walster & Berscheid, 1974; Walster & Walster, 1978) to propose a two-component theory of passionate love. They derive their theory from the work of Stanley Schachter (1964), who proposed that emotional experiences are dependent on both cognitive and physiological factors (see Chapter 3). For example, if we have "butterflies in our stomach," we will seek some explanation of that feeling. Often the situation will provide such explanations for us when we are uncertain of the reasons. An uneasy stomach experienced in the presence of an unpleasant roommate may be interpreted as anger; the same stomach condition at the Super Bowl may be viewed as excitement.

Transferring this model to the area of passionate love, Walster and her colleagues suggest that love may be a combination of physiological arousal and the appropriate cognitive labels. They suggest that if the situation is right and if certain cognitions about another person are present, then almost any situation that increases physiological arousal may be interpreted as romantic love. This theory has some important implications. For example, being caught in a tornado with an attractive blind date would be more likely to elicit romantic feelings than a less arousing encounter. Similarly, some of the exercises of *sensitivity training* may also engender arousal. For example, a male and a female may be blindfolded and asked to become familiar with each other's faces through touching. The arousal in this situation, resulting from a new and unfamiliar experience, may well lead the participants to search for labels. Love, or at least infatuation, is one possible explanation.

Alternatively, however, the person may simply ascribe his or her arousal to the general characteristics of the situation. Particularly when the reasons for the arousal are fairly clear, situational attributions may be preferred. For example, in laboratory studies testing the fear and attraction link suggested by Dutton and Aron, little evidence has been found for misattribution (Kenrick, Cialdini, & Linder, 1979). Instead, male subjects in these experiments correctly attributed their excitement to the shock apparatus and did not transfer any arousal to the female confederate.

In summary, the two-component theory of passionate love points to certain irrational aspects of romance. Under the right conditions, arousal caused by external events may be interpreted as a sign of love. If other explanations are apparent, however, love may not be the answer.

D. Stages in the development of love

Earlier we discussed the distinction between romantic and companionate love, suggesting that the latter state represents more long-term rela-

tionships and focuses on more than the momentary stage of passion. Let's now consider this aspect of love more thoroughly by looking at the development of relationships over time.

Social psychologist George Levinger (1974) has defined a sequence of stages of relationships, which can serve to illustrate the development of companionate love (see Figure 6-4). He begins this sequence with a *zero contact* point—those cases,

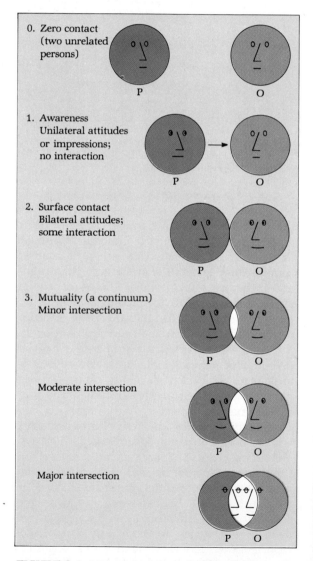

FIGURE 6-4. Levinger's stages of relationships.

representing thousands of instances in our lives, in which we have absolutely no contact with the other person. Obviously, if we paired all the possible people in the world, the majority of relationships could be classified in this zero-contact category. At the next level, Levinger suggests an *awareness stage.* Many of our relationships with other people probably fall into this category: we are aware of another person, perhaps even form an impression, but still have no actual interaction. Much of the material discussed in Chapter 4 concerning impression formation and attribution patterns is illustrative of this stage of a relationship. In addition, many of the variables affecting attraction discussed earlier in this chapter fall into the same category. Studies in which a subject is simply provided with a verbal or visual description of another person, who may be attractive or unattractive, similar or dissimilar in attitudes, are examples of this one-sided form of relationship.

The remaining levels of Levinger's model refer to relationships in which there is actually some form of interaction. *Surface contact* (Level 2) is the beginning stage of these real interactions. Level 2, however, represents only the initial contacts— exchanges that we have with casual acquaintances in which we may exchange names and pleasantries but little else. Many of our relationships are probably limited to this basis and progress no further. The dental hygienist who cleans our teeth, the bus driver on our regular route, and the person we meet occasionally at a neighborhood party are all examples of this level of contact.

Beyond these initial stages, Levinger posits *mutuality,* represented as a continuum of increasing contact and interchange. In the early stages of mutual relationships, we may share only a small portion of ourselves with the other person. Gradually, however, we are willing to open up and share more experiences and feelings.

Although Levinger's model gives us a description of the development of relationships, it is rather general. Just what specific behaviors might be different at different stages in a relationship? Rands and Levinger (1979) approached this question by asking people to rate the likelihood of a set of behaviors for four degrees of closeness: casual acquaintances, good friends, very close relationships, and marriage. In general, the closer the described relationship, the more likely subjects were to believe that the couple would be *behaviorally interdependent*—in other words, would do things with or for each other. Examples of such behaviors include planning a joint project, offering to do an errand, and even showing irritation at the other person's behavior. Not surprisingly, greater amounts of physical contact were also expected with closer relationships, but this factor seemed less important than behavioral interdependence.

Mills and Clark (1982) suggest a distinction between exchange and communal relationships. Surface contact may be characterized by exchange relationships, in which reciprocity is the norm. If I give you something, you will feel obligated to give me something equivalent in return. At the deeper level of mutuality, communal relationships may exist. Here we respond primarily to the other person's need—we care about the person—and we do not feel the need for reciprocity. For example, if a friend is in trouble, you may go to his or her aid but not expect any compensation in return.

In summary, as relationships develop, they change not only in intensity but also in the range of behaviors that are allowed and encouraged. Much more remains to be learned, however, about the sequence of these changes in the development of successful relationships.

■ IV. Falling out of love

In the movies of the 1930s, the story always ended with boy and girl together. Although the Hollywood version of romance has changed even in Hollywood itself, it has surely never been true of all real-life relationships. People do meet and fall in love and live together or marry. Yet, some of these same people fall out of love, break off engagements, and separate or divorce. Jealousy can arise and threaten the foundations of a partnership (see Box 6-2). Why do some relationships work out and others fail? Are there certain factors that influence the course of a relationship, and can we predict the positive and negative outcomes? It is to this side of the attraction coin that we now turn.

BOX 6-2. Jealousy

Jealousy. "Cruel as the grave," it says in the Bible. "The jaundice of the soul," John Dryden declared. And almost inevitable, according to French writer La Rochefoucauld, who stated that "jealousy is always born together with love."

But is it inevitable? And just what is jealousy? As social psychologists have become more interested in the development of love and romance, they have also begun to look at the issue of jealousy. Most definitions of jealousy refer to an emotional state that is experienced when a person perceives that some other person (either real or imagined) poses a threat to an ongoing relationship with a partner.

Are some people more likely to be jealous than others? Recent research suggests that two factors are common to most jealous reactions: a desire for an exclusive relationship and feelings of inadequacy (White, 1981). Beyond these two factors that they have in common, men and women differ in patterns of jealousy. For men, jealousy is often related to a low level of general self-esteem, to dependence on the partner as a source of self-esteem, and to traditionality of sex-role beliefs. For women, high levels of jealousy are associated mainly with a strong dependence on the relationship itself—a belief that it is more rewarding than any available alternative (White, 1981).

Thus, for men, jealousy seems to be more closely related to issues of status, while for women the nature of the relationship is more crucial. These different emphases are also shown in a study that asked men and women to say how they would react to situations that were likely to create jealous feelings (Shettel-Neuber, Bryson, & Young, 1978). Men were more likely to say that they would get angry and involved in activities that would endanger the relationship; women were more apt to say that they would get depressed and do things to improve the relationship. Although jealousy may be nearly universal, then, it is not always experienced in the same way by women and men. ■

A. Breaking up is hard to do

Many relationships that begin with the glow of romantic or passionate love do not go on to fulfill their initial promise; others endure and lead to marriage, children, and golden anniversaries. Can any patterns be detected in those relationships that break up versus those that last? To answer this question, Hill, Rubin, and Peplau (1976) conducted an extensive two-year study, following the course of 231 couples in the Boston area. At the end of the two-year period, 103 couples (45% of the original sample) had broken up; 65 others were still dating, 9 were engaged, 43 were married, and 11 could not be contacted.

To understand the process of breaking up, Hill and his colleagues first looked at the results of the initial questionnaire that each couple had completed at the beginning of the two-year period. Were there any clues at that stage that could predict the course of the relationship? Not surprisingly, those couples who reported feeling closer in 1972 were more likely to be together in 1974. Yet, those reported feelings were not a perfect predictor: many couples who reported feeling close at the initial testing still did break up in the subsequent two-year period. Consistent with our earlier discussion, scores on a love scale were more predictive than scores on a liking scale. In addition, the women's love scores were a better indicator of whether the relationship would last than the men's love scores. Thus, for some reason, the feelings of the woman in the relationship seem to be a more sensitive index of the health of the relationship. Unrelated to the future success of the relationship were whether the couple had had sexual intercourse and whether they had lived together. A couple were equally likely to maintain a relationship whether or not they had engaged in these more intimate forms of interchange.

Similarity of the two partners, discussed earlier as an important factor in attraction, also was important among these Boston couples. As shown in Table 6-1, similarities with respect to age, education, intelligence, and attractiveness were all greater for the couples who stayed together than for those who broke up. However, similarity of religion, sex-role attitudes, and desired family size were not useful in predicting the long-term success of relationships. Nonetheless, on each of these variables, couples were fairly well matched at the beginning of the study, suggesting that these factors may be important in initial partner selection.

Another important predictor of the success of the relationship was the man's need for power (Stewart & Rubin, 1976). As measured by stories told in response to TAT cards, need for power is conceptualized as a stable tendency to seek impact on others, either through direct action or through more subtle influence attempts. Men who scored high in need for power in the Boston couples study were more likely to expect problems in the relationship and were more likely to express dissat-

isfaction with the relationship at the initial stage of testing. True to the expectations of these men, a couple in which the man had a high need for power were much less likely to be together two years later. In fact, 50% of these relationships had broken up, compared with only 15% of those in which the man was low in the need for power. Although need for power was measured for the women partners as well, their scores showed absolutely no association with the success or failure of the relationship.

To gain more understanding of the breakup process, Hill and his colleagues used a second method of data collection: intensive interviews with some of the couples who had broken up. These interviews provided many new insights into the process of breaking up, even including such facts as when the breakup occurred. Considering that the majority of the couples in this study were college students, it may not be surprising to learn that these relationships were most likely to break up at critical points in the school year—at the beginning of the fall semester and at the ends of

TABLE 6-1. Relationship between similarity and breaking up: Couple similarity by status two years later

Correlation of partners	All couples (N = 231)	Together couples (N = 117)	Breakup couples (N = 103)
Characteristics			
Age	.19**	.38**	.13
Highest degree planned	.28**	.31**	.17
SAT, math	.22**	.31**	.11
SAT, verbal	.24**	.33**	.15
Physical attractiveness	.24**	.32**	.16
Father's educational level	.11	.12	.12
Height	.21**	.22*	.22*
Religion (% same)	51%**	51%**	52%**
Attitudes			
Sex-role traditionalism (10-item scale)	.47**	.50**	.41**
Favorability toward women's liberation	.38**	.36**	.43**
Approval of sex among "acquaintances"	.25**	.27**	.21*
Romanticism (6-item scale)	.20*	.21*	.15
Self-report of religiosity	.37**	.39**	.37**
Number of children wanted	.51**	.43**	.57**

*$p < .05$.
**$p < .01$.
NOTE: Significance levels indicated in the table are for chance probabilities.

the fall and spring semesters. Apparently these natural break points in the calendar year allowed couples to break up more easily. However, it was also true that the less involved partner in a relationship was more likely to precipitate a breakup at one of these natural break points. In contrast, when the partner who had reported being more involved chose to end the affair, the timing was more likely to be in the middle of the school year rather than at the end. For the less involved partner, the separation of a summer vacation may provide a good excuse for ending the relationship, testifying to the truth of La Rochefoucauld's maxim "Absence diminishes mediocre passions and increases great ones."

Most of the breakups that occurred were perceived to be somewhat one-sided: over 85% of both men and women reported that one person wanted to end the relationship more than the other. These perceptions were not totally accurate, however. Although there was considerable agreement in many cases, there was also a systematic bias in the reports. People were more likely to say that they were the one who wanted to break off the relationship than to say that their partner wished it. Such a strategy is, of course, self-protective: those partners who did the breaking up were considerably happier, less lonely, and less depressed (but more guilty) than those partners who were the "broken-up-with" ones.

Just who does the breaking up in the typical male/female couple? Although some cases are clearly mutual decisions, when one person initiates the split, it is more likely to be the woman. Rubin and his colleagues (Rubin, Peplau, & Hill, 1978) have suggested that in our society men tend to fall in love more readily than women, and women fall out of love more readily than men. Although such an assertion may contradict many of the stereotypes of the romantic woman and the "strong, silent" man, the data do support the argument. An interesting by-product of men's greater unwillingness to end the relationship is found in the contact that the partners reported having after the

PHOTO 6-7. *The end of a relationship.*

Drawing by Koren; © 1975 The New Yorker Magazine, Inc.

"I'm sorry, but it just isn't working out between us, Jeffrey. You're an orange, and I want an apple."

breakup. If the man broke up the relationship, the couple were very likely to remain casual friends; however, if the woman was the one to end the relationship, staying friends was apparently much more difficult and happened less than half the time.

The end of an affair is probably less traumatic than the end of a marriage. Nevertheless, the factors that contribute to breakups in shorter relationships may have something in common with those that occur in more long-term bonds. Even in itself, however, the breakup of an affair provides important continuity in our understanding of the development of love between two persons.

B. Inequity and impermanence

Earlier in the chapter we discussed the application of equity theory to interpersonal relationships. Whereas we desire equity from our interactions, the perception of inequity may be a factor in ending those relationships. For example, you might feel that you put a lot into a relationship,

giving your partner emotional support and comfort but receiving little in return. If at the same time you felt that your partner was giving little to the relationship in exchange for your kindness, what would you do? Equity theory would predict that if the imbalance were too great, you would probably choose to end the relationship. In a test of this prediction, 511 men and women at the University of Wisconsin were interviewed about their relationships with their dating partners (Berscheid & Walster, 1978). At the initial testing each person was asked to evaluate his or her dating relationship in terms of the contributions and the benefits that each partner was receiving. For example, the person was asked to consider all the things that might contribute to a relationship (such as personality, emotional support, help in making decisions) and to rate his or her own contribution on a scale from $+4$ to -4. Subjects were then asked to make a similar rating of their partners' contributions. Each person was also asked to rate the benefits received from the relationship, such as love, excitement, security, or a good time, again for both the self and the partner. From these four estimates, the investigators were able to determine how equitable the relationship was perceived to be.

Three months later, the people were interviewed again and asked whether they were still going out with the same partner and how long they expected the relationship to last. People who had reported equitable relationships at the earlier session were more likely to be still dating at the second testing period. They were also more likely to predict that the relationship would last than were those persons who reported a less equitable relationship. Hence, although it may be difficult to accurately measure all the factors that contribute to a relationship, it seems clear that our willingness to stay in a relationship is directly related to our perceptions of its costs and benefits.

C. Marriage and divorce

The affair that breaks up probably prevents a marriage that would not have worked. Yet, marriage itself is obviously not a guarantee of lifelong attraction. In the United States, for example, the divorce rate has been increasing quite rapidly in recent years (Levinger & Moles, 1979). What happens in these more extended relationships to cause a split?

A number of personality and demographic factors have been associated with the likelihood of divorce (Newcomb & Bentler, 1981). For example, people who marry young are more likely to divorce. In terms of personality, people with high amounts of ambition and strong achievement needs tend to have less stable marriages. Among men, a need for orderliness is associated with divorce; ambition and intelligence are more common to divorced women.

Yet, these factors are static ones and do not address the dynamics of a marital relationship. In fact, relationships are constantly changing, and it is in the shifting balance between two persons that marriage and divorce must be explored.

Levinger (1979) has offered a descriptive analysis of marital relationships, based on the combination of attractions and barriers that are present. Some of the attractions that he identifies are material rewards, such as family income; others are either symbolic, such as status, or affectional, such as companionship and sexual enjoyment. Barriers are conceived of as the potential costs of divorcing, such as financial expenses, feelings toward children, and religious constraints. Finally, Levinger suggests that people will also weigh the alternative attractions, a concept similar to Thibaut and Kelley's comparison level. Possible alternative attractions that a husband or wife might consider are the values of independence or a preferred companion or sexual partner. This framework is helpful in identifying some of the factors that may come into play when individuals decide whether to continue or to end a relationship. In general, we can predict that when the attractions of the present relationship decrease, the barriers to getting out of the relationship diminish, and the strength of alternative attractions increases, then at that point an individual would choose to get out of the relationship. Although there is evidence that many of the attractions and barriers are indeed related to marital stability, we are still a long way from being able to predict precisely when and how a marital relationship will be ended. Often a single event will precipitate a crisis, providing the final straw for a relationship that was already on shaky ground (Jaffe & Kanter, 1976; Weiss, 1976).

These unresolved questions demonstrate the extensive territory into which future research may go. In 1958, psychologist Harry Harlow wrote "So far as love or affection is concerned, psychologists have failed in their mission. The little we know about love does not transcend simple observations, and the little we write about it has been written better by poets and novelists" (1958, p. 673). We know a great deal more today than we did in 1958. Many more investigators have become interested in the topic of love, and the issue is no longer taboo. Furthermore, the wider variety of methodologies that are now being used by social psychologists make it possible to investigate complex and long-term relationships more fully.

V. SUMMARY

Loneliness is a subjective experience, generally resulting from a lack of social relationships and experienced as unpleasant. Both the causes of loneliness and the reactions to it can vary.

The need to affiliate, or to be with others, is an exceedingly strong one in many people. Reasons for affiliation include the value that other people have in helping us attain goals, the intrinsic value of companionship, and the usefulness of other people in providing a standard for social comparison and self-evaluation. Under conditions of increased situational anxiety, there is a greater desire to be with others, particularly those who are in the same situation.

Studies of real-life affiliation patterns have provided descriptive data on the extent to which people choose to be alone or with others and suggest that same-sex affiliation is important, particularly among women.

The following factors make another person more attractive to us: similarity of beliefs, values, and personality; complementarity of needs; physical attractiveness; competence; pleasant or agreeable characteristics; reciprocal liking; and propinquity. Theories that have been proposed to explain interpersonal attraction include reinforcement/affect theory, social-exchange theory, and equity theory.

Two kinds of love have been defined, both of which differ from simple liking. Romantic (or passionate) love is believed to be more momentary; companionate love represents a longer-term relationship. Measurement of love and liking supports the distinction between these two feelings.

Often situational determinants affect the expression of romantic love. Parental interference is one such factor. Unrelated states of arousal may also be interpreted as signs of love, supporting a two-component theory that proposes that both cognitions and physiological arousal are important factors.

Romantic love is not a static phenomenon. Levinger has proposed a series of stages (zero contact, awareness, surface contact, mutuality) to describe the development of a relationship and has suggested that different factors will be important at different points in time.

People fall in love and people fall out of love. Initial feelings of intimacy and similarity of interests are related to breakups; perceptions of inequality in the relationship are also a factor. Even after couples marry, relationships continue to change. The decision to divorce has been represented as the result of an imbalance among attractions, barriers, and alternative attractions.

GLOSSARY TERMS

complementarity	matching hypothesis	propinquity
equity theory	mere exposure effect	social-exchange theory

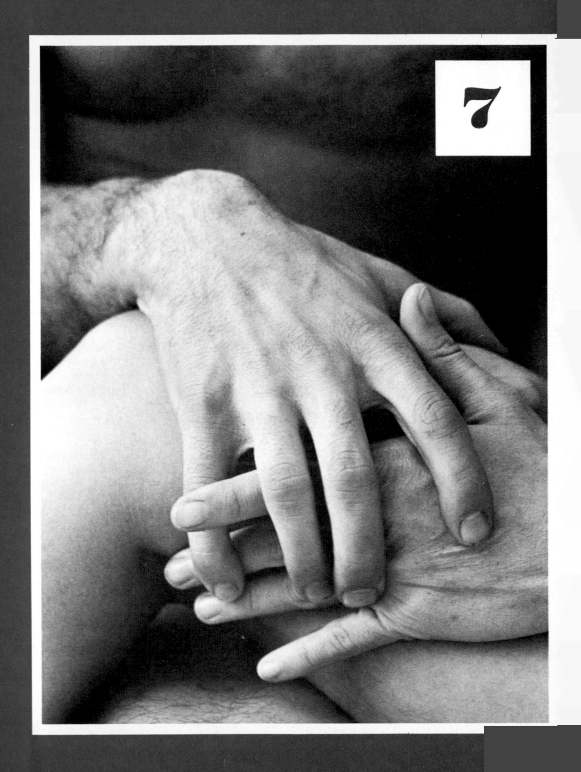

7

The Social Psychology of Sexual Behavior

Sexual relationship is an interpersonal relationship, and as such is subject to the same principles of interaction as are other relationships.
■ LESTER A. KIRKENDALL & R. W. LIBBY

Custom controls the sexual impulse as it controls no other.
■ MARGARET SANGER

Sexual experiences are a part of human social interaction, and sexuality is an obvious part of our lives and of our culture. As romantic love develops and relationships are formed, sexuality generally becomes an issue to be confronted. Most of us remember our first sexual experience; many of us fantasize about future sexual encounters. People joke about sex, worry about sex, and enjoy sex.

At a broader societal level, popular treatments of sexuality become best-sellers, and sex-therapy clinics develop in abundance. In newspapers, magazines, and television commercials, much of the advertising capitalizes on our sexual desires, and in any major city, large numbers of movie theaters offer exclusively X-rated films. Sexual harassment becomes an issue for the courts to deal with.

It is not surprising, then, that the topic of sexual behavior finds a place in a social-psychology text. It is an important part of human interaction, and it relates to our attitudes, to societal norms, and to basic learning processes as well. In this chapter, we will consider a number of facets of sexual behavior: the frequency of various forms of sexual behavior, theoretical models concerning the development of sexual behavior, the role of sexuality in interpersonal relationships, issues of contraception and family planning, the influence of erotic material, and the connection between pornography and aggression.

■ I. A background for the study of sexual behavior

In the Victorian era, when Freud proposed that sexuality was central to human nature, shock waves resounded through the literate world. His ideas were considered not only revolutionary but immoral and evil. Although some people still believe in the immorality of much sexual behavior, many others today, though not necessarily adopting Freudian theory, would nonetheless argue for the centrality of sexuality to human social behavior. Certainly it is difficult to avoid the topic of sex in newspapers, in magazines, or on the streets. Yet, despite our irrepressible sexual habits and their pervasive effects, science has been quite timid in its investigation of sexual attitudes, behavior, and physiology.

For many years, sexual behavior was a taboo topic for the social scientist. Even the teaching of college-level courses on human sexuality has been a development of the last two decades. Other than a course on sex that was taught at Indiana University many years ago by the famous sex researcher Alfred Kinsey, the first university course with a title like "human sexuality" apparently was initiated in 1964 by James L. McCary at the University of Houston. The community hostility toward the public discussion of such topics at that time is reflected pungently in one of the many letters that Dr. McCary received (McCary, 1975, p. 17). It read:

Dear Sir:

I want you to know that as a Christian I resent what you are teaching them boys and girls at that university. Furthermore, I am going to write the school trustees and let them know what you are doing. I hope you burn and suffer on doomsday, you son-of-a-bitch.

Sincerely yours,

Mr. _____

As we saw in the last chapter, even the topic of love was considered taboo for many years. Small wonder, then, that the study of sex aroused considerable antagonism and created innumerable difficulties for those scientists who pursued the topic! Even today, investigators who are concerned with the area of sexual behavior often encounter forms of hostility and antagonism not experienced by those conducting research on less controversial topics.

At the same time, many people are fascinated by the results of sex research, and findings are often quickly publicized and circulated in the mass media. Works by Kinsey and by Masters and Johnson, for example, became best-sellers even though they were written in a technical style and were intended mainly for the professional audience. Such popularity poses an additional problem for the sex researcher, in that findings may be taken for abso-

PHOTO 7-1. *Attitudes toward sexuality have greatly changed since the Victorian era, and physical contact is much more casual today.*

lute truth when they reflect only a preliminary stage of understanding.

The earliest scientific reports of sex were based primarily on the case-history records of practicing psychiatrists. In addition to the obvious example of Sigmund Freud, the work of Havelock Ellis (1899/1936) at the turn of the century was based on clinical practice. In both cases, much of the focus was on abnormal sexual functioning, rather than general descriptions of sexual behavior as a social phenomenon. More recently, some investigators have turned again to the case-study method—but with normal populations—and have shown how rich a source of data that can be (Abramson, 1981).

Apart from the clinical case-history approach, how do investigators study human sexual behavior? Because sex is primarily a private behavior, some of the methods discussed in Chapter 2 are not appropriate for this topic. The most common approach has been the survey, using questionnaires and interviews to investigate the range and frequency of people's sexual activities. Kinsey's studies, for example, were based exclusively on

this method. Kinsey conducted detailed interviews with a large sample of U.S. citizens (Kinsey, Pomeroy, & Martin, 1948; Kinsey, Pomeroy, Martin, & Gebhard, 1953). Similar procedures, often using mailed questionnaires, have continued to be used in recent years (Hite, 1976; Hunt, 1974). The primary advantage of this method, particularly when the questionnaires are anonymous, is that it allows respondents a considerable degree of privacy in discussing intimate aspects of their sexual lives. Potentially embarrassing topics can be dealt with more easily when no face-to-face encounter is involved.

There are some problems with the survey method, however (Byrne & Byrne, 1977). One difficulty concerns the representativeness of the sample of subjects. Subjects in any survey are to some degree self-selected; in other words, after the investigator determines an initial sample, the selected subjects must agree to participate. Particularly in the area of sex research, it is probable that those people who agree to participate are not a random sample. Some people are quite willing to discuss or to describe their sexual experiences, while others are aghast at the very thought. Generalizing the results of surveys to the total population is therefore very risky. A second, related problem concerns the accuracy of the answers themselves. As in any self-report measure, the investigator must be concerned with the accuracy of the subject's information. In the area of sex, where norms and values are so strong, the difficulties of accepting self-report data as completely accurate are particularly acute. On the one hand, people may be reluctant to report behavior that is viewed as nonnormative; on the other hand, some people may exaggerate their reported activities in order to appear exciting, progressive, or even normal in our age of high sexual pressures. Despite these limitations, however, the survey method will continue to be used when the concern is with describing normative patterns of sexual behavior.

A more recently adopted alternative to the survey method is the laboratory experiment. For example, investigators have conducted numerous studies in which subjects are exposed to a variety of erotic films and asked to indicate their reactions to the material or to engage in other forms of behavior, such as aggression toward a confederate. In some instances, most notably the work by Masters and Johnson (1966), subjects engage in intercourse in the laboratory setting. Such approaches gain the advantages of the experimental method but still have some problems (Bentler & Abramson, 1981). Volunteer bias is inevitable, because all potential subjects must be fully informed of the topic of the research before they decide whether to participate in the experiment. People who do not wish to watch pornographic films can choose not to participate, and those who do choose to participate are probably not a random sample. Further, the laboratory is a highly artificial setting for behaviors that typically occur in very private situations. Although this criticism has been applied to many areas of research, it is probably more severe in the case of sexual behavior.

Despite the problems and difficulties inherent in the study of sexual behavior, progress has been made in recent years. We are finally beginning to learn a good deal about sexual behavior—its frequency, its role in intimate relationships, factors that affect its occurrence, and, perhaps most important, the consequences of sexual behavior for social problems such as unwanted births and overpopulation. In this chapter we will consider each of these points as it relates to the social psychology of sexual behavior.

■ II. Forms and frequency of sexual behavior

Who engages in which types of sexual behavior under what circumstances? In seeking the answer to this question, we can look to the results of a number of survey studies completed during the past 30 to 40 years. The original, of course, was the work of Kinsey (Kinsey et al., 1948, 1953). More recently, a large-scale survey by Hunt (1974) has provided an update on Kinsey's data. Other recent surveys have concentrated exclusively on female sexuality (Hite, 1976; Levin & Levin, 1975). In addition, we have detailed information about the sexual attitudes and behavior of college students—a state that reflects the greater ease of access to this population.

A. Kinsey's studies of male and female sexual behavior

Because Kinsey's original investigations are benchmark studies in our society and because they were pioneering efforts in the study of sex in any modern society, their major findings are worth reviewing. A few preliminary comments are in order, however. We must always remember that Kinsey's subjects were volunteers selected from diverse sections of the society; they were not selected in a fashion designed to ensure the representativeness of the sample. Moreover, the data were collected in face-to-face interviews, where subjects may have been reluctant to admit some behaviors. Yet, although there are many possible methodological artifacts in Kinsey's procedures, comparisons between his findings and those of other investigators have produced generally consistent outcomes.

Some of the more general findings of Kinsey and his associates are shown in Figure 7-1. As can be seen, during the late 1940s and early 1950s when these data were collected, higher percentages of men than of women reported engaging in most sexual activities. It is also important to note that although a substantial number of people of both sexes (37% of the males, 28% of the females) reported having had at least one homosexual experience, relatively few people of either sex (4% of the males, 3% of the females) reported themselves as being exclusively homosexual.

For both sexes, socioeconomic status was one of the most significant variables in predicting sexual behavior. College-educated people, when they were children, began most sexual practices later than did children who did not eventually go to college. As adults, however, the college-educated men and women reported less inhibition in most sexual behaviors and were more likely to engage in masturbation, oral-genital sex, homosexuality, and a variety of coital positions. Although differences among religious denominations were not as striking, people who described themselves as nonreligious were more likely to masturbate, to pet to orgasm, and to have premarital coitus and extramarital affairs.

B. Hunt's more recent survey

In the early 1970s, Morton Hunt (1974) conducted a survey of 2026 people in the United States,

generally matching the U.S. adult population in regard to most demographic characteristics. This survey still is subject to some of the methodological problems discussed earlier, particularly in terms of subject self-selection, but the results give us some indication of recent sexual attitudes and behavior.

In considering people's expressed attitudes toward various forms of sexuality, Hunt did not have much basis for comparison, as Kinsey had considered only people's reported behavior, not their reported attitudes. Even without this comparison, however, Hunt's findings suggest a considerable degree of permissiveness in attitudes toward sexuality. For example, more than 75% of his sample believed that schools should teach sex education. The vast majority of the people surveyed believed that the man should not always be the one to initiate sexual intercourse, and nearly as many people reported that nonmarital sex was acceptable. Particular sexual practices, such as cunnilingus and fellatio, also showed wide acceptance.

What about the actual behavior reported by people in this survey? In comparison with Kinsey's data, Hunt's data indicate a number of changes, although not so many as some people might think. For example, extramarital intercourse appears to have decreased slightly for males (from 50% to 41%), while the incidence of extramarital intercourse remained fairly constant for females. However, those who did engage in extramarital affairs

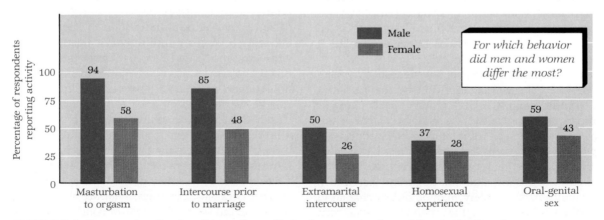

FIGURE 7-1. Frequencies of various forms of sexual behavior among males and females in Kinsey's surveys.

did so earlier in the marriage than did the people in Kinsey's sample. As a possibly related factor, we can consider the results for divorced persons (the frequency of divorce is twice as high as it was at the time of Kinsey's surveys). Divorced males and females both report considerably more sexual activity than did the divorced persons in Kinsey's sample. In Hunt's sample, divorced males reported an average of 8 sexual partners a year, and divorced women reported an average of 3.5.

More women reported nonmarital sex in Hunt's sample (75%, compared with 48% in Kinsey's study), but there was little change in the incidence of nonmarital sex for the men. At the same time, fewer men reported going to prostitutes in the 1970s than in the 1940s and 1950s. Between marriage partners, the frequency of intercourse appears to have increased somewhat; for couples in the 26-to-35 age range, the average was 2.6 times per week, in comparison with the earlier figure of 2.0 times per week. One of the most striking differences was in the frequency of oral-genital contact. Paralleling the permissive attitudes that were expressed, figures showed that more than two-thirds of the people had tried this form of sexual activity.

The incidence of homosexuality does not appear to have changed much since Kinsey's study, despite the considerable publicity given to the gay liberation movement in recent years. Hunt's findings were similar to Kinsey's: 6% of the men and 3% of the women reported having had a homosexual experience within the preceding year. The percentage of people in Hunt's study who reported having had at least one homosexual experience at some time was nearer to 25%.

In summary, Hunt's survey suggests that there has been some relaxation (1) of the pressures operating against sexual activity (particularly in the forms of sexuality), (2) in the sexual activities of women, and (3) in the sexual activity of divorced persons. At the same time, many areas have shown relatively little change between the 1940s and the 1970s, suggesting that the apparent increase in sexuality in our society may be only a change in expressed attitudes, rather than any drastic shift in behavior.

C. Changes in sexual attitudes and behavior among college students

We have looked at changes in the incidence of sexual behavior in the general population over the past three decades. What do we know about the sexual attitudes and behavior of college students during this same period? Here, of course, the majority of sexual activity takes place outside marriage, because the majority of college students are single.

Early surveys (reviewed by Smigel & Seiden, 1968) found that approximately 45% of college men and 12% of college women approved of sexual activity among unmarried people. Later work by Reiss (1960, 1967), using a U.S. sample that included both Black and White high school and college students in both Northern and Southern schools, found that sexual standards had become much more liberal. In 1959, when the first study by Reiss was done, nearly 70% of the males and 27% of the females said that sexual intercourse without marriage would be acceptable to them. By the 1970s, these numbers had shifted again, particularly among women. As many as 70% of college women in these more recent surveys said that nonmarital sexual intercourse would be acceptable to them under some conditions (Kaats & Davis, 1970; Nutt & Sedlacek, 1974).

The attitudes of college students toward nonmarital intercourse are related to a number of factors (Athanasiou, 1973; McCary, 1978). Among college men, acceptance of greater intimacy is related to race, age, semester in college, strength of religious feelings, and region of the country. Older men who are indifferent or hostile to religion and who attend Eastern, Western, or Southern schools have more permissive attitudes than do younger, religious Midwestern males. Among college women, acceptance of intimacy is more closely tied to experience in a relationship. Women who had been in love two or more times or who were currently in a significant relationship were more likely to express acceptance of sexual intimacy.

People's attitudes may not always be expressed in their behavior, however. What are the findings on the actual sexual behavior of college students? Curran (1975) asked 164 U.S. college students at a large, relatively conservative Midwestern university to complete a questionnaire about their sexual experience. Table 7-1 shows the results of his study, which looked at a large variety of sexual behaviors. As indicated in the table, the majority of behaviors show no strong differences between males and females. There is, however, some suggestion from the percentage figures that college men and women may experience some sexual behaviors in different orders. For example, more women have experienced cunnilingus and fellatio than have experienced intercourse, while for males that pattern is reversed. These findings suggest that some women are enjoying various forms of sexual satisfaction while still remaining technically virgins. Similar patterns of results have been found by other investigators as well (Bentler, 1968a, 1968b; Curran, Neff, & Lippold, 1973). Thus, the sequence of behaviors may be somewhat different for males and females, but the overall frequency

of sexual behavior is not terribly different for men and women, suggesting that a double standard of behavior may not be pervasive in the college population.

The overall rates of intercourse for males and females in this Midwestern U.S. sample (44% for males and 37% for females) are somewhat lower than figures reported from other locales. Some other studies suggest that approximately 55% of college females and 75% of college males have engaged in sexual intercourse (King, Balswick, & Robinson, 1977). Similar studies in Canada, done a few years earlier, have shown rates of about 40% for women and 55% for men (Perlman, 1973).

Although frequency differences between college males and females continue to diminish, there are still some male/female differences in the psychological factors that predict sexual activity. Recent research by Keller and his associates (Keller, Elliott, & Gunberg, 1982) considered differences between

TABLE 7-1. Sexual behavior among college students

Have you ever engaged in the following behavior with a member of the opposite sex?	Percentage of males saying yes	Percentage of females saying yes
1. One minute of continuous kissing on the lips?	86.4	89.2
2. Manual manipulation of clothed female breasts?	82.7	71.1
3. Manual manipulation of bare female breasts?	75.5	66.3
4. Manual manipulation of clothed female genitals?	76.4	67.5
5. Kissing nipples of female breast?	65.5	59.0
6. Manual manipulation of bare female genitals?	64.4	60.2
7. Manual manipulation of clothed male genitals?	57.3	51.8
8. Mutual manipulation of genitals?	55.5	50.6
9. Manual manipulation of bare male genitals?	50.0	51.8
10. Manual manipulation of female genitals until there were massive secretions?	49.1	50.6
11. Sexual intercourse, face to face?	43.6	37.3
12. Manual manipulation of male genitals to ejaculation?	37.3	41.0
13. Oral contact with female genitals?	31.8	42.2
14. Oral contact with male genitals?	30.9	42.2
15. Mutual manual manipulation of genitals to mutual orgasm?	30.9	26.5
16. Oral manipulation of male genitals?	30.0	38.6
17. Oral manipulation of female genitals?	30.0	41.0
18. Mutual oral-genital manipulation?	20.9	28.9
19. Sexual intercourse, entry from the rear?	14.5	22.9
20. Oral manipulation of male genitals to ejaculation?	22.7	26.5
21. Mutual oral manipulation of genitals to mutual orgasm?	13.6	12.0

students who were virgins and students who had engaged in considerable sexual activity. They suggest that dominance traits are most closely related to male sexual activity, while the activity of females is more determined by feelings of affection and relationship.

The prevalence of sexual behavior, among the single as well as the married, surely testifies to the importance of sex as one aspect of social interaction. Yet, the frequency data, though interesting, tell us only *what* is being done, not *why*. What are the reasons for sexual behavior? What theoretical frameworks have been offered to explain sexuality?

■ III. Theoretical issues in sexual behavior

Standards for sexual behavior vary widely. If we look across various cultures, we find an incredible diversity of attitudes toward sexual behavior. In some cases, sex is seen as pleasurable, in others as innocuous, and in still others as a potentially dangerous event. Members of one society may say that sex is "the best thing in life," while other groups view sex as "a little like work" (Broude, 1975). How are these variations in attitudes toward sexual behavior explained?

A. Freudian theory of sexuality

Sigmund Freud was perhaps the first person to insist that sexuality is a basic part of the human personality (see Chapter 1). In his theorizing at the turn of the century, Freud proposed that sexual energy is the basic motivator of human behavior, and he described a sequence of stages paralleling supposed changes in the location of sexual tension (Freud, 1938). Infantile sexuality centered on *oral* and then *anal* areas of the body, but at the age of 3 or so, the *genital* area became central to the expression of sexuality. At this stage, too, Freud postulated critical differences between male and female development—differences that he believed contributed to significant variations in the sexual behavior of adult males and females. More specifically, Freud suggested that women could experience mature sexuality only through vaginal

orgasms as a result of penetration by the penis. Other modes of achieving orgasm, such as direct clitoral stimulation, were considered by Freud to reflect inadequate femininity, which he believed derived from the young girl's early penis envy. Although Freud believed that there was a physical as well as a psychological distinction between clitoral and vaginal orgasms, later research has shown that the two forms are identical, both as physiological events and in the sensation they produce (Masters & Johnson, 1966).

Freud also believed that his proposed sequence of the development of sexuality, including the famous Oedipal period, was universal. In other words, he assumed that members of every culture and society go through the same sequence of events in the development of their sexuality. Although the socialization practices of various cultures might modify the expression of sexual energy, Freud for the most part believed that similar sexual motivations and conflicts would be found in every society.

B. Cognitive aspects of sexual behavior

Many people disagree with Freud's theory of sexuality, but few deny that sexual behavior is basic to humans and animals alike. As a necessity for reproduction of the species, sexual intercourse is performed fairly instinctively, although the forms and cycles of sex vary among species (Daly & Wilson, 1978; Ford & Beach, 1951). In human beings, in particular, the variation in forms of sexual behavior is considerable, and it is difficult to account for these differences on the basis of instinct alone. Consequently, many recent theorists in the area of sexual behavior have begun to focus on cognitive factors that surround the choice and experience of sexuality.

As Abramson (1981) states in explaining his model of the sexual system, "The underlying assumption in the present schema is that all decisions regarding sexual expression are controlled by a mechanism which has been represented as a cognitive structure." A careful examination of Figure 7-2 will show how this assumption works. Abramson assumes that a variety of factors influence the cognitive structure: parental standards,

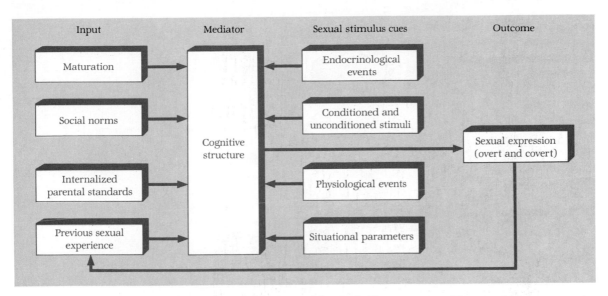

FIGURE 7-2. The sexual system. In this model proposed by Paul Abramson, cognitive structures are a major influence on sexual expression. The structures are formed on the basis of various inputs, and they, in turn, monitor various sexual stimulus cues to determine eventual sexual expression.

social norms, maturation, and previous sexual experience. For example, parents may instruct us in what is proper sexual behavior. Other norms and values may be learned from church or from peers. The process of maturation itself, especially the onset of puberty, can influence our beliefs about sexuality. And finally, actual sexual experience— whether fantasy, masturbation, or intercourse— will play an important role in our beliefs. From the sum of these experiences, we develop a set of principles about sexual behavior. (This idea is similar to the concept of schema discussed in Chapter 3.)

But past experience isn't the only thing that determines our sexual expression. A variety of sexual stimulus cues, both internal and external, can be influential, and these cues too are processed by the mediating cognitive structure. Internally, there are the influences of hormones and the nervous system. Externally, there are a variety of stimuli that may be associated with sexuality, such as erotic movies, racy novels, and particular persons. Certain situations may also encourage sexual expression: environments in which sexual permissiveness is fostered or in which alcohol or other drugs

are being used. On the basis of the principles that people have established, they will then weigh the acceptability of certain forms of sexual behavior and eventually make a choice.

Abramson's model is admittedly complex. Yet, it rests on a couple of very simple assumptions. First, it assumes that we learn from past experience and that principles of learning can be applied as easily to sexual behavior as they can to other forms of social behavior. Second, it assumes that our cognitions about sexuality are important—in other words, that sexual expression is not instinctual but, rather, is the outcome of rational thought. Freud would probably disagree with both assumptions, especially with the latter. Most current investigators of sexual behavior, however, have adopted some combination of learning and cognitive principles to explain sexual behavior (Byrne, 1977; Rook & Hammen, 1977), and the early results appear to justify their assumptions.

C. Heterosexual and homosexual preferences

Evidence that learning plays an important part in our definition of and response to sexual stimuli

PHOTO 7-2. *Greeks and Romans were quite relaxed about all forms of sexual behavior.*

is related to the issue of heterosexual versus homosexual behavior. Why do some people prefer sexual partners of the same sex rather than partners of the other sex? Before discussing this, we must understand the distinction between gender identity and sexual preference. **Gender identity** refers to one's self-awareness of being male or female (Money & Ehrhardt, 1972). Early theories of homosexuality often assumed that, for the homosexual, gender identity was opposite to the biological sex. In other words, some argued that the male homosexual identified himself as a female and hence preferred a male sexual partner. This *sex-role inversion* theory suggested that homosexuals dress, act, and behave as much like the other sex as possible. More recently, it has been recognized that gender identity and *sexual preference* are quite distinct—that homosexuals have no confusion about their gender identity but simply prefer sexual partners of the same sex.[1]

Although there is no society in which homosex-

ual expression is the dominant form (Ford & Beach, 1951), homosexual behavior has been common throughout history. In early Greek times, Sappho, born on the island of Lesbos (from which the word *lesbian* is derived), wrote passionate love poems describing both homosexual and heterosexual love. Romans were fairly relaxed about all forms of sexual behavior, but with the advent of Christianity, the norms regarding homosexual behavior became more restrictive. In the 19th century, Oscar Wilde was jailed and ruined, despite his creative output, when a court found him guilty of homosexual practices (Money & Tucker, 1975). Even in recent years, the majority of people in a national U.S. sample stated that homosexuality is sick and should be outlawed (Levitt & Klassen, 1974). In the United States, numerous initiatives have been proposed (and frequently passed) to limit the civil rights of homosexuals.

The strong feelings aroused by indications of homosexuality and the disagreement about the

---

[1] **Transsexualism,** in contrast, refers to the case in which one's gender identity is in opposition to one's bodily appearance and sexual organs. The writer James Morris, who became Jan Morris after a sex-change operation, described the feelings of a transsexual as follows: "I was born with the wrong body, being feminine by gender but male by sex, and I could achieve completeness only when the one was adjusted to the other" (Morris, 1974).

causes of homosexual behavior obviously have a long history. Freud, for example, did not consider homosexuality an illness but was ambivalent about the normality of such behavior (see Box 7-1). In 1973, however, the American Psychiatric Association officially removed homosexuality from its list of mental disorders, thus endorsing the view that the choice of a sexual partner of the same gender is no more an indication of mental illness than is choice of a partner of the other gender. More recently, an extensive investigation sponsored by the Kinsey Institute (Bell & Weinberg, 1978) indicates that people who prefer a same-sex partner are every bit as well adjusted, on the average, as a comparable sample of heterosexuals. The majority of the homosexuals studied were or had been involved in steady relationships (though often of shorter duration than those of heterosexuals), derived satisfaction from their jobs, had a wide circle of friends, and described themselves as "pretty happy."

The question still remains why some people prefer homosexuality while others prefer heterosexuality. A nature versus nurture debate has raged on this topic for many years, and for most of this period the "nurturists" have had the edge. Theorists from Freud (1930) to Masters and Johnson (1979) have proposed that critical experiences in childhood can determine adult sexual preference. Among the factors suggested to be responsible for homosexuality have been relationships with mothers and fathers, the nature of early sexual experiences, and peer relationships.

Storms (1981) has also pointed to the importance of early experiences, suggesting that sexual orientation is a result of a temporal link between physiological development and social development. According to Storms, if sex drives develop fairly early, then erotic fantasies will be associated with the same-sex peer group. However, if the physiological drives develop at a later age when social interaction with the other sex is more common, then erotic fantasies, and in turn behavior, will be heterosexual. Although this model stresses the importance of social factors, it also invokes a "nature" argument, because Storms suggests that homosexuals generally have an earlier onset of sexual drives.

BOX 7-1. A letter from Freud

April 9, 19_____

Dear Mrs. _____ ,

I gather from your letter that your son is a homosexual. I am most impressed by the fact that you do not mention this term yourself in your information about him. May I question you, why do you avoid it? Homosexuality is assuredly no advantage, but it is nothing to be ashamed of, no vice, no degradation, it cannot be classified as an illness; we consider it to be a variation of the sexual function produced by a certain arrest of sexual development. Many highly respectable individuals of ancient and modern times have been homosexuals, several of the greatest men among them (Plato, Michelangelo, Leonardo da Vinci, etc.). It is a great injustice to persecute homosexuality as a crime, and cruelty too. If you do not believe me, read the books of Havelock Ellis.

By asking me if I can help, you mean, I suppose, if I can abolish homosexuality and make normal heterosexuality take its place. The answer is, in a general way, we cannot promise to achieve it. In a certain number of cases we succeed in developing the blighted germs of heterosexual tendencies which are present in every homosexual; in the majority of cases it is no more possible. It is a question of the quality and age of the individual. The result of the treatment cannot be predicted.

What analysis can do for your son runs in a different line. If he is unhappy, neurotic, torn by conflicts, inhibited in his social life, analysis may bring him harmony, peace of mind, full efficiency, whether he remains a homosexual or gets changed. If you make up your mind he should have analysis with me (I don't expect you will!!) he has to come over to Vienna. I have no intention of leaving here. However, don't neglect to give me your answers.

Sincerely yours with kind wishes,

Dr. Sigmund Freud

PHOTO 7-3. *Lesbian women and gay men are, on the average, as psychologically healthy as heterosexuals.*

The earlier reliance on "nurture" explanations is also questioned in the most recent report on homosexuality from the Kinsey Institute (Bell, Weinberg, & Hammersmith, 1981a, 1981b). In an intensive study of nearly 1000 male and female homosexuals and a comparison group of nearly 500 male and female heterosexuals in the San Francisco Bay area, Bell and his colleagues have questioned much of the conventional wisdom in this area. Their research did show some differences between homosexuals and heterosexuals in feelings toward mothers, toward fathers, and toward the parental relationship and in childhood conformity to traditional gender roles. However, using sophisticated statistical techniques to infer causality, they concluded that these differences did not cause adult sexual preference. Rather, they suggest that "by the time boys and girls reach adolescence, their sexual preference is likely to be already determined" (1981a, p. 186), and thus these socialization differences may reflect an already-established sexual preference.

The recent Kinsey Institute findings also provide an interesting perspective on **bisexuality**—engaging in sexual behavior with both the same and the other sex during similar periods of time. Freud (1930) believed that people are inherently bisexual. Similarly, Kinsey's original studies concluded that sexual choice is best represented as a continuum, from exclusively heterosexual at one end to exclusively homosexual at the other, with many people falling somewhere in between these extremes. In the recent Kinsey Institute study, 8% of the heterosexual males and 13% of the heterosexual females were best considered, on the basis of their self-reports, to be bisexual. For this group of people, social learning and specific sexual experiences appeared to have been much more influential than they had been for the exclusively homosexual groups.

What kinds of experiences might be important in the development of bisexuality? Blumstein and Schwartz (1977) suggest three kinds of circumstances that are common influences: (1) experimentation in a friendship context (particularly common among women), (2) liberal hedonistic environments where group sex and other activities are explored, and (3) erotically based ideological positions wherein sex represents one aspect of a more general philosophy of life. Other situations that may encourage or permit homosexual behavior by persons who generally consider themselves heterosexual include prisons, military camps, and prep schools, where heterosexual outlets are absent or severely limited. The influence of such circumstances underlines the contribution of social factors to sexuality, without denying the contributions that biological factors may make.

■ IV. Sexual behavior in relationships

Thus far we have considered sexual behavior from the perspective of the individual, looking at the frequency with which people report experiencing sexual activities and the theoretical issues involved in an individual's decisions about when and how to engage in sex. Yet, it is clear that sexual behavior is, for the most part, a shared experience—in other words, it is an important social and interpersonal event. Let's look, then, at the role of sexuality in interpersonal relationships.

A. Sexuality in nonmarital relationships

In Chapter 6 we discussed an extensive study of more than 200 dating couples in the Boston area, focusing on the ways in which partners fall in and out of love. This same study included an in-depth investigation of the sexual behavior of these couples and provides us with one of the most thorough reports on the nonmarital sexual behavior of college students in the 1970s (Peplau, Rubin, & Hill, 1977).

The majority of these couples were very positive about sexuality in a relationship. Not only did 80% of the couples believe that it was completely acceptable for couples who love each other to have intercourse, but also their behavior was consistent with these expressed beliefs: 82% of the couples had had intercourse in their current relationship.

This figure does not imply that the number of college students who are sexually intimate is this high; our earlier discussion of the frequency of sexual behavior among college students showed the percentage was somewhat lower. Among students who are "going with" someone, however, the incidence of sexual intimacy is quite high.

Although the majority of the students in the study had experienced intercourse with their current partner, 18% of the couples reported abstention. In these couples, it appeared that the woman was the primary source of restraint. Of the men, 64% reported that it was their partner's desire to abstain that kept them from engaging in sexual activity. Another reason for abstention in these couples, endorsed by nearly half of the men and the women, was a fear of pregnancy. In addition, women said that sex would violate their ethical standards and that it was too early in the relationship to consider sexual activity. The religious background of the woman was also related to the sexual behavior of the couple. Approximately 27% of the Catholic women in the sample refrained from intercourse, compared with 16% of Jewish women and only 2% of Protestant women. Interestingly, the man's religious background had no effect on the presence or absence of sexual intercourse in the relationship.

Among the couples who had engaged in intercourse during their relationship, approximately half had done so within one month after the first date. Comparing these couples with the ones who had begun sexual activity in a later stage in the relationship, Peplau and her colleagues found that characteristics of the woman again were more related to the couple's activities than were characteristics of the man. As shown in Table 7-2, the women in couples who had had sexual intercourse early reported themselves to be less religious, more oriented toward a career, less oriented toward the homemaker role, and higher in self-esteem as assessed by a number of self-ratings.

The three types of couples observed in this study (those who abstain, those who engage in sex fairly early in the relationship, and those who first engage in sex at a later point in the relationship) viewed the relation between sex and emotional intimacy

TABLE 7-2. Characteristics of women in "early coitus" and "later coitus" couples

	Early coitus (N = 90)	Later coitus (N = 92)
Self-rating on religiosity (9-point scale)	3.4	4.2
Preference for being full-time housewife in 15 years (mean rank among 4)	2.8	2.3
Preference for being single career woman in 15 years (mean rank among 4)	3.0	3.5
Authoritarian submission (10 items)	1.8	2.3
Adherence to alternative lifestyle (9-point scale)	6.2	5.3
Self-ratings (all 9-point scales)		
Creative	6.4	5.9
Intelligent	7.0	6.6
Self-confident	5.8	5.0
Desirable as a date	6.8	6.2

NOTE: All early-late differences significant at $p < .05$ or better. Similar analyses for men failed to reach statistical significance. (Early = within one month of first date.)

in rather different ways. Abstaining couples had a traditional view of sexuality, and they believed that a permanent commitment of marriage was a necessary prerequisite for sexual behavior. The women in these relationships were typically virgins, although the men may have had limited sexual experience in other relationships. Those couples who experienced sexual activity very early in the relationship, in contrast, indicated their approval of casual sex. They said that although love is desirable in a sexual relationship, sex without love is also acceptable. Often sexual intercourse for these couples served as a means of developing emotional intimacy, rather than being the result of such feelings. In between these two extremes were the couples that Peplau and her colleagues termed *sexual moderates.* For these couples, sex occurred later in the relationship, after love and emotional intimacy had been established. Ethical reasons did not appear to delay the onset of sexual activity, but romantic concerns were a necessary element.

Despite the diversity in views toward sexuality among these three kinds of couples, the chances for long-term success of the relationship were equal for all three patterns. Two years after the initial interviews, an equal percentage of each type of couple had married (20%), had continued to date (34%), or had broken up (46%).

One final area of interest in this study concerns the differences between men and women in their attitudes toward sexuality. Men were somewhat more positive in their attitudes toward sex in a casual relationship (which is consistent with the attitude surveys discussed earlier), but both men and women agreed that sex was acceptable in a love relationship. Contrary to some assumptions, the relation between love and sexual satisfaction in the relationship was no different for men than for women. For both sexes, reported love was moderately correlated with reported sexual satisfaction.

Perhaps the most striking difference between the sexes in the study concerned the issue of loss of virginity. Many commentators have suggested that the loss of virginity is a more important step for a woman than for a man (Bernard, 1975), and the results of this study of Boston couples support that suggestion. Whether the man was a virgin prior to the existing relationship was not related to the couple's feelings of commitment, but the woman's sexual status prior to the relationship was associated with that commitment. Couples in which the woman had been a virgin prior to the existing relationship reported more love for each other and a higher probability of marriage. In addition, these women reported more closeness and greater satisfaction in the relationship than women who had experienced intercourse prior to the existing relationship. It is interesting, however, that the previous virginity of the woman had no long-term effect on the relationship: couples in which the woman had been a virgin prior to their relationship were no more likely to stay together than couples in which the woman had had prior sexual experience.

In summary, the nonmarital sexual behavior of college students covers a wide range of styles. Although sexual activity of any kind (such as petting or genital manipulation) is most likely to occur when there is a sense of equity in the relationship (Walster, Walster, & Traupmann, 1978), the actual experience of intercourse may happen early, late, or not at all. Its occurrence seems to have little to do with predicting the long-term success of the relationship.

B. Sexuality in marital relationships

Although nonmarital sex appears to have little effect on the stability of dating relationships, we might ask whether it has any long-term effects. Specifically, for the couple who do get married, does their premarital sexual experience have any effect on their subsequent marital satisfaction? Ard (1974) asked this question of a sample of 161 couples who had been married for about 20 years. Of these couples, nearly half reported having had premarital intercourse with their future spouses. (This figure very closely approximates Kinsey's data but may prove surprising to some students. College students, when asked to estimate the extent of their parents' sexual activities, tend to grossly underestimate the levels of such activity, whether it is premarital, marital, or extramarital, as studies by Pocs and Godow, 1977, have shown.) When persons in Ard's sample of married couples were asked whether their premarital sexual experience—either intercourse or the lack of it—had had any effect on their marriages, the majority of couples in both groups reported that there was little effect. More people reported a favorable effect than an unfavorable effect, regardless of the level of activity, although wives who had not experienced premarital intercourse with their spouses were inclined to be most favorable about the effects of premarital abstention on subsequent marital happiness.

Within the marital relationship itself, sex is often believed to be a critical determinant of marital happiness. For example, Golden (1971) has concluded: "There are couples for whom the only good thing in marriage is sex. And there are sexless marriages which are satisfactory to husband and wife. But both these situations are rare. Usually in a discordant marriage the sex life is unsatisfac-

tory, too" (p. 185). Research has tended to support this relation between sexual satisfaction and marital satisfaction (Perlman & Abramson, in press). For example, Thornton (1977) asked married people to monitor the frequency of their sexual intercourse for 35 days and at the end of that period to rate their marital happiness. The two indices were highly related, suggesting that sex and marital happiness do go together. In this same study, Thornton found that marital happiness was negatively related to the frequency of reported arguments, as might be expected, and that the frequency of sex was negatively related to the frequency of arguments as well. Although these latter relationships are not surprising, they are important because they remind us that correlational data cannot demonstrate causality. The frequency of sex and the frequency of arguments both may affect marital happiness; in turn, both of these factors may be affected by some third variable, such as job difficulties, health worries, or the presence of interfering relatives in the home.

The fact that sexual activity and marital happiness are related to a large number of other variables is clearly demonstrated by a large-scale survey conducted by *Redbook* magazine (Levin & Levin, 1975). In this survey, nearly 100,000 women responded to a series of questions about the sexual satisfactions of their marriage. Nearly 70% of these women, regardless of how long they had been married, reported that their marital sex life was either good or very good. Interestingly, women who said that they were strongly religious were more likely to report a satisfying sex life than women who reported not being religious. At the same time, women who said that they were nonreligious were less positive about other aspects of their marriage, and about themselves as well, compared with the more religious women. The sexual satisfaction of these married women appeared to vary directly with the reported frequency of intercourse, consistent with earlier findings. For example, only 9% of those women who reported no sex in their marriage were willing to say that that situation was satisfactory. In a similar vein, sexual satisfaction was reported to be greater when the women had frequent orgasms and when they felt that they could discuss their sexual feelings with their husbands on most occasions.

From these studies, we can conclude that sexual behavior is indeed an important aspect of most marriages. Although it surely is not the sole determinant of marital happiness and may be affected by many other kinds of behaviors and events, sexual behavior is nonetheless central in most people's ongoing relationships.

■ V. Sexual behavior and contraception

As everyone knows, sexual behavior may be more than an end in itself. It can also have future consequences—specifically, pregnancy and the birth of children. Or *does* everyone know? The dramatic increase in teenage pregnancies in the United States, many to unwed mothers, suggests that the connection between sexual intercourse and future pregnancy is not always recognized, at least at the time the intercourse occurs.

Over 3 million births occur each year in the United States. In 1978, over ½ million of these births were to single women (Alan Guttmacher Institute, 1981). In one study of marriage and birth records, 73% of the 16-year-old girls who got married gave birth less than eight months later (Tillack, Tyler, Paquette, & Jones, 1972). Such statistics are startling and certainly provide evidence that contraceptives are often not used during sexual activity.

Lack of information is probably not the major reason. Even among a well-educated college sample at a university with an active contraception information service that provides birth control freely, fewer than a third of the students who acknowledged being sexually active used contraception regularly (Byrne, 1982). In fact, one recent study of college students has suggested that college women are using less effective contraceptive methods now than they did five years earlier, despite an increase in the amount of sexual activity (Gerrard, 1982).

A number of reasons have been suggested for failure to use effective contraception devices. One reason is the appearance of "premeditation" that

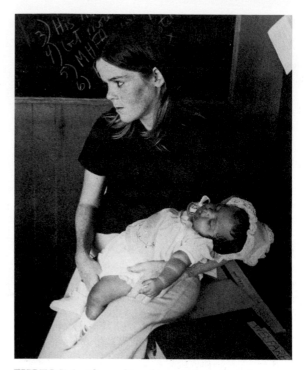

PHOTO 7-4. *The reality of teenage pregnancy.*

the use of contraceptives suggests (Sorenson, 1973). Particularly among young females, the use of contraceptives is believed to reflect negatively on the user, although this belief may not be accurate (Phillis & Allgeier, 1982). Another reason for nonuse of contraceptives has been termed the "personal fable" (Cvetkovich, Grote, Bjorseth, & Sarkissian, 1975). Many young women seem to believe that they cannot become pregnant, that they are somehow exempt from the general laws of probability that apply to other people. "It won't happen to me," unfortunately, is all too often a myth. Other barriers to the use of contraceptives include difficulty of obtaining effective devices and beliefs that pregnancy is desirable or at least acceptable (Allgeier, 1983).

Byrne (1982) has suggested that five steps occur in the decision to use contraception: (1) acquiring factual information about contraception, (2) acknowledging the likelihood of engaging in sexual intercourse, (3) obtaining contraceptives, (4) communicating with the sexual partner about contraception, and (5) practicing contraception. At each step of this sequence, a variety of social and psychological factors can affect the outcome. For the person who wishes to believe that sexual intercourse is an impulsive, romantic occurrence, such a sequence of steps is probably unthinkable. Yet, without taking account of each step, unwanted pregnancies may well result.

One factor that affects this sequence is the person's general attitudes toward sexuality. Byrne (1977, 1982) has discussed individual differences in such attitudes, contrasting people who have generally positive attitudes about sexuality with those who have generally negative attitudes. People who hold more negative attitudes are also less knowledgeable about sex and contraception, are less likely to seek contraceptive services, and are less likely to use contraceptives when they engage in intercourse (Byrne, Jazwinski, DeNinno, & Fisher, 1977; Fisher, Byrne, Edmunds, Miller, Kelley, & White, 1979).

The degree to which people feel guilt, or expect to feel guilt, about sexual activity is also related to their contraceptive use. Gerrard (1982), for example, found that sexually active women who scored high on a measure of sex guilt were more likely to use either ineffective contraceptives or none at all, in comparison with women who scored lower in sex guilt. Even retaining information about contraception can depend on a person's general feelings about sex. Schwartz (1973) presented a lecture on the biological and medical aspects of abortion to a group of college students. Students who were high in guilt about sexual activities retained less information about the lecture than students who were low in guilt, presumably because anxiety about sexual matters interfered with retention of the material. Thus, our general attitudes toward sexuality may have important consequences. Understanding these links can help us in dealing with such problems as overpopulation.

■ VI. Erotic material and sexual arousal

As we noted earlier in discussing theoretical models of sexuality, external stimuli can affect sexual choices and behavior. Such influences are abundant in our society—in books, in films, and on television (see Box 7-2). But just what is sexually arousing? And how does sexual arousal affect other forms of behavior? Are the effects of sexual imagery limited to sexual behavior, or can they influence other forms of behavior, such as aggression, as well? These are some of the questions we will consider in this section.

A. Definitions of sexual stimuli

Defining sexual stimuli is one of the most difficult tasks in this area of study. The terms *erotica*, *obscenity*, and *pornography* have been used interchangeably, but they each have somewhat different meanings. The word **obscenity** is mainly a legal term (as is the term *insanity* in the mental health field). Originally *obscenity* referred to that which was considered publicly offensive and therefore proscribed—primarily derogatory statements about the church or government (Wilson, 1973). The incorporation of sexual terms and activities within the realm of obscenity developed around the middle of the 19th century; more recent developments in the United States have completed the process by limiting legal obscenity to the sexual realm (Bender, 1971). The U.S. Supreme Court set three criteria by which material could be judged obscene: (1) material appeals to prurient interest in the average person, (2) material goes substantially beyond community standards with regard to the depiction of sex, and (3) material is without redeeming social value (Money & Athanasiou, 1973). In subsequent court cases, however, it has

PHOTO 7-5. The first step in the decision to use contraceptives is the acquiring of information.

BOX 7-2. Sex and the media

How much sex is really portrayed in the media? Do best-selling novels and major motion pictures do well precisely because they contain a great deal of explicit sexuality? Has the sexual content of books and movies changed over the past three decades? Abramson and Mechanic (in press) considered these questions in an analysis of the top five novels and top five motion pictures of 1959, 1969, and 1979. The subjects of their archival analysis are listed below.

Novels
1959*
Dr. Zhivago (Pasternak)
Lolita (Nabokov)
Exodus (Uris)
Lady Chatterley's Lover (Lawrence)

1969
Portnoy's Complaint (Roth)
The Godfather (Puzo)
The Salzberg Connection (MacInnes)
The Love Machine (Susann)
Airport (Hailey)

1979
The Women's Room (French)
Bloodline (Sheldon)
The World According to Garp (Irving)
The Holcroft Convenant (Ludlum)
Scruples (Krantz)

Motion Pictures
1959
Auntie Mame
Some Like It Hot
Pillow Talk
Imitation of Life
Shaggy Dog

1969
The Love Bug
Funny Girl
Bullitt
Butch Cassidy and the Sundance Kid
Romeo and Juliet

1979
Superman

*Only four novels were included in the 1959 sample.

Every Which Way but Loose
Star Trek
Alien
The Amityville Horror

In books and in movies, people who engage in sex are generally young, single, attractive, and physically healthy. Rarely are these fictitious characters uninterested in sex or unable to perform, and almost never is there any evidence of concern with contraception. Movies, which are subject to specific moral codes and rating systems, generally depicted less sexual activity than the best-selling novels did.

Changes in sexual activity described in novels are evident over the 20-year period. In the most recent books, compared with the earlier novels, sexual partners are depicted as having known each other for a shorter time and showing less romantic concern. These modern partners are also less communicative. In the 1979 novels, 46% of the characters avoided both verbal and nonverbal communication after sex, compared with only 9% in the 1959 books.

Relatively few sexual scenes were contained in any of the most popular movies, although those sections that did contain sex were more explicit in the most recent films. Certainly there were many highly sexual films in those years (for example, the film *10* in 1979), but they were not necessarily the most widely attended films. One interesting shift between 1959 and 1979 is the presence of alcohol and other intoxicants: in 1959, such substances were always part of the sex scenes, whereas they were absent from the best-selling films of later years.

Perhaps most striking in this analysis of sex in the media is the uniform and somewhat unrealistic presentation of sexuality that seems to dominate. People are not old, people are not married, people do not talk, and no one worries about the consequences. In reality, sexual behavior is far more varied than that. ■

been discovered that these criteria are very difficult to pin down—even though some people may glibly claim that they "know obscenity when they see it."

Erotica is the term most often used by social scientists to refer to any visual or verbal material that is considered sexually arousing. This definition is still somewhat vague, reflecting the fact that relatively little work has been devoted to specifying the content of sexual stimuli (Diamond, 1980). Furthermore, material may be sexually arousing to one person and not to another. However, the definition of *erotica* does attempt to focus on the material as such and is an improvement over definitions that require an inference of prurient interest or social value.

We define **pornography** as a particular type of erotic material—material which combines elements of sexuality and aggression and in which force or coercion is used to accomplish the sexual act. As we shall see, this distinction based on the presence or absence of aggressive themes is an important one.

Until very recently, laboratory research has been limited to the study of nonaggressive erotica. We will consider the results of some of those studies, looking at the effects of sexual arousal on physiological responses, on fantasy and other psychological responses, and on behavior. Then we will turn to the recent research on pornography and consider the effects of that type of material on aggression, particularly toward women.

B. Physiological responses to erotic stimuli

Several methods are used to determine physiological reactions to erotic stimuli. For example, actual measurement of the reactions by sexual organs can be made. A device called the penile plethysmograph can be attached to the penis to measure its volume and size (Freund, Sedlacek, & Knob, 1965; Zuckerman, 1971), and the female's responses can be measured by blood volume and pulse pressure in the genital area (Heiman, 1975).

PHOTO 7-6. *Some communities accept forms of sexual material that would outrage citizens in other communities.*

More recently, investigators have begun to use thermograms, which are essentially temperature maps of the body (Abramson, Perry, Seeley, Seeley, & Rothblatt, 1981). This method can be used for both males and females, thus making direct comparisons possible. Another advantage of the thermogram is that it is nonintrusive, allowing subjects more privacy and reducing recording errors. As an alternative to these more technological methods, other investigators have assessed physiological reactions simply by asking subjects how aroused they feel (Mosher, 1973; Schmidt, Sigusch, & Meyberg, 1969).

Most studies of physiological responses to erotic stimuli find that subjects do report sexual arousal. For example, in a study by Schmidt et al. (1969), approximately 80% of the German male college students who had observed sexually explicit photos reported that they had had an erection, and almost one-fifth reported the emission of some pre-ejaculatory fluid. In a later study that included female college students, most of the women reported some bodily reactions in the genital area (Schmidt & Sigusch, 1970). Similar results were found in a study conducted with U.S. college students (Mosher, 1973).

Although the physiological responses to erotic material are consistent, there is some evidence that the effect diminishes over time, at least for the typical college student. For example, in a study done for the U.S. Commission on Obscenity and Pornography, Howard and his colleagues (Howard, Liptzin, & Reifler, 1973; Howard, Reifler, & Liptzin, 1971) found that exposure to erotic material could be satiating. Each male subject, approximately 22 years of age, spent 90 minutes a day for three weeks alone in a room that contained a large and diverse collection of erotic materials, including books, photographs, and movies, as well as some nonerotic material. All measures—including both penile erections and self-rating of arousal—decreased over time. Subjects spent less and less time with the erotic material and even resorted to reading *Reader's Digest*. However, the introduction of new erotic stimuli heightened the response once more, suggesting that the satiation may be specific, rather than general.

Sexual arousal can also occur without the presence of such erotic materials in the environment. Self-generated fantasies and other cognitive processes can lead to arousal, and their effects on physiological responses can be demonstrated in a laboratory setting (Geer, 1974). In such studies, subjects are asked to sit in a comfortable chair, to imagine a sexual scene, and to "turn themselves on" by doing so. Within two or three minutes, changes in physiological responses have been observed.

C. Psychological responses to erotic stimuli

Responses to erotic material occur at a mental level as well as a physiological one. People often respond to erotic stimuli by engaging in sexual fantasies, for example, imagining future encounters or recalling past events. These cognitive reactions to erotic stimuli clearly are part of what is generally called sexual arousal.

In the original Kinsey studies (Kinsey et al., 1953), it was reported that women were less likely to be sexually aroused by erotic stimuli than men were. Although this sex difference was accepted without question for many years, recent investigations suggest that it is no longer accurate. Both men and women report sexual arousal in response to erotic stimuli, although certain qualitative aspects of the reported fantasies may differ. Fisher and Byrne (1978) asked undergraduate students, who had previously agreed to be involved in an experiment dealing with sexual material, to watch a ten-minute film in which a couple undressed and engaged in heavy petting. Both sexes reported considerable arousal in response to the film, and the investigators found no sex differences in the responses. Interestingly, when the investigators varied the background description for the film—describing the couple as married, as a prostitute and client, or as casual acquaintances—both men and women reported being most aroused by the casual-sex theme.

Other investigators (for example, Carlson & Coleman, 1977) have simply asked subjects to completely relax for a short period and to fantasize about an erotic situation. Reported fantasies during this period again show no quantitative differences between males and females, but there is some evidence that women have more complex and emotionally richer fantasies than men do (Carlson & Coleman, 1977). Similarly, when men and women are asked to describe the thoughts and ideas they've had during sexual activity, women tend to report more imaginary fantasies, while men are more apt to think of past experiences and current behavior (McCauley & Swann, 1978). Again, however, the overall level of fantasy is no different for males than for females, suggesting that Kinsey's conclusions are no longer warranted.

Not all responses to erotic stimuli are positive, however. For many people, guilt can be a primary reaction. For such people, viewing erotic stimuli is more of an aversive situation; in fact, people who score high on a measure of sex guilt are less likely to view erotic material (Schill & Chapin, 1972) and show less physiological arousal when they are exposed to such material (Pagano & Kirschner, 1978). Guilt about sex is stronger among the older generation than the younger, possibly reflecting some changes in general attitudes toward sex (Abramson & Imai-Marquez, 1982).

Sexual arousal can affect the ways we evaluate other people, particularly people with whom some sexual interactions can be imagined. For example, Stephan, Berscheid, and Walster (1971) found that sexually aroused males rated photographs of women as more attractive than nonaroused males did. This perception of the woman's increased attractiveness was particularly strong when the men believed they would actually have a date with the woman. As might be expected in looking at a primarily heterosexual, college-student population, increases in the attractiveness evaluation occurred only with regard to other-sex persons, not with regard to same-sex persons (Griffitt, May, & Veitch, 1974). Presumably, if a similar study were conducted with a homosexual population, stronger effects would be found for same-sex than for other-sex targets.

Sexual arousal and, in turn, fantasy can be affected by a variety of factors. In a recent experiment by McCarty, Diamond, and Kaye (1982), some male and female subjects were given a vodka-and-tonic drink before viewing erotic photographs from *Playboy*, *Playgirl*, *Penthouse*, and fashion magazines. Other subjects drank only tonic water. Subjects who had the alcohol reported more arousal and stronger fantasies than the "teetotalers." Consistent with earlier findings, there were no differences between the fantasy reactions of males and females. In an additional experimental manipulation, McCarty and his colleagues told half the subjects in each group that they would be drinking alcohol and told the other half that they would be drinking neutral tonic water. (Because vodka is tasteless, this deception was effective.) The manipulation had a strong effect. Subjects who thought they had been drinking alcohol reported stronger fantasies than subjects who thought their only drink was tonic, regardless of what drink they actually had. The strongest fantasies of all were reported by those subjects who believed they had tonic but actually had alcohol—presumably because they could not readily explain the actual arousal caused by the alcohol and attributed that arousal to the erotic photographs. (See the discussion of Schachter and Singer's work in Chapter 3 and of Zillmann's work in Chapter 8.)

D. Behavioral responses to erotic stimuli

Exposure to explicit sexual materials leads to a state of physiological arousal, to fantasy, and to more positive evaluation of sexual targets. But does it lead to increased sexual activity?

The assumption generally made is that exposure to erotic material will cause an increase in the sexual activity of the observer. Investigators have tried to test this assumption in the following way. First, the typical sexual activity of subjects (who volunteer for the study) is assessed through a self-report that describes their sexual activities during the previous week or month. Then, the subjects are shown erotic materials (usually films), and at a later time—perhaps a day later, perhaps a week—they are asked to report again on their sexual activities. The procedural problems in this methodology are probably apparent. The use of volunteers may mean that the sample contains too high a proportion of sensation-seeking subjects. There may be demand characteristics that influ-

PHOTO 7-7. *Contrary to what many believe, women and men have very similar reactions to erotic stimuli.*

ence the subjects to engage in or to report more sexual activity after watching the films. Nevertheless, results from these studies are still preferable to uninformed speculation.

The results of such studies show a relatively limited effect of erotic material on subsequent sexual behavior. By way of summary, we can report the following conclusions: (1) Heightened sexual activity occurs for only a brief period, such as on the night the subjects view the film (Cattell, Kawash, & DeYoung, 1972). (2) There are no reports of increased sexual activity over a prolonged period—say, 12 weeks—even in response to four viewings of sexually explicit films (Mann, Sidman, & Starr, 1971, 1973). (3) There is apparently no change in types of sexual activity (Amoroso, Brown, Pruesse, Ware, & Pilkey, 1971). Mosher (1973), in reviewing studies by himself and others, offers the generalization that "erotic films lead to increased sexual activity immediately following the films only if there is a well-established sexual pattern" (p. 109). And even those mild increases are not found in younger and less experienced viewers. Thus, exposure to specifically erotic stimuli appears to have a relatively weak effect on subsequent sexual activity, at least under the conditions studied to date.

However, the effects of erotic material cannot be discussed fully without considering another possible link—that between sexual stimuli and aggressive behavior. Freud was one of the first to suggest that sexual behavior and aggression are closely linked. He stated that "the sexuality of most men shows an admixture of aggression, of a desire to subdue" (1938, p. 659). Recent psychoanalytic theory has continued to argue for this connection, as illustrated in the following statement: "Hostility, overt or hidden, is what generates and enhances sexual excitement, and its absence leads to sexual indifference and boredom" (Stoller, 1976, p. 903).

In the United States, the U.S. President's Commission on Obscenity and Pornography (1970) was appointed to determine whether there is in fact a link between erotic material and violence. The commission concluded that there is not. Later research has modified that conclusion, however. Let us first consider the effects of nonaggressive erotic material on aggression—the kind of material on which the commission based its conclusions.

If a person has not been previously angered, exposure to erotic material seems to have no effect on aggression (Donnerstein, 1982), thus confirming the commission's original conclusions. When anger is involved, however, aggression and exposure to erotica seem to be related, although the linkage is a bit complex. In some cases, exposure to erotic material may actually inhibit the display of aggression. For example, Baron and Bell (1977) found that college males who had seen pictures of women in bathing suits, pictures of nude women, or pictures of acts of lovemaking were less aggressive than men who had seen neutral pictures of scenery. Men who read erotic literary passages, however, showed no decrease in aggression, suggesting that only some forms of erotica will inhibit aggression. Further research has shown that this inhibitory effect is also dependent on a very low level of provocation (Ramirez, Bryant, & Zillmann, 1982).

In contrast, more intense provocation or more arousing forms of erotic material—such as films depicting actual intercourse and oral and anal activities—will increase aggressive behavior (Donnerstein, Donnerstein, & Evans, 1975; Ramirez et al., 1982). Lengthy exposure to these more intense forms of erotic material has also been shown to have other effects, including more leniency in attitudes toward rape and greater callousness in attitudes toward women in general (Zillmann & Bryant, in press). There are a number of competing explanations for these findings, and no single theoretical explanation has prevailed. It is quite clear, however, that the relation between erotic material and aggressive behavior is more complex than the President's Commission realized and that erotic material can often cause an increase in aggressive behavior.

E. Aggressive responses to pornography

Virtually all the research on which the commission's report was based, and much of the subsequent laboratory research, used nonaggressive erotic material. Indeed, at the time that the commission's report was published, pornographic material was relatively infrequent (Malamuth & Donnerstein, 1982). During the past decade, pornographic material that combines sex and violence has become much more common, as scenes of rape, coercion, and the exertion of power pervade both books and films. What effect does this kind of material have on aggressive behavior, toward other people in general and toward women in particular, who are usually portrayed as the victims of aggression?

A widely publicized study in Denmark considered the frequency of sex offenses before and after the removal of all restrictions on the sale of pornographic materials (Kutchinsky, 1973). The initial results of this "natural experiment" suggested that sex crimes declined markedly, and the study gave rise to a "safety valve" theory (Kronhausen & Kronhausen, 1964). Thus, it was argued that potential sex offenders may have obtained sufficient sexual satisfaction through the reading and viewing of pornographic materials. However, more recent figures from Denmark show an increase, rather than a decrease, in rape (Bachy, 1976). Because these data are correlational, we cannot be certain that lifting restrictions on pornography caused the increase in sex crimes in Denmark. These findings do, however, pose questions for the safety-valve theory.

More conclusive answers to the question of pornography and violence come from the extensive research program of Edward Donnerstein and his colleagues (Donnerstein, 1982; Malamuth & Donnerstein, 1982). Their results show very consistently that men who are exposed to pornographic materials will be more aggressive toward women in subsequent interactions. Let's consider one of these experiments by Donnerstein and Berkowitz (1981) in some detail.

Male college students believed they were participating in an experiment on stress and learning, in which they would be paired with either a male or a female student. In the initial stage of the experiment, they were asked to write an essay. Their partner then was asked to evaluate the essay, indicating a judgment by administering shocks to the subject. The partner gave a high number of shocks, indicating a negative evaluation. In the next stage of the experiment, the subjects were exposed to one of four films: a neutral talk-show interview, an erotic film depicting sexual intercourse with no aggressive content, or one of two pornographic films that combined aggression and sexuality, depicting a woman being slapped and sexually attacked. One of these pornographic films had a positive outcome, ending with the woman smiling at her attackers. In the other pornographic film, the outcome was negative, and the woman was clearly suffering at the end of the film. After viewing one of these films, the subject was returned to the "learning task" and given the opportunity to be aggressive toward (that is, to shock) his partner. Figure 7-3 shows the results of this experiment.

As Figure 7-3 shows, aggression levels were quite different, depending on the sex of the target. If the male subject was paired with another male, none of the sexual films significantly affected the level of aggression, compared with the neutral film. With a female partner, in contrast, both pornographic films dramatically increased the male's level of aggression. But what if the male subject had not been angered? Is a state of anger necessary for such a display of aggression against women? Donnerstein and Berkowitz (1981) conducted a second study to answer these questions. Using the same four films, they found that nonangered males did not act aggressively toward a female partner when the pornographic film had a negative ending. But when the pornographic film showed the woman enjoying the sexual violence, nonangered men were nearly as aggressive toward a female partner as were the men who had been angered.

Other current research continues to demonstrate the negative effects of pornography on attitudes and behavior toward women. Men who listen to audiotapes depicting rape, for example, are more likely to believe that women get pleasure from being raped, more prone to have aggressive

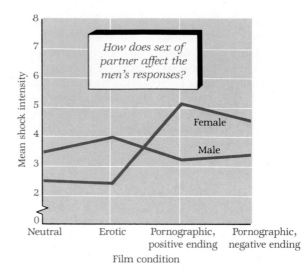

FIGURE 7-3. Aggression by male subjects toward a male or female partner after viewing neutral, erotic, or pornographic films.

sexual fantasies, and more accepting of violence against women (Malamuth, 1981a, 1981b). Not all men respond this way. Many do, however, and for some men, scenes of rape are more arousing than scenes of mutually consenting sex (Malamuth, 1981b).

Thus, to answer our earlier question, the effects of pornography on subsequent behavior appear to be quite strong. Exposure to pornographic materials leads to more aggressive behavior, and this aggression is, for the most part, directed against women.

VII. SUMMARY

Sexual behavior is an important aspect of social interaction, although, until fairly recently, scientific study of the topic was considered taboo. Initial work in this area relied on case studies of clinical patients. More recently, methods have also included survey research and laboratory experimentation.

Kinsey's landmark work provided information on the frequency with which U.S. adults engaged in various forms of sexual behavior. More recently, Hunt has updated Kinsey's information and found a gradual increase in the sexual behavior of U.S. adults, particularly women. Similar studies conducted with college students show that nonmarital sexual activity is fairly frequent.

Freud was among the first to insist that sexuality is a basic part of the human personality. His theories on infantile sexuality and the differences between male and female sexuality were influential for many years. Other theoretical discussions of sexuality point to the importance of cognitive factors. These theories stress the importance of socialization experiences and the role of learning in determining what situations and stimuli will be perceived as sexually arousing.

Explanations for the development of homosexual and heterosexual preferences have stressed both "nature" and "nurture." Recent evidence suggests that homosexual tendencies develop very early and that there may be some biological influences.

Bisexuals are people who engage in sexual behavior with persons of both sexes. Evidence suggests that learning and experience may play a larger role in bisexuality than in homosexuality.

Studies of sexual activity in nonmarital relationships show little connection between the presence or absence of such activity and the future success of the relationship. Those couples who abstain, those who engage in sex in the early stage of a relationship, and those who engage in sex at later stages of a relationship do differ, however, in values and beliefs.

In marital relationships, reports of marital happiness are related to frequency of sexual activity. It is possible, however, that both these variables may be related to some other factors in the marital relationship.

An obvious consequence of sexual activity is pregnancy. Attitudes and behaviors toward birth control are related to more general attitudes toward sexuality.

Studies of the influence of erotic stimuli on sexual behavior must begin with a consideration of the distinctions among the terms *obscenity*, *pornography*, and *erotica*.

Responses to erotic material include physiological changes, fantasy, guilt, and changes in the attractiveness evaluations of other people. Actual sexual behavior may be affected by exposure to erotic stimuli, although the effects are fairly short-term. Exposure to aggressive erotica (pornography) can lead to an increase in aggressive behavior, particularly directed toward women.

GLOSSARY TERMS

bisexuality	gender identity	pornography
erotica	obscenity	transsexualism

8

Aggression & Violence

You cannot shake hands with a clenched fist.

■ INDIRA GANDHI

One of television's great contributions is that it brought murder back into the home where it belongs.

■ ALFRED HITCHCOCK

During the approximately 5600 years that humans have recorded their history, more than 14,600 wars have occurred, averaging out to nearly three wars per year throughout our history (Montagu, 1976). Places such as the Falkland Islands become known to most people only because of warfare. Since the beginning of the 20th century, more than 900,000 civilians in the United States have died as a result of criminal acts. In fact, among stable industrialized societies, the United States has the highest rates of homicide, assault, rape, and robbery.

One could easily conclude from these facts that violence and aggression are integral facets of human society. Indeed, some behavioral scientists assume that aggression is the natural result of a "killer instinct" in human nature. Robert Ardrey (1961) has placed this **instinct** in an evolutionary context, stating that "man is a predator whose natural instinct is to kill with a weapon." Other scientists, however, believe that aggression can be explained

PHOTO 8-1. Violence has become commonplace in some neighborhoods.

completely as a learned social behavior that is predictable and controllable.

Definitions and interpretations of aggressive behavior are determined by theoretical viewpoints; and when we consider the nature of aggression, we find more than enough theories to go around. These theoretical perspectives differ in a variety of ways: in the extent to which they consider aggression innate or learned, in the extent to which the person, rather than situational factors, is considered influential, and in the proposed ways in which aggression might be controlled in the future. In this chapter we will look at three theoretical viewpoints. In addition, we will consider what factors influence aggression. We ask, for example, how alcohol and drugs affect aggressive behavior, whether violence on television and in films affects the observer, how aggression is expressed in the home, and how violence might be controlled in the future.

Before we look at these more complex issues, however, some of the basic questions in the area of aggression need to be addressed. A definition of aggression is first in importance.

■ I. Definitions of aggression

Exactly what is aggression? Although *aggression* is a term used often in everyday language, it can take on some very specific meanings when used by social scientists. Different theories of aggression offer different definitions of aggression and different assumptions about its causes. Let's look at three of those definitions before we consider the theories in greater depth.

A. The psychoanalytic definition

According to traditional Freudian psychoanalytic theory, aggressive energy is constantly generated by our bodily processes. For example, the intake of food leads to the generation of energy. Aggression is thus defined as an underlying urge that must seek expression. Like sexual urges, aggressive urges must be "released"—that is, expressed directly or indirectly. They can be discharged either in socially acceptable ways (such as a vigorous debate or an athletic activity) or in less socially acceptable ways (such as insults or fights). The destructive release of aggressive urges need not be directed against other people; it may be aimed toward the self, as in suicide. However it is discharged, aggression is considered to be innate and inevitable. In fact, Freud believed that one function of society is to keep natural aggression in check.

B. The ethological definition

The noted ethologist Konrad Lorenz (1966) describes aggression as "the fighting instinct in beast and man which is directed *against* members of the same species" (p. ix). According to Lorenz, aggression is not a bad thing in itself; rather, it functions to preserve the species as well as the individual. In other words, aggression has survival value.

Lorenz believes that an organism is far more aggressive toward its own species than toward other species. The basic purpose of such aggression is to keep members of the species separated—to give each member enough area to survive. Intraspecies aggression also affects sexual selection and mating; the stronger are more likely to mate. Thus, aggression assures that the best and strongest animals will carry on the species.

In Lorenz's view, aggression becomes undesirable only when the species—the human species, for example—fails to develop the usual instinctual inhibitions against it. Intraspecies fights do not usually end in death but, rather, in acts of appeasement by the loser (see Photo 8-2). According to Lorenz, all humans' troubles arise from their "being a basically harmless, omnivorous creature, lacking in natural weapons with which to kill [their] big prey, and, therefore, also devoid of the built-in safety devices which prevent 'professional' carnivores from abusing their killing power to destroy fellow members of their own species" (1966, p. 241). Lacking the innate ability to kill without weapons, the human species also has failed to evolve inhibitory mechanisms to prevent aggression. If humans had no weapons at their disposal, they wouldn't be equipped to kill members of their species. What if all killing of other people had to be

PHOTO 8-2. *The agony of defeat. In the photo above, the wolf on the left has accepted defeat, although the signs of her submission are quite subtle. The position of the ears and the tail are two signs of submission.*

done with our hands and teeth? Wouldn't that not only reduce the murder rate but also restrain our desire to kill?

C. The experimental social psychologist's definition

In contrast to the psychoanalysts and the ethologists, most social psychologists consider aggression not as an innate instinct but as learned behavior that may be displayed depending on the circumstances. As we shall see in the next section, social psychologists are not in total agreement on all issues relating to aggression. Most, however, would accept the following definition: *Aggression is any form of behavior directed toward the goal of harming or injuring another living being who is motivated to avoid such treatment* (Baron, 1977, p. 7). This definition focuses on the behavior and does not deal directly with its causes.

This definition has a number of important features. First of all, it limits aggression to those forms of behavior in which the person *intends* to harm a victim. If you accidentally knock someone over while riding your bicycle, for example, that would not be considered an act of aggression. Similarly, when a nurse gives a patient a routine injection, the intention is not to do harm, although pain may be involved. But what if the patient has just insulted the nurse, who then jams the needle in with unnecessary force? Certainly there is a component of aggression in this behavior. If an attempt to harm someone is unsuccessful—for example, if I try to hit someone but miss—that behavior, too, would be considered aggressive, because the intent was to inflict harm. Although it is often difficult to establish intention with complete certainty, as the proceedings of criminal trials well indicate, the concept of intentionality is important in distinguishing aggressive behavior from other forms of behavior that might lead to some harm.

Often, in everyday speech, we talk about an "aggressive manager" or an "aggressive salesperson." Generally, such descriptions refer to a person who is energetic, assertive, and eager to get ahead. These behaviors do not fit the social psychologist's definition of aggression, however, unless the particular manager or salesperson is deliberately trying to harm another person in the process of being successful.

Our working definition doesn't limit aggression to physical harm. Verbal insults are forms of aggression, and even the refusal to give a person something he or she needs can be considered a form of aggression. Our definition does, however, limit aggression to those behaviors that involve other living beings, either human or animal. A person who kicks a wall is probably angry, but this behavior would not be considered aggressive according to our definition. Finally, instances of aggression are limited to those cases in which the other person would prefer to avoid the pain. Behaviors most clearly ruled out by this clause are those of a sadomasochistic nature.

■ II. Theoretical positions on aggression

Definitions are only a starting point. Theorists have developed a number of broad models of aggression, emphasizing different aspects of the cause, the consequences, and the related factors that may affect aggressive behavior. In this section, we consider three major viewpoints on aggression: the instinctual position, the drive (or motivation) position, and the position that emphasizes aggression as a learned behavior.

A. Instinctual and biological explanations of aggression

Sigmund Freud wrote: "The tendency to aggression is an innate, independent, instinctual disposition in man" (1930, p. 102). A number of other theories, though not adopting the psychoanalytic viewpoint, also assume that aggression is biologically based. We will consider two of these—ethology and sociobiology—in addition to the psychoanalytic position.

Freud was a physician, and the psychoanalytic position that he developed was closely tied to his study of bodily functions and human physiology. He believed that an instinct is a mental representation, resulting from tensions created by biological needs. Thus, according to Freud, aggressive energy is generated within the body and must be dissipated. This energy can be either neutralized or discharged (Freud, 1917/1963)—discharged, for example, in the form of aggressive behavior.

Some of Freud's successors—often called **neo-Freudians**—revised his theory, viewing aggression as more of a rational than an irrational process (Hartmann, Kris, & Loewenstein, 1949). According to these neo-Freudians, aggressive drives are healthy; they represent adaptations to the realities of the environment. Like Freud, however, most of these later theorists continued to believe that aggression develops from innate and instinctive forces.

A different biological view of aggression comes to us from the ethologists. As suggested earlier, **ethology** is a subfield of biology concerned with the instincts and action patterns common to all members of a species operating in their natural habitat (Eibl-Eibesfeldt, 1970). Ethologists observe the normal behavior of fish, birds, and other animals in the field and try to identify similarities in and causes of their behavior. It is often assumed that these behaviors (or "action patterns") are under innate, or instinctual, control (Crook, 1973).

According to ethologists, the expression of any fixed action pattern depends on the accumulation of energy. But in order for this energy to be released, it must be triggered by an external stimulus, called a "releasing stimulus" (Hess, 1962). Ethologists use the concept of *releasers* (releasing stimuli) to explain the relationship between internal factors and external stimuli. Specifically, in explaining aggression, ethologists suggest that certain environmental cues allow an organism to express aggressive behavior. Essentially, this is a two-factor theory of the expression of aggression: it has an advantage over orthodox psychoanalytic theory and the neo-Freudian approaches in recognizing that environmental changes contribute to the aggressive response.

Another theory that has developed from animal studies is **sociobiology.** As developed by E. O. Wilson (1975, 1978) and others, this theory assumes that many social behaviors are genetically based. Such genetically based behaviors will be maintained by a population or society "if they increase the genetic fitness (i.e., reproductive success) of the individual or his close relatives who also carry the genes for that behavior" (Cunningham, 1981, p. 71). In the case of aggression, sociobiologists would suggest that there is a biological advantage to be gained in being aggressive. To acquire more resources, for example, or to defend the resources one has, one might show aggressive behavior. If successful, the aggressive individual might thereby strengthen the position of his or her own group relative to others. Thus, for the sociobiologist, aggressive behavior has a clear goal—to preserve one's own species and to increase its chances of future success.

Although the views of psychoanalysts, ethologists, and sociobiologists differ in some important respects, such as the role of the environment in contributing to aggressive behavior, they share some basic assumptions. Most important, all three positions consider aggression to be an innate, instinctual behavior and thus a basic part of the human condition. They may argue about when and where aggression will be displayed, but they all agree that it will be displayed. For the biological theorist, aggression always has existed and always will.

B. Motivational explanations of aggression

Although most social psychologists are not willing to accept aggression as an inevitable and instinctual behavior, the concept of aggression as a general motive, or drive, that can be either learned or innate has been widely accepted. In 1939 a group of psychologists at Yale University (Dollard, Doob, Miller, Mowrer, & Sears, 1939) introduced a hypothesis that has probably influenced more thought and research than any other theory of aggression. These psychologists hypothesized that frustration causes aggression. More specifically, this **frustration-aggression hypothesis** postulated that "the occurrence of aggression always presupposes frustration" (N. E. Miller, 1941, pp. 337–338). Would any frustrating event inevitably lead to aggression? Not necessarily, argued Neal Miller, one of the authors of this hypothesis. "Frustration produces instigations to a number of different types of responses, one of which is an instigation to some form of aggression" (1941, p. 338). In summary, although these psychologists believed that aggression is always a consequence of some frustration, frustration may have other outcomes as well. Does this theory account for the incidence of aggression in society? To answer this question, we must look more carefully at the components of the frustration-aggression theory.

1. *What is frustration?* To say the least, *frustration* is a vague term that is subject to many interpretations (see Berkowitz, 1969). In common usage, *frustration* can refer to the external event that causes a reaction, or it can refer to the reaction itself. Suppose a man is ready to drive to the airport to meet his fiancée when he discovers that his car battery is dead. What is the frustration? Is it the dead battery or the fact that the car won't start (the external instigating conditions)? Or is frustration the man's feelings of increased tension and the pounding of his heart—or does it refer to his pounding on the car? In the original frustration-aggression formulation, the Yale theorists defined frustration as the state that emerges when circumstances interfere with a goal response: "an interference with the occurrence of an instigated goal-response at its proper time in the behavior sequence" (Dollard et al., 1939, p. 7). For example, a rat accustomed to running down a particular path for food might experience frustration if a door suddenly appeared in the middle of what had

previously been a clear path. Although this example is straightforward, it is often more difficult to specify a precise sequence of events in human behavior. As a result, definitions of frustration have often become muddled and have made precise tests of the theory difficult (Berkowitz, 1969).

2. *Is the relation between frustration and aggression innate?* There is a tendency to regard the frustration-aggression relation as inevitable, or instinctual. Dollard and his colleagues fostered this belief when they stated that "the frustration-aggression hypothesis assumes a universal causal relation between frustration and aggression" (Dollard et al., 1939, p. 10). Many critics disagree. These critics suggest that because people can learn to inhibit their aggressive reactions or learn different responses to frustration, the possibility of innate behavior is excluded (Bandura, 1973; Bandura & Walters, 1963; Berkowitz, 1969). For example, if your boss severely criticizes your performance, you might quickly learn to inhibit tendencies to strike back. Does that mean that the frustration/aggression link is not innate? Not necessarily. Evidence of learning does not rule out the possibility of innate causes. Learning can alter or modify built-in patterns. Although frustration might instinctively heighten the likelihood that a certain type of response (such as aggression) will be instigated, learning can alter or disguise the display of this response. The original formulators of the theory appeared to fall back to this position. In 1964, N. E. Miller wrote: "It seems highly probable that . . . innate patterns exist, that they play an important role in the development of human social behavior, and that these instinctual patterns are modifiable enough so that they tend to be disguised by learning, although they may play crucial roles in motivating, facilitating, and shaping socially learned behavior" (p. 160).

3. *Does research support the frustration-aggression hypothesis?* Evidence derived from studies using both human and nonhuman subjects suggests that aggression *may* be caused by frustration (see Azrin, Hutchinson, & Hake, 1966; Rule & Percival, 1971). For example, Buss (1963) subjected college students to three types of frustration: failing a task, losing an opportunity to win

money, and missing a chance to earn a better grade. Each type of frustration led to approximately the same level of aggression, and in each case the level of aggression was greater than in a control condition in which no frustration was experienced. Yet, the level of aggression exhibited was not very great in any case. Perhaps the aggression was minimal because it could not serve to overcome the cause of the frustration. Buss (1961, 1966) suggests that frustration and aggression may be linked only when the aggression has *instrumental value*—that is, when aggressive behavior will help to override the frustration. Other studies also have reported no increase in aggression as a result of the degrees of frustration produced in human subjects in the laboratory (Gentry, 1970; Taylor & Pisano, 1971).

We know less about the possible links between frustration and aggression outside the laboratory. An extensive observational study of children's everyday behavior found little evidence that frustrating behavior leads to aggression (Fawl, 1963). However, some investigators have suggested that most homicides can be interpreted as aggressive acts that result from frustration (Berkowitz, 1974). Although it is true that most homicides are not planned but instead are fairly quick reactions to a situation (Mulvihill & Tumin, 1969), the somewhat automatic nature of the aggressive response does not necessarily prove the existence of frustration. Other precipitating causes, such as direct attack, have been found to be potent causes of aggression in the laboratory (Gaebelein & Taylor, 1971; Rule & Hewitt, 1971) and probably cause aggression outside the laboratory as well.

Most researchers believe that factors other than frustration are necessary to elicit aggressive behavior, and a number of revisions of the frustration/aggression formulation have been suggested. The most influential of these revisions has been proposed by Berkowitz (1965b, 1969, 1971), who emphasizes *the interaction between environmental cues and internal emotional states.*

Berkowitz suggests that the reaction to frustration creates "only a *readiness* for aggressive acts. Previously acquired aggressiveness habits can also establish this readiness" (1965b, p. 308). In other words, Berkowitz maintains that the occurrence

A. *Hurrying to meet a deadline, Louise approaches the copy machine to make duplicates of her report.*

B. *Frustration—the machine doesn't work.*

C. *Louise's tension mounts as her attempts to fix the machine prove unsuccessful.*

Standing in the rain, waiting for a bus to take you to an important interview, you watch the bus pass by without stopping. As you write a final exam answer, the point breaks off your last pencil. Well trained for the final swim match of the season, you sprain your wrist in a friendly game of volleyball. How many occasions like these can you think of—when you have been frustrated, when some event interfered with your reaching some goal? How did you react? It is on events such as these that the frustration-aggression hypothesis is based, predicting that often the response to frustration will be aggressive behavior.

D. *Help from other people could reduce the frustration—if they can get the machine to work.*

E. *No luck. With her report uncopied and the deadline approaching, Louise vents her anger on the office assistant.*

of aggressive behavior is not solely dependent on frustration (a point that Neal Miller also is willing to grant) and that an intervening variable—a readiness—must be added to the chain.

According to Berkowitz, a second important factor is the presence of aggressive cues in the environment that serve as triggers for the expression of aggression. Frustration creates the readiness of anger; stimulus cues can actually elicit aggression. Furthermore, the cues themselves can increase the strength of the aggressive response, particularly when the aggressive response is impulsive in nature (Zillmann, Katcher, & Milavsky, 1972). Although stimulus cues aren't always necessary for aggression to occur, Berkowitz would argue that they generally increase the probability of aggressive behavior.

Do aggressive cues really elicit aggressive behavior? In a systematic research program conducted by Berkowitz and his colleagues at the University of Wisconsin, considerable support for this position has been established. In a typical experiment, a male college student is introduced to another subject, who, in reality, is a confederate of the experimenter. The confederate either angers the subject deliberately or treats him in a neutral manner. Immediately after this phase of the experiment, both persons watch a brief film clip— either a violent prize-fight scene from the film *Champion* or a neutral film showing English canal boats or a track race. After watching the film clip, the subject is given an opportunity to administer electrical shocks to the accomplice. Using this basic paradigm, Berkowitz and his colleagues have developed a variety of tactics to create aggressive cues in the environment. In one experiment, for example, the accomplice was introduced either as a nonbelligerent speech major or as a physical education major who was interested in boxing. When the confederate was introduced as a boxer, the subjects administered more severe shocks (Berkowitz, 1965a). In another experiment, the confederate was introduced either as Kirk Anderson (presumably providing an association with Kirk Douglas, who was the actor in the boxing film) or as Bob Anderson. Once again, the aggressive-cue value of the confederate affected the level of aggression displayed by the subject (see Table 8-1). As shown in the table, subjects gave the most shocks when they were angered, when they had watched an aggressive film, and when the accomplice had the same name as the boxer in the film. In addition, subjects who had been angered were always more aggressive than those who had not been angered.

Other experiments in this series have focused on the aggressive-cue value of weapons (Berkowitz & LePage, 1967). For example, in one such experiment, male university students received either one or seven electrical shocks from a student (confederate) and then were given an opportunity to administer shocks in return. While some subjects participated in the study, a rifle and a revolver were placed on a nearby table; for other subjects, no objects were present. As one might expect, the subjects who had been shocked more by the confederate were apt to administer shocks in return. More important, the presence of the guns increased the average number of shocks administered from 4.67 to 6.07. The results of this experiment have

TABLE 8-1. Mean number of shocks given to accomplice

Accomplice's name	Aggressive film		Track film	
	Angered	Nonangered	Angered	Nonangered
Kirk	6.09_a	1.73_c	4.18_b	1.54_c
Bob	4.55_b	1.45_c	4.00_b	1.64_c

NOTE: Cells having a subscript in common are not significantly different (at the .05 level) by Duncan multiple range test.

PHOTO 8-3. *While some citizens urge gun control, others defend in graphic terms their right to bear arms.*

important theoretical and practical implications. At a theoretical level, they clearly support Berkowitz's hypotheses about the role of aggressive cues in eliciting aggression. At a more practical level, the results suggest the dangers in a society that allows the free display of dangerous weapons. As Berkowitz has phrased it, "Guns not only permit violence, they can stimulate it as well. The finger pulls the trigger, but the trigger may also be pulling the finger" (Berkowitz, 1968, p. 22). Differences between Canada and the United States are consistent with Berkowitz's position. In Canada, where firearms such as revolvers and submachine guns must be registered and may not be owned for purposes of "protection," the homicide rate is considerably lower than in the United States. Similarly, in England, where even the police usually do not carry guns, reported incidents of violence are markedly lower than in the United States. However, there are other differences among these countries as well, and we cannot be certain that the availability of guns is a major cause of homicides. In Canada, for example, imprisonment is more likely than in the United States, and such policies may also be related to the frequency of homicide.

In the laboratory, the link between weapons and violence has also been questioned. Some experiments have demonstrated a similar "weapons effect" (Frodi, 1975; Leyens & Parke, 1975), but others have failed to do so (Buss, Booker, & Buss, 1972; Page & Scheidt, 1971). Some people have suggested that the effect might be due to demand characteristics (recall our discussion in Chapter 2), although Berkowitz and LePage (1967) do not believe that this is a sufficient explanation. Others have suggested that the presence of weapons is not sufficient if the person fails to interpret the weapons appropriately (Fraczek & Macaulay, 1971; Turner & Simons, 1974). At this point, then, it is best to conclude that although weapons sometimes increase the probability of aggressive behavior, we aren't yet certain of the exact conditions under which such effects occur.

To summarize the frustration-aggression theory, we can say with considerable certainty that frustration and aggression are often related. This is not to say that frustration always leads to aggression or that frustration is the only cause of aggression. But it is one possible cause.

Other theories have been developed in social psychology that also rely on motivational factors but do not necessarily involve frustration. Zillmann's **excitation-transfer theory** is one recent example (Zillmann, 1978, 1979). According to Zillmann, the expression of aggression (or any other emotion, for that matter) depends on three factors: first, some learned dispositions or habits of the person; second, some source of energization or arousal; and third, the person's interpretation of the arousal state. Parts of this theory are very similar to the work of Schachter (1964) on self-labeling of emotions, discussed in Chapter 3. Thus, the way we interpret an event is important in determining whether we act aggressively. Zillmann has taken this analysis a step further, however, and suggests that energy may transfer from one situation to another. For example, imagine that you've just jogged five miles around a track. You're lying in the infield, recovering from the run, and a man yells an insult at you as he runs by. What would you do? If you had just settled down in the infield, you might not do anything. You might feel aroused, but you would attribute it to your exercise. However, if the insult were hurled a few minutes later, you might no longer be thinking of the exercise—but there might still be some arousal remaining. In this circumstance, that residual arousal might be transferred to the insulting incident, and you might react aggressively to your tormentor—more aggressively than if you had not just run five miles (Bryant & Zillmann, 1979).

Both frustration-aggression theory and excitation-transfer theory talk about drive or arousal state as a necessary condition for aggression. There are a number of important differences between the two theories, but each stresses the ways in which internal drives and external events or cues may combine to produce aggressive behavior.

C. Social-learning explanations of aggression

Our third theoretical explanation of aggression views aggression as a totally learned behavior. Rather than focusing on a concept of instinct or drive, social-learning theorists look to the environmental conditions that lead someone to acquire and maintain aggressive responses.

Many psychologists believe that although the aggressive behavior of lower animals can be explained by instinctual processes, the aggressive behavior of humans is not regulated by internal drives—rather, it is learned. Psychologist J. P. Scott has concluded that "all research findings point to the fact that there is no physiological evidence of any internal need or spontaneous driving force for fighting; that all stimulation for aggression comes eventually from forces present in the physical environment" (Scott, 1958, p. 98). If aggressive behavior is indeed learned, how does such learning take place? Proponents of this viewpoint have suggested two methods: instrumental learning and observational learning (Bandura, 1973).

The principle of **instrumental learning** says that any behavior that is reinforced, or rewarded,

is more likely to occur in the future. Therefore, if a person acts aggressively and receives a reward for doing so, he or she is more likely to act aggressively on other occasions. The possible range of reinforcements for humans is broad. For example, social approval or increased status can act as a reinforcement of aggressive behavior (Geen & Stonner, 1971; Gentry, 1970). Money can act as a reinforcement for adults (Buss, 1971; Gaebelein, 1973), and candy has proved to be an effective reward for children (Walters & Brown, 1963). For the person who is extremely provoked, evidence of a victim's suffering can serve as a form of reinforcement (Baron, 1974; Feshbach, Stiles, & Bitter, 1967), suggesting a mechanism whereby mass executioners are able to perform their activities.

Although many aggressive responses can be learned through direct reinforcement, most investigators believe that **observational learning,** or social **modeling,** is a more frequent method of acquiring aggressive behaviors. Specifically, we can learn new behaviors by observing the actions of other people (called *models*). Consider the following situation. A child in a nursery school is brought to a room and asked by an experimenter to play a game. The experimenter then takes the child to one corner of the room and shows him or her how to make pictures by using potato prints and colorful stickers. Soon thereafter, the experimenter brings an adult into the room and takes that person to another corner, where a mallet, a set of Tinker Toys, and an inflated Bobo doll are placed.

After the experimenter leaves the room, the adult begins to play with the "adult toys." In a nonaggressive condition, the adult plays quietly with the Tinker Toys for ten minutes. In an aggressive condition, the adult spends most of the time attacking the Bobo doll, hitting it, kicking it, pounding its nose, and yelling aggressive comments such as "Sock him in the nose!" Then the experimenter returns and takes the child to another room with another set of toys. After frustrating the child briefly by telling him or her that play with a favorite toy is not allowed, the experimenter gives the child an opportunity to play with any of the other toys in the room. These include aggressive toys (such as a Bobo doll, a mallet, and several dart guns) and nonaggressive toys (such as crayons, toy bears, a tea set, and plastic farm animals).

In this and similar experiments by Bandura, Ross, and Ross (1961, 1963a), experimenters were interested in the ways in which the observation of an adult's aggressive behavior would affect a child's play choices. The adult's behavior did have an effect (see Photo 8-4). Children who had watched an aggressive adult model were consistently more aggressive than those children who had watched a nonaggressive model. (They were also more aggressive than members of control groups, who had watched no model at all.)

Although these experiments show that children can model behaviors they observe, some critics have suggested that the studies do not really focus on aggression (Klapper, 1968). Recall that our definition limits aggression to behavior directed against another living being. A Bobo doll doesn't seem to qualify. However, recent investigations have shown that attacks directed toward a Bobo doll do relate to other forms of aggression. Nursery school children who behaved most violently toward the inanimate doll were also rated as being most aggressive in general by their teachers and their peers (Johnston, DeLuca, Murtaugh, & Diener, 1977).

Even if an attack on a Bobo doll cannot be considered true aggression, Bandura (1973) has argued for the importance of the experiments in demonstrating the ways in which aggressive behaviors can be acquired. He makes the important distinction between *learning* and *performance* of a response. Presumably, when children observe the attacks, they learn, or acquire, a response; subsequently, when interacting with human beings, they may *perform* the acquired response. Many studies with adults attest to the importance of modeling (Bandura, 1973). Although most adults know how to be aggressive, their willingness to do so is often based on the presence of an aggressive

PHOTO 8-4. *Children playing with Bobo doll after observing an aggressive model.*

model. The model might not serve as an instructional source, but he or she could act as a *disinhibiting* factor—an example that says "It's all right to be aggressive in this situation."

In summary, social-learning theorists focus not only on the ways in which aggressive behavior is learned but also on the conditions under which it is instigated and maintained (Bandura, 1973; Baron, 1977). They focus on the external conditions that lead to aggressive behavior and, on the opposite side of the coin, control aggression. We will return to the issue of control later. At this point, however, it is important to note that if aggression is externally rather than internally determined, the possibilities of controlling aggression may be more promising.

■ III. Conditions that influence aggression

We've examined three theoretical perspectives that differ in the degree to which they believe aggression is caused by innate factors; they also differ in the degree to which they consider environmental factors to be important. Each perspective, however, gives some recognition to the importance of environmental factors: as a releasing mechanism for the ethologists, as a stimulus cue in the revised frustration-aggression hypothesis, and as a direct source of learning and performance for the social-learning theorists. Let us now turn to a consideration of some of these external factors that influence aggressive behavior.

A. Frustration

As we said earlier, an experience of frustration—the blocking of a goal-directed response—can lead to aggressive behavior on some occasions. For example, Geen (1968) asked subjects to work on a jigsaw puzzle. In one condition (task frustration), the puzzle had no solution; in another condition (personal frustration), the task was solvable, but the experimenter's confederate continually interfered with students as they worked, preventing them from completing the puzzle. In both experimental conditions, subjects were more

aggressive toward the confederate than the subjects in a control condition were. Yet, other studies have failed to find a relation between frustration and aggression, suggesting, as discussed earlier, that the relation between the two factors is not an automatic one. Two conditions are important in predicting whether frustration will lead to aggression: (1) the magnitude of the frustration experienced by the potential aggressor and (2) the extent to which the thwarting is arbitrary or unexpected (Baron, 1977).

Frustrations of a fairly mild nature are unlikely to result in aggression; in contrast, intense frustration often leads to aggressive behavior. A field study by Harris (1974) suggests the importance of the level of frustration. Harris had her confederates purposely cut in ahead of people standing at different points in lines at theaters and grocery stores. If the confederate cut in ahead of the person who was second in line, that person tended to become quite aggressive (verbally), whereas a person who was twelfth in line exhibited many fewer aggressive reactions. Presumably, when you are close to the checkout counter or the ticket window, an interference is much more frustrating than when you still have a considerable way to go.

Aggressive responses also depend on how arbitrary the frustration is. In one demonstration of this relationship, Burstein and Worchel (1962) found that group members whose progress was impeded by a member who had a hearing problem were much less aggressive than those group members who had equal difficulty because of one member who appeared to be deliberately blocking the group's progress. Other studies have shown that frustration leads to aggression only when the goal blocking was not expected (Worchel, 1974).

B. Verbal and physical attack

Although frustration occupied early investigators seeking the causes of aggression, recently the focus has turned to an even more obvious determinant of aggressive behavior—direct verbal and physical attacks. When someone yells at you for no apparent reason, are you likely to scream back? Or if someone walked up to you in the street and began to shove you, how would you react? In all probability, you would be tempted (and might well act) to retaliate with some form of verbal or physical aggression.

Attacks are a much more reliable provocation to aggressive behavior than frustration. For example, in the experiment in which Geen (1968) manipulated two types of frustration while students were working on a jigsaw puzzle, a third experimental condition was included in which the subjects were allowed to complete the puzzle (thus eliminating the possibility of frustration). At the completion of the task, however, the confederate proceeded to insult the subject, attacking both his intelligence and his motivation. In this condition, subsequent aggression toward the confederate was stronger than in either of the frustration conditions. In line with these findings, many laboratory investigations of aggressive behavior have included verbal attack prior to the assessment of aggression (Berkowitz, 1965a; Buss, 1966; Rule & Hewitt, 1971).

Taylor and his colleagues (Taylor, 1967; Taylor & Epstein, 1967) have also looked at the effect of direct attack on subsequent aggression. In these experiments, the subjects weren't asked to administer shocks to a passive learner; instead, they engaged in a two-person interaction in which both persons were allowed to administer shocks. (In actuality, the subject's opponent was a confederate of the experimenter or was fictitious—the subject was told that another person was returning the shocks, but in fact the schedule of shocks was arranged by the experimenter.) In general, these experiments provide clear evidence of reciprocity—subjects tended to match the level of shock that their opponent delivered. If the opponent continued to increase the level of shock, the subject also increased the intensity. Although the absolute level of shock can vary with certain factors—for example, both males and females are more reluctant to administer shock to a female than to a male (Taylor & Epstein, 1967)—the general pattern of increases and decreases in response to the partner's pattern holds true.

We do not always retaliate immediately when we are attacked by another person. Remembering the discussion of attribution in Chapter 4, you might suspect that our explanations of an attacker's motives could affect our reactions. Did the person *intend* to harm us? Could he or she have foreseen the consequences of the action? The answers that we give to questions such as these do indeed affect our subsequent aggressive behavior (Ferguson & Rule, 1983).

In one demonstration of the role of attributions, college men received bursts of aversive noise from a male opponent (Dyck & Rule, 1978). The noises were described as either typical of most people (high consensus) or atypical of most people (low consensus). A second variable that the experimenters manipulated was whether the opponent had any knowledge of the consequences of his action— whether he knew the type and level of noise that he was imposing on the subject. Both factors affected the amount of aggressive behavior that subjects showed. Less retaliation was shown when the behavior was believed to be typical (thus leading the attribution away from the particular individual) and when the subject believed that the opponent was not aware of the consequences of his actions. Further demonstrating the crucial role of intent, Greenwell and Dengerink (1973) found that the intentions of the opponent could be more important than the actual amount of harm the opponent caused. What we think the person is trying to do seems to be the more significant influence.

C. Third-party instigation

Aggression doesn't always occur when two persons are in isolation. Often there are witnesses and bystanders who become involved in the interaction. At a prize fight, for example, members of the audience can enthusiastically urge their favorite to pulverize his opponent. Newspapers frequently report incidents in which pedestrians urge a potential suicide victim to jump (see Box 8-1). What are the effects of such third-party instigations on the frequency and intensity of aggressive behavior?

In a famous series of experiments, Milgram (1963, 1964a, 1965, 1974) explored the effect of an experimenter's commands on the willingness of subjects (in this case, men in New Haven and Bridgeport, Connecticut) to administer shock to

BOX 8-1. The baiting crowd

"A Puerto Rican handyman perched on a 10th floor ledge for an hour . . . as many persons in a crowd of 500 . . . shouted at him in Spanish and English to jump. Even as cries of 'Jump!' and 'Brinca!' rang out, policemen pulled the man to safety from the narrow ledge" (*New York Times*, quoted in Mann, 1981, p. 704).

Why would a crowd bait a person to commit suicide? This kind of incident doesn't happen very often, but when it does, serious questions are raised about human behavior. To understand more about this aspect of group behavior, Leon Mann (1981) analyzed newspaper reports of 21 cases in which a crowd was present when someone was attempting to commit suicide by jumping from a building, a bridge, or a tower. In 10 of these cases, the crowd had urged the person to jump.

Two factors were significantly associated with the baiting crowd. First, crowds were more likely to urge the victim on in evening hours—baiting was more common after six at night than earlier in the day. Second, baiting was less likely when the potential suicide victim was higher than the 12th floor of the building. In the few cases when bystanders were very close to the person, baiting did not occur.

Both nighttime and distance from the victim are factors that would increase deindividuation (discussed in Chapter 2). When people are farther away from a victim, aggression is more likely. (If the victim is too far away, however, potential hecklers may realize that their cries will not be heard.) Like distance, the cover of darkness increases anonymity, and, in this case, it made aggression more likely. ■

maximum level, which was labeled highly dangerous (for more details on this experiment, refer to Chapter 12). Many of the subjects agreed to administer this level of punishment. In subsequent studies, Milgram removed the pressure of the experimenter's presence but substituted peers who were instructed to urge the subject on. Once again, the effect of external pressure was clear: subjects who were prodded to be aggressive delivered much greater shock than subjects who acted alone.

Not all bystanders are so intrusive, however. What happens when a witness simply observes the aggressive behavior but neither urges nor condemns it? Borden (1975) has demonstrated that the effect of the observer depends in large part on the implicit values he or she conveys. For example, in one case, male subjects participating in the standard shock experiment were observed by either a male or a female student. Subjects who were observed by a male showed a significantly higher level of aggression than subjects who were observed by a female. After the male observer left, the subjects reduced their level of aggression, whereas subjects' behavior was relatively unaffected by the departure of the female. Why did the sex of the observer have an effect? Borden hypothesized that the norms of our society implicitly suggest that males approve of violence whereas females are opposed to it. To test this hypothesis of implicit values, Borden conducted a second experiment in which the observer belonged either to a karate club (aggressive observer) or to a peace organization (pacifistic observer). In this case, the sex of the observer was also varied, so that both males and females assumed the aggressive and pacifistic roles. With a control over the explicit values of the observer, the sex of the observer had no effect; however, the explicit values were influential. Subjects who were observed by a member of the karate club were more aggressive than subjects who were observed by a member of a peace organization. Once again, the departure of the aggressive instigator led to a decrease in shock levels, but the departure of the pacifist resulted in no increase in shocks.

Let's look at one more aspect of third-party instigation. Turning the tables slightly, let's look

another person. Subjects, who believed they were participating in a learning experiment, were urged to increase shock levels to their partner up to the

at how the aggressor can affect the instigator. Are instigators of aggression influenced by the degree to which someone follows their recommendations? Gaebelein has conducted a series of studies examining the behavior of the person who instigates aggression (Gaebelein, 1973, 1977a, 1977b, 1978; Gaebelein & Hay, 1974; Mander & Gaebelein, 1977; White & Gruber, 1982). Her studies show that instigators will urge more aggression if their recommendations are followed. In contrast, if that person refuses to be aggressive, the instigator will reduce his or her urgings. Thus, cooperation in this situation would lead to an increasing level of violence, whereas noncooperation would tend to decrease the level of hostility. Another way to reduce the instigation is to involve the instigator directly in the situation, allowing that person to both give and receive shock directly. Gaebelein and Hay (1974) found that instigators tend to "cool it" when they themselves are vulnerable to shock.

In summary, direct urging by an observer or audience member will increase the amount of aggression a person displays. Furthermore, an observer who reflects aggressive values can cause increases in aggressive behavior. The instigator is not totally removed—his or her behavior is affected by the cooperation or noncooperation of the aggressor, and the instigations may wane when the recommended aggression is not forthcoming.

D. Deindividuation

When people can't be identified, they are more likely to perform antisocial acts. As we saw in Chapter 2, students who participated in a laboratory experiment that involved administering shock were more likely to be aggressive when they were completely disguised by hoods and sheets than when they were identified by name tags (Zimbardo, 1970). Other experiments have used similar manipulations of anonymity and have found that people are more likely to express both physical and verbal hostility when their own identity is not stressed (Cannavale, Scarr, & Pepitone, 1970; Festinger, Pepitone, & Newcomb, 1952; Mann, Newton, & Innes, 1982). In discussing **deindividuation,** Zimbardo (1970) has suggested that conditions that increase anonymity serve to minimize

concerns with evaluation and thus weaken the normal controls that are based on guilt, shame, and fear. More recently, Prentice-Dunn and Rogers (1982) have pointed to the concept of private self-awareness (see Chapter 3). When focus is shifted to external cues, private self-awareness decreases. No longer as tuned to themselves, people seem more willing to engage in aggressive behavior.

The concept of deindividuation can be applied to the victim as well as to the aggressor. For example, Milgram (1965) found that people were more willing to administer electric shocks when they couldn't see the victim and when the victim couldn't see them. (Also see Box 8-1.) In some ways, aggression under these conditions is dehumanized— because people cannot see the consequences of their actions, these actions may be easier to perform. It is probably significant that the genocide of World War II involved gas chambers that could be controlled from a distance and that hoods are often placed over the heads of execution victims. Even when aggression is not severe (for example, honking your horn at a stalled driver in front of you), a driver who cannot see the "victim" (because a curtain is drawn across the rear window) will be more likely to honk at a stalled motorist (Turner, Layton, & Simons, 1975).

E. Drugs and alcohol

Drugs and alcohol are widely used in our society. Popular wisdom suggests that alcohol facilitates aggression, and cartoons of the hostile drunk are common. Similarly, many people believe that marijuana has the opposite effect—that it tends to "mellow people out" and minimize any tendencies toward aggression. In this instance, the popular wisdom appears to be close to the mark, although research on the topic is still in an early stage. Taylor and his colleagues have conducted a series of studies in which various dosages of either alcohol or THC (tetrahydrocannabinol, the major active ingredient of marijuana) are administered to subjects before they participate in an aggression experiment (Shuntich & Taylor, 1972; Taylor & Gammon, 1975, 1976; Taylor, Schmutte, & Leonard, 1977; Taylor, Vardaris, Rawtich, Gammon, Cranston, & Lubetkin, 1976). In the aggression situation, subjects compete against a partner in a reaction-time experiment; each player has an opportunity to shock the player who loses on a trial. These specific conditions are important to remember, because it appears that effects are found only when a person is provoked or attacked (Taylor, Gammon, & Capasso, 1976). What happens when alcohol or THC is present in the bloodstream of a potential attacker? As shown in Figure 8-1, the two substances have quite different effects. Although low doses of alcohol (.5 ounce of alcohol per 40 pounds of body weight, or the equivalent of one cocktail) actually reduce the level of aggression (compared with a group that has had no alcohol), larger doses of alcohol (1.5 ounces per 40 pounds of body weight) have quite the opposite effect: subjects who had consumed large doses of alcohol gave substantially stronger shocks.

Marijuana has a different effect. Small amounts of THC (1.82 milligrams per 40 pounds of body weight) have virtually no effect on aggressive behavior, whereas larger doses (5.44 milligrams per 40 pounds of body weight) decrease the tendency toward aggressive behavior. Although too little research has been done to regard these results

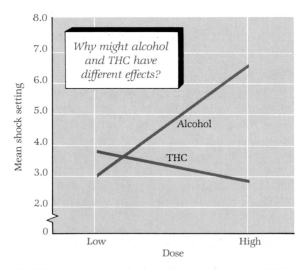

FIGURE 8-1. Mean shock setting as a function of high and low doses of alcohol and THC. Increasing the amount of alcohol in the system leads to greater aggression in the laboratory setting, while THC tends to have the opposite effect.

as conclusive, they certainly suggest that reasonably large amounts of alcohol can cause an increase in aggressive behavior—at least in response to provocation—whereas marijuana inhibits aggressive reactions.

F. Environmental factors

Popular wisdom has also suggested links between the physical environment and behavior. For example, you might complain that you feel grouchy because the air conditioning in your room doesn't work on a hot day or because the noise of construction outside makes you irritable. Do these conditions—specifically, noise and heat—have any demonstrated effect on aggressive behavior?

Research suggests that unpleasant levels of noise can sometimes increase aggressive behavior. For example, Donnerstein and Wilson (1976) found that subjects who were exposed to loud bursts of noise delivered significantly higher levels of shock to a partner than did subjects exposed to either low-level noise or no noise at all. Other investigators have had similar results (Geen & O'Neal, 1969; Konečni, 1975a). In each case, however, increases in aggression were found only when the subjects had been provoked or angered. Like alcohol, the external stimulus in itself is not sufficient to produce aggression, but it does lower the threshold, so that when an instigation to aggression is present, the aggression will be displayed more readily.

The supposed effects of heat on aggressive behavior have been more widely proclaimed than the effects of noise. During the extensive outbreak of civil disturbances in the United States in the 1960s, the mass media frequently emphasized the "long hot summer" effect (see Box 8-2). Heat was cited as a cause of riots. Indeed, the majority of disturbances did occur during summer (U.S. Riot Commission, 1968).

Laboratory experiments do not support a straightforward relation between temperature and aggressive behavior. In a series of experiments, Baron and his colleagues (Baron, 1972; Baron & Bell, 1975, 1976; Bell & Baron, 1976) found that, under some conditions, heat increases the tendency toward aggression, even in subjects who

BOX 8-2. Violence as a function of temperature

Is there a "long hot summer" effect? If so, what is its function? Do riots increase only up to a certain point as the temperature rises? Temperature and aggression are almost certainly related, but the exact form of that relation is still subject to dispute.

Using archival data, Baron and Ransberger (1978) tested the relation between temperature and instances of collective violence. First, they identified the instances of collective violence in the United States between 1967 and 1971. Then they obtained records of the average temperature on the days when the violence occurred. Plotting these two pieces of information on the same graph, they found the results shown below. (Because a number of the riots surrounded the death of Martin Luther King, Jr., two separate curves were calculated, although the two do not differ very much.) In general, the results seem to support Baron's contention that temperature and aggression are related in a curvilinear manner: riots are more likely to occur as the days

get hotter—but only up to a point.

This conclusion has not gone unchallenged, however. Underlining some of the problems of archival studies, Carlsmith and Anderson (1979) have suggested that Baron and Ransberger did not take account of the number of days in different temperature ranges. In other words, if 80-degree days are more common than 90-degree days, simple probability would lead us to expect more riots in the former periods than in the latter. By using simple probability theory, Carlsmith and Anderson calculated the likelihood of a riot for each temperature interval. Their results suggest a simple linear relation—the higher the temperature, the more likely a riot.

Both sets of investigators, however, agree that temperature and aggression are related, and both would probably agree that aggression would be unlikely if the temperature were 130°F. Their disagreement concerns the point at which the downward trend begins. ■

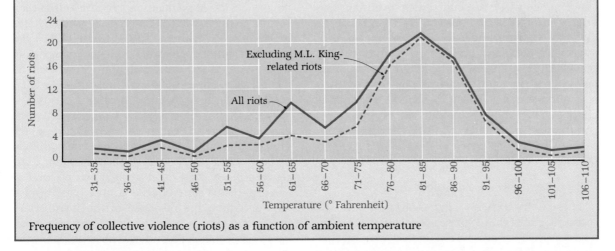

Frequency of collective violence (riots) as a function of ambient temperature

haven't been angered; however, in other cases, higher temperatures seem to decrease the tendency toward aggression. Although the initial set of findings was somewhat confusing, Baron (1977)

has provided an intriguing explanation that appears to incorporate all the findings. Specifically, he suggests that aggression is mediated by the level of negative affect or discomfort that a person experiences and that the relation between this discomfort and aggression is curvilinear. In other words, at very low or very high levels of discomfort, aggression is minimized. Aggression is most likely at intermediate levels of discomfort.

This complex explanation has been supported by other laboratory findings. For example, Palamarek and Rule (1979) either insulted or did not insult college males in a room that was either fairly comfortable (about 73° F) or unreasonably warm (about 96° F). When they were given a choice of tasks to perform, the men who had been insulted were more likely to choose a task that allowed them to aggress against their partners when the temperature was comfortable, but they were less likely to choose the aggressive task when the room was excessively warm. Again, these results support the curvilinear interpretation: moderate arousal, caused by *either* insult or heat, leads to greater aggression, but when both factors are present *or* when both are absent, less aggression occurs.

Let's consider one more kind of environmental influence—in this case, a substance put in the environment by humans. Perfume may seem to be a rather innocuous substance at worst and at best may be more associated with love than with anger. Baron (1980), however, has found that the presence of perfume may increase the level of aggressive behavior, particularly if a subject has previously been angered. Why would such an effect occur? One explanation invokes Zillmann's (1979) excitation-transfer theory, discussed earlier in this chapter. The arousal caused by the perfume may combine with the arousal caused by the provocation, leading to more aggression than would otherwise occur.

G. Cross-cultural comparisons

Those who explain aggression as a learned response claim that if there are societies in which no aggressive behavior is manifested, one can conclude that learning, rather than instinct, plays a dominant role in aggression. Such societies *do* exist. For example, in the United States and Canada, members of isolated communities such as the Amish, the Mennonites, and the Hutterites strive

PHOTO 8-5. *An Amish community.*

to achieve peaceful coexistence. The Hutterites advocate a life of pacifism; aggressive acts in their society go unrewarded (Eaton & Weil, 1955, cited in Bandura & Walters, 1963). Gorer (1968) has reviewed anthropological evidence of societies whose goal is peaceful isolation; these societies include the Arapesh of New Guinea, the Lepchas of Sikkim, and the Pygmies of central Africa.

The societies described by Gorer have several characteristics in common that facilitate the development and maintenance of nonaggressive behavior. First, they tend to exist in rather inaccessible places that other groups do not covet as a living area. Whenever other groups have invaded their territory, the response of the members of these societies has been to retreat into even more inaccessible areas. Second, members of these societies are oriented toward the concrete pleasures of life—such as eating, drinking, and sex—and an adequate supply of these pleasures apparently satisfies their needs. Achievement or power needs are not encouraged in children: "The model for the growing child is of concrete performance and frank enjoyment, not of metaphysical symbolic achievements or of ordeals to be surmounted" (Gorer, 1968, p. 34). Third, these societies make few distinctions between males and females. Although differences between men's and women's roles exist in each of these societies, no attempt is made to project (for instance) an image of brave, aggressive masculinity.

Although the majority of societies in the world exhibit some forms of aggression (Rohner, 1976), the existence of nonaggressive societies reminds us of the malleability of human nature and the great diversity in "normal" behaviors from one society to another (Eisenberg, 1972). Both within and between societies, there are a variety of conditions that encourage or discourage the display of aggression. Any instinctual readiness to aggress, if it exists, can surely be modified by the learning experiences that occur.

■ IV. Violence and the mass media

On March 30, 1981, John W. Hinckley, Jr., stood outside a Washington, D.C., hotel among a crowd of reporters and well-wishers waiting for President Ronald Reagan to appear. When the president came out of the hotel, Hinckley fired, wounding the president, his press secretary, and two other persons. Why did he do it? This disturbed young man apparently identified with the protagonist of the movie *Taxi Driver*, reportedly seeing the movie more than a dozen times and falling in love with the actress who had played the lead. By shooting the president, he somehow thought, he could make part of the film's fiction become his own reality.

Some years earlier, a 15-year-old boy in Florida killed his 82-year-old neighbor for no apparent reason. The lawyers for the defendant claimed that the boy was legally insane at the time of the murder as a result of watching too much television. (Their defense was unsuccessful, however, and the boy was convicted of murder.)

Do presentations of violence in the media encourage the observer to act aggressively? Is aggression in our society greater than it would be if such presentations were not available? We have already seen, in our discussion of pornography in Chapter 7, that pornographic material depicting violence against women does lead to greater aggression toward women by men who have viewed that material. Here we will look even more broadly at the issue of media and violence, particularly at the effects of television, which is watched by millions of people daily.

The existence of violence on television is not subject to dispute. On prime-time television, there are an average of eight acts of violence per hour. On children's Saturday morning cartoons, a violent act occurs every two minutes. It has been estimated that by age 16 the average child will have witnessed more than 13,000 killings on TV (Liebert & Schwartzberg, 1977).

The first evidence that witnessed aggression could lead to aggressive behavior came from Bandura's studies of children's behavior with a Bobo doll, discussed earlier. In some of these studies, the aggressive model was a live actor who was in the room with the child; in others, the model was shown on film or in the form of a cartoon character (Bandura et al., 1961, 1963a). In all cases, children who watched a model acting aggressively were more likely to engage in similar aggression against the Bobo doll.

There were a number of criticisms of these early modeling studies (see Klapper, 1968). Critics suggested that the laboratory setting was artificial, that a Bobo doll is not a real person, and that learning to be aggressive in a laboratory does not mean that one will perform those aggressive acts in other settings (a point that Bandura himself acknowledged). Subsequent studies, however, suggested that the laboratory experience could be a powerful one. Children who observe violence against a Bobo doll do act more aggressively toward a human clown as well (Liebert & Schwartzberg, 1977), and the amount of violence children show in play behavior is related to their level of aggression in other situations (Johnston et al., 1977).

In trying to learn more about the possible link between media violence and subsequent aggression, investigators adopted two strategies. First, they continued to do laboratory experiments, but they began to use actual film and television material rather than the more artificial Bobo-doll sequences. Second, many investigators moved out into the field, conducting field studies and using quasi-experimental designs to analyze the problem.

Within the laboratory setting, investigators were able to define some of the factors that are related to the acquisition and display of aggressive behavior. For example, some investigators have suggested that the observed violence must be justified in the film presentation in order for aggression to result (Berkowitz & Alioto, 1973). Other factors that appear important are the degree to which the observer identifies with the aggressor in the film, the initial aggressiveness of the observer, and the degree to which the villain has some redeeming features (Geen & Stonner, 1973; Liebert & Schwartzberg, 1977; Turner & Berkowitz, 1972). Although not all studies found a relation between media violence and aggression, the majority of studies do suggest that media presentations have an effect.

Field studies, as we know, sacrifice some control, but they allow us to look at people's natural viewing habits. A great many such studies have been conducted in recent years, and most of them confirm the relation between media violence and aggressive behavior (Eron, 1963; Eron, Huesmann, Lefkowitz, & Walder, 1972; Singer & Singer, 1981). Children who watch more violence on television are more aggressive. It is also true that children who are more aggressive are more apt to watch violent programs on TV (Eron, 1982). Not only does this relation hold true for children in

the United States, but it has been found among children in Finland, Poland, and Australia as well (Eron, 1982).

If we had only this kind of correlational data, we might not be so sure that media violence really *causes* aggression. But at least two kinds of evidence suggest that we can talk about causality. Longitudinal studies have looked at the amount of television that children watch when they are, for example, 8 years old and the amount of aggressive behavior they show ten years later. These correlations are statistically significant, often more significant than the two measures assessed at the same point in time. In other words, knowing how much television an 8-year-old watches tells us more about how aggressive that child will be at 18 than it does about how aggressive the child is now (Eron, 1980). Such evidence does not show that television is the only cause of violence, but it has become quite clear that it is one cause.

Another approach used to study the link between television violence and aggression is the field experiment. During a designated "Movie Week" in Belgium, investigators manipulated the amount of violent content that was shown on television (Leyens, Camino, Parke, & Berkowitz, 1975). Teenaged boys who lived in four small dormitories in a boarding school were observed before Movie Week started, and their aggressive behavior was recorded. Aggressive behavior tended to be high in two of the dormitories and relatively low in the other two. During Movie Week, the television sets that the boys normally watched were disconnected, and special movies were shown instead. Boys in two

PHOTO 8-6. *Children may become engrossed in television and adopt the messages it presents.*

of the dormitories (one high in violence, one low) watched only films that were saturated with violence, including *Bonnie and Clyde*, *The Dirty Dozen*, and *Iwo Jima*. The residents of the other two dormitories saw nonviolent films such as *Lili* and *La Belle Americaine*. Leyens and his observers then rated the amount of aggressive behavior shown by each boy during Movie Week and the following week.

The boys who saw the violent films showed increases in physical aggression. The authors concluded that "the films evoked among the spectators the kind of aggression they had been exposed to" (Leyens et al., 1975, p. 353). Verbal aggression, however, increased only among the residents of the aggressive dormitory who were shown violent films. Residents of the nonaggressive dormitory who saw the violent films actually exhibited a decrease in verbal aggression. As might be expected, the effects of the films were much more extreme just after viewing than during later observation periods. Other studies conducted recently in the United States have found similar results (Parke, Berkowitz, Leyens, West, & Sebastian, 1977).

On the basis of the evidence, collected through a variety of research methods, it seems reasonable to conclude that observing violence on television can increase people's tendency to be aggressive, both immediately afterward and at some distance in the future. Yet, it is also important to recognize that this link is not inevitable. Not all children who watch violence on TV will grow up to be aggressive adults. Furthermore, researchers have begun to explore the ways this link can be weakened. For example, it has been found that if a child watches violence on television in the presence of an adult who condemns the violence, that child is less likely to behave aggressively in later situations (Hicks, 1968; Horton & Santogrossi, 1978). (On the other side of the coin, condoning or encouraging comments made by an adult can lead to more aggressive behavior by the child.) The behavior of children's peers may also be influential (Leyens, Herman, & Dunand, 1982). Eron (1982) has experimented with short training sessions in which children are helped to discriminate television fantasy from real-life events, learning, for example,

how special effects are used to simulate violence. His results are encouraging, suggesting that a year later children who had gone through the three-hour training session were less aggressive than a comparable group of children who had not had the training. Programs such as these may serve as important keys to the control of aggressive behavior.

■ V. Violence in society

Questions about the effects of media violence have taken investigators out of the laboratory. In this broader setting, they have found ample evidence of aggressive behavior. Let's look more closely at some real-life aggression—behavior that is, unfortunately, very common in U.S. society and in many others as well.

A. Violence in the home

Apparently, when it comes to aggressive behavior, "there's no place like home." Commuter students, asked to describe episodes of anger that they had had, reported that episodes of verbal or physical aggression were most likely to occur in the home and that relatives (such as parents, offspring, and spouses) were the most frequent targets of aggression (Fitz & Gerstenzang, 1978). Indeed, such terms as *wife beating*, *husband beating*, and *battered children* have become common in recent years. Shelters for battered wives have been created in most major cities. In light of this evidence, some social scientists have described the family as the "cradle of violence" (Steinmetz & Straus, 1973).

Straus and his colleagues have conducted an extensive series of studies to describe and explain the incidence of family violence (Steinmetz & Straus, 1974; Straus, 1973). Their research shows that aggressive behavior in the family is extremely frequent, if not commonplace. For example, in a study of more than 2000 married couples in the United States (see Table 8-2), these investigators found that more than 25% of the couples had engaged in some form of physical violence during their married life. Both husbands and wives

TABLE 8-2. Percentage of couples engaging in each type of violent act

CRT violence item	Percentage	
	In 1975	Ever
Threw something at spouse	6.7	16.7
Pushed, grabbed, or shoved spouse	13.0	23.5
Slapped spouse	7.4	17.9
Kicked, bit, or hit with fist	5.2	9.2
Hit or tried to hit with something	4.0	9.5
Beat up spouse	1.5	5.3
Threatened with a knife or gun	1.0	4.4
Used a knife or gun	0.5	3.7
Any of the above	16.0	27.8

engaged in acts of violence, but the rates for husbands were higher for the more harmful forms of violence, such as beating or using a knife or gun. As seen in the table, some couples admitted engaging in each of the violent behaviors listed in 1975, the year the study was conducted, although in some cases the percentage of people was quite low. When couples were asked whether they had *ever* engaged in these behaviors, the frequency of positive responses increased in every case.

In many such cases, violence may create more violence. Some recent studies have shown that the majority of women who commit homicide (accounting for only 15% of all homicides) do so in self-defense against a boyfriend or husband. Often there is a history of wife abuse (Campbell, 1981; Jones, 1981).

Comparisons of social-class differences tended to challenge some popular stereotypes. Although white-collar workers indicated less approval of marital violence than blue-collar workers did, the reported frequency of actual aggressive behavior did not differ very much between the two groups. The fact that aggression between spouses is so common (and that such incidents are far more frequent than physical attacks between strangers or mere acquaintances) provides support for Straus's somber description of "the marriage license as a hitting license" (Straus, 1975).

Family violence is not restricted to parents. Children, too, become statistics of domestic violence. For example, a survey of university students revealed

that more than half had experienced either actual or threatened physical punishment during their final year of high school (Straus, 1971). Reports of child beating have become increasingly prominent in recent years. Although parent/child aggression is an obvious problem in itself, there are also suggestions that the consequences of such aggression extend far beyond the immediate incident. For example, Owens and Straus (1975) report that persons who experience violence as children are more likely to favor violence as a means of achieving personal and political ends as adults. In other words, through learning and role modeling, people can perpetuate the aggressive behaviors they learned as children.

B. Violence in the streets

Although the home is the most common site of violence, aggressive behavior in our society is by no means limited to the family. Reports of homicides, rapes, and other forms of aggression can be found daily in the newspapers, often as feature articles in some of the more sensational tabloids. According to the Federal Bureau of Investigation and the Royal Canadian Mounted Police, crime rates in the United States and Canada have been increasing yearly.

No single explanation accounts for these forms of aggression and violence. Although "individual criminal tendencies" may explain some occurrences, broader structural explanations are needed also. For example, Sanday (1981) has found that certain kinds of cultural groups are more likely to have a high incidence of rape than others. Looking at a sample of tribal societies, Sanday found that rape was most common in societies that had a high amount of interpersonal violence, generally supported male dominance, and encouraged separation of males and females. In contrast, societies that fostered greater equality between the sexes were likely to have a very low incidence of rape. Sanday's findings, though based on cultures in some ways quite different from our own, suggest that general cultural values may be related to particular forms of aggression and violence.

Exact figures on the incidence of aggression are difficult to obtain, particularly if one wants to make comparisons across countries. Differences in reporting procedures, for example, may exaggerate crime rates in one country while underestimating them in another. Available statistics, however, suggest that the United States has the dubious distinction of leading most of the industrialized nations of the world in crimes of violence. Such evidence certainly testifies to the importance of understanding the causes of aggression and seeing the problem of aggression as more than an academic issue.

C. Collective violence

Aggression is not only the act of a single individual acting alone. Collective violence—violence between nations or between identifiable groups within a nation—has played a role in most civilizations. In the United States, for example, incidents of violence were frequent between 1879 and 1889, whereas rates were low in the following decade (Levy, 1969). Again, in the 1960s, collective violence was frequent in riots by young people, ghetto residents, and others. Canada, too, has had its share of collective violence. Canadians have rioted over unemployment in the 1930s, conscription in the 1940s, and confederation itself in the 1960s and 1970s.

Why does collective violence occur? Davies (1962, 1969) has suggested that dissatisfaction occurs when a long period of rising prosperity is followed by a sharp drop in fortunes. The earlier increase in socioeconomic or political satisfaction leads people to expect the continuation of such improve-ments (thus producing a "curve of rising expectations"). When these expectations are frustrated, collective violence is more likely to occur. Economic trends in both the United States and Canada in the 1980s fit this general pattern, leading some to fear that collective violence will become more common.

Other theorists have developed Davies's ideas further, focusing on the concept of **relative deprivation.** According to this general theory, people compare their conditions with those of others (Crosby, 1976). Relative deprivation is "a feeling of discontent based on the belief that one is getting less than one deserves" (Martin, 1980). In *fraternal deprivation*, the comparison is made between one's own group and another group. For example, Blacks might compare their state with that of Whites, or women might make comparisons with men. In *egoistic deprivation*, the comparison is made on a more individual level, as if you were to compare your general situation with that of your roommate.

A number of factors influence feelings of relative deprivation. Among these are a belief that one deserves the particular outcome and a belief that one is not responsible for the failure to possess that outcome (Crosby, 1976). If a person feels deprived relative to some other person or group, what does he or she do? Martin (1980) suggests that the actions depend on how optimistic or pessimistic a person is about the situation. If there are some grounds for hope, a person may engage in self-improvement efforts at the individual level or constructive

PHOTO 8-7. *The aftermath of an urban riot.*

actions, such as voting, at the system level. If hopes are frustrated, however, less positive outcomes may result. An individual may turn to alcohol or drugs, and at the group level, collective violence may occur.

There is considerable support for this theory, ranging from laboratory experiments to historical analyses of cases as disparate as the French Revolution and the civil-rights protests in the United States. In each case, the evidence suggests that it is not those groups who are most oppressed who engage in collective violence; rather, it is those who have reason to believe that they should and could have something better. Or, as de Tocqueville once commented, "Evils which are patiently endured when they seem inevitable become intolerable when once the idea of escape from them is suggested" (quoted in Crosby, 1976, p. 85).

■ VI. The future: How can aggression be controlled?

Although some form of violence has always existed in our society, we can question whether aggression is inevitable. Can aggressive behavior be controlled or eliminated? The answer to this question depends on the assumptions one makes.

A. The instinctual and biological views

Theorists who believe that aggression is an innate characteristic of human beings are, predictably, the most pessimistic about the possibilities of controlling aggressive behavior. As Freud grew older and witnessed the devastation of World War I, he became increasingly resigned to the inevitability of aggression. His postulation of a death instinct—a compulsion in all human beings "to return to the inorganic state out of which all living matter is formed" (Hall & Lindzey, 1968, p. 263)—represented the culmination of his pessimism. He saw aggression as a natural derivation of the death instinct.

Psychoanalysts who adopt this position see little chance of restraining our violent behaviors. Freud himself wrote that there is "no likelihood of our being able to suppress humanity's aggressive tendencies" (quoted in Bramson & Goethals, 1968, p.

76). However, two procedures might provide some hope. One, at an international level, is a combining of forces to restrain the aggressive actions of powerful nations. At an individual level, the development of the superego can serve as a way of restraining innate aggressive impulses. Additionally, neo-Freudians advocate participation in socially acceptable aggressive activities (sporting events, debates, and the like) as a way of releasing aggressive energy.

According to ethologists and sociobiologists, who believe that aggression is innate, the possibility of eliminating aggression is unlikely. Our task, then, becomes one of channeling aggression into socially acceptable behaviors. Lorenz (1966), for example, believes that Olympic games, space races to Mars, and similar international competitions provide opportunities for the direction of aggressive behaviors into relatively harmless pursuits. The ethologists encourage us to try to identify, and thereby control, the cues that trigger the expression of aggression.

B. The motivational view

According to motivational theorists, frustration is a major cause of aggression, creating a drive or arousal state that will be expressed in the presence of appropriate cues. Consequently, we might look to ways of reducing frustration as a means of controlling aggression. Ransford (1968) interviewed Blacks living in the Watts area of Los Angeles and found that those with intense feelings of dissatisfaction and frustration were more prone to violent action. The attendant violence of Quebec's separatism movement has been attributed to social and economic frustrations. Community leaders can take numerous actions to reduce such frustrations: by providing better services, introducing human-relations training for police, and dealing directly with the causes of frustration, they could reduce aggression and violence.

Motivational theorists have suggested **catharsis** as a means of controlling aggressive behavior. Originally introduced by Freud, the term *catharsis* refers to the release of aggressive energy through the expression of aggressive emotions or through alternative forms of behavior. The role of catharsis in reducing aggressive behavior is stated clearly by Dollard and his colleagues: "The expression of any act of aggression is a catharsis that reduces the instigation to all other acts of aggression" (1939, p. 33). In other words, the concept of catharsis suggests that if you can get the anger "off your chest," you will be less likely to behave aggressively on future occasions.

Proponents of the catharsis hypothesis have suggested that fantasy is one way in which aggression can be reduced. Although investigators have found that aggressive behavior can result in a decrease in aggressive fantasies (Murray & Feshbach, 1978), the more important possibility (if one is interested in controlling aggressive behavior)—that fantasies can serve to reduce aggressive behavior—has not received much support (Hartmann, 1969; Walters & Thomas, 1963). There is somewhat more support for the notion of behavioral catharsis—that the opportunity to express aggression at the time of frustration reduces subsequent aggressive behavior (Konečni, 1975b). Behavioral catharsis, however, does not reduce the overall incidence of aggressive behavior—it simply controls the future expression at the cost of present violence.

More optimistic grounds for control of aggressive behavior concern the role of appropriate environmental cues. Because such cues are important in the elicitation of aggression and might even increase the strength of the aggressive impulse, removal of such cues should reduce aggressive behavior. Therefore, limits on the availability of guns and other aggression-eliciting stimuli could serve as a means of controlling aggressive behavior.

C. The social-learning view

Social-learning theorists are more optimistic about the possibility of controlling aggression. Because they believe that environmental factors control the acquisition and maintenance of aggressive behaviors, they maintain that appropriate changes in environmental conditions can cause a decrease in aggression and violence. For example, social-learning theorists suggest that observation of nonaggressive models leads to the acquisition

of nonaggressive behavior. In an experiment demonstrating this effect, students watched a subject administer shocks to a "victim" before the students were given their turn (Baron & Kepner, 1970). As shown in Figure 8-2, the students who had observed an aggressive model administered more shocks to the "learner" than subjects who had not observed a model. In contrast, students who witnessed a restrained, nonaggressive model were less aggressive. Other investigators have found similar results (see Donnerstein & Donnerstein, 1977), although the success of the model in reducing an opponent's aggression might be an important qualification (Lando & Donnerstein, 1978). Even more important, research has shown that if both types of models are present, the nonaggressive model can effectively negate the influence of the aggressive model (Baron, 1971). Therefore, even if we cannot eliminate the presence of all aggressive models in society, we might be able to reduce aggression by adding more nonaggressive models to the environment.

Learning theorists advocate nonreinforcement of aggressive responses (Brown & Elliott, 1965). If a person is not rewarded for displays of aggression, aggressive behaviors are less likely to be acquired or maintained. Some people have also suggested that punishment or the threat of it might serve as a deterrent to aggressive behavior (see Box 8-3). Actual punishment may be an effective deterrent under certain conditions. Baron (1977)

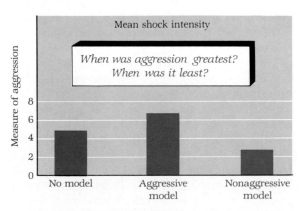

FIGURE 8-2. Impact of aggressive and nonaggressive models on overt aggression.

BOX 8-3. Is capital punishment a deterrent to violent crime?

Policy makers have often argued about the possible deterrent effects of capital punishment. Advocates of capital punishment believe that the threat of the death sentence will reduce homicide; opponents suggest that such threats of punishment will have no noticeable effect. For the most part, these debates have been carried on in the absence of data.

David Phillips (1980) recently conducted an archival study that presents some relevant information. Using reports of murders and capital punishments recorded in London between 1858 and 1921, Phillips found that homicides decreased immediately after a well-publicized execution—and then they increased. As the accompanying graph shows, homicides decreased (by about 35%) during the period just after an execution. During subsequent weeks, however, homicides increased above the rate that would be expected, returning to the base rate about six weeks later.

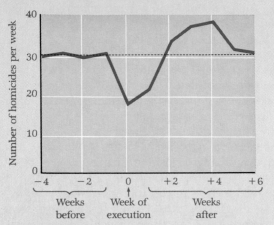

Thus, both advocates and opponents of capital punishment may have some basis for their beliefs. Capital punishment may serve as a deterrent in the short run, but the long-term effects are not evident—at least not in 19th-century England. ■

---

suggests four necessary conditions: (1) the punishment must be predictable, (2) it must immediately follow the aggressive behavior, (3) it must be legitimized by existing social norms, and (4) the persons administering the punishment should not be seen as aggressive models. If these conditions are not met, punishment could encourage aggression.

The conditions under which the *threat* of punishment can reduce aggression are perhaps even more limited. A threat appears to be effective only when the person making the threat is not terribly angry, when the expected punishment is very great and the probability of its delivery is high, and when the potential aggressor has relatively little to gain by being aggressive (Baron, 1977). These apparent limitations suggest that, in general, threatened punishment is not a very effective means of reducing aggressive behavior.

Investigators have pointed to incompatible re-

sponses as a third means of controlling violence. Basically, they suggest that because it is hard to do two things at once, the performance of violent acts should be reduced when conditions induce responses that are incompatible with the expression of aggression. Demonstrations of the effectiveness of this strategy have included the use of humorous cartoons (Baron & Ball, 1974), mild sexual arousal (Baron, 1976), and conditions that foster empathy (Rule & Leger, 1976). In each case, subjects were less aggressive when an alternative response was available than when aggression was their only choice.

Finally, social-learning theorists have pointed to cognitive factors that might inhibit aggressive behavior. Specifically, they suggest that information about mitigating circumstances can lead to reduced aggression. Basically, this theory suggests that explaining a person's aggressive behavior—providing reasons that suggest that the provocation was beyond the person's control—reduces the tendency to counterattack (Zillmann, Bryant, Cantor, & Day, 1975; Zillmann & Cantor, 1976). Of course, such mitigating explanations are not always available; however, to the extent that they can be introduced and accepted as reasonable, they allow people to consciously choose to reduce their aggressive tendencies.

In summary, the social-learning view of aggressive behavior provides some basis for optimism as we look to the future. A belief in innate aggressive tendencies might lead us to throw up our hands and say "There's nothing to be done; war is inevitable and people are naturally violent," but social-learning theorists point to specific environmental factors that can be controlled and changed. Even if such factors do not account for all aggressive behavior, they clearly account for a portion of it. These facts should not be overlooked as we seek a more peaceful human existence.

PHOTO 8-8. *Many people—young and old—believe that a better environment leads to a more peaceful existence.*

VII. SUMMARY

According to Freud and orthodox psychoanalysts, aggression is a physical urge that must eventually find release. Ethologists believe that intraspecies aggression has survival value, because it facilitates selective mating and dispersion of a species. However, most experimental social psychologists believe that aggressive behavior can be learned (much like other social behaviors). We define aggression as any form of behavior that is directed toward the goal of harming or injuring another living being who is motivated to avoid such treatment.

The various theoretical explanations of aggression focus on different causes and consequences. Biological explanations stress the innate character of aggression and consider aggression to be part of the basic human condition. Motivational explanations focus on aggression as a drive (either learned or innate) that can be elicited by environmental cues. The frustration-aggression hypothesis is one statement of this position. Experimental research shows that frustration can lead to aggressive behavior, but frustration is not a necessary condition for aggression to occur.

Social-learning explanations of aggression stress the ways in which aggressive behavior is acquired and maintained as a function of forces that are present in the physical environment. Both instrumental learning and observational learning are important processes in the acquisition of aggressive behavior. By observing aggressive behavior in other people, an observer can learn how to be aggressive; however, other conditions may be necessary in order for the learned behavior to be performed.

Many conditions can influence the occurrence of aggressive behavior. Frustration and direct physical or verbal attack can cause aggression; similarly, instigation by a third party can increase a person's aggressive behavior. Factors such as the level of frustration and the intentions of the person who attacks can affect the amount of aggression exhibited. Aggressive behavior is more likely to occur when the potential aggressor is not readily identifiable—when he or she is in a deindividuated state.

Research also suggests that moderate amounts of alcohol increase levels of aggressive behavior; marijuana, in contrast, appears to act as a deterrent. Environmental factors such as noise and heat can also affect the amount of aggression exhibited.

Cross-cultural comparisons suggest considerable variety in the levels of aggression, supporting the argument for learning as an important determinant of aggressive behavior.

Depictions of violence in the mass media can lead to increases in aggressive behavior. Early experiments with children and Bobo dolls have been followed by more realistic laboratory studies and by longitudinal studies of actual television-viewing habits in children. All these studies point to a link between media violence and aggressive behavior. There are procedures and training that can weaken this effect.

Considerable violence occurs in the home, between spouses and between parents and children. Other forms of violence in our society include homicide and rape, as well as incidents of collective violence—violence between nations or between identifiable groups within a nation. The concept of relative deprivation has been used to explain why some groups decide to revolt or express collective violence.

Prospects for the control of aggression in the future depend in large part on one's theoretical assumptions. A belief that aggression has an innate and instinctual basis leads to relatively pessimistic outlooks. Although aggression might be diverted into socially acceptable forms, its expression is inevitable. Motivational theorists, who believe that catharsis is a means of diverting aggression, point to the added importance of environmental cues. Social-learning theorists rely totally on environmental factors and, as a result, present the most optimistic picture of the control of aggression in the future. Suggested strategies for reducing aggression include the use of nonaggressive models, nonreinforcement and punishment, incompatible responses, and information about mitigating circumstances.

GLOSSARY TERMS

catharsis
deindividuation
ethology
excitation-transfer theory

frustration-aggression
  hypothesis
instinct
instrumental learning
modeling

neo-Freudians
observational learning
relative deprivation
sociobiology

Prosocial Behavior

It is more blessed to give than to receive.
■ ACTS 20:35

If it is more blessed to give than to receive, then most of us are content to let the other fellow have the greater blessing.
■ SHAILER MATHEWS

This chapter was written by Carol K. Sigelman.

Often it seems that all we read about in the newspapers is violence, war, and corruption. Yet, people do behave in more likable ways. They join forces to accomplish positive goals; they do favors for one another; they support charities. Occasionally they even risk their lives to save others:

> A young man, late one Saturday evening, was driving by a dance hall just as the dance was ending and the crowd was beginning to spill out onto the sidewalk. He noticed a lot of people suddenly running toward an area. Then, as he recounts what happened, he saw "this dude carrying a girl by her hair, dragging her and punching her, punching her out like a beanbag." At that point he became involved: "I went over there and I grabbed the dude and I shoved him over and I said lay off the chick. So me and him started going at it. I told him to get out of here, man, look at her, man, the girl's mouth's all bleeding, she got her teeth knocked out, she got a handful of hair pulled out. Everybody was just standing around" [Huston, Ruggiero, Conner, & Geis, 1981, p. 17].

This example of a real-life rescue attempt raises many questions: Why did this young man help, and why did the other bystanders fail to help? What really was his motivation, and what was going on inside him as he sized up the situation and decided to take action? Whatever the answers, we can call his act a clear example of what this chapter is about: **prosocial behavior,** usually defined as behavior that benefits others or has positive social consequences (Staub, 1978; Wispé, 1972). The term *prosocial* contrasts with the term *antisocial*, which applies to aggression and other negative forms of social behavior discussed in Chapter 8. A host of more specific behaviors can be viewed as prosocial—for example, intervention by a bystander, charity, courtesy, cooperation, donation, friendship, helping, rescue, sacrifice, sharing, and sympathy.

Notice that prosocial behavior has been defined in terms of its consequences. This raises some issues. For example, if you unintentionally worsen the condition of an accident victim to whom you are administering first aid, have you acted in a prosocial manner? What if you clearly benefit some-one by giving him or her money but do so in order to get a favor in return? The act has positive social consequences, but wouldn't most of us call it a bribe rather than a prosocial act? Because of such problems, it is often useful to consider not only the consequences of an act but the motives behind it. The clearest instances of prosocial behavior are those that merit the term *altruism*. **Altruism** is a very special form of helping behavior that is voluntary, costly to the altruist, and motivated by something other than the expectation of material or social reward (Walster & Piliavin, 1972). Altruism, then, is selfless rather than selfish, and prosocial acts vary widely in the degree to which they are altruistic.

Although there is much controversy about what prosocial behavior is and about whether true altruism is even possible, these definitions will serve us well in this chapter. We will focus most closely on *helping behavior*—prosocial behavior that clearly

PHOTO 9-1. *Helping behavior takes many forms, from giving aid after a life-threatening accident, as shown below, to the casual response to a request for direction.*

benefits another person rather than oneself, especially intervention by bystanders in emergencies and other helping acts that appear to be at least somewhat altruistic in motivation (see Chapter 16 for a discussion of cooperation, or working with others for mutual benefit).

The study of prosocial behavior has become one of the liveliest areas in social psychology. Although psychologists have always been concerned with negative social behavior, they have recently become more and more interested in positive social behavior (Wispé, 1981). Several recent books on the topic testify to this interest (for example, Derlega & Grzelak, 1982; Piliavin, Dovidio, Gaertner, & Clark, 1981; Rushton, 1980; Rushton & Sorrentino, 1981; Staub, 1978, 1979; Wispé, 1978). The behaviors studied have ranged from the merely considerate to the heroic—from picking up pencils, filling out questionnaires, and turning off the lights of parked cars to stopping a thief and helping the victim of an epileptic seizure. In some studies, the emergencies staged by researchers are so realistic and so intense that ethical issues arise about whether such research should be done (see Chapter 2). Yet, such research has much to say about people's behavior in emergencies.

We will begin our exploration of prosocial behavior by examining the challenge that the very idea of altruism poses to our understanding of human nature. Then we will look at what happens when an individual encounters a situation that calls for prosocial behavior and how social psychologists have tried to explain prosocial acts. Using these explanatory models, we can better interpret a wide range of influences on prosocial behavior—both factors in the situation, such as characteristics of the person in need and the presence of other people who could potentially help, and factors within the person, such as aspects of personality and moods of the moment. Throughout most of the chapter, we will be looking through the potential helper's eyes, but later we will shift our perspective to that of the recipient of help in order to understand why some prosocial acts are appreciated and others are not. Finally, we will try to apply what we have learned to the task of building a more prosocial society.

■ I. Prosocial behavior and human nature

There are many practical reasons for being interested in the study of prosocial behavior. We believe that the world would be a better place if people were more prosocial, and we deplore the cases we read about in which a person in desperate need of help fails to receive it. For psychologists, however, part of the fascination of prosocial behavior is theoretical rather than practical. The very existence of prosocial behavior, especially altruism, poses a challenge to psychology. Most psychological theories assume that human beings are basically selfish. How, then, can those theories account for our selfless actions? Is true altruism even possible? Is it conceivable that altruism is built into the very nature of human beings? These are perhaps the most important questions, and certainly the most fascinating ones, in the study of prosocial behavior.

A. Traditional psychological theories and altruism

Recall the psychological theories presented in Chapter 1. Psychoanalytic theory, for example, rests on an assumption that human nature is instinctively selfish and aggressive. How can it explain altruism? Not very easily. Some psychoanalytic theorists view altruism as a way in which people defend themselves against their own internal conflicts and anxieties, but this approach seems to deny that we can genuinely care for others. Other psychoanalytic theorists have taken a more positive approach and tried to understand how positive influences in personality development could reduce the strength of selfish motives and lead us to internalize more selfless values (Ekstein, 1978). Still, psychoanalytic theory is much better suited for explaining aggression than for explaining altruism (see Chapter 8).

Or consider stimulus-response and social-learning theories. A basic principle of stimulus-response theory is that we repeat and strengthen those behaviors that result in positive consequences for us. How, then, could altruism increase in strength, or even exist, since it is associated with negative consequences such as loss of resources, injury, and even death?

Some stimulus-response or social-learning theorists have dealt with the challenge by denying that true altruism exists. What appears to be altruism, they say, is really egoism, or self-interest. Some argue that there are rewards for seemingly altruistic acts but that they are subtle (for example, Rosenhan, 1978). People may feel better about themselves as a result of rushing to the rescue, or they may expect rewards in the afterlife. It has also been argued that by adulthood we have learned to find prosocial behavior rewarding in itself and no longer need external rewards to make such behavior worthwhile to us (Baumann, Cialdini, & Kenrick, 1981). Researchers acting within a stimulus-response framework have tried to show that helping is in fact reinforcing to the helper (for example, Aronfreed & Paskal, 1965; Weiss, Buchanan, Altstatt, & Lombardo, 1971).

Should we believe, then, that selflessness is really selfishness in disguise? Some of the arguments offered by S-R theorists sound somewhat circular; that is, they seem to assume that because the prosocial behavior occurred, its consequences *must* have been reinforcing. So strong is the belief that people act in their own self-interest that it is impossible for many psychologists to imagine an act that is not selfishly motivated. Stimulus-response theorists do make a useful point when they note that the rewards for altruism may be subtle. Even in the most heroic rescues, it is hard to prove that no selfish motivation whatever existed. At the same time, demonstrations that prosocial behavior can be reinforcing do not prove that prosocial behavior is *always* reinforcing. Like psychoanalytic theorists, S-R theorists still have difficulty explaining why people sometimes help others at huge costs to themselves and with little or no apparent reward.

B. Sociobiological theory and altruism

Recently another approach to understanding human social behavior has emerged, one that has many implications for our understanding of altruism and its place in human nature. **Sociobiology** is defined by Edward O. Wilson (1975) as "the systematic study of the biological basis of all social behavior" (p. 4). Sociobiologists try to account for the social behavior of various species in terms of the genetic makeup of those species as it has been influenced by their evolution over the ages.

If we held to the traditional theory of evolution developed by Charles Darwin and others, we would not get far in explaining altruism. Darwin's "survival of the fittest" view says that if genes contribute to survival and thus allow the individual to reproduce more frequently than less "fit" individuals, they will become more common in future generations of the species. But how could genes that predispose an individual to be altruistic be passed on with any frequency when altruists endanger their very survival for others? Sociobiologists, by revising evolutionary theory, have made some fascinating attempts to answer this question.

Consider an especially puzzling example of altruism among social insects. Female worker bees have evolved so that they are sterile. Instead of producing offspring of their own, they devote their lives to caring for the queen bee's offspring and even sacrifice their lives defending her hive. This is impossible to explain in terms of the survival of the fittest individuals. Sociobiologists have suggested, however, that it can be explained in terms of survival of the fittest *genes* (Hamilton, 1964; Trivers & Hare, 1976). As offspring of a single queen and as sisters, female workers share three-fourths of their genes with other workers and any future workers the queen may produce. By contrast, if a worker were able to reproduce, she would pass on only half of her genes to her own offspring, just as human parents do. At this point sociobiologists introduce the concept of **kin selection,** arguing that what matters in evolution is the survival of genes, which are shared with relatives (kin), rather than the survival of individuals. The worker bees can actually pass on more of their genetic material to future generations by helping the queen to produce more sisters than they could by reproducing themselves. The genes that make worker bees sterile and altruistic do not improve their own chances of survival, but those genes may have been selected through evolution because they enhance the survival of kin. Similarly, when an animal dies to save its offspring or other relatives, its genes are lost, but the genes of the kinship group survive and perhaps become more prevalent in future generations.

As you may have noticed, this is a view that, like so many others, regards altruism as a matter of selfishness—in this case, an interest in passing on as much of the family's genetic formula as possible. Altruism, according to sociobiologists, may be built into the genetic code of humans and other animal species because it has been effective over the ages in increasing the survival of kin.

Kin selection can perhaps explain our special willingness to help kin, but why would anyone help a stranger? Here the concept of **reciprocal altruism** has been introduced (Trivers, 1971). You may well risk your own safety to help someone, the argument goes, if you can expect help in return—help that will pay you back for your original sacrifice and will make both of you gain in the long run. Here selection over the course of evolution would favor those with genes predisposing them to altruism because in the long run altruistic acts are reciprocated and thus benefit the individual. Once again, then, altruism is interpreted as genetic self-interest: we would donate blood, for example, with the idea of getting blood back when we need it.

By applying such concepts as kin selection and reciprocal altruism, sociobiologists paint an unsettling picture of human nature. Taken to its extreme, this view suggests that "we are survival machines—robot vehicles blindly programmed to preserve the selfish molecules known as genes" (Dawkins, 1976, p. ix). At the same time, sociobiology carries a positive message by suggesting that altruism is part of the basic biological nature of human beings, just as self-interest is (Hoffman, 1981).

How strong is the evidence for this view? Almost all of it comes from studies with animals, and critics point out that there are important differences between social insects and humans and that, among humans, cultural influences and learning could account for the evolution of prosocial behav-

ior (D. T. Campbell, 1978, 1979; R. Cohen, 1978). Hoffman (1981), however, has drawn together a range of sociobiological and psychological evidence supporting the idea that altruism is part of human nature. Moreover, he proposes that the genetically influenced quality underlying altruism is **empathy,** or the vicarious experiencing of another's emotions, as when we shed tears with or feel the joy of our favorite movie stars. In support of this hypothesis, some fascinating studies indicate that we are designed from birth to respond to the distress of our human peers. In one recent study, newborns became distressed by the cries of other newborns and apparently could distinguish such cries from their own tape-recorded cries and the cries of chimpanzees, neither of which upset them (Martin & Clark, 1982). Recent research also suggests that individual differences in empathy among adults may have a genetic basis. Similarity on a measure of empathy was found to be greater between identical twins, who share all their genes, than between fraternal twins, who, on the average, share only half their genes (Matthews, Batson, Horn, & Rosenman, 1981). Finally, as we shall see shortly, several researchers emphasize the role of empathic emotion as a motivator of altruistic behavior. Hence, the concept of a genetic basis for altruism seems worth pursuing.

Such controversies over the nature (and even the possibility) of altruism are debates about the very nature of human beings. Psychoanalytic theory, stimulus-response theory, and sociobiology all assume that humans are basically selfish and interpret altruistic behavior as basically selfish, too. No one denies that people sometimes behave in ways that seem very unselfish. The most heated debates center on the motives behind such behavior: some theorists believe that the motives are ultimately egoistic, or selfish, but others argue that genuinely altruistic motivation based on empathy for fellow humans is possible and is distinguishable from more egoistic helping (for example, Batson & Coke, 1981, to be discussed in the next section). As long as altruism continues to challenge major conceptions of human nature, it will continue to fascinate social psychologists.

■ II. Why do we help? Models of prosocial behavior

Think back to the young man described at the beginning of the chapter. Certainly the most important question we can ask about him is why he leaped out to help the woman being assaulted. Why does any of us help? As we shall see, many factors influence whether a person will act pro-socially. Here we are concerned with the basic motivations and processes behind such behavior. In trying to explain why people help, social psychologists have emphasized their emotional reactions, their standards of behavior, and their decision-making processes.

A. Emotional arousal and empathy

Several researchers have proposed that emotional arousal is the key motivator of helping behavior, especially in emergencies. Emergencies are by nature sudden and emotionally involving. Even watching someone drop a pencil may produce mild forms of arousal, such as feelings of concern or obligation.

In their model of intervention in emergencies, Piliavin et al. (1981) emphasize the role of arousal in helping. They suggest that emergencies produce an arousal that bystanders are then motivated to reduce. If a person is aroused to the point of panic and sees little chance of accomplishing anything positive, the most direct way to reduce arousal may be to escape from the situation. However, when the victim's need is clear and severe, and it seems possible to be of aid without huge difficulties, arousal can be reduced by providing help.

Several studies show that emergencies are indeed physiologically arousing and, more important, that people who are more highly aroused are more likely to help or to help quickly. For example, Gaertner and Dovidio (1977) staged an emergency in which a stack of chairs apparently crashed down on a woman in the next room. Bystanders who had the fastest heart rates and reported that they felt the most upset intervened more quickly than those who were less aroused. However, the same study demonstrated that arousal alone is not sufficient

to motivate helping: thoughts are also important, for the arousal one experiences must be attributed to the victim's plight rather than to something else if helping is to occur (see the discussion of attribution theory in Chapter 4). Bystanders who were given a placebo drug that they were told would arouse them were slower to help in an ambiguous emergency than were bystanders who were given a drug that would supposedly give them a dull headache and other symptoms but would not arouse them. Those given the "arousing" drug could attribute the arousal they then felt when the crash was heard to the drug rather than to the crash. Thus, it seems to be important for emotional arousal to be interpreted as some kind of response to the emergency (see Chapter 4).

But what kind of emotional response do people in need elicit? Several theorists have emphasized one particular form of emotional reaction as the basis for helping behavior: *empathy*, or the vicarious experiencing of another person's emotions (Coke, Batson, & McDavis, 1978; Hoffman, 1981; Krebs, 1975). Coke et al. (1978) propose that taking the perspective of a person in need—a cognitive process—produces an emotional response of empathy. Empathy then motivates us to reduce the distress of the person in need. In these studies, college students heard taped broadcasts about people in need. Subjects who were asked to put themselves in the victim's place and who could not attribute any arousal they experienced to a drug they had been given helped more than those who were told to focus on the broadcasting techniques in the tape or who were able to attribute their arousal to a drug.

Batson and his colleagues have gone on to suggest that there is an important distinction between empathically focusing on another person's distress and being motivated to reduce it, on the one hand, and being concerned with one's own discomfort and being motivated to reduce it, on the other hand. Empathic concern may provide a genuinely altruistic motivation for helping (Batson & Coke, 1981). Such altruistic motivation does not appear to be present in lower species. Rats, for example, will respond to another rat's distress, but research demonstrates that their real concern is for themselves rather than for the other rat (Lucke & Batson, 1980). Among humans, however, empathic concern seems to exist, is separable from personal distress, and has different motivational properties than personal distress.

For example, Coke and his associates (1978) asked students who had listened to a plea for help with a research project to complete a scale measuring their emotional reactions. Some adjectives on the scale tapped empathy (for example, *compassionate*), while others measured personal distress (for example, *alarmed, upset*). Those who reported high levels of empathic concern were more helpful than those who felt little empathic concern, but degree of personal distress was unrelated to helping.

In a clever attempt to untangle empathy and personal distress still further, Batson, Duncan, Ackerman, Buckley, and Birch (1981) led some women to think they were experiencing empathic concern and others to think they were experiencing personal distress as they watched a woman apparently being shocked in a learning experiment. (For example, to make half the women experience personal distress but not empathy in response to the victim's plight, the researchers told them that the drug they were being given—actually a placebo—would create feelings of empathy. Any feelings of empathy would then be attributed to the drug, not to the victim's plight, and the primary response to the victim would be seen as personal distress.) Both groups of women were quite willing to help by taking some of the shocks themselves when they had no chance of escaping the situation. However, when escape was easy, the women experiencing personal distress were egoistic rather than altruistic, escaping rather than helping. Escaping, after all, is an easier and quicker way of reducing one's own unpleasant distress than helping is. By contrast, those experiencing empathic concern continued to help spare the woman her agony even when they could easily escape and turn their backs on her (see Figure 9-1). Thus, empathy, but not personal distress, appears to arouse a genuinely altruistic motivation for helping, which can be satisfied only by seeing another person's suffering end.

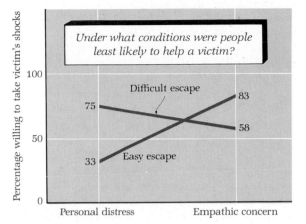

FIGURE 9-1. Empathy versus distress: Percentage of subjects who were willing to help a victim as a function of whether their arousal was labeled as personal distress or as empathic concern and of ease of escape from the situation.

Slowly, then, researchers are beginning to understand the emotions we feel when someone needs help. There is now solid evidence that emotional arousal motivates helping behavior—if that arousal is interpreted as due to an emergency situation or a victim's plight. Special attention has been given to the specific emotional reaction of empathy, for it implies a genuinely altruistic motivation for helping—a desire to reduce suffering that we, through our capacity for empathy, share with the person directly affected. Both empathic concern and personal distress can and do motivate helping behavior, for both are arousing. However, it is one thing to say that we help in order to reduce someone else's distress and another to say that we help in order to get rid of our own unpleasant feelings of disgust, fear, alarm, and so on. Thus, those who emphasize the role of emotion in motivating helping behavior must continue to grapple with the issue of how much of that emotion is altruistic and how much is egoistic.

B. Norms

Normative explanations of helping behavior suggest that we help others because we have internalized **norms,** or societal standards for behavior, and are motivated to act in accordance with those norms. What norms are relevant to prosocial behavior? One that has been proposed is the **social-responsibility norm,** which states that we should help those who need help (Berkowitz & Daniels, 1963). As we shall see, people are indeed likely to help those who appear to be dependent on them. However, we shall also see that there are many instances in which highly needy persons do not receive the help that the social-responsibility norm says they should receive. Most people endorse the norm verbally, but fewer act according to it (Piliavin et al., 1981).

A more powerful norm is the **reciprocity norm.** As conceptualized by Gouldner (1960), it states that people should help those who have helped them and should not injure those who have helped them. It is closely related to *equity theory* (see Chapter 6), which emphasizes the imbalance produced in a relationship when one person helps (or harms) another. Gouldner argued that the norm of reciprocity is universal and is essential to maintaining stable relationships among people. The only people exempt from the obligation to reciprocate are the dependent—young children, the ailing elderly, the sick—the very people whom the norm of social responsibility tells us to help.

There is no doubt that people usually feel strong feelings of obligation to reciprocate when someone does them a favor. Indeed, prison inmates have been known to capitalize on the norm of reciprocity by trying to "buy" and dominate newcomers through the giving of gifts (McCorkle & Korn, 1954). The very power of the reciprocity norm may be one reason that recipients of help are sometimes resentful, as we shall see later. Despite the power of this norm, however, it sometimes fails to operate (see, for example, Schopler & Thompson, 1968).

Even if we refer to both the norm of social responsibility and the norm of reciprocity in explaining helping behavior, normative explanations have been found wanting (see, for example, Latané & Darley, 1970; Schwartz, 1977). First, norms are so general that they may not tell us what to do in particular situations. Second, if most people in a society subscribe to such norms, how can norms explain individual differences in help-ing behavior? Third, two conflicting norms may seem equally applicable in a situation. For example, the norm of social responsibility is contradicted by a norm that says "Don't meddle in other people's affairs." And finally, people often do not act consistently with the norms they hold.

However, new life has been given by Shalom Schwartz (1973, 1977; Schwartz & Howard, 1981) to the normative approach to understanding prosocial behavior. Instead of focusing on general social norms, Schwartz and his colleagues have measured **personal norms**—the individual's feelings of moral obligation to act in a given way in a given situation. These feelings of obligation motivate us to help, and we are then rewarded by the recognition that we have acted according to our moral standards. Schwartz's normative model of helping shows how personal norms are activated in a situation and how additional factors must be considered before it is possible to predict behavior on the basis of normative beliefs.

For example, how would you respond to this question: "If a stranger to you needed a bone marrow transplant and you were a suitable donor, would you feel a moral obligation to donate bone marrow?" The question is a measure of one personal norm studied by Schwartz (1973). Along with it in the survey were questions assessing respondents' tendencies to use defenses to neutralize their personal norms. Specifically, Schwartz measured people's tendencies to accept or deny responsibility for the welfare of others. Three months later, respondents received a mail request to donate bone marrow. People with a strong personal norm motivating them to donate marrow were indeed more likely to act according to their beliefs—unless they also had a strong tendency to deny responsibility for the welfare of others. Those who denied such responsibility sometimes felt an obligation to help, but when it came to deciding, they may have talked themselves out of feeling personally responsible for helping. For them, there was no relation between the norm they verbalized and the way they acted.

In a wide range of studies by Schwartz and others, measures of personal norms, along with measures of defenses against those norms (such as denial of responsibility), have proved very useful in predicting behavior. Endorsement of broad social norms has not been so useful. Schwartz's model is more complex than earlier normative explanations. It specifies how a motivation to help, in the form of a personal norm, is activated in a situation and then how defenses come into play to determine whether a personal norm is acted on (see Figure 9-2). It recognizes that people differ not only in their normative beliefs but also in their tendencies to act consistently with their beliefs. By measuring personal norms relevant to a particular situation and by examining factors that determine whether norms are activated and then acted

on, Schwartz has shown that norms can play an important role in explaining why people act prosocially.

C. Decision making and cost/reward analysis

A third approach to understanding why people help focuses on cognitive processes—on how a potential helper perceives a situation and assesses the consequences of alternative actions. One way to think about the heroic young man at the beginning of the chapter is to view him as an information processor—taking in information, interpreting it, and acting on the basis of his analysis. All of us find ourselves in situations that call for deciding whether to help or whether to refuse, to ignore the victim's plight, or to run away. How does the potential helper size up a situation and decide whether to help?

Latané and Darley (1970) developed a five-stage model for analyzing decision making in emergencies, a model that is applicable in nonemergency situations as well. Each of its elements—noticing the situation, interpreting it as one in which help is needed, assuming personal responsibility, choosing a form of assistance, and implementing the assistance—must occur in some form, or no help will be provided. Obviously, nothing at all will happen if the potential helper never notices the person in need. Once that first step is taken, the potential helper may still fail to interpret the event as one calling for a helping response—or may recognize the need for help but not feel like the right person to provide that help. The photo essay on page 231 illustrates some of the considerations that may enter in at each step.

Viewing helping situations as decision-making situations focuses attention on the costs and rewards of deciding to help or not to help. In their arousal–cost/reward model of intervention in emergencies, Piliavin et al. (1981), as already noted, emphasize that bystanders to emergencies are emotionally aroused and are motivated to reduce that arousal. Decision-making processes enter in as bystanders evaluate the situation and seek to reduce their arousal in the least costly way they can. An analysis of costs and rewards leads to a

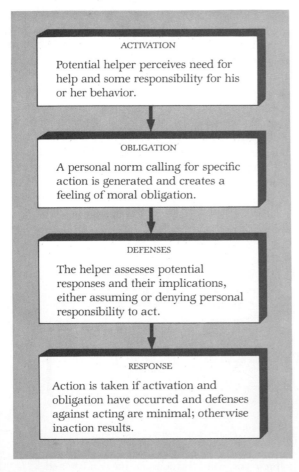

FIGURE 9-2. Schwartz's (1977) normative model of helping.

decision to help or not to help and influences the form that any assistance takes.

This model assumes, as do several social-psychological theories, that people are generally motivated to increase the rewards of their actions and decrease the costs. In emergencies and other helping situations, the focus is on costs, for the rewards are often few. Both the consequences of helping and the consequences of failing to help must be weighed; moreover, potential helpers must consider the consequences of an action not only for themselves but also for the victim.

What costs and rewards are relevant? First, there are the almost inevitable *costs of helping:* effort and time expended, loss of resources, risks of harm, possible embarrassment or disapproval by others, negative emotional reactions to interacting with the victim, and so on. Costs also include rewards one has to forgo in order to help (as when helping means missing an important appointment). To establish the *net* costs of helping, the bystander would subtract from these costs any potential rewards for helping: payments, social approval, increased self-esteem associated with being a helpful person and living up to personal norms, and so on.

But cost/reward analysis does not stop here. The *costs of not helping* must also be considered. Piliavin et al. (1981) break these costs down into personal costs and empathy costs. Personal costs of failing to help include such consequences as guilt, loss of self-esteem, and social disapproval. Empathy costs are tied to the knowledge that the victim will continue to suffer if no help is supplied.

It is essential to recognize that this cost/reward approach is concerned with costs and rewards as perceived by the potential helper. For example, faced with the assault described at the beginning of the chapter, our heroic young man may have perceived himself as capable of taking on the attacker without suffering a scratch, while other bystanders may have thought it would be their last day on earth if they intervened. Not only do different people calculate costs differently, but all of us are motivated to distort costs and rewards when we face a difficult decision. For example, one way out of the dilemma posed by an emergency in which the costs of helping and the costs of the victim's receiving no help are both high is to use cognitive distortion (Piliavin et al., 1981). We might downplay the consequences of failing to help by thinking "It's not so serious" or "Someone else will help, so there's no problem if I don't."

Many of the influences on prosocial behavior that we will discuss later in the chapter work by affecting perceptions of costs and rewards. Figure 9-3 summarizes the predictions that the model of Piliavin and associates makes about how a person is likely to respond when the costs of helping and costs of not helping are either high or low. For example, the model predicts that a person is most likely to help when the costs of helping are low

Costs of direct help

		Low	High
Costs of no help to victim	High	By all means, give direct help! Few costs, many benefits	A real dilemma: Help in an indirect, safe way, *or* distort things to rationalize escaping the situation
	Low	It depends: What are the norms in the situation?	Helping is not a good idea: Distort things or escape

You see a student drop her books. Which cell describes this situation?

FIGURE 9-3. Predicted effects of cost factors. Costs of helping and costs expected if the victim receives no help are considered in making a decision. The decision is especially difficult when both kinds of costs are high. In such situations, people sometimes throw cost considerations out the window and help impulsively.

A. *Summer in the city: some people read, while others engage in more physical forms of relaxation.*

B. *But Bill's exercise suddenly comes to a halt as a leg cramp doubles him up in pain.*

C. *Hearing Bill fall to the ground, Marlene looks up from her reading and sees that he is in pain.*

A CLOSER LOOK:
Deciding to Help

Often, perhaps daily, people around us need help. Sometimes the needs are minor, such as a request for directions or a dropped briefcase. At other times, the need for help may be more pressing and the situation even life threatening. When and why do we decide to help? Sometimes we don't help simply because we aren't aware of the need. Had Marlene been more engrossed in her book or had Bill been on the other side of the street, for example, his need may have gone unnoticed. Once someone becomes aware of a need for help, such things as the costs of helping or not helping, the rewards for doing so, and the person's beliefs about his or her ability to help come into play. Depending on the balance among these factors, help may or may not be offered. In this case, Marlene helped.

D. *"Is he really hurt?" "Should I offer to help?" "What could I do?" Marlene contemplates and then takes action.*

but the costs of not helping are very high. By contrast, little help is to be expected if helping is likely to be highly costly but there is no great cost if one fails to help. Much research supports these predictions.

The decision-making and cost/reward approaches to explaining helping behavior may strike you as too cold and calculating, too rational. Latané and Darley (1970) emphasize, however, that their steps may not occur one by one in a logical way. Emergencies, by their very nature, are dangerous, unusual, unique, unforeseen, and pressing. As a result, they produce arousal or stress which is not present in nonemergencies and which may interfere with rational decision making and action. Similarly, Piliavin and her associates do not call their model the "arousal–cost/reward model" for nothing; they too emphasize the arousing nature of emergencies and the interplay between arousal and cost/reward analysis. Indeed, they demonstrate that some emergencies are so clear and severe, and so arousing, that bystanders act impulsively, ignoring many cues in the situation, failing to weigh costs and rewards, and behaving in ways that look "irrational" to an outsider—much as our heroic young man did. Impulsive help, as the term suggests, is quick help—as when every one of the subjects in one study rushed to aid a workman who apparently crashed off a ladder, within an average of less than 10 seconds after the crash (Clark & Word, 1972). Piliavin et al. (1981) speculate that the impulse to act in such dramatic emergencies may be innate but that we are socialized to pay closer attention to cost and reward factors in less compelling emergencies.

We have now introduced three important aspects of the helping response: the motivational role of emotional arousal, particularly empathy with the person in need; the activation of norms relevant to helping and the motivation to act in accordance with internalized personal norms; and the cognitive processes involved in assessing a helping situation and weighing the costs of alternative actions. Armed with these models, we are now in a position to look more closely at influences on helping behavior. Like all social behavior, prosocial behav-

ior is influenced by characteristics of the situation, characteristics of the person, and the interaction between situational and personal factors. Let us examine some of the situational and personal factors that make prosocial behavior more or less likely to occur.

■ III. Situational influences on prosocial behavior

The situations in which prosocial behavior occurs vary widely, from emergencies to nonemergencies, from ambiguous situations to perfectly clear-cut ones. Accordingly, levels of arousal and empathy, relevant norms, and cost factors also vary widely from situation to situation. In exploring the impact of situational factors on helping, let us begin with what is usually the most prominent element in a helping situation—the person in need of help.

A. The person in need of help

Characteristics and behaviors of the person in need of help are situational cues that a potential helper reads as he or she interprets the situation and decides whether to help. Who receives help and who does not?

Nature of the need. By its very nature, helping is a response to a person in need, but the nature of the person's dependency on others influences the rate of helping behavior. Dependency can be a stable characteristic of a person (for example, a mentally retarded child) that elicits helpful responses from almost everyone. For instance, research suggests that elderly people are viewed as more dependent than younger adults and are helped more often (Weinberger, 1981). Dependency can also result from a temporary plight (for example, a sprained ankle). Finally, dependency can be the function of a relationship between two persons (for example, between parent and child). Berkowitz and his colleagues have shown that if dependency is introduced into the relationship between two persons—for instance, if a supervisor's rewards depend strongly on a worker's productivity—helping behavior is more likely (Berkowitz, 1978; Berkowitz & Daniels, 1963). Thus, the people who receive help seem to be the people who are dependent on others. However, potential helpers look closely at the nature of, and the reasons behind, an individual's dependency.

First, potential helpers weigh the legitimacy of a recipient's need. Imagine how you would react if a woman approached you in the supermarket and asked for a dime to buy milk. Then imagine the same woman asking for a dime for frozen cookie dough. Bickman and Kamzan (1973) found that 58% of the shoppers asked for milk money responded but only 36% were willing to shell out for cookie dough. The more legitimate the need, the more help will be received.

Potential helpers are also influenced by the causes of dependency or need. Bernard Weiner (1980), for one, has placed great emphasis on our attributions about the reasons for an individual's need for help (see Chapter 4). Suppose that you are approached by a fellow student in need of your class notes. Will you be more likely to help the student who claims to be unable to take good notes or the student who just skips class because of lack of motivation? Research suggests that you are more likely to help if the need is due to something uncontrollable, such as lack of ability or the professor's shortcomings, than if it is due to something more controllable, such as lack of effort (Barnes, Ickes, & Kidd, 1979; Weiner, 1980). Perhaps for similar reasons, a "sick man" with a cane who collapses on the subway is helped more than a "drunk" carrying a bottle and smelling of liquor (Piliavin, Rodin, & Piliavin, 1969). Generally, people who are dependent through no fault of their own are helped more than people who can be blamed for their dependency. According to Weiner, our attributions about the cause of dependency influence the nature of our emotional response. When we attribute need to uncontrollable factors, positive emotions such as empathy are aroused, and they, in turn, motivate helping. However, when we attribute need to controllable factors and, therefore, hold a person responsible for his or her plight, negative emotions such as disgust and anger are aroused, and

PHOTO 9-2. *Both this man's condition and his age convey a message of need for help.*

these emotions motivate us to avoid the person.

All this is quite straightforward. The people who receive help are those who are dependent, whose need is legitimate, and whose need is not their fault and not under their control. But a puzzle arises: sometimes the people who should have the greatest claims on us for these very reasons are not given the help they deserve. Consider these findings: a person with a birthmark who collapses receives less help than a person without a birthmark (Piliavin, Piliavin, & Rodin, 1975); a person with a bandaged forearm receives more help picking up dropped envelopes than a nondisabled person, but a person with a bandaged forearm, an eye patch, and a scar receives no more help than a nondisabled person (Samerotte & Harris, 1976). The only way we can account for these curiosities is to consider the costs of helping. People often experience an aversion to persons who are disabled, disfigured, or otherwise stigmatized, and they may be reluctant to pay the extra "costs" of interacting with such persons, despite their dependency. This is especially true when other costs of helping are high. For example, salespersons in shoe stores spent more time helping a customer who limped in with a broken heel than helping a "normal" customer when the store was almost empty, but they spent slightly *less* time helping this more dependent person when the store was busy and the salesperson risked losing business (Schaps, 1972). We must recognize that even the most dependent and worthy persons do not always elicit the help to which they seem entitled, especially as the perceived costs of helping escalate.

Relationship with the potential helper. We cannot consider the characteristics of the person in need of help entirely in the abstract; we must also take into account the relationship between that person and the potential helper. Relationships between relatives or friends imply mutual dependency and a special obligation to help. Indeed, studies of tornadoes and other disasters indicate that people tend to help family members first, then friends and neighbors, and finally strangers (Form & Nosow, 1958). Different norms seem to apply to such close relationships than apply to less intimate relationships (Clark, 1981; Clark & Mills, 1979). Yet, even though intimate relationships are special, even a brief acquaintance or familiarity increases the rate of helping (Latané & Darley, 1970; Pearce, 1980). So does the expectation of future interaction (Gottlieb & Carver, 1980).

Those persons with whom we have some relationship are seen as part of our "we-group." As Hornstein (1976, 1982) and others have suggested, we become more emotionally involved when someone in our "we-group" is in trouble, and we are motivated to reduce the tension we experience. We might also view the rewards of helping and the costs of not helping such a person as greater than if the person were a total stranger.

This suggests that we will be especially helpful to anyone who is similar to ourselves in some important way. Indeed, we generally are. For example, Krebs (1975) led subjects to believe that they were either similar or dissimilar to a person whom they watched receiving rewards and punishments in a roulette game. Those who believed themselves similar to the roulette player not only were more emotionally aroused as they watched but were more likely to help the person at a cost to themselves. "Hippie" and "straight" subjects have been found to be more likely to give dimes to those who resemble them in dress than to dissimilar solicitors (Emswiller, Deaux, & Willits, 1971). People are also more helpful to those who share their opinions and beliefs than to those who disagree with them (Sole, Marton, & Hornstein, 1975).

Similarity is, of course, a major basis for attraction to other people (see Chapter 6). Not surprisingly, other aspects of attractiveness have also been found to influence helping responses. For example, pleasant people are helped more than unpleasant ones (Gross, Wallston, & Piliavin, 1975), and applications for graduate school left in phone booths are more likely to be returned if a physically attractive person's photo is attached than if a physically unattractive person's photo is attached (Benson, Karabenick, & Lerner, 1976).

Characteristics eliciting ambivalence. If we generally help people who are similar to ourselves and attractive, are we more helpful to members of our own racial or ethnic group than to members of other groups? The extent to which Blacks and Whites help members of their own race or the other race has been examined intensively, and the evidence is a bit baffling (see Piliavin et al., 1981). Whites, for example, sometimes help Blacks less than Whites, sometimes help Blacks and Whites equally, and sometimes show reverse

PHOTO 9-3. *Neighborhoods can create a sense of "we-ness" that will promote helping behavior among group members.*

discrimination by helping Blacks more than they help Whites. Similar inconsistencies are found in the helping behavior of Blacks. The simple "Help those who are similar" rule does not hold up well here. Why not?

According to Katz (1981), the reactions of most White people toward Black people are ambivalent. The concept of ambivalence appears to be useful in explaining why both Black and handicapped persons are favored in some situations but treated more poorly than they deserve in others. The result of ambivalent attitudes is inconsistent and extreme reactions. For example, many Whites are aware of the problems created by racial prejudice and do not want to think of themselves as bigoted. Piliavin et al. (1981) suggest that some of the confusion in the literature can be resolved if we understand this ambivalence. Most Whites would bend over backward to help Blacks, or at least would treat them equally to Whites, if denying help to Blacks would smack of racial prejudice. However, if Whites can find a reason other than race for failing to

help Blacks, the negative side of their ambivalence may win out. Consistent with this interpretation, Gaertner and Dovidio (1977) found that Whites helped Blacks as quickly as they helped Whites in an unambiguous emergency in which a fellow research participant was apparently struck by a stack of falling chairs and screamed out from the next room. In this clear emergency, failing to help the Black victim would be inexcusable and racist. However, Whites helped Blacks less quickly than they helped Whites in an ambiguous emergency (the same crashing sounds but no screams to clearly signal injury). Here subjects may have been able to rationalize their failure to help along these lines: "It's not that I'm prejudiced against Blacks; it's just that this person does not seem to be in any serious trouble." We can expect Whites to be most helpful to Blacks when a failure to help would clearly mark them as bigots and least helpful to Blacks when they can avoid such added costs of failing to help by justifying their inaction on more acceptable grounds.

Similarly, our ambivalent attitudes toward handicapped and otherwise stigmatized persons may explain why we sometimes go out of our way to help them and at other times fail to give them as much help as we give nonhandicapped people in the same situation. On the one hand, we feel sympathy and recognize that the norm of social responsibility should guide our behavior, but on the other hand, we are uncomfortable around such people and are motivated to avoid them. Again the result is inconsistent reactions.

Mixtures of sympathy and discomfort in encounters with disabled people lead to strange behavior. In one study, a woman who was either handicapped or nonhandicapped sought volunteers for her research project in either a pleasant or an unpleasant manner (Katz, Farber, Glass, Lucido, & Emswiller, 1978). As one would expect, subjects were more willing to help the nondisabled person when she was pleasant than when she was unpleasant, but, surprisingly, subjects helped the

disabled woman more when she was nasty than when she was nice. The authors suggested that subjects seemed to be annoyed by a disabled person who did not seem to be suffering as much as they thought she should be. In another study, subjects were asked to give feedback to either a disabled or a nondisabled person who did poorly on a task (Hastorf, Northcraft, & Picciotto, 1979). Sympathy for people with handicaps led subjects to go easy on the disabled person. This attempt to be kind is not so kind, however, if we assume that people with handicaps, like other people, benefit from accurate feedback about themselves.

As you can see, the answer to the question of who elicits help is complex. We do tend to help those who are dependent, especially when that dependency is legitimate and is no fault of the victim. In addition, we are especially helpful to people whom we view as part of our "we-group," people with whom we already have some rela-

PHOTO 9-4. *Reactions to handicapped people may alternate between help and avoidance.*

tionship, people who are similar to ourselves, or people who are otherwise attractive to us. At the same time, ambivalent attitudes toward some people cause certain exceptions to these generalizations. Aversive reactions to disabled and disfigured persons sometimes make us less likely to help them than their dependency would warrant, especially as the costs of helping escalate, and ambivalence about members of dissimilar racial groups sometimes makes us particularly helpful to them even though they are dissimilar. Both handicapped persons and members of racial minorities elicit more than their share of help under some circumstances but less than their share of help under other circumstances because of ambivalence. Despite these exceptions, it is clear that characteristics of the person in need are an important influence on prosocial behavior.

B. The influence of other people

At the heart of social psychology is the truth that people influence one another. If you witness an assault or some other emergency, other witnesses become part of the situation from your perspective. They can influence you not only through what they do in the situation but by their very presence.

Presence of others: The bystander effect. Some of the first and most exciting social-psychological research on helping behavior was inspired by a puzzling and disturbing incident in New York City in 1964. The stabbing of Kitty Genovese might have passed for "just another murder" except for some peculiar circumstances:

> For more than half an hour thirty-eight respectable, law-abiding citizens in Queens watched a killer stalk and stab a woman in three separate attacks in Kew Gardens.
> Twice the sound of their voices and the sudden glow of their bedroom lights interrupted him and frightened him off. Each time he returned, sought her out and stabbed her again. Not one person telephoned the police during the assault; one witness called after the woman was dead (*New York Times*, March 27, 1964).

The New York community was appalled by this dramatic failure to help—appalled all the more because the number of potential helpers was so large. Was this a comment on big-city life, a sign that people had become apathetic and unconcerned for their fellow humans, or what? Bibb Latané and John Darley set out to find an explanation, suspecting that the very fact that so many witnesses were present may have contributed to Kitty Genovese's death.

Latané and Darley (1968) arranged a situation in which male college students were completing questionnaires when pungent smoke came wafting through a vent into the testing room. The students were either alone, with two passive confederates of the experimenter who noticed the smoke but shrugged and continued writing, or with two other "naive" subjects. Being with two deliberately nonreactive people considerably reduced the likelihood of reporting the smoke. Whereas 75% of those who were alone acted, only 10% of those with two passive peers did so. Even three naive witnesses together were less likely to act than was a single subject; only 38% of these naive groups responded. This, then, is the **bystander effect:** individuals are less likely to help when they are in the presence of other bystanders than when they are alone.

The emergency in the "smoke" study was ambiguous at first and threatened the subjects themselves. Moreover, subjects who remained seated, coughing and rubbing their eyes, may have misguidedly wanted to appear brave, figuring that if the others could take it, so could they. Another early study (Darley & Latané, 1968) provided a situation more like that of the Genovese murder. Students were in cubicles connected by an intercom system and were to have a discussion of college life. Subjects were led to believe either that they were alone with another participant (who would soon be the victim of an epileptic seizure), that there was one other witness besides themselves, or that there were four other witnesses. The victim explained that he had seizures, and then, the next time he came on the air, he had one, becoming incoherent and crying for help ("I'm gonna die—er—help—err—er—seizure—er").

Again the bystander effect was clear: helping became less frequent and slower as the number of potential helpers increased (see Figure 9-4).

By now the bystander effect has been observed in a variety of emergency situations. It applies in nonemergencies as well. For example, groups of diners in restaurants leave smaller tips per person than do people eating alone (Freeman, Walker, Borden, & Latané, 1975). Reviewing some 50 studies, Latané and Nida (1981) concluded that the bystander effect is very consistent. On the average, in studies in which participants were either alone or in the presumed or actual presence of nonreactive confederates of the experimenter, 75% of the people who were alone helped, but only 53% of those in the presence of others did so.

But does this really mean that there is no "safety in numbers" at all? Even if each individual has a lower probability of helping when he or she is part of a group, isn't it likely that *somebody* in a group will provide help and that the victim will thus be helped more often by groups than by individuals? Not so, according to Latané and Nida. In studies in which bystanders are in full communication, the victim is actually less likely to get help as the number of potential helpers increases. When bystanders cannot communicate, victims are no better off in the hands of groups of bystanders than in the hands of an individual bystander. Thus, the presence of others not only decreases the likelihood that an individual will help but may even decrease, though less consistently and powerfully, the probability that the victim will receive help.

The bystander effect is an important phenomenon that may aid in explaining the Kitty Genovese incident. Why does it occur? Three social processes may account for it (Latané & Darley, 1970; Latané, Nida, & Wilson, 1981). Through a *social-influence* process, bystanders look to others to help them interpret the situation and may conclude that the need for help is not so great if others do not seem alarmed or are not taking action. Second, *audience inhibition*, or what some call evaluation apprehension (see Chapter 2), may contribute to the bystander effect if a bystander is worried about how others will evaluate his or her behavior. The risk of embarrassing oneself—for example, by

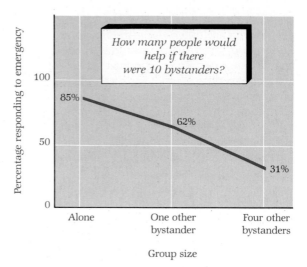

FIGURE 9-4. Percentage of subjects exposed to a "seizure" who intervened by the end of the taped emergency as a function of group size.

acting as though there were an emergency when there is not—may inhibit helping. Finally, there is the process called *diffusion of responsibility:* when several potential helpers are available, responsibility for acting is divided, and so each individual may be less likely to assume personal responsibility for acting. These three processes—social influence, audience inhibition, and diffusion of responsibility—all play a role in explaining the bystander effect. Although the three are sometimes difficult to untangle, closer examination of how they work tells us much about when the bystander effect will occur and when it will not.

For example, social-influence processes that affect a bystander's interpretation of the situation are more important in ambiguous emergencies than in clear and severe emergencies, where there is little need to rely on cues from other people to tell you that you have an emergency on your hands (Clark & Word, 1974; Solomon, Solomon, & Stone, 1978). Indeed, in one study 100% rates of helping were obtained from groups of bystanders when a maintenance man fell and cried out in pain in the next room (Clark & Word, 1972). The presence of others inhibited helping only when the emergency was ambiguous (when the fall but not the cry was heard). If other bystanders are not passive but instead indicate, by the expressions of alarm on their faces or by what they say, that the situation is clearly an emergency, they can encourage the individual to view the situation as serious and to take action (Bickman, 1979; Staub, 1974).

The audience-inhibition process depends on the individual's believing that others will disapprove if he or she treats the situation as an emergency and takes action. When other bystanders seem unconcerned, a person may conclude that the group norm in the situation is inaction and will then worry about negative evaluations if he or she helps. In other emergencies, however, it may be clear that the group views helping as appropriate, and then a person might worry about what others would think if he or she *failed* to act. Schwartz and Gottlieb (1976, 1980) have argued that the critical thing is what an individual believes the group's norm is. If the cues in the situation suggest that help is appropriate, having an audience of other bystanders will increase helping; but when helping appears to be inappropriate, having an audience will inhibit helping. In many of the studies of the bystander effect, people probably concluded that they might be in an embarrassing position in the group if they intervened.

Finally, the diffusion-of-responsibility process appears to depend on whether responsibility is focused on individual bystanders and on whether they feel especially competent to help, compared with other bystanders. Bickman (1972), for example, found that the bystander effect was reduced when another bystander was supposedly in a different building from the one where the subject and the victim were. In this situation, subjects knew that the other bystander was incapable of helping and that if they did not help, no one would. Subjects did diffuse responsibility when they thought the other bystander was in the same building as they were and thus was equally capable of helping. Focusing responsibility on an individual—for example, asking him or her to watch your belongings on the beach in case of theft—makes that person more likely to help than if he or she had no special obligation (Moriarty, 1975). However, an individual is likely to dodge personal respon-

sibility for acting when another witness has special competence—for example, when the other witness is a medical student who could be expected to be more capable and responsible in a medical emergency (Piliavin & Piliavin, 1972; Schwartz & Clausen, 1970).

The bystander effect is most likely to occur when all three processes are operating—for example, when bystanders conclude from one another's impassive behavior that nothing is wrong, when they feel that the group's norm is one of inaction, and when they feel no special responsibility for acting but instead diffuse responsibility among themselves. The social-influence process depends on the individual's ability to see others' reactions, the audience-inhibition process on knowing that others can see you, and diffusion of responsibility on the simple awareness that other bystanders are available. When bystanders can neither see others nor be seen by them, the bystander effect is weak because only diffusion of responsibility can operate to produce it (Latané & Darley, 1976). But won't bystanders who can see one another and communicate freely figure out that the situation is serious and that they should help? Not if no one communicates concern or initiates action. The opportunity to communicate is not sufficient to dampen the bystander effect—and may strengthen it.

To summarize, the social-influence process by which other bystanders inhibit helping behavior can be lessened if (1) someone in the group signals by expressions or words that an emergency is occurring or (2) the incident is difficult to interpret as anything but an emergency. The audience-inhibition process can be lessened if apprehension about being evaluated negatively for helping can be reduced, as when the group norm favors action rather than inaction. Diffusion of responsibility is less likely if bystanders have responsibility to act focused on them as individuals or feel that they are more capable of helping than others are. It is likely that one or more of the three processes underlying the bystander effect was at work the night Kitty Genovese was slain, but research indicates that there are limits to the bystander effect and ways to reduce its power. Many studies underscore people's willingness to get involved in emergencies. However, the Kitty Genovese incident can play itself out time and again if the conditions are right.

Actions of others: Reinforcement and modeling.   As we have just seen, other people, by their very presence, can influence the likelihood of a helping response. As we have also seen, what those people do—their facial expressions, words, and deeds—can have an impact as well. A discussion of the influence of other people on helping behavior would not be complete without reference to more direct ways in which other people affect our prosocial behavior. The basic learning principles emphasized by social-learning theory are highly relevant here. First, reinforcement and punishment are important sources of social influence. If you are reinforced by others for helping, you will help more in the future; if you are punished for your attempts to help, you will help less in the future (Moss & Page, 1972; Rushton & Teachman, 1978). The one drawback of reinforcing people for their attempts to help is that it can undermine altruistic motives under some circumstances (Batson, Coke, Jasnoski, & Hanson, 1978). If a reward is promised in advance, people come to perceive themselves as motivated by the reward rather than by their own altruistic motives, and they are then less likely to behave altruistically in the future when no external reward is offered.

Social-learning theory also alerts us to the effects of observing models of helping behavior. Models can remind us of what is appropriate in a situation, show us how to be helpful, reduce our inhibitions against acting, or inform us of the consequences of acting (Aderman & Berkowitz, 1970). For example, if one bystander in a group of bystanders breaks the ice and begins to take action, others are likely to follow the lead (Wilson, 1976). We are especially likely to imitate a model of helping behavior if we see the model reinforced. For instance, when the collector for the United Fund calls, you may be more likely to contribute if you have already seen your friends do so and know that they have the stickers on their doors and virtuous feelings to prove it. Watching people *fail* to

help influences us through the same basic learning processes. Part of the reason for the bystander effect in groups is that other bystanders serve as models of inaction rather than action. Our own tendencies to help are influenced in many ways, good and bad, by the presence and actions of other people.

■ IV. Personal influences on prosocial behavior

With so many situational factors influencing prosocial behavior, you may begin to wonder whether characteristics of the potential helper matter much. Do some people have traits that make them more likely to be Good Samaritans than others? Do more fleeting characteristics, such as moods, affect willingness to help? Let us consider both the enduring traits and the psychological states of the potential helper.

A. Traits: The search for the Good Samaritan

Mother Teresa of India, like the Good Samaritan in the Bible, is an altruist. She has devoted her life to bettering the life of poor and starving people everywhere. She has sought no reward for her efforts (although she has been honored with a Nobel Prize). Surely she and those rare others like her would be the first to return a lost wallet or lend a stranger a dime. In contrast, most of us have met people who almost literally will not give us the time of day. What makes some people more prosocial than others?

The search for a recipe for the Good Samaritan has been rather frustrating. For example, in their pioneering work, Latané and Darley (1970) tried to predict helping behavior on the basis of several paper-and-pencil personality tests and background variables. The only factor that seemed to matter was size of home town. People who had grown up in small towns tended to be more helpful than those from large towns or cities. Several

PHOTO 9-5. Urban overload.

studies are in agreement, finding lower rates of helping among city-raised people or city-dwellers (for example, House & Wolf, 1978), although not all agree (for example, Korte, Ypma, & Toppen, 1975). Stanley Milgram (1970) has proposed a **stimulus-overload theory** to account for the lower rate of helping sometimes found among urbanites. In the face of high levels of stimulation, he says, city people must be selective, and that sometimes means ignoring people in need, treating people brusquely, and being choosy about whom to help. In support of Milgram's stimulus-overload theory, laboratory studies demonstrate that loud, irritating noise interferes with helpfulness (Sherrod & Downs, 1974; Yinon & Bizman, 1980). Moreover, although Korte et al. (1975) did not find city folks to be less helpful overall than small-town-dwellers, they did find that people in neighborhoods with a great deal of environmental stimulation (noise, traffic, crowded quarters, and so on) were less helpful than people in quieter, less congested neighborhoods. When we are bombarded by too much stimulation, we may fail to notice the needs of other people or be too preoccupied to help them.

Another aspect of a person's background that seems to be related to being a Good Samaritan is having parents who serve as models of altruism. London (1970) conducted interviews with persons who had rescued Jews from the Nazis during World War II. Almost all identified strongly with at least one parent who had high moral standards and was altruistic. This theme of identification with a moral parent was echoed in interviews with persons who committed themselves to the civil-rights cause in the United States (Rosenhan, 1970) and also recurs in studies of prosocial behavior among children (Hoffman, 1975a). Experiences during socialization, then, may underlie some of the differences among adults in their prosocial tendencies.

When we turn from background characteristics to personality traits, we see that people who are highly helpful seem to be highly moral and oriented toward the needs of others. More mature and complex levels of moral judgment, which reflect a concern with broad principles of human rights rather than with self-interest, are associated with a greater willingness to help (Eisenberg-Berg, 1979; Erkut, Jaquette, & Staub, 1981). Just as those who emphasize the role of empathy in prosocial behavior would expect, the ability to take the perspectives of other people and the tendency to empathize with others predict helping behavior (Underwood & Moore, 1982). Moreover, as the work of Schwartz (1977) on norms indicates, the people who tend to be most helpful are those who hold strong personal norms relevant to helping and who tend to ascribe responsibility for others' welfare to themselves. Thus, on several counts the Good Samaritan tends to be concerned about others rather than about self.

Since many religions foster concern for other people, do highly religious people tend to be especially prosocial? Here the evidence is mixed. Simple measures such as church attendance do not predict helping behavior (Latané & Darley, 1970). The nature of a person's beliefs may be more relevant. Batson and Gray (1981), for instance, distinguished between two types of religious students on the basis of paper-and-pencil scales: those who viewed religion as an end in itself and those who viewed it as a quest or process of questioning. Students of both types were confronted with another student, Janet, who confided her great loneliness but indicated either that she wanted company or that she preferred to handle the problem on her own. Those who viewed religion as an end had a high need to be helpful. Unfortunately, they seemed so interested in meeting their own need to be helpful that they offered as much help to Janet when she did not want it as when she did. Quest-oriented students were more sensitive to the victim's needs, helping Janet only when she wanted to be helped. Thus, what matters may not be whether people worship frequently but whether their beliefs make them sensitive to the needs of others.

Finally, willingness to help appears to be related to one's competence and confidence in a particular situation. This was very evident in a comparison of persons who had actually intervened to stop criminals with control subjects similar in basic demographic characteristics (Huston, Ruggiero, Conner, & Geis, 1981). Although men have not been found to be consistently more helpful than women, all but one of these Good Samaritans was a man, possibly because men feel more competent in dangerous situations such as assaults and holdups. Compared with the control interviewees, interveners proved to be taller and heavier, viewed themselves as stronger, and were more likely to have had training in such relevant skills as lifesaving, first aid, and self-defense (see also Shotland & Stebbins, 1980). By contrast, scales measuring humanitarianism and social responsibility failed to distinguish interveners from non-interveners.

This leads us to an important point: relations between prosocial tendencies and the personal factors we have emphasized here—small-town background, parents who model altruism, mature moral judgment, role-taking and empathy skills, personal norms and beliefs supportive of helping, and competence—have tended to be weak and somewhat inconsistent. Most studies relate various measures of background and personality to behavior in a particular situation. The problem is that helping situations differ so greatly that it may be unrealistic to expect the same traits to predict behavior in every situation. For example, the self-defense skills that were highly relevant in the dangerous emergencies that Huston and his associates studied are likely to be totally irrelevant when the task is to fill out questionnaires for a needy graduate student. Similarly, the social-responsibility scale that failed to predict emergency intervention in the Huston study has predicted helping in other situations (see Berkowitz & Daniels, 1964).

The lesson is that characteristics of the situation and characteristics of the person interact in complex ways to influence behavior. Some people do seem to be more consistently prosocial across a range of situations than others are (see Rushton, 1980). Moreover, we have just identified some personal characteristics that fairly consistently underlie prosocial behavior. However, it may be futile to search for traits that predict Good Samaritanism in *all* situations.

B. Psychological states and helping

Suppose you have had a wonderful day, with money, grades, love, and anything else your heart desires all coming your way. Do you want to spread happiness throughout the world, or do you jealously guard your good feelings, refusing to let anyone spoil your good mood? What happens if you are in a bad mood? Temporary moods and feelings do affect prosocial behavior, but how?

Good moods. Isen (1970) administered a battery of tests to teachers and college students, telling some that they had scored very well, others that they had performed poorly, and still others nothing at all. A fourth group was spared from taking the tests. The "successful" subjects were more likely than the others to help a woman struggling with an armful of books. Isen therefore spoke of a "warm glow of success," which makes people more likely to help. This effect has been documented many times, even among professional football players, who are more likely to help other players to their feet when their own teams are ahead than when they are behind (Berg, 1978).

Succeeding on a task, then, increases helping behavior. Might good moods in general, even if they are not a result of recent success, do the same? Isen and Levin (1972) tried to find out. Students who had been given free cookies in the library and students who had had no such good fortune were asked to volunteer for an experiment that required either aiding or distracting subjects. Beneficiaries of cookies were more willing than control subjects to help but less willing to distract. Evidently the good moods produced by cookies did not lead to compliance with just any request but increased helping behavior specifically. To ensure, however, that these students were not just influenced by the model of helping behavior provided by the cookie distributor, Isen and Levin tried a second study. Here people made happy by the seemingly small good fortune of finding a free dime in the coin return of a pay phone were more helpful than those who found no dimes. Even sunshine and other pleasant weather conditions seem to lift people's spirits and make them more helpful (Cunningham, 1979). Good moods consistently produce helpful behavior in a variety of circumstances.

Why is this? In Isen's view, the answer lies in positive thoughts. When a person is made happy, the good mood sets up a "loop" of positive cognitions, which can be added to by engaging in prosocial behavior (Isen et al., 1978). If, in order to be helpful, subjects must do something unpleasant, they are not as likely to help, because helping would interfere with their good mood and break the chain of positive cognitions (Isen & Simmonds, 1978).

Bad moods. If good moods make helping more likely, do bad moods make it less likely? The answer is not simple. First, we are talking about such negative psychological states as sadness, depression, and guilt, not such states as frustration and anger, which, as Chapter 8 indicates, can lead to aggression. Second, the research is very inconsistent. In some studies, bad moods actually increase helping, while in other studies bad moods have no effect on helping or actually decrease it (see Rosenhan, Karylowski, Salovey, & Hargis, 1981). There is support for the idea that either good moods or bad moods (compared with more neutral moods) can increase prosocial behavior, but the link between good moods and helping is far more consistent than the link between bad moods and helping. Why is this?

One reason for inconsistencies among studies is that people in bad moods are very much affected by characteristics of the situation. For example, in one study adults in bad moods were very likely to volunteer to help if helping was easy and potentially very beneficial (Weyant, 1978). However, they were unlikely to help if helping was costly or was for an unimportant cause. In this study, people who were put in good moods were not so greatly affected by the costs and benefits of helping and were generally more helpful than control subjects. People in bad moods also may be less likely to notice a need for help and may be more helpful only if that need is clearly pointed out to them (McMillen, Sanders, & Solomon, 1977). Apparently, then, people in bad moods have to perceive the need for help and perceive helping as likely to improve their mood in order for bad moods to increase helping behavior.

Another reason for the inconsistencies in the literature on bad moods and helping is that subjects of different ages behave differently. Cialdini and Kenrick (1976) noticed that most of the studies in which bad moods increased helping had been done with adults, whereas most of the studies in which bad moods decreased helping had been done with children. They proposed that we come to learn during childhood that helping someone is a way to get relief from a negative mood. They then demonstrated that young children are less helpful than normal when they are in bad moods but that, by high school age, children become more helpful than normal when they are in bad moods. According to the **negative-state-relief model** offered by these researchers, adults have learned that prosocial behavior can be self-rewarding and can alleviate the blues. To the very young child who has not yet learned this, helping involves only a loss of rewards. During the school years, children will be more helpful after being put in a bad mood only if they can get social approval by helping, not if their helping is anonymous (Kenrick, Baumann, & Cialdini, 1979). Finally, by high school age, helping has become self-rewarding and so will occur even when the individual expects no external rewards. In support of their view that helping becomes self-rewarding, these researchers have shown that the same good and bad moods that increase helping among adults also increase behavior that is self-gratifying, such as paying oneself a large number of tokens (Baumann, Cialdini, & Kenrick, 1981). In addition, if people who are put in a bad mood as a result of inflicting or witnessing harm to someone have a chance to escape their bad mood in some way other than by helping, they are less helpful than subjects who are left in a bad mood (Cialdini, Darby, & Vincent, 1973). Helping, then, is not the only way to relieve a negative mood, but it is one way for adults—but not children—to do so.

Finally, some of the confusion about the relation between bad moods and helping can be reduced if we consider more specifically what the person is thinking about rather than only whether he or she is feeling good or bad. Thompson, Cowan, and Rosenhan (1980) found that if students were instructed to imagine the feelings that would be experienced by a friend who was dying, they were more helpful than control subjects who thought neutral thoughts. However, if students were instructed to imagine their own reactions to the friend's dying, they were no more helpful than controls. In short, it mattered what the person was sad about and what he or she was thinking about while sad. Empathic sadness for the friend increased helping, but sadness for oneself did not. Extending this line of study to good moods, Rosenhan, Salovey, and Hargis (1981) found that being happy over the idea of being sent to Hawaii increased helping, while empathic joy for a friend's going to Hawaii actually decreased helping below the level for the control group that imagined more neutral events. The findings of these two studies are shown in Figure 9-5.

These studies suggest that the effects of moods on helping behavior depend on whether people are focusing their attention on themselves or on others—and on how they compare their own condition with that of the person in need of help. If you feel sad about your own state of affairs, you may think *you* are the one who needs help and therefore may be less likely to help someone else than if your thoughts are focused on the misfortunes of someone else. If you feel happiness for yourself, you have set in motion the kind of loop

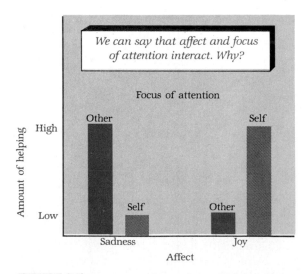

FIGURE 9-5. Amount of helping as a function of joy, sadness, and self versus other as focus of attention.

of positive cognitions that Isen proposed as a facilitator of helping. However, focusing on the good fortunes of others may make you envious or prompt you to consider other people very well off compared with yourself and thus in no great need of help (Rosenhan, Salovey, & Hargis, 1981). Perhaps the most important implication of this research is that not just any bad mood, or for that matter any good mood, increases helping behavior. It is important to consider the role of the thoughts that accompany a mood.

As we have seen, the effects of good and bad moods on helping are complex. Good moods generally make people more likely to help than they would normally be. They may do so by setting in motion a chain, or loop, of positive thoughts, which can be furthered through providing help. Negative moods increase helping only under some conditions. They are most likely to prompt helping when the need for help is clear and when meaningful help can be provided at relatively little cost; when the potential helper is an adult and has come to view prosocial behavior as a self-rewarding activity that can be effective in negative-state relief; and when the individual's attention is focused somehow on the woes of others rather than his or her own woes. Certainly we can conclude that helping behavior is affected by how a person is feeling and what he or she is thinking about when a helping occasion arises.

■ V. Seeking and receiving help: The recipient's perspective

So far in this chapter, the focus has been on giving help rather than receiving help. Implicitly, we have assumed that it is good to help others and that they can only feel deep appreciation afterward. Yet, if our society has norms that call for giving help when needed, it also has norms valuing self-reliance and independence. Most of us certainly would be insulted if we were offered or forced to accept help tying our shoes. But even when you need help, you may be reluctant to seek it and uncomfortable when you get it if it means that you have to admit being needy, incompetent, and

dependent on others rather than self-reliant. Just as helpers want to present themselves as good people, recipients of help want to avoid being seen as incompetent and dependent (Baumeister, 1982).

When does being the target of help make people uncomfortable and perhaps more likely to bite than shake the hand that feeds them? This question has special importance when we consider persons or groups who are frequently in the position of needing and receiving help—welfare recipients, handicapped and elderly persons, and even countries dependent on aid from other nations.

A critical determinant of whether help is appreciated or resented is the extent to which receiving it threatens self-esteem. Fisher, Nadler, and Whitcher-Alagna (1982) have detected two clusters of responses among recipients of help. If help supports a person's self-esteem, he or she will have positive feelings, evaluate the helper and the help positively, reciprocate the help if possible, and seek help again. However, if help threatens self-esteem, the recipient will have negative feelings, dislike the helper and the help, be unlikely to reciprocate, and avoid seeking help again. When self-esteem is threatened, in other words, the recipient of help will show negative and defensive reactions aimed at restoring self-esteem (see Figure 9-6).

What is likely to determine whether help supports or threatens self-esteem? We can begin with the individual's interpretations of why he or she needs help. Suppose, for example, that you are working difficult problems and can get expert help if you need it. If you are under the impression that most people need help with these problems, you can attribute your own need for help to the difficulty of the task, but if you believe that you are one of the few who need any help, you are likely to attribute your dependency to internal causes ("I must be dense"). People are less likely to seek help when they feel personally inadequate than when they can find an external cause for their problem (Tessler & Schwartz, 1972). People with high self-esteem are especially likely to view needing or receiving help as threatening, perhaps because they are not as often in the position of having to admit personal inadequacies (DePaulo, Brown, Ishii, & Fisher, 1981; Nadler, Altman, & Fisher, 1979).

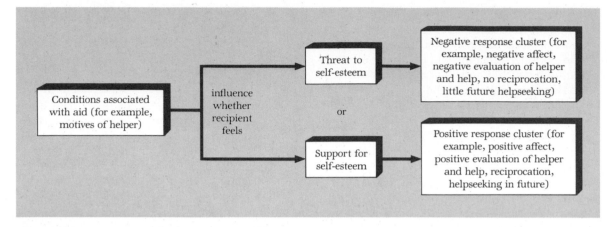

FIGURE 9-6. Recipient reactions to being helped. Reactions to receiving aid depend on whether the conditions of the aid threaten self-esteem or support it.

Similarly, recipients are influenced by the attributions they make about the helper's intentions. For example, in the foreign-relations field, if people in one nation view an aid-giving nation as having unacceptable policies or as being an enemy, aid from that nation is likely to be seen as manipulative and is less appreciated than aid from a friend (Gergen & Gergen, 1974; Nadler, Fisher, & Streufert, 1974). More generally, a favor that seems motivated by selfishness is less appreciated than one motivated by altruism (Tesser, Gatewood, & Driver, 1968).

The way in which a helper makes help available can also influence how threatening it is to receive help. For example, should a helper take the initiative and offer help, or is it better to wait for a request for help? Certainly most of us could agree that it is unwise to force help on people, especially when it is unneeded and unwanted. However, there does appear to be an advantage to offering help, assuming it is needed and can be freely accepted or rejected. When help is offered automatically, more help is received and the helper is better liked than when it must be requested (Broll, Gross, & Piliavin, 1974; Gross, Wallston, & Piliavin, 1979). This effect was demonstrated in a field experiment with welfare recipients, who obtained more needed social services when their caseworkers offered such services routinely than when recipients had to ask for them (Piliavin & Gross, 1977). This is not to say that it is never threatening to self-esteem to be offered help (Fisher & Nadler, 1974). However, the act of asking for help may be especially humiliating, and service providers might reduce negative reactions among their clients if they make it easier for clients to get help.

Finally, another factor that influences whether help recipients react favorably or unfavorably is whether they have an opportunity to reciprocate. Receiving help creates a feeling of indebtedness and an obligation to reciprocate that can be uncomfortable (Greenberg, 1980). What happens when we cannot reciprocate as the reciprocity norm tells us to do? In one study, people in the United States, Sweden, and Japan played a gambling game in which another player gave them ten chips, which saved them from bankruptcy and eventually allowed them to win the game (Gergen, Ellsworth, Maslach, & Seipel, 1975). Consistently, the helper was liked better if he asked for the ten chips back than if he either wanted no repayment or demanded repayment with high interest. A favor that can never be repaid may be no favor at all, for recipients are motivated to reduce their feelings of indebtedness and restore equity in the relationship by reciprocating.

These findings suggest why help is not always appreciated and have many practical implications. For example, to avoid negative reactions to their efforts, helpers in professional roles can avoid making their clients feel personally worthless, can convey their own genuine interest in helping, can offer needed help rather than making the client ask for it, and can give clients chances to reciprocate. When help undermines the self-worth of people with problems, it only adds to their problems.

■ VI. Toward a prosocial society

Although prosocial behavior is not always appreciated, and although some people believe we should value individual initiative and independence more highly than interdependence, most would agree that the world would be a better place if whatever prosocial tendencies people have were strengthened. How might knowledge of prosocial behavior be applied to achieve this goal? Let us conclude by looking briefly at the tasks of fostering prosocial behavior in children, increasing support for charities, and legislating prosocial behavior.

A. Encouraging prosocial behavior in children

Children do not have to be taught to be prosocial. As we saw earlier, newborns are distressed by the cries of other newborns, and older infants seem to show primitive forms of empathy and tendencies to share and help well before the age of 2 (Hoffman, 1975b; Rheingold, 1982; Zahn-Waxler, Radke-Yarrow, & King, 1979). One 13-month-old, for example, recognized that an adult might cheer up a crying friend but, still being somewhat egoistic, brought his own mother rather than the friend's mother (Hoffman, 1975b). Children then become increasingly prosocial with age (Eisenberg, 1982; Moore & Underwood, 1981; Rushton, 1980). Part of this developmental trend has little to do with how children are raised. As children mature cognitively, they are increasingly able to take the perspectives of other people and, by adulthood, to help others on the basis of empathic concern (Underwood & Moore, 1982). Yet, some children become more prosocial than others, and this is where socialization experiences can play a role.

Basic principles of learning can be used to encourage prosocial behavior among children. Children can be reinforced for their prosocial behavior; indeed, before they develop internal motives for helping, children seem to rely on promises of external rewards to motivate them (Bar-Tal, Raviv, & Lesser, 1980). As we have also

PHOTO 9-6. *Early in life, children show signs of prosocial behavior, and these tendencies strengthen as children develop.*

seen, being exposed to models of prosocial behavior can strengthen prosocial behavior. Just as exposure to violence on television can increase aggression, exposure to prosocial programming can increase prosocial behavior (see Rushton, 1979). Preaching charity can be as effective as modeling it, especially if the preaching is strongly stated and points out reasons for giving (Grusec, Saas-Korlsaak, & Simutis, 1978). The problems arise when parents preach charity but practice selfishness. Research suggests that children exposed to this kind of hypocrisy will do just what one might expect: they preach charity but practice selfishness (Bryan & Walbek, 1970a, 1970b). Thus, parents who recognize the importance of practicing what they preach and also reinforce their children's helpful acts will foster prosocial behavior.

Some psychologists have argued that competition and individual achievement are so highly valued in North America that children are not given enough opportunities to learn and practice prosocial behavior (Bronfenbrenner, 1970). Some are attempting to change classrooms to encourage more cooperation and mutual helping among students. Instead of competing, children are put into small groups where each must contribute toward a common goal. The results of such efforts suggest that such cooperative classroom structures promote not only learning but positive relationships among children (for example, Aronson, Blaney, Stephan, Sikes, & Snapp, 1978; Johnson & Johnson, 1975). By providing more of these kinds of experiences to children, we might correct the current imbalance in favor of individualism and competition.

B. Enlisting support for charities

The material presented so far in this chapter also has much to say about how to encourage people to give to worthy charities. As we have seen, appeals to the norm of social responsibility are not very effective. Instead, fund raisers can try to reduce the costs and increase the rewards of donating. Already, they make it easy for people to give at the office, and they highlight the fact that donations are tax-deductible. It is no accident that neighbors are recruited as solicitors. The potential donor,

susceptible to modeling, may think "The Joneses are behind this cause, and look how rewarding it has been for them." Telethons may encourage giving by providing us with prestigious models of giving and by putting us in good moods. In some campaigns, small gifts are given to potential donors, perhaps to make people feel obligated to reciprocate. In these and other ways, many of the influences on prosocial behavior discussed in this chapter can be applied quite directly to increase support for charities.

At the same time, research on the psychology of giving reveals some subtleties and surprises in people's reactions to charity appeals. In one study, door-to-door campaigners who showed people an attractive picture of a handicapped child as they made their pitch actually got fewer donations than those who simply made their pitch (Isen & Noonberg, 1979). The authors suggested that the photo may have distracted people from the appeal itself and from their decision-making processes. In another surprising study, Paulhus, Shaffer, and Downing (1977) found that pointing out the benefits to donors themselves of giving blood—a strategy that would be expected to work well—was not as effective as appealing to altruistic motives in getting experienced blood donors to commit themselves to further donations. The primary motivation for giving blood among these people seemed to be the satisfaction of helping people in need, and so they responded well to a pamphlet that emphasized the altruism of blood donors. Continued research into the complex psychology of giving should help worthy causes obtain the support that seems increasingly difficult to come by today.

C. Legislating a prosocial society

Kaplan (1978) has analyzed laws relevant to prosocial behavior in several countries. He finds laws in North America quick to define and punish antisocial behavior but less concerned with punishing failures to help. True, we do punish the failure to help in apprehending a criminal. We may also hold bystanders accountable if they have a special relationship to the victim, if they are responsible, even accidentally, for the victim's plight, or if they worsen the situation by intervening. But Kaplan would have you imagine sitting on a dock munching a sandwich as the person next to you falls into the water and screams for the nearby life preserver. Under United States and Canadian law, you will suffer no legal penalty at all if you continue to chomp away at your sandwich and watch the person drown! Countries such as France and the Netherlands do hold bystanders accountable if they fail to help strangers in emergencies.

Applying the cost/reward model of helping, we could increase helping not only by punishing failures to help but by reducing the costs and increasing the rewards of helping. Indeed, we already have "Good Samaritan" laws that protect doctors

from liability when they stop to help injured motorists. "Secret witness" programs allow people to call anonymously to report crimes so that they need not fear retaliation by the criminal. Some such programs also offer rewards for useful information. Still, our society's emphasis on individualism stands in the way of legislating prosocial behavior (Kaplan, 1978).

Perhaps the message is that increasing prosocial tendencies in children and adults takes work. The seeds of altruism may be built into our nature, but so are the seeds of selfishness and aggression. As Hornstein (1976) put it, "Human beings are potentially the cruelest and kindest animals on earth" (p. 66).

PHOTO 9-7. *An appeal for blood donations.*

"Give a very personal gift... blood...the gift of life." —Bill Cosby

American Red Cross

VII. SUMMARY

Prosocial behavior—behavior that benefits others or has positive social consequences—takes many forms. The term *altruism* is reserved for prosocial acts performed to benefit another person rather than to gain material or social rewards. Altruism poses a challenge to psychoanalytic and stimulus-response, or social-learning, theories, for both assume that people are basically selfish. Sociobiological theory proposes that altruism may be built into our genetic makeup through kin selection and reciprocal altruism because such behavior contributes to the survival of genes.

Models explaining why we help others emphasize emotional arousal and empathy, internalized norms, and decision-making and cost/reward considerations. Research shows that emotional arousal leads to helping behavior and that empathic concern, which can be distinguished from personal distress, may be especially important as a motivator of altruism. Although general norms such as the social-responsibility norm and the reciprocity norm have limits as explanations of helping, measuring the strength of personal norms, in conjunction with the tendency to accept or deny responsibility for the welfare of others, has proved useful in predicting helping behavior. Finally, it is useful to consider the decision-making process facing potential helpers. In order to help, one must notice an event, interpret it as one requiring help, assume personal responsibility for acting, choose a form of assistance, and implement that assistance. The costs of helping and the costs of the victim's failing to receive help are weighed during this process, and such cost factors influence the likelihood of helping.

Among the situational influences on helping behavior are the characteristics of the person in need of help. Generally, the people most likely to receive help are those who are dependent, whose need is legitimate, and whose need is not their fault and not under their control. In addition, we tend to help people with whom we already have a relationship, who are similar to ourselves, or who are otherwise attractive to us. Ambivalence toward disabled persons and members of minority groups results in some exceptions to these generalizations.

Other important situational influences are associated with the presence and actions of other bystanders. The bystander effect, whereby people are less likely to help when others are present than when they are alone, is brought about by three processes: social influence affecting interpretations of the situation, audience inhibition or evaluation apprehension, and diffusion of responsibility among potential helpers. The bystander effect can be countered if these processes cannot operate—for example, if the emergency is clear, if people can expect social approval rather than social disapproval for helping, and if responsibility is focused on individual bystanders. Other people also influence us more directly by reinforcing and modeling helping behavior.

Personal influences on prosocial behavior include both traits and states. Especially prosocial persons tend to have small-town upbringings, parents who modeled altruism, mature moral judgment, role-taking and empathy skills, personal norms supportive of helping, and competence, but it is difficult to identify traits that predict helping behavior in all situations. Being in a good mood consistently increases the likelihood of helping, while being in a bad mood does so mainly when the helper is an adult, when helping can result in negative-state relief, and when attention is focused on others' woes rather than one's own.

Taking the perspective of the help recipient makes us realize that it is difficult to seek and receive help gracefully because of threats to self-esteem. Threats to self-esteem are reduced and help is more appreciated when help recipients are not made to feel personally inadequate, when they attribute selfless motives to the helper, when help is offered freely rather than being available only on request, and when recipients can reciprocate.

Knowledge of prosocial behavior can be used to build a more prosocial society. For example, although children become more prosocial with age as a result of cognitive maturation, they can be encouraged further through rewards, exposure to prosocial models, preaching (as long as adults do not practice selfishness while preaching charity), and participation in cooperative learning groups in school. Similarly, applying social-psychological findings can increase charitable giving and bystander intervention among adults.

GLOSSARY TERMS

altruism	norms	reciprocity norm
bystander effect	personal norms	social-responsibility norm
empathy	prosocial behavior	sociobiology
kin selection	reciprocal altruism	stimulus-overload theory
negative-state-relief model		

Attitudes, Prejudice, & Discrimination

People are disturbed not by things, but by the views which they take of them.
■ EPICTETUS

You're going to find racism everyplace. In fact, I have never lived a day in my life that in some way—some small way, somewhere—someone didn't remind me that I'm Black.
■ HENRY AARON

With this chapter, we begin the exploration of a different aspect of social psychology—the study of attitudes and attitude change. The concept of attitude has been a central one in psychology. Nearly 50 years ago Gordon Allport (1935) grandly described it as "the keystone in the edifice of American social psychology" (p. 798). For most of us, the concept of attitude is central in daily life as well. Public opinion pollsters report the results of their latest surveys to eager political candidates. A bachelor cook nervously asks for his guests' opinion on the cheese soufflé. And television network executives impatiently await the report on audience response to their new fall programming.

Attitudes serve as an index of how we think and feel about people, objects, and issues in our environment. In addition, they can provide clues to future behavior, predicting how we will act when encountering the objects of our beliefs. At an even more general level, the concept of attitude relates to some of the broadest and most serious social issues in our society: the problems of prejudice and discrimination, racism, and sexism. Consider the following examples:

Aloysius Maloney has grown up in Grates Cove, C.B., Newfoundland, one of the many poor fishing villages of the province. His father, a fisherman, was lost at sea. His mother receives only a small welfare check in addition to the family allowance for the family's livelihood. Aloysius is very intelligent and desperately wants to go to a university on the mainland. But a university admissions officer tells him that he can't be admitted to the university because the academic quality of his school is so low. "Everybody knows that Newfoundland's schools are so inferior that no one from that province could survive in college," he is told.

Patricia Wilson has just completed a Ph.D. in history and is seeking a college teaching position somewhere in the Chicago area. Her husband works for a nationwide company there, but it is possible that he will be transferred to another city in the future. Despite her strong credentials and the fact that there are several openings in the area, Patricia gets no job offers. She learns that many heads of departments believe

that hiring married females is risky because of their childbearing propensities, their domestic responsibilities, and the likelihood that they will follow their husbands elsewhere.

In these examples, behaviors toward a particular individual are being influenced by general attitudes that are held about groups of people. Prejudice and discrimination are very vivid illustrations of the ways attitudes and behaviors are related, and we will begin our consideration of attitudes with an exploration of these issues of prejudice and discrimination. Then we can consider the concept of attitude in finer detail, and finally we will return to the general issue of the relation between attitudes and behaviors.

■ I. Prejudice and discrimination: Some case studies

Prejudice and discrimination, although the terms are often used interchangeably, are actually two distinct concepts. **Prejudice** refers to an intolerant, unfair, or unfavorable *attitude* toward another group of people (Harding, Proshansky, Kutner, & Chein, 1969); **discrimination** refers to specific *behaviors* toward members of that group which are unfair in comparison with behavior toward members of other groups. To illustrate the ways prejudice and discrimination operate, we will consider three "isms": racism, sexism, and the issues surrounding separatism in French-speaking Canada.

A. Racism

The term *racism* is somewhat difficult to define, although most people would agree that it includes both prejudice and discrimination as components. Marx (1970) has suggested that it includes "hostility, discrimination, segregation and other negative actions expressed toward an ethnic group" (p. 101). The U.S. Commission on Civil Rights (1969), in a booklet entitled *Racism in America and How to Combat It*, defines racism as "any attitude, action, or institutional structure which subordinates a person because of his or her color" (p. 1). Thus, racism may exist on an individual level or on an institutional one. In the latter case, we are talking about formal laws and regulations that discriminate against certain ethnic groups as well as about informal social norms that limit the opportunities available to certain ethnic groups (Weissbach, 1977).

Examples of racism are unfortunately all too numerous in our world. In both Great Britain and Canada, for example, attitudes and behaviors toward settlers from India and Pakistan frequently reflect extreme prejudice and discrimination. In South Africa, a minority of Europeans live in domination over a majority of Africans, and segregation of the races is virtually total. Although some policies are at last changing, Africans have been punished for staying overnight in White areas, are jailed for holding meetings and forming political parties, and must produce pass permits on demand to members of the ruling police force. Few newspapers are allowed to print articles critical of the ruling Nationalist party, and it was not until 1975 that the government permitted any television in South Africa.

During World War II, shortly after the Japanese attack on Pearl Harbor, pressure built in the United States to evacuate Japanese-Americans from the West Coast of the United States and confine them to internment camps in the interior. Both the mass media and government officials insisted that these Japanese-Americans, two-thirds of whom were U.S. citizens, were a threat to the country's security. Early in 1942, more than 110,000 Japanese-Americans were moved to hastily constructed camps, where they were detained for three years. Similarly, thousands of Japanese-Canadians in British Columbia were uprooted and resettled in the interior, most of them losing their homes, farms, and businesses in the process.

Although examples of racism are numerous, we will focus on research dealing with Blacks and Whites in the United States because this situation has been studied most extensively.

Stereotypes are often at the heart of racism. As discussed in Chapter 4, **stereotypes** are a form of schema dealing with a particular group of people.

PHOTO 10-1. *This bus in South Africa restricts its passengers to Black Africans, while other buses allow only Whites.*

The contents of such stereotypes are not necessarily negative, but they often are. Stereotypic traits ascribed to Blacks have included laziness, superstitiousness, musical ability, and love of pleasure (Brigham, 1971; Karlins, Coffman, & Walters, 1969; Katz & Braly, 1933). These stereotypes have diminished somewhat in recent years. In some cases, class distinctions appear to be more important than racial classification in the stereotypes of college students (Smedley & Bayton, 1978).

Elimination of stereotypes does not mean the automatic elimination of racism, however. Racism is based on a complex set of attitudes and behaviors at both the individual and societal levels. Brigham and his colleagues, for example, have defined a set of 11 attitude dimensions that can be used to describe the attitudes of Whites toward Blacks (Brigham, Woodmansee, & Cook, 1976; Woodmansee & Cook, 1967). These dimensions include attitudes toward integration, views on interracial marriage, approaches to racial equality, and attitudes toward Black militance. **Social distance** is another aspect of prejudice, referring to a person's acceptable degree of relationship with members of a given group (Westie, 1953). Social distance is usually measured by asking whether the person would accept members of Group X as close friends, whether the person would invite them to a party, whether the person would live in the same neighborhood with them, and so on.

These distinctions are important when we try to understand the attitudes of Whites toward Blacks and vice versa. They are also important in resolving a debate that arose concerning the relative importance of belief similarity in prejudice. In *The Open and Closed Mind*, social psychologist Milton Rokeach (1960) argued that prejudice or rejection can result largely from perceived dissimilarity in values. Rokeach argued that if a White person rejects Blacks, he or she does so not on the basis of their being Black but rather because the person assumes that Blacks have different values. Rokeach and his colleagues have provided data to support this hypothesis, both in laboratory pencil-and-paper studies and in a real employment setting (Rokeach, 1968; Rokeach & Mezei, 1966; Rokeach, Smith, & Evans, 1960).

Other psychologists, however, have argued that people do reject other individuals simply because of their race. As social psychologist Harry Triandis forcefully stated, "People do not exclude other people from their neighborhood . . . because the other people have different [values], but they do exclude them because they are Negroes" (1961, p. 186).

To some degree, both viewpoints are true, as prejudice and discrimination depend on the type of behavior being considered. For some issues, such as whether one is willing to work with a person, recent evidence suggests that beliefs are more important than the person's race. For other behaviors, such as accepting a person as close kin by marriage, race is more influential than beliefs (Moe, Nacoste, & Insko, 1981). Social pressure appears to account for some of these effects: when social pressure favors discrimination, the effect of race is stronger than the effect of beliefs. In contrast,

when such pressure is weak, beliefs may be a more important determinant of attitudes.

The study by Moe and his colleagues also provides information on recent changes in attitudes of Southern junior high school students. In comparing the views of students in 1966 and in 1979, there is evidence that, overall, the race effect is weaker now than a dozen years ago. It is also interesting to note that the attitudes of Black students toward Whites are less negative than those of White students toward Blacks, and Blacks appear less likely to have internalized norms against the other group.

Racism is not just a matter of individual prejudices and attitudes, however. At a societal level, we must consider how the laws and practices of a society can enforce and perpetuate discrimination against one group by another. In South Africa, as noted earlier, there is a wide-ranging body of

PHOTO 10-2. *Changes in Indian law may gradually lead to changes in social practices, including the ability of all citizens to draw water from a well once off limits to members of the "untouchable" caste.*

laws and restrictions that keep the Black South Africans separate from the ruling White minority. Until fairly recently, the Untouchable class in India was controlled by a similar set of policies and long-standing norms; members of that class were not allowed to participate freely in the society. Similarly, in the United States, numerous policies have existed that kept Blacks "separate but equal" and perpetuated institutional racism. Many of these policies have changed in recent years. In 1954 the famous *Brown* v. *Board of Education* case was evaluated by the Supreme Court, which decided that schools could not be separate—that equality could not be gained through separation of Black and White because such separation would always psychologically imply inequality. Yet, despite considerable gains, it is clear that racism still exists in the United States and that the larger social structure must be considered as important a factor in racism as individual attitudes of prejudice (Wellman, 1977; Willie, 1977).

B. Sexism

Sexism operates in much the same way as racism. However, the prejudice and discrimination are directed against people by virtue of their *gender* (their physical identity as male or female), rather than according to ethnic or racial group. Sexism incorporates a host of beliefs and behaviors that result in the unfair treatment of women in society. In many respects, racism and sexism are similar. Kirkpatrick (1963) has discussed these similarities, pointing to more than 30 parallels that can be drawn, including assumptions of biological inferiority, discriminatory practices in education, and stereotypes of typical characteristics.

As in racism, pervasive stereotypes about the differences between two groups—in sexism, women and men—lie at the heart of the prejudice. Many researchers have asked groups of people to describe what the average man and the average woman are like, and they have found a surprisingly high degree of consensus about which traits are typical of each sex. Frequently the ascribed characteristics fall into two general groups—one collection of traits representing competence and independence and a second group focusing on warmth

and expressiveness (Broverman, Vogel, Broverman, Clarkson, & Rosenkrantz, 1972). Men are generally seen as embodying the competence cluster, women as embodying the expressive cluster. Table 10-1 lists some of the traits most frequently associated with males and with females.

Although it might be argued that these two patterns—competency and expressiveness—are different but do not represent more favorable or less favorable impressions, other evidence suggests that the picture is not so optimistic. For example, studies of stereotyping generally find that many more of the characteristics that our Western societies value are associated with men than with women. Perhaps even more indicative of the rather negative stereotype associated with women is a study by Broverman and her colleagues (Broverman, Broverman, Clarkson, Rosenkrantz, & Vogel, 1970). These authors asked 79 practicing mental health clinicians (clinical psychologists, psychiatrists, and social workers) to describe the characteristics of one of three types of persons: a normal adult male, a normal adult female, and a normal adult person with sex unspecified. The clinicians were asked to characterize the healthy, mature, socially competent person in each category. The results, not particularly encouraging if sexual equality is our goal, were quite clear-cut. Both male and female clinicians saw the healthy adult male and the healthy adult person as nearly synonymous; the healthy adult female, in contrast, was significantly different from the healthy adult person. For example, both the healthy adult person and the healthy adult male were described by adjectives from the competency cluster (independent, active, competitive), whereas the healthy adult female was seen as possessing far less of each of these characteristics. The healthy adult female was viewed as more submissive, more concerned about her appearance, and more excitable in minor crises—a set of characteristics not attached to either the healthy adult or the healthy male.

Although the existence of less favorable stereotypes of women has an impact in its own right, it is also important in the effect it can have on other judgments. Beliefs about what men and women are like can have the effect of a *self-fulfilling*

TABLE 10-1. Stereotypic items typically used to describe males and females

Competency Cluster

Feminine	Masculine
Not at all aggressive	Very aggressive
Not at all independent	Very independent
Very submissive	Very dominant
Not at all competitive	Very competitive
Very passive	Very active
Has difficulty making decisions	Can make decisions easily
Not at all ambitious	Very ambitious

Warmth-Expressiveness Cluster

Feminine	Masculine
Very tactful	Very blunt
Very quiet	Very loud
Very aware of feelings of others	Not at all aware of feelings of others
Very strong need for security	Very little need for security
Easily expresses tender feelings	Does not express tender feelings at all easily

prophecy (see Chapter 5). If women are assumed to be less competent, for example, their performance may be judged as less successful than it actually is. Or if women are assumed to be less competent, they may be given less opportunity to assert themselves and prove their competence (with the result that they may be viewed as less assertive!). Like racism, sexism does not stop with the stereotypes; discriminatory behaviors are practiced as well.

In employment categories, females are underrepresented in nearly all professional and prestige occupations. In part, such underrepresentation may stem from the kinds of behaviors that women encounter as they attempt to prepare themselves for these occupations. For example, Harris (1970) reports the following responses given by male faculty members to female applicants for doctoral work: "You're so cute, I can't see you as a professor of anything"; "Any woman who has got this far has got to be a kook. There are already too many women in this department"; "I know you're competent, and your thesis advisor knows you're competent. The question in our minds is are you

really serious about what you're doing?" and "Why don't you find a rich husband and give this all up?" (p. 285).

Such comments may seem frivolous, but the evidence that women are underrepresented in professions and that the full-time working woman has a salary equal to approximately 60% of the salary of the full-time working man are much more serious matters. In fact, it has been estimated that the woman college graduate earns approximately the same salary as the White male with less than a high school education.

Numerous studies have documented the existence of bias in hiring women. For example, Fidell (1970) sent a number of academic résumés to heads of psychology departments at major U.S. universities and asked each head to evaluate the applicant as a potential professor in that department. Two forms—identical except for sex of applicant—were used, each going to half of the selected chairpersons. The results showed that men were generally offered a higher position than women (that is, associate professor rather than assistant professor), despite the equality of their back-

DOONESBURY

by Garry Trudeau

grounds. Lest we infer that only psychologists are biased, it should be noted that Lewin and Duchan (1971) found similar results in physics departments.

Dipboye et al. (1975) asked college recruiters from major organizations to rate the desirability of hiring a number of candidates who varied in both sex and competence. Although the academic qualifications of the candidate were clearly the most important factor in the recruiters' decisions, sex again had an effect. Recruiters showed a significant preference for the male candidate over the equally qualified female candidate. In another simulated hiring study, Terborg and Ilgen (1975) found that women were hired as often as men but were offered lower starting salaries. Once hired, these women were more likely to be assigned to routine tasks, thus further limiting their performance on the job.

Whereas the studies just discussed held the job constant and compared the judgments about males and females, occupations in real life vary tremendously, and men and women are distributed unevenly across various occupations. The majority of doctors, carpenters, and steelworkers, for example, are male, and the majority of elementary school teachers, nurses, and secretaries are female. Perhaps not surprisingly, the average salaries in these occupations vary as well, male-dominated occupations generally carrying higher salaries than predominantly female occupations.

Evidence that jobs are distributed unevenly is buttressed by stereotypes about people who hold

PHOTO 10-3. *Women's entry into traditionally male occupations is a means of redressing the salary imbalance between women and men.*

various jobs. Certain role behaviors and certain traits are associated with various jobs, often reflecting the stereotypes of the sex that typically occupies that job (Deaux & Lewis, in press; Mellon, Crano & Schmitt, 1982). Eagly and Wood (1982) have shown that people make inferences about status on the basis of gender. Thus, when given only general occupational information about individuals in a work situation, people assume that the woman has a lower-status job and that the man has a higher-status job. People also believe that the man will be more influential than the woman. When specific job titles of both the male and the female employee are provided, in contrast, people do not predict any sex differences in influence if the man's and woman's jobs are comparable.

There are many parallels between racism and sexism. In both instances, negative stereotypes are accompanied by discriminatory behavior in a wide range of areas, including education and employment. There are some important differences between the two "isms," however. For example, the social-distance concept that we discussed in reference to racism does not apply to sexism. Women's lives have always been intimately intertwined with the lives of members of the dominant male group, and women have experienced far greater informal power through these liaisons than Blacks have (Cameron, 1977). Historically, too, although both Blacks and women have been denied the vote and treated as property by the dominant male, the record of Black slavery is a more blatant example of discrimination than the marriage contracts and dowries of women.

C. Separatism

In his 1979 New Year's message, Canadian Prime Minister Pierre Trudeau warned of the potential for violence in his country. Among other sources of violence, he cited "the prejudices that French-speaking and English-speaking Canadians harbor against one another." As the third of our "isms," separatism is somewhat different from racism and sexism. The term itself refers to a political movement in Canada, centered in Quebec province. Many of the issues that underlie this movement, however, relate very closely to our discussion of racism and sexism, because a major reason for the movement is the perception by French-speaking Cana-

dians that there is prejudice and discrimination toward them by English-speaking Canadians. In this case, it is not a physical characteristic, such as skin color or gender, that differentiates the groups; it is language and ethnic origin. Nevertheless, many of the problems are similar.

Stereotypes exist about French Canadians. For example, Canadian students described French Canadians as excitable, talkative, impulsive, emotional, haughty, religious, and tenacious (Gardner, Wonnacott, & Taylor, 1968). Some of the students had more negative images, viewing French Canadians as unreliable and uncultured; these students were much less favorable about French Canadians as a group. Evidence of discriminatory practices also exists. Studies of the career advancement of civil servants have shown that French-speaking Canadians make less money, on the average, than English-speaking Canadians when factors of age, education, and seniority are equivalent (Beattie & Spencer, 1971). As with racism and sexism, some attempts to explain these disparities between the two groups have focused on characteristics of the more powerful group; other explanations have looked to traits of the group that is discriminated against (Richer & Laporte, 1973). The nature of the explanation chosen has important consequences for the actions that are taken to reduce prejudice and discrimination.

■ II. The causes of prejudice and discrimination

Many theories have been advanced to explain why prejudice and discrimination occur. In general, these theories represent two levels of analysis—the societal and the individual (Ashmore, 1970). Societal explanations are concerned with situational effects on prejudice in given societies, social systems, and groups and with institutional factors that may encourage and perpetuate discrimination. The individual level of analysis asks why one person is more prejudiced than another. Gordon Allport's classic and readable book *The Nature of Prejudice* (1958) has outlined these various levels (represented in Figure 10-1), and we will discuss each type of theory in turn.

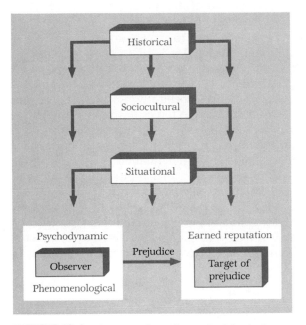

FIGURE 10-1. Theoretical and methodological approaches to the study of the causes of prejudice.

A. Historical and economic emphasis

The historian reminds us that the causes of prejudice cannot be fully understood without studying the historical background of the relevant conflicts. At the societal level of analysis, it is a sad fact that most prejudices have a long history. Allport points out that anti-Black prejudice in the United States, for example, has its roots in slavery and the slave owner's treatment of Black families, in the exploitation of Blacks by carpetbaggers, and in the failure of Reconstruction in the U.S. South after the Civil War.

Some historically oriented theories of prejudice emphasize economic factors. For example, advocates of the theories of Karl Marx see prejudice as a way of letting the rulers exploit the laboring class. As Cox has stated, "Race prejudice is a social attitude propagated among the public by an exploiting class for the purpose of stigmatizing some group as inferior so that the exploitation of either the group itself or its resources may both be justified" (1948, p. 393). Treatment of Black slaves before the U.S. Civil War, of Oriental immi-

grants in California at the turn of the century, and of Chinese laborers brought in to build the Canadian Pacific Railroad are all examples of the haves vilifying the have-nots.

In emphasizing broad patterns, the historical and economic emphasis provides a useful background for understanding prejudice and discrimination. Social psychologists, however, prefer more "micro" explanations.

B. Sociocultural emphasis

Sociologists and anthropologists emphasize sociocultural factors as determinants of prejudice and discrimination. Among these sociocultural factors are (1) the phenomena of increased urbanization, mechanization, and complexity, (2) the upward mobility of certain groups, (3) the increased emphasis on competence and training, the scar-

PHOTO 10-4. *The treatment of Black slaves before the Civil War is one example of the exploitation of one group by another for economic reasons.*

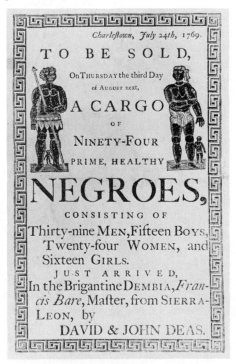

city of jobs, and the competition to get them, (4) the increased population in the face of a limited amount of usable land and a lack of adequate housing, (5) the inability of many people to develop internal standards, leading to reliance on others (individuals, organizations, the mass media, or advertising) and a conforming type of behavior, and (6) changes in the role and function of the family, with concomitant changes in standards of morality.

The overt racism demonstrated in the 1970s by members of the British working class may reflect the threat to full employment posed by the influx of large numbers of Pakistanis, Indians, and West Indians (Esman, 1970). The covert racism of a former Canadian government's "Green Paper" on immigration and a more recent report of the Ontario Royal Commission on Education undoubtedly reflects the concern of many White Canadians over the perceived threat to the "stability" of Canadian society posed by the increased numbers of "nontraditional" immigrants, such as Blacks from the United States and the Caribbean and Orientals from Vietnam. Economic self-interest may influence attitudes toward programs directed at minorities, such as affirmative action employment efforts (Kluegel & Smith, 1982).

Increased urbanization can also be considered a cause of prejudice against ethnic groups. Watson (1947) found that many of the people he studied became more anti-Semitic after they had moved to the New York City area. Supposed urban traits—dishonesty, deceit, ambitiousness, vulgarity, loudness—were, several decades ago, reflected in the stereotype of the Jew. The late sociologist Arnold Rose believed that "the Jews are hated . . . primarily because they serve as a symbol of city life" (1948, p. 374).

This sociocultural emphasis is a plausible explanation of prejudices toward urbanized minority groups as well as toward groups that have not accepted White middle-class values. But it does not explain the hostility toward hard-working Japanese-American and Japanese-Canadian farmers during World War II or the fact that farm-dwellers—isolated from the depersonalized city—may be as prejudiced as city-dwellers.

C. Situational emphasis

Let us now turn to explanations that operate at a more individual level—those that begin to deal with the question of why some people are prejudiced while others are not. The situational emphasis is the most social-psychological in nature, focusing on current forces in the environment as the cause of prejudice. Conformity to others is a strong influence on prejudice, according to theories that look to the situation for the causes of prejudice. We gain social approval by conforming to the opinions held by our friends and associates. During the 1960s in the U.S. South, for example, many restaurant owners claimed that they themselves were not prejudiced but that other customers would object if the owners allowed Blacks to be served.

Changes over time in stereotypes of racial or national groups often reflect this situational emphasis. During World War II, U.S. citizens were exposed to government propaganda that led to an adoption of negative stereotypes of the Japanese and the Germans and to favorable stereotypes of allies, including the Russians. Early in the war most U.S. citizens described the Russians as hard-working and brave. In 1948, as postwar conflicts betweeen the two great powers emerged, the stereotypes were quite different, as Figure 10-2 indicates. Although "hard-working" was still considered an appropriate description of the Russians, more people in the United States in 1948 believed that Russians were cruel. In a world where the Soviet Union was no longer an ally but an adversary, assumptions about the nature of Russians had changed. In recent years a different change has begun to take place in regard to the assumptions held by many U.S. citizens about mainland Chinese: negative attitudes about these people may be moderating with the advent of rapprochement and such things as Coca-Cola franchises in China.

D. Psychodynamic emphasis

In contrast to the situational emphasis is the view that sees prejudice as a result of the prejudiced person's own conflicts and maladjustments. Here we find theories that are essentially psychological, in contrast to the historical, economic, and

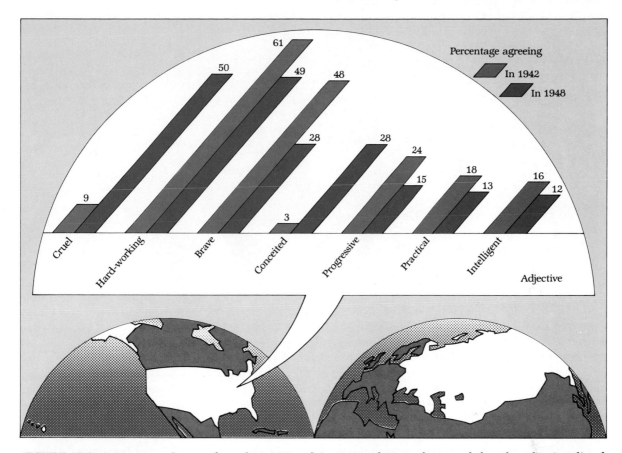

FIGURE 10-2. Percentage of respondents (U.S. citizens) in 1942 and 1948 who agreed that the adjectives listed above described the Russians.

sociological emphases of previous approaches. According to these theories, if you want to alter prejudice and discrimination, you must focus directly on the prejudiced person.

Two types of psychodynamic theories of prejudice are used. One of these assumes that prejudice is rooted in the human condition, because frustration is inevitable in human life. Frustration and deprivation lead to hostile impulses, "which if not controlled are likely to discharge against ethnic minorities" (Allport, 1958, p. 209). In this interpretation, we can see the frustration-aggression hypothesis (discussed in Chapter 8) finding its place in the explanation of discrimination. **Scapegoating**—the displacement of hostility onto less powerful groups—is hypothesized to result from frus-

tration when the original source of the frustration is not available for attack or is not attackable for other reasons. Lynching of Blacks, burning of synagogues, and other assaults on representatives of minority groups are instances of such behavior.

In evaluating frustration theories, Feshbach and Singer (1957) make a very useful distinction between shared threats and personal threats. A shared threat, such as the possibility that one's community might be hit by a hurricane, has the effect of bringing people together; such a threat has been found to reduce anti-Black prejudice. But a personal threat—such as losing one's job—has an escalating effect on prejudice, as frustration theory would predict.

Within the psychodynamic emphasis, a second

PHOTO 10-5. *Members of the Ku Klux Klan and the American Nazi party both advocate White supremacy, expressing hostility toward Blacks and Jewish people. The displacement explanation would suggest that members of these groups are frustrated—by economic conditions, for example—and displace their aggression on easily identifiable or nonpowerful groups.*

approach focuses on the hypothesis that prejudice develops only in people who have a personality defect or a weak character structure. This approach does not accept prejudice as normal; it postulates that prejudice is the result of the strong anxieties and insecurities of neurotic persons. A similar approach derives from research on authoritarianism, which conceptualizes prejudice as a function of the antidemocratic orientation of certain people.

A book called *The Authoritarian Personality* (1950) was a landmark in the history of social psychology (see Chapter 13 for more discussion of authoritarianism). Written by the German social scientists T. W. Adorno and Else Frenkel-Brunswik and their colleagues at the University of California at Berkeley, this huge book (990 pages) included clinical hunches, extensions of psychoanalytic theory, multiple item analyses of various attitude scales,

in-depth interviews, and post hoc theory. Although written more than 30 years ago, this work is still of contemporary interest (Cherry & Byrne, 1977).

The initial focus of the research program conducted by Adorno et al. was an understanding of prejudice and discrimination as they are evidenced in *anti-Semitism*, or negative attitudes and behaviors toward Jewish persons. Gradually, however, the focus of the program shifted toward prejudice, or what the California group chose to call *ethnocentrism*. They preferred the latter term to *prejudice* because *ethnocentrism* refers to a relatively consistent frame of mind—a rejection of all out-groups and aliens. The ethnocentric person has a dislike for anything and everything different. For example, it has been found that highly ethnocentric subjects are less likely to own foreign-made automobiles (Day & White, 1973). This emphasis on ethnocentrism reflected the California group's assumption that prejudice results from some characteristic of the ethnocentric person, rather than from the characteristics of a particular minority group. Adorno et al. looked at prejudice from a psychoanalytic viewpoint—namely, that the authoritarian personality results from a strict and rigid superego, a primitive id, and a weak ego structure (Sanford, 1956), which lead to predictable patterns of behavior toward minority groups.

As Pettigrew (1961) has shown, each of these explanations of prejudice within the psychodynamic approach depicts an externalization process. According to this viewpoint, people interpret external events in terms of their own personal lives. For example, a person who is compulsively neat may view less orderly people not only as messy but also as bad. Such an interpretation may reflect the individual's own psychological "hang-ups." Yet, there exist prejudiced persons to whom the psychodynamic emphasis does not apply. The psychodynamic approach is particularly inadequate to explain cases in which prejudice and discrimination pervade the entire social structure.

E. Phenomenological emphasis

The phenomenological emphasis advances the notion that what should be studied is not the objective world but the individual's perception of the world. Unlike the psychodynamic view, which stresses more durable personality characteristics, the phenomenological emphasis stresses the immediate perceptions of a person. As we saw in Chapter 4, there are many possible interpretations of a single event. Our interpretation can be influenced by a variety of factors: our past experience with the person, the behavior of other people in the same situation, our selective attendance to certain aspects of the situation. The combination of these factors will, in turn, affect our behavior. For example, the assertive behavior of a woman, seen in the context of more passive women, may be interpreted as "too aggressive" and "pushy," even though the behavior may be comparable to that of a man in the same situation. Discriminatory behavior may follow. In contrast, previous experience with that same woman, or comparison of her behavior with that of others in a similar situation, might result in quite different behavior on our part. In other words, the phenomenological interpretation of prejudice and discrimination emphasizes immediate influences and pays little attention to broad historical causes.

With the phenomenological emphasis, we have reached the immediate level of causation as represented in Figure 10-1. But our survey of approaches is not complete until we consider the stimulus object of prejudice.

F. Emphasis on earned reputation

All the previous approaches have localized the source of prejudice in the observer. They have failed to consider that minority groups, by their behavior or characteristics, may precipitate the negative feelings that are directed toward them. The *earned reputation* theory postulates that minority groups possess characteristics that provoke dislike and hostility. There is some evidence to support this theory. For example, Triandis and Vassiliou, in a study of people from Greece and the United States, conclude: "The present data suggest that there is a 'kernel of truth' in most stereotypes *when they are elicited from people who have firsthand knowledge of the group being stereotyped*" (1967, p. 324). A careful review by Brigham (1971) concludes that ethnic stereotypes can have a "kernel of truth" in the sense that different groups of respondents agree on which traits identify a particular object group. Furthermore, at least in some cases, these beliefs about the characteristics of members of another group may be relatively accurate (McCauley & Stitt, 1978).

We have reviewed a variety of explanations for prejudice. Although each has some merits, the reader should realize that none of these theories is sufficient to explain every case; a phenomenon as pervasive as prejudice has many sources. Hence, we must acknowledge the multiple causes of prejudice, while realizing that attempts to identify specific causes for individual cases of prejudice are helpful.

■ III. The nature of attitudes

Prejudice and discrimination are "big" concepts: they involve stereotypes and beliefs about groups of people and about individuals who represent those groups, they involve actions and behaviors toward these people, and they may involve norms and institutional policies that influence beliefs and behaviors. Are all these aspects included in the concept of attitude? In a general sense, yes. Yet, because these phenomena are so complex, social psychologists have attempted to break down their analysis of such events into smaller components. Defining the components more precisely makes it possible to put the pieces back together and look at the broader phenomena of prejudice and discrimination. Let us look, then, at how the basic concept of attitude is conceptualized in social psychology.

A. Definitions of attitude

Because *attitude* can mean so many things to so many people, it is not surprising that social psychologists have entertained many definitions of *attitude*. In one of the earliest uses of the word, it meant a physical posture, a body position. For example, in early experiments on reaction time, experimenters would talk about a subject's attitude when referring to a readiness to respond to the onset of a stimulus (Himmelfarb & Eagly, 1974b). For most of recent history, however, the use of the term has been limited to mental rather than physical states, although the notion of a readiness to respond to objects has often been maintained in the definition (Allport, 1935).

Many theorists have proposed that attitudes have three basic components: the cognitive; the affective, or emotional; and the behavioral (Katz & Stotland, 1959). As McGuire (1969) has noted, the proposition that people take three existential stances in regard to the human condition—knowledge, feeling, and acting—has been advanced by philosophers throughout history. As far back as Plato, the terms *cognition*, *affect*, and *conation* were used to refer to the three components of what we may call attitude (Oskamp, 1977). In this analysis of attitudes, the cognitive component consists of the beliefs and ideas a person has about some attitude object (Harding et al., 1969). For example, the beliefs that women are more intuitive than men, that all cab drivers are talkative, and that Germans are always methodical represent the cognitive aspect of attitudes toward objects. The affective component of an attitude is the emotional feelings one has about the attitude object or one's like or dislike for the object. Positive feelings might include respect, liking, and sympathy; negative feelings might be contempt, fear, and revulsion. The behavioral, or conative, component of an attitude is one's action tendencies toward the object. For example, does a legislator vote for or against a balanced-budget amendment? Does an individual donate money to the cancer society?

Obviously, it causes some confusion to imply three separate things when using the single word *attitude*. Because of this potential confusion, whereby a single concept refers to three separate kinds of response, many recent investigators have become much more precise in the use of the term *attitude*. Fishbein and Ajzen (1972), for example, suggest that the term be used only in reference to the evaluative dimension, to indicate like or dislike toward the object. Most of the measurements of attitudes, which we will discuss in the next section, in fact are simple measures of like and dislike. This approach to the definition of attitudes has considerable merit, and in our remaining discussion we will accept attitude as an indicator of liking and disliking.

If we do accept this definition of attitude, however, then how do we refer to the other components of what has been called an attitude in the past? *Beliefs* is a term that has been used to refer to the cognitive component. In Fishbein and Ajzen's terms (1972), beliefs are probabilistic judgments about whether a particular object has a particular characteristic. For example, if I say that professors are smart people, I am indicating my belief that smartness and professors are related. Other beliefs about the properties of professors might include arrogance, absent-mindedness, and liberalism. Such beliefs may be held with varying degrees of certainty. For example, the person who says that the planet Venus might be inhabitable is indicating a lower probability, or a weaker belief, than the person who swears that life exists on Venus. In and of themselves, such statements do not indicate overall liking or disliking; in other words, they are conceptually distinct from attitudes as an evaluative statement. Together, they may be able to predict some kinds of behavior that relate to a particular attitude object.

To refer to the conative (or behavioral) component, Fishbein and Ajzen (1972) offer the concept of *behavioral intention*. This refers to a person's stated intention to perform a particular behavior with respect to the object of consideration.

In summary, attitudes, beliefs, and behavioral intentions can be used to represent the affective, cognitive, and conative components of attitudes.

There are a couple of other terms that we should mention before we go further into the nature of attitudes, because these terms are sometimes confused with *attitudes* and *beliefs*. *Values* are broader and more abstract goals that an individual may have, and they lack a specific object or reference point. Bravery, beauty, and freedom are values. They serve as criteria for judgments or as abstract standards for decision making, through which the individual may develop specific attitudes and beliefs (Rokeach, 1973). Thus, if beauty is a primary value for you, many of your beliefs may revolve around the issue of whether a particular object is beautiful. In turn, your attitude toward that object may be influenced by the degree to which you think it is esthetically pleasing. For other people, the value of practicality or efficiency may be more important, and so their attitudes and beliefs toward the same object might differ sharply from yours.

Opinion is a less easily defined term that has often been used interchangeably with both *attitude* and *belief*. In fact, McGuire (1969) has suggested that these are "names in search of a distinction, rather than a distinction in search of a terminology" (p. 152). Yet, the term *opinion* continues to be used widely, particularly in reference to public opinion polling, where the focus is on the shared attitudes and beliefs of large groups of people (Oskamp, 1977). Generally these public opinions combine aspects of attitudes, beliefs, and behavioral intentions. For example, a television poll may ask respondents "Do you like Candidate X?" "Do you think Candidate X is interested in the problems of minorities?" and "If the election were held today, would you vote for Candidate X?" In our discussion, we will avoid the use of the term *opinion* and maintain the distinctions among attitudes, beliefs, and intentions. When you next see the results of a public opinion survey, however, you might want to analyze the questions according to this three-way distinction.

B. Measurement of attitudes

Attitudes, like many variables of central interest to social psychology, are not observable entities. You can't see, smell, or touch an attitude; it is an underlying construct that must be inferred. To make this inference, psychologists have developed many methods of measurement, all designed to tap people's underlying attitudes toward various objects and issues in their environment. Most methods of attitude measurement are concerned with the evaluative dimension; in other words, they attempt to determine how much an individual likes or dislikes a particular object. (It is for this reason, among others, that we are comfortable in limiting the term *attitude* to the affective dimension and reserving the term *beliefs* for cognitive aspects.)

Hundreds of methods have been devised to measure attitudes. In the simplest form, a method might consist of open-ended questions—for example, "What do you think about space exploration?" Such questions have the advantage of eliciting a broad range of respondent viewpoints and sometimes more detail than some of the other forms. However, open-ended questions also have the disadvantage of having low reliability (often, a person will answer quite differently on different occasions), and it is difficult to compare the answers of different respondents because their answers may vary so widely. Although open-ended questions can be quite useful in the initial stage of an investigation—when you are not sure of all the issues that may be involved—later stages of attitude research generally use more closed-ended questions that allow more precision.

We cannot detail all the methods of attitude measurement that have been developed. We will, however, briefly discuss three of the most common methods in use in order to provide a sense of the strategies that investigators use in this complex area.

The Thurstone method of equal-appearing intervals. In this method of attitude measurement, developed early in the history of attitude research (Thurstone, 1928), the goal of the investigator is to construct a scale marked off in equal units. Although such a goal might seem relatively easy to attain, the procedure for developing this kind of scale is in fact quite complex. Initially, the investigator develops a large number of statements about the attitude object of interest—abortion, nuclear energy, or violence on television, for instance. These statements are then rated by a large group of people who indicate their favorable or unfavorable attitude toward the topic. The rating is accomplished by asking each person to place each statement in one of 11 piles, the first pile indicating an extremely unfavorable statement and the last pile indicating an extremely favorable statement. For example, if you were a judge in this procedure and the topic were attitudes toward North American Indians, you might place the statement "I would rather see the White people lose their position in this country than keep it at the expense of the Indians" in one of the piles at the favorable end of the continuum. The statement "I consider that the Indian is fit only to do the dirty work of the White community" might be placed in one of the piles at the unfavorable end.

Once this initial group of statements has been judged, the investigator then selects a smaller number of statements (about 20 is typical) for the final attitude scale. Statements that show considerable disagreement in ratings among judges will be discarded, and the statements chosen will represent a spread of scale values (based on the median of the judges' ratings) along the entire dimension of favorable to unfavorable, with approximately equal intervals between pairs of adjacent scale values.

All this work is preliminary to using the scale to measure a person's attitude. Once the items have been selected, they are presented in random order (with no mention of the scale values) to a sample of the population of interest. People are then asked to check those items that they agree with, and the investigator determines a respondent's attitude by calculating the mean or median of the scale values of the items checked. Thus, in the final analysis, a person's attitude will be represented by some number between 1 and 11.

The Likert method of summated ratings. Responding in part to the difficulty of using the Thurstone method, Likert (1932) proposed an alternative procedure for measuring attitudes that is considerably simpler and, as a result, has been more widely used in recent years than the Thurstone method. In the Likert method, there is no effort to find statements that are distributed evenly along a continuum; rather, only statements that are definitely favorable or unfavorable to the object are used. The investigator compiles a series of these statements and then asks subjects to indicate their degree of agreement or disagreement with each statement. An example of this format is shown in Figure 10-3.

A Likert scale will contain a series of such items, and a person's final attitude score will be the sum of the responses to all items. For example, if there are 20 items on the scale, a person's score can

FIGURE 10-3. A sample item from the Likert scale of attitude measurement.

"The policy of encouraging Indians to remain on reservations should be terminated immediately."

Strongly disapprove	Disapprove	Undecided	Approve	Strongly approve
(1)	(2)	(3)	(4)	(5)

range from 0 to 100. In refining a Likert scale, an investigator will generally do an item analysis to determine which questions are the best measures of the attitude being studied. Specifically, the investigator will determine the correlation of each item with the total score and will keep only those items that show a substantial correlation with the total score.

The semantic differential technique of Osgood, Suci, and Tannenbaum. Both the Thurstone and Likert methods, to varying degrees, require the investigator to do considerable initial development before a scale can be used to assess a person's attitude on the topic of interest. In contrast, the semantic differential method uses a scale that is general enough to be applied to any topic and asks the person to evaluate the attitude object directly (Osgood et al., 1957). In this method, which was originally developed to measure the meaning of an object (hence the term *semantic*), the person is asked to rate a given concept on a series of seven-point, bipolar rating scales, as shown in Figure 10-4. Any concept—a person, a political issue, a work of art, or anything else—can be rated using this same format.

In addition to the Thurstone, Likert, and

FIGURE 10-4. A sample item from the semantic differential scale of attitude measurement.

The subject is asked to rate a given concept (such as "North American Indian") on a series of seven-point, bipolar rating scales. Any concept—a person, a political issue, a work of art, a group, or anything else—can be rated. The usual format is as follows. The person places an X to indicate his or her rating on each bipolar dimension.

North American Indian

Fair	– – – – – –	Unfair
Large	– – – – – –	Small
Clean	– – – – – –	Dirty
Bad	– – – – – –	Good
Valuable	– – – – – –	Worthless
Light	– – – – – –	Heavy
Active	– – – – – –	Passive
Cold	– – – – – –	Hot
Fast	– – – – – –	Slow

semantic differential methods, many other attitude measures have been developed. These three, however, are probably the most widely used measures in attitude research today. Furthermore, although the assumptions and characteristics of these methods differ, the responses to all three scales generally have been found to be highly related (Fishbein & Ajzen, 1974). For example, a person whose responses to a Thurstone scale indicate a highly favorable attitude toward North American Indians would probably also show a positive attitude on the Likert and semantic differential scales.

With this variety of measurement techniques in hand, social scientists have investigated a tremendous range of attitudes. Attitudes on virtually every topic—religion, politics, the environment, drugs, sex, and many others—have been investigated with nearly every segment of the population.

C. Development of attitudes

Most of us have attitudes about a great many things. But where do these attitudes come from? There is, as you might suspect, no single answer to this question. However, a number of influences can be identified as possible sources of attitudes and beliefs. Let us look briefly at some of these possibilities.

Classical and instrumental theories of learning. Both classical and instrumental theories of learning have been borrowed from experimental psychology to explain the acquisition of attitudes. The work of Arthur Staats exemplifies the use of basic conditioning principles in developing a model of attitude formation (Staats, 1967; Staats & Staats, 1958). Building on earlier work by Doob (1947), Staats has used a classical conditioning model, like that developed by Pavlov with his dogs, to explain the acquisition of attitudes. In the now-familiar experiments by Pavlov, an unconditioned stimulus (UCS) is paired with a new stimulus, called the conditioned stimulus (CS). Through the process of association, the animal learns to make the same response to the CS as it previously did to the UCS (see Figure 10-5). This new response is called a conditioned response (CR), and Staats defines an attitude as such a response—

a conditioned evaluative response to some object in the environment.

To apply these principles to the acquisition of attitudes, consider your associations to the word *seedy*. Most people would react to this description rather negatively. Now assume that a particular minority group is always described in the same breath with seedy people. Presumably you would learn to evaluate that group negatively as well.

Operant principles of reinforcement have also been applied to the study of attitude acquisition. For example, imagine that you express an opinion about nuclear disarmament and a listener excitedly says "You're right!" Would you be more likely to endorse that opinion in the future?

Insko (1965) attempted to answer this question by conducting a verbal-reinforcement study using the telephone. Students at the University of Hawaii were phoned by an interviewer who sought their opinions about "Aloha Week" (festivities held every fall in Honolulu). For half the students, the investigator responded with "Good" when the student indicated a favorable opinion about Aloha Week; for the other half, a "Good" response followed statements of negative attitudes toward Aloha Week. By this means, verbal conditioning was instituted—for some of the students positive attitudes were reinforced, and for others negative attitudes were reinforced.

About one week after the telephone calls, the same students completed an apparently unrelated "Local Issues Questionnaire" in their regular class meeting, and one of the items in this questionnaire asked for their attitudes on Aloha Week. Students who had been verbally reinforced by the telephone interviewer for positive attitudes expressed more favorable views than subjects who had been verbally reinforced for negative attitudes. The effect of verbal reinforcement thus appeared in another setting one full week later.

Verbal reinforcement has been used to modify such phenomena as wearing clothes of certain colors (Calvin, 1962), expressing prejudiced attitudes (Mitnick & McGinnies, 1958), adhering to certain philosophies of education (Hildum & Brown, 1956), and holding particular attitudes toward capital punishment (Ekman, 1958). In each case, rein-

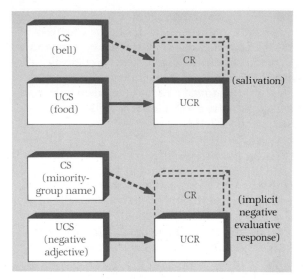

FIGURE 10-5. Classical conditioning model. (CS = conditioned stimulus; UCS = unconditioned stimulus; UCR = unconditioned response; CR = conditioned response.)

forcement of an attitude enhances the future expression of that attitude. There are, however, limitations to these conclusions. First of all, the verbal-reinforcement procedure can cause the respondent to accentuate his or her previously held attitudes, but it will not produce a reversal in the direction of attitudes. In other words, this procedure requires that a person already hold an attitude and express it; then the experimenter is limited to reinforcing and perhaps thereby strengthening the original attitude. A second criticism of this approach to attitude change is that most of the attitudes studied have been rather unimportant or irrelevant ones. Most University of Hawaii students, for example, are probably indifferent whether Aloha Week is held once a year, once a month, or once a century. Even changes in attitude about a more important question, such as capital punishment, may occur without much investment on the part of the changer.

A third concern in this area is the exact nature of the reinforcement. Why does a verbal response such as "Good" lead to changes in expressed attitudes? One possibility is that the response leads the person to believe that conformity to his or her present opinion will result in a variety of future reinforcements; however, this explanation is not totally convincing (Insko, 1967). Other people have questioned whether the reinforcement itself is really the cause of changes in attitudes, suggesting that *demand characteristics* may be a more reasonable explanation. For example, in Insko's study, it is possible that students expressed either more favorable or more unfavorable attitudes toward Aloha Week on the Local Issues Questionnaire because they felt they were supposed to, rather than because any true shift in attitude had occurred (Page, 1969, 1971, 1974).

This issue is not totally resolved. Investigators seem to agree that **contingency awareness** is necessary—in other words, a person must realize that statements such as "Good" are being used in response to particular attitude statements (thus refuting the popular idea of "hidden persuasion")—but they do not agree on whether a person must also realize that a deliberate persuasive attempt is being made (Insko & Oakes, 1966; Page, 1969).

Although conditioning of attitudes may not occur without awareness, it is still true that attitudes can be conditioned. A child who knows that her parents are approving when she says school is good and disapproving when she says school is bad is aware of the contingencies; nevertheless, those parental responses may still lead her to develop a positive attitude toward school, in part because of the reinforcement she receives. In a similar manner, praise and approval from friends and relatives may be effective in molding our attitudes.

Social-learning theory. As we have discussed in previous chapters—for example, in dealing with altruism and aggression—humans learn a great many behaviors from simply observing the actions of others. Attitudes can be learned in the same fashion. Watching a parent endorse the Republican candidates, for instance, may lead to the acquisition of a positive attitude toward Republicans.

Parents are not the only models that may affect the formation of attitudes. Media are another powerful source. There is continuing debate on whether media actually create attitudes or merely reinforce attitudes that already exist (Roberts & Bachen, 1981). Probably both processes occur. In one study, for example, Eskimo children were exposed to television for the first time, witnessing a series about other cultures and values. Children who watched this series showed significant changes in their beliefs about other cultural groups (Caron, 1979). In the case of sex-role stereotypes, amount of television viewing has been shown to affect the sexism scores of adolescent girls. Particularly for girls from middle-class families, more television viewing led to higher sexism scores. Interestingly, this effect was not found for boys. Although boys who initially were more sexist in their views did watch more television, their attitudes were not altered by their viewing experience (Morgan, 1982).

There are many other ways in which attitudes may be acquired. In Chapter 3, for example, we described Daryl Bem's theory of self-perception, which suggests that we come to know our attitudes by observing our own behavior. For example, if I find myself eating snails at a party, I may decide that I like snails. Or, if I volunteer to work on Candidate Golden's campaign, perhaps because my friends are doing so, I may come to the conclusion that I really am in favor of Golden. This model may be as useful in explaining how existing attitudes are strengthened as in describing their initial formation (Fazio, Zanna, & Cooper, 1977).

In summary, there are many ways in which individual attitudes can be formed. Some attitudes may be developed through the operation of basic learning and reinforcement principles; others may be formed as a person acquires information about new topics. As we will see in the next chapter, attitudes are frequently subject to change, and alterations in one attitude may have a "domino" effect on other attitudes.

■ IV. Attitudes as predictors of behavior

A. Do attitudes predict behavior?

The implicit assumption among those who have studied attitudes has always been that attitudes are related to behaviors. In other words, if we measure a person's attitude toward Spanish-speaking Americans and find that it is negative, then we should be able to predict that this person would engage in a number of discriminatory behaviors toward any individual Spanish-speaking American. But can we make this prediction? Fairly early on in the history of attitude research, investigators learned that relations between attitudes and behavior and relations among various behaviors were not nearly so neat as early theoretical work would have predicted. As a result of several studies showing such inconsistencies, many social scientists in the early 1970s began to regard the concept of attitude as nearly useless (Eagly & Himmelfarb, 1978).

The classic study used by critics as evidence for inconsistency was done by Richard LaPiere back in 1934. At that time there were strong feelings against Orientals in the United States, particularly along the West Coast. LaPiere, a highly mobile sociologist, took a Chinese couple on a three-month automobile trip, twice across the United States and up and down the West Coast. The trio stopped at 250 hotels and restaurants during their trip, and only once were they refused service. Later LaPiere wrote to each of these establishments, asking whether it would accept Chinese patrons. Only about half of the proprietors bothered to answer, but of these, 90% said that they would not serve Chinese! In a similar study, Kutner, Wilkins, and Yarrow (1952) arranged for a Black woman to join two White women seated in a restaurant, repeating this procedure in 11 restaurants. In no case was the Black woman refused service. However, later telephone calls requesting reservations for an interracial party produced six refusals and only five grudging acceptances of the reservation.

Although both these studies suggest some discrepancy in behavior, they are not without their problems. For example, in neither case was attitude actually assessed. Instead, an indication of intended behavior (or a *behavioral intention*) was compared with an actual behavior. Dillehay (1973) has argued that these studies are actually comparing types of role behavior, and he notes that "the unit sampled is suprapersonal, the establishment rather than the individual" (p. 888). Simi-larly, there is no way of knowing whether the person who refused the reservation by letter or by phone was the same person who had admitted the Chinese and Black persons when they were at the establishment.

Although the variety of problems in these early studies of discriminatory behavior still might not lead us to discard any notion of attitude/behavior consistency, more recent studies that have eliminated some of the problems have often been no more successful in establishing a relation between attitudes and behavior. Wicker (1969), in a review of many of these studies, concluded that attitudes were a very poor predictor of subsequent behavior.

In the face of numerous failures to find expected relations between measured attitudes and observed behavior, many social psychologists began to believe that the concept of attitude was not useful in their attempt to understand human behavior. Other investigators, however, rather than throwing the baby and the bath water out together, have pointed to a number of reasons that the expected relation may not always be strong and, at the same time, have charted new directions for the investigator of attitudes. Let us consider some of these reasons for the weak relation.

First, consider the *level of specificity* at which attitudes and behaviors are defined. Often, investigators have used a very general measure of attitudes (for example, attitudes toward psychology) and then looked at a very specific measure of behavior (for example, willingness to enroll in a social-psychology course taught at Classic University by Professor Knowlittle). In many ways, it is not surprising that such a general measure of attitude does not fare well in predicting such a specific behavior. In contrast, experiments in which the measure of attitude is more specific have had much more success in predicting specific behavior. For example, Weigel, Vernon, and Tognacci (1974) measured people's attitudes toward general issues, such as the environment, and toward more specific objects, such as the Sierra Club (see Photo 10-6). Later they gave subjects the opportunity to volunteer for activities of the Sierra Club. Although no relation between general environmental attitudes and Sierra Club activities was found (cor-

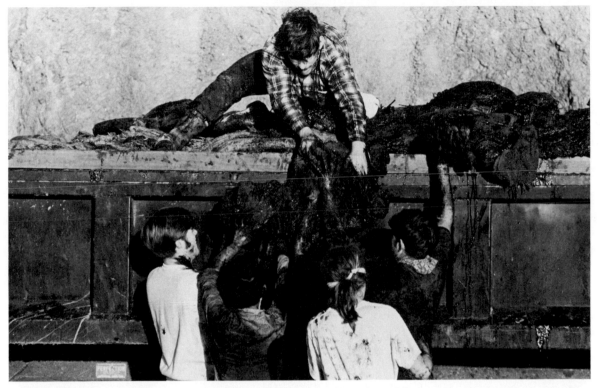

PHOTO 10-6. *These volunteers are cleaning up after an oil spill on the California coast. Such behavior has been shown to correlate more highly with people's attitudes about a specific object (for instance, the Sierra Club) than with their attitudes about more general concepts (such as the environment).*

relations were .06), there was a strong relation between the more specific attitudinal measures and the actual behavior.

A related issue in considering the attitude/ behavior relation is the question of single acts versus multiple acts. Generally, investigators have selected a single behavior to test their predictions. Yet, if we are interested in a general issue, such as attitudes toward women, then it probably makes more sense to look at a series of possible behaviors. In other words, although a person's general attitude toward women may not be an accurate predictor of his or her response to a particular woman in an employment interview, that attitude may be a much more accurate predictor when a whole series of behaviors related to women is taken into account. For any single act, there may be a variety of factors that influence the behavior; over a wide range, however, the general attitude may exert a more powerful influence.

One of the reasons for seeking this broader range of indexes is that behavior is complex and multi-determined. Our attitude toward an object may affect some of our behavior, but other factors may influence our behavior as well. For example, suppose an elderly man tells his friend "the less contact I have with Blacks, the better" and then boards a bus. Noting that all the seats but one are occupied, the man takes the available one—next to a Black. We cannot conclude that his verbal statement is false just because his choice of seats has repudiated it. Even the apparently simple action of taking a seat may be multidetermined. Although it may be upsetting for the old man to sit next to a Black, his feet may be hurting him so much that sitting, under any conditions, is more tolerable

PHOTO 10-7. *Even if we knew these bystanders' attitudes well, it would be difficult to predict whether any of them would come to the man's help.*

than standing. Observation of future behavior, however, might prove more enlightening. Perhaps the man would refuse to take that bus anymore or would change his schedule to avoid crowded-bus hours. Even more broadly, other situations involving the man's interactions with Blacks might show a consistency between expressed attitude and actual behavior. In short, one-shot measures of behavior may not give us much information about the strength of the attitude/behavior relation.

Situational factors may also influence behavior, as we have seen repeatedly in earlier chapters. When situational pressures are strong, people of widely differing attitudes may act in a similar way. For example, if a young Vietnamese child were about to be hit by a car, most people, no matter what their attitude toward Vietnamese, would probably

try to save the child. Yet, in other situations that did not involve life or death, varying attitudes toward Vietnamese might influence one's reaction to a Vietnamese child. In general, we can say that the stronger the situational pressures toward some behavior, the less likely individual differences in attitudes are to affect the behavior. (We shall have reason to return to this general point later on in Chapter 13.)

A related issue in considering the attitude/behavior relation is that a given behavior may be related to more than one attitude. For example, in the case of the Vietnamese child about to be struck by a car, a person might have one set of attitudes toward Vietnamese and another set of attitudes toward children. Which attitude would best predict behavior? Thus, the relation between behavior and a single attitude may appear inconsistent because other attitudes have greater influence (Cook & Selltiz, 1964; Wicker, 1969). In one study, Insko and Schopler (1967) used a person whose attitudes were favorable to the civil-rights movement but who refused to contribute money to the movement. Perhaps this person had stronger attitudes about caring for family needs, maintaining a good credit rating, and the like. Understanding the competing role of different attitude domains may facilitate future prediction of behavior.

B. Resolving the attitude/behavior issue

All the reasons already mentioned tend to diminish the observed relation between attitudes and behavior. Yet, they do not mean that we should throw up our hands in despair and accept the claim that there is no relation. Instead, these problems may point the way to a successful resolution.

Izek Ajzen and Martin Fishbein (1977; Fishbein & Ajzen, 1975) have done exactly that. On the basis of their review of the research, Ajzen and Fishbein (1977) conclude that "a person's attitude has a consistently strong relation with his or her behavior when it is directed at the same target and when it involves the same action" (p. 912). Thus, if we carefully construct our attitude measure and carefully select the behavior to be observed, we can indeed predict behavior from attitudes. In general, these investigators suggest that attitudes toward specific behaviors (for example, a person's attitude toward recycling wastes) will provide the best predictor of *single-act criteria* (for example, the specific act of taking bottles to the local recycling center), while more general attitudes toward objects (such as attitudes about ecology) are more suitable for *multiple-act criteria* (such as a combination of behavioral measures, including taking bottles to a recycling center, reducing the thermostat, and using recycled paper for correspondence). Clearly this is a more complex approach to attitude/behavior assessment than early investigators used, but it appears to be a much more profitable one as well.

Fishbein and Ajzen have also proposed a model for predicting people's behavioral intentions and actual behavior (see Box 10-1). This model includes

BOX 10-1. Intentions and weight loss

According to Fishbein and Ajzen, a person's intentions are the best predictor of his or her behavior. These intentions, in turn, are affected chiefly by two factors: one's personal attitude toward the behavior in question and one's beliefs about what other people expect one to do. These two factors do not necessarily have equal influence. For some people, individual attitudes may be more important, while for other people the opinions of significant other persons may be crucial. These two components may also vary depending on the particular behavior in question.

In one of the many tests of this model, Saltzer (1980) questioned women who were considering joining a weight-loss program. Not all the women entered and subsequently completed the course. For those who did, however, the normative component appeared to be the best predictor of how much weight they lost. Most important were the perceived opinions of close friends; much less important were the perceived opinions of spouses. Personal consequences, such as health, appearance, and energy, seemed to be less related to weight loss, even though the women themselves believed some of these factors to be very important. ■

both a measure of the person's attitude toward the action and a measure of his or her normative beliefs about the desirability of the action (Fishbein, 1967; Fishbein & Ajzen, 1975). With the inclusion of this latter factor, these investigators are able to consider how other people may influence a person's behavior in ways that are or are not consistent with the person's actual attitude toward the specific object. Triandis (1977a) has proposed a similar model that also includes a habit factor, reflecting the number of times the person has performed a particular action in the past. Both these models have received considerable support and testify to the usefulness of taking a more complex view of the relation between attitudes and behavior.

C. Factors affecting attitude/behavior consistency

Confident that attitudes do indeed predict behavior, investigators have recently begun to explore the conditions under which attitudes and behavior will be more or less consistent. Direct experience with the attitude object is one important factor. Attitudes formed through direct experience with the object show more consistent relations to behavior than do attitudes formed less directly (Regan & Fazio, 1977). For example, when a student has participated in several psychology experiments, that student's attitude toward psychology experiments is much more likely to predict his or her future participation than if the student had only read about experiments (Fazio & Zanna, 1978). At a more esoteric level, your attitude toward Martians is far less likely to predict your actual behavior should you ever encounter a Martian than your attitude toward professors is likely to predict your classroom behavior.

The personal relevance of an attitude also influences consistency. When a person has a "vested interest" in an issue—for example, attitudes of younger people toward an increase in the legal drinking age—behavior is more likely to reflect the stated attitude (Sivacek & Crano, 1982).

Individual differences can also be important; in other words, some people are more consistent than others. Recall our discussion of the characteristic of *self-monitoring* in Chapter 3. One characteristic of low self-monitors, according to Snyder (1979), is that they show greater consistency between their internal beliefs and their external actions. High self-monitors, in contrast, are more likely to act in response to the situation, guided less by internal cues. This difference between these two types of people apparently does not lie in the link between attitudes and intentions but, rather, in the connection between intentions and actions (Ajzen, Timko, & White, 1982). High self-monitors may disregard previous intentions when situational cues become strong.

These developments in attitude research are important ones, but they do make life more complicated. Recalling our earlier discussion of racism, for example, we can be much less certain that there is a racist personality, whose attitude can be assessed and whose every behavior toward members of other ethnic groups can be predicted. Although there certainly may be some generality, many of the behaviors that fall into the category of racial discrimination can be predicted only by quite specific attitudes and may occur only in particular circumstances. Knowledge of this complexity does not make us any less concerned about issues of racism, sexism, prejudice, and discrimination, but it should make us realize that these problems are highly complex and that any strategies for solution and change will necessarily be complex as well.

V. SUMMARY

Attitude is and always has been a central concept in social psychology, and it is related to a variety of important phenomena. *Prejudice* refers to an intolerant attitude toward a group of people; *discrimination* refers to specific unfair behaviors toward members of that group.

Racism is a particular form of prejudice and discrimination, directed toward an ethnic group. It may exist at either the individual or the institutional level. Sexism is a similar form of prejudice, but in this case the behavior is directed against a person by virtue of gender, rather than race. *Separatism*, a Canadian political movement, is propelled by evidence of prejudice and discrimination toward French-speaking Canadians. In each of these cases, negative stereotypes are accompanied by discriminatory behavior in a wide range of areas.

Theories about the causes of prejudice make a distinction between prejudice existing in the society at large and the degree of prejudice held by different individuals. The historical emphasis hypothesizes that prejudice is often the result of traditions and relationships that have existed for generations. Economic exploitation of less powerful groups is advanced as one cause of prejudice.

Sociologists and anthropologists emphasize sociocultural factors as causes of prejudice. The situational emphasis states that prejudice is caused by current forces in the environment.

Psychodynamic theories of the causes of prejudice posit that prejudice results from personal conflicts and maladjustments within the prejudiced person. The phenomenological emphasis argues that a person's perception of his or her environment is of crucial importance in understanding that person's behavior.

Throughout the years, many definitions of *attitude* have been offered. Although beliefs, behaviors, and evaluations have all been considered a part of the attitude concept at some time, more recent usage limits the term *attitude* to only the evaluative dimension (liking or disliking). *Beliefs* are cognitions or ideas that one has about an object, apart from any liking or disliking. *Behavioral intentions* are tendencies toward action. *Values* are broader and more abstract goals and lack a specific reference point.

Three major methods for measuring attitudes are the Thurstone method of equal-appearing intervals, the Likert method of summated ratings, and the semantic differential technique.

Attitudes can be formed in many ways. Basic learning theories describe some processes of attitude acquisition. Social learning and modeling are also influential.

A major question has always been the relation between assessed attitudes and observed behaviors. Many early investigations found little relation between the two. Some of the factors that may affect the relation are the level of specificity of the attitude measured, the question of single-versus multiple-act criteria for behavior, the influence of situational factors, and the fact that several attitudes may be relevant to one specific behavior. Recent investigations have shown considerable correspondence between attitudes and behaviors when these various factors are taken into account and when both the attitude and the behavior are assessed carefully.

GLOSSARY TERMS

contingency awareness	prejudice	social distance
discrimination	scapegoating	stereotypes

Theories of Attitude Change

The world is not run by thought, nor by imagination, but by opinion.
■ ELIZABETH DREW

Some praise at morning what they blame at night, but always think the last opinion right.
■ ALEXANDER POPE

Our attitudes and the ways they are related to behavior are a topic of interest in their own right. Perhaps even more interesting, however, are the ways we alter our attitudes, our beliefs, and our actual behavior. Virtually every day, some of our attitudes are challenged by pressure from others or by questions from ourselves.

Consider, for example, a few moments in the life of a young woman named Joan Siegel. It is a dreary Monday morning. Joan drags herself out of bed and flips on the television. She hopes the early morning program will provide some provocative piece of news that she can share with people at the office. Instead, a commercial praises a new hair rinse that promises to transform her into the essence of charm, popularity, and sexuality. That's the last thing she needs, Joan thinks—to heighten her sexuality. The phone rings—it's Ernie, still trying to persuade her to go away with him for the weekend. But Joan is resistant; she's never *done* that before. She finally terminates the conversation by telling Ernie that she'll see him at lunch and discuss it further then. She sighs for a moment, then quickly prepares her breakfast, swallows her sugar-coated corn flakes, and scans the front page of the newspaper. The headlines are about efforts to persuade Congress to pass a new nuclear arms agreement. Joan wonders how persuaded her own congressional representative has been. As she leaves for work, the mail arrives, but it contains nothing but some throwaway ads.

If Joan had nothing else to do all day, she might be able to keep track of the number of efforts made to change her attitudes or behavior. On this particular morning, she has already been inundated by advertisements emanating from several media—including even the cereal box! It may seem to her that every story in the newspaper is concerned with changing attitudes or behavior—whether it's pressures on a president or prime minister, a local petition campaign to build a new park, or a terrorist's threats to destroy a hijacked plane unless certain demands are met. And then there's always Ernie and his constant persuasion campaign. When we consider these events as typical of the ever-present assault on our sensibilities, it's no wonder that social psychologists have taken an immense interest in attitude change.

There are a number of theories of how attitude change takes place. Each of these theories has a different focus and may explain only some types of attitude change. We will consider four of the major theoretical approaches in this chapter. The first, *learning models* of attitude change, reflects the stimulus-response orientation derived from basic experimental psychology. The second and third models, *social-judgment theory* and *consistency theories*, represent more-cognitive approaches to understanding attitude change. *Functional theory*, our fourth major model, is somewhat eclectic, although it draws mainly on psychoanalytic theory and other orientations that emphasize personal needs.

Each of these theories rests on certain assumptions about human nature—often quite different assumptions, as we shall see. In discussing each theory, we will assess these assumptions as well as describe the major concepts and principles that the theory offers. In addition, we will look at some of the research generated by each model and at how its principles have been applied in such areas as advertising, health care, and political opinion. Finally, we will discuss an equally important issue—when attitudes *don't* change.

■ I. Learning models of attitude change

A. Assumptions about human nature

As indicated in Chapter 1, stimulus-response theory focuses on the relation between specific stimuli and responses. Behavior is analyzed by being broken down into units of habits and other separable responses. A response is more likely to be made again if it is reinforced (rewarded). It follows from this analysis that a stimulus-response theory of attitude change will place great emphasis on the characteristics of the communications (message, appeals, and so on) that try to make us change our attitudes and on the rewards that we may derive from doing so.

It has become fashionable to state that stimulus-response and reinforcement theories assume that humans respond to stimuli in a rather passive, robotlike fashion. A careful reading will indicate, however, that such a notion does not reflect S-R theory fairly. Although it is true that researchers using the S-R approach are interested primarily in aspects of the stimulus and the communicator, they also recognize that the recipient's characteristics can influence the extent of attitude change. Contemporary S-R theories are more accurately called S-O-R theories, in that they recognize the place of the organism that intervenes between stimulus and response.

Basic to S-R and reinforcement approaches is the notion that incentives for change must be stronger than incentives for maintaining the status quo. Behind this notion may be a recognition of each person's individuality, in the sense that to predict the person's response, his or her past history of reinforcements must be understood and accounted for. Underlying this recognition, however, is an assumption that if the past history of reinforcements is known by the communicator, it can be used to manipulate the recipient's attitudes. Reinforcement theorists will claim that if they had enough information about the recipients and if they had sufficient resources at hand, they could bring about attitude change in every recipient through the same general techniques.

With these general assumptions in mind, let us look at one particular approach to attitude change that is based on these assumptions.

B. Hovland's Communication Research Program

During the late 1940s and 1950s, a highly energetic and productive group of social psychologists gathered at Yale University under the direction of Carl Hovland. Together they developed a model of attitude change that used learning principles to suggest critical factors in the attitude-change process. They believed that the principles applicable to acquiring verbal and motor skills could also be used to understand attitude formation and change (Hovland, Janis, & Kelley, 1953).

In the learning of new attitudes, three variables were believed to be important: attention, comprehension, and acceptance. Figure 11-1 shows how

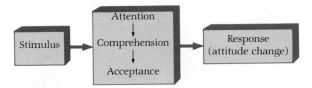

FIGURE 11-1. Steps in the attitude-change process, according to the Hovland/Janis/Kelley model.

these factors are related. The first factor, *attention*, recognizes the fact that not all message stimuli that we may encounter are noticed. Driving down a highway lined with billboards, for example, you may notice only a fraction of the persuasive messages that you pass by. Lacking your attention, the attempted persuasion will very likely not be successful. But even when an appeal is noticed, it may not be effective. The second factor posited by Hovland and his colleagues, *comprehension*, recognizes that some messages may be too complex or too ambiguous for their intended audience to understand. A highly complex treatise on the balance-of-payments deficit, for example, may be totally ineffective in persuading the economic novice to vote for or against a particular bill. Finally, in the third step, a person must decide to accept the communication before any real attitude change takes place. The degree of *acceptance* depends largely on the incentives that are offered: the message may provide arguments or reasons for accepting the advocated point of view, or it may engender expectations of rewards or other pleasant experiences. For example, the billboard on the highway may tell you that a nationally known restaurant is only minutes off the highway, thus promising you something better than you had planned to get at the next truck stop. More than any other approach, the stimulus-response and reinforcement theories regard this assumption as basic—that attitudes are changed only if the incentives for making a new response are greater than the incentives for making the old response.

A major contribution of this theory is the specification of factors that may influence the acceptance of a persuasive communication. As journalism students are often told, a good news article should identify "who said what to whom under

PHOTO 11-1. *A billboard's effectiveness depends not only on its attracting attention but also on its message being understood and accepted.*

what circumstances." In a similar fashion, the Communication Research Program at Yale identified four elements that are involved in most persuasive situations: (1) the source of the persuasive communication, (2) the characteristics of the message, (3) the context in which the message is delivered, and (4) the personality of the recipient of the message. Interest in these four elements has motivated considerable research, both by the original Yale group and by investigators who have followed their lead.

C. Representative research

In discussing research related to the learning model, we will consider each of the elements just identified.

Source. *Who* says something may be just as important as what is said. Hovland et al. (1953) suggested that the credibility of a source would affect the incentives for changing one's attitude. Therefore, the more believable a source, the more likely is attitude change. In the early research that tested this hypothesis, the manipulations of credibility were quite strong. For example, Hovland and Weiss (1951) contrasted the effectiveness of U.S. physicist Robert Oppenheimer with that of the Russian newspaper *Pravda*. Not surprisingly, U.S. subjects were more persuaded by a message from Oppenheimer.

Recent research has considered more-specific components of a communicator's credibility, including expertise, trustworthiness, attractiveness, and similarity to the recipient (Petty & Cacioppo, 1981). Each of these factors has been shown to affect attitude change. For example, a message advocating a certain number of hours of sleep was more effective when the source was a Nobel Prize-winning physiologist than when the source was a YMCA director. A communicator may also be more effective when we believe that the person is arguing *against* his or her best interest (Walster, Aronson, & Abrahams, 1966), presumably because the person is seen as more trustworthy. Eagly, Chaiken, and Wood (1981) have discussed this process in terms of attribution theory, noting two kinds of bias that the recipient may perceive. In *knowledge bias*, we believe that the source's knowledge is inaccurate and biased. For example, I might suspect that a millionaire does not know how poor people live. A second form of bias is *reporting bias*, in which we suspect that the source is simply not willing to report the known facts. Politicians are often accused of showing this latter bias. In either case, we are making attributions about the source, and our attributions will determine how effective the source will be. Messages that seem unlikely to reflect the communicator's self-interest are much more credible and therefore much more apt to change attitudes.

Both the physical appearance of communicators and their similarity to us can also affect attitude change. After the 1960 U.S. presidential election, many commentators attributed John Kennedy's victory to the fact that he appeared more attractive on the televised debates than did his opponent, Richard Nixon (McGinniss, 1970). Closer to home, Chaiken (1979) asked students to persuade other undergraduates to sign a petition. Physically attractive sources were more effective than less attractive sources. In trying to explain this effect, Chaiken found that the more attractive student sources had a number of other characteristics as well, such as better communication skills and higher SAT scores, all of which may have contributed to their greater effectiveness.

We are also more easily persuaded if the source is similar to us in ways that are relevant to the issue (Berscheid, 1966). Race of the source may be an additional influence, especially for listeners who are prejudiced against a particular ethnic group (Aronson & Golden, 1962).

Message. Imagine that you were asked to persuade an audience of the virtues of yearly medical checkups. Assume that you know everything there is to know about the topic and that you have been designated as the source. How would you organize your arguments? What medium would you use? What particular appeals would you stress? These questions deal with the communicated message itself. Considerable research has been conducted to isolate those factors of communication that are most effective. In general, we can place these factors in three categories: the content, the organization or format, and the medium used.

One of the major concerns in considering the content of persuasive messages has been the effectiveness of fear-arousing appeals. In our example of yearly medical examinations, for example, would it be wise to describe serious diseases? Or would it be better to stress the positive effects of having a medical exam—improved health, greater self-assurance, and the like?

In an early experiment, Janis and Feshbach (1953) presented subjects with a message designed to encourage proper dental care. The level of fear-arousing content in the message ranged from low (some small cavities might occur) to high (pictures of advanced gum disease were included). These investigators found the greatest reported change among those subjects who had been exposed to low levels of fear-arousing material. More recent evidence contradicts this conclusion, however, often

finding greater attitude change following high-fear appeals (Higbee, 1969; Leventhal, 1970).

These contradictions suggest the need to look more carefully at the content of fear-arousing messages. Rogers (1975) has proposed that three factors are important in any fear appeal: the magnitude of unpleasantness of the event described, the probability that the event will really occur if the recommended action is not taken, and the perceived effectiveness of the recommended action. For example, most people probably see the chances of developing severe gum disease as slim, even though they may forget to brush their teeth for days. Other people may disregard antismoking campaigns that warn of lung cancer and heart attacks, assuming that they are not going to die in the near future whether or not they quit smoking. In summary, a message that arouses fear may not be effective unless the source focuses on the specific behavior that is desired and considers the beliefs that relate to that behavior (Fishbein & Ajzen, 1975).

Another issue in the content of persuasive messages is the question of one-sided communications versus two-sided communications. For example, if you are arguing in favor of reduced television time for children, should you present only arguments that are favorable to your position, or should you acknowledge and attempt to refute an opposing viewpoint? In answering this question, we again see that few answers are "all or none"; instead, specific conditions must be considered in each case. As Karlins and Abelson put it:

> When the audience is generally friendly, or when your position is the only one that will be presented, or when you want immediate, though temporary, opinion change, present one side of the argument. [But when] the audience initially disagrees with you, or when it is probable that the audience will hear the other side from someone else, present both sides of the argument [1970, p. 22].

If there are occasions in which it is most effective to present both sides of an argument, which side should be presented first for maximum impact? Here we face the issue of primacy versus recency effects, also discussed in regard to impression for-

PHOTO 11-2. *Fear-arousing messages may stress the most severe consequences (as in the ad on the left) or consequences that are less serious but more immediate for the target audience (as in the ad on the right).*

mation in Chapter 4. In general, the answer to this question depends on the time intervals involved— the time between the two messages and the time between the messages and the measurement of attitude (Petty & Cacioppo, 1981). Figure 11-2 shows how these factors interact. As can be seen, sometimes there is a primacy effect, sometimes there is a recency effect, and sometimes there is no effect at all.

A third question, in addition to the content and organization of the persuasive message, concerns the medium by which the message is delivered. In Chapter 5 we considered the ways in which communication can be either encouraged or hampered by various modalities. In the present instance, we are concerned with a one-way aspect—how persuasive a communication can be, depending on the modality of transmission. Again, the answer is not a simple "one is better, one is worse." Although some early investigators reported that live or video-taped messages were more effective than audio-taped messages, which were more effective than written messages, recent evidence is less clear-cut (Eagly & Himmelfarb, 1978). One resolution of the confusion (Chaiken & Eagly, 1976) has proposed that we consider the separate stages of comprehending and yielding to a message. A written communication may be more effective in conveying information, particularly information that is complex and difficult to grasp. In contrast, more direct communications, such as videotaped or live presentations, may be more effective when the focus is on yielding rather than comprehension. Therefore, if you want to present a complex proposal to your supervisor at work, written communication might be preferable in the initial presentation stage. Later, however, when the options have been reduced to "yes" and "no," a face-to-face presentation should be more effective.

Context. Up to this point, we have discussed persuasive communications as though they took place in a vacuum. Although some laboratory experiments have structured situations in just that way, it is evident that, in a real-life persuasion context, many factors may be operating at the same time. For instance, a television commercial suggesting that you buy a particular brand of aspirin may have to compete with a family argument, the stereo in the next room, and a knock at the door. What effect do distractions have on the effectiveness of a persuasive message?

Although one might think that any distraction would automatically reduce the effectiveness of a persuasive message, that is not necessarily true. Apparently, distraction inhibits the thoughts that we have and mentally rehearse while we listen to a communication (Petty, Wells, & Brock, 1976). If a message is one with which we are in sympathy, distraction prevents us from rehearsing supportive arguments; therefore, the communication

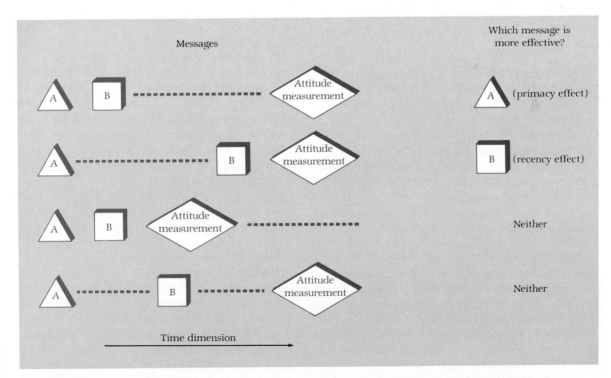

FIGURE 11-2. Effects of order of presentation of two messages and of timing of attitude measurement.

PHOTO 11-3. *The heckler as a distraction in the communication context.*

proves less effective than it would under more neutral circumstances. However, if a message contradicts our beliefs, distraction reduces our ability to generate arguments.

Distractions in laboratory experiments generally involve asking a subject to do two tasks simultaneously. A more natural version of distraction can be seen in the political heckler, who makes comments from the audience while a speaker tries to present an argument. Studies of heckling have found, in contrast to the laboratory situation, that this form of distraction generally reduces the persuasiveness of a message (Silverthorne & Mazmanian, 1975; Sloan, Love, & Ostrom, 1974) among listeners who are initially neutral, although it may serve to moderate positions of listeners who were originally extreme. Why do these results differ from the results of laboratory-based studies of distraction? One reason may be that a heckler not only serves as a distractor (as a competing laboratory task does) but also provides information and an

opposing viewpoint. When uninvolved members of an audience are presented with another side of an argument, the speaker's position may seem much less convincing than it otherwise would. Consistent with the research on two-sided communications, however, a speaker who responds to hecklers in a calm and relevant manner apparently can overcome their effects (Petty & Brock, 1976).

Recipient. Are some people, by the nature of their personalities, more responsive than others to an attempt to change their attitudes, regardless of the source, the content, or the context of a message? Conversely, are some people able to resist efforts—even the best-designed and most appropriate ones—to change their attitudes? The answer is yes, to a slight degree (McGuire, 1968a, 1968b). However, in the majority of cases, the personality of the recipient interacts with other factors to determine whether a change in attitude will take place.

Early attempts to relate personality to persuadability focused on single variables, such as intelligence, self-esteem, the need for social approval, and gender. Generally, these simple approaches met with little success. For example, despite the frequently held belief that women are more apt to be persuaded than men, recent reviews find that, in the standard attitude-change setting, men and women have nearly equal tendencies to change their attitudes (Eagly & Carli, 1981). Although early research suggested that people low in self-esteem would automatically be more prone to change their attitudes (Janis & Field, 1959), this assumption proved to be inaccurate when subjected to a wider range of tests (Bauer, 1970; Cox & Bauer, 1964).

One alternative to this simple but unsuccessful approach has been proposed by McGuire (1968b). As we noted earlier, the learning model considers three distinct stages in the attitude-change process—attention, comprehension, and acceptance, or yielding to the message. If we look at each of these stages separately, we may find that a personality variable has different effects at different stages. For example, people of high intelligence might be able to comprehend a complex message more easily than persons less intellectually endowed; or more intelligent people might be less prone to yield to persuasion, because they have greater confidence in their own critical abilities. In testing this hypothesis, Eagly and Warren (1976) found that high intelligence is related to attitude change when a message is complex—people higher in intelligence changed their attitudes more than less intelligent people. When a message is weak and unsupported by arguments, only people of lower intelligence are likely to change their attitudes.

Up to this point, we have dealt with attitude change in a static way that is reminiscent of the Shannon and Weaver model discussed in Chapter 5. We have viewed the source as having a set of stable characteristics and the recipient as having a set of stable characteristics, and we have looked at the possible matches, or persuasive tendencies, between these units. In fact, attitude change, like communication in general, is an active and dynamic process; the source and the recipient can greatly affect each other. For example, communicators have been shown to shift their message toward the position of the audience if they know what that position is (Crawford, 1974; Newtson & Czerlinsky, 1974). Observers of political campaigns are well aware of this tendency. Speakers often shift the content and organization of their message when they perceive an unfriendly or unfavorably disposed audience, stressing problems and issues (a two-sided approach) rather than simple solutions (Hazen & Kiesler, 1975). Therefore, recipients of a persuasive communication not only receive—they can actively shape the content and the organization of the persuasive message as it is being delivered.

D. Applications

There are many ways that the principles of the learning model can have practical applications. In seeking to use this model, one might first consider the various stages in the attitude-change process. For example, the political adviser planning a media campaign must first be certain that the potential audience is attending to the message. Politicians do not always gain such attention: flyers are thrown into the wastebasket, commercials are aired while the television viewer goes to the kitchen for a snack, and even billboards are ignored. Having gained some attention, however, candidates should try to present messages that will be understood by a wide audience. Two-sided messages may be more effective in persuading the audience that is aware of the issues. For less informed audiences, one-sided messages may be more successful. At the same time, however, most evidence shows that those voters who have the least interest in the campaign are the ones most likely to change (Oskamp, 1977). Such evidence suggests that attention may be a major factor in political campaigns, reinforced by the effects of mere exposure (see Box 11-1).

Advertisers have also used principles developed by the learning model. It is, for example, quite common for a famous person from the world of sports or entertainment to be presented endorsing a particular product. Here the attempt is clearly to use the credibility or trustworthiness or attractiveness of the source to make a message more convincing.

Within the field of health, fear appeals have often been used to persuade an audience. For example, in one recent study, dental patients viewed slide

PHOTO 11-4. *The athlete as persuasive source: Joe Di Maggio makes a pitch for Mr. Coffee.*

BOX 11-1. Effects of mere exposure on voting behavior

Because of the increased use of television in recent political campaigns, many investigators have begun to focus on the effects that exposure alone can have on voting behavior. Laboratory research by Zajonc (1968) has shown that mere exposure to a stimulus can increase our positive feelings about that stimulus (see Chapter 6). In other words, the more we see something, the more we are apt to like it. Apparently, this simple principle applies to political elections. Grush, McKeough, and Ahlering (1978) predicted 83% of the winners in the 1972 U.S. congressional primaries by calculating the amount of media coverage devoted to each candidate. In light of this finding, it isn't surprising that Grush and his colleagues have found that wealthy candidates are very likely to win elections (Grush & Schersching, 1978). With money, a candidate can buy extensive television coverage. The frequency of exposure in the media apparently provides a strong force for attitude change—specifically, a vote for the candidate on election day.

Yet, there may be some limits to this effect. In the 1982 U.S. elections, for example, more candidates spent more money than ever before. But many of the highest-spending candidates did not win, suggesting that there may be a limit to the effectiveness of mere exposure— at some point, every candidate is seen often enough. ■

presentations that described gum disease as either high or low in severity. In the high-severity condition, patients heard about throbbing pain, bleeding gums, facial disfiguration, and eating difficulties. In the low-severity condition, only mild annoyances were described. Contacted three to four weeks later, these two groups of patients reported differences in the recommended action of flossing

their teeth: the higher-fear message apparently was more effective (Beck & Lund, 1981).

Another important factor in changing health-related behaviors is the similarity of the source to the target audience. In another study of the effect of fear appeals on behavior, Dembroski, Lasater, and Ramirez (1978) found that the content of a communication had no effect on toothbrushing behavior of high school students. Among the Black students, however, a Black communicator was much more effective than a White communicator, suggesting that similarity of the source is an important variable in eliciting attitude and behavior change.

Many other examples, of course, could be offered showing the relevance of learning models to practical change efforts. In each case, the emphasis would be on the sequence of stages and the importance of source, message, context, and recipient.

■ II. Social-judgment theory

A. Assumptions about human nature

Social-judgment theory is a more cognitive and more individualistic approach to the study of attitude change. This theory emphasizes the individual's perception and judgment of a persuasive communication, and it views such judgments as mediators of attitude change. Viewing the human as a cognitive being, this theory assumes that people know what their attitudes are, where they stand along a continuum, what other attitudes they are willing to accept, and which attitudes they would reject. These cognitive judgments are assumed to precede any actual changes that occur. At the same time, social-judgment theory assumes that emotional involvement in an issue can affect attitudes and attitude change. Thus, cognitive and affective components are intertwined in this theory, and each may affect the other.

B. Basic concepts of social-judgment theory

The major developer of the social-judgment approach to attitude change has been Muzafer Sherif (Sherif & Hovland, 1961; Sherif, Sherif, &

Nebergall, 1965). To understand the principles of social-judgment theory as developed by Sherif, we need to look briefly at some issues in psychophysics, from which the theory was developed. In their early work, Sherif and his colleagues were interested in the basic question of how simple judgments are affected by the context. First they asked subjects to judge the heaviness of a series of weights (ranging from 55 to 141 grams) on a 6-point scale, where 1 was to be used for the lightest weight and 6 for the heaviest. Sherif and his colleagues (Sherif, Taub, & Hovland, 1958) found that, with only this set of weights on which to base their judgments, subjects tended to distribute their judgments equally across the 6-point scale (see the top panel of Figure 11-3).

In the next stage of the experiment, Sherif and his colleagues altered the judgment context by introducing an **anchor**—a reference point used in making judgments. They did this in two ways. First, they gave subjects a weight of 141 grams and told them that this weight should be rated as a 6. With this weight as an anchor, subjects showed **assimilation effects**: judgments tended to pile up toward the anchored (heavier) end of the scale, rather than being equally distributed as they had before (see the middle panel of Figure 11-3). In a second demonstration of judgment effects, the investigators gave subjects an anchor weighing 347 grams and told them that this weight should be rated as a 6. In this case, when judging the original series of weights, subjects showed a **contrast effect**—their judgments tended to pile up at the lighter end of the distribution, as they rated the weights as being much lighter in contrast to the anchor stimulus (illustrated in the bottom panel of Figure 11-3).

Although weights may seem a bit abstract, we all make these kinds of judgment shifts fairly regularly. Consider, for example, the resident of snowbound Minneapolis or Ottawa in the winter, who would probably rate a winter day when the thermometer went above 32 degrees Fahrenheit as warm and balmy, showing a contrast effect in judgment—comparing it with the below-zero anchor points that are typically experienced. However, that same temperature in the summer (or in

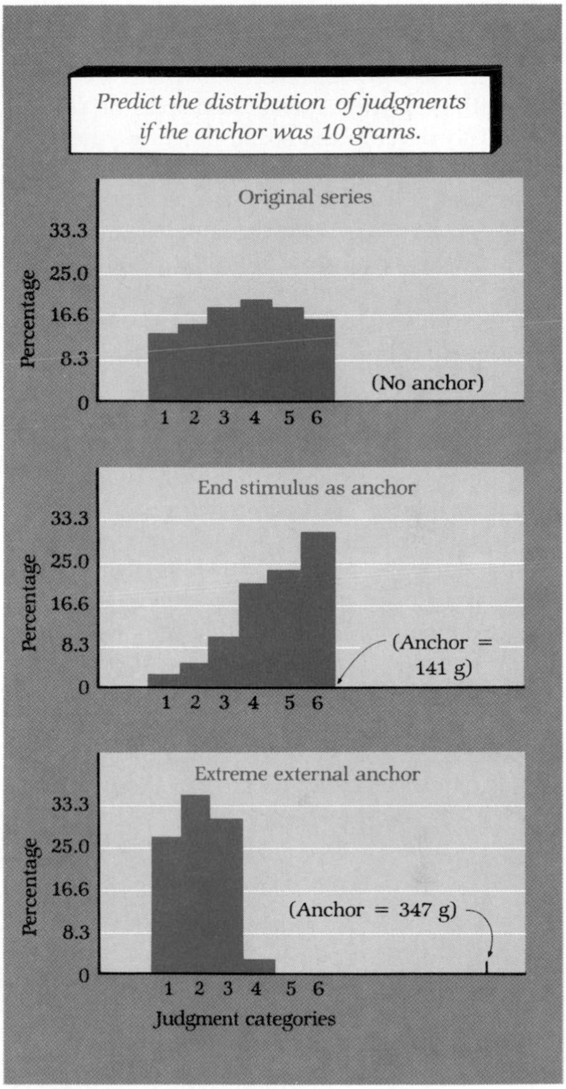

FIGURE 11-3. Distribution of judgments of weights without anchor (top) and with anchors (middle and bottom). In Sherif's study, there were an equal number of stimuli at each of the six weight levels. In the absence of an anchor, subjects made an equal percentage of judgments to each of the six categories. When an anchor was introduced, judgment patterns changed. In the middle panel, we see that nearly 30% of the weights were judged to be heaviest, showing assimilation toward the 141-gram anchor. A contrast effect is evident in the lower panel. None of the weights was judged as heaviest when the anchor was much heavier, and a high percentage of judgments were made to the lighter categories.

a Florida winter) might be judged as cold, in comparison with the anchor-point days with temperatures in the 60s and 70s.

Sherif used these basic principles of psychophysics to develop his social-judgment theory of attitude change. Persuasive communications that are similar to our own view (an internal anchor) will be judged as more similar than they really are, whereas communications at some distance from our own position will be contrasted, or judged as farther away than they actually are. To explain how these judgments of assimilation and contrast are related to actual attitude change, Sherif introduced three new concepts: *latitude of acceptance, latitude of rejection,* and *latitude of noncommitment* (Sherif & Hovland, 1961; Sherif et al., 1965). The principle of latitudes reflects Sherif's belief that a person's attitude cannot be represented by a single point on a scale; rather, an attitude consists of a range of acceptable positions. For example, if you were presented with a set of statements on a particular issue (using, for example, a Thurstone scale as described in Chapter 10), you would be asked to indicate all the statements that you felt were consistent with your attitude on the issue. These statements would constitute your latitude

of acceptance (see Figure 11-4). The range of statements that a person finds unacceptable or objectionable is defined as the latitude of rejection, and statements that are neither acceptable nor unacceptable constitute the latitude of noncommitment.

When a person encounters a persuasive communication, his or her first reaction is to make a judgment on where this communication falls on the dimensions in question and, specifically, whether it falls inside or outside the latitude of acceptance. Once this judgment is made, then attitude change may or may not occur. Social-judgment theory states that attitude change is most likely to occur when a communication falls inside a person's latitude of acceptance (Atkins, Deaux, & Bieri, 1967). Attitude change has also been shown to occur when the message falls within an individual's latitude of noncommitment, approaching but not within the latitude of rejection (Peterson & Koulack, 1969).

C. Representative research

Research done within the framework of social-judgment theory has concentrated on two issues:

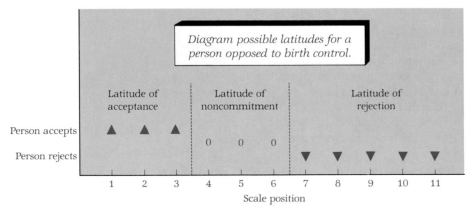

FIGURE 11-4. Latitudes of acceptance, rejection, and noncommitment. Each number represents a particular statement that the person is asked to accept or reject. For example, if the issue were birth control, a statement at 1 might be "Birth-control devices should be available to everyone, and the government and public welfare agencies should encourage the use of such devices." A statement at the other extreme might be "All birth-control devices should be illegal, and the government should prevent them from being manufactured." In the example depicted here, our hypothetical person favors pro-birth-control positions and rejects anti-birth-control positions.

(1) What are the effects of ego involvement in an issue on the latitudes of acceptance and rejection and hence on attitude change? (2) How much is attitude change influenced by the discrepancy between the communication and the recipient's position?

Ego involvement and the latitudes.   A question of major concern to Sherif and his colleagues has been how the size of a person's latitudes of acceptance, rejection, and noncommitment may differ as a function of that person's involvement in the issue at hand. In other words, if you are extremely committed to an issue, will you be apt to find a smaller range of positions acceptable than if your concerns are less intense? Surprisingly, Sherif and his colleagues found no difference in the size of the latitude of acceptance as a function of a person's involvement in an issue. People who were strongly committed to either a Republican or a Democratic position did not differ from uncommitted or neutral people in the size of their acceptable range of positions (although obviously the content of statements within those ranges did differ considerably). Differences did occur in the width of latitudes of noncommitment and rejection. People at either extreme of the scale found considerably more positions unacceptable and were neutral or uncommitted on far fewer items. In other words, the person who is a fanatic about some issue, such as gun control, will not necessarily find any fewer positions acceptable than will a less ego-involved advocate—but that person will reject more positions at the opposite end of the gun-control spectrum and be neutral about very few positions. Not all research is consistent with Sherif's findings, however, and the exact relation between ego involvement and size of latitudes is still uncertain (Eagly & Telaak, 1972; N. Miller, 1965).

The question of the size of the latitude of acceptance is important in Sherif's theory because it serves as the basis for predictions of attitude change. A person with a narrow latitude of acceptance would not be expected to change his or her position easily, whereas the person with a wider range of acceptance should find more persuasive mes-

PHOTO 11-5. *Commitment to an issue: Canadians rally against "acid rain" caused, they believe, by smoke from U.S. industries.*

sages falling in or near the boundaries of acceptability.

Effects of discrepancy between communication and recipient's position.   On the basis of the principles of the latitudes, social-judgment theory predicts a curvilinear relation between discrepancy and attitude change. If you consider the implications of the various latitudes, the reasons for this prediction become clear. Messages that fall very close to the person's own position should be assimilated, and no real change would be necessary. At the other end, messages that are highly discrepant with one's own position would probably fall within the latitude of rejection and would not be acceptable or effect any change. Between these two extremes, when messages fall somewhere in the latitude of noncommitment, their persuasive impact should be the greatest. Research results generally support this prediction (Hovland, Harvey, & Sherif, 1957; Peterson & Koulack, 1969).

Social judgment has also attempted to incorporate other variables, such as the credibility of a persuasive source, into its models. For example, social-judgment theorists have suggested that if the persuasive agent is highly respectable and highly credible, attitude change will be more likely to occur. Although other theorists, such as those in the Yale Communication Research Program, have predicted similar effects, the rationale for the social-judgment prediction is slightly different. Social-judgment theorists argue that source credibility affects the perception of the message and thus effectively broadens the latitudes of acceptance and noncommitment, thus making attitude change more likely.

D. Applications

The major applications of social-judgment theory have dealt with definition of attitudes rather than with attitude change. Perhaps the most frequent application has been in the area of political attitudes. As we saw earlier, the attitudes of Republicans and Democrats can be distinguished in terms of their latitudes of acceptance and rejection. Other investigators have also been interested in political attitudes, although not always using the exact procedures of Sherif. For example, Free and Cantril (1967) attempted to find out where voters stood on a general liberal/conservative dimension. They sampled over 3000 respondents in the United States, asking them general questions about such issues as federal interference, government regulation, and individual initiative. On the basis of these results, they reported that 50% of the citizens in the United States considered themselves completely conservative, 34% considered themselves middle-of-the-road, and only a small percentage could be identified as completely or predominantly liberal. A second set of questions, which focused on *operational* liberalism and conservatism, produced quite different results. (The questions dealt with specific issues, such as Medicare, urban renewal, and federal aid to education.) In this case, the majority of people were found to be liberal in their political ideology (see

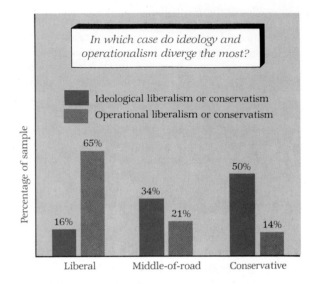

FIGURE 11-5. Ideology versus operationalism in political beliefs.

Figure 11-5). These results underline the importance of knowing the specific positions that people are willing to endorse, a notion that is consistent with the social-judgment approach.

Although there have been some applications of social-judgment theory, it has not been used so extensively in the practical arena as some other models. Although Sherif himself often dealt with practical issues, the theory itself is somewhat limited, dealing only with the variables of message discrepancy and a person's ego involvement in the issue. Furthermore, because the measurement procedures are somewhat cumbersome, other methods and theories are often preferred. The main attraction of social-judgment theory is its recognition of an optimum distance between the subject's attitude position and the position of the persuasive communication. As we shall see in the next section, however, other theories with a broader range of coverage make this same prediction from a different theoretical stance.

■ III. Consistency theories

A. Assumptions about human nature

Theories of the third type, consistency theories of attitude change, share with social-judgment theory an emphasis on cognitive processes. They assume that we are aware of our attitudes and behaviors and, more important, that we want these various aspects of ourselves to be consistent with each other. Holding inconsistent attitudes is assumed to be an uncomfortable experience that leads to attitude change.

Although consistency theory assumes that we are thoughtful, it does not necessarily posit that we are rational. Indeed, Abelson and Rosenberg (1958) have coined the term *psycho-logic* to refer to the process whereby we may alter our beliefs so that they are psychologically consistent without necessarily following the strict rules of formal logic. For example, if you know that cigarettes can cause cancer and yet continue to smoke, the belief and the behavior are inconsistent. To resolve this uncomfortable state of inconsistency, you may deny that cigarettes have anything to do with disease. Such a choice is not totally rational; yet, the denial allows your continued smoking behavior to be consistent with your beliefs.

There are a variety of cognitive consistency theories, but we will limit our discussion to two: Heider's balance model and Festinger's cognitive dissonance theory. Both these theories assume that people are motivated to be and to appear consistent; both assume that a person's awareness of his or her own inconsistency produces tension and cannot easily be tolerated; and, finally, both assume that attitude change is a principal tool for resolving inconsistencies.

B. Balance theory

Fritz Heider (1946, 1958) was the first to develop a theory, based on a principle of consistency, about the ways people view their relationships with other people and with their environment. For simplicity, Heider limited his analysis to two persons (P and O) and to one other entity (X). The person P is the focus of analysis, and O represents some other person; X can be an idea, a person, a thing, or any attitude object. Heider's goal was to discover how the relationships among P, O, and X are organized in P's cognitive structure. Heider proposed that two possible relationships could exist among these three elements—a *unit relationship*,

which refers to the extent to which two elements belong together, as in ownership or similar-group membership, and a *liking relationship*. We will concentrate on the liking relationship, which includes all forms of positive or negative sentiments, or affect, between two or more elements.

In formulating **balance theory,** Heider proposed that the relations among P, O, and X may be either balanced or unbalanced, depending on the pattern of like and dislike links among elements. Consider the following example. Paul (P), who has spent all summer as a volunteer worker for the Republican presidential candidate, enters the state university as a freshman in the fall. He is assigned to Professor O'Hara (O) as his faculty adviser. When they meet to plan a first-semester schedule, Paul observes that Professor O'Hara is wearing a campaign button for the Democratic candidate. Will Paul like Professor O'Hara? Will Paul think much of the professor's recommendations about which courses to take? Probably not—because Paul does not feel comfortable in unbalanced relationships. If X in this example stands for the Democratic candidate, a balanced state exists when Paul likes Professor O'Hara, Paul likes Democrats, and O'Hara likes Democrats. The only way a balanced state can exist within Paul's cognitive structure, as long as Paul dislikes Democrats and the professor disagrees, is for Paul to dislike Professor O'Hara. Paul can say, in effect, "Professor O'Hara is no good, which fits because she's a big supporter of the Democratic candidate."

Heider proposed that balanced states exist either when all three relations are positive (as in liking) or when two relations are negative (disliking) and one is positive (see Figure 11-6). The preceding example fits the latter possibility. Of course, if Paul had found that his adviser was a Republican supporter and if he had come to like her, then balance theory would describe the relationship as "P likes O, P likes X, and O likes X." As seen in Figure 11-6, unbalanced states do occur; people do like other people who differ in their attitudes toward important issues or objects. The reverse situation is also possible: you may discover that someone you hate intensely likes the same rather obscure art works that you do. What do you do about such a state?

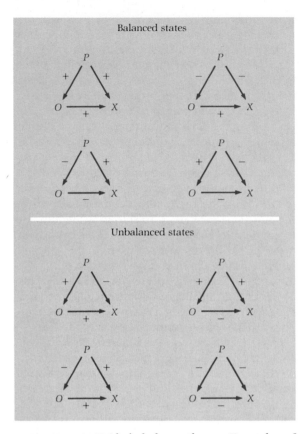

FIGURE 11-6. Heider's balance theory: Examples of balanced and unbalanced states according to Heider's definition of balance. In each case, P is the person whose attitudes are of concern. P can either like or dislike O, and both P and O can have either positive or negative attitudes toward X. Can you find any pattern in the definition of balanced and unbalanced states?

Heider proposes that such unbalanced states produce tension and generate forces to achieve or restore balance.

Heider's approach is highly simplified. This simplicity is intriguing, and the idea of balance can be applied to many situations (Cialdini, Petty, & Cacioppo, 1981). Yet, the model's greatest limitation may be that it's *too* simplified, for the approach fails to consider degrees of liking, relationships that consist of more than three elements, or more than one direction of liking—for example, it does not consider whether O likes P but only whether P likes O.

C. Cognitive dissonance theory

Cognitive dissonance theory, as first proposed by Leon Festinger (1957), has been the most influential consistency theory, not only in the area of attitude change but in a wide variety of other areas of social psychology as well. The basic assumptions of the theory are quite simple (see Figure 11-7). Cognitive dissonance is said to exist when a person has two cognitions that contradict each other. Cognitions are thoughts, attitudes, beliefs, and also behaviors of which the person is cognitively aware. For example, the following statements could be considered cognitions: "It's a nice day today," "I am a thoughtful person," "I believe that schools are repressive institutions," and "I forgot my father's birthday." According to Festinger, such cognitions can be either relevant or irrelevant to each other. For example, "It's a nice day today" and "Schools are repressive institutions" would probably be considered irrelevant, in that the one cognition does not imply anything about the other. In contrast, "I am a thoughtful person" is relevant to "I forgot my father's birthday" because the one cognition relates to the other in a psychological sense. Two relevant cognitions

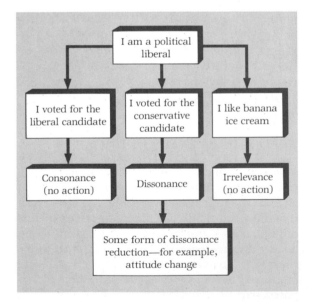

FIGURE 11-7. Elements of cognitive dissonance theory.

may exist either in a state of *consonance* or in a state of *dissonance*. In dissonance, exemplified by "thoughtful person" and "forgetting father's birthday," the two elements do not fit with each other—or, to use a term of Festinger's, the one element implies the obverse of the other.

A basic assumption of dissonance theory is that a state of dissonance motivates the person to reduce or eliminate the dissonance. Dissonance, the theory says, is uncomfortable and produces a state of psychological tension. Just how uncomfortable this state is or how great the magnitude of the dissonance depends on two factors: (1) the ratio of dissonant to consonant cognitions and (2) the importance of each cognition to the person. In other words, two cognitions may exist in a state of dissonance, but if neither is terribly important or central to your beliefs, then the tension experienced will be only minimal. When important beliefs or behaviors are at stake, however, dissonance theory would predict considerable tension and considerable effort to reduce that tension.

How is dissonance reduced? One method is to decrease the number or importance of the dissonant elements. If a man has forgotten his father's birthday, he may convince himself that celebrating birthdays is meaningless or that his father would just as soon not be reminded that he's getting older. Or the man may increase the number or importance of the consonant cognitions. To reaffirm that he is a thoughtful person, for example, he may buy his father tickets for the Super Bowl, ask him out for dinner, or engage in other behaviors that are consistent with being a thoughtful person.

A third way of reducing dissonance is, of course, to change one of the dissonant elements so that it is no longer inconsistent with the other cognitions. Often this reduction involves changing one's attitude so that it is consistent with a behavior already performed. In our example, the man might change his self-perception and no longer consider himself an extremely thoughtful person. This latter example underlines one of the unique aspects of dissonance theory. Because the theory proposes that any of the elements in the relationship may change when dissonance is experienced, it allows one to treat the attitude/behavior relationship from both

directions. A change in one's cognitions about the self, for example, may lead to future changes in behavior. But it is equally possible that a change in one's behavior may lead to a change in one's attitudes—thus, attitude change may result from behavior as well as cause behaviors.

What is dissonant for one person may not be dissonant for another, and recent formulations of dissonance theory have often stressed the self. Cognitions may be dissonant but will not necessarily create tension unless some element of personal responsibility is involved (Aronson, 1968; Greenwald & Ronis, 1978). Commitment to a decision is also important, and dissonance will be greater when a person freely chooses a particular behavior (Brehm & Cohen, 1962).

The flexibility of this theory has made it extremely popular, and it has been applied to a wide variety of situations, ranging from controlled laboratory experiments on attitude change to participant observation of religious cults. At the same time, the openness of the theory has presented certain problems as well; for example, it is often difficult to specify with any precision just what elements are relevant to a particular situation and how important those elements may be to a particular person. Nonetheless, the theory has generated a huge body of research and, as any good theory should, has suggested many new and significant questions.

D. Representative research

Both balance theory and dissonance theory have been subjected to empirical tests. Studies of the relation between attitude similarity and attraction, for example (as discussed in Chapter 6), are basically derived from Heider's model. If you like pizza with pepperoni and mushrooms and your new roommate has the same preference in pizza, then you are more apt to like your roommate than if the person is an anchovy freak. Similarly, a rave movie review from a friend will make you more inclined to rate that movie positively than you would if your friend had pronounced the movie a dud.

However, the research on balance theory (see Mower-White, 1979) has been only a trickle compared with the hundreds of studies deriving from dissonance theory. For that reason, we will focus on dissonance research, looking at just a few of the major issues.

Consequences of decision making. More than most other theories of attitude change, dissonance theory has been concerned with the consequences of making a decision for subsequent attitudes and behavior. According to the theory, any time one is forced to choose between two attractive options, postdecisional dissonance exists (Festinger, 1957). The more difficult or important the decision, the more likely a person is to find reasons that support the choice that was made and to minimize the attractive qualities of the forgone choice. For example, if you are undecided about which of two persons to invite to the Super Bowl game, dissonance theory predicts that once you have made your choice, you will find many ways of "spreading apart" the alternatives—your chosen date will seem more attractive than he or she did before, and the rejected date will seem less attractive than before. This same strategy has been evidenced in a variety of settings, including election polling areas and race tracks (see Box 11-2).

Counterattitudinal advocacy. When a person is forced to take a public position contrary to his or her private attitude, dissonance theory proposes that the conflict will lead to attitude change (usually in the private attitude). The theory also makes the somewhat surprising prediction that the less a person is induced to advocate a public position that violates the private attitude, the more likely the person is to shift the privately held attitude. The now-classic study that first tested this prediction (Festinger & Carlsmith, 1959) paid male students either $1 or $20 to lie to other students. After participating for an hour in a series of dull, meaningless tasks (for example, putting 12 spools in a tray, emptying the tray, and then refilling it, time and time again), the student was paid to tell a prospective subject that the experiment was interesting, educational, and highly worthwhile. Later, under the guise of a survey not part of the experiment, each subject who had lied for either

$1 or $20 answered a questionnaire about his private attitudes toward the experiment. Festinger and Carlsmith found that students who had been paid only $1 rated the experimental task as more enjoyable than did students who were paid $20. Presumably, the students who were paid $20 for the lie could easily justify their behavior—money did talk, in this instance. The other students, who received only $1 in payment, had to find some other reason for their behavior—hence the attitude change, whereby they said that the experiment was enjoyable because they believed it was.

Not everyone has accepted this conclusion. The methodology of cognitive dissonance studies, particularly those that involve deception, has been severely criticized, and questions have been raised about the validity of some of the results (Chapanis & Chapanis, 1964). Critics have also questioned the plausibility of some of the manipulations and suggested that the subjects may have been suspicious. Rosenberg, for example, has argued that paying large monetary rewards in cognitive dissonance experiments has led to an increase in the subject's **evaluation apprehension,** defined as "an active, anxiety-toned concern that he win a positive evaluation from the experimenter, or at least that he provide no grounds for a negative one" (1965, p. 29). This apprehension, presumably greater when more money is involved, might cause the subject who was paid $20 to resist admitting any change in private opinion.

Controversy surrounding the effects of counterattitudinal advocacy continued for more than a decade after Festinger and Carlsmith's original experiment, resulting in dozens of studies and numerous lively debates. In the aftermath of this debate, it seems clear that Festinger's basic hypothesis does indeed hold true, when certain conditions are met. In brief, these conditions are the following: (1) there is low incentive (for example, money) to perform the behavior; (2) the person has a high degree of perceived choice to perform the behavior; (3) the action has unpleasant consequences for someone; and (4) the person believes that he or she has a high degree of personal responsibility for the action and its consequences (Kiesler & Munson, 1975; Oskamp, 1977).

BOX 11-2. Postdecisional dissonance reduction at post time

"Put your money where your mouth is" was an admonition followed by Robert Knox and James Inkster (1968), who were not content to test cognitive dissonance theory only under controlled laboratory conditions. These researchers went to a race track in Vancouver and interviewed bettors at the $2 window about the chances of their horse's winning. Subjects who were interviewed as they stood in line waiting to place their bets thought their horse had a little better than fair chance to win. In contrast, subjects interviewed right after they had placed their bets were significantly more confident, rating their chances as good. These results suggest that the act of committing oneself by placing the bet creates dissonance and leads to the dissonance-reducing rating of greater confidence in one's choice. A similar process was observed by Frenkel and Doob (1976) at polling areas in a Toronto election. Voters polled after they had cast their ballot were more likely to believe that their candidate was best and that he or she would win than voters polled before they entered the polling area. ■

Furthermore, some degree of arousal related to the inconsistency is necessary as well. Subjects who are administered a tranquilizer in the forced-compliance situation, for example, show little attitude change (Cooper, Zanna, & Taves, 1978). Although the behavior of these subjects is still counter to their attitudes, the tranquilizer presumably reduces any tension that might arise from the dissonance between attitude and behavior—and, without tension, there is no pressure to change the attitude. Thus, as is true of the consistency notion in general, some behaviors that are discrepant with previously held attitudes will not cause any subsequent attitude change; however, those that are more important, more personal, and less readily justified may indeed lead us to modify our attitudes.

E. Applications

Consistency theories have had dozens of practical applications, in areas as diverse as politics, marketing, and health. As we have already seen, postdecisional dissonance reduction is alive and well at both polling stations and betting windows (Box 11-2). Let us look at just a few of the other applications of these far-reaching theories.

In the realm of political opinion, balance theory can often explain how voters view candidates and their positions. Kinder (1978) studied voters' perceptions of the 1968 U.S. presidential candidates —Nixon, Humphrey, and Wallace. At the same time, he asked the voters about their own stands on a number of current issues, such as the problem of urban unrest. In line with balance theory, voters who thought that the solution to urban unrest was the use of more force, for example, also tended to see their preferred candidate as having similar views on the issue. Other voters who were opposed to the use of force saw the same candidate as sharing their views. In other words, people were attempting to achieve a balanced relationship among the triad consisting of (1) their attitude toward an issue, (2) their attitude toward a candidate, and (3) the candidate's attitude toward that issue.

As we suggested earlier, dissonance theory has been one of the most widely applied theories. In the marketing context, for example, investigators have considered how consumers would react to products introduced at special low prices (Doob, Carlsmith, Freedman, Landauer, & Tom, 1969). Although marketing people often assume that such a lure would be enticing, dissonance theory predicts that people would be more likely to endorse a product if they had paid *more* money for it. Thus, according to the dissonance prediction, greater investment causes greater liking. Testing this prediction at a series of discount houses, Doob

and his colleagues introduced a new product either at a discount price or at the regular price. After a period of one to three weeks, the regular price was adopted at all stores. Consistent with the predictions of dissonance theory, subsequent sales were higher when the initial price had *not* been discounted.

Alcoholism has also been studied in the context of dissonance theory. Recall that dissonance theory assumes that the experience of dissonance is both arousing and unpleasant. If this is so, Claude Steele and his colleagues reasoned, then drinking might serve as a way to reduce dissonance—even if it could not effectively change the cognitions that lead to dissonance (Steele, Southwick, & Critchlow, 1981). In this experiment, college students who were at least 21 years old and who had experience with alcohol were recruited for a study of beer tasting. Dissonance was initially created by asking these students to write a counterattitudinal essay—an essay in favor of increased tuition, which most students in fact opposed. Having created this inconsistency between behavior and belief, the experimenters then gave subjects the opportunity to sample a variety of beers. Although dissonance did not affect the amount of beer that students drank, it did affect their subsequent attitudes. Students who drank beer after writing the counterattitudinal essay were less likely to change their attitudes than subjects who indicated their attitudes immediately after completing the essay, before drinking any beer. In a further demonstration of the specific effect of alcohol, these investigators found that neither water nor coffee had any noticeable effect on attitudes. Thus, for many people, alcohol may serve as a way to reduce uncomfortable tension and to avoid recognizing the contradictions between one's behaviors and one's beliefs.

There are dozens of other ways that dissonance theory has been applied. A major concern for the practitioner, however, is to determine the ways in which people are most likely to reduce dissonance. Because so many alternatives are possible, it is necessary to evaluate the situation carefully to understand which route of dissonance reduction is most apt to be followed.

■ IV. Functional theories

A. Assumptions about human nature

The fourth type of attitude-change theory, functional theory, emphasizes individual differences in human nature. Whereas other theories tend to emphasize the common factors in attitude change, **functional theory** looks at the ways in which individual attitudes are based on different assumptions and needs. In part, functional theories base their analysis of needs on the assumptions of psychoanalytic theory, looking for underlying motivations that may explain more superficial attitudes.

B. Basic concepts of functional theory

The basic proposition of a functional theory of attitude change is simple: people hold attitudes that fit their needs, and in order to change those attitudes, we must determine what their needs are. The functional approach is a phenomenological one; it maintains that a stimulus (for example, a television commercial, a new piece of information, or an interracial contact) can be understood only within the context of the perceiver's needs and personality. Different people may have quite different needs, and consequently the same persuasive message may not be equally effective for all people.

Two rather similar functional theories have been developed, one by Katz (1960, 1968; Katz & Stotland, 1959) and one by Smith, Bruner, and White (1956). Each theory proposes a list of functions that attitudes serve. The two theories have some differences, but Kiesler, Collins, and Miller (1969) have helpfully synthesized the functions of each, as shown in Table 11-1. We will describe each general function, drawing heavily on the analysis of Kiesler and his associates.

First, attitudes may serve an *instrumental, adjustive,* or *utilitarian* function. According to Katz, a person develops a positive attitude toward those objects that are useful in meeting his or her needs or are effective in preventing negative events. If an object or another person thwarts the person's needs, he or she develops a negative attitude toward that

TABLE 11-1. The functions of attitudes

Katz	Smith, Bruner, and White
Types:	
1. Instrumental, adjustive, utilitarian	Social adjustment
2. Ego defense	Externalization
3. Knowledge	Object appraisal
4. Value expressive	Quality of expressiveness

object or person. As we can see, this particular basis of attitudes draws heavily on learning principles, suggesting that a person's past history of reinforcement or punishment with a particular attitude object will serve as the basis for attitude formation and change.

Second, attitudes may serve an *ego-defensive* or *externalizing* function. Here, Katz's functional theory is influenced by psychoanalytic thought. An attitude may develop or change in order to protect a person "from acknowledging the basic truths about himself or the harsh realities in his external world" (Katz, 1960, p. 170). For example, derogatory attitudes toward out-groups and minority groups may serve as a means of convincing oneself of one's own importance. Without utilizing psychoanalytic supports, Smith, Bruner, and White see attitudes as functioning in a similar way, permitting the externalization of internal reactions.

The *knowledge* function, or *object appraisal*, is a third function of attitudes. Attitudes may develop or change in order "to give meaning to what would otherwise be an unorganized chaotic universe" (Katz, 1960, p. 175). This will happen particularly when a problem cannot be solved without the information associated with the attitude. Smith et al. see attitudes as a "ready aid in 'sizing up' objects and events in the environment from the point of view of one's major interests and going concerns" (1956, p. 41). Some of the consistency notions are relevant here, as we may view new situations in terms of the previous beliefs that we have about the situation. Object appraisal "stresses the role that gathering information plays in the day-to-day adaptive activities of the individual" (Kiesler et al., 1969, p. 315).

PHOTO 11-6. *Agreements in international relations, as acknowledged here by the late Anwar Sadat, Jimmy Carter, and Menachem Begin, require recognition of the various functions that specific attitudes may serve.*

Value expression is a fourth function of attitudes. According to Katz, people gain satisfaction from expressing themselves through their attitudes. For example, one's attitude toward the latest Porsche may be a reflection of a general self-image, one that in this case is centered on fast cars and new trends. Beyond this, the expression of attitudes may help people form their own self-concepts. Smith, Bruner, and White diverge most widely from Katz at this point. To them, the expressive nature of attitudes does not mean that any need for expression exists but, rather, that a person's attitudes "reflect the deeper-lying pattern of his or her life" (Smith et al., 1956, p. 38). In other words, they do not see this fourth type of attitude as serving any real function or satisfying any real need but, rather, as being simply a reflection of some general aspects of the personality.

If we consider that attitudes may be serving any one of these four different functions, we can see why the process of attitude change is sometimes very difficult. First of all, different conditions may arouse different attitudes. For example, posed threats or a rise in frustration may activate ego-defensive needs. In contrast, new information presented in an intellectual way may arouse attitudes based on the knowledge function. In turn, different types of influences are predicted to be effective in changing each type of attitude. The promise of social approval from an important peer group, for example, might be effective in changing an instrumentally based attitude. Attitudes based on ego-defensive needs would probably be unaffected by such a strategy but might be more influenced by some form of self-insight therapy.

C. Representative research

A straightforward test of functional theory would be to select two subjects whose attitudes toward an object are similar but are based on different needs and then to determine the effectiveness of various kinds of attitude-change techniques. Unfortunately, however, this straightforward approach has not been used, largely because of the difficulty in determining just what function a particular attitude serves for a particular individual.

A more general approach is demonstrated in a study by McClintock (1958), in which groups of subjects were assessed on two general personality measures (need for conformity and ego defensiveness) and then presented with one of several messages concerning prejudice. One message, for example, was informational, stressing the cultural-relativism arguments against prejudice; another was interpretational, focusing on the internal dynamics that can lead to prejudice. McClintock predicted that subjects high in conformity would be more susceptible to the informational appeal, whereas subjects high in ego defensiveness would be more persuaded by the interpretational appeal. (Notice that the investigator is assuming that, for a person high in ego defensiveness, any attitude is presumed to have that basis. Such an assumption is very risky, and an experiment based on it does not really test the individual approach of functional theory.)

Despite a number of methodological problems in this study, one of the hypotheses was confirmed. Among subjects who read the informational message, more high-conformity subjects than low-conformity subjects changed their attitudes. In contrast, high-ego-defensive persons were less likely to show attitude change than low-ego-defensive persons. Results for the interpretational message were much less consistent. Conformity showed no relation to change, and for the ego-defensiveness measure, greatest change was shown by those in the middle range of the scale. Although Katz would argue that those high in ego defensiveness are simply too rigid to make any changes, at least in such an impersonal setting, we must conclude that the results are not wholehearted support for functional theory. Furthermore, later attempts to demonstrate the utility of functional theory have also not been very successful (Katz, Sarnoff, & McClintock, 1956; Smith & Brigham, 1972; Stotland, Katz, & Patchen, 1959).

A functional theory of attitudes is appealing to anyone who recognizes that attitude change is a function of both the message and the recipient of that message. More than any other approach, this one recognizes individual differences in persuasion, and for that reason it should not be dismissed lightly. But the development of the theory is hampered by a lack of adequate measurement of needs. Until such measures are better developed, we must conclude that the theory has little practical use. As a general heuristic model, it may be more widely accepted than as a specific and testable theory.

■ V. When attitudes don't change

Discussions of theories of attitude change often convey the impression that all people change their attitudes almost all the time. That is not the case. Often, shifts in attitude are quite temporary; sometimes, strong resistance to change is exhibited. Let us look more carefully at some of the cases in which attitudes do not change.

A. Anticipatory attitude change

Attitudes may change even before a person receives a persuasive message. In the initial demonstration of this *anticipatory attitude change*, McGuire and his colleagues observed that people who expected a persuasive message shifted their attitudes in the direction of the forthcoming message before it was even presented (McGuire & Millman, 1965; McGuire & Papageorgis, 1962).

Are such changes in attitude real? If so, why do they occur in the absence of any actual persuasion? Early explanations of this phenomenon stressed self-esteem, suggesting that people change their attitudes in advance of a communication in order to avoid appearing gullible later (Deaux, 1968; McGuire & Millman, 1965). More recently, investigators have stressed two factors in attitude change. First, as Cialdini and his colleagues have described it, there is "elasticity" in a person's attitudes (Cialdini, Levy, Herman, & Evenbeck, 1973; Cialdini, Levy, Herman, Kozlowski, & Petty, 1976). In response to various pressures, people may moderate their position within a limited range (perhaps comparable to the latitude of acceptance); however, when the outside pressures disappear (for example, when the promise of a persuasive speech is withdrawn), their attitudes "snap back" to their original positions. Cialdini and his colleagues raise the possibility that most of the attitude change observed in the laboratory reflects this principle of elasticity rather than any real change.

At a more general level, we can think of these anticipatory changes as a form of impression management (Hass, 1975; Hass & Mann, 1976). In other words, when people anticipate a persuasive message, they may try to manage the impression that others are forming, and in an attempt to appear broad-minded, they may moderate their original position. Such strategies are no doubt common in real life as well as in the laboratory. Consider the way you would state your opinion about a longer school year if you were discussing that issue with a friend who was in favor of the extension. Such concerns with appearing moderate and reasonable may occur, however, only when people are not personally invested in an issue. Indeed, Cialdini and his colleagues (Cialdini et al., 1976) found that when an issue is of great importance to a subject, anticipatory shifts are in the direction of greater polarization rather than greater moderation. Furthermore, these subjects who had initially polarized their attitudes maintained this more extreme position even when the threat of persuasion was removed, suggesting continued vigilance on their part.

B. Resistance to persuasion

Although a forewarning of persuasion may lead to some initial shifts in the direction of the forthcoming communication, some evidence suggests that, in the long run, forewarning may encourage resistance to the persuasive attempt—or, in the words of Petty and Cacioppo (1977), "forewarned is forearmed."

In an experiment conducted during the months preceding President Truman's announcement that the Soviet Union had produced an atom bomb, Lumsdaine and Janis (1953), members of the Yale Communication Research Program, considered the effects of one-sided and two-sided messages. Their special focus was on which of these two types of messages would be more likely to encourage resistance to subsequent counterpropaganda. Their results showed that two-sided communication was more effective in inducing resistance to propaganda, and they suggested that the presentation of counterarguments initially serves to "inoculate" subjects against later persuasive attempts.

McGuire (1964) pursued this explanation in a more elaborately designed set of studies. Before hearing a persuasive message, his subjects were presented with arguments that supported their initial beliefs, arguments that refuted the counterarguments that would be used in the subsequent persuasion, or arguments that refuted counterarguments that would not be used in the actual communication. Subjects who had heard only the arguments that supported their initial position showed the least resistance to subsequent persuasion. In contrast, subjects who had already been exposed to a weakened form of the counterarguments showed resistance when the actual message was presented (see Figure 11-8). Using a medical analogy, McGuire suggests that exposure to weakened forms of a message can be effective in producing defenses. In other words, the exposure inoculates a person against the subsequent attack. Presumably, this strategy is most effective when a person's initial position is relatively "germ-free"—when it hasn't been questioned.

Applying this same rationale to a marketing context, Szybillo and Heslin (1973) studied the effectiveness of various defenses when people were exposed to arguments favoring the installation of inflatable air bags in cars. Once again, they showed that prior arguments could increase resistance to persuasion and that refutational arguments were more effective than supportive arguments in building up resistance.

Even when counterarguments are not supplied, forewarning can be effective in allowing people to provide their own counterarguments and become more resistant to later attacks. For example, Petty and Cacioppo (1977) have shown that when people are warned of a forthcoming message and are given time to think about the issue, they consider their own positions and alternative positions, and

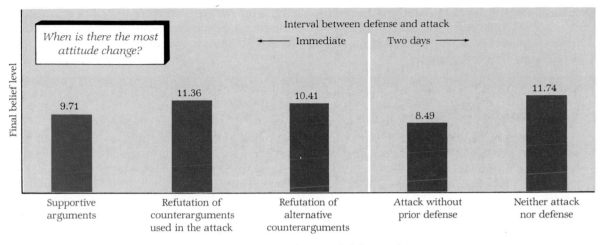

FIGURE 11-8. Persistence of the resistance to persuasion conferred by three types of prior belief defense. Numbers represent level of belief, with 15 representing complete endorsement of the initial belief and 1 complete acceptance of the persuasive message.

they generate cognitive defenses against the impending assault. Therefore, one of the most effective ways of encouraging resistance to persuasion is to warn a person that a persuasive attempt is about to be made and to identify the specific content of a message (so that counterarguments can be rehearsed). Given these findings, it isn't surprising that commercials are often introduced with little warning or that government leaders often call "surprise" press conferences to announce new policy initiatives.

C. Central and peripheral routes to persuasion

The diversity of findings indicating change on some occasions and no change on others can be more easily understood if we consider two different routes to persuasion (Petty & Cacioppo, 1981). In the first route, which has been termed the *central route*, people are motivated to think about an issue. Arguments in a message are comprehended and learned, as the learning model suggests, and people rationally evaluate the implications of a position. A second route, termed the *peripheral route*, presents a more ephemeral picture of change.

In this type of attitude change, not so much thought is given to the message itself. Instead, tendencies to change are more affected by other external characteristics, such as the attractiveness of a source or the rewards associated with the attitudinal position.

The distinction between these two routes is clearly shown in an experiment by Chaiken (1980). Half the subjects in this experiment expected to be interviewed about a particular topic in the future. For these subjects, attitudes were most affected by the number of issue-relevant arguments contained in the persuasive message. The remaining subjects did not expect a future interview on the topic and therefore could be assumed to be less involved and less motivated to attend to the arguments. For these subjects, issue-relevant arguments had little effect on attitudes; instead, the likability of the persuasive source was more influential.

These findings support the view that there are two quite different forms of attitude change. The peripheral route makes change rather easy, although such change is also likely to be short-lived. Many laboratory experiments that deal with uninvolving issues may simply be showing this peripheral form of change. In contrast, the central route suggests that change is more difficult to achieve. Only when a person is motivated to learn about an issue and able to process the arguments will change be achieved—but in this case the change is likely to persist over time.

VI. SUMMARY

Persuasive attempts are pervasive in society, and social psychologists have developed a number of theories to explain attitude change. Four of the major theoretical approaches are learning theories, social-judgment theory, the consistency theories, and functional theories. Each theory has different assumptions about human nature, and each has had a variety of practical applications.

The Yale Communication Research Program stressed a three-stage process of attitude change—attention, comprehension, and acceptance. This program of research also identified four general factors that may influence attitude change: the source, the message, the context, and the recipient.

Social-judgment theory represents a more cognitive approach to attitude change and emphasizes the individual's perception and judgment of a communication as prerequisites to predicting attitude change. Attitudes are described by a range of positions along a scale, called the latitude of acceptance. Other opinion points on the scale may fall either in the latitude of rejection or in the latitude of noncommitment. Attitude change is believed most likely to occur when a persuasive communication falls in or near a person's latitude of acceptance. Research within the social-judgment framework has focused on two major variables: (1) the effects of a person's ego involvement in an issue and (2) the amount of discrepancy between a persuasive communication and the person's own position.

The consistency theories of attitude change include Heider's balance theory and Festinger's cognitive dissonance theory. Common to these is an assumption that people change their atti-tudes in order to reduce or remove inconsistency between conflicting attitudes and behaviors. Although these theories assume that we are thoughtful, they do not require that we be rational either in our perception of inconsistency or in its resolution.

Heider's balance theory deals with the relationship among a person P, another person O, and some object X. Festinger's cognitive dissonance model has generated the most research. Dissonance is said to exist when a person possesses two cognitions that are contradictory. Such dissonance is believed to be uncomfortable and to motivate the person to eliminate the dissonance by changing either the behavior or the attitude. Research within the cognitive dissonance framework has focused on the consequences of decision making and the effects of counterattitudinal advocacy.

Functional theories of attitude change assume that people hold attitudes that fit their needs and that to change these attitudes, we must determine what the particular needs are. Among the functions that attitudes may serve are (1) the instrumental, adjustive, or utilitarian function, (2) the ego-defensive or externalization function, (3) the knowledge or object-appraisal function, and (4) the value-expressing function. These theories have not generated much research.

Although emphasis has been placed on the factors that bring about change, we also should consider the factors that increase resistance to change. Studies of anticipatory attitude change suggest that some changes may simply reflect an "elasticity," with people consciously presenting their opinions as moderate in order to appear flexible. When a person is forewarned of a persuasive communication, he or she may be inoculated against subsequent change as a result of that warning.

It is helpful to think about attitude change in terms of two different routes—central and peripheral. Central routes emphasize involvement in the issue and active learning of the arguments. Changes occurring through this route are apt to be relatively permanent. In contrast, attitude change via the peripheral route is more apt to occur when a person is not particularly motivated to understand the issue. Such changes may be more susceptible to situational factors such as the attractiveness of a source, but they are less likely to endure.

GLOSSARY TERMS

anchor	cognitive dissonance theory	functional theory
assimilation effects	contrast effects	social-judgment theory
balance theory	evaluation apprehension	

12

Social Influence & Personal Control

*As for conforming outwardly, and living
your own life inwardly, I do not think
much of that.*
■ HENRY DAVID THOREAU

*Don't compromise yourself. You are all
you've got.*
■ JANIS JOPLIN

Attitude change is one example of social influence, one that relies on verbal comprehension and generally assumes that human behavior has a cognitive basis. Yet, there are many other ways in which we can be influenced and even controlled by others—through the use of power strategies, direct orders, requests, and even simple example. In many cases, succumbing to social influence is adaptive: driving on the right side of the road in the United States and Canada, for example, is a simple matter of safety, just as doing the opposite in Great Britain is wise. In other cases, conformity behavior may be questionable, as when members of a junior high school clique determine what clothes are acceptable to wear and reject people who choose a different dress style. How we respond to the requests or orders of others will vary across a wide range of situations; we do not respond the same way to a friend who asks us for a favor, a door-to-door salesperson who's pressuring us to buy a gadget we don't need, and a dictator in a repressive society.

Each time we encounter an attempt by a person or persons to influence our behavior or attitudes, we must decide whether to comply or resist. At the heart of this process is the issue of control—the degree to which we feel we have control over our own lives versus the degree to which others have the power to affect our behavior.

This very basic issue of influence and control is the focus of this chapter. First we will consider the various forms of control—conformity, compliance, and obedience. Then we will look more carefully at why control is an important issue and how people respond to a loss of control in their lives.

■ I. Conformity

A. The Asch situation

A male college student has volunteered to participate in a research project. He is to be a subject in a visual-perception experiment. Along with six other "subjects" (who are in fact confederates of the researcher), he is seated at a round table. The group members are shown a vertical line and then asked which of three other vertical lines match it in length. (All lines are in view at the same time.) One of these lines is identical in length to the first line; the others are different enough so that in controlled tests (done individually, not in groups) more than 95% of subjects make correct judgments about the length of the lines. In the group experiment, the subjects are asked to state their choices out loud, one at a time. The real subject is seated so that he is always the next-to-last person to respond. On the first and second trials, everyone gives the same response, and this response is the obviously correct one. (The volunteer begins to think that this task is easy.) The same outcome occurs on several more trials. Then, on a subsequent trial—where the choice appears as clear-cut as those before—the first confederate gives a response that is obviously incorrect. All the other confederates follow suit, giving the wrong response. When it is the subject's turn to respond, all the preceding respondents at the table have given an

PHOTO 12-1. *Conformity in dress and appearance often suggests conformity in attitudes and beliefs as well.*

answer that he believes is wrong. What does he do? Does he stick to his convictions, remain independent, and give the correct response? Or does he conform to the group, giving an answer that he knows is wrong? Or does he convince himself that he must be wrong and that the group's answer is correct?

This was the procedure used in an early set of studies on conformity by social psychologist Solomon Asch (1951, 1956, 1958), and it illustrates some of the basic characteristics of the process of influence and control. In its most basic sense, **conformity** refers to a yielding to group pressures when no direct request to comply with the group is made. Thus, in the Asch situation, the confederates did not directly ask the subject to go along with their judgment. Nevertheless, the subject undoubtedly perceived some real pressures to have his judgment be consistent with those of the other group members.

How did Asch's subjects respond? In Asch's standard procedure, there were 12 critical trials on which confederates gave the wrong response, interspersed with a large number of trials on which all confederates gave the correct answer. The conformity behavior of 50 subjects is shown in Figure 12-1. When we consider the responses of subjects on all the critical trials, we find that 32% of the responses were conforming: subjects, on the average, conformed on 3.84 out of 12 possible trials. But the averages are deceiving; in Asch's study the distribution of conforming responses is important because of the great range of individual differences. Notice in Figure 12-1 that 13 of the 50 subjects never yielded to the majority on any of the critical trials, whereas 4 subjects yielded on 10 or more of those trials. Thus, although some conformity was certainly shown in Asch's procedure, many subjects showed little or no conformity.

Asch's work on conformity was influenced by the even earlier studies of Sherif (1935) on the **autokinetic effect.** If you look at a stationary light in an otherwise completely dark room, the light will appear to move, because your eyes have no other reference point (Levy, 1972). Sherif capitalized on this autokinetic phenomenon to study the effects of another person's response and found that

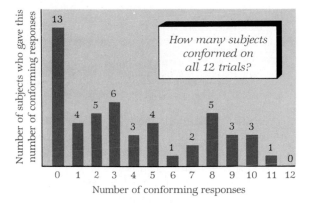

FIGURE 12-1. Distribution of conformity responses in Asch's study.

a subject's reports of movement were highly influenced by other people's estimates. In this case, it is not surprising that some conformity occurred; the stimulus was ambiguous, and there was no other source of information. In contrast, the results of the later studies by Asch are more surprising, because in the absence of group pressure, the correct response was so clear.

B. Situational influences on conformity

Since these early pioneering investigations, many additional studies of conformity behavior have been conducted. These later studies show that many situational factors influence the degree to which an individual will conform to group pressure. For example, what is the effect of group size? One might expect that the larger the number of persons who form a unanimous majority, the more often the subject will conform. This is true, but only to a degree. Asch and others have studied the extent to which people yield to unanimous majorities (varying from only 1 to 15 persons). More conformity occurs when two confederates give false answers than when only one does (see Table 12-1). Groups of three or four confederates are most influential; groups of eight or more persons are somewhat less effective, indicating the possible limits of increasing numbers (Stang, 1976). In the real world, however, further increases in group size may continue to increase conformity; Krech,

TABLE 12-1. Extent of conformity with unanimous majorities of different sizes

Size of majority	1	2	3	4	8	10–15
Mean number of conforming responses	0.33	1.53	4.00	4.20	3.84	3.75
Range in number of conforming responses per subject	0–1	0–5	1–12	0–11	0–11	0–10

Crutchfield, and Ballachey (1962) suggest the greater possibility of threats of reprisal as one reason that conformity may increase with increases in the size of real-life groups.

Another important factor in considering the effect of the group is the extent to which members of the group are regarded as a single unit (Wilder, 1975). Consider the difference between a situation in which four individuals all give the wrong answer, apparently independently, and one in which those four persons are viewed as a single group or club. In the latter case, conformity pressures are apparently less effective and may more closely approximate the pressure exerted by only a single individual. In other words, the four opinions are actually considered to represent only one voice, and hence the size of the majority becomes less important.

C. Issues in the study of conformity

Conformity in behavior does not always reflect a private acceptance of the position. A person may conform to the group's opinion without believing that position to be true. Put in another situation, this person might behave quite differently. For example, we can quite easily imagine a person who says she dislikes rock music when among friends who are devoted to classical music but who also dances up a storm when in the presence of other friends at a disco. For such a person, public conformity would tell us very little about her private beliefs.

If conformity is public behavior that yields to group pressure, what is the opposite of conformity? We may think of two different types of opposing, nonconformity responses. One is *independence*, defined as the expression of behavior without regard to group norms. The person who wears blue jeans when they are popular and continues to wear them when the styles change is

showing independence—a person who "does his or her own thing." In contrast to this type of behavior, which is independent of group pressure, the term **anticonformity** or *counterconformity* is used to label the response that is opposed to the majority response on all occasions. The anticonformist might choose to wear blue jeans when more formal clothes are in style but switch to more formal wear when blue jeans become popular. Thus, the actions of two persons may appear similar in some situations but may actually reflect quite different motives. For example, in studying the reasons that some U.S. soldiers who were prisoners of war did not collaborate with their Communist Chinese captors during the Korean war, psychologists identified two types of resisters. Some soldiers resisted because they knew that admitting guilt for the war and broadcasting peace appeals were wrong; these men were labeled independent resisters. Another group of men had a long history of unwillingness to accept any kind of authority; they did not conform to commands from officers in the U.S. Army *or* to orders from the Chinese (Kinkead, 1959; Schein, 1957). These men displayed anticonformity, or counterconformity.

Use of terms such as *conformist, anticonformist,* and *independent* suggests that we can classify people into one of these categories, implying that someone who conforms in one situation will conform in every other. The wide variation in responses to Asch's task led many investigators to explore the various personality types that might accompany conformity. A number of differences were reported. Crutchfield (1955), for example, in studying a group of businessmen and military officers, reported that independent subjects showed "more intellectual effectiveness, ego strength, leadership ability, and maturity of social relations, together with a conspicuous absence of inferiority feelings, rigid and excessive self-control, and authoritarian attitudes" (p. 194). Other studies have found that conforming subjects have a stronger need for affiliation (McGhee & Teevan, 1967), stronger tendencies to blame themselves (Costanzo, 1970), and lower self-esteem (Stang, 1972). Yet, none of these characteristics could predict all conformity behavior. Furthermore, evidence for the consistency of conformity behavior across a variety of situations has been much weaker, and the search for a single conforming type of person has proved somewhat futile (McGuire, 1968b).

At a more general level, popular social critics such as David Riesman (1950) and William H. Whyte, Jr. (1956), considering the society as a whole, have argued that conformity has increased. In *The Organization Man*, Whyte argued that the complexities of modern society have increased the need to rely on others. A social ethic that emphasized "getting along with others" as a norm or standard was replacing the Protestant ethic that had valued individual effort and hard work. Riesman's discussion of the prevalence of the "other-directed" person in our society reflects a similar viewpoint. As Riesman sees it, U.S. citizens several generations ago were more "inner-directed," meaning that they determined their own values and goals. "Other-directed" persons, in contrast, look to peers to determine their behavior, and Riesman believed this orientation was increasing in the society.

However, such global depictions of conformity are inevitably oversimplified. If the laboratory research on conformity has demonstrated anything, it is that situational factors are of great importance in eliciting conformity behavior. Furthermore, it is undoubtedly a mistake to consider conformity a reflexive reaction to group pressure. Rather, it is important to consider the reasons for individual choices. Some have argued that a person in the typical conformity situation is simply seeking to resolve uncertainty. For example, if a person is unfamiliar with the topic being discussed or if the required judgments are ambiguous, that person will be more likely to go along with the opinions of other people than when the topic is familiar and the required decision is clear. With this perspective, we may view conformity as simply one outcome of an attempt to solve prob-

lems and reach conclusions about one's surroundings. Such a perspective is important and should be considered before one too quickly adopts a value stance that conformity is always and forever bad. As Collins has stated:

> It would be a mistake to oversimplify the question and ask whether conformity is good or bad. A person who refused to accept anyone's word of advice on any topic whatsoever . . . would probably make just as big a botch of his life . . . as a person who always conformed and never formed a judgment on the basis of his own individual sources of information [1970, p. 21].

■ II. Compliance

The term **compliance** has often been used interchangeably with *conformity*. Here, however, we will use the term more specifically, limiting its use to situations in which a direct request is made and the person agrees to behave in accord with that request. In contrast to conformity, in which the pressure to comply is indirect, in the compliance situation there is some direct pressure to comply (although these two influence tactics may be combined, as Box 12-1 shows). Such demands are made of us daily. For example, a professor may ask you to stop by after class, a door-to-door salesperson may suggest that you buy a new vacuum cleaner, or a panhandler may stop you on the street and ask for a quarter. Many experimental studies of compliance have, in fact, taken their lead from these common events.

A. The "foot in the door" effect

The **"foot in the door" effect** has been developed from the sales lore that suggests that once the seller has his or her foot in the door, a subsequent sale will be no problem. Phrased in other terms, a person who complies with one small request is much more likely to comply later with a larger and more substantial demand.

In an initial test of this hypothesis, Freedman and Fraser (1966) arranged for two undergraduate experimenters to contact suburban women in

BOX 12-1. Are two tactics better than one?

Peter Reingen (1982) tested a procedure for inducing compliance that combined a direct request with a conformity manipulation. In one study, for example, students at the University of South Carolina were asked to donate money to the heart association. In some cases, only the request was made; in other cases, a list of eight donors was presented while the request was made. When there was evidence that others had also donated, 43% of the subjects approached donated money, compared with only 25% when such information was not provided. Adult residents contacted at their homes showed the same pattern of compliance: 73% donated when they knew others had, compared with 47% who did not receive the conformity manipulation. Thus, for the practical strategist, a combination of techniques may be more effective than any single tactic alone. ■

their homes—first with a small request and later with a larger one. The women were first asked either to place a small sign in their window or to sign a petition about driving safely or keeping California beautiful. Two weeks later, a different experimenter returned to each home and asked each subject to place a large and unattractive billboard promoting auto safety on her lawn for the next couple of weeks—a rather substantial request. A second group of homemakers (the control group) was contacted only about the second, large-billboard request. The results showed a very strong foot-in-the-door effect—those subjects who had complied with the earlier trivial request were much more likely to comply with the larger request several weeks later. More intriguing yet was the apparent generality of the effect; signing a petition to "keep California beautiful" led to greater compliance with a different experimenter on a different issue.

Why does the foot-in-the-door effect occur? One explanation offered by social psychologists stresses people's perceptions of themselves (see Chapter 3). Having once agreed to help, a person may decide that he or she is basically a helpful person. A second request—even a burdensome one—may then be granted because the person wishes to maintain that image of helpfulness. Considerable evidence supports this interpretation (DeJong, 1979). However, at least two conditions are apparently necessary for the effect to occur. First, the initial request must be large enough to cause people to think about the implications of their behavior. Offhandedly telling someone the correct time, for example, might not be enough to cause you to think about yourself, whereas giving a set of complicated directions to someone who was lost might lead to self-perceptions. A second necessary condition is a perception of free choice. If a person feels forced to comply, then there is no reason to make attributions to internal dispositions. In fact, any external justification for the compliance will weaken or eliminate the foot-in-the-door effect. For example, homemakers who were offered money for agreeing to a 5-minute telephone interview were no more likely to comply with a later request for a 25-minute interview than women who did not receive the initial request. Demonstrating the foot-in-the-door effect, women not offered the monetary justification were more likely to agree to the later request (Zuckerman, Lazzaro, & Waldgeir, 1979).

What about people who refuse the initial request? The self-perception explanation would suggest that these people would be *less* likely to comply with subsequent requests. In contrast to people who agree to help, these noncompliers should view themselves as nonhelpful people and act accordingly on future occasions. Labels can also be provided by others, as Kraut (1973) has shown. In this experiment, subjects who gave to charity were either labeled as charitable or not labeled. For example, after their donation, subjects in the labeling condition might be told "You are really a generous person. I wish more people were as charitable as you are." Similarly, subjects who refused to give to charity were either labeled as uncharitable or not labeled. All subjects were later asked by another canvasser to contribute to a second charity. Subjects who had been labeled as charitable gave more, and subjects labeled as uncharitable gave less, than their respective unlabeled peers.

Thus, consistent with sales lore, there is considerable evidence for the foot-in-the-door effect. A "foot in" makes future compliance more likely, but "no foot in" should reduce future compliance. But does the latter reduction in compliance always occur?

B. The "door in the face" effect

Coining the term *"door in the face" effect,* Cialdini and his coworkers (Cialdini, Vincent, Lewis, Catalan, Wheeler, & Darby, 1975) suggested that on some occasions people who refuse an initial request may be *more* likely to agree to a subsequent request. These researchers approached college students with a socially desirable but highly demanding request: Would they serve as voluntary counselors at a county juvenile detention center for two years? Virtually everyone politely refused, thus in effect slamming the door in the face of a demanding request for compliance. However, when a second and smaller request was made—specifically, to chaperone juveniles on a trip to the zoo—many subjects readily agreed.

Why wasn't there less compliance in this case, as the self-perception explanation would predict? Apparently, investigators have concluded, the door-in-the-face effect depends on a particular set of circumstances (DeJong, 1979). First, the initial request must be very large—so large that the person who refuses does not make any negative inference about the self. Thus, the person who declined two years of voluntary service would probably conclude that hardly anyone would agree to such a large request and would not have to form a self-perception of unhelpfulness. Second, for the door-

PHOTO 12-2. *A foot in the door or a door in the face?*

in-the-face effect to occur, the second request must be made by the same person who makes the first request. According to Cialdini and his colleagues, subjects view the toned-down request as a concession by the experimenter, and they then feel pressure to reciprocate that concession. If a different person makes the second request, however, such conciliatory behavior is not necessary.

The door-in-the-face technique has been applied in a business context as well (Mowen & Cialdini, 1980). Pedestrians selected randomly were more likely to agree to fill out an insurance-company survey when the initial request had been for a much longer survey. In this case, however, the second request had to be part of the first request for the tactic to be successful. In other words, a door slammed in the face could be reopened only if the topic of the second survey was the same.

C. The "low ball" procedure

Yet another investigation of compliance that was inspired by a practitioner's rule of thumb is the "low ball" procedure (Cialdini, Cacioppo, Bassett, & Miller, 1978). Presumably widespread (especially among new-car dealers), the technique of "throwing a low ball" consists in inducing the customer to buy a car by offering an extremely good price (for example, $500 below what competitors are offering). Once the customer has agreed to buy the car, the conditions of the deal are changed, resulting in a higher purchase price than the customer originally agreed to. Reported techniques include a refusal to approve the deal by the salesperson's boss, a reduction in the trade-in figure given by the used-car manager, or the exclusion of various options from the purchase price offered.

As Cialdini and his colleagues demonstrated, this technique of inducing compliance works beyond the new-car showroom. University students, for example, were more likely to show up for an experiment at 7 A.M. if they had first agreed to participate in a general way than if they were initially told of the early hour. Although this technique of compliance is in many ways similar to the foot-in-the-door procedure, there is at least one important difference. In "low balling," the ini-

tial commitment is to the behavior to be performed; in the "foot" procedure, the commitment is first to a different and less demanding behavior.

D. The generality of compliance

In a normal day, many requests are made of each of us. Research such as that just described has concentrated on showing different conditions under which compliance to a request is more or less likely. In some instances, a decision to comply with a request may be a rational choice, in which we consider the pros and cons of agreeing with the request. Often, however, our willingness to comply with a request may be much less considered. Langer, in fact, has argued that many such behaviors are essentially "mindless"—in other words, we go along with the request without much thought. To demonstrate that people may comply without giving much thought to their actions, Langer and her colleagues (Langer, Blank, & Chanowitz, 1978) conducted a series of studies in which people were asked to comply with requests with little or no justification. For example, people about to use a copying machine were interrupted by an experimenter who asked to go first, either for no reason, for a noninformative reason ("I have to make copies"), or for a real reason ("I'm in a rush"). As long as the request was a small one, people were equally likely to comply with the latter two requests—even though "I have to make copies" provided no real reason for letting the other person go first. (Less compliance occurred when no reason at all was offered.)

Although such "mindless" compliance may be common, studies of power strategies suggest that we may at times be quite sensitive to the form in which compliance is requested. French and Raven (1959) have identified five bases of power, or ways in which one person can induce compliance by another. These five strategies are defined in Table 12-2. You can probably think of instances when others have sought your compliance with each of these types of power. The parent who promises use of the car for some behavior, for example, is using reward power, while the parent who threatens "grounding" is using coercive power. A pro-

TABLE 12-2. Forms of power or potential influence

Types of power	Bases of power
Coercion	Ability of agent to mediate punishment
Reward	Ability of agent to mediate rewards
Expertise	Attribution of superior knowledge or ability to influence agent
Reference	Agent is used as frame of reference for self-evaluation
Legitimacy	Acceptance of relationship in power structure such that agent is allowed to prescribe behaviors

fessor may gain compliance through the use of expert power, whereas a friend may be powerful because he or she is someone you would like to emulate (reference power). Corporate officers and elected officials often have legitimate power and may gain compliance because it is agreed that they have a right to have such influence. Of course, it is possible that one person may have several bases of power; an admired professor, for example, may be able to reward and punish by means of grades and may be an important role model and source of expertise as well.

The likelihood of compliance will vary depending on which form of power is used. Coercive power may be quite effective if the power source is present, for example, but may be less effective if that person is not present when the behavior is to be performed. Furthermore, people will attribute the reasons for compliance differently depending on the power strategy chosen. For example, when either referent or reward power is used, compliance is generally explained by looking at characteristics of the person who performs the compliant behavior. In contrast, when either coercive or legitimate power is used, explanations for compliance generally focus on the person making the request (Litman-Adizes, Raven, & Fontaine, 1978). Thus, recalling the discussions in Chapters 3 and 4, we see that attributional patterns may influence the extent of future compliance once the agent mak-

ing the request is no longer present.

Willingness to comply with the request of another person may occur for many reasons: At one extreme, there may be the "mindless" response, in which we comply almost automatically, giving little thought to the reasons we should or should not agree to carry out the behavior. This form of compliance is most likely to occur when the response is overlearned, not requiring much conscious monitoring on our part. At the other end of the spectrum, there may be situations in which we carefully weigh the reasons for compliance and act accordingly. Yet, although rationality may contribute on many occasions, the sheer force of the request often determines our response. As we shall see in the case of obedience, once legitimate power has been established, a person may refuse to question the reasons for the agent's request and simply carry out orders because they are given.

■ III. Obedience

A special form of compliance, in which the request is made in the form of an order, is **obedience.** All of us feel some degree of pressure to obey certain symbols of authority, such as parents, police officers, and traffic lights. But can obedience lead us to take extreme actions against our better judgment? Can destructive obedience occur? The cases of Lieutenant Calley and Adolf Eichmann are relevant. When he was tried for killing 100 Vietnamese villagers, U.S. Army Lieutenant Calley stated that he was simply following orders. Adolf Eichmann, in charge of exterminating 6 million Jews (as well as gypsies, homosexuals, political prisoners, and others deemed unworthy by the Third Reich) also did what he was told. At his trial for war crimes, Eichmann denied any moral responsibility. He was, he said, simply doing his job.

A. Milgram's laboratory studies of destructive obedience

Are Eichmann and Calley unusual cases? Stanley Milgram, a social psychologist, attempted to determine whether people will also obey an au-

PHOTO 12-3. *Lieutenant William Calley, Jr., on trial for killing Vietnamese villagers.*

thority under more normal conditions, even when they believe they are endangering the life of another person.

Through advertisements and direct-mail solicitations in New Haven, Connecticut, Milgram (1963) gathered 40 males of various ages and occupations for paid participation in a research project at Yale University. When each subject arrived for the experiment, he was introduced to the experimenter and another subject (actually an accomplice of the experimenter). The subjects were told that the purpose of the experiment was to determine the effects of punishment on learning. Subjects drew lots to determine who would be the teacher and who the learner, but the drawing was rigged so that the true subject was always the teacher and the accomplice was always the learner. Then the learner was strapped to a chair, electrodes were attached to his wrist, and the subject was instructed in his task.

The lesson to be "taught" by the subject was a verbal learning task. The "teacher" was told to administer a shock to the "learner" in the next room each time he gave a wrong answer, using a shock generator with 30 separate switches. These switches increased by 15-volt increments from 15 to 450 volts and were labeled from "Slight Shock" at the low end to "Danger: Severe Shock" and finally an ominous "XXX" at the highest end. In fact, this equipment was a dummy generator and the confederate never received an actual shock, but its appearance was quite convincing.

After each wrong answer (of which the accomplice intentionally gave many), the experimenter instructed the subject to move one level higher on the shock generator. When the subject reached 300 volts, the accomplice began to pound on the wall between the two rooms, and then, from that point on, he no longer gave any answer to the questions posed by the subject. At this point, subjects usually turned to the experimenter for guidance. In a stoic and rather stern way, the experimenter replied that a failure to answer should be treated as a wrong answer and that the learner should be shocked according to the usual schedule.

Milgram's basic question was simply how many subjects would continue to administer shocks to the end of the series, following the experimenter's orders. Table 12-3 presents the results. Of the 40 subjects, 26 (65%) continued to the end of the shock series. Not a single subject stopped before administering 300 volts—the point at which the learner began pounding on the wall. Five refused to obey at that point; at some point 14 of the 40 subjects defied the experimenter. Milgram concludes that obedience to commands is a strong force in our society, since nearly two-thirds of his subjects obeyed the experimenter's instructions even though they were led to believe that they were hurting another human being.

TABLE 12-3. Distribution of breakoff points in Milgram's study of obedience

Verbal designation and voltage indication	Number of subjects for whom this was maximum shock
Slight shock	
15	0
30	0
45	0
60	0
Moderate shock	
75	0
90	0
105	0
120	0
Strong shock	
135	0
150	0
165	0
180	0
Very strong shock	
195	0
210	0
225	0
240	0
Intense shock	
255	0
270	0
285	0
300	5
Extreme-intensity shock	
315	4
330	2
345	1
360	1
Danger—severe shock	
375	1
390	0
405	0
420	0
XXX	
435	0
450	26

Milgram (1965, 1974) then extended his research program to study some of the situational factors that may lead subjects to obey or to refuse to obey when the experimenter (the authority figure) tells them to hurt another person. He found, for example, that the closer the victim was to the subject, the more likely subjects were to refuse the command of the experimenter. Thus, when the victim was in the same room as the subject and only 1½ feet away, only one-third of the subjects were willing to go to the maximum shock level. Milgram also found that obedience was less frequent when the experimenter was not physically present but, rather, presented his commands either by telephone or by tape recording. In fact, when the experimenter was absent, several subjects administered shocks of a lower voltage than was required, thus defying the authority of the experimenter. The situation in which the authority figure is absent is probably more typical of everyday living, and so defiance of authority may be more common than Milgram's results suggest. Rada and Rogers (1973), however, also found that when the authority figure had previously issued a strong command to obey, the subjects tended to obey whether the authority figure was present or not.

B. Criticisms of Milgram's obedience studies

Provocative as these findings are, Milgram's research program has not gone without criticism. Perhaps the strongest of the critics is Baumrind (1964), who believes that the studies were not only unethical but also lacking in generalizability to real-world obedience situations. Let us look at these two lines of criticism.

Ethics of the experiment. One criticism of Milgram's studies is that the subjects' rights were not protected. No prior permission was obtained from the subjects allowing the experimenters to place them in distressful conflict situations. In fact, it is unlikely that the exact procedures of Milgram's studies could be replicated today. In most cases, experimenters are required to give subjects more information before they consent to participate than Milgram gave his subjects.

A second claim is that participation could have had long-term effects on the subjects. Among these effects could be the subjects' loss of trust in future experimenters, the university, or science in general. Another type of long-term effect might have been on the subjects' self-concepts. Until the experiment, most subjects probably saw themselves as persons who would not deliberately inflict pain unless the circumstances were extreme. As a result of the experiment, they would have to believe otherwise. One can certainly argue that such self-education might be beneficial, but it is probably not within the province of the experimental social psychologist to force such education on a subject.

Milgram has argued that debriefing at the end of the experiment was sufficient to eradicate any tensions, doubts, or resentment that subjects experienced. In describing the debriefing procedure, Milgram stated: "After the interview, procedures were undertaken to assure that the subject would leave the laboratory in a state of well-being. A friendly reconciliation was arranged between the subject and the victim, and an effort was made to reduce any tensions that arose as a result of the experiment" (1963, p. 374). Milgram further reports (1964b, 1968, 1974) that interviews by psychiatrists and follow-up questionnaires completed by the subjects indicated no long-term deleterious effects.

Lack of generality. People have also questioned whether the extreme degrees of obedience found in Milgram's subjects can be generalized to the real world. For example, trust in and obedience to the authority figure may be demand characteristics that are especially salient for subjects in experiments (Orne & Holland, 1968). In other words, subjects who will do as they are told in an experiment might disobey another authority figure, such as the physician who tells them to exercise daily or the employer who tells them to fire a popular coworker. Along with the criticism is the claim that the prestige of Yale University contributed to the high obedience rate; subjects may have assumed that anything carried out at Yale must be scientifically and socially acceptable—hence, they were more inclined to obey. However, the available evidence contradicts this last claim. Milgram repeated the experiment with another group of men in a run-down office building in a deteriorating area of Bridgeport, Connecticut. Here he found that almost 50% of the men obeyed the experimenter to the end of the shock series. Although the prestige of Yale apparently accounted for some obedience, the phenomenon still occurred in a blatantly nonuniversity setting.

The use of "prods" by the experimenter in Milgram's task may have contributed significantly to the high rate of obedience. If a subject was unwilling to continue, the experimenter used four verbal prods to urge him to continue, beginning with "Please continue" and advancing in strength to "You have no other choice—You *must* go on." We do not know what the rejection rate would have been if the prods had not been used, but it is probable that more subjects would have terminated their participation earlier. However, in real-world situations where prods or similar devices are used to keep people at tasks that are personally abhorrent, Milgram's findings may well be applicable.

Despite the legitimate criticisms, Milgram's work has demonstrated that obedience is a much more pervasive phenomenon than had been thought. Neither a group of undergraduates nor a group of psychologists and psychiatrists, when told of the procedures, predicted that subjects would continue to obey when the high voltage levels were reached. Assumptions about human nature were more favorable than the actual outcomes.

■ IV. The sense of control

Theories of human behavior differ in their assumptions about human nature and hence are divided on the issue of personal control. Humanistic approaches to social behavior often rest on the assumption that, as humans, we have almost complete control over our behavior. In contrast, Skinner and his followers take the position that stimuli in the environment determine our behavior—that we are controlled by external rewards and punishments and that free will is merely a figment of our imagination (Skinner, 1971). Between these two positions lie a number of variations, although it is certainly fair to say that experimental social psychology has emphasized external influences more than individual choice.

The issue of control is particularly relevant when we talk about social influence. As we have seen, people will, under a variety of circumstances, conform to group pressure, comply with requests, and obey orders. In each of these cases, external forces appear to regulate the behavior, and the element of individual control seems peculiarly absent. Yet, many people fervently believe that we do have nearly complete control over our behavior, and even those, like Skinner, who would disagree nevertheless admit that most people believe in a sense of personal control.

The remainder of this chapter will consider the general issue of control—how we develop illusions of control, how a belief in control affects our behavior, and how we react to a loss of control in our lives.

A. The illusion of control

Magicians entertain by appearing to control events that we cannot explain. Although most of us cannot make rabbits appear out of hats or people float in air, we do believe in our ability to control more mundane events. Even for events that objectively are determined purely by chance, we often develop an "illusion of control" over the outcome. Ellen Langer and her colleagues have presented the most persuasive evidence for these beliefs (Langer, 1975, 1978a; Langer & Roth, 1975).

The lottery is a situation in which the likelihood of winning is determined solely by chance—the "luck of the draw" allows little room for an individual to influence the outcome. To illustrate the illusion of control, Langer (1975) gave people the opportunity to buy $1 football lottery tickets with the chance of a $50 prize. To vary the illusion of control, the experimenters allowed one group of people to select the ticket they wanted. Other participants received randomly selected lottery tickets from the experimenter (identical to those chosen by the first group). Before the random drawing of the prize ticket, the experimenter approached all subjects and asked whether they would be willing to sell their ticket to someone who would pay

more than the going price for the ticket. Subjects who had not been given a choice in the ticket they held were willing to sell it for an average of $1.96. In contrast, subjects who believed that they had had some choice demanded an average of $8.67 for their ticket, presumably because they believed they had a better chance of winning the random draw than did those subjects who had not exercised a choice.

Many factors can increase our belief in control. In general, the more similar a purely chance situation is in appearance to a real skill situation, the more likely we are to believe in our own ability to control the outcome. For example, competition increases our belief in control. Paired with a seemingly incompetent competitor, we will be much more confident of our success than when the competitor appears competent, even though the task itself is purely chance-determined (Langer, 1975). For example, playing a slot machine with a 5-year-old at the next stand would probably lead us to believe that we had greater control over our outcome—even though the machines themselves are obstinately beyond our control. Similarly, involvement in the task, knowledge about the procedures involved, and practice in performing the task all lead us to believe that we have more control than we in fact possess. Success at a task may also create the illusion of control. In another study, Langer and Roth (1975) asked subjects to predict coin tosses and structured the outcome so that people experienced either early success and later failure, early failure and later success, or a purely random order of outcome. In each case, however, the number of correct predictions was the same and did not differ from what could be expected by chance. People who experienced early success were much more confident of their ability on the task, predicting more future successes for themselves and viewing themselves as more skilled. Early experience with success apparently created a belief in the ability to control the outcome, a finding that is probably quite similar to the case of the novice gambler who hits the jackpot the first time around—and then proceeds to lose far more than was initially won!

Findings such as these do not mean that we never have real control over situations and out-

PHOTO 12-4. *An illusion of control.*

comes. However, it is apparent that our belief in control may range far wider than the actual boundaries of our control.

B. Consequences of a belief in control

Why do we believe so strongly in our ability to influence events, often in the face of evidence suggesting that we in fact have little or no control? One reason is that a belief in such control makes the world seem more predictable. If we are expecting to interact with someone in a competitive situation, for example, we would like to be able to predict that person's behavior and, in turn, our own outcomes. Experiments have shown that we may exaggerate our ability to make such predictions. In one study, subjects who expected to compete with another subject were more certain that they would be able to infer the personality of their competitor than were subjects who expected only to observe the interaction (Miller, Norman, & Wright, 1978). Yet, the belief in control is not

something that exists only in our fantasies. Behavior, too, is altered when we believe that we have control over our circumstances.

Performance on routine tasks is better when we believe that we had control over loud noise that was present before the performance, even when that control was not actually exercised (Glass & Singer, 1972). People who have control over their environment perceive conditions as less crowded than do those who feel that they have no control; further, they judge their surroundings as more pleasant and their own mood as more positive (Rodin, Solomon, & Metcalf, 1978). In general, over a wide range of circumstances, we react more positively when we believe we have some control than when we do not.

Perhaps one of the most dramatic demonstrations of the power of a belief in control is a study of aged people in institutions by Ellen Langer and Judith Rodin (Langer & Rodin, 1976; Rodin & Langer, 1977). These investigators suggested that one of the reasons for the debilitated condition of many elderly residents of institutions was their perception of having no control. In contrast to their lives in their own homes, where dozens of decisions are required daily, these residents of institutions were placed in a decision-free environment where all the control resided in others. Such psychological factors might be as important as physical factors, or more so, in determining well-being.

To test this hypothesis, Langer and Rodin (1976) gained the cooperation of the staff of a Connecticut nursing home, divided the residents into two groups, and administered one of two communications. Residents of one floor received a message that stressed the staff's responsibility for them and for their activities. Residents were given a plant but were told that the nurses would care for the plant; they were informed that they would be allowed to see a movie but that the staff would determine what day the movie would be shown. In contrast to this message that minimized the resident's sense of control (and probably paralleled the situation in most nursing homes), members of the other group were given a communication that emphasized their own responsibility. The message stressed the number of things that residents could do for themselves, from arranging the furniture in their room to deciding how to spend their time, and encouraged the people to make their complaints known if they were not satisfied with the current arrangements. Members of this group were also given a plant, but they were allowed to pick which plant they wanted and were told that it would be their responsibility to take care of it. Finally, these residents were also told that a movie would be shown and that they could decide when and whether they would view it.

In many respects, the communication provided to the experimental group seems quite weak. The defined areas of responsibility are, after all, ones that most of us take for granted. It may be difficult to believe that a specific reminder would have much effect. But it did. Members of the group in which personal control had been stressed reported significant increases in happiness when questioned

PHOTO 12-5. Training in self-defense can give older people a psychological sense of control as well as actual physical skills to protect themselves from attacks.

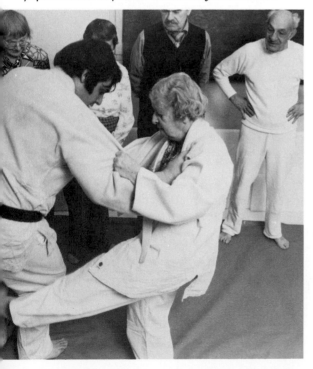

three weeks later. Nurses judged these same residents to be improved in their mental outlook and reported substantially increased activity among the residents—talking with other patients, visiting people from outside the nursing home, and talking to the staff. Even attendance at the promised movie was greater for those residents who had control over the time that they would see the film.

More dramatic evidence of the effects of control was found when Rodin and Langer (1977) returned to the nursing home 18 months later. Nurses continued to rate the responsibility-induced group of residents as more active, more sociable, and more vigorous; physicians rated these same patients as being in better health. Most striking of all was the difference in mortality rates. Whereas 30% of the patients in the control group had died in the months intervening, only 15% of the residents in the responsibility group had died. These results provide graphic and powerful evidence for the importance of control in a person's life.

C. Individual differences in perceptions of control

Although situational factors can forcefully affect the extent to which we believe we have power over events, it is also true that people differ widely in their general beliefs about control. The general question of individual differences in behavior will be discussed much more extensively in Chapter 13. Here, however, we should give some notice to the idea of **locus of control,** as originally proposed by Rotter (1966). Rotter suggested that people have a general tendency to believe that control of the events in their lives is either internal or external. Internal people tend to believe in their own ability to control events; external people believe that other people or events are the primary influences on their own circumstances. Table 12-4 shows some items from the scale that Rotter developed to measure these general orientations. More-recent research has suggested that Rotter's ideas, though accurate in a general sense, may be too simplified. A belief in external control, for example, can imply a number of different dimensions: belief in fate, belief in powerful others, belief in a difficult world, and belief in a politically unresponsive world (Col-

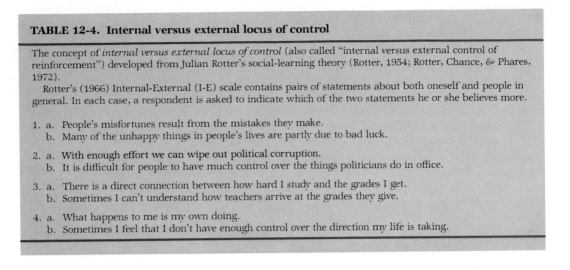

TABLE 12-4. Internal versus external locus of control

The concept of *internal versus external locus of control* (also called "internal versus external control of reinforcement") developed from Julian Rotter's social-learning theory (Rotter, 1954; Rotter, Chance, & Phares, 1972).

Rotter's (1966) Internal-External (I-E) scale contains pairs of statements about both oneself and people in general. In each case, a respondent is asked to indicate which of the two statements he or she believes more.

1. a. People's misfortunes result from the mistakes they make.
   b. Many of the unhappy things in people's lives are partly due to bad luck.

2. a. With enough effort we can wipe out political corruption.
   b. It is difficult for people to have much control over the things politicians do in office.

3. a. There is a direct connection between how hard I study and the grades I get.
   b. Sometimes I can't understand how teachers arrive at the grades they give.

4. a. What happens to me is my own doing.
   b. Sometimes I feel that I don't have enough control over the direction my life is taking.

lins, 1974; Gurin, Gurin, Lao, & Beattie, 1969; Mirels, 1970).

In addition to the multidimensional nature of beliefs in control, other investigators have suggested that we have different beliefs about positive than about negative outcomes (Crandall, Katkovsky, & Crandall, 1965). A person may, for example, believe that he or she has considerable control over positive outcomes while feeling that negative events are beyond personal control. Other people might believe just the opposite. At least one study suggests that the major difference between people who are internal or external in the general sense proposed by Rotter lies in their reaction to negative outcomes. Subjects in this experiment were asked to perform a difficult task that was described as dependent on skill (Gregory, 1978). When a reward was promised for successful performance, internal and external persons behaved similarly. When the instructions were changed, stressing the avoidance of punishment if performance was successful, only internal subjects performed well. People who believed in external control, in contrast, seemed to default their responsibility and accept the inevitability of punishment from an outside agent.

Although the concept of a person's locus of control is not without ambiguity, considerable research has shown that people do differ, often dramatically, in their approach to the world and in their feelings of effectiveness over their environment (Phares, 1976; Strickland, 1977). Individual differences in such beliefs must ultimately be considered in conjunction with those situational factors that make us feel more or less in control of our world.

■ V. Reactions to a loss of control

Although most of us would like to believe that we have control over events, such control is not always possible. Often we are faced with situations in which someone else or something else appears to be in control of our fate, and our own freedom of choice is severely limited. In some cases, this sense of another's control may simply be exasperating or frustrating. Social observer L. Rust Hills (1973), for example, discussed the roles of social life in the contemporary United States and concluded that there are several "social cruel rules." One of these is the following: "(a) Whenever you really feel like going out you don't have an invitation; and in converse: (b) whenever you are invited to go out, you feel like staying at home" (p. 15). In this case, although the belief in control by others may not be overpowering, it can be a source of some annoyance—especially on a Saturday night. In other cases, a perception that others have control over our lives may be much more pervasive. Citizens living under a repressive dictatorship, for example, may feel that they have little control over their daily activities, their conversations, and even their thoughts.

Illness may also cause feelings of no control. One of the reasons for severe depressions following major illnesses such as heart attacks, for example, is the feeling that one has lost control over one's life (Glass, 1977). A heart attack is a dramatic example of an event that is both undesirable and to a large degree uncontrollable. Yet, events that share these two properties and are much less serious than heart attacks can also lead to depression and feelings of no control (Suls & Mullen, 1981). How do people cope with these perceptions of a loss of control?

A. A theory of reactance

Social psychologist Jack Brehm (1966; Brehm & Brehm, 1981) has proposed the concept of psy-

chological **reactance** to explain some of our reactions to a loss of control or freedom of choice. According to Brehm, reactance is a motivational state that is aroused whenever a person feels that his or her freedom has been abridged or threatened. Consider the following fairly commonplace example offered by Brehm:

Picture Mr. John Smith, who normally plays golf on Sunday afternoons, although occasionally he spends Sunday afternoon watching television or puttering around his workshop. The important point is that Smith always spends Sunday afternoon doing whichever of these three things he prefers; he is free to choose which he will do. Now consider a specific Sunday morning on which Smith's wife announces that Smith will have to play golf that afternoon since she has invited several of her lady friends to the house for a party. Mr. Smith's freedom is threatened with reduction in several ways: (1) he cannot watch tele-

PHOTO 12-6. *Unemployment and reliance on charitable soup kitchens for food severely diminish a person's sense of control.*

vision, (2) he cannot putter in the workshop, and (3) he must (Mrs. Smith says) play golf [1966, p. 2].

Given this threat to his freedom, reactance theory would predict that Mr. Smith would attempt to restore his personal freedom. He might choose to stay in his workshop, for example, perhaps creating a clamor of protest in the process. Threats to freedom, according to this theory, create a psychological state of reactance, and this motivational state leads the person to take actions that will help to retain control and personal freedom.

The exact actions that the person chooses will, of course, depend on the nature of the threat and the freedom being threatened. For example, in the face of a threatening communication, a person might change an attitude in a direction opposite to that advocated, thus confirming a sense of independence and control. Another example of reactance is a situation in which certain alternatives are eliminated, so that our ability to choose freely is threatened. In one experiment, for example, subjects were initially given a choice of record albums and then later told that certain albums would not be available. Reacting to this threat to their freedom, these subjects showed increased positive feelings toward the threatened options (Brehm, Stires, Sensenig, & Shaban, 1966). Perhaps an even more relevant example of the effects of restrictions on people's feelings is the case of limitations on the availability of pornography. According to reactance theory, material that is restricted or censored would take on greater appeal; and, in fact, Worchel, Arnold, and Baker (1975) found that censorship of a message caused a potential audience to change their attitudes in the direction of the position advocated by the communication, as well as to develop a greater desire to hear the communication.

Censorship is only one example of the application of reactance theory. Clee and Wicklund (1980) have reviewed a wide variety of areas of consumer behavior in which feelings of reactance may play a role. The high-pressure salesperson, for example, may create reactance by pushing a particular product too hard, thus leading the consumer to prefer an alternative product. Similarly, govern-

ment regulations or bans may lead to a greater desire for the prohibited product or policy.

Many other examples of reactance can be imagined, in which a threat to freedom or a perception of external control may lead to actions geared to restoring a sense of personal control. Children who are told not to touch certain furniture, for example, often make a game of touching the forbidden objects. Teenagers show similar behavior when they break a parent's imposed curfew, not because they lost track of time or were involved in anything of interest but simply as a means of demonstrating that they, not their parents, control their activities. Thinking back on your own behavior, you can probably easily think of cases when reactance may have been operating and when the sheer act of exerting a sense of control was more important than the particular action that you took.

Of course, it is not always to our advantage to be perceived as in control of a situation. For example, if a man pointed a gun in your face and demanded your money, would you try to show that you were in control by wrestling with him? In such cases, in which an attempt to reestablish control could lead to personal injury, people are often content to acknowledge the other person's control (Grabitz-Gneich, 1971). In still other cases, personal harm may not be likely, but the responsibility for harm to someone else may be equally discomforting. "Passing the buck" is a case in point. Here people may voluntarily relinquish control in order to avoid the responsibility for some unpleasant outcome (Feldman-Summers, 1977). Thus, in situations in which negative outcomes and personal responsibility for those outcomes are involved, we are willing to abrogate a sense of control; in many other cases, however, in which outcomes are positive or simply neutral, we actively attempt to reassert control and preserve our sense of personal freedom.

B. The case of learned helplessness

One aspect of our belief in personal control rests on the fact that outcomes are predictable—the issues of predictability and control are very closely related. Many routines in our life are based on a sense of predictability. For example, if you live in a city that has a subway system, you have probably learned to expect that every time you put a token in the subway stile, it will click, turn, and allow you to board the next train. A failure of the stile to turn when the coin is dropped almost inevitably results in frustration. Such a break in the normal routine may involve threats to both predictability and control. On the one hand, the subway stile did not react as you predicted it would, and, on the other, its recalcitrance casts doubt on your ability to control your own outcomes.

Consider the adventures of Alice in Wonderland. Finding herself in a strange environment, Alice quickly discovers that all is not as she has learned it to be. On one occasion she drinks the contents of a bottle and quickly shrinks to a mere ten inches in height. Trying another bottle similarly labeled "Drink me," Alice grows to gigantic proportions. Such adventures, though fictional, illustrate the

PHOTO 12-7. *The adventures of Alice in Wonderland: Experiences with noncontingency.*

CHAPTER II.

THE POOL OF TEARS.

"Curiouser and curiouser!" cried Alice (she was so much surprised, that for the moment she quite forgot how to speak good English); "now I'm opening out like the largest telescope that ever was! Good-bye, feet!" (for when she looked down at her feet, they seemed to be almost out of sight, they were getting so far off) "Oh, my poor little feet, I wonder

principle of *noncontingency:* similar actions do not lead to similar outcomes. There are many situations in life in which people may experience a similar fate.

The result of such experiences is a state that psychologist Martin Seligman (1975) has termed **learned helplessness,** defined as a belief that one's outcomes are independent of one's actions. The first research on this problem was done with animals. Here it was found that animals that were first exposed to shock that they could not avoid were later unable to learn how to avoid shock when it actually could be avoided. Seligman suggested that three kinds of deficits result from experiences with uncontrollable outcomes. First, there is a motivational deficit, whereby the animal does not *try* to learn new behaviors. Second, there is a cognitive deficit because the learning does not take place. Finally, the learned-helplessness hypothesis suggests that there is an emotional deficit as the animal becomes depressed because outcomes are uncontrollable.

Although this phenomenon would seem to be applicable to humans as well, we cannot make the transfer without considering one additional element—the causal attributions that a person makes for his or her situation. Imagine that you have taken two biology exams and failed them both. In one case you studied hard, and in the other you just glanced at your notes. Nevertheless, you failed both times. Would you experience a state of learned helplessness and depression? The answer depends on the attributions that you make for your failure. If you made external attributions—for example, the tests were unfair and everyone else failed, too—then you might feel helpless, but you would not take the failure personally. However, if you made an internal attribution, seeing the failure as specific to yourself and not shared by others, then your reaction would probably be more severe. Such attributions to personal helplessness lead to a fourth deficit—lowered self-esteem—and make depression more likely (Abramson, Seligman, & Teasdale, 1978).

Thus, the experience of learned helplessness in humans seems to depend on a complicated pattern of explanations. Depression will be most severe if attributions are made to internal causes, making helplessness more personal; to stable causes, making helplessness more chronic; and to global causes, making helplessness general to more situations. In the case of the exam failure, an attribution to general stupidity might lead you to avoid not only biology courses but the college curriculum in general.

Crowded environments may affect a person's ability to regulate social control and thus contribute to a feeling of learned helplessness. Rodin (1976), for example, found that children living in a high-density residence were less likely to assume control of outcomes than children living in less dense settings, and they performed more poorly on puzzles. Patients in hospitals, who have little control over their environment, show greater deficits in performance as their length of hospitalization increases, even though their physical condition may be improving (Raps, Peterson, Jonas, & Seligman, 1982).

But why do people fall, with such apparent ease, into a state of learned helplessness? Why don't they react against the situation, as reactance theory suggests they would? Sometimes they do. In a situation in which the person had no initial beliefs in control, learned helplessness may be the imme-

diate response (see Figure 12-2). In contrast, Wortman and Brehm (1975) predict that "reactance will precede helplessness for individuals who originally expect control" (p. 308). In a field study of this hypothesis, Baum, Aiello, and Calesnick (1978) selected residents of college dormitories who lived either in large or in moderate-sized groups and for whom the architecture of the building (long- or short-corridor design) either facilitated a sense of control and predictability in their interactions or diminished this sense of control. Taking these subjects into the laboratory to perform a standard social task that allows either cooperation or competition, the experimenters considered the performance of subjects as a function of how long they had lived in the residence halls—either one, three, or seven weeks. Students who had lived in the long-corridor dormitories for shorter periods of time (either one or three weeks) reported negative feelings about their living conditions, but at the same time they showed highly competitive behavior, which suggested an attempt to assert control. However, after living in the low-control situation for several more weeks, the students seemed to relinquish some of their attempted control. They became less negative and more accepting of the conditions, and their play in the game became less

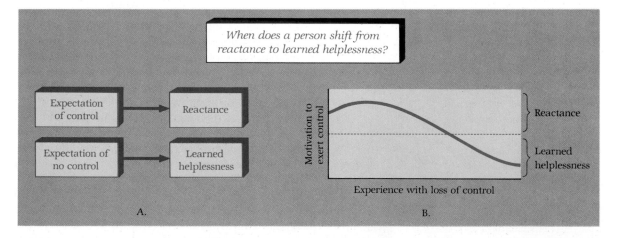

FIGURE 12-2. Reactance and learned helplessness. The basic principle, as shown in panel A, is that the person who expects to be able to control a situation will experience reactance, while the person who does not have such expectations will experience learned helplessness. As the graph in panel B shows, this shift from reactance to learned helplessness may be gradual.

PHOTO 12-8. *When we label someone as dependent, we may help create that very dependence.*

competitive, less involved and motivated, and more withdrawn. Thus, in the initial weeks, the students appeared to show reactance—attempting to restore their belief in freedom and their feeling of control. But because their attempts were presumably for the most part unsuccessful, regulated by the facts of the dormitory design, attempts to gain control were replaced with feelings of resignation and helplessness. In contrast, residents of short-corridor dormitories did not perceive any problems of control, and their behavior was more adaptive than the other residents' and did not change over the course of the study.

C. Self-induced dependence

Although learned helplessness is initially generated by an experience with uncontrollable outcomes, a feeling of loss of control may be caused by other factors as well. Langer (1978b, 1979) has suggested that a number of situations may create an illusion of incompetence. Other people, for example, may imply or suggest directly that a person is incompetent, and that belief may be incorporated by the person himself or herself. Langer has suggested that part of the apparent dysfunction of the elderly may result directly from others'

labeling them as incompetent. As a society, we tend to disparage the elderly, assuming that they are past their prime, incapable of any significant physical or mental activity, and generally dependent on the aid of friends, relatives, and institutional personnel. Although such assumptions may not be totally unfounded, it is certain that they are vastly overdrawn. Such assumptions not only are inaccurate, Langer argues, but may also create the conditions that they presuppose. The elderly themselves, labeled as dependent, may come to believe the label.

The reality of such self-induced dependence is made clear in a study by Langer and Benevento (1978). In this study, male high school students were given the opportunity to perform a set of word-hunt problems and experienced success on the task. In a second phase, each boy worked in a team with another male (actually a confederate of the experimenter). By a predetermined draw, the student was assigned the role of assistant, and the confederate was assigned the role of boss. After working on a second task in this role of assistant, the subjects then took part in the third phase of the experiment, in which they were once again allowed to work individually on the word-hunt task they had performed during the first phase. As Figure 12-3 shows, the performance of these boys dropped by 50%—they located only half as many words—after they had experienced a dependent role. In contrast, boys who had not participated in the assistant role showed little change in their performance level.

Perhaps the most surprising aspect of this experiment is how strong the performance effects were after only a brief experience in the role of assistant. If we imagine the elderly, or other groups who are frequently put in the role of dependents, we can easily see how pervasive and powerful self-induced dependence effects can be.

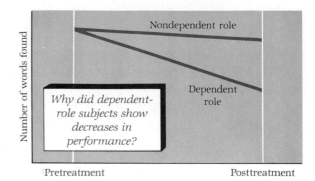

FIGURE 12-3. Effect of experience in a dependent role on performance on a word-hunt task.

VI. SUMMARY

The issues of social influence and personal control are central to human behavior and are evident in everyday interactions as well as in more global issues of government and politics.

Conformity is a yielding to group pressure when no direct request to comply with the group is made. Asch conducted some of the earliest studies demonstrating the effect of a group's judgments on the behavior of the individual. Later investigators have shown that a variety of situational factors—such as group size, number of persons who agree with the individual, status of the group members, and type of task—can affect the degree of conformity behavior.

Nonconformity behavior can be of two types. Independent behavior is that which occurs with no reference to the group position. In anticonformity behavior, in contrast, an individual does exactly the opposite of what the group does, thus showing that the group is still serving as a reference point for the individual's behavior. Conformity itself, though sometimes regarded as a purely negative type of behavior, can serve a positive function by reducing a person's uncertainty in an unfamiliar situation.

Compliance is behavior that occurs in response to a direct request. In the "foot in the door"

technique, a small request is followed by a substantially larger one. Agreement with the first stage will increase the probability of compliance with the second request. The "door in the face" effect works in the opposite way. In this case, the person who initially refuses a fairly large request will be more likely to agree to a subsequent smaller request. A third technique for inducing compliance is the "low ball" procedure, in which initial commitment to a behavior correlates with increased probability of compliance when the costs are increased.

Although compliance with some requests appears to be relatively "mindless," occurring without conscious thought, other acts of compliance evidence considerable thought, as when we evaluate the kind and amount of power that the agent has over our own situation.

Obedience studies show that people readily follow orders even when their compliance may cause harm to another person. Less obedience occurs when the victim is nearer to the subject, and more obedience occurs if the experimenter is nearer.

Criticisms of Milgram's obedience studies focus on ethical questions and on their generalizability.

In the face of pressures for conformity, compliance, and obedience, people maintain a pervasive belief in their own control. Even in situations that are obviously determined by chance, people have an illusion of control. Some of the factors that strengthen this illusion are competition, involvement in the task, knowledge and practice, and the similarity of the situation to a skill task.

Belief in personal control results in better performance and more positive affect than the lack of such belief. Individual differences in perceptions of control exist; some people are inclined to believe in external control, and others believe strongly in internal control.

Because beliefs in personal control are so pervasive, people often react strongly to a perceived or real loss of control. Psychological reactance is a motivational state that is aroused whenever a person feels that his or her freedom has been abridged. According to reactance theory, people will attempt to restore their sense of freedom when such threats are perceived. In some cases, however, as when harm to oneself or to others is involved, people show a willingness to relax their control and accept control as being in the hands of others.

Learned helplessness can be induced by exposing a person to a situation in which outcomes occur in a manner that is noncontingent on one's own behavior (apparently random). People who experience such outcomes may develop beliefs that their own responses have no effect on subsequent outcomes. A variety of deficits may result—motivational, cognitive, emotional, and loss of self-esteem, depending on which attributions are made.

Self-induced dependence may develop even without such outcomes. Labeling people as dependent can cause decrements in subsequent behavior, apparently because the labeled person begins to believe that his or her own behavior is dependent primarily on the actions of others.

GLOSSARY TERMS

anticonformity
autokinetic effect
compliance

conformity
"foot in the door" effect
learned helplessness

locus of control
obedience
reactance

13

Group & Individual Differences

We must recognize that beneath the superficial classifications of sex and race the same potentialities exist.
■ MARGARET MEAD

Each individual ego is endowed from the beginning with its own peculiar dispositions and tendencies.
■ SIGMUND FREUD

In *Gulliver's Travels*, the wandering Captain Gulliver visits a series of imaginary societies, encountering the Lilliputians, the Blefuscudeans, the Houyhnhnms, and a variety of other people and nations (Swift, 1726/1960). In each case, he finds a group of people whose appearance, values, and behaviors are radically different from his own. In similar scenarios, science fiction writers describe human beings whose behaviors and thoughts are often quite different from those of the people we all know. Do these kinds of differences among groups represent mere fictional license, or do groups of people really differ in their behavior?

Many social psychologists assume that people are basically alike and that the primary causes of behavior are external to the person. This argument suggests that different situations produce different behaviors and that, given the same conditions, all people would generally have the ability to behave in the same way. In contrast, other observers of human behavior assume that various groups of people behave differently. For example, in the year 1909, newly inaugurated President William Howard Taft told a group of Black college students in Charlotte, North Carolina, "Your race is adapted to be a race of farmers, first, last and for all times" (quoted in Logan, 1957, p. 66). Taft was not alone in making this kind of assumption. As we saw in earlier chapters, there are stereotypes of many groups. People maintain beliefs about men and women, Blacks and Whites, old people and young people, and the citizens of various countries. But to what extent do these beliefs reflect the truth?

In this chapter, we will provide an answer to this question. First, we will look at the field of cross-cultural psychology, which attempts to determine the generality of basic psychological principles across a variety of countries and cultural groups. Then we will turn to the more specific factors of race and gender, asking whether they predict differences in social behavior.

The chapter will also explore the issue of personality differences. Although the categorization of people may begin at a highly visible level, most of us pursue a system of classifying people that goes beyond obvious physical characteristics such as gender or race. Implicit personality theories (discussed in Chapter 4) may guide us in categorizing the people we know. For example, we may see Tony and Harriet as being very similar in their extroverted, friendly personalities, whereas Jeannette and Peter may be quiet and introverted. In trying to select workers for a community project, we may consider a dimension of efficiency and favor Alice and Al over Joan and Jim. In doing so, we are identifying a particular personality characteristic (efficiency), and we are assuming that personality can affect behavior (in this case, work on a community project).

Psychologists have attempted to systematically conceptualize and measure the ways individuals differ. Many of these differences have implications for social behavior, and we will look at some of these patterns. In addition, we will look at some of the broad issues involved in relating personality constructs to situational variables.

■ I. Similarities and differences among groups

Throughout recorded history, people have made comparisons between their own racial or geographical group and other groups (Gossett, 1963). For example, Aristotle believed that Greece's benign climate enabled the Greeks to develop physical and mental characteristics that were superior to those of other Europeans. This *chauvinistic* stance (a belief that one's own group is better than other groups) is certainly not unique to Aristotle. Often, when people make comparisons between their own country and other countries, between their own sex and the other sex, or between their own class and other classes, they tend to imply that their country, sex, and so on are superior. The possibility of such biases is one of the issues that must concern the investigator of group differences. Often, people fail to recognize how strongly their own experience may influence what they see.

When we consider possible differences among groups, several important issues emerge. First, as a backdrop, there is the tradition of social psychology, in which situational factors have been given far more attention than person factors. A second issue is the nature of differences—are differences absolute, or are we simply talking about more or less? Third, and perhaps most important, we must consider the causes of any differences that are found. Let's review some of these issues in more detail before moving on to specific comparisons among groups.

A. The social-psychological tradition

Traditionally, social psychology dates its heritage to Kurt Lewin, who stressed the person's present psychological life space as a source of behavior (Lewin, 1935, 1936) and disdained past determinants. Although Lewin clearly recognized that both the person and the environment are important, most of his followers have tended to stress the environment, rather than the person. (Lewin's original formulation that B (behavior) $= f(P,E)$, where P and E represent the person and the environment, respectively, clearly shows that he himself regarded personality and individual differences as important.)

As Helmreich has pungently stated, "Classic, laboratory social psychology has generally ignored individual differences, choosing to consider subjects as equivalent black boxes or as two-legged (generally white) rats from the same strain" (1975, p. 551). In other words, social psychologists did

PHOTO 13-1. *"Boys will be boys and girls will be girls" — but on the Little League playing field, similarities may be more apparent than differences.*

not give much thought to possible differences among individuals or groups. What was true of one group, it was assumed, would probably be true for any other group.

This assumption has been challenged, however, as more and more social psychologists have begun to explore the nature of group differences at a variety of levels. Cross-cultural psychologists have asked whether behaviors observed in the United States can be generalized to people in other cultures. Within the United States, many people have begun to look at the role of gender, often questioning earlier assumptions that what was true of males would be true of females as well. Personality variables have begun to appear more frequently in the theorizing of social psychologists, and debates on their importance have been waged with increasing fervor.

Thus, assumptions that the empirical relationships emerging from one laboratory with one kind of subject in one country or culture will be true of all people are not held as strongly as they once were. Some social psychologists still hold to the "universal" position; but for many others, the patterns of variation among groups are important keys to understanding human social behavior.

B. The principle of overlapping distributions

Terms such as *cultural differences* or *sex differences* can be misleading. Often, they convey the assumption that there are differences to be found— and that is a question we should ask, rather than a conclusion that we can assume.

In looking for differences, investigators can become blind to similarities between members of different groups. In anthropology, the term **exotic bias** has been coined to refer to the tendency of investigators to focus only on those aspects of a group or society that differ from their own society. North American social scientists visiting a South Seas island may first notice differences in style of dress and diet. If the society is a matrilineal one, in which status descends through women's lineage, this feature also may command the attention of investigators who are accustomed to a patrilineal system. However, aspects of the culture that correspond to the culture of the investigators may go unnoticed—since they aren't exotic or different, they may be taken for granted.

The effects of biases are not restricted to the anthropological field study. Whenever we set out to explore the ways in which two groups may differ (Blacks and Whites, or women and men, for example), we run the risk of ignoring the similarities between those groups, which may far outweigh the differences between them.

Even when we do observe differences between two identifiable groups, precautions are in order. For example, if you found a statistically significant sex difference in aggression, you wouldn't be able to assume that all men are more aggressive than all women. If you were to study aggressive behavior in young children, you would find many little girls who are potential sluggers and many young boys who tend to shy away from physical confrontation. This concept of *overlapping distributions* is illustrated in Figure 13-1. Most studies that find differences between races, cultures, or sexes exhibit this type of distribution. Although one group may differ from another, there are many people within each group who do not fit the pattern.

C. Causes of group differences

Perhaps the most difficult problem of all in the study of possible differences between various groups is in determining why differences occur. Recalling our discussion of methods in Chapter 2, we can speak of the independent variable in an experiment as one that is manipulated by the experimenter and randomly assigned across conditions. In such experiments, the assumption is rather safely made that the independent variable (for example, the number of bystanders present in an emergency) does not systematically vary with any other characteristics of the subjects. When our quasi-independent variable is race or sex or culture, however, we can't make such assumptions. The experimenter has not randomly assigned race, for example, and many other factors could be associated with such a characteristic. In seeking to determine what these other factors are, psychol-

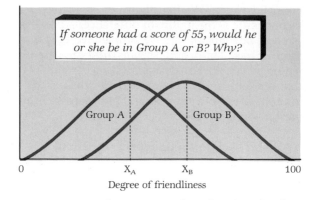

FIGURE 13-1. The concept of overlapping distributions. The curve on the left represents the distribution of "friendliness" scores for members of Group A, and the curve on the right represents the scores for members of Group B. Assume, for arbitrary purposes, that the highest score is 100 and the lowest is 0. If we look at the group averages, indicated by an X, we see that members of Group B are, on the average, friendlier than members of Group A; however, many members of Group A have higher scores than some members of Group B, and some members of Group B are quite unfriendly. (Many members of A and B are alike on friendliness.) Most psychological traits and social behaviors exhibit this kind of overlap when two groups are compared.

ogists have encountered innumerable obstacles and have often become embroiled in controversy.

Traditionally, investigators have looked to hereditary factors as one possible cause of group differences and environmental factors as another possible cause. Hereditary explanations stress the importance of genetic factors and often assume the inevitability of observed group differences. Sociobiologists provide one example of the hereditary perspective. Sex differences in behaviors such as aggression and caring for children are assumed to be genetically based, according to the sociobiological position. Other investigators with a biological bent have pointed to a variety of possible genetic and hormonal determinants of postulated differences between women and men in a variety of intellectual behaviors, such as verbal abilities and problem solving (for example, Broverman, Klaiber, Kobayashi, & Vogel, 1968).

Most often, questions of genetic determinants have been concerned with the issue of intelligence.

For example, considerable controversy was raised during the 1970s surrounding racial differences in intelligence. Numerous studies indicate that Black children, on the average, score approximately 15 points lower than White children on standard IQ measures (Loehlin, Lindzey, & Spuhler, 1975). Both "hereditarians" and "environmentalists" recognize that such differences in test scores occur; the difference between the two perspectives lies in the interpretation of the differences. For the genetically based interpreter, such differences are evidence of innate racial differences (Herrnstein, 1973; Jensen, 1969, 1973).

Similar hereditary arguments have been posed to explain assumed sex differences in intelligence, particularly in the early part of the century. As Shields (1975) has vividly shown, these investigations were not without their problems. Shifts in theory regarding which area of the brain controlled intelligence were often followed by dramatic reversals in findings concerning which sex possessed a larger area of the supposed "seat of intelligence." According to these turn-of-the-century investigators, male dominance in social life was paralleled by, and indeed the result of, male superiority in intelligence. In subsequent years, some investigators took a different stance and assumed that there were no sex differences in intelligence. In fact, the standard Stanford-Binet test of intelligence was constructed so that only items showing no sex differences were included (McNemar, 1942).

Individual differences in specific personality traits have also been explained on the basis of genetic influence. The British psychologist Hans Eysenck (1967), for example, has defined introversion/extroversion as a basic personality dimension and has pointed to its roots in physiological processes.

Other investigators have looked to socialization experiences for the causes of observed differences between groups. These explanations cover a broad range, including economic and environmental conditions, specific socialization practices of parents, and more general issues of racism and sexism (as discussed in Chapter 10). Thus, cultural differences may be seen as the result of different norms and cultural beliefs. Racial differences may be explained by patterns of socialization, economic and social-class differences, or differences in the reactions of Blacks and Whites to the testing situation itself. Similarly, sex differences may be attributed to differences in the learning experiences of boys and girls and to the continued pervasiveness of **sex-role norms**—beliefs about appropriate behavior for women and men.

Rather than focusing exclusively on either heredity or environment, many investigators prefer to consider the possible influence of both factors—although they may still differ considerably in the weight they attach to each factor. As just one example of this strategy, from hundreds that might be considered, we can look at a recent study by Price, Vandenberg, Iyer, and Williams (1982). They studied 138 pairs of Swedish twins, as well as the spouses and children of these twins. Height, clearly a genetically based physical characteristic, was measured, as were a variety of personality traits. Although similarity of height between twins and relatives showed a strong influence of heredity, personality was not so strongly related. In fact, the authors suggest that personality was influenced mainly by the environment, especially from influences outside the home (experiences not shared by the family as a whole).

Other studies have shown a stronger effect of heredity. Overall, however, it is probably safe to conclude that although both heredity and environment may be influential, environment and experience probably have more to do than heredity with determining the kinds of social behaviors discussed in this book.

■ II. Cross-cultural comparisons

Much of the research reported in this book has been based on samples of U.S. citizens. Social psychology is, in the words of one critic, both "culture bound and culture blind" (Berry, 1978). In part, this focus reflects an ethnocentric bias, and, in part, it reflects that the majority of social psychologists are located in the United States. In fact, it is estimated that 80% of all psychologists who are living now or who ever have lived are from the United States (Triandis & Lambert, 1980).

Often, investigators from the United States make generalizations to other cultures without much thought. For example, it is frequently assumed that the United States and Canada are quite similar in attitudes, behaviors, and values. However, the governments of these two countries differ, as do their basic constitutional premises and many of their social customs. In recent years, Canadians have pointed out that such differences do exist and that past generalizations are not warranted (Berry, 1974; Sadava, 1978). If there are important differences between these two neighboring countries, then it is easy to see how cultural differences can be quite substantial if we compare the United States with, for example, countries in Asia or Latin America.

It is the aim of cross-cultural psychology to study and understand these potential differences. More specifically, in the words of Harry Triandis, "Cross-cultural psychology is concerned with the system-atic study of behavior and experience as it occurs in different cultures, is influenced by culture, or results in changes in existing cultures" (1980, p. 1). We cannot do justice to all the work that has been done in this area. Nonetheless, we will briefly describe some of the major principles of cross-cultural research and give a few examples of the areas of study.

A. Some principles of cross-cultural psychology

Investigators outside the United States have often questioned how applicable the theories and principles of American social psychology are to their own countries. Moscovici (1972), for example, has argued that the concept of equity theory (see Chapter 6) is particular to capitalistic systems and may play only a small role in the interpersonal behavior of people who live under different forms of government. Similar arguments have been voiced

PHOTO 13-2. *The interdependence of nations underlines the importance of understanding cultural similarities and differences.*

regarding other U.S.-derived principles, such as those relating similarity and attraction or those dealing with the content of particular communications (Brislin, 1980).

Recognizing these potential problems, social scientists distinguish between what they call etic constructs and emic constructs. **Etic** constructs refer to universal factors—those that hold across all the cultures we know or have investigated. For example, the concept of the family can be considered an etic construct, although the various forms of family life certainly differ across cultures (Triandis, 1977b). In contrast, an **emic** construct is one that is culture-specific—that exists or has meaning only within a particular cultural framework. "Generation gap," for example, might have meaning only in the United States and in societies that are similar to the United States. To take another example, research has shown that social distance (see Chapter 10) is a construct that can be measured etically. However, certain forms of social distance may be found only in certain cultures. Triandis (1980) suggests that the concept of *philotimo*, referring to conformity to the expectations of an in-group, is an emic construct unique to Greece.

The problem arises when truly emic constructs are assumed to be etic—in other words, when findings from one culture are assumed to be true of the larger society. The term *pseudoetic* has been applied to this type of conclusion. For cross-cultural psychologists, one of the challenges is to distinguish the etic from the pseudoetic.

How does the cross-cultural psychologist go about making this distinction? There are no easy answers to this question, but some strategies are more productive than others. Of course, research has to be carried out in more than one culture in order to determine whether there is any commonality. For the investigator exploring another culture, it is also important to become familiar with that culture. Through this familiarization process, the investigator may realize that certain concepts taken for granted in one's own country are not assumed in the other country. For much the same reason, an experimenter cannot always take a methodology and apply it intact in another setting. Procedures

may have different meanings in other countries: an operationalization of "crowding" in the United States, for example, might be seen as luxurious space in an overpopulated country.

Although the problems of cross-cultural research are considerable, the rewards may also be great. Cultures themselves may be considered as independent variables, allowing the investigator a far greater range of conditions than would be possible within a single setting (Mann, 1980). For example, investigators have studied patterns of sex-role development by looking at cultures that vary widely in the degree to which physical strength is required in the society's activities (Whiting & Edwards, 1973). Particular cultures may also offer situations not easily duplicated, such as the civil disturbances and consequent deaths in Northern Ireland (see Box 13-1). By extending our horizons in these ways, we stand to gain a great deal more understanding of human behavior.

B. Some examples of cross-cultural research

The scope of cross-cultural research is too broad to describe easily in a few pages. Cross-cultural psychologists have explored a great range of issues, ranging from perception to cognition to emotion (Triandis & Lonner, 1980). Even limiting the range to social-psychological processes, the variety of endeavors is impressive. Let us consider just a few examples.

As we saw in Chapter 5, facial expressions are an important form of nonverbal communication. Do such expressions constitute an etic principle? Extensive research suggests that expressions of emotions are indeed innate and universal (Izard, 1980). However, the *display rules* that govern the particular expression of an emotion may vary widely among cultures, suggesting emic principles with regard to a particular expression. A similar combination of etic and emic principles can be found in the social-distance literature, discussed earlier. Triandis and his colleagues have found, for example, that citizens of different countries use cues of race, occupation, religion, and nationality to rate the favorability of other group members, but the

BOX 13-1. Reactions to stress in Northern Ireland

Northern Ireland has been the site of violence for centuries, and civil disturbances have been particularly intense during the past 15 years. Between 1969 and 1976, over 1500 people were reported killed and another 17,800 injured. Such persistent conditions of violence allow us to study reactions to stress in an environment not found in many parts of the world. William Mercer and his colleagues have conducted a number of investigations in Northern Ireland, exploring some of the consequences of this strife (Mercer, Bunting, & Snook, 1979, 1980). Comparing students in Northern Ireland with those in the Republic of Ireland, these investigators found

greater fear and anxiety among the students of Northern Ireland. Within Belfast itself, however, students living in comparatively safe areas were no less afraid than those living in less secure areas. Actual experience with a bombing had more complicated effects: for men, the experience seemed to cause some withdrawal, while feelings of aggression appeared to be more common among females. Through all these analyses, the influence of religion appears to be quite minimal: Protestants and Catholics react to the stress in similar ways, despite the divergence of their beliefs that perpetuate the struggles. ■

relative importance of these cues varies among cultures. In the United States, for example, a person's race was found to be more important than his or her occupation or religion; in Germany, occupation and religion were more important than race (Triandis, Davis, & Takezawa, 1965).

Gergen and his colleagues have suggested that social exchange may be a basic principle of human interaction (Gergen, Morse, & Gergen, 1980). Yet,

the resources that are exchanged may differ widely among cultures. Foa and Foa (1974) have suggested that there are six basic classes of resources, as shown in Figure 13-2. According to these investigators, resources that are adjacent to each other in this diagram should be most easily interchangeable, and their research supports this prediction. However, when we move across various cultures, we may find shifts in the preferences for certain

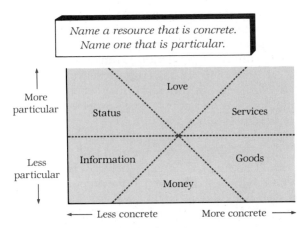

FIGURE 13-2. Basic classes of resources in social exchange. These classes vary on two dimensions: how concrete they are (goods, for example, are concrete, while information is more symbolic) and how particular they are, or how important one's identity is to the specific exchange.

sectors of this exchange pattern. Some societies may stress the concreteness of rewards, while others may stress particularism. Although the patterns of preferences may vary, however, the overall structure of resources may be an etic construct.

■ III. Demographic categories

Moving closer to home, in this section we will look at similarities and differences between groups of people within our own society. Specifically, we will ask whether people from different racial and ethnic groups differ and whether men and women differ, focusing on social behaviors. Both race and sex are considered *demographic* variables—categories that can be used to classify people on the basis of "vital statistics" such as age, geographic region, race, or sex. Such categorization systems are not perfect. In the case of race, for example, both scientists and citizens have often debated the means of classifying someone's racial status. (South Africa's distinction between Blacks and Coloureds is a graphic illustration of political debates on this question.) Sex is somewhat clearer, although even here there are people whose physical and genetic characteristics may make them anomalous in the

typical categorization systems. Although these are important questions, they are not our interest here. Instead, we will accept the categories as they are typically defined and will look to possible differences in social behaviors that parallel these distinctions.

A. Race and ethnicity

Just as psychologists have tended to concentrate on people in the United States, so they have tended to focus on Whites. In an illustration of this trend, Guthrie's (1976) summary of the history of psychological research is entitled *Even the Rat Was White*. In this volume, Guthrie deals not only with the assumptions made about the differences between Blacks and Whites but also with the often-unrecognized contributions of Black psychologists to scientific knowledge.

Much of the research comparing Blacks and Whites has focused on issues of intelligence, reflecting social and political concerns with education. This issue is somewhat outside the domain of social psychology. Nonetheless, we should note that although the issue is not totally resolved, it is generally accepted that both heredity and environment contribute to intelligence. With regard to the specific issue of Black intelligence, Scarr and Weinberg's conclusion seems most acceptable: "The social environment plays a dominant role in determining the average IQ level of Black children and . . . both social and genetic variables contribute to individual variation among them" (1976, p. 739).

More social-psychological in nature are investigations dealing with self-esteem of Blacks and Whites (see Chapter 3). It has often been hypothesized that Blacks would have lower self-esteem than Whites, as a result of continued experience with prejudice and discrimination. Early research seemed to support this hypothesis (Gurin, Gurin, Lao, & Beattie, 1969; Proshansky & Newton, 1968). In the 1970s, the emergence of the message that "Black is beautiful" in the United States suggested an alteration in this pattern, as Blacks began to adopt their own standards of evaluation. In the process of "becoming Black" (a process that Cross, 1980, calls "nigrescence"), self-esteem may increase. There are a number of factors that can influence

PHOTO 13-3. *Pride in their African heritage has led many Black Americans to adopt styles, such as this head scarf, that reflect that heritage.*

measures of self-esteem among Blacks (as well as Whites). In reviewing a series of recent studies, Gray-Little and Appelbaum (1979) found that studies reporting higher self-esteem scores among White students than among Black students, as well as studies reporting no difference, were most apt to have been conducted at integrated schools. In contrast, studies conducted at segregated schools and desegregated schools with Black majorities generally indicated more positive self-concept scores among Black students than among Whites. Desegregated schools may have other effects on Black children as well. Although the evidence is not conclusive, it appears that Black children in such schools may have a greater sense of internal control, even though they do not always find the atmosphere congenial (Epps, 1980).

As in cross-cultural research, investigators are often hampered by unfamiliarity with the group they are studying. Paradigms developed in a middle-class White culture may be no more appropriate to Black culture than they are to Asian cultures (see Boykin, Franklin, & Yates, 1979). Jones (1979) has suggested five areas in which patterns of difference may emerge: time, rhythm, improvisation, oral expression, and spirituality (see Box 13-2).

To take a more concrete example, we can look at the area of nonverbal communication. As we saw in Chapter 5, differences between Blacks and Whites have been observed in the amount of gazing behavior shown while talking or listening to someone else speak. Other nonverbal behaviors may show characteristic differences between Black and White society. Cooke (1980) has discussed a variety of hand gestures and stances that may be unique to the Black culture, communicating very specific meanings to the people involved. Although some of these gestures have made their way into other parts of the culture—such as "giving skin," now prominent in sports—they are aspects of the Black experience that have typically been ignored by social psychologists.

In trying to determine how racial group may relate to various forms of social behavior, investigators must always be aware that race may be confounded with other variables (see Jones, in press). In the United States, Blacks typically have higher unemployment rates, lower incomes, lower education levels, poorer housing, and more health problems than Whites (Pettigrew, 1964). In addition, as we have seen in Chapter 10, Blacks are subject to the pressures and practices of racism. Any and all of these factors can contribute to observed differences between Blacks and Whites. As a consequence of this multidetermined reality, we really know rather little about racial differences in social behavior.

B. Gender

Whereas social-psychological research on Blacks and Whites has been relatively sparse, research comparing women and men has been abundant. Although concern with possible sex differences in a variety of behaviors has been evidenced since the

BOX 13-2. Understanding TRIOS

Psychologist James Jones (1979) suggests that an understanding of bicultural dynamics in the United States may require new concepts and theories. He offers TRIOS, a set of five dimensions that may be different in the Black and White experience. These dimensions are *Time*, *Rhythm*, *Improvisation*, *Oral* expression, and *Spirituality*.

1. *Time* can be divided into units of different sizes, from the milliseconds used by physicists to the years and seasons calculated by ancient astronomers. People, too, may differ in their perception and sense of time. Although psychologists tend to ignore the time dimension, looking instead at static moments in time, we might learn a great deal by studying how people conceptualize time and what units they use in interpreting the flow of their life. As just one example, cited by Jones, consider the difference between the executive who blocks time by a series of 15-minute appointments and the native of Trinidad who says that "any time is Trinidad time."

2. *Rhythm*, often assigned to the Black stereotype, has a broader meaning than the musical patterns it often describes. Related to time in Jones's definition, rhythm is seen as "an organization of time into recurring patterns" (p. 417). Ideas of rhythm can also be used to describe the relationship between individuals and social systems. Blacks and Whites may differ in their basic rhythms, and the introduction of a member of one group into the system of another may highlight these different tempos.

3. *Improvisation* can take many forms, from playground basketball to American jazz. Both of these particular examples are rooted in the Black experience. Improvisation may occur when a person confronts an unstable or unknown environment or when one's own qualities are not the ones sought by a particular system. Jones

suggests that "Black people could not have survived the American experience without improvisation" (p. 423). Not having access to the dominant system, Blacks have been forced to improvise and develop new systems. Psychologists tend to focus on the dominant systems in their research, and they may fail to notice the many forms that differ from those dominant patterns.

4. *Oral expression* may form the basis for rich traditions when a group is excluded from the written exchange of a society. In Ireland, for example, traveling storytellers preserved accounts that might have been destroyed by warfare had they been written. The popular television series *Roots* depicted the important role that oral tradition played in African society. Oral expression requires personal contact and therefore engenders certain forms of communication while eschewing others (see Chapter 5). Language itself may show differences among groups; the status of Black language has been a widely debated topic in recent years (see Smitherman & McGinnis, 1980).

5. *Spirituality* is a topic that psychologists have often avoided, but it is clearly central to the lives of many people. Whether one thinks in terms of a particular religious creed or a more general worldview, spirituality may be as important to some lives as the notion of individual achievement is to others.

These five concepts—time, rhythm, improvisation, oral expression, and spirituality—are not the only dimensions of importance when we talk about differences between Blacks and Whites or among peoples of many other ethnic groups. Yet, they do suggest some important perspectives that may need to be taken into account when we look at members of different racial and ethnic groups. ■

turn of the century, research has been given new impetus by the growth of the women's movement during the 1970s and society's debates over the appropriate roles for men and women. This concern with gender in research has taken many forms. Here we will consider the possibility of sex differences in just three areas of social behavior: aggression, conformity and social influence, and nonverbal behaviors.

Aggression. Are men more aggressive than women? In the frequently lively debates over possible differences between women and men, it is often conceded that men tend to be more aggressive than women. Some people argue that although men are more aggressive physically, women excel in verbal aggressiveness. In a lengthy review, Maccoby and Jacklin (1974) concluded that men are indeed the more aggressive sex, and they suggested that this difference may have a biological base that creates a greater readiness for aggression in men than in women.

Subsequent analysis shows that this simple conclusion may be too simple. From a social-psychological standpoint, we need to consider the various situational factors that may affect aggressive behavior, and in doing so, we find that the differences between men and women are somewhat complex. For example, although men are more likely than women to describe themselves as aggressive, actual behavioral measures show few differences between the sexes (Frodi, Macaulay, & Thome, 1977). When aggression has been provoked directly, through insult or previous attack, there is no evidence that women are less likely to react aggressively than men are. However, women are less likely than men to instigate aggressive behavior or to act as third-party instigators of aggression (Frodi et al., 1977; Gaebelein, 1977b). Further, as noted in Chapter 8, the forms of aggression chosen by men may be considerably more violent than those chosen by women. It has been suggested that women may consider aggression to be inappropriate in many situations and may associate anxiety and guilt with aggression when direct provocation is not present (Frodi et al., 1977). Finally, contrary to popular belief, there is no evidence that women are more aggressive than men verbally.

Conformity and social influence. Another area in which sex differences are often assumed is conformity and persuadability. Although several generations of textbooks have supported this assumption, sex differences are much less striking than was previously thought (Eagly, 1978; Eagly & Carli, 1981). Reviewing dozens of studies, Eagly found that there are no general differences between men and women in susceptibility to persuasive communications. In contrast, women are somewhat more conforming than men in situations that involve face-to-face interaction. One possible explanation for this difference is that women are more concerned with group harmony—when group pressure is exerted, they may be more willing to go along with the group rather than exert their own judgment and risk disharmony. Yet, even in these situations in which sex differences are found, the difference is quite small. Referring back to Figure 13-1, we would find considerable overlap if we diagrammed the conformity scores of women and men.

Perceiving nonverbal cues.   As we saw in our discussion of communication patterns in Chapter 5, men and women often differ in their nonverbal behaviors. In the amount and patterning of eye contact, in body position and gestures, in touching behavior, and in interpersonal distance, men and women exhibit reliable and often substantial differences (Henley, 1977; LaFrance & Mayo, 1978). In interpersonal interactions, women are more able to elicit warmth, whereas men elicit anxiety (Weitz, 1976).

Beyond these differences in actual behavior, women have been found to be more able to judge the affective, or emotional, state of other people (Hall, 1978). In other words, in situations that require an interpretation of another person's mood or intentions that is based on nonverbal cues, women prove to be superior to men. However, there are limits to this superiority. If a message is very brief, women seem to lose their advantage, suggesting that a certain minimal amount of information is necessary in order for the sex difference to appear (Rosenthal & DePaulo, 1979).

Sex differences also appear in the reception of deceptive messages. Women are more likely than men to believe a deceptive message rather than grasping the true state of affairs that underlies a cover-up. On the other side of the coin, women are more revealing senders of emotional cues. Men may be less expressive than women, who convey their moods and sentiments more clearly than men do (Rosenthal & DePaulo, 1979).

Several hypotheses have been offered to explain these differences. One hypothesis suggests that women have been better trained to read cues and have been socialized to respond in a more emotionally expressive way. Another suggestion is that because women have less power than men in many social situations (Henley, 1977), they learn by necessity the importance of interpreting the behaviors of others, going beyond the obvious verbal messages and seeking nonverbal cues of intentions. Finally, a third hypothesis suggests that such sex differences are innate. Hall (1978), in fact, has postulated that the early experiences of mothers with their infants may require them to be extremely sensitive to external threats to their young; there-fore, women develop the ability to perceive the outside world more accurately than men. Although each of these suggestions remains a possibility, there is no one hypothesis that has amassed the amount of evidence necessary for us to discard the others. In fact, it is quite possible that each of the hypotheses offers some insight into the causes of observed sex differences.

C. Difficulties with demographic variables

The use of demographic variables to describe differences in social behavior can provide us with some useful information. At the same time, their use is ultimately limited, particularly when we seek *explanations* for any observed differences. Let's briefly consider some of these problems.

First, neither race nor sex is a "pure" variable. In the case of race, possible genetic differences are often submerged by differences in education, social class, and other aspects of life-style. Thus, we say that race in the United States is *confounded* with other variables; that is, its effects can't be separated out. Similarly, in the case of sex, possible genetic differences cannot be separated from the very strong influence of socialization. Few people would argue with the contention that boys and girls are raised quite differently and that early experiences are important in the development of adult differences. Social structures, opportunities, models, and the specific reinforcements provided by parents, teachers, and peers all provide possible sources for learning patterns of behavior. As the philosopher John Stuart Mill stated more than 100 years ago, "I deny that any one knows, or can know, the nature of the two sexes, as long as they have only been seen in their present relation to one another." His message is still true today. Hence, both race differences and sex differences, although they may be observed, are very difficult to explain.

A second limitation of the demographic approach is that the overlap between the two selected groups is often considerable (see Figure 13-1). Observed sex differences in aggression and conformity, for example, have been shown to account for very little of the total variation in people's behavior

(Eagly & Carli, 1981; Hyde, 1982). In other words, the influence of race or sex, though statistically significant, may be practically quite small (Deaux, in press).

A third issue is that Blacks and Whites, and men and women, do not act in a vacuum. As we have seen in earlier chapters, people tend to form expectancies about other people, and in acting on these expectancies, they may confirm them. In the case of gender, sex-role norms—beliefs about appropriate behavior for women and men—are pervasive (Spence, Deaux, & Helmreich, in press). Similar norms may affect interactions between Blacks and Whites. Thus, social-interaction situations may actually create differences between women and men, or between Blacks and Whites, rather than being a neutral stage for their display.

■ IV. Personality variables

Because demographic variables often create as many questions as they answer, psychologists have often preferred to look at differences among people in terms of psychological characteristics, rather than demographic characteristics. The concept of personality differences has not been entirely absent from our earlier discussions. Chapter 3, for example, examined the characteristics of self-monitoring and self-consciousness. We looked at locus of control in Chapter 12. And our extensive discussion of attitude change implies that there are individual differences in people's beliefs and values. In this section we will consider two other personality dimensions that have been used widely by

social psychologists, and we will consider the more general issue of personality and social behavior.

First, however, we should look briefly at some of the central concerns in the study of personality.

A major concern is the extent to which we can classify all individuals on a single dimension, as opposed to the extent to which each individual must be viewed as a unique combination of characteristics (Allport, 1937; Mischel, 1977; Murray, 1938). In taking the former approach, termed the **nomothetic** approach, investigators isolate a single dimension of concern and try to categorize people in terms of one variable. In other words, the focus is on one trait, and the assumption is that all people have some "amount" of that trait. For example, a researcher interested in the concept of achievement behavior may develop a scale to measure need for achievement. With this scale in hand, the researcher can assess people's achievement needs, eventually developing a rank ordering of people, from those who score very high on need for achievement to those who score very low. Then the researcher will try to determine how individuals with different scores on the measure will perform in selected situations.

In contrast, the **idiographic** approach to personality focuses on the interrelationship of events and characteristics within an individual—it is a person-centered focus. Here the focus is not on making comparisons among individuals but, rather, on understanding the complexity of a single individual and the way in which the component parts of a person fit together. Idiographic personologists are also interested in the concept of choice and the

ways in which individuals determine the environments in which they are found (Tyler, 1978). In other words, there is more interest in how people shape their environments than in how environments mold people.

The implications of these differences are numerous—they involve basic assumptions, methodologies, and goals—and the development of these positions goes far beyond the bounds of a social-psychology textbook. For the social psychologist, the trait-centered (or nomothetic) approach has clearly been dominant (to the extent that personality has been considered at all). We will focus our attention on traits that exemplify this approach.

The number of personality traits and personality measures is staggering. We will select two: (1) authoritarianism and (2) the interrelated concepts of masculinity, femininity, and androgyny. In each case, we will try to explain the rationale behind the development of the concept and describe several of the social behaviors to which the concept has been related. Then we will return to the more general issues of predicting behavior on the basis of personality characteristics.

A. Authoritarianism

As discussed briefly in Chapter 10, the concept of authoritarianism was the product of a group of social scientists, led by T. W. Adorno and E. Frenkel-Brunswik, who attempted to assess degrees of anti-Semitism. Clearly instigated by events in Germany during the 1930s under the reign of Hitler, this concept initially was seen as a series of separate components, including anti-Semitism, ethnocentrism, and political and economic conservatism (Adorno et al., 1950).

Aiming to develop a general measure of individuals' susceptibility to antidemocratic ideology (without specific reference to any particular group), the research team headed by Adorno and Frenkel-Brunswik constructed a measure of **authoritarianism,** popularly referred to as the F scale (*F* denoting Fascism). In developing their conceptualizations, the California group relied on the theory of psychoanalysis and Freud's concepts of the ego, the superego, and the id (discussed in

PHOTO 13-4. *Authoritarianism in action. A rigid belief in traditional standards and the acceptance of authority to enforce those standards may lead to extreme action, such as this book burning in Ohio.*

Chapter 1). They postulated nine components of authoritarianism: conventionalism, authoritarian submission, authoritarian aggression, power and toughness, anti-intraception, superstition and stereotypy, destructiveness and cynicism, projectivity, and overconcern with sex, which illustrates authoritarianism in action. Each of these components is defined, with sample items from the original F scale, in Table 13-1. Although some items have been altered as the scale has gone through a set of revisions, the third and final version of the scale contains many of the items listed in Table 13-1 (Cherry & Byrne, 1977).

How does authoritarianism relate to social behavior? Investigators have approached this question in two ways. In the first approach, scores on the authoritarianism scale are correlated with other variables in an attempt to see how a package of variables might fit together. In the second approach—a more social-psychological approach—an investigator manipulates specific situations and

TABLE 13-1. Components of authoritarianism

1. **Conventionalism.** *Rigid* adherence to and *over*emphasis on middle-class values, and overresponsiveness to contemporary *external* social pressure.
   Sample item: "A person who has bad manners, habits, and breeding can hardly expect to get along with decent people."
   Sample item: "No sane, normal person could ever think of hurting a close friend or relative."

2. **Authoritarian submission.** An exaggerated, emotional need to submit to others; an uncritical acceptance of a strong leader who will make decisions.
   Sample item: "People should have a deep faith in a supernatural force higher than themselves to whom they give total allegiance and whose decisions they obey without question."
   Sample item: "Obedience and respect for authority are the most important virtues children should learn."

3. **Authoritarian aggression.** Favoring condemnation, total rejection, stern discipline, or severe punishment as ways of dealing with people and forms of behavior that deviate from conventional values.
   Sample item: "Sex crimes, such as rape and attacks on children, deserve more than mere imprisonment; such criminals ought to be publicly whipped, or worse."
   Sample item: "No insult to our honor should ever go unpunished."

4. **Anti-intraception.** Disapproval of a free emotional life, of the intellectual or theoretical, and of the impractical. Anti-intraceptive persons maintain a narrow range of consciousness; realization of their genuine feelings or self-awareness might threaten their adjustment. Hence, they reject feelings, fantasies, and other subjective or "tender-minded" phenomena.
   Sample item: "When a person has a problem or worry, it is best for him or her not to think about it, but to keep busy with more cheerful things."
   Sample item: "There are some things too intimate and personal to talk about even with one's closest friends."

5. **Superstition and stereotypy.** Superstition implies a tendency to shift responsibility from within the individual onto outside forces beyond one's control, particularly to mystical determinants. Stereotypy is the tendency to think in rigid, oversimplified categories, in unambiguous terms of black and white, particularly in the realm of psychological or social matters.
   Sample item: "It is entirely possible that this series of wars and conflicts will be ended once and for all by a world-destroying earthquake, flood, or other catastrophe."
   Sample item: "Although many people may scoff, it may yet be shown that astrology can explain a lot of things."

6. **Power and toughness.** The aligning of oneself with power figures, thus gratifying both one's need to have power and the need to submit to power. There is a denial of personal weakness.
   Sample item: "What this country needs is fewer laws and agencies, and more courageous, tireless, devoted leaders whom the people can put their faith in."
   Sample item: "Too many people today are living in an unnatural, soft way; we should return to the fundamentals, to a more red-blooded, active way of life."

7. **Destructiveness and cynicism.** Rationalized aggression; for example, cynicism permits the authoritarian person to be aggressive because "everybody is doing it." The generalized hostility and vilification of the human by highly authoritarian persons permit them to justify their own aggressiveness.
   Sample item: "Human nature being what it is, there will always be war and conflict."

8. **Projectivity.** The disposition to believe that wild and dangerous things go on in the world. In the authoritarian personality, the undesirable impulses that cannot be admitted by the conscious ego tend to be projected onto minority groups and other vulnerable objects.
   Sample item: "The sexual orgies of the old Greeks and Romans are kid stuff compared to some of the goings-on in this country today, even in circles where people might least expect it."
   Sample item: "Nowadays when so many different kinds of people move around so much and mix together so freely, people have to be especially careful to protect themselves against infection and disease."

9. **Sex.** Exaggerated concern with sexual goings-on and punitiveness toward violators of sex mores.
   Sample item: "Homosexuality is a particularly rotten form of delinquency and ought to be severely punished."
   Sample item: "No matter how they act on the surface, men are interested in women for only one reason."

observes the ways in which the personality variable leads to different behaviors in various situations. We will consider the evidence related to authoritarianism in each of these approaches.

Relation between authoritarianism and other variables. Investigators of the authoritarian personality were interested in determining (1) the conditions that might lead to the development of an authoritarian personality and (2) the characteristics that could accompany authoritarianism. In seeking answers to the first question, investigators turned to a consideration of the parents of highly authoritarian people. They found, for example, that highly authoritarian persons tend to have a more traditional family ideology, which includes strong parental control over family decisions, clear-cut roles for each parent, and restrictions on the rights of children to dissent. Less authoritarian persons appeared to prefer a more democratic family structure (Levinson & Huffman, 1955).

The search for other characteristics that describe the authoritarian personality has been a prolific area of research. Literally hundreds of studies have been conducted that point to a number of features that provide a broad picture of the authoritarian personality. Prejudice, for example, has been shown repeatedly to relate to authoritarianism, from the

PHOTO 13-5. *People high in authoritarianism are more likely to see the world in oversimplified terms and may take actions that are consistent with their clear dichotomy between good and bad. In* The Great Santini, *Robert Duvall's character exemplified many of these characteristics.*

time of the early California studies that related F scores to a general measure of ethnocentrism to a host of later studies that consistently show the high-F person to be more prejudiced against minority groups. This holds true whether the focus is White prejudice against Blacks (Martin & Westie, 1959), Arab prejudice against Jews (Epstein, 1966), or Israeli prejudice against Arabs (Siegman, 1961). Hanson (1975) has provided a thorough summary of these findings.

Highly authoritarian persons are often uncomfortable in ambiguous situations (Zacker, 1973); in such situations, they try to impose a simplified structure. Steiner and Johnson (1963a) found that authoritarian persons were reluctant to believe that "good people" can possess both good and bad attributes.

Highly authoritarian people also avoid some kinds of situations. For example, they aren't likely to complete mail questionnaires sent by psychologists (Poor, 1967) or volunteer for psychological experiments (Rosen, 1951; Rosenthal & Rosnow, 1975). This avoidance of personal involvement by high authoritarians is not limited to their interaction with psychologists. By interviewing a representative sample of adults in Philadelphia, Sanford (1950) found that authoritarian interviewees reported less interest in political affairs, less participation in politics and community activities, and more characteristic preferences for strong leaders (in other words, let someone else do it) than low authoritarians. In contrast, highly authoritarian people are more likely than less authoritarian people to attend church (Jones, 1958).

Preferences for political candidates can also be predicted by scores on the F scale: highly authoritarian people generally prefer the more conservative candidate. Most recently, Byrne and Przybyla (1980) found that supporters of Ronald Reagan in the 1980 U.S. presidential election had significantly higher F scores than did supporters of either Jimmy Carter or John Anderson. Similar results were found for the New York senatorial election: supporters of the Conservative party candidate (Alfonse D'Amato) were more authoritarian than supporters of either Jacob Javits (a Republican) or Elizabeth Holtzman (a Democrat).

PHOTO 13-6. *People low in authoritarianism are less likely to support military involvement by a government—an attitude symbolically enacted here by war protestors placing flowers in gun barrels.*

Persons high in authoritarianism are also more supportive of specific military involvement by the government. For example, during the Vietnam War, students who actively protested the war scored lower in authoritarianism than students who supported U.S. involvement in Vietnam (Izzett, 1971). In a related study, an attitude scale toward Lieutenant Calley and the My Lai massacre was constructed by Fink (1973), who administered the attitude scale, along with the F scale, to a group of college students. The subjects who believed that Calley's actions were excusable and that he shouldn't have been court-martialed were more authoritarian than those who were critical of Calley's actions. Defenders of Calley during that period were more apt to believe that Calley had no choice but to obey orders and that, therefore, he was not personally responsible for the outcome of actions carried out under his instructions (Kelman, 1973). Such opinions are highly consistent with the gen-

eral belief in authority that is held by the authoritarian personality.

In summary, the search for correlates of authoritarianism has given us a picture of a person who is generally conservative in political and social attitudes, deferent to authority, and prone to look askance at deviations from the conventional moral order.

Authoritarian behavior and situational factors. As Kirscht and Dillehay (1967) have noted, "Authoritarian deeds have more social consequence than authoritarian thoughts" (p. 2). Therefore, it is important to look at specific behaviors and determine whether the authoritarian personality is as easily predictable as the neat pattern of correlates would suggest. First, we should consider situations that are likely to elicit differences in behavior between highly authoritarian and less authoritarian people. Logically, we should predict that behavioral differences would be most apparent in those areas that relate to the specific construct—for example, conformity to authority and judgments of right and wrong.

Overall, studies that have attempted to relate authoritarianism to conformity behavior have been inconsistent (Cherry & Byrne, 1977). Perhaps this set of findings is surprising, but we must consider the source of conformity pressure more carefully. If that source is a clearly recognized figure of authority, we might expect highly authoritarian persons to conform more readily than less authoritarian persons. In contrast, if the source of conformity pressure has little authority, is there really any reason to expect the authoritarian to exhibit substantial conformity? When we look at the evidence from this more reasoned perspective, the results seem to fall into place. Highly authoritarian people are more conforming and less hostile to high-status sources, compared with people who are low on authoritarianism (Roberts & Jessor, 1958; Steiner & Johnson, 1963b).

Behavioral differences between high-authoritarian and low-authoritarian personalities have been observed in their perception of information. For example, Levy (1979) asked a sample of registered voters in Detroit to evaluate the evening news commentators (who at that time were Cronkite on CBS, Chancellor on NBC, and Reasoner and Smith on ABC) and to indicate how often they believed what their preferred source of information told them about race relations and Vietnam. Highly authoritarian listeners were much more likely to believe in the source that they had designated as an authority than less authoritarian listeners.

There is also evidence for differences between high and low authoritarians in their ability to recall information. Using one of the most famous trials of the 1970s, Garcia and Griffitt (1978) compared high and low authoritarian persons in their recall of evidence in the Patricia Hearst case. The subjects did not differ in the number of prosecution arguments they recalled; however, high authoritarians recalled significantly fewer arguments presented by the defense attorneys than low authoritarians did. Moreover, high authoritarians

were more likely than low authoritarians to infer guilt.

Further studies indicate that high authoritarians may have a general bias against the defendant in a criminal trial. Not only are they more likely to recommend conviction, but they also are more influenced by incriminating evidence (Werner, Kagehiro, & Strube, 1982). In a mock trial situation, students were asked to determine the guilt of a defendant in a robbery/murder trial. In addition to the general testimony, subjects heard incriminating evidence about the defendant that had been obtained by wiretapping. In some cases, the trial transcript showed that the judge had declared the evidence inadmissible; in other cases, the evidence was allowed by the judge. Authoritarian "jurors" were more likely to be influenced by the incriminating evidence, whether or not it was declared admissible. In contrast, when the wiretap evidence exonerated the defendant, they were relatively uninfluenced by the information.

To summarize, high and low authoritarian persons do behave differently in some situations—but not all. As we will discuss in more detail later in this chapter, it is important to consider the characteristics of the situation, as well as the characteristics of the person. Certain situations may trigger an authoritarian response; in such situations, the behavior of a high-F person will be predictably different from that of a low-F person. Other situations may simply be irrelevant to the authoritarian character; in those situations, personality characteristics may tell us nothing about the behaviors that might occur.

B. Masculinity, femininity, and androgyny

Earlier in this chapter, we discussed differences and similarities between males and females—we treated sex as a demographic variable that can be used to divide the population roughly in half. For dozens of years, psychologists have been dissatisfied with such a gross dichotomy; they have sought to develop personality measures of masculinity and femininity that presumably could be found among males *and* females. In other words, they have assumed that, psychologically, some men and women may be more similar to than different from each other. They believe that a consideration of these psychological dimensions could be more fruitful than a reliance on the obvious physical characteristics of males and females.

The early research in this area has been ably reviewed by Constantinople (1973). As she has pointed out, although the early investigators differed in some of the details of their measurement procedures, they made two common assumptions: (1) that masculinity and femininity represent two opposite points on a scale and (2) that the dimension of masculinity/femininity is unidimensional (rather than a complex conglomerate of characteristics). More recently, investigators who examined male/female differences began to argue that masculinity and femininity are quite separable sets of characteristics and that both men and women can possess varying degrees of each set (Bakan, 1966; Block, 1973; Carlson, 1971).

These theoretically based arguments were followed by a number of specific scale developments, in which investigators devised separate scales to measure masculinity and femininity (Bem, 1974; Berzins, Welling, & Wetter, 1975; Heilbrun, 1976; Spence, Helmreich, & Stapp, 1974). The assumption underlying each of these investigations is that there is a set of characteristics that can be considered masculine (or *agentic*, in Bakan's terms) and another set that can be considered feminine (or *communal*). Typically, the masculinity scales contain items such as *independent, competitive,* and *self-confident,* whereas the femininity scales contain items such as *kind, gentle,* and *warm.* Although males, in general, score higher on the masculinity scale, and females, in general, score higher on the femininity scale, the two scales are unrelated (Bem, 1974; Spence & Helmreich, 1978). In other words, a person may score high on both scales, low on both, or high on one and low on the other. Statistically, this means that the correlation between the two scales approaches zero. In more descriptive terms, it means that both males and females can be either high or low in either masculinity or femininity; the presence of one set of characteristics does not imply the absence of the other, as earlier investigators had assumed.

To categorize people who have these varying combinations of characteristics, investigators have borrowed the term **androgyny** (originally used by the ancient Greeks to refer to individuals who combined the physical characteristics of both sexes). In its present use, the term refers to a combination of *psychological* characteristics. The classification of individuals according to their scores on masculinity and femininity scales is shown in Figure 13-3.

Using this method of categorization, Spence and Helmreich (1978) have examined the masculinity and femininity scores of different groups of people. Table 13-2 shows some of the results of their work. As you can see, among an average college-student sample, approximately one-third of the males are masculine sex-typed, and one-third of the females are feminine sex-typed. One-fourth to one-third of the students score as androgynous; the remaining students are either undifferentiated or reverse sex-typed (masculine-sex-typed females and feminine-sex-typed males). Other groups deviate somewhat from these patterns, as shown by the data in Table 13-2.

Although it is easy to place people in one of these four categories, there is considerable disagreement over what these categories mean. For Bem (1974), whose work was the first to be widely recognized in this area, the androgynous person is an ideal toward which we should strive. By combining positive masculine and feminine charac-

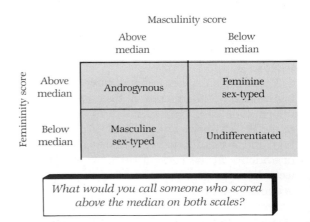

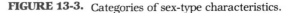

What would you call someone who scored above the median on both scales?

FIGURE 13-3. Categories of sex-type characteristics.

TABLE 13-2. Percentage of populations in the four sex-type categories

	Masculine	*Feminine*	*Androgynous*	*Undifferentiated*
Female college students	14	32	27	28
Male college students	34	8	32	25
Female high school students	14	32	35	18
Male high school students	44	8	25	23
Female homosexuals	22	13	33	32
Male homosexuals	9	23	18	50
Female scientists	23	23	46	8
Male scientists	43	5	32	20

teristics, the androgynous person, in Bem's view, can function effectively in a wide variety of situations that call for either masculine or feminine behavior. She believes that sex-typed persons, in contrast, are more limited, because they are able to operate effectively in some situations but not in others. Other investigators take a more cautious approach, arguing that the personality characteristics of masculinity and femininity may or may not relate to what we typically consider sex-role behaviors. For example, the personality characteristic of femininity may not be related to homemaking skills; rather, running a home may be related to both masculine and feminine (or agentic and communal) characteristics (Spence & Helmreich, 1978).

Still other critics have argued that the notion of androgyny is a phenomenon that is peculiar to the United States, where individuality is valued and interdependency is scorned (Sampson, 1977). According to this view, traditional sex roles and characteristics may be functional in most societies and at most times—or, at minimum, the advantages of the androgynous personality remain to be demonstrated. As we can see, the notion of androgyny has gathered its share of controversy since it was introduced into the psychological literature.

Theoretical controversy has been accompanied by abundant research, and we are continually learning more about what it means to be androgynous. It is important to remember, however, that *androgyny* is just a convenient label for a combination of high scores on both masculinity

(instrumental) and femininity (expressive) scales. Looking at the scales separately, we find that they are related to different kinds of behavior. People who score high on the masculinity scale generally have higher self-esteem. They are also more likely to have high achievement needs, to be dominant, and to be aggressive, compared with people who score low on masculinity (Taylor & Hall, 1982). High scores on the femininity scale are related to different kinds of behavior. For example, high femininity is related to the ability to show empathy, sociability, and skill in decoding nonverbal communications (Spence & Helmreich, 1978; Taylor & Hall, 1982).

The androgynous person, by definition, has both these kinds of skills, and in many situations this combination may be advantageous. In conversations, for example, both instrumental and expressive skills may be useful. Being instrumental may allow you to initiate discussion and introduce new topics; being expressive may allow you to relate to the other person and interpret his or her mood. Research has shown that androgynous people are more comfortable in conversational settings (Ickes, 1981). In one set of studies, male and female subjects representing various combinations of masculinity and femininity scores met each other in a waiting room (Ickes & Barnes, 1977, 1978). Their conversations were recorded on videotape and analyzed, and each member was also asked how much he or she had enjoyed the conversation. The results may contradict some common assumptions. The lowest levels of interaction and the lowest levels of reported enjoyment were found among pairs in which the male was traditionally masculine sex-typed (high in masculinity and low in femininity) and the female was feminine sex-typed (high in femininity and low in masculinity). In contrast, when both persons were androgynous, levels of interaction and mutual enjoyment were high. These results support the hypothesis that the possession of both instrumental and expressive skills leads to more rewarding encounters.

Although masculinity (instrumentality) and femininity (expressiveness) relate to some behaviors that we typically associate with men and women, androgyny is not associated with all aspects of gender-related behavior. Thus, it is incorrect to assume, for example, that an androgynous person is more likely to favor equal rights or feminist stances (Spence & Helmreich, 1980). Nor is an androgynous person necessarily likely to enjoy both cooking and fixing cars. Consider a traditional woman living on a Midwestern farm, for example. She may score high on warmth and expressiveness as well as on independence and assertiveness but display these characteristics only in the context of her family relationships. She may have opposed the Equal Rights Amendment to the U.S. Constitution and may never have repaired a tractor. We must be careful not to assume that a personality characteristic reflects a particular political stance or a preference for certain specific behaviors.

■ V. The relation between personality and social behavior

As a result of our discussion to this point, you may wonder why there is any question about the ability of personality traits to predict social behavior or the fact that individual differences can contribute to a broad understanding of human behavior. However, we have, admittedly, been selective in our coverage, choosing to focus on examples that have been successful in showing the relation between personality measures and social behavior. Meanwhile, in the closets of personality psychology and social psychology, there are numerous

PHOTO 13-7. *Masculinity and femininity may not necessarily relate to what are typically considered sex-role behaviors.*

examples of failure. How can we explain the successes and failures—why something that works on one occasion may not work on another occasion? To answer these questions, let us look at some of the basic issues that personality psychologists and social psychologists have been discussing (often with great intensity) in recent years.

A. Some questions about personality

Some years ago, many people were discouraged about the ability to predict behavior from personality, pointing to numerous failures and weak correlations (Mischel, 1968). In recent years, however, the picture has been more encouraging as psychologists have begun to analyze the role of personality traits more carefully. Among the issues discussed are the methods of measuring both traits and behaviors and the importance of particular traits to particular individuals.

The most common way to assess personality is to ask people to describe themselves, often using a scale that has been designed by psychologists to assess a particular characteristic. Yet, questions have been raised about the accuracy of people's reports of their own behaviors (Fiske, 1978). Instead of asking people to state how dominant, authoritarian, or unique they are, some investigators have argued strongly for straightforward observations of behavior. In other words, we would decide whether or not a person was friendly by observing the person's behavior in a variety of situations in which friendliness or unfriendliness might be displayed. As you might guess, the avoidance of this particular technique has not been based on rational grounds alone; it is obviously much more difficult to make a series of observations than to administer a simple paper-and pencil questionnaire. Some investigators have found that by combining a number of personality-assessment techniques—for example, biographical information, trait questionnaires, and behavioral sampling methods— they can predict actual behavior much more effectively than when they use only a single measure of personality (Alker & Owen, 1977).

One side of the coin of the argument regarding the relation between personality and social behavior concerns the method of assessing personality traits; the other side, of course, concerns the kinds of social behavior that we are trying to understand. Often, an investigator will spend a great deal of time refining the personality instrument and then choose the social behavior with haste and little thought.

The issue at stake here is similar to the one faced by investigators of attitudes, who have been attempting to predict behavior from measures of individual attitudes. As we saw in Chapter 10, there are a number of reasons to believe that such prediction can be achieved, if certain factors are taken into account and certain pitfalls are avoided. The same strategy can be applied here. For example, Jaccard (1974, 1977) has suggested that personality measures should be related to multiple-act criteria but not to single-act criteria. In other words, if we measure a person's achievement motivation and set up a number of situations in which achievement traits might be exhibited, we should find that, overall, high-achievement individuals exhibit more achievement behavior than low-achievement individuals. At the same time, in any single situation, results may not be clear—some situations may result in little difference, whereas other situations may even show a reversal. A similar point has been made by Epstein (1979), who has pointed out that any single observation of behavior can involve considerable error and have limited generality. However, if we observe a person's behavior over a period of time, general personality measures become much more capable of predicting overall behavior.

Suppose that your friend Joe is someone you think of as extroverted, outgoing, and friendly. Yet, at a party on one particular Thursday evening, Joe (for any of a number of reasons) stays pretty much to himself, talking to a few close friends and avoiding most of the people at the party. As a personality psychologist who believes that assessing personality should allow you to predict every single behavior, you might feel that your theory about Joe was wrong. It is more likely, however, that you would consider how Joe had acted in all the other situations in which you had seen him—you would keep your assessment of his character intact.

So far, we have used the nomothetic approach, assuming that all people can be assessed on all traits. But perhaps that assumption is not true. Bem and Allen (1974) argue that some people will be consistent on some traits, but others will not. In other words, each personality dimension devised by psychologists does not necessarily apply to every person. A particular dimension may be relevant to some individuals but not to others. How can we find out whether people are consistent on a particular dimension? Again, Bem and Allen propose a simple answer—just ask them. For example, by asking people whether they are friendly in general and how much they vary from situation to situation in their friendliness, researchers were able to show that people who perceive friendliness as one of their stable characteristics are consistent across a variety of situations. Those people who reported that they were less consistent in their display of friendliness were, in turn, less consistent across situations. The psychologist, in attempting to predict behavior, can at least predict some of the people some of the time.

Can psychologists do better than that? Is it possible to predict all of the people all of the time? Kenrick and Springfield (1980) suggest that it is possible, but only if we recognize that various traits have differing degrees of relevance from one individual to another. Extending Bem and Allen's reasoning, these investigators asked each individual subject to select a personality dimension on which his or her behavior was most consistent. Not surprisingly, the particular dimensions selected differed widely among the subjects. However, in analyzing the selections of subjects individually, the investigators found that there was a consistency of reported behavior—one that was reported by subjects themselves and seen by parents and friends.

Another way of viewing the issue of consistency is to think in terms of prototypes (see Chapter 4). Mischel and Peake (1982) have suggested that some behaviors are highly prototypic for a person. For example, if I want to evaluate how compulsive I

am, I may think about the neatness of my bookshelves, the arrangement of my filing system, and the cleanliness of my kitchen—and ignore the state of my closet or the piles of junk in the basement. For me, then, the former behaviors would fit my prototype of compulsiveness, and one might expect greater consistency in those behaviors. For the latter behaviors, less consistency might be shown because I do not consider them basic to my prototype of compulsiveness.

Thus, the issue of consistency in personality and behavior is complicated, and analysis must consider the trait, the representativeness of the behavior, and the particular individual who is being assessed. In short, there is consistency in personality—and there is inconsistency. A Chinese philosopher would smile at the thought!

B. Some questions about situations

Another question raised in the debate about personality and behavior is the role of situations. Despite social psychologists' considerable involvement with the situational determinants of action, we do not have an adequate taxonomy of situations. Situations can vary on a number of dimensions: their location, the kinds of activities that go on, the number and kinds of people involved in them, to name only a few (Magnusson, 1981). In addition to these objective characteristics, we can also look at the way people perceive situations. From this more subjective perspective, we may ask people how similar various situations seem to them. Once again, we find greater consistency in behavior when we take this individual perspective into account (Lord, 1982).

In considering the influence of personality on behavior, we also need to assess how "weak" or "strong" the situation is (Mischel, 1977). As defined by Snyder and Ickes (in press), strong situations are ones that "provide salient cues to guide behavior and have a fairly high degree of structure and definition" (p. 60). In a typical laboratory experiment, for example, the choices that a subject can make are typically quite restricted. In such cases, we might not expect personality differences to have much effect, because the possible behaviors are

PHOTO 13-8. Situations may be strong or weak. In the structured (or strong) classroom setting pictured on the left, students taking an exam show little variation in their behavior. In contrast, unstructured (or weak) situations like the one below allow more room for individual personalities to have an effect.

quite limited. In contrast, situations that are less structured (or "weak") may allow for a much greater range of behavioral choices, and hence personality variations may become more influential (Monson, Hesley, & Chernick, 1982). To illustrate this distinction, consider the behavior of students in a classroom compared with the behavior of students in their own apartments or dormitory rooms. We would expect much more variation in the second situation than in the first, variation that would probably relate to many personality traits.

Finally, in thinking about situations, we need to consider the concept of choice (Snyder, 1981; Snyder & Ickes, in press). In real life, people are not randomly assigned to situations; rather, they choose to enter some situations and avoid others. Some people may frequent church socials, while others seek out X-rated movies. What situations people choose probably indicates a great deal about basic personality traits, and social psychologists are beginning to look more closely at such choices.

C. Interaction between personality and situations

The consensus that has evolved—confirming Kurt Lewin's early formulation—is that personalities *and* situations must be considered in order to completely understand human social behavior. This *interactionist* position probably represents the views of most social psychologists today; however, there is controversy about the exact meaning of the term *interaction.* The interactionist position maintains that, in most instances, we can explain some behavior by considering only personalities and some behavior by considering only situations, but we can explain more behavior by considering the interface between personalities and situations. Many psychologists have come to adopt this position (Endler & Magnusson, 1976; Magnusson & Endler, 1977).

If we adopt the interactionist position, we will probably begin to think of human behavior in active terms (Endler & Magnusson, 1976), considering the interaction between personalities and situations. As we saw in Chapter 5, communication is not a stable process, nor is the interaction of any single individual with his or her environment. Situations constantly change, often in very subtle ways, and a person's behavior may reflect subtle changes. Human behavior is more complex than we had originally thought, and understanding that behavior is a far more exciting endeavor than we had imagined.

VI. SUMMARY

Social psychologists have traditionally been more interested in situational determinants of behavior than in individual differences among people. However, it is possible to compare groups divided on the basis of sex or ethnicity. Although such comparisons often reveal group differences, it is important to remember that many similarities exist as well. Furthermore, the concept of overlap is important. When trying to explain observed differences between groups, psychologists consider both hereditary and environmental explanations, although the latter are generally weighted more heavily.

Cross-cultural research attempts to determine how general our knowledge of human behavior is—whether our constructs are etic (truly universal) or emic (specific to a particular culture).

Research comparing Blacks and Whites demonstrates the need for a broader understanding of human behavior. It is often difficult to interpret racial differences, however, because so many other factors vary with race.

Some sex differences have been found in the areas of aggression, conformity, and nonverbal communication, although in each case the effects are fairly small. In the absence of direct provocation, men are more aggressive than women, but there are few sex differences when aggression is provoked. Women conform more readily than men in face-to-face situations and are better able to interpret nonverbal messages.

Psychologists often prefer to describe people in terms of personality variables, rather than demographic characteristics. The nomothetic approach to the study of personality stresses general dimensions and norms that apply to all people; the idiographic approach focuses on the interrelationship of events and characteristics within an individual.

The concept of authoritarianism was developed by a group of social scientists who wanted to understand anti-Semitism during World War II. They developed the F scale to measure authoritarianism and defined nine components of authoritarianism. High- and low-authoritarian people differ in many respects, including family ideology, political preferences, prejudice, and attitudes toward authority figures and criminal defendants.

Early researchers considered masculinity and femininity to be opposite poles of a single dimension; recent investigators have shown that the concepts are separate and independent. *Androgyny* is a term used to describe people who are high in both masculinity (instrumentality) and femininity (expressiveness). The concept of androgyny has generated much controversy and much research. The two dimensions of masculinity and femininity are related to different kinds of behavior. In some situations, a person who has both kinds of skills will be more successful than a person who is high on only one of the dimensions.

The relation between personality variables and social behavior is complex. How a trait is measured and to whom it is applied are important issues in understanding the consistency of personality. Consideration of the situation is also important. According to the dominant interactionist view, personality and situations must be studied jointly.

GLOSSARY TERMS

androgyny	etic	nomothetic
authoritarianism	exotic bias	sex-role norms
emic	idiographic	

14

Behavior in Groups

No man is an island, entire of itself.
■ JOHN DONNE

It takes two flints to make a fire.
■ LOUISA MAY ALCOTT

Stuck in an elevator that is stalled between floors, seven strangers begin to notice one another, then start to compare reactions and share stories of past experiences, and then develop a plan of action to get out of the elevator. Returning for the second part of the marathon play *Nicholas Nickleby,* members of the Broadway audience who were formerly strangers begin to chat with their neighbors, share their box lunches, and cheer heroes and boo villains together. In both these instances, individuals become involved with a group of persons, and their actions are influenced by the group.

In citing these examples, we are no longer focusing strictly on the individual but, rather, on the behavior of a number of persons. According to many people, this is the essence of social psychology. However, social psychologists often prefer to work at the level of the individual, stressing each person's perceptions, beliefs, and actions and ignoring the interaction that takes place in groups. Some social psychologists have even suggested that groups are not real. The late Floyd Allport used to say "You can't stumble over a group," proposing that groups exist only in the minds of people. According to Allport, groups are no more than shared sets of values, ideas, thoughts, and habits that exist simultaneously in the minds of several persons. Others have argued just as impressively that groups are entities that should be treated as unitary objects in our environment (Durkheim, 1898; Warriner, 1956). Such advocates renounce the suggestion that all social behaviors can be explained adequately at the individual level; they stress the unique aspects of the group process in and of itself.

Clearly, there are a number of perspectives that one can adopt regarding the influence of more than one person in a situation. Most of us would probably agree that many of the activities of our lives involve other people. Football teams, families, faculties, and fishing crews all involve the interaction of a group of people. But groups also may be composed of individuals who don't come into close proximity with one another or see one another often. The national sales manager for Frisbees, along with his or her field representa-

tives, may constitute a group; likewise, all the members of an audience at the latest Woody Allen movie may constitute a group.

A basic question is "How can we define the term *group?*" Although many definitions have been offered, perhaps a simple working definition of a group is "two or more persons who are interacting with one another in such a manner that each person influences and is influenced by each other person" (Shaw, 1981, p. 8). A more comprehensive definition of the term includes the following properties: "interaction between individuals, perceptions of other members and the development of affective ties, and the development of interdependence or roles" (DeLamater, 1974, p. 39). In other words, members of a group have some relationship with one another, often complex and extended over time.

We can apply the term *aggregate* to collections of individuals who do not interact with one another. Persons standing on a street corner waiting for the light to change, passengers on an uneventful elevator ride, and, in many cases, the members of a large college class—these people typically do not interact or share feelings to such a degree that they influence one another. However, as the case of the passengers in the stalled elevator illustrates, an aggregate can become a group.

In this chapter, we consider the ways in which groups act—how they perform, how members of groups communicate with one another, and how they draw together or split apart. Our survey will look at both the carefully contrived laboratory group, which participants join on an involuntary basis, and real-life groups, such as juries, families, and experiential groups. First, however, let us turn our attention to a simpler question—how does the presence of other people influence the behavior of the individual?

■ I. The influence of other people

Reaching back in the history of social psychology (and to our memories of the early chapters of this text), we can recall the experiment of Norman Triplett, who was interested in the effects of other

PHOTO 14-1. *The impact of an audience depends on a variety of factors, including its size and distance from the performers.*

people on individual performance. Creating an analogy to bicycle racing (see Chapter 2), Triplett (1897) asked children to wind fishing reels and compared their performance when alone with their performance when another child was present. This experiment marks the earliest attempt to understand how the mere presence of other people—not necessarily acting as a group—can influence behavior. Considerable investigation has followed the initial venture by Triplett.

A. The effects of an audience

On many occasions, we may act individually but, at the same time, be aware that others are watching us. For example, on entering a room full of strangers, we may be painfully (or gleefully) aware that many eyes are focused on us. A guest lecturer may present a talk and have no interaction with the members of the audience. How does awareness of an audience affect behavior?

Many people experience fear and anxiety in the presence of an audience. For example, a survey of people's fears showed that speaking in front of a group is feared more than height, darkness, loneliness, sickness, and even death (Borden, 1980). However, on some occasions, the presence of an audience can give us an extra "charge." For example, athletes report that they perform better before a crowd than in an empty stadium (Davis, 1969), and many actors comment on the difference between playing for a full house and playing in a

theater that is nearly empty. What accounts for these differences?

First of all, let us define the basic characteristics of the audience situation. The individual is acting or performing a behavior in the presence of a group of people; however, there is no direct interaction between the individual and the audience—rather, the members of the audience are passive observers of the action (Geen, 1980).

The influence of the audience depends on a number of factors. Latané (1981) has suggested three major factors: the number of people in the audience, the immediacy of the audience, and the strength (or status) of the members of the audience (see Figure 14-1). In describing his model of *social impact*, Latané uses the analogy of a light bulb. Just as the amount of light falling on a surface depends on the number of bulbs, their closeness to the surface, and the wattage, so does social impact represent the joint contribution of *numbers*, *immediacy*, and *strength*. Let's consider how each of these audience factors affects an individual's performance.

First, as the number of people in an audience increases, so does the impact. However, increments in impact tend to decrease with the addition of each observer; for example, the difference between 3 and 4 observers would be much greater than the difference between 30 and 31. (This relationship can be plotted as a mathematical power function.) In considering the effect of immediacy, Latané and others have found that audiences that

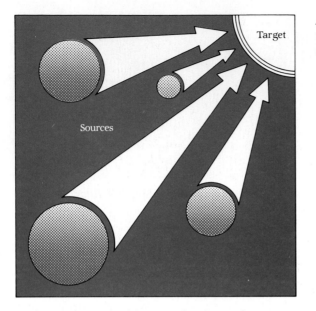

FIGURE 14-1. A model of social impact. The impact of an audience is determined by the number of sources (or circles, in this illustration), their strength (or size, in this illustration), and their immediacy, or nearness to the target.

are physically present have more impact than those that are at some distance—for example, audiences that are separated from the performer by a one-way mirror through which only the audience can see. Finally, the strength or status of an audience is important. Latané and Harkins (1976) found that students who expected to sing before an audience of high-status people reported more tension than those who expected a low-status audience.

Alone or in combination, each of these three factors can affect how we are influenced by an audience.

B. Social facilitation

We have seen that an audience can influence performance. But just what kinds of effects does an audience have? In some cases, an audience acts to increase the level of performance; in other cases, it decreases performance. Such contradictions beg for a theory. **Social facilitation,** a term coined by Floyd Allport (1920), refers to the improvement of individual performance in the presence of other people. (Remember, we are concerned with the effect of the *mere presence* of other people, not with interaction between a person and an audience.) In contrast, **social inhibition** refers to a decrease in an individual's performance in the presence of other people.

Many years after Allport made his observations, Zajonc (1965) proposed a theoretical model to account for discrepant findings for the effects of an audience. Relying on a drive model of learning, Zajonc suggested that the presence of others is a source of general arousal, or drive (see Figure 14-2). Such arousal occurs because other people can be unpredictable, thus creating feelings of uncertainty in the individual. In the case of responses that are well learned (or *dominant*, in the terminology of the model), this drive results in increased levels of performance. In contrast, responses that are not well learned suffer from increased arousal, since well-learned responses interfere with their

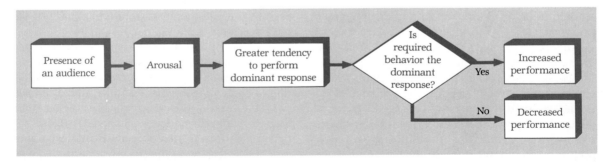

FIGURE 14-2. Arousal model of social facilitation.

PHOTO 14-2. *Whether these dancers' performance will be enhanced or inhibited by the audience depends, among other things, on their skill.*

performance (Zajonc & Sales, 1966). For example, if you are asked to act in a community play, and it is your first experience with acting, the presence of an audience may be detrimental—you may drop lines, forget your entrance, or suffer a severe case of stage fright. In contrast, an experienced and well-rehearsed actor appearing before a similar audience should show improved performance, because arousal leads to an increase in well-learned behaviors. This explanation, which is based on rather simple assumptions, has been quite successful in accounting for many of the findings regarding the effects of an audience on performance (Cottrell, 1972; Geen & Gange, 1977).

Although there is considerable agreement that the presence of an audience can affect performance—sometimes for better, sometimes for worse—we are not totally sure why those effects occur. Zajonc himself assumes that the arousal properties of an audience are innate, or wired into the organism, and has, in fact, shown that cock-roaches, as well as people, are subject to social-facilitation effects. Yet, there may be other causes of this arousal state as well. Cottrell (1972), for example, has argued that the presence of others is a *learned* source of drive. According to Cottrell, it is not the mere presence of others that causes arousal but, rather, the expectation that an audience will be judging one's performance. Consequently, if subjects are asked to perform in front of a group of people who are blindfolded, they should show less arousal than when performing in front of a group of clear-sighted evaluators. Studies using this approach have supported the distinction, finding more arousal in subjects (and the predicted effects on performance of simple and complex tasks) when an audience is expected to be capable of evaluation (Cottrell, Wack, Sekerak, & Rittle, 1968; Sasfy & Okun, 1974).

Others have suggested that increased arousal is a result of conflict between possible responses and that distraction is an important mediator of social facilitation (Sanders, 1981). For example, when giving a lecture to a large audience, you might shift your attention to the man sleeping in the back row, distracting yourself from your speech and creating arousal. Still others have relied on the concept of self-presentation (see Chapter 3), pointing to the possible role of embarrassment in causing performance decrements (Bond, 1982). There is not necessarily one right answer to this controversy. The state of arousal that leads to social-facilitation effects may be caused by a variety of factors, and although each one may be sufficient, no single cause may be a necessary condition. For each explanation, however, the end result is the same: arousal leads to an increase in the performance of well-learned responses and a decrease in the performance of poorly learned responses. As Box 14-1 shows, these effects can be found in the pool hall as well as in the psychology laboratory.

C. The coacting audience

So far, we have concentrated on the effects of a passive audience that merely observes while the actor performs. However, if we look back to the initial experiment of Triplett, we see that the audience was not passive; it performed a task. How does the situation involving the coacting audience differ from those we've described earlier?

How would you react in the Triplett situation, winding a fishing reel and being acutely aware of the person next to you engaged in the same task? Many people, particularly in Western societies,

would see the situation as a challenge and attempt to do better than their companion. These competitive attitudes were pointed out in early research by Dashiell (1930), who found that people in a coactive situation performed faster but less accurately than people working alone.

A coacting audience provides a basis for social comparison (see Chapter 3) and may contribute to the development of competition. By observing others' behavior, we can establish a basis for evaluating our own performance. If another person is doing somewhat better than we are, that person's performance may serve as a competitive cue, and our own performance will improve. But what if the other person is doing about the same, or even worse? Then, the coacting audience seems to have little effect. There is also little effect when the other person is vastly superior; the person's great distance from us may make him or her an invalid source of comparison, and we will continue to perform at our standard rate (Seta, 1982).

Characteristics of the task and the situation may also affect performance with a coacting audience. When the task is a simple or well-learned one, competition may improve performance, consistent with the predictions of social-facilitation theory. On more complex or less familiar tasks, however, competition may impair performance. To counter this tendency, specific instructions encouraging cooperation on a complex task have been found to improve the performance of coactors (Laughlin & Jaccard, 1975).

Performers in a coacting audience can also use

PHOTO 14-3. *Coacting performers can create a sense of competition.*

BOX 14-1. Social facilitation in the poolroom

Do you ever play pool? What happens to your game when someone is watching? According to social-facilitation theory, your performance should improve if you are a good player but should get worse if your typical play is only mediocre. James Michaels and his colleagues tested this prediction in the pool center of a college union (Michaels, Blommel, Brocato, Linkous, & Rowe, 1982). During the initial stage of this study, observers unobtrusively watched the action and identified pairs of players who were either above average or below average in their play. During the second stage, teams of four observers stood next to the table where one of the pairs was playing and observed the next several rounds of play. Six different pairs of above-average players and six different pairs of below-average players were observed in this manner.

Did the presence of observers make a difference? Yes, and in exactly the way that social-facilitation theory would predict. Above-aver-

age players increased their shot accuracy from 71% when not being closely observed to 80% when group members stood by. In contrast, below-average players got worse, their accuracy decreasing from 36% to 25%. ■

one another as a source of new information. This modeling effect, discussed in earlier chapters, suggests that new responses can be learned simply by observing the other participants. If the other participants seem to be successful in their actions, a person is most likely to learn and perform these same responses (Bandura, 1965). At a sorority or fraternity rush party, for example, the would-be pledge may spend part of the time observing how other people interact with the group members, hoping to gain clues to the appropriate behavior.

■ II. Qualities of groups

We have begun our consideration of people in interaction by looking at a relatively simple situation in which an individual is observed or accompanied by one or more persons. However, a group (as defined at the beginning of this chapter) involves

more than people performing the same activity at a particular time and place. Groups involve interaction, the development of shared perceptions and affective ties, and interdependence of roles.

In their form and structure, groups are as varied as individuals. There are several major issues that we can consider when attempting to describe the character of a particular group. First, we can talk about *group composition*. Here we are looking at characteristics of the group, such as size, that can describe what a group "looks like." Other aspects of group composition that might be of interest include the sex and ethnic identity of the members or the particular abilities and personalities of individuals in the group.

A second way to look at groups is in terms of their *structure*. For example, what channels of communication are available within the group—who can talk to whom? What status systems develop within a group? Leadership, discussed in Chapter 15, is another example of a structural concern. A third issue in considering groups is the actual process that occurs, sometimes called *group dynamics*. How do members of a group respond to and influence one another? And what are the emotional ties that bind a group together? Finally, a fourth issue for groups is the issue of *performance*—how well or poorly does a group do in achieving its goals?

Although we can separate these factors for discussion, in reality they are interdependent. The composition of a group, for example, may affect the level of performance that can be accomplished. Structures that have been established may determine the kinds of influence that take place.

In this section we will consider three ways in which groups can differ: in their size (a composition variable), in the opportunities they present for communication (a structural variable), and in their cohesiveness (an issue of group dynamics). In the following section we will take a more detailed look at the fourth issue of group performance.

A. Size of the group

Even within the limits of the definition of *group* that we introduced at the beginning of the chapter, it is possible to conceive of groups that range in size from a couple on their honeymoon to all the members of the U.S. Congress or the Canadian House of Commons. Most experimental research, however, has concentrated on small groups, generally varying from 3 to 10 persons. The most frequently studied topic has been the relation between a group's size and its performance. As shown in Box 14-2, more people may result in less individual effort.

There have been some efforts to specify the "ideal size" of problem-solving groups. For example, P. E. Slater (1958) concluded that groups of five were the most effective for dealing with mental tasks in which group members collect and exchange information and make a decision based on the evaluation of that information. Osborn (1957), the developer of brainstorming, suggested that the optimum size of such groups ranges from five to ten members.

Yet, conclusions regarding the ideal size of problem-solving groups are probably oversimplifications. First, there are varying criteria for determining what is successful. Smaller groups may be more satisfying to participants, because they have a chance to express their opinions fully. The addition of a few more members may add essential skills and make for a better solution to the task, but it can hurt members' participation and morale. Second, task structure can interact with group size. Some tasks may require only one person, whereas other tasks can be performed only by several individuals. Third, the amount of structure in the group interacts with its size. Although groups composed of more than five persons are often less satisfying than small groups, larger groups can be effective without any major loss of morale when the task is structured.

The effects of group size are important in everyday life. We know that the traditional jury in England, the United States, and Canada consists of 12 persons who must come to a unanimous decision. However, a number of U.S. states are experimenting with smaller juries and majority verdicts (Kalven & Zeisel, 1966). Several other countries already use trial juries of fewer than 12 persons (Saks & Ostrom, 1975). What are the effects of these variations on group process and outcome? Do smaller juries spend less time in deliberation than 12-member juries? Are smaller juries more likely to reach guilty verdicts? Are their verdicts less likely to be correct?

A recent study used mock juries to examine some of these questions (Davis, Kerr, Atkin, Holt, & Meek, 1975). Juries composed of either 6 or 12 undergraduates listened to a 45-minute recording of a trial—an abbreviated version of the transcript of an actual rape trial. Some "juries" of subjects were instructed to come to a unanimous decision about the guilt or innocence of the accused rapist within 30 minutes. Others were told that their jury should reach a two-thirds-majority decision.

It was found that 89% of the 6-person juries and 83% of the 12-person juries judged the defendant not guilty. Moreover, the judgments of the groups forced to unanimity were similar to those of the two-thirds-majority groups (81% and 92%, re-

BOX 14-2. Many hands make light the work: The case of social loafing

To remove debris from a California highway after a major mud slide, several persons would probably be more effective than a single individual. But would each person work harder in such a situation than alone? Two experiments by Latané, Williams, and Harkins (1979) suggest that "social loafing," rather than increased effort, takes place in group endeavors. In one situation, subjects were asked to clap as loud as they could; in the second instance, they were asked to cheer as loud as they could. In each case, subjects performed the task alone, in pairs, in groups of four, and in groups of six. As shown in the graph, individual effort drops precipitously as group size increases. Presumably because each individual believes that his or her own performance cannot be identified, less effort is invested.

Is it inevitable that functioning in groups will reduce individual effort? Not necessarily, report Harkins and Petty (1982). Two ways to counter the social-loafing tendency—and thus to increase

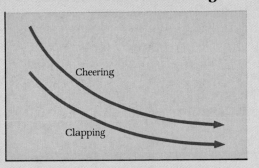

group productivity—are (1) to make the overall task more challenging and difficult and (2) to give each person a somewhat different task to do. In both of these cases, the individual still may not believe that his or her contribution can be identified in the total outcome, but the feeling of making a unique contribution eliminates social loafing. ■

---

spectively, returned a verdict of not guilty). The major differences were found in the group *processes* rather than the verdicts. Table 14-1 shows that unanimous juries needed a larger number of poll votes before reaching a verdict, as well as a longer deliberation time. On the basis of this study, it would first appear that Supreme Court decisions permitting majority decisions are safe enough. Unanimous juries and majority juries appear to produce about the same results. But this is not the whole story. Further analyses by Davis and his colleagues indicated that, of the 36 juries operating under the two-thirds rule, 26 had a two-thirds majority on their first poll (but did not have unanimity). Of these 26, a total of 9 juries (35%) decided *immediately* on the majority position, and several more deliberated only a short time after the first vote. The nonunanimous rule may lead to a "cur-

sory consideration of dissenting views" (Davis et al., 1975, p. 12).

B. Communication opportunities

Group size is meaningless when group members have difficulty in communicating with one another. Real-world groups sometimes establish restricted channels through which messages may go. For example, members of a large faculty may not be allowed to speak about problems with the university president directly but instead may have to communicate through a dean. Relationships between individuals may affect communication channels; there may be two members of the church's board of deacons who "haven't spoken to each other for years." Location of some group members in a different building may inhibit com-

TABLE 14-1. Mean number of polls and mean time (in minutes) to verdict in each experimental condition

Assigned social-decision scheme	Jury size 6 persons	12 persons	Total
Unanimity			
Polls	2.39	2.89	2.64
Time	13.28	19.22	16.25
Two-thirds majority			
Polls	1.94	1.78	1.86
Time	11.83	7.61	9.72
Total			
Polls	2.17	2.33	2.25
Time	12.56	13.42	12.99

munication between them. (In Chapter 17, we consider some of the effects of the physical environment on group members' interactions.)

We refer to prescribed patterns of communication as **communication networks** (Shaw, 1964, 1978). A number of communication networks are represented schematically in Figure 14-3. Although these representations are abstract, it is relatively easy to think of concrete examples of each. On a football team, for example, the quarterback is generally the center of communication. Other players direct most of their comments to him, and he speaks to everyone on the team. This would be an example of the wheel. In the circle, each person can talk only to adjacent persons. The children's party game of "telephone" illustrates this pattern. Organizational hierarchies represent more complex communication networks; these networks often involve hundreds of people, but they can usually

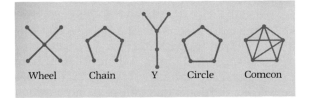

FIGURE 14-3. Some examples of communication networks. The dots represent positions of persons in the networks, and lines represent the permissible channels of communication.

be broken down into these simpler patterns.

Communication networks are important because they produce different processes in a group. For example, the "wheel" gives great control to the person in the middle; he or she can communicate with each of the other four members, but they (in *peripheral positions*) can communicate only with the *central person* and not with each other. If such a communication network were established as the ground rules at the formation of a new group, the central-position person would probably emerge as the leader (Hirota, 1953; Shaw, 1954; Shaw & Rothschild, 1956). In such cases, possession of information leads to power.

Both the "Y" and "chain" networks in Figure 14-3 also lead to centralized organization as the central person becomes pivotal. In contrast, "circle" networks do not facilitate the emergence of a dominant leader (Leavitt, 1951). In groups that have a "circle" communication network or a "comcon" network, in which every member is able to communicate with everyone else, it is impossible to predict which position will lead to leadership and dominance. In these networks, the individual personalities and skills of group members are the determining factors.

What effects do communication networks have on productivity? Which networks are most satisfying to group members? The second question can be answered simply. People prefer positions in which they have greater opportunities for communication and participation. "Silent" partners do not like to remain quiet. The central position in the "wheel," the "chain," and the "Y" is rated as a satisfying one, whereas the peripheral positions in these same networks lead to poor morale (Leavitt, 1951). Networks that permit decentralized communication lead to higher morale for persons at each position.

The efficiency of various communication networks depends on the task faced by the group. Leavitt found that a centralized network—such as a "wheel" or a "Y"—was most efficient as judged by the time required for the solution of a problem, the number of errors made, and the number of messages communicated. However, Leavitt used a simple symbol-identification task that required only the collection and straightforward assembling of information by one person, analogous to collecting the pieces of a simple jigsaw puzzle and putting them together.

Shaw (1954) used tasks that drew on the problem-solving abilities of group members and the active manipulation of information. Shaw found

that, in dealing with complex problems, the "circle" was most efficient, whereas the "wheel" was least efficient, as measured in time required to reach a solution. The decentralized networks were able to detect and correct errors more rapidly than the "wheel" or the "Y." There is yet another aspect of the story. The "wheel" groups required fewer messages to find a solution. The difference in outcomes for simple and complex tasks is consistent, as Table 14-2 indicates. Once again, we see how important it is to consider the nature of the task when we ask questions about group composition.

C. Cohesiveness

The spirit of closeness—or lack of it—in a group can have an important effect on the behavior of its members. For example, sportswriters are fond of observing that certain athletic teams have the "best material" or "personnel" but that they "just can't put it together." In such cases, it is likely that the absence of closeness—or even the presence of hostilities among team members—is influential in the team's less-than-expected performance. A

TABLE 14-2. Number of comparisons showing differences between centralized ("wheel," "chain," "Y") and decentralized ("circle," "comcon") networks as a function of task complexity

	Simple problems[a]	Complex problems[b]	Total
Time			
Centralized faster	14	0	14
Decentralized faster	4	18	22
Messages			
Centralized sent more	0	1	1
Decentralized sent more	18	17	35
Errors			
Centralized made more	0	6	6
Decentralized made more	9	1	10
No difference	1	3	4
Satisfaction			
Centralized higher	1	1	2
Decentralized higher	7	10	17

[a]Simple problems: identification tasks involving symbols, letters, numbers, and colors.
[b]Complex problems: arithmetic, word-arrangement, sentence-construction, and discussion problems.

PHOTO 14-4. *Cohesiveness among group members can lead to higher levels of performance.*

number of terms have been used to describe the variable of closeness, including "we-feeling" and "emotional climate" (Vraa, 1974). The most frequently used term is group **cohesiveness,** defined as a "characteristic of the group in which forces acting on members to remain in the group are greater than the total forces acting on them to leave it" (Davis, 1969, p. 78). In other words, groups in which members like one another and want to remain in one another's presence are cohesive; groups in which members are unattracted to one another and groups that are breaking up are said to be low in cohesiveness. Because group members who are attracted to the group work harder to achieve its goals, cohesiveness usually leads to higher productivity. A close-knit fraternity, for example, is more likely to make elaborate house decorations for the homecoming weekend and engage successfully in intramural sports than a less cohesive fraternity. However, this example assumes that the goals or norms of the group favor productivity; in contrast, if the group norm is to

avoid work, we could expect the highly cohesive group to be less productive.

Highly cohesive groups are more likely than less cohesive groups to agree on a common goal (Schachter, Ellertson, McBride, & Gregory, 1951). One reason for this agreement is that uniformity is stressed in cohesive groups. Back (1951) found that members of cohesive dyads (pairs) changed their opinions in the direction of their partner's opinions more than members of less cohesive dyads. Similar findings with larger groups have been reported by Festinger, Gerard, Hymovitch, Kelley, and Raven (1952) and by Lott and Lott (1961). When you like the other members of a group, you may have a greater tendency to go along with their opinions, believing that harmony will enhance the good feelings that are present.

■ III. Interaction in groups

In dealing with selected properties of groups, such as size, networks, and cohesiveness, we have often referred to the performance and outcomes of the group process. Now let's look more directly at this fourth aspect of groups—group performance.

A. Group problem solving and performance

One question of major interest in the history of group research is whether individuals working together in a group perform more successfully or efficiently than individuals working alone. The reason for such interest is not hard to discover: any organization seeking to maximize its output needs to know how to structure its tasks. Although this question is straightforward, the answer is complex. To begin to formulate an answer, let us first consider two types of group performance: judgment and problem solving.

Judgments and observations. If your car is rammed from behind, is it better to have one witness or a group of onlookers if you seek accurate testimony? If a decision is to be made on which of your paintings is the best entry in an art show, is it better to have a single judge or a team of judges? To answer these questions, we need to consider both the particular individuals and the particular task. On a purely physical task, such as pulling a car out of a ditch, the group performance should be better than any individual's. Although each person may exert less effort than he or she would if alone (see Box 14-2), the combined force will still be greater than any one person's. For judgments and mental tasks, however, we can't assume that a group's performance will be better or more accurate than the performance of the most proficient group member acting alone. A single genius may easily outperform a more average group.

Comparison of an individual with a group can take a number of forms (Hill, 1982). One can, for example, compare an average individual with an average group; or one can compare the group with the best individual acting alone. Or if one wanted to look specifically at the contribution of interaction within the group, one could compare an actual group with the pooled responses of an aggregate

(called the *statisticized group technique*). Each of these methods will yield a somewhat different answer. The judgment of a highly trained or highly skilled individual, for example, will often be more accurate than the combined group judgment. The other methods tend to point toward the superiority of the group. As Shaw (1981) has noted, "Group judgments are seldom less accurate than the average individual judgment and are often superior" (p. 59). The group often has the advantage of a wider range of knowledge and the greater probability of including someone who will have accurate information. Yet, even though the group is often better than the *average* of individual members, there may be a single member whose judgment is better. At the same time, a dominant member of a group may be able to lead all the other members astray, resulting in deficient judgments by the collective body.

Problem solving. The term *problem solving* has been used to refer to a wide variety of tasks, varying from counting dots to solving the problems faced by the managements of large business organizations. The requirements of these tasks frequently vary. Some tasks are easily divisible, so that the overall problem can be broken down into specialized subtasks, each of which may be performed by one person. Other tasks cannot be broken down into subtasks. Even when subtasks can be defined, they may or may not be obvious to the participants; if they aren't obvious, considerable judgment and negotiation may precede the actual problem-solving attempt (Steiner, 1972). An example of a problem-solving task in which subtasks are not easily defined is described in Box 14-3.

On the basis of a number of studies, we may conclude, along with Shaw, that "groups produce more and better solutions to problems than do individuals, although the differences in overall time required for solution are not consistently better for either individuals or groups" (Shaw, 1981, p. 63). However, when the person-hours required for solution are considered, individuals have to be judged as superior.

BOX 14-3. Do groups solve problems better than individuals?

You may recall the mental problem involving the missionaries and the cannibals. In the task, three cannibals and three missionaries must be transported across a river in several trips, since the boat holds only two persons. One of the cannibals and all three of the missionaries know how to operate the boat. The crossing must be carried out so that the cannibals on either shore never outnumber the missionaries. In a classic study, Marjorie E. Shaw (1932) used puzzles and problems like this one to compare group and individual problem solving. Subjects worked either in five groups of four persons each or as individuals. In solving such problems, 5 individuals out of 63 produced correct solutions (8%), compared with 8 out of 15 groups (53%). The groups took about 1½ times as long to solve the problems, however. The cost in person-hours was thus greater in the groups. Shaw concluded that the major advantage of the group was its ability to recognize and reject incorrect solutions and suggestions. ■

TABLE 14-3. Rules for brainstorming

1. Given a problem to solve, all group members are encouraged to express whatever solutions and ideas come to mind, regardless of how preposterous or impractical they may seem.
2. All reactions are recorded.
3. No suggestion or solution can be evaluated until all ideas have been expressed. Ideally, participants should be led to believe that no suggestions will be evaluated at the brainstorming session.
4. The elaboration of one person's ideas by another is encouraged.

Brainstorming is another example of a group problem-solving task in which subtasks may be developed but are not immediately apparent. About 25 years ago, an advertising executive named Osborn (1957) began to advocate brainstorming as a device by which groups could come up with new or creative solutions to difficult problems. The ground rules for brainstorming are shown in Table 14-3. Such a technique could be applied to a wide range of problems. For example, an advertising agency might use brainstorming to develop a new slogan, a government agency might use it to predict the effects of a policy change, or a school board might use it to discover ways of handling a financial deficit.

Osborn claimed great success with the brain-storming procedure. Empirical evaluations, however, have not consistently produced results to indicate that brainstorming is worth its time (Bouchard, Barsaloux, & Drauden, 1974). For example, Taylor, Berry, and Block (1958) found that the number of suggestions made by groups did in fact exceed the number made by any given individual working alone. However, when the suggestions of four separate individuals operating under brainstorming instructions were combined, they produced almost twice as many ideas per unit of time as did the face-to-face brainstorming groups of four persons each. This was also true when the subjects were research scientists who had worked together to solve problems (Dunnette, Campbell, & Jaastad, 1963). Lamm and Trommsdorff (1973) have summarized brainstorming research in the following way: "The empirical evidence clearly indicates that subjects brainstorming in small groups produce fewer ideas than the same number of subjects brainstorming individually. Less clear evidence is available on measures of quality, uniqueness, and variety" (p. 361).

Much of the research on brainstorming groups has been criticized because it brings together individuals who do not know one another—individuals who, for the purpose of the experiment, are formed into "groups," which are then disbanded (Bouchard, 1972). Members of such groups might be reluctant to express some of their wild flights of fancy in front of strangers, even under ground rules that prohibit criticism of any idea. Moreover, such transitory groups may not be highly motivated. It has been shown that training and practice can improve the performance of brainstorming groups (Cohen, Whitmyre, & Funk, 1960; Parnes & Meadow, 1959). One of the critical factors may be the degree to which separate subtasks can be defined. If members are selected who readily select subtasks, or areas of specialization, group brainstorming may not involve the mismanagement of time that it is often claimed to generate.

To summarize the work on group problem solving, we must consider both the task and the nature of the individuals engaged in the task. Under many circumstances, a group may be better able than an individual to solve a problem—for example, when a task can be divided into subtasks and individuals' skills can be matched with those particular subtasks (Steiner, 1972). However, when the division of tasks is unspecified or when the members of a group lack the necessary skills, group performance may fall well below its potential (and even below the level of an individual performing the task alone).

B. The perils of groupthink

The group, as we have described it so far, appears to be a very rational creature: individuals come together, seek the best solution to a problem, and proceed to perform tasks to the best of their ability. However, from experience, we know that such an ideal state does not always exist. Groups often make bad decisions and then go on to defend those decisions with ardor. Social psychologist Irving Janis, in analyzing a number of case studies in which government policy makers made serious errors, has coined the term **groupthink,** which he defines as "a mode of thinking that people engage in when they are deeply involved in a cohesive in-group, when the members' strivings for unanimity override their motivation to realistically appraise alternative courses of action" (Janis, 1972, p. 9). More recently, Janis has defined *groupthink* more simply as a tendency to seek concurrence (Longley & Pruitt, 1980).

Among the situations (or *fiascoes*, to use Janis's own term) analyzed were the U.S. invasion of the Cuban Bay of Pigs, U.S. involvement in North Korea, the escalation of the Vietnam War, and the lack of

preparedness on the part of the United States for the attack on Pearl Harbor during World War II. When is groupthink most likely to occur?

As shown in Figure 14-4, Janis has pointed to five conditions that are likely to foster groupthink. Groups that are cohesive among themselves and isolated from the judgments of qualified outsiders are likely victims. Add a highly directive leader, in a context where procedures for debate are not established, and groupthink becomes even more likely. Finally, immediate pressures to reach a solution will intensify the tendency toward groupthink (or the concurrence-seeking tendency). Janis goes on to describe symptoms that are typical of the groupthink situation, as also shown in Figure 14-4. Among these symptoms is the emergence of "mindguards"—members who protect the group from information that might shatter its complacency. Finally, Janis describes the characteristics of the decision-making process thought to take place in this situation, a process that generally is highly selective in both information search and the evaluation of alternatives.

In a constructive vein, Janis goes on to suggest ways in which groupthink can be prevented. A leader should encourage dissidence, call on each member of the group to be critical, and reinforce members who voice criticism of a favored plan. Furthermore, a leader should not present a favored plan at the outset; initially, he or she should describe a problem, not recommend a solution. Finally, Janis suggests that routine procedures should be established by which several independent groups could work on one problem. With such dispersion of energies, it is unlikely that a consensus will develop prematurely. Of course, in order to reach a final decision, the groups must merge.

Despite the fascinating nature of Janis's analysis, relatively few direct tests of his hypotheses have been conducted (Longley & Pruitt, 1980). One archival study used the public statements of leading decision makers involved in five U.S. foreign-policy crises, three of which Janis described as examples of groupthink (Tetlock, 1979). Consistent with Janis's hypothesis, groupthink decision makers made more positive references to the United States and to its allies than did the non-

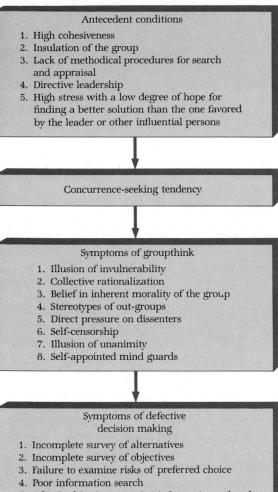

Antecedent conditions

1. High cohesiveness
2. Insulation of the group
3. Lack of methodical procedures for search and appraisal
4. Directive leadership
5. High stress with a low degree of hope for finding a better solution than the one favored by the leader or other influential persons

Concurrence-seeking tendency

Symptoms of groupthink

1. Illusion of invulnerability
2. Collective rationalization
3. Belief in inherent morality of the group
4. Stereotypes of out-groups
5. Direct pressure on dissenters
6. Self-censorship
7. Illusion of unanimity
8. Self-appointed mind guards

Symptoms of defective decision making

1. Incomplete survey of alternatives
2. Incomplete survey of objectives
3. Failure to examine risks of preferred choice
4. Poor information search
5. Selective bias in processing information at hand
6. Failure to reappraise alternatives
7. Failure to work out contingency plans

FIGURE 14-4. A model of groupthink.

groupthink participants. Moreover, groupthink policy makers were more simplistic in their perceptions of the basic issues. However, in contrast to Janis's suggestion, groupthink members were no less negative than nongroupthink members toward Communist states and their allies.

One laboratory test of groupthink involved the experimental manipulation of group cohesiveness and leadership style (Flowers, 1977). Once again,

Janis was partly supported; a closed-leadership style was found to lead to few suggested solutions and a limited use of available facts. Contrary to Janis's hypothesis, however, evidence of groupthink was apparent in both high-cohesive and low-cohesive groups.

Although many aspects of the groupthink model remain to be clarified, it offers a fascinating perspective on group decision making.

C. The polarizing effects of group interaction

Observations of group discussions reveal that pressures toward uniformity (or concurrence-seeking tendencies) often occur during the decision-making process (Festinger, 1950). In a classic study of the group problem-solving process, Schachter (1951) arranged for one member of a group to maintain a position on a discussion topic that was quite at odds with the positions of the other group members. Initially, this person, who was called a *deviate* because of his position on the issue, received a great deal of attention. Other members directed more of their communications toward him than toward one another. However, after it began to be clear that his position on the topic was not going to shift, the others terminated their communications to him and concentrated on resolving their own minor differences.

One very strong outcome of group discussions is a *polarization* of responses; that is, the consensus judgments and opinions resulting from group participation are more extreme than those of the individual participants beforehand (Myers & Lamm, 1976). Initial research in this area focused on the specific question of whether groups are more or less conservative in their decisions than individuals are. This question generated more than a decade of research on what was termed the *risky shift*. This research began with the initial finding by Stoner (1961) that group decisions were riskier than individual decisions, countering the common belief that groups tend to be more conservative than their individual members. (The view that groups are less productive and produce less satisfactory solutions than individuals still pervades

A. *As the group convenes to solve a problem, each member offers his or her opinion about the best solution.*

B. *One member turns out to have a very different opinion from those of the other group members.*

C. *Attention is directed toward that deviate, as members try to convince him to change his opinion.*

D. *The pressure toward uniformity can become intense, especially if the issue is an important one to the group.*

Groups are often faced with a need to make decisions in spite of disagreement among their members. When the majority of the group agrees on a single option, pressure is often placed on the one or two members who favor a different course of action. Once their position is known, these "deviates" will generally get a lot of the group's attention, as efforts are made to change their opinion. Reason, threats, and promises may all be used in an attempt to gain unanimity. But what if the deviate remains unconvinced? Rejection may be the outcome, as the group decides to ignore the deviate and focuses on resolving any minor differences that the majority members have among themselves.

E. *Unconvinced, the deviate faces a choice: go along with the group or risk rejection by maintaining his position.*

popular wisdom—consider the description of a camel as "a horse designed by a committee.")

Most of the research studies that followed Stoner's employed the choice-dilemma questionnaire developed by Kogan and Wallach (1964), one item of which is shown in Figure 14-5. Note that the definition of a risky choice is rather specific in this figure. Subjects are not asked whether they would recommend a risky or a conservative decision; instead, they are asked to estimate what the odds for success would have to be in order for them to choose a risky action. In the typical risky-shift experiment, members of a group respond to the questionnaire individually. Then they form a group to discuss each hypothetical choice and arrive at a unanimous group decision. Each subject is then asked to go back over each item on the question-

FIGURE 14-5. A choice-dilemma questionnaire item.

Mr. A., an electrical engineer who is married and has one child, has been working for a large electronics corporation since graduating from college five years ago. He is assured of a lifetime job with a modest, though adequate, salary and liberal pension benefits upon retirement. On the other hand, it is very unlikely that his salary will increase much before he retires. While attending a convention, Mr. A. is offered a job with a small, newly founded company which has a highly uncertain future. The new job would pay more to start and would offer the possibility of a share in the ownership if the company survived the competition of the larger firms.

Imagine that you are advising Mr. A. Listed below are several probabilities or odds of the new company proving financially sound. *Please check the lowest probability that you would consider acceptable to make it worthwhile for Mr. A. to take the new job.*

_____ The chances are 1 in 10 that the company will prove financially sound.
_____ The chances are 3 in 10 that the company will prove financially sound.
_____ The chances are 5 in 10 that the company will prove financially sound.
_____ The chances are 7 in 10 that the company will prove financially sound.
_____ The chances are 9 in 10 that the company will prove financially sound.
_____ Place a check here if you think Mr. A. should *not* take the new job no matter what the probabilities.

naire and, once again, indicate an individual decision. Most studies that used this method found that group decisions were indeed riskier, and a variety of theoretical formulations were offered to explain this initially unpredicted finding (Cartwright, 1971; Clark, 1971; Dion, Baron, & Miller, 1970; Pruitt, 1971a, 1971b; Vinokur, 1971). In a group, the shift toward risk is dependent on three conditions: group discussion, "a certain divergence between the individual positions, and a certain normative quality in the material on which the discussion is based" (Moscovici & Doise, 1974, pp. 271–272). In other words, the members of the group must show some disagreement at the beginning of the discussion, and the topic itself must have some implications for socially accepted values.

More recently, investigators have realized that although group discussion often produces a shift in individual opinions, such a shift is not necessarily in the direction of greater risk. If the initial opinions of the group tend toward conservatism, then the shift resulting from group discussion will be toward a more extreme conservative opinion (Fraser, 1971; Myers & Bishop, 1970). Therefore, the term **group polarization** has effectively replaced the term *risky shift* as a general description of this particular phenomenon.

Given the apparent pervasiveness of group polarization, we should ask *why* such polarization occurs. What causes the members of a group to shift their opinions toward an extreme position? Three general kinds of explanations have been offered. These explanations are based on group-decision rules, interpersonal comparisons, and informational influence (Myers & Lamm, 1976).

Explanations based on group-decision rules focus on statistical prediction of the group product, using specific combinations of individual preferences. Although a variety of social-decision schemes exist (Davis, 1973), most investigators have examined the principle of majority rule; that is, a group will shift toward that pole favored by the majority of members, because initially deviant members fall in line with the majority. Some investigators have argued that group polarization effects are a statistical artifact rather than the outcome of a real, internalized change in opinions; others, however, have simply tried to predict specific changes without a concern for psychological underpinnings.

Although attempts to predict specific changes are laudable, we would like to have a better understanding of the psychological mechanisms involved in these changes. Explanations based on interpersonal comparison and informational influence provide this understanding. According to the *interpersonal comparison* explanation, individuals in a group shift their opinions in order to conform to the opinion of the group (see Chapter 12). Motives suggested for this behavior include the desire for a favorable evaluation by others and a concern for self-presentation. This explanation focuses on the characteristics of the group members, not on information that might develop in the course of group discussion. As stated by Myers and Lamm (1976), the interpersonal-comparison explanation suggests that "group polarization is a source effect, not a message effect" (p. 613). Andrews and Johnson (1971) have called one variation of this position the "climb on the bandwagon" effect, believed to be particularly evident when members of the group expect future interactions with one another in other settings.

Informational influence explanations stress the cognitive learning that results from exposure to persuasive arguments during the course of group discussion. Here the emphasis is on the actual content (or the "message") of the group discussion and on the degree to which members are persuaded by the new information presented. This persuasion may involve mutual reinforcement. For example, Myers and Bishop (1971) found that 76% of the arguments in a group were in support of the position held by most of the members. Therefore, a shift toward extremity occurs because the tendency to accept dominant positions is reinforced by statements of attitudes that reflect one's own attitudes.

The adoption of a more extreme position is not caused solely by being exposed to arguments. In addition, when group members hear such arguments, they generally process the information, rehearse their arguments, and then actively commit themselves to the position of the group. Moscovici and Zavalloni (1969) believe that group discussion leads to an enhancement of participants' involvement with the issues and their confidence that their position is the correct one.

In summary, group polarization effects are indeed real; they may cause a group to become either more conservative or more risky, depending on the initial opinions of the majority of group members. When emphasis is placed on reaching a consensus, group members are more likely to shift their positions. Moreover, polarization is most likely to occur during active group discussions.

■ IV. Group socialization

We have looked at a number of characteristics of groups, illustrating their composition, structure, dynamics, and performance. So far, however, we have considered only intact groups, studied at one particular time and often constituted by the social psychologist for one occasion. In actuality, groups are not static. People join groups and they leave groups; groups accept members and they reject members. To truly understand the nature of groups, we need to look more closely at this process of socialization and at the changes that occur in the composition of groups and the status of members.

Social psychologists Richard Moreland and John Levine (1982) have provided an insightful account of the process of group socialization, and we will rely on their model to discuss the relation between groups and their members.

A. Basic processes of group socialization

People belong to many kinds of groups—sports teams, fraternities and sororities, church groups, political parties, and work groups, to name only a few. Although groups differ in focus and purpose, within any group we can spot a number of common characteristics. According to Moreland and Levine (1982), three processes are basic to group socialization: evaluation, commitment, and role transitions.

1. *Evaluation.* Evaluation is a process by which members of the group assess the rewards that members and the group as a whole provide. In

evaluating a group, for example, you might consider what you get out of what it costs you, and how important the group goals are to you. Further, recalling the ideas of social-exchange theory (see Chapter 6), you might also compare the rewards of the group with the possibilities for rewards in other groups. Would you rather be in sorority A or sorority B? Would you rather be a member of the chess club or the skydiving club?

Members of a group also make such assessments about individual members. Does Blair really make a contribution to our group? Is Sonny fun to have around? These evaluation processes continue through the life of a group and can incorporate many different dimensions. Furthermore, these evaluations take into account past rewards and costs and expected future rewards and costs as well. For example, a manager might look at her team and decide that although Robin has been an important contributor in the past, his ability to contribute to the next project is doubtful. Once again, these evaluations will probably take into account other possible members that the group might have.

2. *Commitment.* If the individual or the members of a group evaluate the relationship as a positive or rewarding one, then commitment is likely to result. As Moreland and Levine state, "Groups are more committed to individuals who help them attain group goals, and individuals are more committed to groups that help them satisfy personal needs" (1982, p. 145). In making such a commitment, both the group and the individual again take into account a variety of temporal perspectives—past, present, and expected future rewards, as well as a comparison with other situations that might offer more. The more rewarding the present member or group, and the less rewarding other available groups, the greater will be the commitment.

Commitment has a number of consequences, some of which we discussed in describing the group interaction process. Here we can point to four specific consequences: (1) consensus agreement on the group goals and values, (2) positive affective ties, both of the individual to the group and of the group to the individual, (3) a willingness to exert effort on behalf of the group or the individual, and (4) a desire for continuance of membership in the group (Moreland & Levine, 1982). Again, we look at these consequences from two perspectives—from that of the individual who is committed to the group and from that of the group that is committed to the individual member.

3. *Role transitions.* Groups are not stable over time, and the role of any individual within the group can change. We may think of the various roles as lying on a dimension from nonmembers at one end to full members at the other end. A nonmember of a bowling team, for example, could be either someone who has never joined or someone who quit the team last month. Full members of a group are those who are closely identified with the group and are fully established in their roles. In between these two extremes, we can think about so-called quasi members—newcomers to the group who are not yet fully accepted or marginal members who have lost some of their former status.

As the group changes over time, individual members may have different roles within the group. Often the transition from one role to another is marked by formal ceremonies, or rites of passage. Bar mitzvahs and bat mitzvahs, for example, mark the transition of Jewish children to adulthood. Other role transitions may be marked in more personal ways. On becoming a member of an honorary society, for example, you may be toasted by your friends at a party. After getting promoted to a more desirable team in the organization, you may buy yourself a present. These and other activities may serve as markers of a social-psychological transition in the life of a group.

B. Stages of group socialization

Having considered the major processes that occur in the life of a group and in the lives of its members, let us turn to the actual process of group socialization. As shown in Figure 14-6, we can think of the life span of a group in terms of five general periods, with four specific points marking the transition between one stage and another. As we analyze each of these stages, you may want to think about your own experiences in groups as

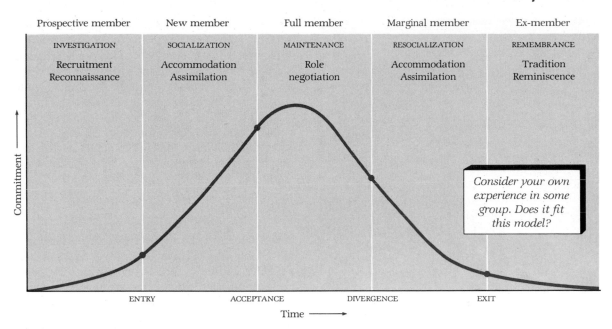

Prospective member	New member	Full member	Marginal member	Ex-member
INVESTIGATION	SOCIALIZATION	MAINTENANCE	RESOCIALIZATION	REMEMBRANCE
Recruitment Reconnaissance	Accommodation Assimilation	Role negotiation	Accommodation Assimilation	Tradition Reminiscence

Consider your own experience in some group. Does it fit this model?

Commitment →

ENTRY   ACCEPTANCE   DIVERGENCE   EXIT

Time →

FIGURE 14-6. The stages of group socialization.

possible illustrations of the process. Bear in mind that this curve is only a general model—the exact shape of the curve may vary in different groups.

1. *Investigation.* Fraternity or sorority rush provides an excellent example of the investigation stage. From the perspective of the individual who wants to join a group, the rush period is one of reconnaissance. As the person goes through rush, he or she is assessing the various groups, trying to decide which one would be most compatible with personal needs and values. Individuals' reasons for joining a group, of course, can vary widely, just as their actual choice of a group will be different. People may seek groups that have similar interests, have attractive members, promise status, or provide the means to some other desired goal.

At the same time, groups are engaging in recruitment activities, looking for persons who will "fit in" with their goals and activities. Fraternities and sororities, for example, use various criteria to decide on the suitability of a prospective member. Not all groups are as formal and closed, of course. Many groups do very little evaluation at this stage and are willing to accept anyone who wishes to be a member. Political organizations, for example, are relatively open groups. In part, a group's willingness to accept new members depends on its past success. Successful groups are often more restrictive in their policies toward new recruits. Unsuccessful groups, in contrast, often actively seek new members. A good example of this latter state is the famous study by Festinger et al. (1956), looking at the behavior of a group that predicted the end of the world on a particular date. When the prediction proved false, members of this group became active proselytizers, seeking new recruits wherever they could find them.

2. *Entry.* The entry stage (indicated by the first dot in Figure 14-6) marks the role transition between investigation and socialization. At this point, the individual moves from being a prospective member to being a new member of the group. In formal groups, this transition is usually marked by some kind of ceremony or initiation rite, designed in part to increase the member's commitment to the group. In less formal groups, this transition may occur without much notice, and the commitment to the group and by the group may be less as a result.

PHOTO 14-5. *For this Jewish boy, the bar mitzvah ceremony marks the transition from childhood into adulthood.*

3. *Socialization.* The period of socialization is one in which the individual and the group attempt to merge their respective goals and norms. From the group's perspective, there is an attempt to assimilate the individual to the group, instructing the person in the ways of the group, its rituals, procedures, and expectations. At the same time,

the individual may attempt to shape the group so that it is compatible with his or her own needs.

This socialization period can vary in length and can take many forms. In the sorority or fraternity, for example, the pledge period represents a stage of socialization. Many corporations have an initial training program for prospective managers that serves much the same function. In less formal organizations, the socialization stage may be less clearly defined but can still be viewed in terms of gradual assimilation of the member to the group and gradual accommodation of the group to the new member.

4. *Acceptance.* Acceptance marks the transition between being a new member and being a full member, or between being an outsider and an insider within the group. At this point, as the curve in Figure 14-6 indicates, commitment of the group to the member and commitment of the member to the group are both high. Again, rites of passage may mark this second transition. The full benefits of the group are now available to the member, and questions of loyalty or contribution are no longer raised.

5. *Maintenance.* Role negotiation is most clearly seen during the maintenance period of a group. Now a full member, the individual tries to see where he or she will fit most clearly into the structure of the organization. At the same time, the group is trying to restructure itself, taking into account the potential contributions of the new member. Leadership roles evolve in this stage (see Chapter 15), and members of the group negotiate complex and interdependent relationships with one another.

6. *Divergence.* Role negotiation is not always successful. Sometimes workable relationships do not develop; in other cases, relationships that once worked may be altered by the addition of new members to the group. When the group no longer satisfies the individual, or the individual no longer satisfies the group, a third transition point (termed "divergence") may be marked. Sometimes this transition is expected. For example, when you graduated from high school and went to college, your departure (at least in part) from your group of high school friends was an expected divergence.

Similarly, when you graduate from college, memberships in college clubs or activities will be predictably terminated. In these cases, movement on the curve in Figure 14-6 is toward exit.

In other cases, the divergence may be unexpected. An individual who veers from the group position on some important issue may be labeled

PHOTO 14-6. *College graduation represents a divergence in group membership, moving the person away from the group.*

a deviant by the group, and that person's status in the group will be questioned. From the individual's perspective, the group may shift its focus, diminishing the commitment that the individual feels toward the group.

7. *Resocialization.* If the divergence was expected, resocialization efforts are usually minimal. Instead, both the group and the member may engage in efforts to prepare for the eventual exit of the member. Going-away parties, for example, are one means of preparing for a transition that is inevitable.

If the divergence was unexpected, efforts at resocialization may be much stronger. As discussed earlier, responses to a deviant often involve a great deal of attention and communication, attempting to change the person's position to be more consistent with the group's (Schachter, 1951). Both the individual and the group may negotiate and compromise, trying to regain the prior levels of commitment. Should these efforts be successful, the individual will return to full membership status, essentially moving backward on the curve shown in Figure 14-6. If the efforts are unsuccessful, then this individual, like the expected divergent, will move toward the exit transition point.

8. *Exit.* At the point of exit, the individual's and the group's commitment to each other have diminished. An evaluation of the rewards of the situation has led to a conclusion that such rewards are minimal, either in themselves or in comparison with the rewards that another group or another member would offer. The exit transition may be executed very quickly, as when an employee resigns or is fired outright. In other cases, negotiating this transition point may take more time as both the individual and the group prepare for the new situation. The individual may show a gradual decline in his or her commitment to the group—first missing a few meetings, then failing to carry out some responsibilities, then being a member in name only. On the other side, the group may gradually shift the individual to a marginal position where there is less involvement in decisions and less interaction with members.

Rites of passage may mark the exit transition as well. Retirement ceremonies mark the end of ser-

PHOTO 14-7. *Although all groups share certain properties, each type has characteristics of its own.*

vice for the employee. Angry public statements may be made by the individual who was expelled from the group. These, like the rites that preceded them, testify to the importance of such transition points in the relationships between individuals and groups.

9. *Remembrance.* Finally, when the relationship between the individual and the group has been severed, there is a period of remembrance. The individual may reminisce (with either favorable or unfavorable thoughts) about his or her relationship to that group and what it means for the future. From the group's perspective, recall of events involving that person may take the form of tradition. "Remember what Todd did on that occasion" may be the basis of consolidating the memories of Todd, either favorable or unfavorable, depending on the basis of the exit. Although commitment is now weak or absent, evaluations of the member or the group may persist and may provide a basis for future evaluations by groups and by prospective members.

This model of group socialization can be applied to nearly every kind of group, from formal to informal, from large to small, from short-lived to long-lived. Although the length of various stages and the forms of various transition points may vary, the model captures important aspects of the socialization processes in groups.

■ V. Groups in action

As you read about the ways that people enter and exit from groups, you may have considered a variety of groups to which you now belong or have belonged in the past. Indeed, it is hard to think of a society without also noting the number of groups that operate. The jury system is an important part of the judicial process; although their demise is often forecast, families continue to form the basis of most societies; and new forms of group therapy are discussed in the pages of psychiatric journals and the popular press. In this section we consider some of these groups.

A. Juries

Juries are an important example of groups in action. Although they are a potentially rich area for social-psychological investigation, legal restrictions preclude the study of actual juries in operation. Perhaps the closest approach to an actual jury situation is found in the work of Strodtbeck and his colleagues (James, 1959; Strodtbeck, James, & Hawkins, 1957; Strodtbeck & Mann, 1956), who drew their subjects from actual jury rosters, assembled them in a courtroom, and asked them to listen to a recording of a real trial in the presence of court officials. The subsequent jury deliberation process was conducted in as realistic a manner as possible. Overall, Strodtbeck came as close as an investigator can come to observing jury behavior without intruding on the actual judicial process.

One focus of Strodtbeck's research was the roles that develop during the course of jury deliberations. High-status members participated more than low-status members, and they were perceived as being more influential. The foreman of the group was likely to be a high-status person. Sex differences appeared as well. Women expressed more positive reactions to other jurors during the deliberation phase, whereas men were more likely to attempt to give answers. Overall, the groups felt that the members who had offered the most answers were the most helpful, suggesting that the males were somewhat more valued in the group than the females.

James (1959) examined the specific content of jury deliberations and found that a surprising 50% of the discussion was devoted to personal experiences and opinions. About 25% of the discussion was devoted to procedural issues, 15% to the actual testimony, and 8% to the judge's instructions to the jury. Highly educated jurors emphasized procedure and instructions, whereas members with only a grade school education were more likely to focus on opinion, testimony, and personal experiences (Gerbasi, Zuckerman, & Reis, 1977).

In contrast to these studies of jury process, studies of the outcome of jury deliberations have considered the ways in which various compositions of juries affect their ultimate decision regarding the accused. For example, in the study conducted by Davis and his colleagues that we discussed earlier, it was shown that the size of the jury (6 versus 12 persons) had little effect on their ultimate decision. Group polarization effects have been found in simulated jury settings. When the evidence for guilt is weak, individuals tend to shift toward a more lenient decision after their deliberation; however, when the evidence for guilt is strong, deliberation leads to harsh judgments (Myers & Kaplan, 1976). The decision rules that are imposed on a jury can also have an effect (Davis, Bray, & Holt, 1976). For example, a hung jury is, not surprisingly, more likely to occur when unanimity is required than when only a majority decision is needed (Kerr, Atkin, Stasser, Meek, Holt, & Davis, 1976).

Jury behavior provides an exciting area of investigation for the social psychologist. Although many studies of the judicial process have focused on individual decision making (Davis, Bray, & Holt, 1976), there is a growing recognition that group behavior must be studied in context and that the factors of duration and commitment present in a real jury may create a situation that is quite different from the simulated jury situation in the laboratory experiment.

B. Families

In contrast to the jury, in which members initially are strangers, the family shows us a group in which members maintain extensive and long-term interaction. The dynamics of the family are more intensive, and more complex, than those of the jury. This complexity has caused many investigators to shy away from the family as a focus of investigation, whereas others have attempted to create "simulated" families, in which specific factors can be controlled (Waxler & Mishler, 1978). Although certainly no one would argue that such an artificial family is the same as the real thing, such attempts have pointed to certain consistent factors that may operate in both simulated and real families. For example, Bodin (reported in Waxler & Mishler, 1978) found that artificial fam-

PHOTO 14-8. *Families exemplify long-term, complex group interactions.*

chal nature of Navajo society; and the Protestant Texan couples exhibited equality in their decision-making process. Expanding the dyad to a triad (including a mother, a father, and an adolescent son) and considering two other cultures (Jewish and Italian), Strodtbeck (1958) again found evidence for cultural differences. Italian fathers were much more powerful than their wives and their sons; in Jewish families, parents shared power and had more power than their sons.

Although Strodtbeck's findings are intriguing, they tell us little about the causes of cultural differences. One way to circumvent this problem would be to conduct studies of families over their life cycle—observing a number of families over many years, noting changes in structure (for example, the birth of a child or the death of a grandparent), and relating these structural changes to differences in the process of family interaction. Such an approach is incredibly time-consuming, and a full project could outlive the investigator. Alternatively, one can, at a single point in time, select couples who are at different points in the family life cycle and make comparisons among the groups.

Recently, many investigators of family structure and process have introduced experimental interventions, attempting to show clearly how particular variables affect family interaction (Waxler & Mishler, 1978). For example, Bandura, Ross, and Ross (1963b) experimentally varied the status of parents' roles and their reward power and then looked at the imitation behavior of children. They found that children are more likely to imitate the behaviors of the high-status parent, regardless of who is giving or receiving rewards.

Many people would, of course, question whether such experimental situations have much to do with real-life families, with their complex histories of interactions, joys, and sorrows. This question must be answered cautiously. On the one hand, it is quite likely that some of the characteristics of artificial groups and the results of laboratory group experiments are relevant to the family; they will help to point out some of the critical variables in family interaction. On the other hand, there may

ilies and real families used the same general modes of resolving problems; however, mothers in the real families were less compromising than the "mothers" in the ad hoc groups. After comparing real and artificial husband/wife dyads, Ryder (1968) concluded that "the differences between married and split dyads seem much better described by noting that subjects treat strangers more gently and generally more nicely than they do their spouses" (p. 237)!

Other investigators have preferred to study real families exclusively; for example, they investigate the ways demographic variables affect the pattern of family interaction. Strodtbeck (1951) studied husband/wife decision making among Protestant Texan, Navajo, and Mormon couples. He found that Mormon husbands were much more powerful than their wives; Navajo wives were more powerful than their husbands, reflecting the matriar-

be no real substitute for more intensive, longitudinal studies of actual family interaction. The challenge of this kind of investigation is great, but its potential for expanding our understanding of group behavior is equally great.

C. Experiential groups

During the past 25 years, we have witnessed an increase in the number of experiential groups, in which individuals have sought to improve their own skills or life-styles through participation in groups. Through the group experience itself, individual changes are sought (Shaw, 1981). Such groups take many forms and have a variety of names: T-groups, sensitivity groups, encounter groups, *est*, and consciousness-raising groups, to cite only a few.

T-group (which stands for "training group") is a technique originally developed by Kurt Lewin and his colleagues. They developed the technique while leading a workshop on the use of small groups as a vehicle for personal and social change (Lippitt, 1949). The methods they used in their workshop were rather traditional. During the evenings, the staff would meet to discuss the daily events. One evening, to the surprise of all, three trainees wanted to listen to the staff's discussion. In an interview obtained by Back (1972), Lippitt later described what happened:

> And on this particular night, three of the trainees, three school teachers who hadn't gone home that evening, stuck their heads in the door and asked if they could come in, sit and observe and listen, and Kurt [Lewin] was rather embarrassed, and we all were expecting him to say no, but he didn't, he said, "Yes, sure, come on in and sit down." And we went right ahead as though they weren't there, and pretty soon one of them was mentioned and her behavior was described and discussed, and the trainer and the researcher had somewhat different observations, perceptions of what had happened, and she became very agitated and said that wasn't the way it happened at all, and she gave her perception. And Lewin got quite excited about this additional data and put it on the board to theorize it, and later on in the evening the same thing happened in relation to one

of the other two. She had a different perception on what was being described as an event in that group she was in. So Lewin was quite excited about the additional data, and the three at the end of the evening asked if they could come back again the next night, and Lewin was quite positive that they could; *we* had more doubts about it. And the next night the whole fifty were there and were every night, and so it became the most significant training event of the day as this feedback and review of process of events that had gone on during the work sessions of the day. And as Ken Benne, Lee Bradford, and I discussed this, actually it was at a hamburger joint after one of these evenings, we felt the evidence was so clear that the level of our observations of the phenomena about these sessions were a major basis for reorganizations of perceptions and attitude change and of linking up to some degree attitudes and values with intentions and behavior [Back, 1972, pp. 8–9].

From this accidental beginning, a huge industry of group experiences has developed that uses the group as a basis for individual change. The original National Training Laboratory, developed by Lewin and his associates, generally does training with a specific purpose (Hare, 1976). Based in Washington, D.C. (with summer workshops in Bethel, Maine), NTL engages in work for personnel departments and government agencies, and it conducts sessions for individuals who are concerned with personal growth.

What are the effects of participation in experiential groups? Since such groups vary in composition, duration, purpose, and procedures, it's difficult to answer this question. Moreover, systematic research on the phenomenon of experiential groups is still in its infancy (Lieberman, 1976). The problems in establishing control groups are similar to those encountered in research on the effectiveness of psychotherapy. Changes in actual behavior are often difficult to detect, and they are difficult to measure after participants have returned to their homes. Much research falls back on the use of participants' self-reports regarding the benefits of experiential groups—a procedure that is rife with demand characteristics. (Someone who has paid $500 for a weekend group encounter will be unlikely to admit that it was a flop.)

Despite the weak basis for drawing conclusions, Shaw (1981, p. 426) has offered four tentative hypotheses about the effects of experiential groups:

1. The discrepancy between the perceived self and the ideal self decreases as a function of participation in experiential groups.
2. Participants in experiential groups perceive changes in their feelings and behavior as a consequence of the group experience.
3. Observers report perceived changes in members' behavior following participation in experiential groups.
4. Under some conditions, participation in experiential groups results in severe psychological disturbances.

In summary, it is difficult at this time to validate (in accepted scientific fashion) the exact effects of experiential groups. The structural elements present in the many varieties of these groups are only beginning to be identified (Lieberman, 1976). Nonetheless, experiential groups are popular and powerful, and they underline the pervasiveness of the group process.

VI. SUMMARY

A *group* has the following properties: interaction between individuals, development of shared perceptions, presence of emotional ties, and development of interdependence and roles. Collections of people that do not possess these characteristics are called *aggregates*.

Other people may influence our behavior, even when we are not part of a group. The *social impact* of an audience is determined by the number of people, their status, and their immediacy to the target.

Zajonc's drive theory of *social facilitation* suggests that the presence of others is a source of general arousal that will result in increased performance of simple or well-learned responses and decreased performance of more complex tasks. A variety of social and cognitive concerns can lead to greater arousal.

Coacting audiences create a feeling of competition. In addition, they provide a source of modeling and of social comparison.

We can analyze groups in several ways—in terms of composition, structure, the dynamics of the group, and group performance. Group size is one example of a composition variable; communication networks illustrate an aspect of structure; and cohesiveness is an element of group dynamics.

Group performance can be affected by each of these factors. Whether a group will perform better than an individual depends both on the nature of the task and on the characteristics of individual members. *Groupthink*, defined as a tendency of members to seek concurrence, illustrates the process by which groups may come to poor decisions.

In general, group interaction tends to lead to a *polarization* of responses: opinions resulting from group discussion are more extreme than the opinions of individuals prior to the group discussion.

Over the life span of a group, three processes appear particularly important: evaluation, commitment, and role transition. The socialization of a group can be described in terms of five general periods, separated by four specific transition points. These periods and the transition points are investigation, entry, socialization, acceptance, maintenance, divergence, resocialization, exit, and remembrance. Both the individual and the group engage in characteristic activities at each stage of this socialization process.

Real-life examples of groups in action include juries, families, and experiential groups. Each of these types of groups has a set of unique properties; each, too, shows the applicability of social-psychological principles.

GLOSSARY TERMS

cohesiveness	group polarization	social facilitation
communication networks	groupthink	social inhibition

Leadership

The question "Who ought to be boss?" is like asking "Who ought to be the tenor in the quartet?" Obviously, the man who can sing tenor.
■ HENRY FORD

You can take people as far as they will go, not as far as you would like them to go.
■ JEANNETTE RANKIN

Groups, as we have described them, are collections of people interacting and working together toward a common goal. Yet, not all members of a group play the same role in directing the group toward that goal. In nearly every group, whether it is a wolf pack or a society, a single individual or group of individuals takes greater responsibility for getting things done. This individual or group of individuals is considered the leader(s), and leadership can be viewed as one particular aspect of group structure (see Chapter 14).

Leadership has long been a topic of interest to many. Business firms and consulting organizations sponsor leadership training workshops, attempting to instill the qualities of leadership in the novice manager. National magazines declare a vacuum of leadership in the country and search for potential leaders of the future. Social and organizational psychologists have, over the years, continued to explore the question of **leadership**—that "process of influence between a leader and followers to attain group, organizational, or societal goals" (Hollander, in press, p. 4).

Many of the psychological concepts that we have covered earlier in this book are related to leadership—social influence and power, for example, as discussed in Chapter 12. However, the leadership role cannot be fully described by any single set of processes; indeed, many writers have resorted to the more magical quality of *charisma* in seeking to explain how leaders are different.

The study of leadership has changed from a search for simplicity to a recognition of complexity. In early attempts to study leadership, researchers tried to identify the qualities that "made" a leader—characteristics that all leaders, but no followers, possessed. Implicit in this approach was the assumption that certain traits—or even a single trait—would guarantee the emergence of a leader, whether it be the election of a captain of the church bowling team, the promotion of a company vice-president, or the selection of a jury foreman. But that simple approach didn't work. It failed to recognize the numerous functions that leaders play, the variety of tasks performed by groups, and the characteristics of the system in which leaders and groups operate. More complex analyses followed that took into account some of these broader issues.

In this chapter we will explore the issues of leadership, considering what it means to lead, what it means to follow, and how organizations deal with the interactions between leaders and subordinates.

■ I. The search for leadership traits

What makes one person a successful leader, while another person fails in the same position? How have some revolutionary leaders—for example, Napoleon, Hitler, and Mao Zedong—been able to control the destiny of thousands of people, while other leaders come and go? Why does one person consistently become the class president, the director of the local city council, or the occupant of other leadership positions? Patterns of this kind have led people to look for the limited set of traits or characteristics that can distinguish the leader from the follower.

A. Do leaders possess certain traits?

The earliest approach to studying leadership, and one that is still used to a small extent today, was to find a group of leaders and followers, give them a series of personality measures, and try to determine which characteristics distinguish the leaders from the followers. Although researchers were initially enthusiastic about this approach, it has become considerably less popular in recent years.

In part, the disillusionment with this approach resulted from the rather simplified assumptions that were made. Often, for example, investigators assumed that a single characteristic would be sufficient to separate leaders from followers. For example, Bird (1940) analyzed the results of 20 studies that had considered 79 different leadership traits. In these studies, leadership was usually defined in terms of school activities, but with great variation in the settings; for example, they included student councils, scout troops, speech and drama groups, and athletic teams. Bird found little con-

PHOTO 15-1. *Even when leaders are the same sex and participate in the same political system, their personality characteristics may be very different.*

sistency in the results from one study to another. Of the 79 traits, 51 made a difference in only one study each. Although the lack of consistency was partly the result of using different, but almost synonymous, terms in different studies (for instance, *more reliable* versus *more accurate in work*), the general result was a disappointment for those who assumed that leaders were somehow "special" in regard to many traits. High degrees of only four characteristics—intelligence, initiative, sense of humor, and extroversion—were identified often enough in leaders for Bird to consider them "general traits of leadership" (1940, p. 380).

Later reviews of studies of leadership characteristics (Jenkins, 1947; Stogdill, 1948) tended to arrive at the same conclusion: there is no single trait that consistently characterizes leaders. Even high intelligence, which many academic investigators assumed should be a mark of the successful leader, did not turn out to be of overwhelming importance as a general leadership trait. For example, Mann's (1959) review concludes: "Considering independent studies as the unit of research, the positive association between intelligence and leadership is found to be highly significant. . . . However, the magnitude of the relationship is less impressive; no correlation reported exceeds .50 and the median r [correlation coefficient] is roughly .25" (p. 248). In other words, although intelligence is frequently related to good leadership, the association is quite weak.

Korman (1968), in his review of managerial performance, suggested that although the intelligence levels of first-line supervisors could be related to their performance levels, there was little connection between intelligence and the success of higher-level managers. In part, the lack of connection between intelligence and performance of leaders at higher levels may be the result of a selection process: at these levels, perhaps all managers have relatively high intelligence, and so other variables become more important in determining leadership. Gibb (1969) suggested that if there is too much discrepancy between a potential leader's intelligence and the intelligence of other group members, his or her success in initiating and maintaining leadership is hampered. Leaders can be too bright for their followers. "The evidence suggests that every increment of intelligence means wiser government, but that the crowd prefers to be ill-governed by people it can understand" (Gibb, 1969, p. 218). In short, available evidence does not support the assumption that any *single* variable— be it a personality trait such as extroversion, a demographic variable such as height or age, or a cognitive characteristic such as intelligence—distinguishes leaders from followers.

More recent research has shown, however, that certain *clusters* of behaviors do reliably separate leaders from their followers, as well as distinguish effective leaders from ineffective leaders. As summarized by Stogdill (1974), these clusters include "a strong drive for responsibility and task completion, vigor and persistence in pursuit of goals, venturesomeness and originality in problem solving, drive to exercise initiative in social situations, self-confidence and sense of personal identity, willingness to accept consequences of decision and action, readiness to absorb interpersonal stress, willingness to tolerate frustration and delay, ability to influence other persons' behavior, and capacity to structure social interaction systems to the purpose at hand" (p. 81). Note that this list describes rather specific behaviors and processes, rather than very general traits. It thus represents a greater level of specificity and recalls the issues of personality and behavior prediction discussed in Chapters 10 and 13.

Analysis of the personality of leaders has also benefited by considering a variety of situational factors. A pattern or cluster of traits that predicts leadership in one setting may not be relevant in a different kind of setting. A recent study by McClelland and Boyatzis (1982) provides one example of this variation. On the basis of previous research, these investigators identified a pattern of motives that are characteristic of effective managers: a high need for power, a lower need for affiliation, and high self-control. Managers high in power motivation are interested in having impact on others; managers lower in affiliation are less concerned about being disliked when unpopular decisions must be made; and high self-control allows the person to be organized and disciplined in his or her actions.

Assessing a group of male managers on these characteristics in the late 1950s, the investigators then checked back 8 and 16 years later to determine the progress of the managers within the company. Men who had the defined pattern of scores in earlier years were significantly more likely to be at higher levels of management at the later period—but only if they were in nontechnical fields, such as customer services, marketing, accounting, and personnel. In contrast, the pattern was not at all predictive of the advancement of managers in technical fields, such as engineering and construction.

Hence, trait approaches should not be abandoned entirely. The early "simple and sovereign" approach, however, has been replaced with a more complex version of trait models, recognizing the interaction of persons and situations (and echoing the message of Chapter 13).

B. The "great man" theory of leadership

The "great man" theory of leadership, in its boldest form, proposes that major events in national and international affairs are influenced by the people who hold positions of leadership "and that all factors in history, save great men, are inconsequential" (Hook, 1955, p. 14). Perhaps the greatest exponent of the "great man" theory was the historian Thomas Carlyle, who believed that genius would exert its influence wherever it was found.

A sudden act by a great leader could, according to this theory, change the fate of a nation. Thus, Germany became overtly nationalistic and belligerent in the 1930s solely because Adolf Hitler was in power; had there been no Hitler, says the theory, there would have been no World War II. The extreme form of the theory would go on to propose that, had a "great man" been in power in Great Britain or the United States at that time, World War II could have been averted in spite of Hitler's belligerence. Implicit in the "great man" theory is the assumption that leaders possess *charisma*, a set of personality characteristics that facilitate the accomplishment of their goals, even in the face of great obstacles.

Can this theory of leadership be tested by relating the personal qualities of ruling monarchs to the extent of growth or decline in their countries during their reign? Frederick Adams Wood (1913), an early-20th-century American historian, thought so. He made a detailed study of 386 rulers in 14 Western European countries who lived between A.D. 1000 and the time of the French Revolution. All the rulers whom he studied had absolute power over their kingdoms. Each was classified as strong, weak, or mediocre on the basis of knowledge about his or her intellectual and personal characteristics (presumably independent of the strength or weakness of the nation at that time). The condition of each country was also classified by whether it exhibited a state of prosperity, a state of decline, or no clear indication of either. (This classification was based on the country's economic and political status, not on its artistic, educational, or scientific development.)

Wood found a relation between the monarchs' personalities and the state of their countries: "Strong, mediocre, and weak monarchs are associated with strong, mediocre, and weak periods respectively" (1913, p. 246). Although the correlation coefficient was reasonably strong (between +.60 and +.70), as with any correlation, we cannot infer a direct relation between cause and effect. However, Wood clearly favors the interpretation that strong leaders cause their countries to flourish. It is equally possible, though, that a state of prosperity in a country permits brilliant rulers to emerge or to reign successfully with little strain. The interpretation that Wood favors can also be doubted because of the problems in establishing independent and objective measurements of the quality of a monarch and his or her country's development. King Charles I of England is an example. It is not enough that King Charles lost his crown and his head; the final indignity is that Wood called him two-faced and obstinate. Yet, other observers, as Hook notes, might describe Charles as "shrewd and principled." Although we admire Wood's exhaustive approach to the study of "great men," we must conclude that his data do not permit an answer to his question.

An opposing viewpoint: The *Zeitgeist* and social determinism. A strong rebuttal to the "great man" theory is found in approaches that place emphasis on social forces, social movements, and changing social values as determinants of historic events. *Zeitgeist* means "spirit of the times" or "temper of the times." According to the *Zeitgeist* theory of history, leaders are like actors who play out the roles designed for them by broad social forces. This theory sees the leader's temperament, motives, and ability as having little real influence in the face of social movements. As Victor Hugo wrote, "There is nothing in this world so powerful as an idea whose time has come"— a statement reflecting the perspective of the *Zeitgeist*, or social determinism.

Which is more nearly correct, the "great man" or the *Zeitgeist* theory? Let's first discuss the historical evidence. Study of the history of scientific discovery gives rather weak support to the "great man" hypothesis. Although certain scientists rise notably above their peers, an analysis by Simonton

(1979) of scientific accomplishments suggests that sheer chance and the influence of the *Zeitgeist* (and of previous technological discoveries) are more important determinants of scientific eminence than personal qualities.

Can the conflict between the "great man" theory and the *Zeitgeist* hypothesis be resolved? We have emphasized throughout this book that no one theory is always correct and that conflicting theories can each make a contribution to the understanding of complex social phenomena. Simonton (1979) concurs with this point in his analysis of scientific eminence, and Hook believes the "great man" plays a unique and decisive role "only where the historical situation permits major *alternative* paths of development" (1955, p. 109). Even if Christopher Columbus had not set sail in 1492, another explorer would have "discovered" the New World soon thereafter. The forces at work gave no alternative. Only when choices exist does the great man or woman influence history.

What may arise out of a clash between a particular leader and his times is a new set of values; for example, one effect of the nonviolent protest for Black rights led by Martin Luther King, Jr., was the consciousness among many Whites that certain citizens in the United States were being unfairly treated. This effect cannot be attributed to the man alone or to his times; it resulted from a creative interaction between the two (Elkind, 1971).

Furthermore, both the times and people change. In fact, Suedfeld and Rank (1976) have suggested that the most successful revolutionary leaders were those who could change their behavior with the demands of the situation (see Box 15-1).

The "great man" theory in the laboratory. A quite different approach to the "great man" theory of leadership involves using manipulations and experimental controls to determine how the behavior of the single person in the top position affects organizational performance. Borgatta, Couch, and Bales (1954) used this approach with three-man groups of military recruits. Each man participated in four sessions of 24 minutes each, with two new participants in each session. "Great men" were selected on the basis of their performance in the first session; the top 11 of 123 men were so classified. These 11 men were followed through the subsequent sessions so that their productivity could be assessed. (Productivity was measured by the number of acts initiated per time unit and the leadership and popularity ratings given each man by his coparticipants.) "Great men" selected on the basis of the first session continued to have an influence that led to relatively superior performance in their subsequent groups. Of the 11 top men, 8 were in the top 11 productivity ranks in the second and third sessions. In the fourth session, 7 were still in the top rank. Groups in the second, third, and fourth sessions with "great men" as participants demonstrated smoother functioning, with fewer cases of anxiety or withdrawal from participation.

Supportive as these findings are, we are still a long way from verifying a "great man" theory of leadership in practice. The study by Borgatta et al. (1954) does indicate some consistency in group performance across groups with different leaders classified as "great"—over a 96-minute period. It does not, however, show the degree to which a charismatic leader can manipulate the content of eventful decisions over the course of months or years.

C. Where is the "great woman" theory?

Throughout history there have been famous women leaders in addition to famous men. The queens of France, Russia, and England can be matched with more recent counterparts such as Golda Meir, Indira Gandhi, and Margaret Thatcher. Yet, most of the research on leadership has focused primarily or entirely on men as leaders. Indeed, a major bibliography of leadership research (Bass, 1981) does not even include sex in the index, although other variables such as race, age, and social class have numerous references. In the past, some researchers have justified this gap by pointing to the absence of women leaders in business, industry, politics, and academics, although the absence of women in these positions has never been as total as some commentators suggest. Accompanying this lack of attention is evidence that pervasive stereotypes exist to the effect that

BOX 15-1. Long-term success of revolutionary leaders

Social psychologists Peter Suedfeld and A. Dennis Rank (1976) hypothesized that, during the phase of initial struggle, revolutionary leaders would need to be cognitively simple—categorical and single-minded in their approach to problems. After the revolution, however, the successful leader might need a broader, more complex view of the world. In an archival study, these investigators tested their hypothesis by analyzing the prerevolution and postrevolution writings of 19 leaders throughout history.

Their hypothesis was supported. Leaders who continued to be prominent after the revolution (such as Cromwell in England, Thomas Jefferson in the United States, Lenin and Stalin in Russia, and Castro in Cuba) showed a shift toward greater complexity. Their themes became more varied and their ideas more complex. In contrast, leaders who did not continue in power after the revolution (such as Alexander Hamilton in the United States, Trotsky in Russia, and Guevara in Cuba) showed little change in their more single-minded statements. ■

women do not make good leaders (Bass, Krusell, & Alexander, 1971; Massengill & DiMarco, 1979; Shein, 1973, 1975). Thus, in the trait approach to leadership, a common, though rarely tested, assumption is that being male is one of the characteristics essential to the good leader.

With the increasing appearance of women in leadership positions in many fields, it has become clear that the assumption of a sex difference in leadership ability must not remain untested. As the research begins to emerge, results are somewhat contradictory (Brown, 1979; Hollander & Yoder, 1980). However, the contradictions seem to fall into place if we consider the difference between assigned leaders and self-selected leaders. Studies that randomly assign men and women to leadership roles frequently find differences, men being more effective in this role than women. Different amounts of experience may be one explanation. In contrast, studies of actual leaders who have emerged naturally in those roles typically show no differences (Hollander, in press). Thus, for people who choose to be leaders, individual differences may be more important than gender.

Also important in considering the influence of gender on leadership behavior is more careful consideration of actual leadership behaviors and the interaction of the leader's personality with the situation. A variety of situational factors may affect a leader's behavior, such as the task demands, the success or failure of the group, and the gender composition of the group (Hollander & Yoder, 1980). Some of these factors may affect men and women differently. Attitudes of subordinates, for example, may be critical to the leader's success, and prevailing stereotypes about women's ineffectiveness as leaders may influence the group outcome. Subordinates may also react differently to the same behavior when performed by a man than by a woman. For example, Jago and Vroom (1982) found that men who were perceived to be autocratic managers were evaluated favorably by group members, whereas autocratic women were viewed negatively. Participative styles of leadership were

PHOTO 15-2. *Indira Gandhi and Margaret Thatcher, two women in leadership position.*

rated favorably, whether performed by a male or a female manager. Thus, male leaders may have greater latitude in their behaviors, being able to gain acceptance from subordinates for a variety of practices. Women, in contrast, may have fewer acceptable options and hence may be more constricted in the behaviors that they can display.

In summary, what leaders do may be as important as who they are. Therefore, let's leave the question "Who is a leader?" and consider "What do leaders do?"

■ II. Leadership behavior

A. Leadership versus the designated leader

The relative futility of the quest for distinguishing traits of leaders had several ramifications. One was a rethinking of the difference between a designated leader and a person who exercised leadership (Stogdill, 1974). During the 1940s and 1950s,

research focused on the *functions* of leaders. The result of these efforts was a new focus on *influence* as the salient aspect of leadership.

From this viewpoint, almost every member of every group has some leadership responsibility. Certainly all members of a football team have some such function—even the water carrier, if the provided refreshment really renews energy, effort, and efficiency. Of course, some group members exert much more influence toward goal attainment than others do. Members of a group, team, or organization can often be rank-ordered according to the amount of influence they exert on each aspect of the group's task. For a football team, the coaching staff and the quarterback may exert the most influence when it comes to selecting plays that are successful in moving the team toward the goal line. When considering inspiration and motivation, some other player may be more important.

An emphasis on goal-oriented functions of leaders is a far cry from the earlier search for personality characteristics that were unique to leaders.

In studying the functions of leadership, the initial research efforts examined what kinds of things leaders actually do. For example, the United States Army adopted 11 "principles of leadership" (Carter, 1952), which Gibb (1969, p. 228) has converted into seven possible behaviors: (1) performing professional and technical specialties, (2) knowing subordinates and showing consideration for them, (3) keeping channels of communication open, (4) accepting personal responsibility and setting an example, (5) initiating and directing action, (6) training people as a team, and (7) making decisions. Similarly, the survey by the Ohio State leadership group (Hemphill & Coons, 1950) proposed nine basic dimensions of the leader's behavior; these are listed in Table 15-1.

B. Actual dimensions of the leader's behavior

So much for analysis; what does a leader actually do? Halpin and Winer (1952) set out to identify empirically the dimensions of a leader's behavior. After constructing questionnaire items and administering them to various sets of group members, the Ohio State researchers did a factor analysis of the responses (Stogdill, 1963). Two major factors of leadership, or clusters of behaviors, emerged: **consideration** and **initiating structure.** These two factors are independent of each other; in other words, a person's standing on one dimension is not related to his or her standing on the other.

Consideration. This dimension of leadership behavior reflects the extent to which the leader shows behavior that is "indicative of friendship, mutual trust, respect, and warmth" in relationships with the other group members (Halpin, 1966, p. 86). Genuine consideration by the leader reflects an awareness of the needs of each member of the group. Leaders high in this behavioral characteristic encourage their coworkers to communicate with them and to share their feelings (Korman, 1966). In Halpin and Winer's study, consideration accounted for almost half of the variability in behavior among different leaders.

TABLE 15-1. Nine proposed dimensions of leader behavior

1. **Initiation.** Described by the frequency with which a leader originates, facilitates, or resists new ideas and new practices.
2. **Membership.** Described by the frequency with which a leader mixes with the group, stresses informal interaction between himself or herself and members, or interchanges personal services with members.
3. **Representation.** Described by the frequency with which the leader defends his or her group against attack, advances the interests of the group, and acts in behalf of the group.
4. **Integration.** Described by the frequency with which a leader subordinates individual behavior, encourages pleasant group atmosphere, reduces conflict between members, or promotes individual adjustment to the group.
5. **Organization.** Described by the frequency with which the leader defines or structures his or her own work, the work of other members, or the relationships among members in the performance of their work.
6. **Domination.** Described by the frequency with which the leader restricts individuals or the group in action, decision making, or expression of opinion.
7. **Communication.** Described by the frequency with which a leader provides information to members, seeks information from them, facilitates exchange of information, or shows awareness of affairs pertaining to the group.
8. **Recognition.** Described by the frequency with which a leader engages in behavior that expresses approval or disapproval of group members.
9. **Production.** Described by the frequency with which a leader sets levels of effort or achievement or prods members for greater effort or achievement.

Initiating structure. A second dimension was called *initiating structure*, which was defined as "the leader's behavior in delineating the relationship between himself and members of the work group and in endeavoring to establish well-defined patterns of organization, channels of communication, and methods of procedure" (Halpin, 1966, p. 86). Thus, initiating structure refers to the leader's task of getting the group moving toward its designated goal. (A part of initiating structure may be identifying and agreeing on the goal.) Initiating structure accounted for about one-third of the variability among leaders.

Other analyses of leadership have produced similar results. Bales (1953), for example, has concluded that leadership has two functions: *task orientation* (or thrust to achieve the group's goals) and *socioemotional orientation* (support of group members' morale and cohesiveness). Because the results of studies by Bales (1958) and others have been independently confirmed, we conclude that *initiating structure* and *consideration* (or similar factors) are two major dimensions of leadership behavior, not simply mutually exclusive leadership patterns (Gibb, 1969). In other words, the leadership process generally involves both of the leadership dimensions or orientations, and people may exhibit both in various degrees.

The most common method of assessing a leader in terms of leadership dimensions is to ask the group members to rate him or her on a set of descriptive statements, reprinted in Table 15-2. These form the Leader Behavior Description Questionnaire (LBDQ), devised by the Personnel Research Board at Ohio State University (Halpin, 1966; Schriesheim & Kerr, 1974; Stogdill, 1963, 1969).

In any organized group—whether it is a professional hockey team, the teaching staff at an elementary school, or a firefighting crew for an oil company—an evaluation can be made of the leader's behavior in terms of initiating structure and showing consideration. It may be difficult for the same person to fulfill both these functions successfully in a single setting. The achievement-oriented leader must often be critical of the group members' ideas or actions; such a leader may constantly turn the members' attention back toward the goal when they digress. At the same time, another member of the organization may become the group-maintenance expert, concerned with arbitrating task-oriented disputes, relieving tensions, and giving every person a pat on the back or a chance to be heard. However, sometimes a particular behavior may achieve both functions; a leader who helps a group solve a difficult problem

---

TABLE 15-2. The leader behavior description questionnaire*

Initiating structure	*Consideration*
1. He makes his attitudes clear to the staff.	1. He does personal favors for staff members.
2. He tries out his new ideas with the staff.	2. He does little things to make it pleasant to be a member of the staff.
3. He rules with an iron hand.[a]	3. He is easy to understand.
4. He criticizes poor work.	4. He finds time to listen to staff members.
5. He speaks in a manner not to be questioned.	5. He keeps to himself.[a]
6. He assigns staff members to particular tasks.	6. He looks out for the personal welfare of individual staff members.
7. He works without a plan.[a]	7. He refuses to explain his actions.[a]
8. He maintains definite standards of performance.	8. He acts without consulting the staff.[a]
9. He emphasizes the meeting of deadlines.	9. He is slow to accept new ideas.[a]
10. He encourages the use of uniform procedures.	10. He treats all staff members as his equals.
11. He makes sure that his part in the organization is understood by all members.	11. He is willing to make changes.
12. He asks that staff members follow standard rules and regulations.	12. He is friendly and approachable.
13. He lets staff members know what is expected of them.	13. He makes staff members feel at ease when talking with them.
14. He sees to it that staff members are working up to capacity.	14. He puts suggestions made by the staff into operation.
15. He sees to it that the work of staff members is coordinated.	15. He gets staff approval on important matters before going ahead.

Each item is answered by checking one of five adverbs: *always, often, occasionally, seldom,* or *never.*
*This questionnaire, developed 20 years ago, fails to recognize that leaders may be female.
[a]Scored negatively.

PHOTO 15-3. *The success of a TV managing editor depends in large part on the person's ability to fulfill the leadership functions of consideration and initiating structure.*

may also, by that action, develop solidarity and better morale (Cartwright & Zander, 1968).

In general, the challenges of successfully fulfilling both leadership functions are considerable. (You may wish to consider, for example, how many presidents of the United States or prime ministers of Canada were successful in "getting the country moving again" at the same time that they were "bringing people together.") However, although the combination of behaviors may be difficult, leaders are rated as being most effective when they rank high on both dimensions (Stogdill, 1974).

Group performance level has also been shown to relate to leadership-skill ratings. For example, pupils of Canadian teachers who were rated highly on both consideration and initiating structure scored higher on provincewide examinations (Greenfield & Andrews, 1961). Even the rank of the school principals on these two dimensions was related to the performance of the students (Keeler

& Andrews, 1963). In another study, Hemphill (1955) asked faculty members at a liberal arts college to name the five departments in the college that had the reputation of being the best led or administered and the five departments that were least well administered. Faculty members in each department then rated their department head on the LBDQ. As shown in Figure 15-1, the department's administrative rating was consistent with the ratings that its staff gave the leader. In an entirely different setting, Korean War aircraft commanders were rated on overall effectiveness by their superiors (including a performance assessment of each commander's group), while their crews completed the LBDQ (Halpin, 1953, 1954). Once again, the relation between leadership effectiveness rating and group performance level held. Of the nine commanders who were rated in the upper 10% of overall effectiveness by their

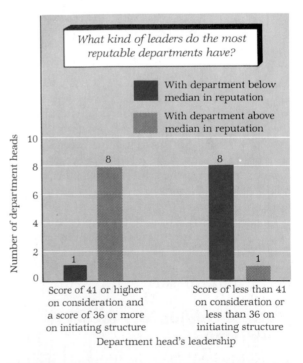

FIGURE 15-1. Relation between the reputation achieved by college departments and the consideration and initiating-structure scores of department heads taken conjunctively

superiors, eight were above the mean on both consideration and initiating structure, according to their crews. Of the ten commanders who were rated least effective, more fell below the mean than above the mean on both dimensions of leader behavior.

However, despite the results of the preceding studies, some questions remain. Stogdill, for example, summarizes the findings of these studies as follows: "The significance of consideration and structure is to be explained, not in terms of leadership, but in terms of followership. The two patterns of behavior emerge as important, not because they are exhibited by the leader, but because they produce differential effects on the behavior and expectations of followers" (1974, p. 141). Others have argued that the LBDQ does not provide ratings of actual leader behavior but instead reflects the *implicit leadership theories* of the person doing the rating (Lord, Binning, Rush, & Thomas, 1978; Rush, Thomas, & Lord, 1977). According to this explanation, most of us have an idea of what "appropriate" leadership behavior is, and even with minimal information about the leader, we will give high ratings when performance is good and low ratings when performance is poor. Such an explanation does not mean that real leader behaviors are not the source of *some* of the findings for the LBDQ ratings, but it does caution us against assuming that the questionnaire ratings are a completely accurate representation of behavior. One obvious solution to the problem of whether ratings reflect actual behavior or people's ideas about ideal leader behavior is to observe actual leadership behavior, rather than to rely solely on questionnaire ratings by group members. Although this approach is difficult and time-consuming, it is necessary if we are to fully understand the dynamics of leadership behavior.

■ III. A contingency theory of leadership

The early research on basic personality traits of leaders was followed by a more functional approach to the topic, in which leadership *behaviors* became more important than the leaders' personality traits.

But a functional analysis was not enough to fully understand leadership behavior. Not until the 1960s—beginning with the work of Fred E. Fiedler—was attention directed squarely at both the leader *and* the situation in which that leader must operate. (Box 15-2, pp. 402–403, presents an analysis of U.S. presidential effectiveness that considers both the leader and the situation.)

Fiedler (1967) defines the leader as the individual in the group who is given the task of directing and coordinating task-relevant activities or who—in the absence of a designated leader—carries the primary responsibility for performing these functions in a group. Fiedler's theory is called a *contingency theory of leadership* because it relates the effectiveness of the leader to aspects of the group's situation. Specifically, the theory predicts that the leader's contribution to group effectiveness depends on both the characteristics of the leader and the favorableness of the situation (Graen, Alvares, Orris, & Martella, 1970). To Fiedler, there is no one successful type of leader; task-oriented leaders may be effective under some circumstances but not under others. A permissive leader who is oriented toward human relations and who has been successful with one group may not be successful in a different group.

A. Elements of Fiedler's contingency model

There are four basic components in Fiedler's contingency model. One of these refers to the personality of the leader, whereas the other three describe characteristics of the situation in which the leader must lead. Let's consider the personality component first. To Fiedler, this means leadership style, which is defined as "the underlying need-structure of the individual that motivates his behavior in various leadership situations" (Graen et al., 1970, p. 286). Leadership style is assessed by the extent of the leader's esteem or liking for his or her "least preferred coworker," called the LPC measure. Each leader is asked to think of all the people with whom he or she has ever worked and then to select the one with whom it has been most difficult to cooperate. This person is the "least preferred coworker," or LPC. The leader is then given a set of bipolar rating scales and is asked to rate this least preferred coworker on each of the dimensions listed. Examples of these dimensions include pleasant/unpleasant, friendly/unfriendly, and rejecting/accepting (Fiedler, 1967).

The LPC score may be thought of as an indication of a leader's emotional reaction to people with whom he or she could not work well (Fiedler, 1972). Low-LPC leaders, who rate their least preferred coworker quite negatively, are considered to be task-oriented administrators, who gain satisfaction and self-esteem from the group's completion of its tasks, even if the leader personally must suffer unpleasant interpersonal relationships for the tasks to be completed. For these leaders, a poorly performing coworker is a major threat to self-esteem. In contrast, high-LPC leaders (who rate their least preferred coworker more favorably) are more concerned about interpersonal relationships. To high-LPC leaders, satisfaction comes from happy group relationships; they are more relaxed, compliant, and nondirective. Low performance by a coworker is not terribly threat-

ening, and hence that worker is not rated as negatively. Thus, high-LPC and low-LPC leaders seek to satisfy different basic needs in a group. In a review of the LPC research, Rice (1978) describes the two types of leaders as differing in their basic value orientation. High-LPC leaders value interpersonal success more than low-LPC leaders do, and they tend to base a wide range of judgments about themselves, others, and the environment on interpersonal success. Low-LPC leaders, in contrast, value task success more than high-LPC leaders do, and their judgments are correspondingly based on task considerations.

As we noted before, the contingency model does not consider just the personality of the leader. Rather, contingency theory is important because it assumes an interaction between the situation and the characteristics of the leader; both of these factors, according to Fiedler, play a role in determining the nature of the leader's influence as well as the extent of the leader's effectiveness. The three basic situational components of the contingency model are (1) leader/member relations, (2) task

PHOTO 15-4. *An orchestra conductor, like any other kind of leader, may be effective in some situations and less effective in others.*

BOX 15-2. Leadership: The case of presidential effectiveness

In recent U.S. history, presidents have often been in trouble. Elected with mandates of varying strengths, presidents inevitably decline in popularity as their terms progress. Every modern U.S. president has been endorsed less favorably at the end of his term than he was at the beginning.

Why are evaluations of presidential effectiveness so negative? The most popular explanation is a dispositional one, reflecting the *fundamental attribution error* (see Chapter 4). Both the citizens and the media are most likely to explain events in terms of the person—in this case, in terms of the president. In contrast to this dispositional explanation, Wrightsman (1982) has suggested that we consider the nature of the task as well as the character of the president.

structure, and (3) leader position power.

1. *Leader/member relations.* The leader's personal relations with members of his or her organization can range from very good to very poor. Some leaders are liked and respected by their group, whereas others may be disliked, distrusted, or even completely rejected. Fiedler proposes that this general group atmosphere is the most important single factor determining the leader's influence in a small group (Fiedler, 1964).

2. *Task structure.* The amount of structure in the task that the group has been assigned, often on an order "from above," can vary widely. Some tasks have a great deal of *goal clarity*; that is, the requirements of the task are clearly known or programmed. For example, the factory team assembling a car or a refrigerator has little doubt about what it is supposed to do. Other tasks, such as those of ad hoc committees, policy-making groups, and creative groups, often lack goal clarity and structure—no one knows exactly what the group purposes are or how the group should proceed. A second element of task structure concerns *solution specificity*—that is, whether there is more than one way to complete the task. A third element of task structure is *decision verifiability*: once a decision has been made, how clearly does the group know that the decision is a correct one? All these aspects of task structure play a role in determining

The modern presidency is far more complex than its predecessors were. For example, F. D. Roosevelt had a White House staff of 37, whereas recent presidents have had staffs of as many as 600. The role of the media has become much more important, highlighting even minor actions of an incumbent president. The numbers of government agencies and private lobbyists have both increased as well. This increasing complexity may mean that no single person could do the job well. The person who can do well on some aspects of the job may be a dismal failure at others—and all failures will undoubtedly be noted by at least some segments of the population!

Wrightsman (1982) has suggested that ten task dimensions are central to presidential leadership:

1. Persuading the nation
2. Providing moral leadership
3. Appearing "presidential"
4. Identifying goals and priorities
5. Maintaining the ongoing activities of the executive branch
6. Getting legislation passed
7. Determining and conducting foreign policy
8. Managing the White House staff
9. Crisis decision making
10. Providing political-party leadership

In the spirit of Fiedler's contingency model, Wrightsman suggests that both situational and personal factors may determine effective leadership. Consider the fourth goal, for example. Identification of priorities may be easier in a situation in which the electoral mandate was strong or at a time when conflicts within the country are minimal. On the personal side, identification of priorities may be easier for the leader who has strong internal values, who has considerable experience in government, or who can easily see the "big picture." If *either* the situation is not right *or* the leader is not able to define these priorities, effectiveness may be low.

We can also identify in these ten dimensions aspects that may be incompatible. For example, to maintain the ongoing activities of the executive branch, a president may need to be concerned with detail and bureaucracy. In contrast, identifying goals may require the sacrifice of detail for the broader picture. Rarely will a single individual have both sets of skills developed to a high degree.

What can be done? There are no easy answers, no quick resolutions. Recognition that task and situation are indispensable elements of leadership, however, may allow a clearer conception of what presidential effectiveness can be. ∎

the effectiveness of different types of leaders.

3. *Position power.* A third major component of the contingency model is the power and authority inherent in the leadership position. Does the leader have the authority to hire and fire? Can the leader reward persons by giving raises in pay or status, or is he or she limited in means of regulating the behavior of group members? Does the organization back up the leader's authority? For example, the person in charge of a group of volunteer workers in a political campaign would ordinarily have little position power over the volunteers. A football coach, an owner of a small business, and a police chief will often carry high degrees of position power.

B. Putting the elements together

Now that we have defined each of the four components of Fiedler's contingency model, how do we fit the parts together? For purposes of simplification and analysis, Fiedler considers each of the last three components to be dichotomous. Leader/member relationships are either good or poor; task structure is either clear or unclear; and position power is either strong or weak. Because there are two categories in each of these situational components, we may conceive of a system of eight classifications (2 × 2 × 2), which would encompass all their possible combinations. Fiedler has then arranged these eight classifications on a dimension of favorability to the leader, as shown in Figure 15-2, on the basis of his specific assumptions about the importance of each classification.

Favorable conditions emerge from situations that permit the leader to exert a great deal of influence on the group. For example, good leader/member relations, strong position power, and clear task structure are considered favorable for the leader in a general sense. In contrast, poor leader/member relations, an unstructured task, and weak position power are considered unfavorable.

This is only the first part of the story, however. The second part concerns how the personality style of the leader relates to the different conditions of favorability. Fiedler hypothesizes that low-LPC leaders (the task-oriented, controlling types) are most effective under group conditions that are either *very favorable* (classes I, II, and III) or *very unfavorable* (classes VII and VIII). In other words, the low-LPC leader is most effective when he or she has either a great deal of influence and power or

almost no influence or power. In contrast, high-LPC leaders (the relationship-oriented types) are most effective under conditions that are *moderately favorable or unfavorable* and in which the leader's influence and power are mixed or moderate (classes IV, V, VI). These predictions are also shown in Figure 15-2, where the predicted correlations between leader LPC score and group performance are graphed.

Many studies have supported Fiedler's contingency model of leadership (Strube & Garcia, 1981). In perhaps the strongest of these studies, Chemers and Skrzypek (1972), using West Point cadets as subjects, composed four-man groups that differed in leader position power, leader/member relations, and LPC scores. The investigators designated the leaders and asked each group to perform one structured and one unstructured task. These investigators found that the eight conditions of favorability and the LPC scores corresponded almost perfectly to the model. In a more limited

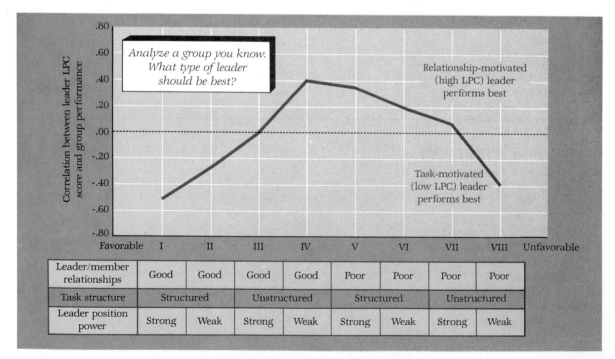

FIGURE 15-2. The contingency model of leadership and group performance.

test of the model, focusing only on class II, Schneier (1978) observed students enrolled in a personnel management course and allowed leaders to emerge naturally. As Fiedler's model would predict, those persons who emerged as leaders had lower LPC scores than the average group member; in fact, in 74% of the groups, the eventual leader had the lowest score among the four or five persons in the group. It is also of interest that this study found similar patterns for both male and female leaders, thus extending the general validity of the model.

The most basic conclusion of Fiedler's massive research program is that there is no such thing as a good leader for all situations. "A leader who is effective in one situation may or may not be in another" (Fiedler, 1969, p. 42). For example, consider a laboratory group in a chemistry class where the task structure is very clear (the instructor has made a definite assignment) but the position power of the group leader is weak (he or she has little authority to make decisions or assign grades). Who would be the best type of leader in this situation? It would depend on the leader/member relations, defining the group as either a class II or a class VI. If leader/member relations were good, a task-oriented leader (with a low LPC score) would probably do the best job. In contrast, if leader/member relations were poor, a high-LPC leader should elicit a better performance from the group. Just these kinds of comparisons have been made in testing the model. For example, high school basketball teams (defined as having a structured task and weak position power) with good relationships between the captain and the other team members win more games if the captain is a task-oriented leader (Fiedler, 1964). You might want to analyze some of the groups that you belong to in terms of these dimensions and consider how the style of the leader leads to effective or ineffective performance of your group.

C. Leadership and change

What if a leader is not effective? Are there ways to change the situation or the leader in order to improve group performance? Fiedler believes it is more fruitful to try to change the leader's work environment than to try to change his or her personality or leadership style. In fact, Fiedler and his colleagues (Fiedler, Chemers, & Mahar, 1976) have developed a leadership training program (called "LEADERMATCH") that helps leaders define and create situations in which they are most effective. For example, a leader can volunteer for structured or ambiguous task assignments and thus achieve the preferred level of task structure; power in a group can be shifted according to autocratic or participatory principles; and a leader can influence leader/member relationships by either socializing or remaining aloof. Fiedler reports that in a series of validation studies using Army cadets, middle managers, police sergeants, and leaders of Latin American volunteer public health organizations, leaders trained by the LEADERMATCH system are consistently more effective than untrained control-group leaders (Fiedler, 1978). Although this approach probably represents a more direct attack on the problem of training effective leaders, other social scientists report that the application of positive reinforcement, dissonance, reactance, and other psychological principles can be successful in modifying the personality and behavior of the leader (Varela, 1969). In fact, the distinction between leadership style and specific leader behaviors may not be as clear as Fiedler's model suggests, and consequently certain changes may alter the characteristics of both the leader's personality *and* the leader's group situation.

Fiedler's contingency model is static; it appears to assume that leaders influence the group but that the group or organization has little or no effect on the leader. Recently, however, Fiedler (1978) has begun to deal with this issue and is formulating a more dynamic theory of the leadership process. One example of this new approach is provided by a study of ROTC students at the University of Utah before and after training in a cryptogram task (Chemers, Rice, Sundstrom, & Butler, 1975). At both times, the leader/member relationships were poor and the leader position had little power. However, as a result of training, the task structure shifted from weak to strong. Correspondingly, as shown in Figure 15-3, the effectiveness of the two types of leaders changed as well. Although rela-

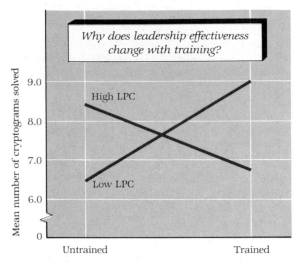

FIGURE 15-3. Task performance by high- and low-LPC leaders with and without task training.

tionship-oriented leaders performed better in the untrained condition, task-oriented leaders were superior after the task was learned. These results point out the importance of recognizing that groups and organizations are not static but instead may be constantly changing.

■ IV. Interaction of leaders and followers

Leadership is not a one-way street. As Fillmore Sanford noted more than 30 years ago, "Not only is it the follower who accepts or rejects leadership, but it is the follower who *perceives* both the leader and the situation and who reacts in terms of what he perceives" (1950, p. 4). Any complete understanding of leadership must therefore include knowledge of followers as well as leaders—knowledge of how the followers perceive the leader and how their behavior may alter the leader's behavior. This is a much more process-oriented approach than that of the contingency model. Like the critics who rejected the Shannon and Weaver model of communication (see Chapter 5), critics of the traditional models of leadership emphasize *process* and *transaction* in their attempt to define their topic of study.

A. Perceptions of leadership

Although the investigator of leadership may specify certain dimensions of leadership and manipulate those dimensions with some precision in the laboratory, it does not necessarily follow that people will perceive leaders according to those dimensions. Pfeffer (1978), in fact, suggests that leadership may be an ephemeral phenomenon—that much of what we call *leadership* is based on the attributions of observers rather than on any real behavior of the designated leader. Pfeffer argues that in any real organization there are innumerable constraints on the leader's effectiveness. In analyzing the effects of individual mayors on city budgets, for example, Salancik and Pfeffer (1977) found that characteristics of the government structure and the particular year had more influence on budget allocations than the individuals who occupied the position of mayor.

Despite evidence to the contrary, however, we tend to think that the leader's personality is important. Why? Pfeffer suggests that we tend to attribute events to the leader because the leader is a more visible cause; the environment may be so complex that it is difficult to pinpoint environmental causes of events. As an example, Gamson and Scotch (1964) noted how the manager of a baseball team serves as a scapegoat when the team is performing poorly. It's unlikely that the owner would fire the whole team, or even a substantial portion of it, even if there were evidence that many players were performing poorly. In contrast, it's easy, if not always effective, to focus on the manager as the cause of the poor performance.

Recalling our discussion of implicit personality theories and schemata in Chapter 4, we may think about the kinds of images people have of leaders. These images may or may not be based on actual performance, but it is likely that they influence the evaluation of any particular leader. Foti and her colleagues, for example, have found that people have rather clear **prototypes** of the effective political leader (Foti, Fraser, & Lord, 1982). Characteristics associated with an *effective* political leader differ from the more general category of political leader in a number of respects. For example, the effective political leader is viewed as more intelligent, as displaying better judgment, and as more sympathetic to the problems of the poor, more likely to side with the average citizen, and more likely to have a well-defined program for moving the country ahead. In another comparison, this time between political leaders and the even more general category of leader, other characteristics were found to differentiate the two categories. Political leaders were seen as more likely to be religious and more sympathetic to the poor than leaders in general were.

It is quite likely that there are also distinct prototypes for other types of leaders—for religious leaders, for athletic coaches, and for business executives. Knowing more about the content of these prototypes might allow us to understand how subordinates evaluate their leaders in different settings.

B. Reactions to a leader's behavior

Followers may react to a leader's behavior because that behavior does or does not fit their prototype of a good leader. Other factors can affect the reactions of subordinates as well. One important facet is the basis of the leader's authority—specifically, whether that leader was appointed by some outside agent or elected by the members. In general, it appears that an elected leader will create a greater sense of responsibility and higher expectations in subordinates (Hollander, in press). In such cases, the leader must be competent and the group must be successful in order for the group to endorse his or her performance. For the appointed leader, either individual competence *or* group success may be sufficient for group endorsement. Further, research by Hollander and Julian (1970, 1978) suggests that the elected leader is also more apt to be deposed—for example, when group failure violates the expectations that were held.

Similar kinds of expectations may also affect perceptions of behavior by female and male leaders. Fallon and Hollander (1976), for example, found that female leaders were perceived as less influential than male leaders, although the actual performance of the group was the same in both cases. Sometimes, however, the different expectations that people tend to have of male and female

leaders may work against the male. Jacobson and Effertz (1974) found that when a group failed, male leaders were judged more harshly than female leaders, presumably because more was expected of the male leader. At the same time, female *followers* were evaluated more negatively than male followers. Again, if we can assume that people think women are better followers, then their failure in such a role is judged more stringently than a similar failure by a male.

Followers evaluate their leaders not only by outcomes but by procedures as well. Hence, it is important that the follower see the actions of the leader as fair. Laboratory studies show that outcomes and procedures are equally important. In an experiment by Tyler and Caine (1981), residents of Evanston, Illinois, were asked to evaluate the actions of a hypothetical councilman with regard to a controversial housing rule. Residents were given information on how the councilman voted (the outcome) and the basis for his decision. In the unfair condition, the vote was described as being based solely on the councilman's personal feelings about the issue. In the fair condition, the vote was presumably based on the feedback received at a town meeting. As Figure 15-4 shows, both

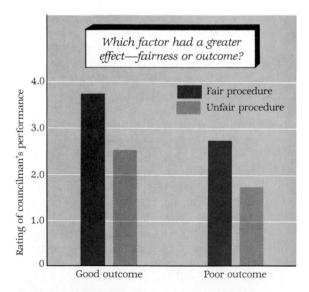

FIGURE 15-4. Effects of procedure and outcome on the evaluation of a leader.

outcome and procedure affected subjects' ratings of the councilman's performance. Thus, even when the outcome was good—in other words, consistent with the respondent's own views—performance was devalued if the procedure to reach that outcome was perceived to be unfair.

Although these subjects took both outcome and fairness into account when evaluating the leader, further studies by Tyler and Caine suggest that fairness may be even more important than outcome in some situations. Asking students to evaluate actual political leaders and actions of the government, these investigators found that perceptions of fairness outweighed the value of the outcome. In other words, although people are capable of taking both factors into account, actual judgments of leaders may depend more on perceptions of justice in the actions of those leaders. Anecdotal support of this conclusion is found in a statement by former British Prime Minister Harold Macmillan, who was asked to evaluate the performance of General Eisenhower during World War II. The one indispensable quality that Eisenhower had, according to Macmillan, was fairness (Hollander, in press).

Perceptions of the leader may affect future actions by group members. For example, suppose that the members of a group perceive the leader's behavior to be inequitable. Perhaps the leader takes more of the credit for a group performance than he or she deserves, or perhaps when salaries are determined, the leader allocates an unfairly small proportion of the total resources to the group and a large proportion to himself or herself. Not surprisingly, followers in such a situation reduce their endorsement of the leader (Hollander & Julian, 1970; Michener & Lawler, 1975). They may also go further—acting on their perceptions of inequity by revolting against the leader and forming coalitions to counter the leader's behavior (Lawler & Thompson, 1978). Such revolts are much more likely to occur when the group members see the leader as responsible for the inequitable decision, rather than when the responsibility can be attributed to someone else—for example, when organizational policy is seen as constraining the lead-

er's options (Lawler & Thompson, 1978). Group members may even choose to depose their leader. Although a crisis may temporarily increase the influence of the leader, particularly if that leader was elected by the group, continued failure will lead to dissatisfaction and an eventual ouster, if the group has the power to depose the leader (Hollander, Fallon, & Edwards, 1977).

C. Influence of followers on the leader's behavior

It is clear that a good leader must pay attention to reactions of the group members. In fact, Weick (1978) has suggested that a good leader should act as a medium, able to take in messages of various types from various sources and to reflect an understanding of those messages in subsequent behavior.

Even if the leader is not aware of all the messages coming from subordinates and the general system, there is considerable evidence that these messages can still significantly influence the leader's behavior. For example, Fodor (1978) found that supervisors adopted a more authoritarian style of control when they were faced with a stressful situation than when the situation involved less stress. Other studies have shown that situational demands will cause different effects, depending on the personality characteristics of the leader. When the situational demands of the situation increase, task-oriented leaders show less structure and instead begin to increase their consideration and concern for people. In the same situation, interaction-oriented leaders will show a decrease in social behaviors and an increased concern for task considerations (Stogdill, 1974).

Leadership is not a static process. There is a constant interchange between leaders and followers (Katz & Kahn, 1978), and each is influenced by the other in an ongoing process. Neither events nor leadership styles are static, and the shifting patterns that exist in an organizational setting provide a fascinating testing ground for the social scientist interested in dynamic, transactional processes.

V. SUMMARY

In the early search for characteristics that distinguished leaders from nonleaders, little consistency was found from one study to another. Although no single leadership trait has been consistently identified, there is a cluster of behaviors that are more typical of leaders than nonleaders: drive for responsibility, vigor and persistence, originality, initiative, self-confidence, willingness to accept consequences and to tolerate stress and frustration, ability to influence, and capacity to structure tasks.

Attempts to explain the emergence of great political leaders have considered both the charismatic qualities of the leader and the *Zeitgeist*, or the temper of the times.

Designated leaders of groups have two major functions: initiating structure and consideration. *Initiating structure* refers to the leader's behavior in identifying the group's goal and moving the group toward the goal. *Consideration* refers to the leader's concern with relationships between himself or herself and other group members. Leaders are rated as more effective when they are considered to fill both functions well.

Fiedler's contingency theory of leadership emphasizes that there is no one successful type of leader. The four basic components of Fiedler's model are the personality of the leader, leader/member relations, task structure, and position power. Depending on the favorability of the situation, either a task-oriented or an interaction-oriented leader may be more effective. Changes in the situation may allow a particular leader to become more effective.

Leaders and followers must be viewed as interacting in order to understand group behavior. The attributions that subordinates make about the leader's behavior will affect the group process and can alter the leader's behavior as well.

GLOSSARY TERMS

consideration

leadership
initiating structure

prototype

16

Intergroup Relations

We must try to trust one another. Stay and cooperate.
■ JOMO KENYATTA

We were wedded together on the basis of mutual work and goals.
■ JUDY CHICAGO

Groups, as we noted in the previous chapter, are numerous in our society—families, athletic teams, clubs, and work organizations. Each of these groups has its own goals, which members pursue with varying degrees of motivation and commitment. Yet, just as individuals are not isolated, neither are groups. Often groups come into contact with one another, and sometimes conflict is the result.

Examples of such conflict are all too numerous, both in literature and in reality. Shakespeare's Montagues and Capulets find more modern descendants in the 19th-century Hatfields and McCoys, who waged a 50-year feud over the theft of some pigs. Wars between the Spartans and the Athenians are echoed in current conflicts, whether they be between the United States and the Soviet Union, the Iranians and the Iraqis, or numerous other parties to international conflict. Within many Western countries, labor and management exemplify two groups that must continually negotiate to accomplish their sometimes shared and often opposing goals. Evidence of such negotiations can be seen in groups as diverse as professional athletes, steel and auto workers, and elementary school teachers, each engaged in recurrent negotiations with their respective managers. In other cases, negotiation may be less formal but the conflicts as great or greater, as in relations among Whites, Blacks, and other ethnic groups or between women and men.

These situations of conflict and potential conflict, so readily found in our society, present a real challenge to those who wish to understand human behavior. As the late British psychologist Henri Tajfel stated, "Intergroup relations represent in their enormous scope one of the most difficult and complex knots of problems which we confront in our times" (1982, p. 1). It is those problems that we will consider in this chapter.

First, however, we should specify exactly what is meant by the term **intergroup behavior.** Following the lead of Sherif and Sherif (1979), we offer the following definition: "Whenever individ-

PHOTO 16-1. *Intergroup conflict often takes place in a very public arena.*

uals belonging to one group interact, collectively or individually, with another group or its members in terms of their group identification, we have an instance of intergroup behavior" (p. 9). The emphasis on *group* in this definition is important, for it alerts us to some of the critical issues in the study of intergroup relations. If I as an individual dislike management or am frustrated with my boss, this would not be an example of intergroup relations. However, if I as a union member take up particular issues with my boss, conscious both of my union membership and of his or her role as a representative of management, then *intergroup relations* would be an appropriate term. In other words, individual actions may be an important part of intergroup relations, *if* those actions are influenced by the stance or values of some larger group.

For a situation to be an example of intergroup relations, each group must recognize the existence of the other (Tajfel, 1982). Thus, a group must have its own sense of identity and must be recognized by outsiders as a group as well. To take the union/management example one step further, if my boss does not recognize the existence of unions and will deal with me only as an individual, then a true state of intergroup relations does not exist, even though I may feel strongly identified with a union.

In this chapter we will explore a variety of issues related to intergroup behavior. First we will consider the influence of minority-group members within a larger group. Then we will look at how different groups view each other and how intergroup conflict develops. Strategies of interaction between groups will be considered, including cooperation, competition, negotiation, and third-party intervention. Finally, on a more optimistic note, we will consider how conflict can be reduced, reviewing some of the strategies that have proved successful in different arenas.

■ I. The role of the active minority

Although the major focus of this chapter is on relations between two separate and identifiable groups, we should give some notice to the situation in which a minority within a group challenges the majority. Such cases fall in between the individual group, in which all members are united on a single goal or set of goals, and the true case of intergroup relations, in which both groups have clear and separate identities.

A. How do minorities form?

Although a group may clearly define goals for itself, it often happens that not all members agree with those goals. As we saw in Chapter 14, the process of group socialization is one in which individual members assimilate to the group goals and the group accommodates to the individual. However, particular stances or changes in policy may cause some members of the group to feel at odds with the group goals. If these members band together, forming a social identification with one another and distinguishing themselves from the larger group, then a process similar to the intergroup situation occurs.

On other occasions, visible signs may make one or more members of a group distinct from the others. As we saw in Chapter 4, certain characteristics of individuals may make them salient— easily distinguishable from the other members of the group. Blacks in a predominantly White organization, for example, or women in predominantly male organizations may be viewed by members of the majority as a recognizable subgroup. Further, as Kanter (1977) has described, people who are viewed this way by others may themselves become more aware of their differences from the majority group members, thus defining themselves as a minority group.

A person may be in the minority for more than one reason. Maass, Clark, and Haberkorn (1982) have made a distinction between "single" and "double" minorities. In their terms, a "single" minority is someone who deviates from the majority only in terms of belief. As an example, they suggest the antiwar students of the middle 1960s, most of whom were from the White middle class of the United States. A "double" minority is a person who differs both in beliefs and in category membership—as an example, a member of the

Black Panthers during the same mid-sixties period.

The person who is in the minority by virtue of some ascribed characteristic, such as race or gender, has little choice about being seen as a minority, at least initially. In stating their beliefs, these minority members may choose to increase or decrease the distance between themselves and the dominant group. For the person who is similar in ascribed characteristics but who differs in values, minority status may not be labeled so quickly by the majority group. Whatever the basis of minority status, the member of the minority must choose whether to adopt the goals and principles of the majority, to try to influence the majority, or to leave the group. In some cases, however, if the constraints in a situation are strong, leaving the group may not be an easy alternative. For Black Americans, as an example, it is not easy to completely avoid participating in the White system, even though partial avoidance may be possible.

B. Minority-group influence

Students of social influence have long recognized the possibility of discrepant views among members of a group. In Chapter 12, for example, we considered how a minority could be influenced by the majority, as the naive individual frequently conformed to the majority members' judgments of lengths of lines even though those judgments were incorrect. Only recently, however, has attention been given to the influence that a minority can exert on the majority. The French social psychologist Serge Moscovici (1976) has been the major contributor to this awareness.

How can a minority influence a majority? Latané and Wolf (1981) suggest that minority influence operates in much the same way as majority influence. Recalling the model of *social impact* discussed in Chapter 14, we can think of minority influence as being determined by the strength, the immediacy, and the number of minority-group members. A minority will be more effective when its members have higher status or greater ability, when they are closer to the majority in space or time, and when their numbers are larger.

According to Moscovici, the success of a minority depends on the inferences that members of the majority group make about the minority members and their alternative position. A minority that presents a united front may cause the majority to attribute strong beliefs and commitment to the minority group. Having made such an inference, the majority group will be less resistant to change. In order for the minority group to create this impression, Moscovici suggests, the *behavioral style* of the members is important. According to Moscovici, they should appear to be consistent, to be invested in their position, to have autonomy and to be able to stand up for their beliefs, to be somewhat rigid, and to be fair. A tall order, it would seem, and one that has not been adequately tested in research to date.

Most research dealing with behavioral style has focused on the idea of behavioral consistency, predicting that a minority that consistently stated its position would be more successful in influencing the majority. There is some support for this prediction (Nemeth, 1979). However, research also suggests that particular situational factors can moderate this effect (Mugny, 1975; Wolf, 1979), and on some occasions a negotiating style may be more effective than inflexible presentation. Sometimes, for example, an active and consistent minority may "go too far," alienating the majority and resulting in exclusion of the minority from the group—becoming a definite out-group in the eyes of the majority (Di Giacomo, 1980).

The specific determinants of the majority's reaction to a minority—whether it is accepting, rejecting, or disregarding—are still a long way from being clearly identified. The questions are interesting, however, as they provide a bridge from the case of one group containing different factions to the true case of intergroup relations, in which the members belong to two distinctly different groups.

■ II. The nature of intergroup relations

When two groups come in contact, there are a number of predictable consequences. Some of these effects can be seen in the way that members of one group view the other, often simplifying and distorting the characteristics of the other group.

Other effects can be seen in the internal workings of each individual group. Let us look in more detail at some of these patterns.

A. Views of the in-group and out-group

As we learned in Chapter 4, people often form stereotypes about members of other groups—schemata that may include a variety of traits and behaviors expected to be characteristic of members of a particular identifiable group. Further, in the case of a distinction between in-groups and out-groups, we have seen that people tend to simplify their view of members of the out-group, seeing all members of that group as being rather similar (Linville, 1982; Park & Rothbart, 1982). To state this in more formal terms, Tajfel suggests that we see members of the out-group as "undifferentiated items in a unified social category" (1982, p. 13).

In intergroup relations, the in-group's views often serve as a reference point whereby an out-group is judged. This phenomenon is known as **ethnocentrism.** As originally defined by the sociologist William Sumner in 1906, ethnocentrism is the "view of things in which one's own group is the center of everything, and all others are scaled and rated with reference to it" (quoted in Brewer, 1979b, p. 71). In a descriptive passage, Sumner goes on to say: "Each group nourishes its own pride and vanity, boasts itself superior, exalts its own divinities, and looks with contempt on outsiders. Each group thinks its own folkways the only right ones, and if it observes that other groups have other folkways, these excite its scorn" (quoted in Brewer, 1979b, p. 71).

Subsequent research has shown ethnocentrism to be somewhat more complex than Sumner so eloquently described it. Sometimes, there is a decided in-group bias, reflecting Sumner's position. Cross-cultural studies, for example, have shown that there appears to be a universal tendency to view one's own group as morally superior and more worthy of trust (Brewer, 1979b). On numerous other dimensions, however, in-groups do not necessarily describe the out-group in more negative terms than they describe themselves (Brewer, 1979b; Tajfel, 1982). In some cases, members of an in-group may recognize that their own position is less favorable than the out-group's. Rather than deny that distinction, the in-group may instead choose simply to minimize the difference between the two groups, seeing them as less dissimilar than outsiders perhaps would (Brewer, 1979b).

Because an in-group recognizes that it is not necessarily better on *all* dimensions, there is often a tendency to choose those dimensions for comparison that favor one's in-group over the out-group. In concluding a discussion of this issue, Brewer accordingly suggests that "perhaps the essence of ethnocentrism is this tendency to expect that the outgroup will share the ingroup's definition of the conflict or distinction between them and will be willing to make comparisons in terms that favor the ingroup" (1979b, p. 84).

To look more specifically at perceptions of in-groups and out-groups, let's consider the views of Blacks and Whites. This in-group/out-group distinction is often associated most closely with the United States, but in fact its existence is more widespread. Recently in Great Britain, for example, Hewstone and Jaspars (1982) looked at people's explanations of racial discrimination. Both Black (mostly West Indian) and White male working-class adolescents were asked to answer questions about race-related situations in England. For example, one item on the questionnaire stated "Many more Black people than White people get arrested on suspicion charges." The boys were then asked to what degree this situation (a true one) was the result of (1) Black people's making more trouble than White people and (2) the police's being racist. Other questions dealt with unemployment rates, proportion of managerial jobs, and educational opportunities. The results of this study, summarizing across the four areas questioned, are shown in Figure 16-1. As can be seen, Black subjects were very strong in their tendency to see White representatives of "the system" as the chief cause of racial discrimination. White subjects tended to divide the blame evenly, although they saw Blacks as more responsible, and Whites as less responsible, than the Black subjects did.

Within the United States, numerous studies have considered the views that Blacks and Whites have

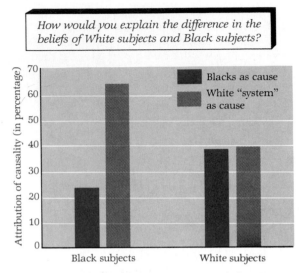

How would you explain the difference in the beliefs of White subjects and Black subjects?

FIGURE 16-1. Perceived causes of racial discrimination in England.

of each other. Most recently, some investigators have looked at the perceptions of equal opportunity for Blacks, following the efforts in recent years to create greater opportunities and to implement affirmative action programs. Some of these perceptions seem inconsistent. For example, in a recent survey of more than 1300 White people in the United States, 18 years and over (Kluegel & Smith, 1982), the majority believed that there was some discrimination against Blacks and other minorities, but a majority also believed that the chances for Blacks and other minorities to get ahead, compared with the average person in the country, were average or better (see Figure 16-2).

Kluegel and Smith's findings (1982, 1983) suggest that the majority of White citizens do not believe that there are important structural limits to Blacks' opportunities and that many, in fact, think the chances for Blacks are better than they are for the average citizen. Kluegel and Smith suggest that many White citizens see their own opportunities as plentiful and regard the U.S. opportunity structure as a fair one. In considering an issue such as poverty, for example, Whites therefore tend to deny structural causes for such a state. Consequently, when seeking explanations for the cause of Black poverty, Whites often see the other person's posi-

tion in the stratification system as the result of individual ability and effort—or the lack thereof. Further, as a result of such beliefs, Whites may feel that specific affirmative action programs are not needed, given the equality of opportunity that they believe exists (Kluegel & Smith, 1983).

B. Differences in power between in-groups and out-groups

In Chapter 12 we discussed forms of power that may be in effect between two individuals. In intergroup relations, issues of power also come into play (Apfelbaum, 1979). Often, though not always, two groups confront each other with different levels of power and potential influence or with different kinds of power. For example, in labor/management conflicts, management typically has the financial resources, but labor can shut down operations. As we will see in Section III of this chapter, groups that have equal power are generally more effective in bargaining and negotiation.

When groups do not have equal power, negotiation is generally more difficult. Unequal power also has certain effects on each of the groups in question, perhaps more notably on the group with lesser power. Often it has been found that the group with lesser power is more aware of the power and status differentials (Tajfel, 1982). Thus, whereas Kluegel and Smith (1982) found that White U.S. citizens did not view structural factors as terribly serious barriers to Black advancement, we might suspect that Blacks would have seen the barriers as more severe.

Early in the study of intergroup relations, Kurt Lewin observed that "the privileged group . . . usually offers its members more and hinders them less than does the less privileged group," further noting that "the member of the underprivileged group is more hampered by his group belongingness" (quoted in Apfelbaum, 1979, pp. 194–195). More recently, research has suggested that differences in status between two groups will increase the tendency in both groups toward in-group bias—particularly if the difference in status is perceived as unreasonable or illegitimate (Tajfel, 1982). Thus, power differences between groups may affect one's perceptions both of one's own group and of the

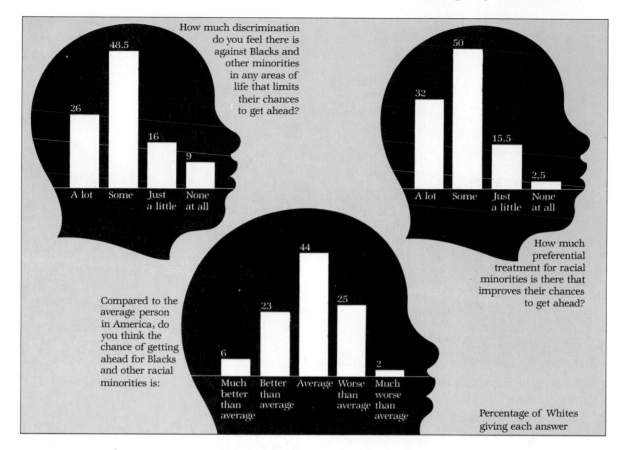

FIGURE 16-2. White perceptions of Black opportunity.

other group, typically accentuating actual differences that exist between two interacting groups.

C. In-group cohesiveness

When two groups come in contact, we have seen that their judgments of both their own group and the other group may shift. Does intergroup conflict have other effects on the functioning of each individual group? A central question in this regard has been the issue of cohesiveness. As defined in Chapter 14, cohesiveness is conceptualized as a force that holds the group together, based on the attractiveness of the group for each member and the attractiveness of the members to the group as a whole. In general, research does suggest that conflict with another group will increase the cohesiveness of the in-group (Dion, 1979). As a recent

example, we can look at the rise in British morale after Argentina invaded the Falkland Islands.

A number of explanations have been offered for this increase in cohesiveness. In terms of balance theory, for example (as discussed in Chapters 6 and 11), sharing a common fate with other members of one's group, in contrast to members of another group, would lead to stronger unit relationships among members of the in-group. Another explanation comes from reinforcement theory (see Chapter 1), suggesting that shared group experiences and rewards will be reinforcing, creating greater liking for the group as a whole. Both these explanations, however, rest on the assumption that the group experiences some degree of success in its activities. Without such success, neither unit relationships nor reinforcements may be present.

PHOTO 16-2. *British citizens cheer the troops, as the refitted* Queen Elizabeth 2 *sets sail for the Falklands.*

■ III. Strategies of interaction

There are many ways that groups can deal with each other. The situation itself may foster certain approaches; for example, certain situations may encourage cooperation between groups, while others, where resources are limited, may engender competition. Often groups approach situations with very different goals in mind, and the achievement by one group of its goal might mean the loss by the other group of its. In such situations, negotiation and bargaining often become necessary, aimed at resolving conflicts in such a way that both groups will be at least partly satisfied with the outcome. Groups cannot always resolve their conflicts, however, and sometimes a third party must be brought into the situation to work for a resolution.

In this section we will discuss these various strategies of interaction. Some of the studies of these strategies and processes have been done with a minimal situation—for example, with two-person "groups," called dyads. Yet, even though these studies do not match the complexity of intergroup relations, they can point out some fundamental aspects of the interaction process.

A. Cooperation and competition

Cooperation and competition are two very different approaches to interaction, whether we are considering the interaction between two individuals or two groups. **Cooperation** can be generally defined as working together for mutual benefit. **Competition,** in contrast, is activity directed toward achieving a goal that only one of the persons or groups can obtain.

Whether an individual or group chooses to cooperate or to compete depends in large part on the *reward structures* inherent in the situation. Reward structures are characteristics of the situation that essentially "set the stage," influencing the kinds of actions that will be taken. We can define three basic types of reward structures:

a cooperative reward structure, a competitive reward structure, and an individualistic reward structure.

In the **cooperative reward structure,** the goals of the situation are linked so that one individual or group can attain its goals only if the other individuals or groups attain theirs. (Deutsch, 1973, has also used the term *promotive interdependence* to describe this kind of situation.) In the contrasting **competitive reward structure,** goals for the participants are negatively linked, such that success by one party necessarily means failure for the other. (Deutsch's term for this situation is *contriently interdependent.*) More graphically describing the distinction between these two situations, Deutsch has stated: "In a cooperative situation the goals are so linked that everybody 'sinks or swims' together, while in the competitive situation if one swims, the other must sink" (1973, p. 20). A third type of reward structure, the **individualistic reward structure,** operates when individual or group goals are independent of one another—that is, what one group does has no influence on what the other group does.

The distinction among these three kinds of reward structures may be clearer if we shift to the individual level, looking at the familiar situation of the college classroom and grading procedures. For example, if a professor announces that grades will be determined on a curve, allowing 15% As no matter what the absolute scores are, that professor is setting up a competitive reward structure. The success of one student in attaining an A actually decreases the chances that another student will receive an A. An even stronger example—and a more competitive reward structure— would be the case in which the professor says that only one A will be given. Within this same classroom setting, a cooperative reward structure might be set up by developing team projects. In this case, the professor might say that grades were dependent on the group's efforts—if the group did well, everyone in the group would get an A, and if the group did poorly, everyone in the group would suffer accordingly. Finally, as an example of the individualistic reward structure, the professor might say "I reward competent work. If you complete your assignments successfully, you will receive an A. There are no curves or quotas; in fact, I would be happy to see all of you produce high-quality work and receive As." In this case students' outcomes are not interdependent, since reward attainment by one has no effect on the probability of reward attainment by another.

The reward structures that prevail in a situation can sharply alter the behavior of people in that situation. Recently, some researchers, convinced of the advantages of cooperation, have tried to alter reward structures in some public schools. In one case, there was a concern about the consequences of racially integrating the schools in Austin, Texas. Attempting to avoid a situation in which minority students would become one separate group and White students another, competing for the same rewards, Elliot Aronson and his colleagues developed the *jigsaw method* of learning (Aronson et al., 1978).

In one demonstration, fifth-graders were asked to study the biography of Joseph Pulitzer. In the jigsaw classroom, students were divided into heterogeneous, multiethnic teams. Each child on the team was given one section of the material on Pulitzer and, after mastering it, had to teach it to the others in the group. Thus, each child depended on others in the group for parts of the "jigsaw."

In studies conducted over six-week periods, the jigsaw method was compared with traditional classrooms run by teachers identified as good teachers by their colleagues (to put the jigsaw method to the hardest test). The experiments were preceded by workshops to train teachers and by "team building" exercises to help students put aside their competitive motives. The teams met for about 40–45 minutes a day, at least three times a week.

At the end of the six-week period, comparisons between jigsaw classes and control classes showed the following results: (1) jigsaw students grew to like their groupmates, (2) Anglo and Black children, although not Mexican-Americans, developed more favorable attitudes toward school, (3) students' self-esteem increased, (4) Black and Mexican-American students tended to master more material, while Anglo students did no worse in the jigsaw classes than in traditional ones, and (5) children in the jigsaw groups were more likely to express cooperative attitudes and to see their classmates as learning resources. Thus, the jigsaw method changed the reward structure in the class, substituting a cooperative goal for what might have been intergroup rivalry.

Competitive reward structures, in contrast, foster intergroup rivalry. As a graphic example of these consequences, let's consider the classic field study at Robber's Cave, conducted by Muzafer Sherif and his associates (Sherif, 1966; Sherif, Harvey, White, Hood, & Sherif, 1961).

The boys at Robber's Cave camp were a normal group of 11- and 12-year-old boys, participating in a summer camp with its typical swimming, hiking, and camping-out activities. What was different about this camp—and what the boys did not know—is that the camp was staffed by researchers who observed their behavior and specifically structured the situation. Two groups of boys were brought to separate cabins on the first day of camp, unaware that the other group existed. To develop cohesiveness within each group, the researchers planned activities that required the boys to cooperate for mutual benefit (for example, camping out or cleaning up a beach). The boys soon came to recognize one another's strengths and weaknesses; leaders emerged on the basis of their contributions to the group. Each group developed a name for itself (the "Rattlers" and the "Eagles"), group jokes, standards for behavior, and sanctions for those who "got out of line." Thus, during this phase, the reward structure between groups was essentially an individualistic one: what one group did had no effect on the other group—in fact, each group was totally unaware of the other's existence.

Then the researchers shifted to a competitive reward structure and created intergroup conflict as a result. They did this by bringing the two groups together and creating situations in which only one group would win—for example, by setting up tournaments with desirable prizes for only one group. When the groups were brought together for this series of contests, fair play was replaced by an ethic akin to that of the former Green Bay Packer coach Vince Lombardi: "Winning isn't everything,

it's the only thing." The groups began to call each other derogatory names, pick fights, and raid each other's camps. "Rattlers" downgraded all "Eagles," and vice versa, to the extent that neither group desired further contact with the other group. Muzafer Sherif remarked that a neutral observer who had no knowledge of what had happened would have assumed that the boys were "wicked, disturbed and vicious bunches of youngsters" (1966, p. 58).

We will return to the boys of Robber's Cave later. For the moment, however, it is important to point out how easily intergroup conflict can begin. Competitive reward structures often foster the development of such conflict, mandating that rewards given to one group will automatically be unavailable to the other. Deutsch (1973) has outlined a number of typical consequences of the competitive process, which are shown in Box 16-1.

On the surface, it sounds easy to avoid intergroup conflict: simply substitute a cooperative reward structure for a competitive one, and groups will work in harmony. But the solution is not that simple. Often there is a real conflict between group interests, as a shortage of resources may make it impossible for both groups to achieve what they want. In industry, labor unions often want higher wages, while managers want to lower costs. In warfare, both nations may want a single piece of territory. In other cases, religious or cultural values may be inherently contradictory. In fact, most conflicts between groups involve elements of both cooperation and competition—the parties must cooperate with each other in order to achieve at least a portion of their own goals. (Such interactions are often called *mixed-motive* interactions.) Bargaining and negotiation become the means for attempting resolution and compromise.

B. Bargaining and negotiation

Bargaining and *negotiation* are terms that are used often, both in conversation and in media reports. We may talk about bargaining with a car dealer for a good price, for example, or reporters may keep us abreast of the latest negotiations in the Mideast. Although there is some tendency to

BOX 16-1. The consequences of competition

Social psychologist Morton Deutsch, who has extensively studied the workings of cooperative and competitive groups, has outlined three common characteristics of the competitive situation (Deutsch, 1973).

1. Communication is unreliable and impoverished. Available communication channels either are not used or are used in a way to deliberately mislead the other group. Consequently, neither group trusts the information it receives from the other.

2. Perceptions of the other group are distorted. Sensitivity to differences between the groups is often increased, while awareness of similarities is minimized. Groups may also see their own behavior toward the other group as benevolent while viewing the actions of the other group as hostile and ill intentioned. Suspicion of the other's motives, in turn, may lead to negative responses to any request made by the other group and to a greater willingness to exploit the other group's needs.

3. Groups develop the belief that the only solution to the conflict is for one side to impose a solution through the use of superior force. Each side tries to enhance its own power and minimize the legitimacy of the other group. In this process, the scope of the conflict is often expanded, moving from a specific issue to a concern with moral principles and general superiority. ■

PHOTO 16-3. *Bargaining takes many forms, from formal labor/management negotiations to informal shopping at a produce market.*

settle what each shall give and take, or perform and receive, in a transaction between them" (Rubin & Brown, 1975, p. 2).

Rubin and Brown (1975) go on to specify a number of features of bargaining relationships that can be derived from this basic definition. First, the core of a bargaining relationship is that at least two parties are involved and that these two parties have a conflict of interest with regard to one or more issues. In labor/management negotiations, for example, the two parties may disagree on a number of issues—wages, fringe benefits, hours, or job security, to name only a few. To begin to negotiate, both parties must voluntarily enter into the bargaining relationship. If one group refuses to negotiate, then no bargaining can take place. If a teacher's union goes on strike, for example, but the board of education refuses to hear the union's demands, then intergroup conflict is at a stalemate, and bargaining cannot begin (see Box 16-2 for two perspectives on strikes).

Once both parties have agreed to negotiate, the

use the term *bargaining* when we talk about interactions between individuals, and *negotiation* when we talk about larger social units, such as unions or nations, we will follow the lead of Rubin and Brown (1975) and consider the terms interchangeable. Further following their lead, we will define **bargaining** (or negotiation) in this way: "the process whereby two or more parties attempt to

BOX 16-2. Two perspectives on strikes

How do strikes affect labor and management? In this classic consequence of intergroup conflict, both groups have a stake in reaching the best agreement. Two recent studies give us some information about the effects of a strike on the perceptions of each side.

The U.S. auto industry has a coordinated collective bargaining arrangement, whereby a strike is conducted at only one of the "big three" automakers (Ford, General Motors, and Chrysler) but the agreement reached in that settlement is generally applicable to all three companies. The existence of such an arrangement allowed psychologists Ross Stagner and Boaz Eflal (1982) to conduct a quasi-experimental study of the effects of a strike on attitudes of union members, comparing workers at the plant that went on strike with those at the plants that did not. Actually being on strike made a substantial difference. Strikers evaluated both their union and their leadership more positively than nonstrikers did, and they were more willing to engage in union activities. During the strike, the striking workers showed more militant and negative attitudes toward management; after the strike, they were more satisfied with the settlement package. Thus, actual involvement in the strike intensified positive attitudes toward the in-group and negative attitudes toward the out-group, demonstrating some of the effects of intergroup conflict that we discussed earlier.

What does management think about strikes? We do not have a parallel study that considers attitudes of management toward workers. However, a recent study by Shirom (1982) gives us some insight into the reactions of managers to a strike settlement and their beliefs about its "goodness" as a resolution of the conflict. In this study, Shirom questioned 51 management negotiators, each of whom had been involved in a strike in which at least 100 workers participated. Under what conditions did the managers think the strike had been advantageous to their

side? Two factors stood out: the size of the striking work force and the ability of management to keep the plant in operation during the strike. With a large work force or with continued operation, managers tended to rate the settlement as advantageous. Perhaps surprisingly, the duration of the strike, which should be related to costs, did not appear to influence managers' opinions.

From both these studies, we can see that the outcome of bargaining is not totally objective. Although it is possible to objectively state dollars or territories, reactions to agreements have a strong psychological component as well. ■

give-and-take process that we have identified as bargaining can begin. If the issues that separate the two parties are numerous, the bargaining process can be extremely complex, although the stages in the process may be predictable. Pruitt (1981, p. 14), drawing on previous work by Druckman (Druckman, 1978; Druckman & Mahoney, 1977), has listed six steps in the negotiating process:

1. Agreement about the need to negotiate.
2. Agreement on a set of objectives and principles (for example, in arms-control negotiations, the principle that the agreement should permit neither side to coerce the other).
3. Agreement on certain rules of conduct.
4. Defining the issues and setting up an agenda.
5. Agreement on a formula (in other words, agreement in principle).
6. Agreement on implementing details.

Reflecting on examples of international negotiation, such as those in the Mideast or those conducted at the end of the Vietnam War, one can fairly easily recall incidents that marked the bargaining at each of these stages.

More generally, we can think of a variety of activities taking place during the course of bargaining (Rubin & Brown, 1975). During the course of negotiations, each side will present demands or proposals, which will, in turn, be evaluated by the other party. Often counterproposals will follow, accompanied perhaps by some concessions, and the process is characterized by a sequence of such exchanges. Usually there is some division or exchange of resources. For example, in a labor/management dispute, labor might agree to accept a somewhat lower wage increase in return for greater job security.

Although the basic bargaining process can be described rather simply, a great many factors affect its outcome, and social scientists have invested considerable effort in the attempt to understand more about particular characteristics of the bargaining process. (For summaries of this work, see Chertkoff & Esser, 1976; Miller & Crandall, 1980; Pruitt, 1981; Rubin & Brown, 1975). Let us look at just some of the factors that can play a part in this complex process.

The nature of demands that each party makes—both the size and the timing—can affect the ultimate outcome of the bargaining process. For example, assuming that an agreement is eventually reached, the party that makes larger initial demands and smaller concessions generally achieves a larger outcome (Pruitt, 1981). However, if both parties make lower initial demands and faster concessions, resolution is usually achieved more rapidly. There are some exceptions to this seemingly obvious statement, however. If one party makes extremely low demands or concedes very quickly, agreement is more difficult to reach (Bartos, 1974; Hamner, 1974). Presumably, the other party in this case decides that it will do much better to sit and wait for additional concessions, without feeling a need to make any concessions of its own (Pruitt, 1981).

Often, in formal bargaining situations, each group is represented by one selected individual, who is termed the *representative bargainer*. For example, the union president may represent the total union membership, and management may similarly appoint one individual to represent the broader management group. In general, studies of this process show that representative bargainers are more competitive, make smaller concessions, and are less likely to reach agreements than individual bargainers who are representing only themselves (Davis, Laughlin, & Komorita, 1976). Surveillance of the representative bargainer by his or her constituents intensifies this effect. For example, in a laboratory study of bargaining conducted by Carnevale, Pruitt, and Britton (1979), some bargainers were told that their behavior would be constantly observed by the "owner" of the company, who was seated behind a one-way mirror. In other cases, bargainers were told that the "owners" would receive only a final report of the negotiated agreement. Surveillance made a difference. When they believed they were being observed, bargainers made more statements about their own role, made more threats and putdowns of the other negotiator, and were less likely to indicate an understanding of the other bargainer's priorities. Not only did surveillance affect the behavior of bargainers, but it affected the outcome as well.

As Figure 16-3 shows, bargainers under surveillance settled for lower profits than bargainers who were not being observed.

Accountability to one's constituents can have similar effects. Knowing that one is accountable may make a bargainer reluctant to give in, fearing the appearance of a loser to the constituency. "Saving face" may become more important than achieving a good agreement (Brown, 1977). Carnevale, Pruitt, and Seilheimer (1981) found that bargainers who were held accountable showed more pressure tactics and gained lower outcomes. Interestingly, however, this pattern held only when the bargainers had face-to-face contact with each other. Perhaps, the authors suggest, the greater range of nonverbal communication possible in the face-to-face situation (see Chapter 5) created stronger messages of dominance and thus impeded the bargaining process more severely.

A myriad of other factors can affect the bargaining process. Differing personalities of individual bargainers, for example, may facilitate or hinder the process (see Rubin & Brown, 1975). Different kinds of strategies and different types of communication will alter the process as well (Putnam

& Jones, 1982). Events external to the bargainers themselves that create stress and tension make bargaining more difficult and outcomes less favorable (Hopmann & Walcott, 1977). Publicity in the mass media, for example, can "leak" critical information, narrowing the options that bargainers have.

At least two general kinds of agreements can be reached in a bargaining process (Pruitt, 1982). In the *compromise*, both parties concede to a middle ground on some obvious dimension. For example, if the teacher's union wants salaries of $20,000 a year and the school board initially offers $16,000, a settlement of $18,000 would represent a compromise agreement. Alternatively, compromise agreements may involve trade-offs, whereby one party concedes in one area while the other concedes in another. For example, the school board might hold fast on salaries while agreeing to the teachers' demands for job security.

A second type of agreement suggested by Pruitt is the **integrative agreement,** one that reconciles both parties' interests and thus yields a high payoff for both groups. In general, the basis for integrative agreements is less obvious initially and may require the development of new alternatives. In this respect, Pruitt has likened integrative agreements to creative problem solving. Both compromise and integrative agreements have been termed "win/win" outcomes (Filley, 1975), in that both parties in the conflict may gain in the eventual resolution.

There are many occasions, however, when conflicting groups cannot reach any agreement, be it compromise or integrative agreement. In these cases, a third party is often sought to reconcile the differences. Let us look more closely at how third-party intervention works.

C. Third-party intervention

Third parties often enter negotiations when the bargaining process has failed to produce an agreement. There are several forms of third-party intervention, differing in their authority and in the rules of procedure that are set for them. Two of the most common forms are *mediation* and *arbitration*. In mediation the third party works along with

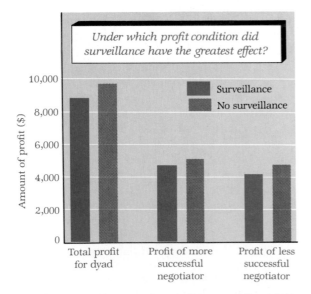

FIGURE 16-3. Effects of surveillance on bargaining outcomes.

the two conflicting groups, trying to get them to reach a satisfactory agreement. In arbitration the third party has the power to make final decisions that are binding on the conflicting groups (Pruitt, 1981).

Once mediation is expected, the bargaining process often slows down. In what has been described as a "chilling effect," bargainers tend to resist making additional concessions until the third party has arrived. Why should this happen? One speculation is that the bargaining groups, hesitant to lose face, resist making final concessions until the mediator has arrived, at which point an external attribution will be available. More practically, some have suggested that bargaining groups expect an arbitrator to "split the difference"—hence any advance weakening of their position will make their final settlement less. Both these reasons may help to explain why movement toward an agreement when expecting third-party intervention is slower when the conflict of interest is large rather than small (Hiltrop & Rubin, 1982)—there is less "face" to be lost and more payoff to be gained by moving slowly.

The major function of a third-party mediator is to create pressure toward agreement (Rubin & Brown, 1975). To do this, the mediator must have a number of characteristics—characteristics that resemble those of the credible source that we discussed in relation to attitude change (Chapter 11). Primary among these characteristics are trustworthiness and perceived ability (Rubin & Brown, 1975). It is also likely that a good mediator is able to see creative solutions to an apparent impasse—in other words, to be capable of formulating the integrative agreement that we discussed earlier.

■ IV. Reduction of intergroup conflict

Bargaining and negotiation are formal procedures that may be used to reduce intergroup conflict when both parties recognize the disagreement and are willing to enter into negotiations in order to resolve the conflict. These procedures work best when specific issues can be defined and the parties are interested in resolving those issues.

Other cases of intergroup conflict are less easily resolved. Sometimes the issues are not capable of being limited in such a way that bargaining could proceed. At other times the groups may not have any formal relationship with each other, making specific negotiation more difficult. In the case of Black/White relations in the United States, for example, intergroup conflict is both less defined and more general than a bargaining situation could handle.

For those concerned with intergroup relations, it is important to identify situations that will prevent conflict, as well as to develop means for its reduction. In this section we will consider a variety of principles and procedures that have been found effective in decreasing intergroup conflict.

A. Superordinate goals

When we left the boys at Robber's Cave, they were "wicked, disturbed and vicious"—the outcome of a competitive reward structure that had been fashioned by the researchers. These investigators did not wish to let the state of intergroup conflict persist, and they tried a variety of methods aimed at reducing the hostilities (Sherif, 1966; Sherif et al., 1961). Several strategies were tried and found wanting. The boys attended religious services that emphasized love and cooperation, but this appeal to moral values did not stop them from going right back to their warlike strategies when the services ended. Introduction of a third group, which served as "a common enemy," only widened the scope of conflict. Conferences between the leaders of the two groups were rejected, because concessions by the leaders would be interpreted by their followers as traitorous sell-outs of the groups' interests. Intergroup contact under pleasant circumstances, such as going to the movies or shooting off fireworks on the Fourth of July, only provided more opportunities for the expression of hostility.

The resolution of this conflict was finally made possible through the introduction of a **superordinate goal**—an important goal that can be achieved only through cooperation. First, the researchers arranged for a breakdown in the water-supply line. The boys joined forces in order to find the leak, but they resumed their conflict when the

PHOTO 16-4. *These boys, busy clearing a lot to make room for a neighborhood vestpocket park, could be an example of a group resolving conflict by working toward a superordinate goal.*

crisis had passed. The researchers then instigated a series of such joint efforts to achieve a superordinate goal: the groups pooled their money to rent a movie, and they used a rope to pull and start the food-supply truck. As a cumulative effect of these joint projects, the groups became friendlier with each other, began to see strengths in each other, and developed friendships across group lines. In fact, the majority of the boys chose to return home on the same bus, and the group that had won $5 as a prize used the money to treat the other group. The introduction of superordinate goals apparently permitted conflict-reduction strategies (such as communication and increased knowledge of the other group) to become effective.

An important element in the effectiveness of superordinate goals, however, is the success of the group in achieving that goal. As Worchel and his colleagues have shown, groups with a previous history of competition that work together on a project and fail may like each other less than they did before work on the superordinate project began (see Figure 16-4). As Worchel summarizes this strategy, "Anyone wishing to reduce intergroup conflict through intergroup cooperation must pay careful attention to the conditions surrounding the cooperative encounter" (1979, p. 271).

B. Intergroup contact

Can simple contact between two groups lead to improvement of intergroup relations? Many people have made the optimistic assumption that if two racial or religious groups could be brought together, the antagonism often expressed by each group toward the other would erode, and positive attitudes would develop. This, in essence, is the **intergroup-contact hypothesis.**

The optimism expressed in this hypothesis has proved to be unwarranted, or at least in need of considerable qualifications. Some of these qualifications can be described briefly. First, one must

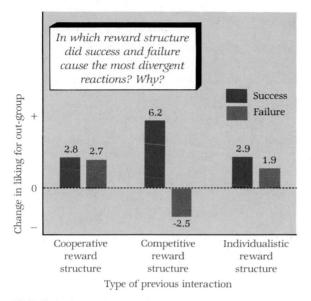

FIGURE 16-4. Change in liking for out-group as a function of group reward structure and the outcome of intergroup cooperation. This experiment by Worchel and his colleagues had two phases. In the first phase, two groups interacted under one of three reward structures—cooperative, competitive, or individualistic. In the second phase, the two groups worked together cooperatively and either succeeded or failed at the task.

consider the opportunity that members of the different groups have for acquaintance (Amir, 1976; Cook, 1970). Casual or superficial contact—such as between two persons who work on the same floor of a building but have no real interaction—has little effect on intergroup attitudes. Further, contact between groups may be difficult to establish because people generally prefer to interact with members of their own group, a tendency that is most pronounced among those who have the most prejudicial attitudes toward the other group (Amir, 1976).

The relative status of participants in a contact situation is important. Positive attitude change is more likely to occur when members of the two groups occupy the same social status. In other words, equal status implies equal power among the people who interact (Ramirez, 1977). Even within the laboratory, the importance of equal status has been demonstrated. In a recent exper-

iment by Norvell and Worchel (1981), two groups first worked separately on a task and then joined with each other for work on a cooperative task. To examine the effect of "historical" status differences, these experimenters created two conditions. In one condition both groups were told that they had done equally well on the first task, creating equal status between them. In the other condition both groups were told that one of the groups (Group A) had done better on the first task, creating unequal status between the two groups. In the second, cooperative phase of the experiment, the researchers introduced an additional factor into the experiment. In half the cases in which a winner had been declared, the experimenters gave additional information to the other group (Group B), thus redressing the balance of their status. Similarly, in half the cases in which no winner had been declared, the experimenters gave additional information to members of one of the subgroups—information that would be useful in performance on the second task—thus creating a new imbalance in their relative power within the larger group. How did these manipulations of status affect people's liking for members of the other group? Figure 16-5 provides the answers.

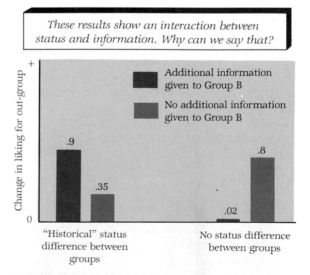

FIGURE 16-5. Change in liking for out-group as a function of previous status difference between groups and additional information provided to one of the groups.

In the no-winner/no-additional-information condition, equal status did increase attraction to members of the other group. In contrast, when an "historical imbalance" existed (based on the previous group experience), it was necessary to restore the balance between the two groups in order for greater attraction to result. One other interesting finding that emerged from the study concerned perceptions of fairness. None of the groups felt that it was particularly fair for the experimenter to provide additional information to one of the groups during the second, cooperative task, even if the purpose was to rebalance the status difference between the two groups. Yet, this perception of unfairness did not prevent members from changing their perceptions of the out-group, as Figure 16-5 shows. Norvell and Worchel (1981) speculate that affirmative action programs may have similar effects: although members of the in-group do not see affirmative action programs as fair, the increased contact that results from such programs may lead to more positive intergroup attitudes.

Investigators today, however, are generally far more cautious about claiming positive effects for the intergroup-contact hypothesis than they were 20 years ago. As Tajfel (1982) has stated, the change may reflect a "loss of innocence." Intergroup contact may have positive or negative results, depending on the conditions that surround the contact. Equal status, a need for cooperation, a social climate that favors intergroup contact, and rewards from the contact itself will all work to support the intergroup-contact hypothesis. In contrast, situations that foster competition, produce frustration, or emphasize status differences between the participants will tend to strengthen, rather than reduce, prejudice between two groups (Amir, 1976).

C. Reduction of threat

In the area of international relations, interactions between major powers—for example, the United States and the Soviet Union—deal not at the level of individual contact but, rather, at the level of the perceived balance of power between the nations. Considering the arms race in partic-

ular, we can search for a strategy to reduce this particular form of intergroup conflict. Psychologist Charles Osgood (1966, 1974) has offered one such strategy, which he terms **GRIT**—standing for "graduated and reciprocated initiatives in tension reduction." The basic principles of this strategy are as follows:

1. Set the atmosphere for conciliation by stating your intention to reduce tension through subsequent acts, indicating the advantages for the other party in reciprocating.
2. Publicly announce each unilateral initiative in advance, indicating that it is part of a general strategy.
3. With each announcement, invite some form of reciprocation.
4. Carry out each initiative as announced, without requiring reciprocation.
5. Continue the initiatives for some time, even in the absence of reciprocation.
6. Make each initiative unambiguous and open to verification.
7. Initiatives should be risky and vulnerable to exploitation, but they should not reduce the capacity to retaliate with nuclear weapons if an attack is launched.
8. Also maintain capacity to retaliate with conventional arms.
9. Once the other party begins to reciprocate, the initiator should reciprocate as well, exposing itself to at least as much, or slightly more, vulnerability.
10. Diversify unilateral initiatives by type of action and geographical location.

Osgood's GRIT strategy is based on a belief that the arms race must be deescalated. His recommended procedure is a gradual one, maintaining strength while gradually reducing the level of conflict. During the initial stages of this sequence, the aim is to put pressure on the target party, both through one's own actions and, presumably, through a buildup of world public support. Later stages in the sequence (for example, steps 4, 5, and 6) are intended to establish an image of credibility and predictability. Later stages—assuming the initial stages are successful—recommend a mixture of resistance and yielding.

The ultimate success of this model cannot be

tested experimentally; it could await the actions of world leaders. Nonetheless, considerable laboratory experimentation has supported the validity of many of the points (Lindskold, 1979). Laboratory research also suggests, however, that participants in intense conflict are often reluctant to use conciliatory techniques, preferring to use threat instead (Deutsch, Canavan, & Rubin, 1971). Generalizing from such research to the current world situation, it may be unlikely that GRIT will be adopted as a means of managing conflict.

V. SUMMARY

Intergroup behavior occurs whenever individuals belonging to one group interact, collectively or individually, with another group or its members in terms of their group identification. Examples of intergroup behavior are numerous, including ethnic relations, labor/management negotiations, and international conflict.

Within a single group, active minorities may constitute a special case of intergroup relations. The ability of minorities to influence the majority is thought to be influenced by a variety of factors, including the behavioral style of the minority.

In-groups and out-groups have predictable views of each other; the in-group often emphasizes its moral superiority and stresses its differences from the out-group. Groups in conflict are often unequal in power. Conflict between groups often increases the *cohesiveness* of each individual group.

There are three basic types of reward structures: cooperative, competitive, and individualistic. Competitive reward structures are most apt to lead to intergroup conflict.

Bargaining is a process used to reduce conflict and resolve differences between groups. A variety of conditions can affect the outcome of the bargaining process, including the timing and size of demands, the accountability of a representative bargainer to his or her constituents, and surveillance by the constituency. Often a third party must be called in when bargaining parties cannot resolve their differences.

Numerous strategies have been used to reduce or avoid intergroup conflict. Establishing a *superordinate goal* is one such strategy. The *intergroup-contact hypothesis* suggests that simple contact will reduce antagonism. Research has suggested that the contact process is more complicated, and its success depends on a variety of factors.

GRIT (graduated and reciprocated initiatives in tension reduction) is one strategy that has been suggested for the problem of arms control.

GLOSSARY TERMS

bargaining	ethnocentrism	intergroup behavior
competition	GRIT	intergroup-contact
competitive reward structure	individualistic reward	hypothesis
cooperation	structure	superordinate goal
cooperative reward structure	integrative agreement	

Physical Environment & Social Behavior

We shape our buildings and afterwards our buildings shape us.
■ WINSTON CHURCHILL

Living organisms never submit passively to the impact of environmental forces.
■ RENÉ DUBOS

This chapter was written by Eric Sundstrom.

With fall term approaching, new first-year students at the State University of New York at Stony Brook moved into their rooms in one of two types of dormitories, the "corridor design" or the "suite design." Both types of dormitories contained double bedrooms and provided just over 150 square feet of floor space per person. As shown in Figure 17-1, however, the dormitories differed in other ways. In the corridor-design dorms, students entered their rooms from long, double-loaded corridors that served 33 other students, all of whom shared the same bathroom and lounge. In contrast, the suite design had small units, each consisting of three bedrooms grouped around a small lounge and bathroom, with the rooms opening onto the lounge instead of the corridor.

Social psychologists Andrew Baum and Stuart Valins (1977) conducted a survey among occupants of the two types of dormitories and found striking differences, despite the equivalence of floor space. Corridor residents reported greater crowding, complained of more unwanted social contact, and expressed a greater desire to avoid people. This seemed to reflect differences in the architecture of the dorms: when residents of suites left their rooms, they might encounter any of their five suite-mates—but when corridor residents went into the hall, they could expect to run into any of more than 30 other residents. Corridor residents with rooms near the bathroom were in the center of the traffic pattern and felt particularly crowded. (The different responses at the two dorms could not be attributed to characteristics of the students, and the findings were later repeated with students randomly assigned to the different types of dorms—see Baum & Valins, 1979.)

Observations in the dormitories where students had completed surveys revealed that corridor residents spent less time there than suite residents. Social encounters of corridor residents generally occurred in hallways and lounges, where suite residents were frequently observed in nonsocial activities, such as studying. Corridor residents typically stayed in their rooms for nonsocial activities, apparently avoiding interaction and perhaps protecting themselves from unwanted social contact.

Students' experiences in the two types of dormitories illustrate the importance of the physical environment for social behavior. In keeping with Winston Churchill's observation that "our buildings shape us," the occupants of the corridor-design dorms felt crowded and avoided the areas in the dormitory where social encounters usually occurred. But they did not submit passively to the influences of their environments. Instead, they coped—by spending little time in the dormitories, by retreating to their rooms while in the dorms, and generally by withdrawing from social contact in an environment that forced them into interaction with too many people.

This chapter explores the relevance of the physical environment to social behavior, including the effects of architecture and other elements of our physical surroundings. The organization of the chapter reflects a view of the relationship between people and their physical surroundings as one of mutual influence, or give and take. We begin by emphasizing the physical setting as a resource that people use in their dealings with one another—for instance, to regulate their accessibility to others. So, in the first two sections, we discuss concepts that refer to the social use of the environment—privacy and territory—and explore some of the ways in which people organize their encounters and relationships through use of their physical settings. Then we change perspectives and emphasize the capacity of the physical environment to influence or determine interpersonal behavior. We begin the third section by describing the concept of environmental stress and then outline the conditions that can precipitate it, such as heat or noise, and their effects on social behavior. Then we explore crowding, a form of stress that sometimes arises when too many people share a space. The last section discusses the impact of architecture and buildings, including research on the corridor- and suite-design dormitories.

■ I. Privacy

The term **privacy** means an intentional retreat from contact with other people by an individual or group (see Margulis, 1977). It can involve delib-

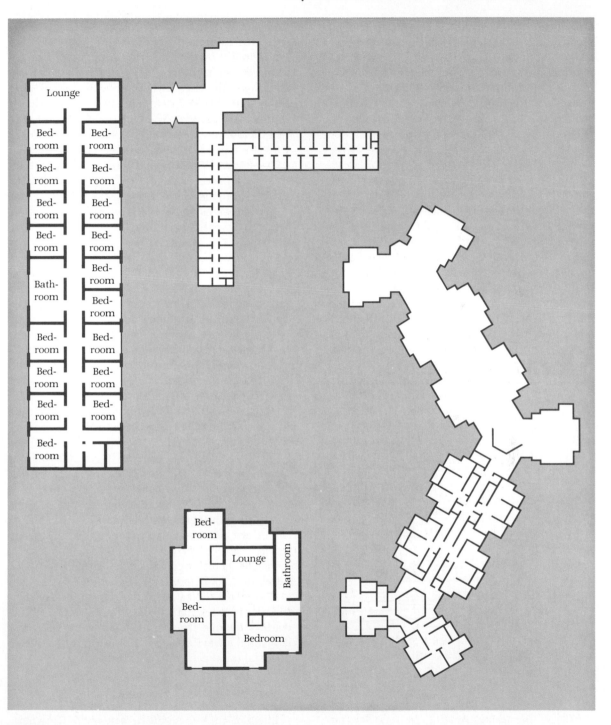

FIGURE 17-1. Corridor-design and suite-design dormitories.

erate limitation of access to oneself, restriction of incoming stimulation, or withholding of information about the self. The physical environment provides a resource for obtaining privacy by allowing us to regulate our accessibility to others. For example, students who live in dormitories can open their doors to encourage visitors and open their curtains to see and be seen by passing students, or they can close doors and curtains for privacy.

Theorists distinguish several types of privacy, notably the four categories identified by Westin (1970): (1) *Solitude* involves the physical isolation of an individual by his or her own choice. (Involuntary isolation, described in Chapter 6, is not a form of privacy.) Solitude allows personal reflection, self-evaluation, emotional release. (2) *Intimacy* refers to the physical isolation of a couple, family, or group, which provides protected communication within the social unit. Intimacy allows the free expression of emotions not intended for other audiences and can be found in residences

DUNAGIN'S PEOPLE

"HELLO, I'M TAKING A POLL ON HOW PEOPLE FEEL ABOUT INVASION OF THEIR PRIVACY..."

and certain other places, such as isolated campsites. (3) *Anonymity* refers to the experience of being in a crowd and having no distinct identity with respect to others. Anonymity depends only slightly on the environment. (Social psychologists have sometimes created anonymity in experiments by dimming the lights; recall the study of deindividuation described in Chapter 2.) (4) Westin's last type of privacy, *reserve*, refers to individual restraint in discussing personal information; it also depends little on the environment (see Chapter 5 regarding self-disclosure).

Privacy gains some of its importance from its links to impression management (discussed in Chapter 3). To influence the impressions that other people form, an individual may act out different roles for different audiences and may be selective in the behavior that certain audiences are allowed to see or hear. For instance, a young man whose date is nearby may not want her to overhear a telephone conversation he is having with his father to ask for money. In fact, he probably prefers that the conversation have no audience at all. (In offices, where many confidential encounters take place, an individual's workspace provides *speech privacy* to the extent that confidential conversations cannot be understood outside it; see Sundstrom, Herbert, & Brown, 1982.)

In Erving Goffman's (1959) theory of role behavior, people act out their roles in "front" regions open to audiences, but between performances they retreat to "back" regions inaccessible to audiences. Here the actors can relax and do things they might not want seen; in other words, they have privacy.

Privacy is an important facet of the process of regulating social contact, described in Altman's (1975, 1976) theory of **privacy regulation.** The theory proposes that a person's desires for social contact change from time to time but that the individual always tries to maintain an optimal level of social contact. Altman writes:

If a person desires a lot of interaction with another person and gets only a little then he feels lonely, isolated, or cut off. And if he actually receives more interaction than he originally desired, then he feels intruded upon, crowded, or overloaded. However, what is too much, too little, or ideal shifts with time and circumstances, so what is optimum depends on where one is on the continuum of desired privacy. If I want to be alone, a colleague who comes into my office and talks for fifteen minutes is intruding and staying too long. If I want to interact with others, then the same fifteen-minute conversation may be far too brief [1975, p. 25].

Altman claims that whenever we want more or less interaction than we experience, we use "privacy regulation mechanisms," including resources supplied by the physical setting, to try to achieve the optimum state of affairs.

We can use any of several strategies for regulating social contact by using the physical environment. First, we can adjust the environment itself—through temporary measures, such as opening or closing a door or window shade, or more permanent adjustments, such as moving a file cabinet into a double dormitory room to separate the beds. Second, we can negotiate the use of a place with other users—for example, by inviting someone to visit, suggesting that someone leave, or working out a schedule of times for using a place. Third, we can regulate social contact by changing locations—for example, by retreating to a private place or by going someplace where people are likely to be found. A fourth strategy is the regulation of one's position in a room, which involves *immediacy behaviors* (discussed in Chapter 5). A person's position in relation to another person establishes interpersonal distance, opportunities for eye contact, or the presence of intervening barriers, which can signal the desired degree of involvement.

Some of the most obvious environmental resources for privacy appear in places labeled "private," such as residences, bedrooms, offices, and clubs. Occupants can literally regulate their boundaries by opening or closing gates, doors, window shades, drapes, and so on. Sometimes the boundaries are largely symbolic, as in the parking lot marked "private," and succeed because of social norms.

Even an environment only partly set off by physical boundaries can provide some privacy. Research from offices points to an association between physical enclosure and privacy, shown in Figure 17-2. In this correlational study, office employees rated their workspaces on privacy; social psychologists measured the amount of physical enclosure of each workspace by noting how many of its four sides were bounded by a wall, partition, or barrier at least six feet high. Privacy was greatest in fully enclosed offices with doors, but in such offices managers rated their privacy higher than clerical employees did, perhaps because people felt freer to walk into a secretary's office (Sundstrom, Town, Brown, Forman, & McGee, 1982).

The failure to obtain needed privacy may have important consequences. In a correlational study at a university (Vinsel, Brown, Altman, & Foss, 1980), first-year students who lived in a dormitory completed a survey, and 18 months later researchers noted which students had dropped out for nonacademic reasons. Responses by the dropouts suggested that they had failed to develop the effective means of regulating interaction that other students had found. Dropouts were less likely than others to shut the doors of their rooms, find a quiet place, or arrange their rooms for privacy. At the same time, dropouts were unlikely to use their environments in certain ways to seek the company of others, such as using the bathroom at busy times or inviting people to their rooms.

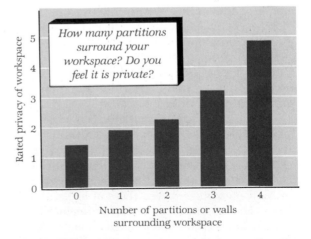

FIGURE 17-2. Ratings of privacy of workspaces by office employees as a function of number of sides bounded by a wall or barrier at least six feet high.

In summary, privacy is important in carrying out social roles and in regulating social contact; the physical environment can help provide privacy, especially in residences and offices. But our ability to obtain privacy in such places may depend to some extent on our treatment of them as territories.

■ II. Territories

In Altman's theory of privacy regulation, a **territory** delineates interpersonal relationships, defines zones of control, and provides a basis for regulating social contact. However, the use of the term *territory* to describe the way people use their environments is controversial, because it implicitly invokes an ethological model of human behavior (see Chapter 8 for the ethological view of aggression).

To an ethologist, *territory* means a particular place that an animal marks with calls, scents, or other signs and uses for nesting and as a base for hunting or foraging. If a member of the same species crosses the boundary, a conflict usually ensues, along with posturing, threatening gestures, or ritualized combat. The intruder usually retreats from such encounters. The behavior is instinctive, but not all species are territorial, and each territorial species has its own biologically based pattern of territorial activity (see Wynne-Edwards, 1962).

Territoriality seems to serve many useful functions that promote the survival of a species as a whole. It disperses animals evenly over a habitat (which prevents overgrazing or overhunting); it supplies places for mating and for caring for the young; and it provides a basis for social organization (Carpenter, 1958). One ethologist observed cats and discovered that when two cats met outside their territories, the animal with a lower rank in the local dominance hierarchy usually retreated. Cats in their own territories, however, nearly always drove away intruders, even those of higher dominance (Leyhausen, 1965). Such **territorial dominance** allows even a low-ranked animal to keep its territory.

Are people territorial? Some claim we are. They argue that violence stems in part from instinctive responses to territorial encroachment (Ardrey, 1966; Lorenz, 1966; see also Chapter 8). Humans clearly do form attachments to places. However, human use of space is much more complex than the stereotypic behavior observed in some species. And if humans are territorial, we are unique in entertaining guests (Edney, 1974). Although observations of nonhuman territoriality obviously do not generalize directly to humans, we still show behavior analogous to territoriality: we maintain homes, work at prescribed work stations, and temporarily claim tables in restaurants, spaces in parks, benches at bus stops, and spots in other public places. Anybody who has strayed onto a farmer's field only to confront the owner's shotgun will probably think twice before completely dismissing the idea that humans have territories.

Social psychologists have adopted a modified version of the ethologist's concept of territory to describe the complex ways in which people use and control places. They have distinguished several types of territories (for example, Goffman, 1971; Lyman & Scott, 1967). Altman (1975) reviewed the theories and identified three types of territories, shown in Table 17-1.

Primary territories are defined as places "owned and exclusively used by individuals or groups, . . . clearly identified as theirs by others, . . . controlled on a relatively permanent basis, and . . . central to the day to day lives of the occupants" (p. 112), such as homes and some private offices. Primary territories are used for relatively long periods of time and are decorated and personalized by the occupants to express their individual or group identity. These places typically provide considerable privacy. **Secondary territories** are "less central, pervasive, and exclusive" (p. 114) and are used by a group to control access to its turf. One example is the neighborhood bar, where regular users sometimes glare at outsiders and make hostile remarks (Cavan, 1963). Another example is the turf defended by a juvenile gang. **Public territories** are temporarily established in spaces available to virtually anyone, such as telephone booths, public beaches, tables at libraries, and picnic tables at parks. However, occupants are expected to conform to local norms. For example,

TABLE 17-1. Three types of human territories

Type of territory	Occupants	Use	Control and privacy	Examples
Primary	Individual; family; primary group	Regular, frequent use; long-term occupancy; personally important activities	High degree of control over access; high degree of privacy	Private room; residence; private office
Secondary	Group	Regular use for varying periods	Moderate control over access by nonmembers	Neighborhood bar, church, or park; classroom; apartment building; fraternity house
Public	Individual; group	Temporary use for limited periods	Limited control; limited privacy	Table in restaurant; bench at bus stop; seat in theater

some restaurants refuse to serve men without jacket and tie (though waiters usually have extras). Public territories generally allow very little privacy.

A fourth kind of territory recognized by some theorists is called an **interaction territory,** the area around two or more persons as they talk. Analogous to an individual's "personal space," these areas are like invisible bubbles that last only as long as the conversations within them. People hesitate to invade a conversation space; intruders typically show signs of discomfort and submissiveness; the "permeability" of an interaction territory depends on such things as the size of the group, their apparent status, and their race (Brown, 1981; Cheyne & Efran, 1972; Efran & Cheyne, 1972, 1973, 1974; Knowles, 1972, 1973). Members of cohesive dyads in one experiment were more likely to go out of their way to avoid intrusion into a conversation space than members of less cohesive dyads were (Knowles & Brickner, 1981).

A. Interactions in primary territories

Like nonhuman species, humans seem to exhibit a form of territorial dominance, in which people dominate encounters on their own turf. A physician noticed that patients appeared submissive in his office, but when he called at their homes, they were confident and assertive (Coleman, 1968). The idea was tested more formally in a college dormitory, where pairs of students debated about the appropriate jail sentence for a hypothetical criminal while in one student's room. One student argued for the prosecution, the other for the defense. Whether they were prosecuting or defending, those in their own rooms argued more persuasively and spent more time talking than their visitors (Martindale, 1971). In another experiment (Conroy & Sundstrom, 1977), pairs consisting of a dormitory resident and a visitor worked on a cooperative task in the resident's room. Half the pairs held similar attitudes, and half had dissimilar attitudes. When attitudes were dissimilar, residents exerted more "dominant speech patterns," as expected. However, when attitudes were similar, residents deferred to the visitors in the cooperative task, exhibiting a "hospitality effect." A later study (Taylor & Lanni, 1981) explored territorial dominance in triads of college men—one member with a low score on personal dominance, one with a moderate score, and one with a high score. The triads worked together on a task in one member's room. Regardless of the resident's personality, the group solutions reflected greater influence by the resident than by either visitor, even though the resident was outnumbered.

Territorial dominance may account for the home-team advantage in competitive sports. For instance, a study of the 1979–80 teams in professional baseball, football, and basketball and college football and basketball found a significant "home field" advantage in all sports, especially basketball (Hirt & Kimble, 1981). As shown in Figure 17-3, professional teams won more home games than they lost (the same was true of college teams).

Whether the home-field advantage reflects a form of dominance that derives from the home team's attachment to its playing field is an open question. A team's home field may be viewed as a group territory because of frequent, exclusive practices there, and it is possible that visitors feel intimidated by their status as visitors. But the home team is also more familiar with the field and gets a boost from its more numerous fans (Hirt & Kimble, 1981).

Territories are typically marked or decorated to reflect the occupants' personalities and perhaps to assert control. In studying "personalization" in university dormitory rooms, Hansen and Altman (1976) counted such things as posters, rugs, stereos, and other personal objects and later found out which students had dropped out of the university for nonacademic reasons. Dropouts had displayed fewer personal items than students who remained on campus. In contrast, another study in the same dormitories (Vinsel et al., 1980) found more personal objects in the rooms of students

who later dropped out than of those who stayed. However, dropouts' markers concerned other localities, such as former residences, in contrast to the markers of students who stayed in school. Through personalization, or lack of it, students who eventually dropped out had failed to demonstrate a commitment to their current environment.

Another characteristic of primary territories is the maintenance of boundaries. A field study (Edney, 1972) found that residents of houses with boundaries marked by fences, hedges, retaining walls, and other such borders had lived in their houses longer and intended to stay longer than neighbors whose boundaries were less clearly defined. Residents of marked houses also answered their doors faster, suggesting greater surveillance of boundaries. Elderly residents in another study (Patterson, 1978) who had boundaries or outdoor decorations felt relatively safe from crime.

B. "Defensible space"

Apartment buildings number among the spaces occupied by groups that try to restrict access by outsiders. In a controversial book entitled *Defensible Space*, urban planner Oscar Newman (1973) argued that crime in multiple-dwelling buildings is minimized by well-defined "zones of influence" that allow limited access by outsiders and surveillance by residents over entries and exits (see Figure 17-4). Newman cited the widely publicized Pruitt-Igoe housing project in St. Louis as an example of nondefensible space. (The project consisted of 33 high-rise buildings with 2764 apartments for low-income families. After only three years it was a crime-ridden wreck, with a vacancy rate of up to 70%. The city eventually demolished the buildings.) The Pruitt-Igoe buildings each contained over 80 dwellings, and so recognition of outsiders was difficult. The buildings stood on featureless grounds with neither physical nor symbolic separation, and so territorial boundaries were unclear. Each building had several entrances through which people could come and go with minimal surveillance. However, one building stood out as an exception. Workers had erected a chain-link fence around the building to protect construc-

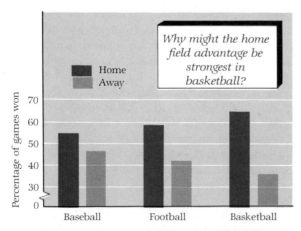

FIGURE 17-3. Percentages of "home" and "away" games won by professional baseball, football, and basketball teams during the 1979–1980 season.

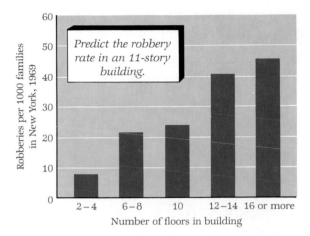

FIGURE 17-4. Frequency of robberies as a function of building height. According to the controversial book *Defensible Space*, occupants of high-rise apartments have trouble controlling access to their buildings by outsiders, which may explain the greater prevalence of robberies in tall buildings, as shown here.

tion material. When the workers left, residents persuaded them to leave the fence up. Two years later the building enjoyed a vandalism rate 80% below that of the other buildings and a vacancy rate below 5%, as residents tended their yard and watched their gate. The fence apparently provided a zone of influence that seems to fit the definition of a group territory. The empirical basis of Newman's theory on the deterrence of crime has been questioned, but his ideas have been influential (R. B. Taylor, 1978).

C. Temporary territories in public places

For temporary claims on public space, people seem to depend more on interpersonal distance than on boundaries. Observations in a library (Sommer, 1966) showed that most students who entered alone sat at tables by themselves (64%); those who sat at tables already occupied by other students usually took the most distant chair (diagonally across the table). Data from other libraries suggested that students maximized their distance from others or the belongings of others (Sommer, 1966) and stayed longest at tables where nobody else was seated (Becker, 1973).

Research in a game arcade suggested that new-comers claimed machines as their temporary territories by touching or manipulating them. Users of machines reacted to potential intruders by prolonged touching of their machines; a confederate touching a machine deterred use of it by others. Touching apparently acted as a "symbolic territorial marker" (Werner, Brown, & Damron, 1981).

A sense of control over a public territory may depend on the length of time the occupant has been there. In an experiment in a campus snack bar, a confederate approached people who had been seated for varying lengths of time and said "Excuse me, but you are sitting in my seat." Those who had been seated for only a few minutes tended to leave apologetically, but those who had been there longer tended to resist the would-be intrusion (Sommer, 1969). Another study found that the longer a party of people had been on a beach, the larger the circular area they viewed as "theirs" (Edney & Jordon-Edney, 1974).

One way to assert a claim on a public territory is to mark it with personal belongings, particularly if the occupant is going to leave for a while. In an experiment on territorial "markers" in a campus snack bar, either a newspaper, a paperback, or a sweater was left to hold a chair. Someone sat at the chair in only 14% of the trials (Sommer, 1969). Another experiment in a crowded study hall used several kinds of markers, as shown in Figure 17-5. Each evening an observer recorded how long it took before someone sat in the marked chair and in a randomly chosen, unmarked chair. The unmarked chair was occupied after an average of 20 minutes, but personal markers deterred students from using the marked chair (Sommer & Becker, 1969). When someone approached a marked chair, he or she usually asked whether it was taken. But would a neighbor actively defend a marked territory? Apparently not, unless the intruder specifically asked whether the marked seat was taken (Sommer & Becker, 1969). Another study found that people sometimes used their own belongings to mark an absent neighbor's territory (Hoppe, Greene, & Kenny, 1972), but only the exceptional neighbor challenged an intruder.

Even the "owner" of a public territory may hesitate to confront an intruder (Becker & Mayo, 1971).

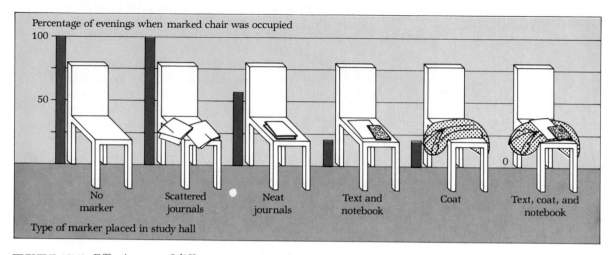

Percentage of evenings when marked chair was occupied

100

50

0

No marker

Scattered journals

Neat journals

Text and notebook

Coat

Text, coat, and notebook

Type of marker placed in study hall

FIGURE 17-5. Effectiveness of different types of markers in establishing public territory.

In a study conducted in a classroom during the break in a long class, an invader took a seat that another student had occupied. Only 27% of invaded students confronted the invader and asked for their seats back, although those whose chairs were in the center of the room were more likely to defend them (Haber, 1980). Fortunately, such invasions of public territories may be uncommon—except perhaps by social psychologists. Respondents to a survey unanimously claimed that they would not invade a marked territory (Becker, 1973).

D. Territories in organizations and groups

The physical environment can indicate a person's rank or position in an organization through the use of status symbols. For example, executives in the CBS building in New York City work in offices of different sizes and furnishings; a promotion brings a larger office with more and nicer furniture. This practice is common. Many features of offices may operate as status symbols, and people with supervisory responsibility are more likely to have them: a private office, a closable door, a receptionist, a large workspace, a large or expensive desk, and other furnishings (Konar, Sundstrom, Brady, Mandel, & Rice, 1982).

In a small group that shares an environment, members may use their setting in accord with their positions in the **dominance hierarchy** (the ranking of members in terms of influence or power). In one group of patients on a mental ward, high-ranked members of the group tended to move freely over the entire ward, while those of lesser rank claimed specific places (Esser, Chamberlain, Chapple, & Kline, 1964). In a group of prison inmates, highly dominant group members were most mobile and had the most desirable bunks as their territories (Austin & Bates, 1974). These groups organized their use of the physical environment so that those with higher status enjoyed more space, better space, or both.

A longitudinal study of a group of boys in a reform school also found highly dominant members in the most desirable places—but only as long as the group's membership remained stable. When the group changed (two highly dominant boys left and two new boys entered), territorial behavior of the entire group dropped, and the boys tended to rove about the cottage instead of using specific locations; the tendency for dominant boys to use desirable places disappeared. At the same time, cottage supervisors reported a 50% increase in aggressive incidents. Within a few weeks the group regained equilibrium, as territorial behavior increased and aggression subsided (Sundstrom & Altman, 1974). Other research also suggests a link between a smoothly functioning group and

A. *A primary territory: Rebecca's office is used exclusively by her and is recognized by others as her domain.*

B. *A secondary territory: Rebecca and her friends regularly occupy the corner table at a local restaurant.*

During the course of a day or a week, we may find ourselves in many different places—at home, in an office, at a friend's apartment, on a crowded bus, or in an empty field. These locations differ in many ways, one of which is the degree of territoriality they imply. In our homes or in our private office at work, we have a great degree of control and privacy. These primary territories, such as the office pictured in the first photograph, are *ours*. In secondary territories, such as a sorority house or a neighborhood café, we have somewhat less control; we use the space regularly, but we generally share it with others. Public territories give us very little control. Although we may stake out a picnic table for the afternoon, the table will "belong" to someone else tomorrow. Even in public, however, we can establish territorial "bubbles" by engaging in intense conversations that others are unwilling to interrupt. In this special case, however, the territory moves with the people and is not defined by physical features.

C. *A public territory: picnic tables at the park can be staked out on a temporary basis.*

D. *Interaction territory: even in a public setting, individuals can create some private territory while they talk.*

orderly use of space by its members (Altman, Taylor, & Wheeler, 1971).

In summary, people may not defend territories as nonhuman animals do, but we apparently form attachments to places and use them to regulate encounters with others. We define places for our use as individuals and as groups and organize our use of the environment within a group or organization to complement their structures.

■ III. Environmental stress

One of the most important ways in which the physical environment can influence its occupants is by creating **stress,** defined as a physiological and psychological response to demand, challenge, or threat that includes both arousal and mobilization of the individual's capacities for coping (see McGrath, 1970; Selye, 1971). Physical surroundings can produce stress through aversive conditions such as loud noise or uncomfortable heat. Environmental stressors are most disturbing when intense, unpredictable, and uncontrollable (Baum, Singer, & Baum, 1981). However, the degree of stress produced by the physical environment depends to a considerable extent on the individual's subjective judgment that the environment poses a potential threat to his or her comfort or well-being (Cohen, 1980b).

Stress is important to social behavior because it can lead to insensitivity to some social cues and overreaction to others. For example, a pedestrian on a sidewalk may experience stress as a consequence of the bustling crowds, the noise from passing traffic, and the afternoon heat. In consequence, the pedestrian may overlook or ignore a person nearby who has just dropped a load of packages. The same pedestrian may react with unusual anger at an accidental collision with another pedestrian.

Stress may bring insensitivity to social cues for several reasons. First, people under stress sometimes show a "narrowing of attention," focusing on cues most salient to their immediate tasks, to the exclusion of other cues (for example, Hockey, 1970; Solly, 1969). This reaction may represent a diminished capacity to handle information under stress (Berkun, 1964). Second, people sometimes cope with sources of stress by trying to avoid *overload* (more information or stimulation than they can process) and by ignoring "low-priority inputs" (Milgram, 1970; see also J. G. Miller, 1964). Third, stress may exact a "psychic cost" due to efforts expended in trying to cope, resulting in diminished cognitive capacities (see Cohen, 1980a).

Stress may also create an unusual responsiveness to instigations to aggression. Because stress includes arousal, it may intensify our reactions to frustration, provocation, or insult (see Chapter 8). However, the impact of environmental stress may be modified by adaptation.

A. Adaptation

Adaptation refers to the many processes that allow organisms to adjust to their environments (Dubos, 1980). Among other things, adaptation by humans brings changes in perceptions of the environment after continued exposure (see Wohlwill, 1974). For example, a person who lives near a busy freeway is bombarded by a constant din of passing motor traffic. It may seem loud at first but in time becomes background—no longer consciously noticed. (Adaptation involves physiological as well as psychological processes. Examples include the inability of most people to smell a strong odor for more than a few seconds and the automatic adjustment of the eye to bright light.) In consequence, environmental stressors may seem most intense and disturbing to newcomers to a physical setting.

Through adaptation each of us establishes his or her own personal standard for evaluating environments. For example, the urbanite who visits a busy suburb may find it quiet—at least by comparison with the city. But a visitor from a rural environment, accustomed to more peaceful surroundings, may find the same suburb noisy. The standard of comparison developed through exposure to an environment is called an **adaptation level** (Helson, 1964). Wohlwill and Kohn (1973) examined adaptation levels by asking residents of small cities (24,000 or fewer people), medium cities (152,000 to 753,000), or large cities (over

1,000,000) to rate the degree of crowding and congestion in a series of color slides that depicted scenes from cities of various sizes. Residents of large cities rated the slides as least crowded and congested; residents of small cities, who were least accustomed to crowding and congestion, rated the slides as highest on both these features (see Figure 17-6).

Despite our ability to adapt in our perceptions of potentially stressful environments, we still suffer adverse effects from them even after the source of stress is gone. These are called *aftereffects*. An experiment on loud, unpredictable, uncontrollable noise found that people could adapt: they performed clerical tasks with unimpaired speed and accuracy even during noise. However, when participants went to a different, quiet room, those who had earlier worked in unpredictable, uncontrollable noise caught fewer errors in proofreading a manuscript and were less persistent in a task designed to assess their tolerance for frustration (Glass & Singer, 1972). Later research (reviewed by Cohen, 1980a) has confirmed the adverse aftereffects of unpredictable, uncontrollable noise and

has found the same effects for other kinds of stressors as well.

Aftereffects of stress are important for social behavior in that insensitivity to social cues—or other effects of stress—may linger after the stressor has been removed. Furthermore, because of adaptation, these effects may occur without conscious awareness. In consequence, stressors such as noise and heat may have interpersonal effects both during and after exposure, perhaps unnoticed by those affected.

B. Noise

Noise is unwanted sound. One of its consequences is a decreased likelihood of altruism, both during and after the noise. In one study (Sherrod & Downs, 1974), students worked on a laboratory task while exposed to loud or soft (uncontrollable) noise. When they finished and began to leave, another student (actually a confederate) asked for help in a project that involved solving arithmetic

PHOTO 17-1. *The noise of construction work inhibits prosocial behavior.*

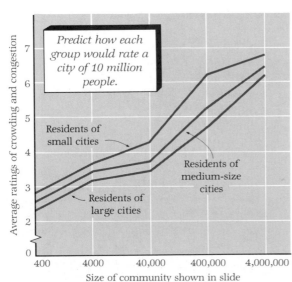

FIGURE 17-6. Ratings of crowding and congestion in slides viewed by residents of small, medium, and large cities.

problems. Those who had earlier been exposed to loud noise helped less. Another researcher staged an accident in which a pedestrian dropped packages near a construction area during jackhammer noise of varying loudness. Fewer passersby stopped to help in noisy conditions, especially when the noise was loud (Page, 1977; see also Wiener, 1976; Yinon & Bizman, 1980).

One explanation for lower rates of altruism during noise is that discomfort impels people to keep moving rather than help. Another explanation is based on overload: noise may occupy so much of an individual's attention that none is left for someone who might need help (S. Cohen, 1978). To test this idea, researchers staged incidents on a city street in which a pedestrian dropped a box of books. In half the incidents, the pedestrian's arm was in a cast. In some cases a noisy power lawnmower was running nearby. When the mower was quiet, people gave more help when it was needed most— when the pedestrian's arm was in the cast. But when the mower was making noise, passersby helped less frequently regardless of the cast, as shown in Figure 17-7 (Mathews & Canon, 1975). As expected, noise led these people to overlook an important social cue.

To demonstrate that noise creates inattention to social cues, Cohen and Lezak (1977) showed color slides to students as they learned lists of nonsense syllables in either quiet or noisy conditions. The slides depicted people in everyday activities or in dangerous situations. For instance, one slide showed a man paying for oil at a gas station; another showed a man holding up a gas station. When the students were unexpectedly quizzed about the slides, those in the noisy condition were able to describe fewer of the dangerous situations. In another experiment on the same hypothesis (Korte & Grant, 1980), researchers placed "novel objects" near a sidewalk, including a female research assistant holding a large yellow teddy bear. Pedestrians who had passed two such objects were interviewed when traffic noise was measured as either quiet or loud. As expected, fewer pedestrians had noticed the novel objects when traffic noise was loud. They also walked faster and looked straight ahead in noisy conditions.

Noise also increases the chances that people will respond to an instigation to aggression. In one study (Geen & O'Neal, 1969), volunteers saw either an aggressive or a nonaggressive film. Then, in a room that was either noisy or quiet, they had an ostensible opportunity to shock another person (an accomplice who did not actually receive the shock). As expected, participants gave more shocks in the noisy condition. In a similar study, college students heard random bursts of noise, either loud or soft, and then had an opportunity to give another person a "shock." Some participants had been angered earlier by an accomplice. Those who had been angered and exposed to loud noise gave more intense "shocks." However, when the participants were given a button that they were told would stop the noise, they were not more aggressive, even when they did not use the button (Donnerstein & Wilson, 1976; see also Geen, 1978). Apparently, if noise is loud and uncontrollable, it intensifies a person's responses to conditions that can lead to aggression (see Chapter 8).

C. Heat

Like noise, heat can create discomfort or stress, depending on its intensity. Following the urban riots of the 1960s, social psychologists speculated

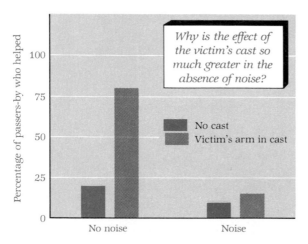

FIGURE 17-7. Helping behavior as a function of whether the victim's arm was in a cast and presence or absence of loud noise.

that uncomfortable summer heat had triggered the violence. There is some evidence for this view (see Carlsmith & Anderson, 1979), but it is controversial; and a laboratory experiment suggested that heat contributes to aggression only up to a point—when extremely uncomfortable, it simply makes people want to leave the situation (Bell & Baron, 1976; see Chapter 8).

Other researchers have hypothesized that heat leads to disliking, but the evidence leaves doubts that it does. Groups of volunteers were placed in either a comfortable or a "hot" environmental chamber (100° F with 60% relative humidity), where they performed simple tasks for 45 minutes. After seeing an attitude scale supposedly completed by a stranger, they indicated how well they liked the stranger. People said they liked the stranger less in the "hot" condition (Griffitt, 1970; Griffitt & Veitch, 1971). Kenrick and Johnson (1979), however, pointed out that other research on stressful circumstances had found people drawn together, just the opposite of disliking. These researchers questioned the generalizability of results of the "bogus stranger" technique and conducted an experiment to compare these results with liking for an actual person in adverse conditions. Using loud noise instead of heat as the stressor, they found that people under stress expressed greater attraction for a real person in a stressful environment, but less liking for the fictitious stranger, as shown in Figure 17-8. These findings suggest that the adverse effect of heat on liking may apply only to reactions to strangers absent from the stressful situation and that sharing a stressful environment may even draw people together.

In summary, environmental stress in response to noise can lead to insensitivity to social cues and decreased likelihood of altruism, during or after the noise, and can create unusual sensitivity to instigations to aggression. We turn next to another form of stress, which seems to have similar effects.

■ IV. Crowding

Crowding is a form of stress that sometimes occurs in a densely populated environment. It may be triggered by riding on an elevator jammed with

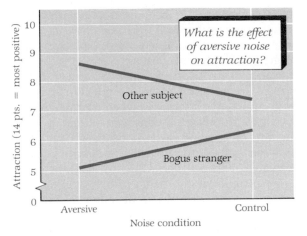

FIGURE 17-8. Liking for a "bogus stranger" and for another person in the same room as a function of environmental stress in the form of loud unpredictable noise.

passengers, by walking on a downtown sidewalk at rush hour, by trying to reach a bargain table at a busy department store, or by spending the intermission of a popular movie with a capacity crowd in a small lobby. But crowding is subjective, so that one person's reactions to these situations may differ from someone else's. And many densely populated environments are not stressful but, rather, pleasant and stimulating, such as cocktail parties, football games, concerts, revivals, and political rallies.

A. The social-pathology hypothesis

Early research on crowding focused almost exclusively on **population density** in cities (the number of people per unit of space, or the number of square feet per person). Many correlational studies associated high population density (measured as the number of residents per acre) with high rates of crime and mental illness. This evidence encouraged the idea that crowding—which was equated with high population density—led to a variety of social ills. A review of popular literature of the 1960s found dozens of articles that subscribed to the **social-pathology hypothesis** (Zlutnick & Altman, 1972). The idea prevailed despite a critical flaw in the correlational research: it overlooked the fact that densely populated areas of cities are usually the poorest, and pathologies found there could result from poverty. One of several tests of this idea used census data from Chicago, which showed positive correlations of the number of persons per acre with rates of death, tuberculosis, infant mortality, public assistance, and juvenile delinquency. When such factors as occupation, income, education, ethnicity, and quality of housing were statistically controlled, however, the relationships disappeared or became negative (Winsborough, 1965).

Proponents of the social-pathology hypothesis have pointed to evidence from nonhuman animals to support their views. One of the best-known studies of nonhuman crowding is called the "behavioral sink," a project in which high density created many pathologies in a colony of rats. Calhoun (1962) placed 48 Norway rats in four connected pens that could comfortably accommodate them, allowed the population to increase to 80, supplied sufficient food and water, and observed. The crowded rats soon began to exhibit abnormalities in nestbuilding, courting, mating, rearing of the young, and social organization. Some males became aggressive and disregarded ritualized signals of submission that usually end a fight. Females often neglected their young, and as many as 75% of the infant rats died. Territories were ignored or were maintained through force. Autopsies revealed signs of prolonged stress, such as enlarged adrenal glands.

A study in a natural setting (Christian, Flyger, & Davis, 1960) showed similar results. Sika deer on an island near the Maryland coast had developed an unusually high density of about one deer per acre, or about 300 deer. During the winter two years later, over half of the herd died even though food was plentiful. Autopsies showed enlarged adrenal glands, indicating prolonged stress. More died the next winter, and the herd stabilized at around 80. Other research has associated high population density with stress and pathology in many nonhuman species (Freedman, 1972).

Social psychologists interested in establishing whether the social-pathology hypothesis applies in urban populations have tried to take account of such factors as income, occupation, and ethnic background. They have also looked more closely at population density, which varies greatly within census tracts or districts of a city. Galle, Gove, and McPherson (1972) distinguished four types of density: persons per room within a dwelling, rooms per dwelling, dwellings per structure, and structures per acre. Their analysis of Chicago census data included statistical controls for differences in socioeconomic status and ethnicity. Results showed that the number of *persons per room* was associated with rates of mortality, public assistance, and juvenile delinquency. A similar study of New York data failed to show the same connection of household density and social pathology (Freedman, Heshka, & Levy, 1975; see also Kirmeyer, 1978). Other studies did link household density with violent crime. In an analysis of census data from 65 nations (including Canada and the United States), Booth and Welch (1973) controlled statistically for socioeconomic factors and found a correlation between density within households and homicide rate. A similar study (Booth & Welch, 1974) used data from U.S. cities with populations over 25,000 and statistically controlled for race, education, and income. In cities of over 100,000, persons-per-room density accounted for significant increments in crimes against persons, such as murder, assault, and rape, especially among poor families. In smaller cities, where a crowded household is perhaps more easily escaped, the relationship of crime and household density was weaker.

Unfortunately, even the best studies of census data are correlational—they can discover only associations between variables, not causal relationships—and their use of aggregate data makes it impossible to uncover the social-psychological basis of the findings. If high population density is associated with "pathologies" such as crime—and the evidence is not compelling—we still need to understand the underlying processes.

B. Theories of crowding

Ideas about crowding have gone considerably beyond the social-pathology hypothesis. The conception of crowding as a form of stress has inspired five general models that identify sources of crowding in high density and predict responses to them, as shown in Table 17-2.

1. The *overload model* applies the concept of **overload** (receiving inputs faster than they can be processed) to crowding. The model predicts that too much social interaction, or excessively close proximity of other people, leads to the avoidance of social contact through such actions as nonverbal compensation for excessive immediacy (see Chapter 5). For instance, the passengers in a crowded elevator stand silently with their arms clenched to their sides, avoiding eye contact, until they reach their floors. Frequent crowding, which could occur in a large city, might lead to a habit of withdrawal and the screening out of social cues (Milgram, 1970).

2. The *interference model* of crowding emphasizes the possibility that in densely populated environments other people block the attainment of one's goals or one's use of scare resources (Schopler & Stockdale, 1977; Sundstrom, 1975b). For instance, a teenager in a crowded home may be thwarted in his attempts to study in a bedroom shared by three brothers. This may result in frustration. A long-term consequence may be aggression (see Chapter 8).

3. In the *control model* of crowding, stress arises from the inability to influence events the individual tries to control (Baron & Rodin, 1978; Rodin & Baum, 1978). For example, a city-dweller on a crowded sidewalk may shun eye contact and try to ignore and avoid people but still get bumped and jostled. The bumping and jostling is less important than the failure of efforts to avoid it. Responses to a loss of personal control may include withdrawal and hostility and, if it continues, *learned helplessness*. In contrast to the overload model, which predicts how people cope with crowding, the control model predicts what happens when coping fails.

4. Altman's (1975) theory of *privacy regulation* predicts that someone who experiences too much social contact will choose from the many strategies available for regulating social contact, including physical withdrawal, avoidance of nonverbal immediacy, and assertion of territorial control. If these efforts at "boundary control" meet with repeated failure, the person may eventually experience stress and may even have difficulty differentiating self from others.

5. The *overstaffing model* derives from Barker's (1968) theory of the "behavior setting," an identifiable place with boundaries, characteristic physical features, and a recognized set of roles for participants (see Wicker, 1979). Crowding may arise when a behavior setting contains more people than necessary to fulfill its roles (Stokols, 1978), a situation called overstaffing, which may lead to

TABLE 17-2. Models of crowding

Theory	Sources of stress in high density	Immediate response	Possible long-term outcome
Overload	People in close proximity; too many people	Avoidance of social contact; inattention to social cues	Habitual withdrawal
Interference	People blocking access to resources or interfering with activities	Frustration; hostility	Aggression
Control	Inability to control sources of overload or interference	Withdrawal; hostility	Learned helplessness
Privacy regulation	Excessive social contact	Seeking of privacy through verbal, nonverbal behavior	Symptoms of stress; indistinct self-identity
Overstaffing	More people than roles in a behavior setting	Lack of involvement; low motivation	Alienation

feelings of alienation among those who have no role.

Importance of the setting. According to a theory of crowding by Daniel Stokols (1976, 1978), crowding is most intense and difficult to resolve in *primary environments*, or places where "an individual spends much time, relates to others on a personal basis, and engages in a wide range of personally important activities" (1976, p. 73)— for example, one's residence. (This concept resembles the "primary territory" discussed earlier.) Stokols suggests that, in primary environments, sources of crowding such as overload, "thwarting," and overstaffing threaten an individual's "psychological security." In *secondary environments*, in contrast, "encounters with others are relatively transitory, anonymous, and inconsequential" (1976, p. 73). Shopping centers, sidewalks, corridors in schools, and elevators are examples. Crowding may be less threatening in such places because people can usually leave when they want to.

Importance of perceptions. Some theorists contend that crowding depends on the way a situation is perceived. Patterson (1976) proposes that crowding can occur when people experience arousal due to the close proximity of others—but only when they label their reaction as a negative response to the other people (see Chapter 3). Other theorists agree, arguing that attribution of arousal to something besides the people in a room may lessen the experience of crowding (Worchel & Esterson, 1978). Drawing from social-comparison theory, Baum, Fisher, and Solomon (1981) suggest that accurate information about a high-density situation can reduce stress due to crowding.

C. Current research evidence

Short-term crowding in the laboratory. Social psychologists have studied the effects of high

PHOTO 17-2. *Residents of this apartment building may be particularly sensitive to crowding in their immediate environment.*

density by packing people into rooms with about four to eight square feet of floor space per person (think of a crowded classroom or concert). This has usually created discomfort and even physiological arousal (Aiello, Epstein, & Karlin, 1975a; see also Evans, 1978). However, high density seems to affect men and women differently: whereas men usually react negatively to others in high density, women often react positively. For example, when groups of eight men or eight women worked on a task in a large or small room, the small room created crowding for everyone, but men made more hostile comments under conditions of high density, whereas women made more hostile remarks in low density (Stokols, Rall, Pinner, & Schopler, 1973). Parallel findings appear for cooperation versus competition (see the review by Sundstrom, 1978).

As predicted by the overload model, people experience greater discomfort and arousal in high-density settings that foster eye contact (Patterson, Roth, & Schenk, 1979; Schaeffer & Patterson, 1980). Occupants of crowded settings cope with excessive eye contact or physical contact by withdrawing from interaction (Greenberg & Firestone, 1977; Sundstrom, 1975a). Researchers have even observed withdrawal among people waiting with one or two persons in *anticipation* of being crowded (Baum & Greenberg, 1975; Baum & Koman, 1976).

Early laboratory research looked for, but failed to find, adverse effects of high density on task performance. Groups of students worked in cramped quarters on math problems, crossing out certain letters in a text, forming words from collections of letters, and many other duties. High density had no adverse effects even after several hours of work (for example, Freedman, Klevansky, & Ehrlich, 1971).

Performance of highly complex tasks or tasks sensitive to interference by other people does deteriorate under crowded conditions. For instance, people did more poorly at tracing a three-dimensional maze in crowded conditions (Paulus, Annis, Seta, Schkade, & Matthews, 1976). Another study reported similar results but only immediately after participants had entered a crowded situation (Paulus & Matthews, 1980). Similarly, high den-

sity led to poorer performance on a task that called for doing two things at once (Evans, 1979) and impaired performance on tasks that called for assembling things in cramped quarters where people get in the way (Heller, Groff, & Solomon, 1977; Saegert, 1974). In a project involving a search for items in a single file cabinet, an increase in group size produced the drop in individual performance expected because of interference. However, performance in high density was improved by paying people on a piece rate, although their reported stress also rose (McCallum, Rusbult, Hong, Walden, & Schopler, 1979).

Like noise, crowding produces negative after-effects. In an experiment modeled after Glass and Singer's studies on noise, groups of eight women worked on several tasks in a small or large room. Some groups were told they were free to leave any time, to give them a sense of control. Results indicated that neither density nor control affected performance. However, when participants later worked on another task in a more spacious room, those who had been crowded and had had no control did more poorly on measures of tolerance for frustration (Sherrod, 1974; see also Cohen & Spacapan, 1978; Evans, 1979).

Crowding in neighborhoods and public places. Urban residents surveyed in one study (Baum, Davis, & Aiello, 1978) reported that, on streets containing stores, they felt more crowded, encountered unfamiliar people more often, and experienced more unwanted social contact. People in crowded areas were less likely to use sidewalks or public places for interaction. Consistent with the overload model of crowding, people in a store noticed fewer details when it was busy (Saegert, MacIntosh, & West, 1974).

Crowding in residences and institutions. Not surprisingly, crowding increases with the number of persons per room in a household (Eoyang, 1974) or in an institution (Paulus, Cox, McCain, & Chandler, 1975). Prolonged residential or institutional crowding may have serious consequences, including physical symptoms (Paulus, McCain, & Cox, 1978). For example, after spending a semester in dormitory rooms designed for two persons but used to accommodate three (by random assignment), "tripled" students felt more crowded and showed poorer performance on complex tasks in a laboratory; tripled women had more health problems (Aiello, Epstein, & Karlin, 1975b). Other research found lower grades among tripled students, despite these students' greater withdrawal (Glassman, Burkhart, Grant, & Vallery, 1978; see also Karlin, Rosen, & Epstein, 1979). Members of the triads apparently tended to contain an alliance, or coalition, of two students and one "isolate," who had particularly severe problems (Aiello, Baum, & Gormley, 1981; see also Baum, Shapiro, Murray, & Wideman, 1979; Reddy, Baum, Fleming, & Aiello, 1981). These findings point to the debilitating effects of crowding in dormitory rooms and perhaps in other residential settings as well.

■ V. Architecture and the built environment

The physical environment can influence people in many other ways besides creating stress, and some of its influences have implications for social behavior. For instance, pleasant surroundings may predispose people to respond favorably to others.

A. Pleasant places

In a test of the idea that a comfortable setting leads to positive responses to other people, college students were ushered into one of three equal-sized rooms to rate a series of photographs (Maslow & Mintz, 1956). The "average" room was a professor's office, well kept but obviously a place of work. The "beautiful" room was carpeted, well lit, pleasantly furnished, and tastefully decorated. At the other extreme, the "ugly" room looked like a janitor's storeroom. Its walls were gray, its windows half-covered with dirty shades; light came from an unshaded overhead light bulb. Pails, mops, and brooms lined the walls, and the bare floor badly needed cleaning. A student interviewer asked each participant to rate ten photographs of faces on "fatigue versus energy," "displeasure versus well-

being," and other properties. Ratings were most positive in the "beautiful" room and most negative in the "ugly" room. The researchers unobtrusively observed the two interviewers and found that they finished their interviews more quickly in the "ugly" room. Asked to rate the photos, the interviewers themselves gave lower ratings in the "ugly" room (Mintz, 1956). Participants in another project viewed color slides of faculty offices at a university; the addition of such decorative items as a potted plant or an aquarium with fish led to higher ratings of the offices on expected comfort and welcomeness (D. E. Campbell, 1978).

Further evidence of an association between positive reactions to the environment and favorable responses to people came from an experiment in which participants wrote down either the positive or the negative features of their residences. Then they "ran into" another student (an accomplice), who asked for help in a project that involved doing arithmetic problems. Those who had focused on positive features of their environments helped more. A second experiment revealed a similar effect on altruism after participants viewed color slides of attractive or unattractive settings (Sherrod, Armstrong, Hewitt, Madonia, Speno, & Teruya, 1977).

In hopes of creating an atmosphere conducive to classroom discussion, two environmental psychologists arranged for the remodeling of a traditional classroom on a university campus. Before renovation it had rows of plastic desk-arm chairs facing toward a blackboard and two large tables. The remodeled classroom had three-tiered benches lined with fabric-covered cushions and arranged in a hexagon. Wooden paneling was added to round the sharp corners of the room, lighting was made adjustable, and decorative items were added. Observations of ten different classes in the new, "soft" classroom, containing up to 20 students, revealed that an average of 79% of the students participated in discussions, compared with 37% participation observed in other classrooms similar to the experimental room before its renovation (Sommer & Olsen, 1980). On another university campus one of two identical 40-student classrooms was remodeled by painting it in attractive colors and adding posters, area rugs, plants, and other decorations. The undecorated room had gray walls and white chairs and was described as "sterile." Introductory psychology classes each used one of the rooms for half a term, then switched. Ratings of the teachers (who were not informed about the hypotheses) were higher in the remodeled room, and grades were higher, although class participation was unaffected in these relatively large classrooms (Wollin & Montagne, 1981).

On the whole, the evidence points to a positive effect of a pleasant environment on an individual's responses to other people. This is consistent with the practice of business executives, clinical psychologists, and other professionals of carefully decorating their offices to create pleasant settings for interviews.

B. "Sociopetal" spaces

Some settings encourage conversation, and the psychiatrist Humphrey Osmond (1957) called them **"sociopetal" spaces.** They place people at comfortable conversational distances (see Chapter 5), facing toward each other to allow eye contact. An example occurred in a new geriatric ward for women at a Saskatchewan hospital. The wardroom was cheerfully decorated and furnished; it was the showplace of the hospital. However, the patients seemed depressed and sat in their new chairs staring into space. The hospital's consultants, Sommer and Ross (1958), noticed that the chairs were lined up along the walls, side by side, all facing in the same direction. They persuaded the staff to rearrange the chairs in circles around small tables. The patients resisted the change, possibly because it disrupted territorial habits, but after a few weeks the frequency of conversations had nearly doubled.

In a more formal experiment (Mehrabian & Diamond, 1971a), students entered a well-furnished room in pairs to listen to music and give opinions about it. They sat in chairs arranged so that they were oriented directly toward each other or at angles of 90° or 180°. They were separated by distances from three to nine feet, all within the range for comfortable conversation. As participants waited for the music to begin, observers surreptitiously recorded affiliative behavior, such as

the number of statements and the amount of positive verbal content. The more directly the chairs faced, the more affiliative the students were. In a similar experiment (Mehrabian & Diamond, 1971b), groups of four strangers could choose their own seats in a room that allowed various seating arrangements. The more directly the participants faced each other, the more time they spent talking.

The opposite of "sociopetal" space is called "sociofugal"—a setting that discourages conversation by arranging people within conversational distance so that they have difficulty making eye contact (Osmond, 1957). An example is a typical airport waiting area, like the one shown in Photo 17-3. Other such spaces include bus depots, some classrooms, and reception areas in clinics and hospitals. The use of sociofugal arrangements in such places may reflect deliberate attempts to create conditions in which people can go about their business without having to attend to one another. However, we go to places like cocktail lounges and bars seeking conversation. These places are usually at least partly sociopetal, with chairs grouped around tables.

People who try to visit in environments unsuited to conversation may blame their discomfort not on the setting but on each other. A recent experiment called for conversations among pairs of people in uncomfortably distant chairs—11 feet apart—or at a comfortable distance. Participants in the distant arrangement felt more ill at ease. However, even though the environment clearly allowed no choice in seating distance, participants in the distant condition held their partners responsible for their own negative feelings (Aiello & Thompson, 1978). Perhaps people in sociofugal settings misconstrue the distance created by the environment as aloofness by the occupants.

Office designers have tried to capitalize on the impact of the physical environment on conversations in the "office landscape" (or, more recently, the "open-plan office"). The idea is that office employees located in close proximity to their coworkers, with few intervening physical barriers, will communicate more frequently and handle work more efficiently than those separated by distance or walls (see Pile, 1978). The result: offices

PHOTO 17-3. *Waiting areas, like this airport concourse, are typically designed to discourage conversation.*

with huge, open work areas containing many desks and few, if any, walls. Workspaces are not separated at all in some installations; in others they are separated by screens, furniture, bookcases, and potted plants. Some offices incorporate shoulder-high interlocking panels from which desks and files are hung (see Photo 17-4). In a field study of an early office landscape (Hundert & Greenfield, 1969), two sections of a manufacturing firm simultaneously moved to new buildings, one to an open office and the other to a conventional office. Six months later the employees in both sections completed a questionnaire. Those in the office landscape said they spent more time talking but cooperated less with coworkers and accomplished less than before. They found the open arrangement more noisy and less private. Other studies of people who moved to open offices reveal a consistent decline in privacy but mixed results on communication, which has improved in some ways, such as convenience of job-related contacts and informal conversation, but declined in another—

ability to hold confidential conversations (see Sundstrom, Herbert, & Brown, 1982).

C. Seating arrangements and group discussion

Seating arrangements also influence group discussions. One experiment found that people in group discussions at circular tables addressed most remarks to those seated directly across the table (Steinzor, 1950). A related study (Strodtbeck & Hook, 1961) simulated jury deliberations in groups of 12 persons, who were asked to elect their own leaders. The "juries" sat at rectangular tables with five chairs on the long sides and one at each end. Those at the ends of the table, who could most easily make eye contact with all the others, were most often elected leader. People in end positions were also seen as most influential and participated more than other members in the group discussions. Perhaps dominant people chose end positions, or perhaps end positions facilitated leadership.

PHOTO 17-4. *In the open office, barriers between workspaces are minimized in order to facilitate communication.*

The idea that people address those whom they face may apply directly in classrooms, where research reveals that students facing the instructor participate in discussions more than other students. Similarly, in rooms with chairs arranged in rows, students in the front rows and in the middle sections of the classroom tend to participate most, as shown in Figure 17-9 (Sommer, 1967; see also Adams, 1969). One explanation is that the students most likely to participate chose front or center seats; or perhaps students in these seats feel compelled to participate because of greater opportunity for eye contact with the instructor (Koneya, 1976). In another study, students at first selected their own seats but later were randomly assigned to seats; results showed greater participation in the front half of the room only after random assignment of seats (Levine, O'Neal, Garwood, & McDonald, 1980). Apparently, greater participation in the front and center of the room is at least partly due to the environment.

Students who sit in the front or center of a classroom tend to get high grades (Becker, Sommer, Bee, & Oxley, 1973; Sommer, 1974). A later study found highest grades in the front half of the room only when students selected their own seats (Levine et al., 1980). These findings are consistent with greater participation in the front and center sections of the room. However, an early study involving over 20,000 students found higher grades in the center of the room than in the rear, sides, *or* front (Griffith, 1921), and the evidence pointed to social facilitation as the best explanation (Knowles, 1982; see also Chapter 14). A recent study also found better grades in the center section of a class where students had been randomly assigned to seats (Stires, 1980). This suggests a second environmental influence that may operate in a classroom: for those in the center section surrounded by classmates, better performance might reflect the motivating influence of their neighbors.

D. Proximity and friendship

Physical proximity of residences apparently makes the occupants likely to meet as they go to and from their houses or apartments, which can

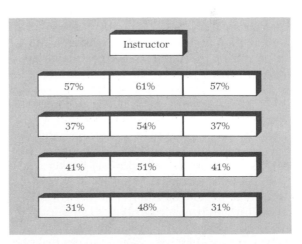

FIGURE 17-9. Classroom participation as a function of seating positions. Students who sat in the front row or center section of a classroom were more frequent participants in class discussion, perhaps because of greater opportunity for eye contact with the instructor.

lead to friendship if the neighbors are compatible. As mentioned in Chapter 6, Festinger et al. (1950) conducted a field study in a housing complex for married students to test the hypothesis that neighbors tend to become friends. In a part of the project called Westgate West, couples lived in two-story buildings with five similar apartments on each floor, all with doors facing in the same direction. Couples had been assigned to apartments as vacancies arose. Researchers asked them to name the three other couples with whom they socialized most. The closer the residents' apartments were on the same floor, the more often they mentioned each other. Of all next-door neighbors who could have been mentioned, 41% were chosen. Only 22% of the possible choices two doors away were chosen. Couples on the same floor selected each other as friends much more often than those on different floors; couples on second floors were often friends with first-floor couples who lived next to the stairs.

Other research also associates friendship and physical proximity of residences. For instance, a study of a Chicago suburb found that parties consisted mainly of neighbors from the same block (Whyte, 1956). Other researchers found similar results (see Rosow, 1961). However, most of these studies involved people who had recently moved into a new neighborhood. If proximity contributed to interaction and friendship, it apparently did so mainly during the initial phases of residents' relationships. Other research found that new dormitory residents formed friendships at first on the basis of proximity but later sought out people with attitudes similar to their own (Newcomb, 1961). Proximity apparently does not contribute to long-term friendship unless other conditions also hold, such as similarity of attitudes and backgrounds (Athanasiou & Yoshioka, 1973; Gans, 1970) or the necessity of mutual assistance (Michelson, 1970).

Proximity may also contribute to animosity. In a field study conducted in an apartment complex in California, researchers asked residents to name the couples they liked most and least. Friendships increased with proximity, but people most disliked were typically even closer than friends (Ebbesen, Kjos, & Konečni, 1976).

E. Social overload in dormitories

In the program of research on corridor- and suite-design dormitories described at the beginning of this chapter, the occupants of rooms on long corridors experienced unwanted social contact in the hallways and bathrooms. Baum, Harpin, and Valins (1975) observed that corridor residents coped by withdrawing from social contact. To test this idea, a laboratory experiment was conducted among first-year students from the two types of dormitories. On arriving at the laboratory, each student was asked to sit in a waiting room. Another student (actually an accomplice) was already there. Corridor residents sat farther away, looked less toward the student's face, and initiated fewer conversations than suite residents did. Corridor residents apparently did all they could to avoid social contact with a stranger. In a group task, corridor residents also showed less inclination than suite residents to rely on group consensus.

An experiment in another dormitory (Reichner, 1979) confirmed that corridor residents prefer to minimize social contact. Corridor and suite residents each worked on a group task with two other persons (actually accomplices), who either included them in group discussion or ignored them. In contrast to suite residents, corridor residents were actually more comfortable when ignored.

Unfortunately for corridor residents, withdrawal could have only a small effect on the overload they experienced at the dormitory, since avoidance of eye contact and conversation could hardly change the numbers of people they encountered near their rooms. In consequence, corridor residents probably experienced pervasive, continued stress from an uncontrollable source. One result could be *learned helplessness* (see Chapter 12), in which the individual becomes passive.

To find out whether corridor residents develop learned helplessness, Baum, Aiello, and Calesnick (1978) conducted a study among first-year students who had been randomly assigned to either suite- or corridor-design dormitories. The students participated during their first, third, or seventh week on campus in an experiment that called for them to play a game with three choices: a cooperative response, a competitive response, or a withdrawal response (in which neither party won). Reliance on withdrawal was thought to show helplessness. Corridor residents consistently gave more competitive and fewer cooperative responses than suite residents, although both groups decreased in competitiveness over the three testing periods. By the end of the seventh week, suite residents had become more cooperative; corridor residents increasingly resorted to withdrawal. In postgame interviews, corridor residents indicated that their competitive responses were designed to express disliking. They explained their choice of withdrawal by saying things like "I don't really care what happens in the game." Corridor residents apparently did develop signs of learned helplessness in an environment that promoted uncontrollable social contact.

It is possible to remedy the problems created by the corridor-design dormitory, as demonstrated in a study of environmental intervention. On a campus where students lived in dormitories with long corridors or short corridors, Baum and Davis (1980) arranged to modify one floor of a long-corridor dorm by dividing it in the middle with a lounge area entered through doors from both sides, as shown in Figure 17-10. Students from the long, short, and modified corridors completed surveys and were observed for 15 weeks. The three groups were comparable at first, but as predicted, the long-corridor residents soon began to report crowding and unwanted social contact, while, in contrast, the short-corridor and modified-corridor residents reported few such problems. After ten weeks the long-corridor residents tended to avoid social encounters in the dormitory and to close their doors. They also avoided social contact in the laboratory. The relatively simple architectural change in the modified-corridor design apparently prevented such outcomes.

F. Urban overload

Large cities expose people to many potential sources of stress all at once: noise, heat, air pollution, crowds, automobile traffic, and complex visual scenes including flashing signs and display windows. City-dwellers probably adapt to such intense stimulation after a while and develop ways

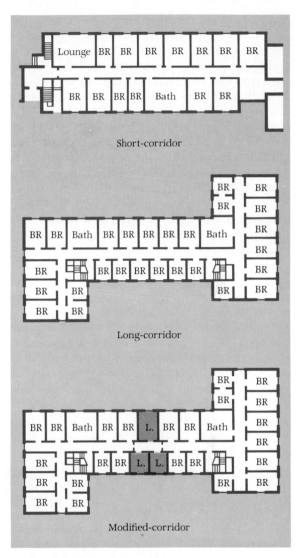

Short-corridor

Long-corridor

Modified-corridor

FIGURE 17-10. In the short-corridor dormitory design (top), residents experienced little of the crowding and social overload found in the long-corridor dorm (middle), where 40 students shared one corridor and two baths. One long-corridor was modified by dividing it at the center with a lounge made up of three former bedrooms and a section of the hallway (bottom; lounge area shaded). As hoped, residents of the modified-corridor experienced little of the unwanted social contact found in the long-corridor.

of insulating themselves from overload, such as habitual inattention to social cues and withdrawal from involvement with other people. This is predicted by the **urban-overload hypothesis** (McCauley & Taylor, 1976), which, unfortunately, is difficult to study. When city-dwellers do show patterns of behavior different from those of people in small towns, the differences could be due to the different norms of cities or to the different personalities of people who choose to live in cities. For instance, Milgram (1970) found urban residents less helpful than suburbanites to strangers asking for assistance. This agrees with the overload hypothesis, but perhaps it reflects big-city norms.

Recent research has confirmed the urban-overload hypothesis through procedures that avoid comparing urban and suburban populations. A study conducted in Holland involved the identification of "high-input" and "low-input" areas in certain neighborhoods of cities and rural towns by measuring noise, automobile traffic, and pedestrian traffic. Researchers stationed a person in each area who looked like a stranger in need of assistance. The person received more help in "low-input" areas of both cities and small towns (Korte, Ypma, & Toppen, 1975). Another study extended an earlier finding that people in cities are less willing to make eye contact with strangers than people in suburbs or small towns (McCauley & New-

man, 1977). To obtain a rural/urban comparison involving the same people, McCauley, Coleman, and DeFusco (1978) observed commuters from a quiet suburb to a busy area of Philadelphia. Male and female experimenters stood in commuter-train stations in Philadelphia in the mornings and in suburban stations in the evenings, recording the number of people leaving the trains who returned their gaze. Eye contact was consistently lower in the city. In a study of altruism using the "lost-letter technique," researchers measured the density of pedestrian traffic in three towns in areas where a stamped, addressed letter was dropped. As predicted by the overload hypothesis, the density of pedestrian traffic was strongly correlated with the number of passersby who ignored the letter (Kammann, Thomson, & Irwin, 1979).

If the urban-overload hypothesis applies to relationships with acquaintances and friends, perhaps city dwellers have more acquaintances, but less involvement with each, than suburbanites. A study designed to test this idea found just the opposite. City-dwellers reported fewer and longer conversations with friends and acquaintances, both by telephone and face to face (McCauley & Taylor, 1976). Apparently the urban-overload hypothesis applies only to involvements with strangers.

VI. SUMMARY

The physical environment provides a resource for regulating and organizing interpersonal interaction and at the same time can influence social behavior. People use their physical settings to obtain *privacy*, an intentional retreat by an individual or group from contact with others. Privacy allows control over the aspects of the self or the group's interaction seen by various audiences, and it also allows the regulation of social contact. Research indicates that privacy in office environments depends on the degree of physical enclosure.

People also regulate social contact through

the establishment of *territories*, analogous to the bounded regions claimed and defended by some nonhuman animals. However, human attachments to places are complex and may better be described in terms of several types of territories. A *primary territory* is central to the individual's daily life and allows considerable control over the boundaries; in a primary territory the occupant has an advantage in a competitive encounter, in a phenomenon called *territorial dominance*. A *secondary territory* is controlled by the members of a group. A *public territory*, temporarily claimed in a public place such as a library or cafeteria, seems to give its occupant little control. People choose public territories as far from others as possible and mark them through nonverbal cues and personal belongings but often hesitate to defend them against intrusion. Territorial patterns among the members of a group who share an environment depend on the group's dominance hierarchy; groups that fail to establish orderly territorial habits tend to function poorly.

The physical environment can create *stress*, a physiological and psychological response to a demand, challenge, or threat that includes arousal and mobilization of resources for coping. Environmental sources of stress such as noise are evaluated against personal standards of judgment called *adaptation levels*. Stressors are most disturbing when a person first encounters them; after continued exposure the individual may become accustomed to the stressor through *adaptation* in perceptions. Loud, uncontrollable noise has been shown to cause inattention to social cues; noise also brings overresponsiveness to instigations of aggression. Noise leads to decreased altruism, apparently because in noisy conditions people protect themselves from *overload* (more stimulation or information than can be processed) by ignoring strangers and avoiding social involvement.

Crowding is a form of stress that sometimes occurs in conditions of high *population density*. At one time high density in large cities was regarded as a source of social pathologies, but the evidence for this causal relationship is weak. Theorists have identified several sources of stress in high-density environments, including overload, interference, and inability to control one's environment. Recent research in dormitories suggests that crowding can adversely affect even physical health and performance in school.

Architecture can influence social behavior by providing a pleasant environment; research evidence suggests that people in pleasant places tend to respond favorably to others. *"Sociopetal" spaces* encourage conversation through seating arrangements that bring people into comfortable conversational distance while facing each other directly enough to allow eye contact. Other settings, such as airport waiting areas, discourage conversation. In group discussions people are apt to address those whom they face most directly. Similarly, participation in classrooms is greatest in the front and center seats, where eye contact between student and instructor is most likely, and in center sections of the room, where social facilitation can occur. People choose friends from among their closest neighbors, apparently because physical proximity encourages social interaction. But some residences create too much social contact, such as "corridor-design" dormitories, whose occupants cope by withdrawing and eventually show signs of learned helplessness.

According to the *urban-overload hypothesis*, city-dwellers react to the many sources of overload in a big city by avoiding involvement with people. Research confirms this idea but only for involvements with strangers, not friends or acquaintances.

GLOSSARY TERMS

adaptation	population density	sociopetal spaces
adaptation level	primary territory	stress
crowding	privacy	territorial dominance
dominance hierarchy	privacy regulation	territory
interaction territory	public territory	urban-overload hypothesis
noise	secondary territory	
overload	social-pathology hypothesis	

18

Social Psychology & Society

Research that produces nothing but books will not suffice.
■ KURT LEWIN

One faces the future with one's past.
■ PEARL S. BUCK

Social psychology has discovered a great deal about human behavior—how people love and hate, how they help and harm, how they perceive as individuals and how they relate in groups. However, the more cynical reader might still ask "What good does this knowledge do?" After all, much of the research of social psychology has been conducted in laboratories, in a rarefied atmosphere removed from the currents of everyday life. Yet, astronomy laboratories have put people on the moon, biological laboratories have developed vaccines to prevent polio, and physics laboratories have produced nuclear energy, with both good and ill effects. Can social psychology match this record of contribution to society?

Some people argue that social psychology has done little. Virulent critics claim that social psychology *can't* do anything—that it has little to contribute to solving the problems of society. But there is evidence to the contrary. Although errors have been made and applications have not been as rapid as many people would like, there is substantial evidence of social-psychological contributions to understanding and solving social issues. And the potential for contribution is even greater.

Many have recognized the need for social-psychological contributions. Although technological developments in the past several decades have been tremendous, it often seems that humanity has made little headway over centuries. Yet, we may be on the brink of changing that assessment—of using social psychology not to control people but to help them run their own lives in more profitable ways. In his presidential address to the American Psychological Association, George A. Miller (1970) urged an extension of this viewpoint. He said "I can imagine nothing that we could do that would be more relevant to human welfare, and nothing that could pose a greater challenge to the next generation of psychologists, than to discover how best to give psychology away" (p. 21).

Miller, reflecting a theme of this book, notes that each of us makes assumptions about human nature. All people routinely "practice psychology" as they attempt to cope with the problems of their everyday lives. But, Miller states, they could practice it better if they knew which assumptions were sci-

entifically verified—if the valid principles of psychology were "given away" to them. For some social psychologists Miller's words have served as a beacon. Throughout this textbook we have tried to show how psychological knowledge can be applied to your own behavior—not only to interpersonal behaviors but also to the larger problems that our societies face now and in the future. The aim is an ambitious one, to be sure, but the potential consequences are substantial and possibly even critical to our future.

■ I. Pure science or applied science—or both?

The ideal of social scientists applying their knowledge to the solution of social problems sounds quite sensible. You may be surprised, however, to learn that many social psychologists have not tried to put their findings to any practical use. Moreover, considerable debate and controversy have raged about whether social psychologists *should* become involved in applied research, much less in social intervention. Some basic-research scientists have felt that it is not part of their role as scientists to point out the practical value of their findings. In fact, some have held that "the pursuit of scientific knowledge is a good activity in its own right, and even better since scientific knowledge is an absolute good apart from its consequences" (Baumrin, 1970, p. 74). This position has been commonly called *knowledge for knowledge's sake.* Other basic scientists, although they do not doubt that scientific findings will eventually prove useful, argue that application at this time is premature. Applied scientists, in contrast, advocate that science should study human problems now in order to work out solutions and determine what the consequences of any action might be. Although arguments have flourished between these two polar positions, social psychology has, throughout its history, produced representatives of both camps, as well as individuals who conduct both basic and applied research, either simultaneously or in alternation. The brief look at the history of social psychology in the next section will confirm this statement.

A. The waxing and waning of applied interests

The earliest work in social psychology, such as the experiments by Triplett described in Chapter 2, consisted mainly of laboratory ventures. Although the problems were often inspired by real-world events (in Triplett's case, by bicycle racing), the objective was to understand basic principles rather than to solve applied problems. Throughout the first 40 years of this century, research encompassed both laboratory and field settings, although the laboratory took increasing precedence in the work of many social psychologists. Still, the problems were often very realistically defined, such as Floyd Allport's work on groups or the early work of Likert, Murphy, and Sherif on stereotypes (Deutsch, 1975).

During World War II, social psychology blossomed and was very often applied as well. Much of the early work on attitude change, as developed by the Yale Communication Research Program (see Chapter 11), was aimed at very practical problem solving—how to maintain good morale and high performance in soldiers during the war. During this same period, Kurt Lewin was making major and highly influential contributions to the field of social psychology, and his program of **action research** (which we will discuss in more detail) was explicitly aimed at fusing basic and applied research into a single pursuit.

Despite Lewin's effort, however, many of his followers became more and more attracted to the laboratory. The research of the 1950s and 1960s focused increasingly on developing sophisticated theoretical models within a laboratory setting and disdaining any concern with real-life application (Ring, 1967). The reasons for this shift are numerous (Bickman, 1980; Deutsch, 1975). In part it reflected a belief among social psychologists that, by doing rigorously controlled laboratory experiments, more credibility would accrue to the discipline. In other words, the more controlled and "pure" the research was, the more scientific its practitioners could claim to be. Other external factors also played a part in this retreat to the ivory tower during the 1950s and early 1960s. Universities tend to reward the specialist—particularly the specialist who is highly productive in terms of papers and reports. Applied problems, in contrast, often require a more interdisciplinary emphasis and a much greater span of time for completion than the more controlled laboratory experiment. During this period, applied psychologists more often worked in industry or for government organizations, whereas theoretically oriented psychologists remained in the university. Communication between the two camps was, unfortunately, often meager at best.

The past decade has witnessed a noticeable shift in the concerns of social psychologists (Reich, 1981). Although many continue to pursue primarily laboratory research, many others are actively engaging in problem-oriented research—choosing problems of high relevance, developing strategies to analyze those problems, and involving themselves in the implementation and evaluation of social programs. Lewin's legacy is having a rebirth.

B. Kurt Lewin and action research

Kurt Lewin was probably the strongest early advocate of combining applied and theoretical social psychology within a single structure. In developing his **field theory** (discussed in Chapter 1), he argued that behavior must always be viewed in relation to the environment. And although he was a passionate advocate of the importance of theory, he also argued that theory must deal with those variables in society that make a difference (Cartwright, 1978).

Lewin's statement that there is nothing so practical as a good theory has often served as the byword of the social-psychological enterprise. Yet, ironically, the context of this statement is often ignored, as investigators justify their exclusive laboratory experimentation and exclusion of applied problems. The full text of Lewin's statement gives a much more revealing picture of his beliefs:

> [Close cooperation between theoretical and applied psychology] can be accomplished . . . if the theorist does not look toward applied problems with highbrow aversion or with a fear of social problems, and if the applied psychologist realizes that there is nothing so practical as a good theory [1951, p. 169].

Thus, although Kurt Lewin was interested in the development of theories, he was also interested in *doing* something with them. Lewin tried to resolve social conflicts such as marital friction, management/worker disputes, and the psychosociological problems of minority groups. Describing his work in these areas as action research, Lewin noted that community organizations and agencies that are concerned with eliminating and preventing social problems are often unsuccessful, no matter how hard they seem to try. His goal was to transform such good will into organized, efficient action by helping community groups answer three questions: (1) What is the present situation? (2) What are the dangers? And, most important of all, (3) what shall be done? To Lewin, action research consists of "analysis, fact-finding or evaluation; and then a repetition of this whole circle of activities; indeed, a spiral of such circles" (Sanford, 1970, p. 4). In short, the action researcher obtains data about an organization, feeds these data into the organization, measures the change that occurs, and then repeats the process.

Lewin's goals were indeed lofty. They aimed at focusing on significant problems, developing solid social-psychological theory, and acting as change and intervention agents as well. Perhaps it is not surprising that such an ambitious program could not be realized in his lifetime. Yet, as we shall see, the roots were good ones, and although the soil was inhospitable for some period and germination was slow, the products of Lewin's ideas are finally beginning to flourish.

■ II. Research on significant problems

Applied research represents a significant shift in thinking for most social psychologists. Bickman (1981) has pointed to differences between basic and applied social psychology in four areas: the purpose of the research, the methods used, the context in which the research is done, and the role of the individual researcher (see Table 18-1). Not all these distinctions apply to every single situation, but they do provide a general picture of the differences between the two endeavors. In broader

TABLE 18-1. Some differences between basic and applied research

Basic	*Applied*
Purpose	
Knowledge	To solve problems
To understand causes	To predict outcomes
Methodological concerns	
Internal validity	External validity
Single level of analysis	Multiple levels of analysis
Experimental	Quasi-experimental
High precision	Low precision
Research context	
Not time-bound	Real time
Self-initiated	Initiated by sponsor
Disciplinary	Multidisciplinary
Autonomous	Hierarchical
Stable	Unstable
Role of the individual researcher	
Specialist	Generalist
Peer orientation	Client orientation
Average social skills	Special social skills
Evaluation based on publications	Evaluation based on experience

terms, we can view the major objective of theoretical research as increasing knowledge, while the major objective of applied research is solving problems. This comparison, of course, is stated in the extreme—applied research may tell us a great deal about theoretical issues, and theoretical research, as Lewin suggested, may provide answers for social problems.

In recent years, social psychologists have become involved in a wide variety of applied areas: health care, energy conservation, judicial processes, consumer protection, welfare policies, and the like. The list is lengthy, and we can deal with only a few of these issues. But these selections will, we hope, show that social psychology can and does contribute to society. In effect, they answer the question "But what good is it?"

A. Health care and medical practice

Health care is a major industry in many countries and a major concern in most countries throughout the world. In the United States, for example, more than 10% of personal income is spent for health care, and the health industry is the largest service industry in the country (S. E. Taylor, 1978). In developing countries, health care often focuses on the young and on problems concerning birth and malnutrition. In more developed countries where zero population growth exists, more and more concern is being given to adult disease and the problems of the elderly.

Traditionally, problems of health were the province of medical personnel—of the doctors, nurses, and paramedics whose training is geared specifically toward health and illness. More recently, contributions from many other disciplines have been recognized, and the field of **behavioral medicine** has developed. Most simply, behavioral medicine can be defined as a field that integrates behavioral and biomedical science, focuses on health and illness, and concerns itself with the application of

PHOTO 18-1. Health care ranges from the treatment of minor wounds to broad-based prevention programs.

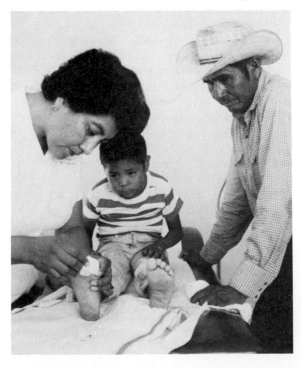

knowledge to the prevention, diagnosis, and treatment of illness. This field is an interdisciplinary one, and social psychologists are not alone in contributing to it. However, social psychology's contributions—both actual and potential—to the field of behavioral medicine are considerable, ranging from analysis of the causes of illness and the recognition by patients that they are ill to the procedures whereby services are delivered (S. E. Taylor, 1978). We will consider just a sample of the research done by social psychologists, looking at examples in four general categories: the causes of illness, the identification of illness, the prevention of illness (or the maintenance of health), and the treatment of illness.

Causes of illness.   The causes of physical and mental illness are numerous and vary for each particular disease under consideration. Causes for disease may be external to the person, residing in environmental conditions, or they may be rooted in individual biological conditions or behavior patterns.

Environmental causes of disease have frequently been the focus of public attention in recent years. Possible effects of radiation from atomic-bomb tests in Nevada have led citizens of St. George, Utah, to file suit against the government. Some years ago, a hotel in Philadelphia became famous as the site of "Legionnaire's disease." Pollution standards for industry have been widely debated as scientists learn more about the harmful effects of various chemical substances. In some cases, such environmental events have direct, measurable effects on physical health. In other cases, environmental events may have their initial impact on people's psychological sense of well-being, which, in turn, can affect their physical health. Such was the case at Three Mile Island, Pennsylvania.

Following the initial accident at the nuclear power plant at Three Mile Island, decisions had to be made about the best method of removing the radioactive gas trapped inside the installation. After considerable debate, it was decided to vent the gas directly into the atmosphere. Contributing to this decision, in addition to the physical scientists, were social psychologists who had been

PHOTO 18-2. *Seemingly peaceful surroundings at Three Mile Island.*

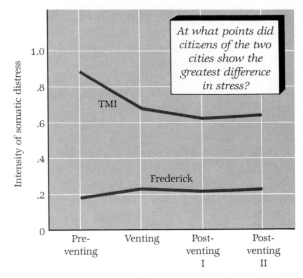

FIGURE 18-1. Somatic distress among citizens of Three Mile Island and citizens of Frederick, Maryland.

assessing stress in the residents of Three Mile Island (Baum, Fleming, & Singer, 1982). Their recommendation was based in part on psychological findings showing that chronic stress (such as would be predicted if the release of gas continued over an extended period) is more debilitating than acute stress, which focuses on a limited point in time.

To study residents' reactions to these events, Baum and his colleagues collected a variety of measures from the residents at four times: before the venting took place, during the venting period, three to five days after the venting, and again six weeks after the venting period. As a basis of comparison, the researchers also surveyed residents of Frederick, Maryland, a town 80 miles away that was similar in many respects to Three Mile Island. Among the measures collected were self-reports of somatic stress—the degree to which the residents reported being bothered by a variety of physical symptoms. Figure 18-1 shows the results of this study. As the graph indicates, residents of Three

Mile Island reported more physical stress symptoms at all four points in time than citizens in Frederick, Maryland. However, the graph also indicates that the frequency of reported symptoms was most intense before the venting began and decreased later.

In interpreting such data, one needs to be concerned about self-reports. Aware of the publicity and the researchers' interest, Three Mile Island residents could have inflated their reports of the symptoms they were actually feeling. However, other information collected by Baum and his colleagues suggests that the self-reports may be reliable. Both performance on a proofreading task and biochemical measures of stress showed similar patterns.

While some psychologists have looked at the effects of environmental events on health, others have turned to particular characteristics of people that may predispose them to illness. One of the most popular areas of investigation has been the **Type A behavior pattern**—a set of behaviors associated with increased risk for coronary heart disease. Among the behaviors that constitute the Type A pattern are intense achievement strivings, a heightened pace of living, strong tendencies to challenge and compete with others, impatience with slowness, and frequent hostility (Matthews, 1982). Research has shown that Type A people overestimate the passage of time, are likely to show greater aggression when frustrated, and react negatively to situations in which they have no control (Glass, 1977). A great deal remains to be learned about Type A people, both concerning the causes of their behavior and concerning the means of reducing coronary risk for them. In these endeavors, social psychologists are contributing to the overall effort.

Identification of medical problems. Identification of a medical problem requires at least two steps: first, the prospective patient must recognize that there is a problem and seek medical help, and, second, the medical personnel must make a correct diagnosis. In both phases, principles of social psychology may be applied.

Recognition of physical symptoms may vary with different individuals. Recalling the concept of private self-consciousness, introduced in Chapter 3, we find that people who score high on this dimension are more likely to detect physical symptoms (Scheier, Carver, & Gibbons, 1979). Situations that focus attention on the body may lead to an increased awareness of physical problems (Pennebaker, 1982). As just one example, national publicity given to public figures (such as Betty Ford) with breast cancer may make the individual woman more prone to perform self-examinations and/or seek medical expertise.

Awareness of one's symptoms does not always lead to an immediate search for medical attention. Often, the attributions that a person makes for the cause of his or her disability may hinder the quest (Rodin, 1978; Taylor, 1982). A person may notice strange pigmentation of the skin, for example, but simply dismiss it as a bad case of sunburn rather than a potential skin cancer. Frequent stomach pains may be self-diagnosed as a minor case of nerves rather than a severe ulcer. Mistaken attributions such as these may cause delay in seeking treatment, often leading to more serious disease.

Attributional processes may also come into play when the doctor makes a diagnosis. Snyder and

PHOTO 18-3. *People showing a Type A pattern are hard-driving, impatient, and high in achievement strivings.*

Mentzer (1978) have suggested that the concept of availability may sometimes bias a physician's diagnosis. This principle of judgment suggests that people estimate the probability of an event on the basis of the psychological availability of that event (Tversky & Kahneman, 1973). In other words, if a number of cases of a particular symptom are readily in mind (such as cyanide poisoning, perhaps), then a physician may be predisposed to make that diagnosis quite readily—even if the likelihood of that disease is quite low.

Medical personnel may also make judgments about patients that are influenced by prevailing stereotypes. For example, Wallston and her colleagues have found that nurses have generally negative perceptions of alcoholics (DeVellis, Wallston, & Wallston, 1978). When asked to evaluate an alcoholic patient, nurses responded much more negatively than they did to patients with other illnesses of comparable severity. Sex discrimination (see Chapter 10) has been shown in hospital wards as well. Licensed practical nurses were asked to rate male and female patients who had identical illnesses. Nurses viewed the female patients more negatively and considered them less mentally healthy than the men—even though the illnesses were primarily physical rather than psychological.

Prevention of illness. The psychological approaches to the prevention of illness have also used a variety of strategies, ranging from a concern with individual differences to broad-scale intervention programs. At the individual level, one variable that has captured the interest of a number of investigators is the concept of health locus of control. In Chapter 12 we discussed the general concept of **locus of control**, referring to the belief that events are internally or externally controlled. **Health locus of control** is a more specific form of this concept, referring to people's beliefs that they can exert control over their state of health or illness (an internal health locus of control) or that prevention of illness is beyond their control (external health locus of control).

Richard Lau and his colleagues have developed a scale to measure this specific form of perceived control (Lau, 1982). The following are sample items from this scale:

1. People who take care of themselves stay healthy.
2. Many times illness results from carelessness.
3. Regular doctor check-ups are a key to health.
4. Basic health principles prevent illness.
5. I can cure myself when sick.

In further studying this measure, Lau found that people who receive high scores on the health-locus-of-control scale are, as we might expect, more likely to actually perform self-care behaviors, such as eating proper foods, getting regular physical exercise, wearing seat belts, and controlling their weight. Other investigators have found that health locus of control relates to such behaviors as the ability to stop smoking, knowledge of disease, and effective use of birth control (see Wallston & Wallston, 1978, for a review).

As an example of a broad-scale intervention program aimed at preventing one particular health-threatening behavior, let us consider the antismoking program conducted by Richard Evans and his colleagues at the University of Houston (Evans, 1980; Evans, Rozelle, Mittelmark, Hansen, Bane, & Havis, 1978). The goal of this program was to train adolescents to resist social pressures to begin smoking. Thus, rather than trying to get adults who are already addicted to cigarettes to stop

PHOTO 18-4. *Regular exercise is one effective means of preventing illness.*

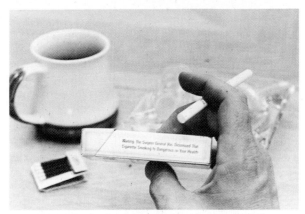

A. *"Cigarettes are not good for me. Can I quit?"*

B. *"Vitamins, minerals, natural sugar, less salt ... Will this food make me healthier?"*

C. *Concern for one's health takes many forms, from regular exercise to periodic checks of blood pressure.*

People differ in the concern they show for their health. Think of friends who smoke, drink, never exercise, and eat banana splits regularly, as compared to others who jog daily, take six kinds of vitamin pills, and shudder at the thought of red meat. Social psychologists interested in behavioral medicine have identified one personality dimension that relates to some of these behaviors—the health locus of control. Individuals scoring high on this dimension believe that they can exert control over their state of health, and they engage in a variety of preventive behaviors. For example, they are likely to eat properly, get regular exercise, and control their weight. Individuals who score low on the health-locus-of-control scale are less likely to take these actions, perhaps because they believe that one's own activities have little effect on the ultimate state of health or illness.

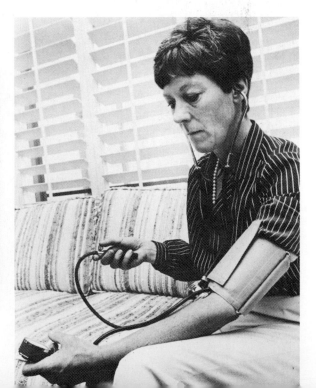

smoking, this program focused on young people who hadn't yet started.

In initial interviews with a group of fifth-, sixth-, and seventh-grade students, the investigators learned that most of the children believed that smoking was dangerous to their long-range health. Nevertheless, more immediate pressures in the environment often encouraged them to smoke. Three pressures that were particularly strong were peer influence, parents who smoked, and media presentations of smokers.

To counteract these specific pressures, Evans and his colleagues designed a program to help children deal with the situation. Through a structured videotaped presentation, children were presented with information about the dangers of smoking, as well as illustrations of the pressures that peers, parents, and media can exert. Sessions followed in which students discussed each of these points, with posters placed in the room to remind students of the filmed messages (see Figure 18-2).

To determine the effectiveness of the program, the investigators used not only self-reports of smoking behavior but also a saliva test that can detect the presence of nicotine in the body. The results of this multifaceted approach are encouraging. Ten weeks later, only 10% of students in the treatment group had begun to smoke, compared with 18% of students in a control group. Thus, although the treatment did not prevent all students from beginning to smoke, it reduced the number by almost 50%.

Treatment of illness. Social, cultural, and emotional factors are important in the treatment of illness, and "healing is seen as a process that is partially interpersonal" (Friedman & DiMatteo, 1979, p. 4). For this part of the process, social psychology is particularly well equipped.

Communication patterns between doctors and patients may be critical to the treatment process. For example, it may be important for the physician to be able to decode the patient's nonverbal messages (as discussed in Chapter 5), especially messages that convey fear and resistance. In turn, physicians need to be aware of the nonverbal messages that they themselves are sending, because patients may rely more heavily on these—particularly when the verbal message is garbed in technical jargon not understood by the average patient.

A thorough understanding of the patient's perceptions is essential for successful treatment. These perceptions are often inaccurate. For example, Taylor and Levin (1976) found that many women blame premarital sex for their breast cancer, suffering guilt and remorse about their illness. Even victims of serious accidents often unreasonably attribute the misfortune to their own actions (Bulman & Wortman, 1977). Such attributions may cause the patient to engage in self-recrimination instead of self-help during the recovery period.

Providing the patient with sufficient information about his or her illness and treatment is one means of reducing stress. Langer, Janis, and Wolfer (1975) found that patients given both information and particular techniques for coping with stress recovered more rapidly than patients who were less involved in the process. Even in less severe or nonemergency situations, such as giving blood, it has been shown that having both information and choice (for example, choosing which arm to

**Even if your parents smoke, you don't have to imitate them.
YOU can decide for yourself.**

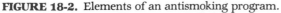

FIGURE 18-2. Elements of an antismoking program.

shortages has vacillated as oil has become more readily available, most scientists assume that there will eventually be an energy shortage. Some of the solutions to this potential shortage are outside the province of the social sciences: developing alternative sources of fuel, for example, is a problem for geologists, chemists, and engineers. Yet, the adoption of these new technologies is a question of human behavior, as are efforts to conserve energy sources now available. (For an example of individual actions that can save energy, see Table 18-2.)

What are the possible solutions to the energy problem? Some would argue that the political process is the only means of solution, with enforced controls by an external authority. *Mutually-agreed-upon coercion* is the term used by Garrett Hardin (1968). Others have argued that voluntary conservation is the preferred approach. In part, people's belief in which strategy is best depends on their explanations of the problem (Belk, Painter, & Semenik, 1981). Those who attribute the energy shortage to actions by the government, by oil producers, or by the oil companies are most apt to favor government pressure as a solution—either

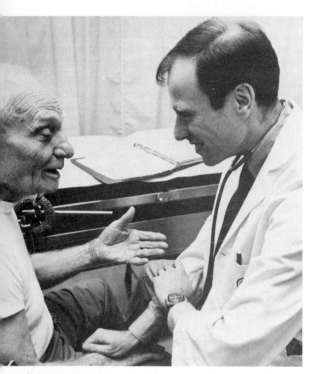

PHOTO 18-5. *The interpersonal relationship between doctor and patient is critical to the healing process.*

use for the blood donation) will reduce the stress (Mills & Krantz, 1979).

In summary, social psychology has much to contribute to the field of behavioral medicine. Until recently, the concern of medicine was technological advancement, a trend that "created an array of tools with which to do things *to* people, thus resulting in less and less time to do things *with* people" (Wexler, 1976, p. 276). Although technological advances are still important, increasing recognition is being given to the human element and to the psychological processes that mediate between health and illness.

B. Energy conservation

When the Arab countries imposed an oil embargo in 1973–1974, many people began to recognize that energy use was an important societal issue. Although public belief in the possibility of severe

---

TABLE 18-2. Ways to conserve energy

Each of the conservation behaviors listed below would save an estimated percentage of the total energy used in a typical household. Some of these actions involve reducing current usage; others involve taking advantage of energy-saving products that are now available.

Action	Percentage of energy saved
Car pool to work with one or two other persons	4–6
Buy a more efficient car (27.5 versus 14 mpg)	20
Get frequent tune-ups for car	2
Set back thermostat from 72° to 68° in the day and to 65° at night	4
Insulate and weatherize house	10
Install more efficient water heater	2
Change half of incandescent bulbs to fluorescent bulbs	1

pressure directed at the oil companies or restrictions imposed by the government on the population. In contrast, people who see energy shortages as caused by the actions of the general public are more likely to favor voluntary conservation as a solution.

Much of the work of social scientists in this area has focused on finding ways to encourage individuals to decrease their energy usage. Among the psychological principles that have been used are goal setting, feedback, commitment, and incentives. Each of these tactics requires some behavioral commitment by the individual, reflecting the knowledge gained from early studies of race relations (see Chapter 16) that simple information is not enough—a lesson that has been relearned in some of the energy-conservation research (Geller, Ferguson, & Brasted, 1978).

One reason that a simple information campaign may not be effective in reducing people's energy consumption is that people hold a variety of beliefs about energy use—and, as we discussed in Chapter 11, unless the persuasive communication is directed at the beliefs in question, little attitude or behavioral change can be expected. Even if communication is tailored to provide specific information about energy usage, however, it may not be effective. Seligman and his colleagues administered a survey about energy that included questions related to beliefs in science, the legitimacy of the energy crisis, efforts to conserve energy, and concern for personal comfort (Seligman, Kriss, Darley, Fazio, Becker, & Pryor, 1979). People's concern for comfort was found to be most closely related to their energy usage. For example, one of the items on the questionnaire was "It's essential to *my* health and well-being for the house to be air-conditioned all summer." Another item was "While others might tolerate turning off the air conditioner in the summer, my own need for being cool is high." People who agreed with statements such as these were unlikely to show strong conservation behavior, even if they endorsed the reality of the energy shortage.

In contrast, some behavioral techniques have been found to be reasonably effective in reducing individual energy consumption, often for long periods. Pallak and Cummings (1976), for example, studied a group of homeowners who committed themselves to reducing energy consumption, both of natural-gas heating in the winter and of electrical air conditioning in the summer. Half of these homeowners were told that their efforts would be made public—their names would be listed in the paper—and the remaining participants were assured that they would not be personally identified. Public commitment proved to be a more effective incentive, compared with either the private commitment of the other group of homeowners or no commitment at all (there was a control group that had no communication with the experimenters). In a further exploration, these same authors asked an additional group of subjects to keep an energy log, monitoring appliance usage, thermostat settings, and utility-meter readings. This procedure proved nearly as effective as the public-commitment condition, a result that suggests the value of self-controlled procedures.

These monitoring procedures provide direct feedback to the consumer and have frequently been shown to be effective in reducing energy consumption (Becker, 1978; Seligman & Darley, 1977). Having information readily available on just how well you're doing in your efforts can be much more effective than shutting off lights or turning down the air conditioner without knowing whether your efforts are really making a difference. Specific goals have proved useful as well. Becker (1978) gave families a goal of 20% reduction in electricity usage during a several-week period in the summer, providing feedback as well, and although those families did not quite meet the goal, their energy consumption did decrease by nearly 15%. In contrast, a group given a relatively easy goal of 2% reduction showed little change in energy use, not differing from a control group that had no goal.

Borrowing from learning and reinforcement models, other investigators have explored the use of financial incentives for reduced energy consumption. This straightforward approach, suggested by Platt (1973) and based on an economic model of human behavior, assumes that rewarded behavior will be maintained whereas behavior that is punished or not rewarded will decrease. Using this approach, McClelland and Cook (1980) set up a contest among groups of apartment residents in a University of Colorado housing complex. In each of a series of two-week periods, the group that had conserved the most energy won $80 to use as it wished. The results of this competition were positive: over a 12-week period, energy savings averaged over 6%. It was clear that "money talks." In designing a large-scale energy-saving plan, however, it would be important to consider whether the incentives awarded for energy savings exceeded the savings themselves! Furthermore, there are some serious questions whether energy-saving behavior will continue once the rewards are removed, and even the money itself (assuming the amounts are conservative) may lose its appeal after a short time (McClelland & Canter, 1978).

Energy conservation, on a national or international scale, depends on more than a single individual's effort. This interrelationship between the individual's behavior and the consequences for society has become a focus of interest in recent years. Instigated by Garrett Hardin's paper on the tragedy of the commons (see Box 18-1), social scientists have begun to discuss the concept of a **social trap.** As described by Platt (1973), social traps are situations that provide immediate individual incentives for behaviors that in the long run may have unfortunate consequences for society if those behaviors are performed by large numbers of people. In the short run, each individual may benefit; in the long run, the society will suffer. Many of the problems of energy conservation can be related to

PHOTO 18-6. *Use of solar energy is expected to increase as we approach the year 2000.*

this dilemma. Individuals may benefit from air-conditioned 65° temperatures in summer and from heated 75° temperatures in winter, but the ultimate outcome of hundreds and thousands of individuals' adopting that same policy is a heavy use of energy and an eventual shortage for everyone.

The energy question will continue to be a major one for decades to come. For the problem-oriented social psychologist, it is certainly an area of challenge and of potential benefit for the society.

C. The legal system

More than 12 million crimes were reported in the United States in 1979 (Greenberg & Ruback, 1982). Figures for other years and other countries vary but in all cases indicate the extent of the criminal justice problem. Unreported crimes would undoubtedly magnify these numbers even further. The criminal justice system is a complex one, involving various levels of jurisdiction (federal, state or provincial, and local) and a variety of agencies (including police, courts, attorneys, corrections officers), as well as the plaintiffs, defendants, and witnesses involved in individual cases. Within this complex setting, social psychologists have taken a growing interest in the processes of the legal system.

Psychologists have become involved in a number of areas. In the most general terms, we can consider three basic areas: substantive law, the legal process, and the legal system (Monahan & Loftus, 1982). In the area of *substantive law*, psychologists have begun to test some of the basic assumptions underlying legal codes and conventions. For example, should children be allowed to testify in criminal cases? Are they able to distinguish fact from fantasy, and would their testimony be reliable? In 1979 the U.S. Supreme Court stated that "most children, even in adolescence, simply are not able to make sound judgments concerning many decisions" (quoted in Monahan & Loftus, 1982, p. 443). Psychologists have begun to test some of these assumptions, using data from both developmental psychology and cognitive psychology to assess children's capacities for understanding and decision making.

Research directed at the *legal process* is concerned with the actual proceedings of conflict res-

BOX 18-1. The tragedy of the commons

The tragedy of the commons is an example of a problem with no technical solution (Hardin, 1968). Consider the example offered by Hardin. A number of people are raising cattle in a common pasture. For years, perhaps centuries, the pasture has provided more than enough food for all the cattle. Any number of events—for example, poaching, disease, or war—may allow each cattle herder to maintain his or her herd without infringing on the stock of others. Yet, at some point this utopia may end, and the land may no longer support all the cattle. How does this change occur?

Let us assume that each herder wants to maximize profit, raising as many cattle as possible for the meat or milk or hides that they can provide. A single herder may decide to add one additional animal to the stock. That herder will realize considerable profit from the addition. The common pasture, at the same time, will have to be divided more ways—yet our individual herder may notice less loss than gain. Eventually, however, as many herders increase their herds, the commons will be depleted. Or, as Hardin has stated, "Freedom in a commons brings ruin to all" (1968, p. 1244).

Such problems are essentially human problems, and they require human solutions. Social scientists have begun to study these problems. Early research suggests that neither information alone nor the knowledge of interdependence will be effective in reducing the exploitation of a resource. More promising results, using a laboratory analogue, have been obtained when communication is encouraged and when subjects develop a sense of participating in the determination of how the resource is to be managed. Solutions such as these and others will have to be developed if we are to halt the depletion of common resources. ■

olution. A major interest in this area is the trial process itself—characteristics of jurors and defendants, rules of evidence and procedures for decision making, and jury deliberation. By far the greatest amount of work by social psychologists has been centered in this area. A third focus of psychological research has been on the *legal system* itself: what factors affect sentencing decisions, how does the parole system operate, and what are the interactions between the criminal justice system and the mental health system?

It is not surprising that social psychologists have been intrigued by the operation of the legal system. It is essentially an interpersonal context, and many of the processes that occur can be interpreted using basic social-psychological principles. Greenberg and Ruback (1982), for example, have interpreted a wide range of legal phenomena in terms of two basic theoretical models: attribution theory and social-exchange theory.

In making attributions, people are trying to explain why a particular event occurred (see Chapter 4). Let's think about just a few of the ways that this process could occur in the legal system. If you saw one person hit another, would you choose to call the police? Part of your decision to help (see Chapter 9) would be based on your explanation of the event. Were the two persons just friends who were kidding around? Or was one person a mugger, intent on robbing the other? Attributions continue to be made throughout the legal process. In setting bond, a judge makes some inferences about the character of the accused. In listening to testimony, jurors make inferences about the character of the plaintiff, the defendant, and other witnesses. In deciding on parole, parole boards make assumptions about the character of the convicted person and try to predict future behavior.

Social-exchange theory (see Chapter 1) can also be used to interpret many of the interactions in the legal system. In plea bargaining, for example, an exchange between the prosecutor and the defendant may take place: "If I reduce the charge, will you agree to testify against X?" In determining a sentence, a judge may try to follow a principle of equity (see Chapter 6), ensuring that the penalty imposed on the convicted criminal matches the damage done to the victim. These and many other examples testify to the relevance of social-psychological theory to the criminal justice system. (For a much more extensive discussion of the application of these principles, see Greenberg & Ruback, 1982.)

Because the applications of psychology to the law have been so numerous, we can discuss only a few examples in depth. We will limit our discussion to three general issues: the setting of bail, the process of jury selection, and procedures in the trial process itself.

Setting bail.   After a suspect has been arrested, he or she must appear before a judge for what is termed the "initial appearance." For minor offenses, the judge may decide the case at that time. For a traffic violation, for example, the case is usually decided quickly and a fine often levied. For more serious offenses, this initial appearance may be the occasion for the judge to set bail, an exchange in which the accused puts up a certain amount of money in return for release from custody until a final hearing takes place (Greenberg & Ruback, 1982).

How is the amount of bail determined? Ebbesen and Konečni (1975) tried to answer this question using two methodological approaches. In the first study, they used a classic experimental design, manipulating the levels of four variables that they believed might be important: the prior record of the accused, the local community ties of the accused, the amount of bail recommended by the prosecuting attorney, and the amount of bail recommended by the defense attorney. Municipal- and superior-court judges in California were asked to make recommendations for bail after reading case descriptions that varied each of these factors. In their second study, Ebbesen and Konečni (1975) used the field-study method, in which observers attended bail hearings and recorded the events that took place, including the actual levels of the four variables that had been manipulated in the earlier study. The observers kept records of other kinds of information as well, including the age and sex of the accused and the severity of the crime

(these variables had been held constant in the experimental study).

What factors proved to be important in the judges' decisions? In the experimental study, three of the four factors emerged as important determinants. Most important were the local ties of the defendant to the community. When the accused was described as having lived in the area for four to six years, being employed in the area, and having family there, bail was set at a significantly lower level than when local ties were weak (living in the area only a couple of months, unemployed, and with family in another part of the state). Also important were the recommendations of the prosecuting attorney and the prior record of the accused. Higher bail was recommended if the prosecuting attorney had asked for higher bail and if the accused had a prior criminal record. In this experiment, the recommendation of the defense attorney had no effect.

The second study, based on actual bail decisions, showed somewhat different results and underlines the importance of testing experimental findings in a less controlled setting. In this "real life" setting, the judges' decisions on bail were influenced primarily by the recommendations of the prosecuting attorney. Much weaker was the influence of the defense attorney's recommendation, and local ties and prior record had no direct effect at all. Both the presence of local ties and the severity of the crime did play an indirect role, however, influencing the recommendation that the prosecuting attorney made. In more severe crimes, prosecuting attorneys requested higher bails, and higher bails were awarded. Somewhat surprisingly, local ties worked in just the opposite direction than in the previous experimental study: when the accused person had strong local ties, prosecuting attorneys tended to recommend higher bail than when such ties were weak.

This study is important because it shows quite clearly just what factors affect the bail-setting process. Further, it testifies to the importance of multiple strategies in research and the need for social psychologists to move outside the laboratory in their search for accurate diagnoses of social problems.

Jury selection. The selection of a jury for any particular trial begins as a process of random selection, as some number of people are called to court from a list of eligible jurors. (Even that original list is not totally representative of the population, however, because certain requirements must be met. For example, jurors must be 18 or older, understand English, and have no felony record.) From this larger group, 12 persons (plus some number of alternates) are selected for the actual jury, after an examination procedure that is known as *voir dire*. In the voir dire, the presiding judge or the opposing attorneys question prospective jurors and are allowed to remove certain potential jurors from the case.

For a number of years, social psychologists have shown interest in the jury-selection process. Beginning in the early 1970s, some social psychologists began to consult with defense teams in the selection of a jury. The aim of these efforts was to select a jury that would be sympathetic to the cause of the defense and hence would make acquittal of the defendant more likely. Although lawyers have always engaged in this strategy in the use of the voir dire, social psychologists brought a variety of systematic measures of attitudes and values to the process. Yet, despite the publicity that accompanied trials such as those of the Harrisburg Seven and of John Mitchell and Maurice Stans, many scientists have concluded that the composition of a jury "is a relatively minor determinant of the verdict" (Saks & Hastie, 1978, p. 66).

Although attempts to match general attitudes of prospective jurors with particular characteristics of defendants have not proved very successful, more recent work on one specific aspect of jury selection has shown some intriguing results. In capital-punishment cases it has often been the policy to exclude jurors who state in advance that they are unwilling to impose a death penalty. (The juries that result from this exclusion are called "death qualified" juries.) A number of people, from both the legal and social science communities, have suggested that this exclusion may result in a bias against the defendant, constituting a "conviction prone" jury rather than a neutral one. Phoebe Ellsworth and her colleagues have recently conducted two studies that test this assumption, and the studies have been cited in recent California court decisions.

In the first of two studies (Fitzgerald & Ellsworth, in press), over 800 eligible jurors in California were contacted by telephone and asked to assume that they were on a jury that was to decide on a sentence for a convicted defendant. They were then asked about their willingness to vote for the death penalty, as well as their attitudes about other aspects of the trial process. About 17% of this sample said they would never vote for the death penalty, a position that would make them unacceptable for jury service in capital cases. The people who voiced this opinion were not a random sample, however. Significantly more women than men, and significantly more Blacks than Whites, would be excluded from capital cases on this basis. In addition, jurors who were opposed to capital punishment differed from other respondents in several other ways. In contrast to the death-qualified jurors, these excluded jurors were less punitive, less mistrustful of the defense, and more concerned with maintaining guarantees of due process. Thus, the death-qualification procedure would seem to create a jury that is not totally representative of the citizenry.

Pursuing this question further, Cowan, Thompson, and Ellsworth (in press) contacted a random group of adults who were eligible for jury service and designed a jury-simulation experiment in the laboratory. Two types of 12-person juries were formed: one in which all members were death-qualified and one in which at least two members were opposed to the death penalty (mixed juries). Each mock jury watched a 2½-hour videotape of a homicide trial, gave an initial verdict, and then deliberated as a group for an hour. The results of the study again show the pattern of differences between the juror who is death-qualified and the one who is not. Both in their initial ballot and after the group deliberation, death-qualified jurors were more likely to vote guilty. Furthermore, analysis of the deliberations of the two types of groups showed that mixed juries seem to benefit from their diversity of opinion. Members of these mock juries were more critical of witnesses and better able to remember the evidence, although they were also less satisfied with their jury experience. These two studies are important contributions by social scientists to an understanding of jury selection. Although the findings have not yet been incorporated into the judicial process, there is reason to believe that they will cause changes in the future (Gross, 1980).

Many other aspects of the jury have been studied. Jury size, for example, has been the subject of both study and controversy (see Box 18-2 on p. 476). In addition, many investigations have considered the various procedures that take place during the trial itself.

Trial procedures. Many of the procedures that occur during a typical trial have been subject to the scrutiny of social psychologists. Judicial instructions, the use of confessions, and the form of opening statements by prosecution and defense attorneys are only a few of the topics investigated.

In their opening statements, both attorneys introduce themselves and their clients and provide the jury with a broad overview of their cases. Although the stated purpose of these opening statements is mainly informational, many attorneys believe that they can serve a persuasive function as well, influencing the jury to be favorable to a particular verdict. To explore the effectiveness of opening statements, Pyszczynski and Wrightsman (1981) set up a simulated trial in which mock jurors heard one of two types of opening statement from both the prosecuting attorney and the defense attorney. In the brief opening statement, only a short introduction was given, in which the attorney promised that convincing evidence would be provided later. In the extensive opening statement, a full summary of the evidence was presented. After the opening statements by both lawyers, the mock jurors then read a full transcript of a criminal trial and made judgments about the defendant's guilt or innocence. Did the form of the attorneys' opening statements affect the final verdicts? Figure 18-3 shows the results. The effectiveness of a particular strategy on the part of one attorney depends on the strategy used by the other. Verdicts of guilty were least likely when the defense

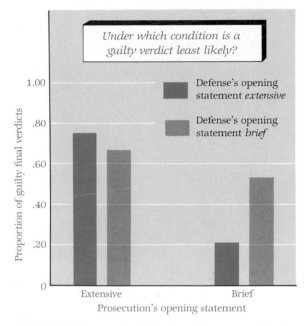

FIGURE 18-3. Length of opening statements and guilty verdicts.

attorney made a lengthy opening statement and the prosecuting attorney spoke only briefly. In general, the authors suggest that jurors may be influenced by the first strong presentation they receive.

There is a risk for the defense attorney, however, in making an extensive opening statement if he or she promises evidence that is not subsequently provided. In a second study, Pyszczynski and his colleagues set up three different conditions (Pyszczynski, Greenberg, Mack, & Wrightsman, 1981). In one condition the defense attorney promised in the opening statement that convincing evidence of innocence would be provided. In a second condition the same promise was made, but later in the trial hearing the prosecution attorney pointed out to the jury that the promise had not been fulfilled. In a third (control) condition neither the promise nor the reminder was included. A promise of convincing evidence did influence the mock jurors, making them more favorable toward the defendant. However, when the prosecution reminded jurors that the promise had not been fulfilled, the effectiveness of the promise diminished sharply.

BOX 18-2. Studies of jury size: A misuse of social science?

Juries are typically composed of 12 members. Why 12? Scholars are not sure, although some suggest that the number derives from Christ's 12 apostles (Wrightsman, 1978). After centuries of 12-person juries, the U.S. Supreme Court ruled in 1970 (in the case of *Williams* v. *Florida*) that juries as small as 6 would be acceptable. In formulating its decision, the Supreme Court referred to social science literature, citing six "studies" that supported its conclusion. These "studies," however, were not in fact well-conducted experiments; rather, the reports were based on casual observation or unsupported assertions (Saks, 1977; Saks & Hastie, 1978).

In rendering its decision, the Court also suggested that proportionality, rather than absolute size of a jury, was critical to a decision. Thus, it suggested, a jury that was split 5 to 1 would exert the same pressure on its minority as would a jury that was split 10 to 2. Yet, as we have seen in discussing the research on conformity in Chapter 12, that is simply not true.

Social scientists did not remain content as their findings were misinterpreted. Numerous studies have been conducted during the subsequent years, exploring the consequences both of jury size and of the unanimous-decision rule. The results of these later studies may not make court decisions any easier. In large part, the answer depends on what question is asked. For example, a unanimous rule leads to longer deliberations; a unanimous rule is also more likely to lead to a hung jury. Quorum juries (requiring some specified majority) are more likely to produce a verdict, but their verdicts are more prone to error. With regard to size, large juries spend more time deliberating and have better recall for testimony; small juries are more variable in their decisions (Saks, 1977; Saks & Hastie, 1978).

The research on jury size and decision rules illustrates some of the perils when two disciplines converge. For greater understanding, both sides must clearly define their questions and correctly interpret their answers. ■

Another question that has been addressed in jury research is the use of coerced confessions. The U.S. Supreme Court has ruled that only voluntary confessions may be admitted as evidence; coerced confessions have been ruled out. Within the legal system, coercion has been defined primarily in terms of a threat of harm. But what if coercion takes the form of the promise of some reward? To explore some of the issues surrounding confessions, Kassin and Wrightsman (1980) presented mock jurors with a trial transcript that included testimony about the defendant's confession. In some cases, testimony showed that the defendant had confessed voluntarily; in other cases, the confession had been in response to either a threat or a promise of leniency. In a control group, no evidence of a confession was presented. The results showed that subjects were willing to discount a confession if it was made under threat. However, a confession made under the promise of leniency was treated in the same manner as a voluntary confession, leading to a greater likelihood of a guilty verdict. Further studies by these authors have shown that even explicit instructions by the judge to discount coerced confessions do not diminish the effect when the coercion is positive in nature (Kassin & Wrightsman, 1981).

Social psychologists have been active in a great many other areas of law. As we saw in Chapter 4, for example, accuracy of eyewitness testimony has been a major interest. Other investigators have focused on the processes of group deliberation, a topic that was considered in Chapter 14. Some of these investigations have dealt mainly with theoretical issues that *might* be relevant to judicial proceedings; others have been aimed at more directly applicable features of the process. There has been a great deal of debate about the degree to which psychology can contribute to the law (Loh, 1981; Saks & Baron, 1980). Too often, it is suggested, psychologists have been concerned solely with the trial process, when in fact fewer than 5% of cases actually go to trial. As in all areas of applied research, it is important for the investigator to establish ties with practitioners in that field. For research to be most useful, the acquired wisdom of the practitioner must be used both to shape questions and to interpret findings, creating a truly interdisciplinary approach to the problems.

■ III. From problems to solutions

Health, energy conservation, and law are all areas of concern to applied social psychologists. But are they necessarily social problems? Leonard Bickman and his associates have suggested that four criteria are needed to define a situation as a social problem (Ovcharchyn-Devitt, Calby, Carswell, Perkowitz, Scruggs, Turpin, & Bickman, 1981). First, the situation must exert a negative impact on some people. Second, one must consider the number of people who are affected. Generally, the more people are affected, the more serious we would consider the social problem. Third, Bickman and his colleagues suggest that we consider the "intractability" of the problem. Social problems, unlike temporary situations that may be unpleasant, generally have a long history, and many previous solutions may have been attempted. Fourth, a social problem is defined by consensus—the society as a whole, or some significant portion of it, agrees that a particular situation is a problem.

A. Documenting problems

Identifying a situation as a social problem is only the first stage in problem solving. Once a problem is recognized, it must be analyzed carefully so that solutions can be devised that fit the problem. In the model for research on social problems that Bickman and his colleagues have proposed (see Figure 18-4), at least five kinds of information are believed to be necessary when documenting a social problem. A general scenario of the situation is suggested as a first step so that

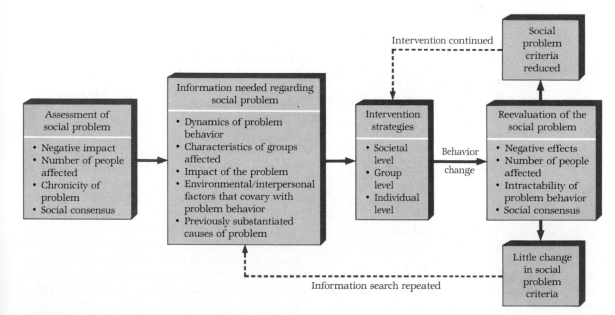

FIGURE 18-4. Stages in research on social problems.

the investigator will understand exactly what is happening. For example, in studying the effects of affirmative action in the steel industry, investigators would want to know how and when women were hired, what groups within the steel mills might be sources of discriminatory actions, and what impact the policies were having both on women and on other workers (see Deaux & Ullman, 1983).

Having become familiar with the basic situation, the investigator should then gather more specific information about the group of people affected by the problem and how great the impact of the problem is. Other environmental and interpersonal factors need to be explored, as the causes of most social problems are complex. Finally, an investigator should gather as much information as possible on the causes of the problem.

Once a problem is thoroughly defined, solutions can be attempted—solutions that focus on either the societal, the group, or the individual level. Solutions must, in turn, be evaluated using the original criteria. Not all solutions resolve the problems that were initially defined, as described in Box 18-3.

B. Evaluating solutions to social problems

Most often the solution to a social problem is devised by politicians, bureaucrats, and other persons directly involved in the problem. In the past, social scientists were often content to maintain their role as citizens and observe the outcomes of such programs. But in 1969 Donald Campbell issued a challenge:

> The United States and other modern nations should be ready for an experimental approach to social reform, an approach in which we try out new programs designed to cure specific social problems, in which we learn whether or not these programs are effective, and in which we retain, imitate, modify, or discard them on the basis of apparent effectiveness on the multiple imperfect criteria available [p. 409].

In effect, he argued for an experimenting society, and in the years since his challenge **evaluation research** has become one of the most active fields of social science (Guttentag & Struening, 1975; Saxe & Fine, 1981; Struening & Guttentag, 1975).

Although the term *evaluation research* has been used in many ways, a basic definition of the term is "research which is aimed at assessing or evaluating the effects of a given social action or program" (Hornstein, 1975, p. 214). This strategy has been applied to a myriad of areas: college courses, mental health programs, compensatory education, and income maintenance, for example. It is applicable to virtually any other social program, large or small, in which the effects of action or change can be measured. The evaluation program can serve a few persons or a few million people; it can focus on a single classroom, an entire nation, or several nations; it can last a few hours or go on indefinitely (Weiss, 1972).

Although the aim of evaluation research is quite simple, the process itself can be quite complex. Weiss (1972), in her definition of evaluation research, begins to hint at some of these complexities: "The purpose of evaluation research is to measure the effects of a program against the goals it set out to accomplish as a means of contributing to subsequent decision making about the program and improving future programming" (p. 4). Evaluation research must begin with specific questions, phrased in terms of the goals that an organization has set for itself. Again, this process might appear to be a simple matter, but in practice it often turns out to be more complex. "Program goals are often hazy, ambiguous, hard to pin down" (Weiss, 1972, p. 25). Officials of a program may have a general sense that they want their program to be better, but exactly how they want it to be better is often left vague and undefined. "Better" or "more modern" or "more effective" is a general description that must be translated into specific criteria before the evaluation research can proceed.

As one example, the announced goals of Operation Head Start, a program in compensatory education conducted in the United States during the late 1960s, were to compensate for the alleged educational disadvantages of poor children that caused them to have difficulties when they entered the first grades of school (Rossi & Williams, 1972). Yet, the major evaluation showed that the program produced no noticeable improvement in

BOX 18-3. Segregation: Problems and solutions

An early and very famous example of research aimed at documenting existing problems is the work of Clark and Clark (1947), who administered projective tests to Blacks and Whites and demonstrated the effects of social prejudice. In the famous *Brown v. Board of Education* case of 1954, Kenneth Clark testified to the court as follows:

I have reached the conclusion . . . that discrimination, prejudice, and segregation have definitely detrimental effects on the personality development of the Negro child. The essence of this detrimental effect is a confusion in the child's concept of his own self-esteem—basic feelings of inferiority, conflict, confusion in his self-image, resentment, hostility towards himself, and hostility towards Whites [Kluger, 1976, p. 353].

As those familiar with U.S. history know, the result of this case was the order to desegregate schools in the United States, under the assumption that separate educational facilities are inherently unequal. The Clarks and other investigators had defined a problem—racial prejudice. Yet, it is important to note that although they advocated a particular solution, their re-

search had focused on the problem, not on the effectiveness of various solutions.

Later assessments have, in fact, suggested that the solution was far less beneficial than proponents would have hoped. Stephan (1978) has systematically reviewed the evidence for desegregation in terms of the hypotheses implicitly or explicitly offered by social scientists in their testimony during the *Brown v. Board of Education* case. Disappointingly, he concludes that desegregation generally has not reduced the prejudices of Whites and Blacks toward each other and that the self-esteem of Blacks has rarely increased in desegregated schools. However, achievement levels of Blacks have increased in desegregated schools, providing support for the decision if not for all the hypothesized effects of desegregation. In this review, however, Stephan is careful to note that these conclusions are tentative. Much of the research had problems, and rarely were either the conditions of desegregation or the measures of effects constant across conditions. A clear moral of this case study is that defining problems is not enough for the concerned social scientist—solutions must be assessed as well as problems. ■

cognitive skills. If the specific goal was a concrete improvement in cognitive skills, then the program evaluation, for the most part, showed the program to be a failure. However, in the swirl of controversy that surrounded this project (Hellmuth, 1970; Williams & Evans, 1972), many advocates argued that other goals were established by the project—for example, the physical health of the children may have been improved. Alternatively, cognitive skills may have improved in ways not tapped by the measures used. These controversies illustrate some of the problems involved in the specification of goals in a social program—and the care that the evaluation researcher must take to specify the exact objectives and to devise appropriate methods of

measuring the outcomes of the program.

Once the exact objectives are specified, an evaluation-research program must devise methods to measure the desired effects. In such an effort, a vast arsenal of methods (as discussed in Chapter 2) may be used—interviews, questionnaires, existing records, observations, and any other available forms of data that appear to be relevant to the questions posed. Often, however, a true experiment, whether of a laboratory or field variety, is impossible. As a result, methodologists, most notably Donald Campbell and his colleagues, have been active in developing a number of **quasi-experimental research** designs that will approximate some of the experimental controls while allowing for the "messiness" of real live data (see Campbell & Stanley, 1966). As illustrated in Figure 18-5, considerable precautions must be taken when interpreting data in evaluation research. Because the investigator has little control over most of the independent variables and only some control over the data collection (the dependent variables), alternative explanations for the effects observed must be considered carefully.

Still another feature of evaluation research is that it takes place in what Weiss (1972) has called a "turbulent setting." Social psychologists accustomed to the calm of their laboratory may find the activity of an on-site evaluation somewhat dis-

quieting. Furthermore, the evaluation-research project is often of secondary concern to the members of the organization that is being evaluated. In most cases, these personnel are concerned mainly with giving service or producing a product. Often they are not concerned with the needs of the researchers and may, in fact, find their presence an annoyance or an inconvenience to the jobs they are performing. Evaluation itself may affect the behavior of the personnel. Personality conflicts may develop between the researcher and key personnel; the organization may suffer a crisis in some other aspect of its operation that will, in turn, affect the evaluation program; or the program itself

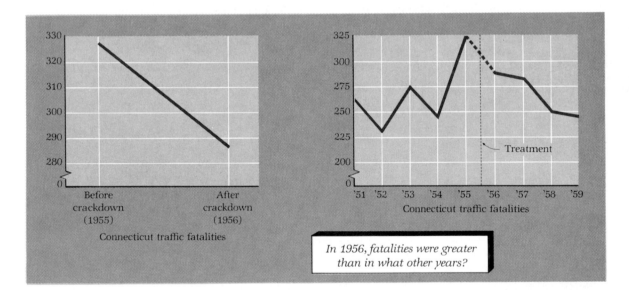

In 1956, fatalities were greater than in what other years?

FIGURE 18-5. Reforms as experiments. Donald T. Campbell, distinguished social scientist, makes a strong appeal for an experimental approach to social reform. He presents several research designs for evaluating specific programs of social amelioration, one of which is the interrupted time-series design. A convenient illustration comes from the 1955 Connecticut crackdown on speeding. After a record high of traffic fatalities in 1955, the governor instituted a severe crackdown on speeding. At the end of one year of such enforcement, there had been 284 traffic deaths, compared with 324 the year before. These results are shown in the left-hand graph above, with a deliberate effort to make them look impressive. The right-hand graph includes the same data as the graph to the left, except that those data are presented as part of an extended time series. Campbell acknowledges that the crackdown did have some beneficial effects, but he advocates the exploration of as many rival hypotheses as possible to explain the decline in traffic fatalities from 1955 to 1956. For example, 1956 might have been a particularly dry year, with fewer accidents due to rain or snow. There might have been a dramatic increase in use of seat belts. At least part of the 1956 drop is the product of the 1955 extremity. (It is probable that the unusually high rate in 1955 caused the crackdown, rather than, or in addition to, the crackdown's causing the 1956 drop.) Campbell asks for a public demand for hardheaded evaluation and for education about the problems and possibilities involved in the use of socially relevant data.

may change during the course of its operation as a result of other pressures and needs. These are only some of the factors that make evaluation research a much more "turbulent" arena than the more traditional social-psychology setting.

Yet, despite the difficulties of evaluation research, its benefits can be substantial. Only through knowing how existing programs are actually working can we begin to develop the means for better solutions to the society's problems.

C. Providing means for change

Research need not be limited to evaluation of existing programs. In addition, social psychologists can contribute to the solution of society's problems by providing the means for change—by actually developing and testing procedures that can be used to change outcomes in a particular setting. Many of the research projects discussed in the sections on health, energy, and the law represent a beginning effort at this form of research. The studies by Langer and Rodin, discussed in Chapter 12, that attempted to increase the perceived control of residents of homes for the aged are another example of this strategy. Thus, social psychologists are using their experimental tools to compare various approaches to a particular problem—and, in the process of their interventions, they are creating the basis for a new social technology (Hornstein, 1975).

There is still another way in which research can contribute to the solutions of problems and provide the means for change to occur. Consider the situation when one or more strategies have been shown to be effective in improving education, in reducing welfare rolls, or in reducing energy consumption. The translation of such knowledge into actual practice may be helped if we understand more about the policy-making process itself. Decisions are not made in a vacuum, and social conflict often results when a variety of opinions clash with one another. The practitioner of social change (see the next section) may have to deal with these issues as they arise; but the researcher may be able to contribute some information by studying the actual judgment process that occurs in a typical policy decision. Hammond (1965), for example,

has suggested the use of a basic model of human judgment (the Brunswik "lens model") to explore the bases of judgmental conflict—how different policy makers may arrive at different positions on the same issue. Using this basic strategy, Summers and his colleagues (Summers, Ashworth, & Feldman-Summers, 1977) have explored people's solutions to the problem of overpopulation. They found that two dimensions were considered important to their respondents: (1) the voluntary or involuntary nature of a solution and (2) the economic or noneconomic nature of the proposed solution. In turn, they showed that conflicts among their subjects, and presumably among real policy makers as well, could be understood more clearly in terms of these basic dimensions. Thus, not only are the solutions of problems a target for social-psychological research, but the ways in which solutions can be developed and carried out can be a focus of research as well.

■ IV. The nature of social change

Research can define the problem, evaluate alternative solutions, and provide the means for change. But the change process itself may go beyond research. As Hornstein (1975) has discussed this issue, the individual can confront a social problem and ask "Is more information needed?" If the answer is yes, then research such as we have discussed can be conducted. However, if the answer is "No, we have enough information" or even "Yes, more information is needed, but we don't have time to get it," then direct social change may be the chosen route.

A. Strategies for change

The term **change agents** is applied to persons who are engaged in the planning and application of change methods in the society. Change can be brought about through the use of various strategies. Three major types of change strategies are (1) the empirical-rational strategy, (2) the normative-reeducative strategy, and (3) the power-coercive strategy.

The empirical-rational strategy. This strategy assumes that people are rational and that they will act on the basis of the best information available. Therefore, in order to improve people's ability to make decisions, one need only present them with the facts. The **empirical-rational strategy** clearly is congenial with many Western values, such as willpower and educability. Because of our belief in this strategy, we maintain public schools, write letters to our legislators, read newspapers regularly, and give money for cancer research. Of course, there are limits to how much we accept this strategy; that is, we also smoke, drive at excessive speeds, refuse to exercise, and often pick a new car by kicking its tires and slamming its doors instead of consulting a consumer-guide magazine. In short, we often act irrationally; hard facts have limited power to change behavior.

The professional role demanded by the empirical-rational strategy has been described as that of an analyst (Vollmer, 1970)—that is, one who tries objectively to diagnose a problem and to bring appropriate data to bear on its solution. Etzioni (1978) advocates this strategy when he calls for "social scientists to make it their business to publicize data policymakers have repeatedly ignored" (p. 26). Expert testimony in front of government committees also represents a form of empirical-rational strategy. To take the argument a step further, one could easily argue that all governmental research is based on the empirical-rational strategy; that is, government agencies fund research that will produce facts, which can then be disseminated for the purpose of effecting change.

The empirical-rational strategy is limited in that no guarantee exists for what kind of people will read the information or put it to use. As just one example of the limitations of the empirical-rational strategy, consider the outcomes of the work of the Federal Commission on Obscenity and Pornography, appointed by President Lyndon Johnson in 1968. Even before the Commission's report was published in the fall of 1970, then-President Richard Nixon renounced many of its conclusions. Moreover, several U.S. legislators denounced the report on national television, although these legislators admitted that neither they nor their staffs

had read it! Obviously, the empirical-rational strategy is often insufficient, in and of itself, to promote extensive change.

The normative-reeducative strategy. A second strategy for social change is based on different assumptions about human nature. The **normative-reeducative strategy** assumes that people are intelligent and rational, but it also assumes that they are bound up in their own particular culture. As a result, they have definite behavioral responses and patterns that are based on attitudes, values, traditions, and relationships with others. Before trying to change a person, group, or community, the change agent must take these cultural or normative determinants into account.

As we mentioned earlier, Kurt Lewin was one of the first to address the issue of using the normative-reeducative strategy in resolving social conflicts (Lewin, 1948), by reeducating groups through professional participation in the groups. Many police training programs that have developed since the 1970s reflect the normative-reeducative strategy. In response to riots and accusations of police brutality, analyses of activities by the police were conducted in many communities. Time-and-motion studies revealed that less than 20% of the working hours of police officers was spent in law-enforcement activities, whereas increasing portions of time were spent in a wide range of social-service activities. Bard (1970) has referred to the New York City police as a "human resource agency without parallel" and has pointed out that "maintaining order and providing interpersonal service—not law enforcement and crime suppression—are what modern police work is all about" (p. 129). Social scientists rediscovered what the police already knew—that crime in the streets is much less common than crime *off* the streets. One of the riskiest activities for police officers is handling family disputes (Driscoll, Meyer, & Schanie, 1973). In brief, the police were being trained in traditional law enforcement or property surveillance but were being called on to serve a wide range of social-service functions.

To bring about change in this system, many social scientists adopted a normative-reeducative strategy for working police officers. They began riding in patrol cars, observing training programs, and generally acquainting themselves with the norms of law enforcement. Actual entry into the system was slow. Social psychologists first performed specific services for the police, such as improving the ways of selecting new recruits. Next came lectures and sensitivity training that dealt with such matters as the emotionally disturbed, ways to deal with aggression, and the general area of interpersonal relations (Diamond & Lobitz, 1973). Gradually, the social scientists became more involved in all aspects of police training—and more acceptable in the eyes of the police (Carlson, Thayer, & Germann, 1971).

The normative-reeducative process moves slowly; change depends on a great deal of agreement and collaboration between the agents of change and the people in the selected system. But there have been payoffs. Bard (1970) has trained a special squad of patrol officers in the use of mediation and referral in handling domestic disturbances. This project has been highly successful in preventing homicides, reducing the number of assaults, reducing the number of arrests, and preventing injury to the police themselves. A central characteristic of this approach has been the predictability of change, which has been in the desired direction and has been approved by both the change agents and the police.

The power-coercive strategy.   This strategy differs from the first two in its use of power. The **power-coercive strategy** is based on political, economic, and social uses of power that have been both popular and effective in bringing about change. Federal legislation of civil rights has moved integration forward in the United States and has promoted bilingualism in Canada; labor strikes have affected economic policies; and boycotts have changed discriminatory hiring practices. Similarly, Martin Luther King, Jr., César Chavez, and Saul Alinsky became famous for their power-coercive strategies in their quests for constructive change (Sharp, 1970, 1971).

In employing power-coercive methods, change agents have been concerned primarily with non-

PHOTO 18-7. *César Chavez, a leader in the organization of farm workers.*

violent strategies of change. Opposition to violent strategies is based on at least two principles. One is that the use of violence means denying human worth and that even the most favorable short-term outcome does not justify using violent methods. A second reason is that violent strategies introduce much more unpredictability into a social system than nonviolent approaches do (Fairweather, 1972). *Predictability* in this context refers to (1) whether one accomplishes one's desired goals, (2) how long one's accomplishments last, and (3) whether any unexpected negative side effects result. When evaluated according to these three criteria, nonviolent strategies are found to be much more effective in establishing planned change throughout a broad social system. (For another point of view, see Box 18-4.)

Nonviolent power-coercive methods have brought about much planned social change during the last two decades. Demonstrations have been accompanied by legal sanctions and class-action suits.

BOX 18-4. The use of violent strategies

Some social scientists would argue that violent strategies may be successful as well. William Gamson (1975) analyzed the outcomes of a sample of 53 groups that sought change in the United States during the late 19th and early 20th centuries and concluded that violence was often a successful tactic when used by groups that possess a sense of confidence and a rising sense of power. Gamson's advocacy of violence as a successful tactic is qualified, however. He finds it used successfully when it is a secondary tactic, backing up primary nonviolent power-coercive strategies such as strikes, bargaining, and propaganda. "Violence, in short, is the spice of protest, not the meat and potatoes" (Gamson, 1974, p. 39). ■

One of the more interesting aspects of the power-coercive strategy is that it can take many forms. The case history described in Box 18-5 summarizes an unusually innovative approach to problem resolution by one of the masters of the power-coercive stategy.

Despite their frequent effectiveness, power-coercive strategies are seldom sufficient change methods in and of themselves. Often they must be coupled with a normative-reeducative approach to maximize change. In fact, in most social-change endeavors, there will be occasion to use all three of these strategies in various ways at various times. Indeed, it is most difficult to use only one strategy. Yet, to be successful, the change agent must be aware of which strategy is being used, as well as how others perceive the strategy.

B. The role of the social scientist in change

Just as the form of social change can vary, so can the role of the social scientist vary in his or her relationship to the change process. Hornstein (1975) has discussed three roles that the change agent may play: the expert, the collaborator, and the advocate.

The expert relationship. A prototype of the expert relationship is the physician/patient interaction. In the analogous change situation, the social scientist plays the role of an outside expert, not directly collaborating with the change makers but, instead, offering advice from a distance. In such a role, the social scientist is most influential in the early stages of the change process, when plans are being formulated. Any single social scientist may, of course, be only one voice among many recommending directions or procedures for change. In congressional testimony, for example, many experts are called in, and the final decision represents some composite of the testimony of these experts, political pressures, and other factors.

For the expert's advice to be taken most seriously, Hornstein (1975) suggests that three con-

BOX 18-5. Use of power-coercive strategies

The late Saul Alinsky was one of the foremost organizers of community-action groups; he trained such minority-group leaders as César Chavez, who organized California's agricultural workers and then precipitated a national consumer boycott against California grapes. Alinsky was a proponent of the power-coercive strategy and used this strategy in quite different ways. One of the more novel uses of this approach was his Rochester, New York, battle with Eastman Kodak. Following a Rochester race riot that was partly due to a conflict over Kodak's inadequate training and job programs for Blacks, the local churches invited Alinsky to work in their Black ghetto. He accepted and soon founded a community-action group called FIGHT (Freedom, Integration, God, Honor, Today). Instead of depending on community-action tactics such as picketing and demonstrating, FIGHT began soliciting stock proxies from churches, individuals, and organizations as a direct power challenge to Kodak's policies. Enough proxies were turned over to FIGHT to enable the group to force Kodak to improve its policies concerning minority groups. ■

ditions are necessary: (1) policy makers must be experiencing a need for change; (2) proposed solutions must fall within the perceived capabilities and goals of the organization; and (3) policy makers must have the motivation to take action as required. Without all three conditions, the expert's advice may fall on deaf ears. Many factors can prevent these ideal conditions from existing. The motivation to comply with suggestions, for example, can be hindered by an inability to translate the suggestions into action. Even when action is possible, organizations may be reluctant to take what they perceive as risks in following the recommendations. On some occasions, the organi-

zation may fear the results of the study or the publicity that might be given to those results. In the United States, for example, organizations are often reluctant to engage in studies of sex and ethnic discrimination, fearful that the results will reflect badly on the company and expose them to potential lawsuits.

The collaborative relationship. As Lewin recognized early on, many of the fears or motivational problems that may occur in the expert relationship are minimized when the social scientist takes a collaborative role. Indeed, it has been argued that "the adaptation of research findings is primarily determined by the motivational byproducts of collaboration rather than by the technical expertise of a research effort" (Hornstein, 1975, p. 223). Kurt Lewin's concept of action research exemplified the collaborative relationship between the social scientist and the target of change. Technical expertise is not sufficient in this kind of relationship; in addition, the social scientist must have interpersonal skills to help the group move toward its goal.

The advocate relationship. In both expert and collaborative relationships, the agent of change (the social scientist) and the object of change (the organization) tend to agree on the goals to be pursued. In contrast, in an advocate relationship, the social scientist may disavow collaboration and instead pursue a path of action aimed at changing the organization from outside. This role of the change agent is most evident in the use of the power-coercive strategy, although the extent of involvement and the forms of power used may vary widely. In some instances, for example, the social scientist may simply present the results of a study in a forceful and well-publicized manner: the use by Clark and Clark of their data on self-concept among Blacks is an example of this strategy (see Box 18-3).

The work of social psychologist Hannah Levin (1970) exemplifies the advocate role. While working as a consultant to a community health center, Levin was dismayed that the people who lived near the health center had little or no say in its operation. The health authorities told the people that they could have an advisory board, but those who actually administered the health program would have to be physicians. However, the people wanted the operating policies to be determined by the local residents. In the confrontation that followed, Levin became a professional advocate for the people. Levin and the people's groups were informed that they could advise, or even participate, but not control. The health authorities were unable to see the difference between participation and control. According to Levin, the people's retort was "If you don't see any real difference between participation and control, then you can participate and the community will control!" (1970, p. 123). Through Levin's advocacy, the people were able to establish influence over the policies of the health center. One outcome of community control was a shift in priorities from programs that emphasized treatment of suicidal and acutely disturbed patients to programs that focused on young people. The people in the community declared that it was irresponsible of the health center to ignore the many health needs of schoolchildren for the sake of a "few suicides" and "psychotics."

C. The development of social technology

Although most social psychologists believe that their research will eventually have practical applications, many resist applying current knowledge to current problems. Our knowledge is imperfect and our understanding inadequate, they claim. Yet, as we have seen, some other social psychologists are much more inclined to apply our findings now, believing that we already have a good deal

of basic technology to use in the solution of social problems. Jacobo Varela (1971, 1977, 1978) has been perhaps the most passionate advocate of such a **social technology.** From his background in engineering, Varela moved to social sciences, attempting to use many of the same strategies but with a different set of tools. His arguments are persuasive:

> The fact is that we already have most of the technology we need to solve an enormous range of social problems, from personal miseries to organizational conflict, from the marriage bed to the conference table. If we wait for pure research to come up with real-world answers, though, we will be waiting for Godot. . . . Engineers and physical scientists cannot wait for theoretical perfection. If the Romans had waited for the elegance of the Verrazano-Narrows Bridge instead of fooling around with stone arches, the course of civilization would have changed. The Roman arches had their faults, but they have lasted nineteen centuries [1978, p. 84].

Many would disagree with Varela's analysis. Yet, just as there are many methods for doing research, there are also many responses to the outcomes of research, and no single response or tactic has an exclusive claim on the truth. It is imperative that social psychologists continue to do basic theory-oriented research, both in the laboratory and in natural settings, for such research will add to our knowledge and form the basis for future social technologies. At some point, however, we may be obligated to use the knowledge that we have in the solution of social problems. And many would argue that the time has come.

V. SUMMARY

The contributions of social psychology do not stop with an increase in theoretical understanding of human behavior. Social-psychological knowledge has been applied to the solution of a variety of social problems. This emphasis on

application began early in the tradition of social psychology, with Kurt Lewin's concept of action research. Although social psychologists became more interested in pure laboratory research during the 1950s and 1960s, much more applied research has been conducted in recent years. Three significant areas of applied social research are health care, energy conservation, and the legal system.

Behavioral medicine is a field that integrates behavioral and biomedical science. Social psychologists are studying many aspects of illness, including causes, identification, prevention, and treatment. Causes of illness may be internal to the person or may, as in the case of Three Mile Island, be a result of environmental stressors. Identification of illness, both by the patient and by the physician, illustrates basic psychological principles of social cognition and attribution. Prevention of illness has been studied in a number of ways, including the general trait of *health locus of control*. Programs to discourage cigarette smoking are another example of social-psychological principles in practice.

Studies of energy conservation have used such principles as goal setting, feedback, commitment, and incentives. Psychologists have also looked at *social traps*, situations that provide immediate rewards to individuals for behaviors that may have negative consequences for a society in the long run.

In applying their knowledge to an understanding of the legal system, social psychologists have looked at substantive law, the legal process, and the legal system itself. Many basic principles, such as attribution theory and social-exchange theory, can be applied throughout the legal system. The specific processes that have been studied include the setting of bail, the process of jury selection, and procedures in the trial process itself.

For a situation to be defined as a social problem, that situation must have negative impact on a substantial number of people, and there must be consensus that there is a problem.

Social psychology can contribute to the process of social change in three ways: by documenting problems that exist, by estimating the costs and benefits of alternative kinds of change, and by providing the means for change.

Social scientists may also be involved in the process of change itself. Three strategies for planned change are the *empirical-rational strategy*, the *normative-reeducative strategy*, and the *power-coercive strategy*. The empirical-rational strategy assumes that people will act on the basis of the best available information and hence focuses on dissemination of information as a means to change. The normative-reeducative strategy assumes that our behavior is based on attitudes, values, and interpersonal relationships, and it takes these factors into account when planning change. The power-coercive strategy uses political, social, and economic pressures to bring about desired social change.

The social scientist can have three roles in the change process: as an expert, as a collaborator, or as an advocate. These roles vary in their level of involvement with the change process itself. *Social technology* is the application of social science principles to the solution of social problems.

GLOSSARY TERMS

action research
behavioral medicine
change agents
empirical-rational strategy
evaluation research

field theory
health locus of control
locus of control
normative-reeducative
   strategy

power-coercive strategy
quasi-experimental research
social technology
social trap
Type A behavior pattern

Glossary

Action research. Research whose goal is the understanding or solution of social problems.

Adaptation. Shift in perception of one's environment that occurs with continued exposure, often involving decreased sensitivity to aversive conditions, such as noise.

Adaptation level. Personal, cognitive standard for evaluating new conditions, such as the noisiness of a city street.

Altruism. A special form of helping behavior that is voluntary, costly, and motivated by something other than the expectation of reward.

Anchor. A reference point that is used in making judgments.

Androgyny. A term referring to a high degree of masculine (or agentic) traits and a high degree of feminine (or communal) traits; currently used by investigators to refer to psychological, rather than physical, characteristics.

Anticonformity. Behavior that is directly antithetical to the normative group expectations. Also called counterconformity.

Archival research. Analysis of existing documents or records, especially those contained in public archives.

Assimilation effects. In social-judgment theory, shifts in judgments toward an anchor point.

Attribution theory. A theory, stemming from the work of Fritz Heider and from Gestalt theory, concerning the way in which people assign characteristics or intentions to other persons or to objects.

Authoritarianism. A basic personality dimension that includes a set of organized beliefs, values, and preferences, including submission to authority, identification with authority, denial of feelings, and cynicism.

Autokinetic effect. The tendency for a stationary light, when viewed in an otherwise completely dark room, to appear to be moving.

Balance theory. A theory of attitude change based on the principle of consistency among elements in a relationship. Heider, who proposed this model, stated that unbalanced states produce tension, which a person will try to reduce by changing some attitude.

Bargaining. The process whereby two or more parties try to settle what each shall give and take, or perform and receive, in a transaction between them.

Behavioral medicine. A field that integrates behavioral and biomedical science, focuses on health and illness, and is concerned with the application of knowledge to the prevention, diagnosis, and treatment of illness.

Belief in a just world. A belief that there is an appropriate fit between what people do and what happens to them.

Bisexuality. Engaging in sexual behavior with both sexes during similar periods of time.

Bystander effect. The finding that a person is less likely to provide help when in the presence of witnesses than when alone.

Catharsis. Release of aggressive energy through the expression of aggressive emotions or through alternative forms of behavior.

Causal attribution. The process of explaining events, or inferring their causes.

Causal schema. A conception of the way two or more causal factors interact in relation to a particular kind of effect; an assumed pattern of data in a complete analysis-of-variance framework.

Central trait. A personal characteristic that strongly influences a perceiver's impressions of the person possessing the trait. Asch showed that the *warm/cold* personality dimension was such a central trait.

Change agents. Persons who are engaged in the planning and application of change methods in the society.

Cognition. Knowledge acquired through experience.

Cognitive dissonance theory. A theory of attitude change developed by Leon Festinger and based on the principle of consistency. Cognitive dissonance exists when two cognitions contradict each other. Such dissonance is uncomfortable, and it is predicted that a person will reduce dissonance by one of several means—for example, by changing an attitude.

Cognitive structure. A set of principles and processes that organizes cognitive experience.

Cohesiveness. The attractiveness that a group has for its members and that the members have for one another; the force that holds a group together.

Communication networks. Representations of the acceptable paths of communication between persons in a group or organization.

Competition. Activity directed toward achieving a goal that only one of the persons or groups can obtain.

Competitive reward structure. A reward structure in which not all people striving for a reward can attain it and in which movement toward the goal by one person decreases the chance that others will attain that goal.

Complementarity. A principle proposed by Winch to explain interpersonal attraction; refers to a pairing of different (and sometimes opposite) needs, such as dominance and submission.

Compliance. Behavior in accordance with a direct request.

Conformity. Yielding to group pressures when no direct request to comply is made.

Consideration. A dimension of leadership; the leader's concern with relationships between himself or herself and other group members and the maintenance of group morale and cohesiveness.

Construct. A concept, defined in terms of observable events, used by a theory to account for regularities or relationships in data.

Contingency awareness. Recognition of the connection or dependency between event and a subsequent event.

Contrast effect. In social-judgment theory, a shift in judgment away from an anchor point.

Cooperation. Working together for mutual benefit; a prosocial behavior.

Cooperative reward structure. A reward structure in which everyone in the group must achieve the reward in order for it to be attained by any one participant. Each person's efforts advance the group's chances.

Correlational method. A study of the interrelation between two or more sets of events. Such a method does not allow conclusions about the causal relation between the two events.

Crowding. A psychological state of stress that sometimes accompanies high population density. (A similar term, *crowded*, refers to situations in which population density is relatively high.)

Debriefing. Discussion conducted at end of an experiment in which experimenter reveals complete procedures to subject and explains the reasons for any deception that may have occurred.

Defense mechanisms. Devices used by the ego, operating at an unconscious level, that transform libidinal impulses into less threatening expression.

Deindividuation. A state of relative anonymity, in which a group member does not feel singled out or identifiable.

Demand characteristics. The perceptual cues, both explicit and implicit, that communicate what behavior is expected in a situation.

Dependent variable. A variable whose changes are considered to be consequences, or effects, of changes in other (independent) variables.

Discrimination. Any behavior that reflects acceptance or rejection of a person solely on the basis of membership in a particular group.

Display rules. Socially learned rules for controlling the expression of emotions.

Dominance hierarchy. In a group, the ranking of the members in terms of influence or power. The most powerful or dominant member is highest in the hierarchy.

Ego. In Freudian theory, that part of the personality that is oriented toward acting reasonably and realistically; the "executive" part of personality.

Emblems. Body gestures that are substitutes for the spoken word.

Emic. Referring to culture-specific constructs that have meaning only within a particular cultural framework.

Empathy. The vicarious experience of another person's perceptions and feelings.

Empirical-rational strategy. A strategy of planned change that holds that publishing the facts that support change is sufficient to initiate that change.

Equity theory. A theory that specifies how people evaluate relative contributions to a relationship. Specifically, the theory suggests that ratios of inputs and outcomes should be equal for both participants.

Erotica. Visual or verbal material that is considered sexually arousing.

Ethnocentrism. The tendency to judge other people or groups by the standards of one's own group.

Ethology. The study of the behavior of animals in their natural settings.

Etic.   Referring to universal factors; constructs that are not culture-specific.

Evaluation apprehension.   A concern on the part of a subject in a study that he or she is performing correctly and will be positively evaluated by the researcher.

Evaluation research.   Research that assesses or evaluates the effects of a particular social action or program.

Excitation-transfer theory.   A theory proposed by Dolf Zillmann that suggests that arousal generated in one situation may transfer and intensify a subsequent emotional state.

Exotic bias.   A tendency, in observing another group or society, to focus on aspects that differ from one's own group or society and to ignore similar features.

Experimental realism.   Arrangement of the events of an experiment so that they will seem convincing and have the maximum possible impact on the subjects. This is sometimes accomplished through deception.

Experimenter expectancies.   Beliefs held by the experimenter and reflected in his or her behavior that may cause changes or distortions in the results of an experiment.

External validity.   The "generalizability" of a research finding (for example, to other populations, settings, treatment arrangements, or measurement arrangements).

Facial affect program.   The connection between an emotional experience and a particular pattern of facial muscles.

Field theory.   A social-psychological perspective developed by Kurt Lewin that proposes that one's social behavior is a function not only of one's own attitudes, personality, and other intrapersonal factors but also of one's environment, or "field."

"Foot in the door" effect.   A psychological effect whereby compliance with a small request makes it more likely that the person will comply with a larger (and less desirable) request.

Frustration-aggression hypothesis.   A theory that assumes that aggression is always motivated by frustration, although frustration may have other consequences as well.

Functional theory.   A theory of attitude change that emphasizes the basis of attitudes in different individual needs. To change someone's attitude, one must understand why that attitude is held.

Fundamental attribution error.   The tendency of observers to overemphasize the actor as a cause of events.

Gender identity.   One's self-awareness of being male or female.

GRIT.   Graduated and reciprocated initiatives in tension reduction; a strategy of arms reduction proposed by the psychologist Charles Osgood.

Group polarization.   A shift in opinions by members of a group toward a more extreme position.

Groupthink.   A mode of thinking, as defined by Janis, in which group members' strivings for unanimity override their motivation to realistically appraise alternative courses of action; or a tendency to seek concurrence.

Health locus of control.   A personality dimension—the belief that one can exert control over one's health (internal health locus of control) or that prevention of illness is beyond one's control (external health locus of control).

Hedonic relevance.   As used by Jones and Davis, the extent to which a person's actions are rewarding or costly to the observer.

Hypothesis.   A tentative explanation of a relationship between variables, or a supposition that a relationship may exist. A hypothesis generates some scientific method (such as an experiment) that seeks to confirm or disprove the hypothesis.

Id.   In Freudian theory, a set of drives that is the repository of our basic unsocialized impulses, including sex and aggression.

Idiographic.   Approach to the study of personality that focuses on the interrelationship of events and characteristics within a single individual.

Illusory correlation.   An overestimation of the strength of a relationship between two variables. Variables may not be related at all, or the relationship may be much weaker than believed.

Illustrators.   Nonverbal behaviors that are directly linked with spoken language.

Implicit personality theories.   Assumptions people make that two or more traits are related so that, if a person has one of the traits, it is believed that he or she will have another one as well.

Impression management.   The conscious or unconscious attempt to control images that are projected in real or imagined social interactions.

Independent variable.   A variable that is manipulated in an experiment; a variable whose changes are considered to be the cause of changes in another (dependent) variable.

Individualistic reward structure.   A reward structure in which goal attainment by one participant has no effect on the probability of goal attainment by others.

Initiating structure. A dimension of leadership; the leader's behavior in identifying the group's goal and moving the group toward its goal.

Instinct. An unlearned behavior pattern that appears in full form in all members of the species whenever there is an adequate stimulus.

Instrumental learning. A type of learning in which a response is followed by a reward or reinforcement, resulting in an increase in the frequency of the response.

Integrative agreement. An agreement that reconciles the interests of both parties in a negotiation, yielding high payoff for both groups.

Interaction. A joint effect of two or more variables such that the effect of one variable is different for various levels of the other variables.

Interaction territory. The area around two or more persons as they are talking, comparable to an individual's personal space.

Intergroup behavior. The interaction of members of one group with members of another group, where such interaction is based on the group identification of the individuals.

Intergroup-contact hypothesis. The assumption that prejudice will be reduced and favorable attitudes will develop when members of two groups with negative attitudes toward each other are brought together.

Internal validity. The conclusiveness with which the effects of the independent variables are established in a scientific investigation, as opposed to the possibility that some confounding variable(s) may have caused the observed results.

Interview. A research method that involves asking another person a set of questions according to a predetermined schedule and recording the answers.

Kinesics. A scheme developed by Birdwhistell for classifying body motions, intended to parallel linguistic categories.

Kin selection. In sociobiology, the concept that genes will become more common in a species if they contribute to the survival of relatives, even if those genes decrease the individual's chances of survival. Used to argue that altruism might be biologically based.

Leadership. The process of influence between a leader and followers to attain group, organizational, or societal goals.

Learned helplessness. The belief that one's outcomes are independent of one's actions, learned through exposure to situations in which outcomes are noncontingent and resulting in behavior deficits and feelings of depression.

Life space. In field theory, the person plus his or her environment, all of which is viewed as one set of interdependent factors.

Locus of control. A construct developed by Julian Rotter, referring to a person's belief that events are within his or her own control (internal) or that outside forces are in control (external).

Main effect. The effect that levels of a single independent variable have on a dependent variable, not considering any other variables that may be affecting the results.

Manipulation check. One or more questions posed to the subject(s) by the experimenter to assess the effectiveness of the experimental manipulation.

Matching hypothesis. The proposition that people will be attracted to others who are approximately equal in physical beauty.

Mere exposure effect. The finding that repeated exposure to an object results in greater attraction to that object.

Modeling. The tendency for a person to reproduce the action, attitudes, and emotional responses exhibited by a real-life or symbolic model. Also called "observational learning."

Mundane realism. Arrangement of the events in an experiment so that they seem as similar as possible to normal, everyday occurrences.

Negative-state-relief model. A hypothesis explaining the relation between negative moods and helping behavior as a learned way of escaping negative psychological states.

Neo-Freudians. Followers of Freud who depart in various ways from some of Freud's doctrines.

Noise. Unwanted sound; a psychological evaluation of a physical stimulus.

Nomothetic. Approach to the study of personality that focuses on differences between people on a single norm or dimension selected by an investigator.

Normative-reeducative strategy. A strategy of planned change that assumes that, before trying to change a person or group, one must take the cultural or normative factors into account (such as the past history of the person or group).

Norms. Socially defined and enforced standards of behavior that concern the way a person should interpret the world and/or behave in it.

Obedience. A special form of compliance in which behavior is performed in response to a direct order.

Objective self-awareness. A psychological state in which individuals focus their attention on and evaluate aspects of their self-concepts, particularly discrepancies between "real" self and "ideal" self.

Obscenity. That which is considered offensive to the mass populace and therefore proscribed. Recent definitions have limited the meaning of *obscenity* to offensive sexual materials.

Observational learning. A type of learning in which responses are acquired simply by observing the actions of others.

Overload. A concept derived from information-processing that refers to a situation in which a person receives inputs at a faster rate than they can be processed. Overload is often a source of stress.

Paralanguage. Vocalizations which are not language but which convey meaning; examples include pitch and rhythm, laughing and yawning.

Participant observer. An investigator in a field study who participates in the activities of the group being observed and maintains records of the group members' behaviors.

Personalism. As used by Jones and Davis, the perceived intentionality of a person's behavior; the degree to which a perceiver believes that another's behavior is directed at him or her.

Personal norms. An individual's feelings of obligation to act in a given way in a certain situation; internalized norms.

Phenomenological approach. A point of view in social psychology stating that the environment, as the person perceives it, is an important influence on behavior.

Philosophies of human nature. Expectations that people possess certain qualities and will behave in certain ways.

Population density. The number of persons (or other animals) per unit of space; for example, the number of persons per acre.

Pornography. Erotic material which combines elements of sexuality and aggression and in which force or coercion is used to accomplish the sexual act.

Power-coercive strategy. A strategy that uses either violent or nonviolent pressures (lobbying, petitions, strikes, riots, and so on) to bring about social change.

Prejudice. An unjustified evaluative reaction to a member of a racial, ethnic, or other group, which results solely from the person's membership in that group; an intolerant, unfair, or unfavorable attitude toward another group of people.

Primacy effect. The tendency for the first information received to have the predominant effect on one's judgments or opinions about persons, objects, or issues.

Primary territory. An area that an individual or group owns and controls on a relatively permanent basis; such areas are central to the everyday lives of the occupants.

Priming effect. The finding that a schema is more likely to be activated if it has recently been used in the past.

Privacy. Ability to control access to the self or information about the self, especially when one wants less involvement with others.

Privacy regulation. A process of controlling the amount of social interaction that we have with others.

Propinquity. Proximity, or geographical closeness; considered an important factor in interpersonal attraction.

Prosocial behavior. Behavior that has positive social consequences and improves the physical or psychological well-being of another person or persons.

Prototype. An abstract representation of the attributes associated with personality types that is stored in memory and used to organize information about a person.

Public territory. A space in a public place that is temporarily used by an individual or group (for example, a bench, cafeteria table, or bus seat).

Quasi-experimental research. Social research in which the investigator does not have full experimental control over the independent variable but does have extensive control over how, when, and for whom the dependent variable is measured.

Questionnaire survey. A research method in which the experimenter supplies written questions to the subject, who provides written answers.

Randomization. Assignment of conditions (for instance, assignment of subjects to treatment conditions) in a completely random manner—that is, a manner determined entirely by chance.

Reactance. A motivational state that is aroused whenever a person feels that his or her freedom to choose an object is severely limited and that results in the object's increased desirability.

Reactive measure. A measurement of a variable whose characteristics may be changed by the very act of measuring it.

Recency effect. The tendency for the most recent information received to have the predominant effect on one's judgment or opinion about persons, objects, or issues.

Reciprocal altruism. In sociobiology, the concept that natural selection would favor those with genes predisposing them to altruism because altruistic acts are eventually reciprocated and thus benefit the individual. Used to argue that altruism might be biologically based.

Reciprocity norm. A standard of behavior that says that people should help, and should refrain from injuring, those who have helped them.

Reinforcement. A consequence of a response that increases the probability that the response will be made again under the same stimulus conditions.

Reinforcement theory. A theory that emphasizes that behavior is determined by the rewards or punishments given in response to it.

Relative deprivation. One's perceived state in relation to the perceived state of others or in relation to unfulfilled expectations.

Reliability. Consistency of measurement. Stability of scores over time, equivalence of scores on two forms of a test, and similarity of two raters' scoring of the same behavior are examples of three different kinds of reliability.

Response. An alteration in a person's behavior that results from an external or internal stimulus.

Role. The socially defined pattern of behaviors expected of an individual who is assigned a certain social function, such as spouse, clergyman, or baseball umpire.

Role expectations. Assumptions about the behavior of a person who holds a particular role.

Salience. The distinctiveness of a stimulus relative to the context.

Scapegoating. The displacement of hostility onto less powerful groups when the source of frustration is not available for attack or not attackable for other reasons.

Schema. An organized configuration of knowledge, derived from past experience, that we use to interpret our experience.

Secondary territory. A physical area often claimed by a person or group, even though it is recognized that others may occupy that area at times.

Self-concept. Thoughts that we have about ourselves.

Self-consciousness. A disposition to focus attention inward on the self. Two forms are private self-consciousness and public self-consciousness.

Self-disclosure. The revealing of personal information about the self; self-revelation.

Self-esteem. The evaluation of oneself in either positive or negative terms.

Self-fulfilling prophecy. The process whereby a perceiver's beliefs about a target person can elicit behavior from the target person that will confirm the expectancy.

Self-handicapping strategies. Strategies by which individuals manufacture protective excuses for anticipated failures in order to preserve and enhance their self-concept of competence.

Self-monitoring. The use of cues from other people's self-presentations in controlling one's own self-presentation. High self-monitoring individuals, as identified by the Self-Monitoring Scale, use their well-developed self-presentational skills for purposes of impression management in social relations.

Self-perception theory. A theory that proposes that we infer our attitudes, emotions, and other internal states from observing our own behavior.

Self-presentation. The process of impression management as it deals with aspects of the self (see **impression management**).

Self-schema. A set of cognitive generalizations about the self that organizes and guides the processing of self-related information.

Self-serving attribution bias. The tendency to accept greater personal responsibility for positive outcomes than for negative outcomes.

Sex-role norms. Beliefs about appropriate behaviors for females and males.

Simulation. A research method that attempts to imitate some crucial aspects of a real-world situation in order to gain more understanding of the underlying mechanisms that operate in that situation.

Situated-identities theory. A theory proposing that for each social situation there is a certain pattern of behavior that conveys an identity appropriate to that setting.

Social-comparison theory. A theory, developed by Festinger, that proposes that we use other people as sources for comparison so that we can evaluate our own attitudes and abilities.

Social distance. The degree of physical, social, or psychological closeness to members of an ethnic, racial, or religious group that a person finds acceptable.

Social-exchange theory. A general theoretical model that conceptualizes relationships in terms of rewards and costs to the participants.

Social facilitation. The state in which the presence of others improves the quality of an individual's performance.

Social inhibition. A decline in individual performance in the presence of other people.

Social-judgment theory. A theory of attitude change that emphasizes the individual's perception and judgment of a persuasive communication. Central concepts in this theory are anchors, assimilation and contrast effects, and latitudes of acceptance, rejection, and noncommitment.

Socialization. A process of acquiring behaviors that are considered appropriate by society.

Social-learning theory. A theory that proposes that social behavior develops as a result of observing others and of being rewarded for certain acts.

Social-pathology hypothesis. The idea that high population density leads to a variety of social ills.

Social-responsibility norm. A standard of behavior that dictates that people should help persons who are dependent or in need of help.

Social technology. The application of social science principles to the solution of social problems.

Social trap. A situation that provides immediate individual incentives for behaviors that in the long run may have negative consequences for society if large numbers of people perform the behaviors.

Sociobiology. A new discipline concerned with identifying biological and genetic bases for social behavior in animals and humans.

Sociopetal spaces. Settings that encourage interaction by placing people at comfortable conversational distances and facing one another.

Spontaneous self-concept. Self-descriptions that a person gives without any guidelines from the experimenter indicating what dimensions might be important.

Stereotype. A schema about members of an identifiable group.

Stimulus. Any event, internal or external to the person, that brings about an alteration in that person's behavior.

Stimulus discrimination. The process of making distinctions between similar stimuli.

Stimulus generalization. A process whereby, after a person learns to make a certain response to a certain stimulus, other similar but previously ineffective stimuli will also elicit that response.

Stimulus-overload theory. Stanley Milgram's concept of an excess of sensory and cognitive inputs; used to account for the behavior of people who live in cities, who are sometimes found to be less helpful than town-dwellers.

Stress. A complex physiological and psychological response to a demand or challenge, involving arousal and mobilization of capacities for coping.

Superego. In Freudian theory, the part of personality oriented toward doing what is morally proper; the conscience. The superego includes one's ego ideal, or ideal self-image.

Superordinate goal. An important goal that can be achieved only through cooperation.

Territorial dominance. The phenomenon in which an individual dominates interactions with others when the interactions occur in the individual's own territory.

Territory. For many nonhuman species, a specific geographic region that an animal marks with scents or calls, uses as a nesting place, and defends against intrusion by other animals of the same species. For humans, an area that is perceived by its occupant(s) as being under their own control.

Transsexualism. A gender identity opposite to one's bodily appearance and sexual organs. A person with male sex organs whose gender identity is female, or vice versa, is a transsexual.

Type A behavior pattern. A set of behaviors associated with increased risk for coronary heart disease.

Unobtrusive measures. A measurement that can be made without the knowledge of the person being studied. An unobtrusive measure is also nonreactive.

Urban-overload hypothesis. The idea that city-dwellers react to excessive stimulation by avoiding involvement with people.

Vividness. The intensity or emotional interest of a stimulus.

References

Abelson, R. P., & Rosenberg, M. J. Symbolic psycho-logic: A model of attitudinal cognition. *Behavioral Science*, 1958, *3*, 1–13.

Abramson, L. Y., Seligman, M. E. P., & Teasdale, J. D. Learned helplessness in humans: Critique and reformulation. *Journal of Abnormal Psychology*, 1978, *87*, 49–74.

Abramson, P. R. *Sexual lives.* Unpublished manuscript, University of California, Los Angeles, 1981.

Abramson, P. R., & Imai-Marquez, J. The Japanese-American: A cross-cultural, cross-sectional study of sex guilt. *Journal of Research in Personality*, 1982, *16*, 227–237.

Abramson, P. R., & Mechanic, M. B. Sex and the media: Three decades of best selling books and major motion pictures. *Archives of Sexual Behavior*, in press.

Abramson, P. R., Perry, L. B., Seeley, T. T., Seeley, D. M., & Rothblatt, A. B. Thermographic measurement of sexual arousal: A discriminant validity analysis. *Archives of Sexual Behavior*, 1981, *10*, 171–176.

Adams, R. S. Location as a feature of instructional interaction. *Merrill-Palmer Quarterly*, 1969, *15*(4), 309–321.

Aderman, D., & Berkowitz, L. Observational set, empathy, and helping. *Journal of Personality and Social Psychology*, 1970, *14*, 141–148.

Aderman, D., Bryant, F. B., & Donelsmith, D. E. Prediction as a means of inducing tolerance. *Journal of Research in Personality*, 1978, *12*, 172–178.

Adorno, T. W., Frenkel-Brunswik, E., Levinson, D., & Sanford, N. *The authoritarian personality.* New York: Harper, 1950.

Aiello, J. R. A test of equilibrium theory: Visual interaction in relation to orientation, distance, and sex of interactants. *Psychonomic Science*, 1972, *27*, 335–336.

Aiello, J. R. A further look at equilibrium theory: Visual interaction as a function of interpersonal distance. *Environmental Psychology and Nonverbal Behavior*, 1977, *1*, 122–140. (a)

Aiello, J. R. Visual interaction at extended distances. *Personality and Social Psychology Bulletin*, 1977, *3*, 83–86. (b)

Aiello, J. R., Baum, A., & Gormley, F. P. Social determinants of residential crowding stress. *Personality and Social Psychology Bulletin*, 1981, *7*, 643–649.

Aiello, J. R., & Cooper, R. E. Use of personal space as a function of social affect. *Proceedings, 80th Annual Convention, American Psychological Association*, 1972, *7*, 207–208.

Aiello, J. R., Epstein, Y. M., & Karlin, R. A. Effects of crowding on electrodermal activity. *Sociological Symposium*, 1975, *14*, 43–57. (a)

Aiello, J. R., Epstein, Y., & Karlin, R. Field experimental research on human crowding. Paper presented at convention of Eastern Psychological Association, New York, April 1975. (b)

Aiello, J. R., & Jones, S. E. A field study of the proxemic behavior of young school children in three subcultural groups. *Journal of Personality and Social Psychology*, 1971, *19*, 351–356.

Aiello, J. R., & Thompson, D. E. When compensation fails: Mediating effects of sex and locus of control at extended interaction distances. Paper presented at the annual convention of the American Psychological Association, Toronto, Ontario, 1978.

Ajzen, I., & Fishbein, M. Attitude-behavior relations: A theoretical analysis and review of empirical research. *Psychological Bulletin*, 1977, *84*, 888–918.

Ajzen, I., Timko, C., & White, J. B. Self-monitoring and the attitude-behavior relation. *Journal of Personality and Social Psychology*, 1982, *42*, 426–435.

Alan Guttmacher Institute. *Teenage pregnancy: The problem that hasn't gone away.* New York: Alan Guttmacher Institute, 1981.

Alexander, C. N., & Knight, G. W. Situated identities and social psychological experimentation. *Sociometry*, 1971, *34*, 65–82.

Alexander, C. N., Jr., & Lauderdale, P. Situated identities and social influence. *Sociometry*, 1977, *40*, 225–233.

Alexander, C. N., Jr., & Sagatun, I. An attributional analysis of experimental norms. *Sociometry*, 1973, *36*, 127–142.

Alinsky, S. *Rules for radicals.* New York: Random House, 1971.

Alker, H. A., & Owen, D. W. Biographical, trait and behavioral-sampling predictions of performance in a stressful life setting. *Journal of Personality and Social Psychology*, 1977, *35*, 717–723.

Allgeier, E. R. Ideological barriers to contraception. In E. R. Allgeier & N. B. McCormick (Eds.), *Gender roles and sexual behavior: Changing boundaries.* Palo Alto, Calif.: Mayfield, 1983.

Allport, F. H. The influence of the group upon association and thought. *Journal of Experimental Psychology*, 1920, *3*, 159–182.

Allport, G. W. Attitudes. In C. Murchison (Ed.), *Handbook of social psychology.* Worcester, Mass.: Clark University Press, 1935.

Allport, G. W. *Personality: A psychological interpretation.* New York: Holt, 1937.

Allport, G. W. *The nature of prejudice.* Garden City, N.Y.: Doubleday Anchor, 1958. (Originally published, 1954.)

Allport, G. W. *Pattern and growth in personality.* New York: Holt, Rinehart & Winston, 1961.

Allport, G. W. The general and the unique in psychological science. *Journal of Personality,* 1962, *30,* 405–422.

Allport, G. W. The historical background of modern social psychology. In G. Lindzey & E. Aronson (Eds.), *The handbook of social psychology* (Vol. 1) (2nd ed.). Reading, Mass.: Addison-Wesley, 1968.

Altman, I. Reciprocity of interpersonal exchange. *Journal of the Theory of Social Behaviour,* 1973, *3,* 249–261.

Altman, I. *The environment and social behavior: Privacy, personal space, territory, and crowding.* Monterey, Calif.: Brooks/Cole, 1975.

Altman, I. Privacy: A conceptual analysis. *Environment and Behavior,* 1976, *8,* 7–29.

Altman, I., Taylor, D., & Wheeler, L. Ecological aspects of group behavior in isolation. *Journal of Applied Social Psychology,* 1971, *1,* 76–100.

American Psychological Association. *Ethical principles in the conduct of research with human participants.* Washington, D.C.: American Psychological Association, 1973.

Amir, Y. The role of intergroup contact in change of prejudice and ethnic relations. In P. A. Katz (Ed.), *Towards the elimination of racism.* New York: Pergamon Press, 1976.

Amoroso, D. M., Brown, M., Pruesse, M., Ware, E. E., & Pilkey, D. W. An investigation of behavioral, psychological, and physiological reactions to pornographic stimuli. *Technical Reports of the Commission on Obscenity and Pornography* (Vol. 8). Washington, D.C.: U.S. Government Printing Office, 1971.

Anderson, C. A., Lepper, M. R., & Ross, L. The perseverance of social theories: The role of explanation in the persistence of discredited information. *Journal of Personality and Social Psychology,* 1980, *39,* 1037–1049.

Anderson, N. H. Application of an additive model to impression formation. *Science,* 1962, *138,* 817–818.

Anderson, N. H. Averaging versus adding as a stimulus-combination rule in impression formation. *Journal of Experimental Psychology,* 1965, *70,* 394–400.

Anderson, N. H. A simple model of information integration. In R. P. Abelson, E. Aronson, W. J. McGuire, T. M. Newcomb, M. J. Rosenberg, & P. H. Tannenbaum (Eds.), *Theories of cognitive consistency: A sourcebook.* Chicago: Rand McNally, 1968. (a)

Anderson, N. H. Likableness ratings of 555 personality-trait words. *Journal of Personality and Social Psychology,* 1968, *9,* 272–279. (b)

Anderson, N. H. Cognitive algebra: Integration theory applied to social attribution. In L. Berkowitz (Ed.), *Advances in experimental social psychology* (Vol. 7). New York: Academic Press, 1974.

Andrews, I. R., & Johnson, D. L. Small-group polarization of judgments. *Psychonomic Science,* 1971, *24,* 191–192.

Apfelbaum, E. Relations of domination and movements for liberation: An analysis of power between groups. In W. G. Austin & S. Worchel (Eds.), *The social psychology of intergroup relations.* Monterey, Calif.: Brooks/Cole, 1979.

Ard, B. N., Jr. Premarital sexual experience: A longitudinal study. *Journal of Sex Research,* 1974, *10,* 32–39.

Ardrey, R. *African genesis.* New York: Delta Books, 1961.

Ardrey, R. *The territorial imperative.* New York: Atheneum, 1966.

Argyle, M., & Dean, J. Eye contact, distance, and affiliation. *Sociometry,* 1965, *28,* 289–304.

Argyle, M., & Ingham, R. Gaze, mutual gaze, and proximity. *Semiotica,* 1972, *6,* 32–49.

Argyle, M., Ingham, R., Alkema, F., & McCallin, M. The different functions of gaze. *Semiotica,* 1973, *7,* 19–32.

Arkin, R. M. Self-presentation. In D. M. Wegner & R. R. Vallacher (Eds.), *The self in social psychology.* New York: Oxford University Press, 1980.

Arkin, R., Cooper, H., & Kolditz, T. A statistical review of the literature concerning the self-serving attribution bias in interpersonal influence situations. *Journal of Personality,* 1980, *48,* 435–448.

Aronfreed, J., & Paskal, V. Altruism, empathy, and the conditioning of positive affect. Unpublished manuscript, University of Pennsylvania, 1965.

Aronson, E. Dissonance theory: Progress and problems. In R. P. Abelson, E. Aronson, W. J. McGuire, T. M. Newcomb, M. J. Rosenberg, & P. H. Tannenbaum (Eds.), *Theories of cognitive consistency: A sourcebook.* Chicago: Rand McNally, 1968.

Aronson, E., Blaney, N., Stephan, C., Sikes, J., & Snapp, M. *The jigsaw classroom.* Beverly Hills, Calif.: Sage, 1978.

Aronson, E., & Carlsmith, J. M. Experimentation in social psychology. In G. Lindzey & E. Aronson (Eds.), *Handbook of social psychology* (Vol. 2) (2nd ed.). Reading, Mass.: Addison-Wesley, 1968.

Aronson, E., & Cope, V. My enemy's enemy is my friend. *Journal of Personality and Social Psychology,* 1968, *8,* 8–12.

Aronson, E., & Golden, B. W. The effect of relevant and irrelevant aspects of communicator credibility on attitude change. *Journal of Personality,* 1962, *30,* 135–146.

Asch, S. E. Forming impressions of personality. *Journal of Abnormal and Social Psychology,* 1946, *41,* 258–290.

Asch, S. E. Effects of group pressure upon the modification and distortion of judgments. In H. Guetzkow (Ed.), *Groups, leadership, and men.* Pittsburgh: Carnegie Press, 1951.

Asch, S. E. Studies of independence and conformity: A minority of one against a unanimous majority. *Psychological Monographs,* 1956, *70*(9, Whole No. 416).

Asch, S. E. Effects of group pressure upon modification and distortion of judgments. In E. E. Maccoby, T. M. Newcomb, & E. L. Hartley (Eds.), *Readings in social psychology* (3rd ed.). New York: Holt, Rinehart & Winston, 1958.

Ashmore, R. D. Prejudice: Causes and cures. In B. E. Collins (Ed.), *Social psychology.* Reading, Mass.: Addison-Wesley, 1970.

Ashmore, R. D., & Del Boca, F. K. Conceptual approaches to stereotypes and stereotyping. In D. L. Hamilton (Ed.), *Cognitive processes in stereotyping and intergroup behavior.* Hillsdale, N.J.: Erlbaum, 1981.

Athanasiou, R. A review of public attitudes on sexual issues. In J. Zubin & J. Money (Eds.), *Critical issues in contemporary sexual behavior.* Baltimore: Johns Hopkins University Press, 1973.

Athanasiou, R., & Yoshioka, G. A. The spatial character of friendship formation. *Environment and Behavior*, 1973, *5*, 43–65.

Atkins, A., Deaux, K., & Bieri, J. Latitude of acceptance and attitude change: Empirical evidence for a reformulation. *Journal of Personality and Social Psychology*, 1967, *6*, 47–54.

Austin, W. T., & Bates, F. L. Ethological indicators of dominance and territory in a human captive population. *Social Forces*, 1974, *52*, 447–455.

Averill, J. R., & Boothroyd, P. On falling in love in conformance with the romantic ideal. *Motivation and Emotion*, 1977, *1*, 235–247.

Azrin, N. H., Hutchinson, R. R., & Hake, D. F. Attack, avoidance, and escape reactions to aversive shock. *Journal of Experimental Analysis of Behavior*, 1966, *9*, 191–204.

Bachy, V. Danish "permissiveness" revisited. *Journal of Communication*, 1976, *26*, 40–43.

Back, K. W. Influence through social communication. *Journal of Abnormal and Social Psychology*, 1951, *46*, 9–23.

Back, K. W. *Beyond words: The story of sensitivity training and the encounter movement.* New York: Russell Sage Foundation, 1972.

Backman, C. W., & Secord, P. F. The effect of perceived liking on interpersonal attraction. *Human Relations*, 1959, *12*, 379–384.

Bakan, D. *The duality of human existence.* Chicago: Rand McNally, 1966.

Baker, N. J., & Wrightsman, L. S. The *Zeitgeist* and philosophies of human nature, or where have all the idealistic imperturbable freshmen gone? In L. S. Wrightsman (Ed.), *Assumptions about human nature: A social-psychological approach.* Monterey, Calif.: Brooks/Cole, 1974.

Bales, R. F. The equilibrium problem in small groups. In T. Parsons, R. F. Bales, & E. A. Shils (Eds.), *Working papers in the theory of action.* Glencoe, Ill.: Free Press, 1953.

Bales, R. F. Task roles and social roles in problem-solving groups. In E. E. Maccoby, T. M. Newcomb, & E. L. Hartley (Eds.), *Readings in social psychology* (3rd ed.). New York: Holt, Rinehart & Winston, 1958.

Bandura, A. Vicarious processes: A case of no-trial learning. In L. Berkowitz (Ed.), *Advances in experimental social psychology* (Vol. 2). New York: Academic Press, 1965.

Bandura, A. *Aggression: A social-learning analysis.* Englewood Cliffs, N.J.: Prentice-Hall, 1973.

Bandura, A., Ross, D., & Ross, S. Transmission of aggression through imitation of aggressive models. *Journal of Abnormal and Social Psychology*, 1961, *63*, 575–582.

Bandura, A., Ross, D., & Ross, S. Imitation of film-mediated aggressive models. *Journal of Abnormal and Social Psychology*, 1963, *66*, 3–11. (a)

Bandura, A., Ross, D., & Ross, S. A comparative test of the status envy, social power and secondary reinforcement theories of identification learning. *Journal of Abnormal and Social Psychology*, 1963, *67*, 527–534. (b)

Bandura, A., & Walters, R. *Social learning and personality development.* New York: Holt, Rinehart & Winston, 1963.

Bard, M. Alternatives to traditional law enforcement. In F. F. Korten, S. W. Cook, & J. I. Lacey (Eds.), *Psychology and the problems of society.* Washington, D.C.: American Psychological Association, 1970.

Barker, R. G. *Ecological psychology: Concepts and methods for studying the environment of human behavior.* Stanford, Calif.: Stanford University Press, 1968.

Barker, R. G., & Schoggen, P. *Qualities of community life.* San Francisco: Jossey-Bass, 1973.

Barnes, R. D., Ickes, W., & Kidd, R. F. Effects of the perceived intentionality and stability of another's dependency on helping behavior. *Personality and Social Psychology Bulletin*, 1979, *5*, 367–372.

Baron, R. A. Reducing the influence of an aggressive model: The restraining effects of discrepant modeling cues. *Journal of Personality and Social Psychology*, 1971, *20*, 240–245.

Baron, R. A. Aggression as a function of ambient temperature and prior anger arousal. *Journal of Personality and Social Psychology*, 1972, *21*, 183–189.

Baron, R. A. Aggression as a function of victim's pain cues, level of prior anger arousal, and exposure to an aggressive model. *Journal of Personality and Social Psychology*, 1974, *29*, 117–124.

Baron, R. A. The reduction of human aggression: A field study of the influence of incompatible reactions. *Journal of Applied Social Psychology*, 1976, *6*, 260–274.

Baron, R. A. *Human aggression.* New York: Plenum Press, 1977.

Baron, R. A. Olfaction and human social behavior: Effects of pleasant scents on physical aggression. *Basic and Applied Social Psychology*, 1980, *1*, 163–172.

Baron, R. A., & Ball, R. L. The aggression-inhibiting influence of nonhostile humor. *Journal of Experimental Social Psychology*, 1974, *10*, 23–33.

Baron, R. A., & Bell, P. A. Aggression and heat: Mediating effects of prior provocation and exposure to an aggressive model. *Journal of Personality and Social Psychology*, 1975, *31*, 825–832.

Baron, R. A., & Bell, P. A. Aggression and heat: The influence of ambient temperature, negative affect, and a cooling drink on physical aggression. *Journal of Personality and Social Psychology*, 1976, *33*, 245–255.

Baron, R. A., & Bell, P. A. Sexual arousal and aggression by males: Effects of type of erotic stimuli and prior provocation. *Journal of Personality and Social Psychology*, 1977, *35*, 79–87.

Baron, R. A., & Kepner, C. R. Model's behavior and attraction toward the model as determinants of adult aggressive behavior. *Journal of Personality and Social Psychology*, 1970, *14*, 335–344.

Baron, R. A., & Ransberger, V. M. Ambient temperature and the occurrence of collective violence: The "long hot summer" revisited. *Journal of Personality and Social Psychology*, 1978, *36*, 351–360.

Baron, R. M., & Rodin, J. Perceived control and crowding stress: Processes mediating the impact of spatial and social density. In A. Baum & Y. Epstein (Eds.), *Human response to crowding.* Hillsdale, N.J.: Erlbaum, 1978.

Barron, N. Sex-typed language: The production of grammatical cases. *Acta Sociologica*, 1971, *14*, 24–42.

Bar-Tal, D. *Prosocial behavior: Theory and research.* Washington, D.C.: Hemisphere (distributed by Halsted Press), 1976.

Bar-Tal, D., Raviv, A., & Lesser, T. The development of altruistic behavior: Empirical evidence. *Developmental Psychology*, 1980, *16*, 516–524.

Bar-Tal, D., & Saxe, L. Perceptions of similarly and dissimilarly attractive couples and individuals. *Journal of Personality and Social Psychology*, 1976, *33*, 772–781.

Bartlett, F. C. *Remembering: A study in experimental and social psychology.* Cambridge, England: Cambridge University Press, 1932.

Bartos, O. J. *Process and outcome in negotiation.* New York: Columbia University Press, 1974.

Bass, B. M. *Stogdill's handbook of leadership* (Rev. ed.). New York: Free Press, 1981.

Bass, B. M., Krusell, J., & Alexander, R. A. Male managers' attitudes toward working women. *American Behavioral Scientist*, 1971, *15*, 221–236.

Batson, C. D., & Coke, J. S. Empathy: A source of altruistic motivation for helping? In J. P. Rushton & R. M. Sorrentino (Eds.), *Altruism and helping behavior: Social, personality, and developmental perspectives.* Hillsdale, N.J.: Erlbaum, 1981.

Batson, C. D., Coke, J. S., Jasnoski, M. L., & Hanson, M. Buying kindness: Effect of an extrinsic incentive for helping on perceived altruism. *Personality and Social Psychology Bulletin*, 1978, *4*, 86–91.

Batson, C. D., Duncan, B. D., Ackerman, P., Buckley, T., & Birch, K. Is empathic emotion a source of altruistic motivation? *Journal of Personality and Social Psychology*, 1981, *40*, 290–302.

Batson, C. D., & Gray, R. A. Religious orientation and helping behavior: Responding to one's own or to the victim's needs? *Journal of Personality and Social Psychology*, 1981, *40*, 511–520.

Bauer, R. A. Self-confidence and persuasibility: One more time. *Journal of Marketing Research*, 1970, *7*, 256–258.

Baum, A., Aiello, J. R., & Calesnick, L. E. Crowding and personal control: Social density and the development of learned helplessness. *Journal of Personality and Social Psychology*, 1978, *36*, 1000–1011.

Baum, A., & Davis, G. E. Reducing the stress of high-density living: An architectural intervention. *Journal of Personality and Social Psychology*, 1980, *38*, 471–481.

Baum, A., Davis, G. E., & Aiello, J. R. Crowding and neighborhood mediation of urban density. *Population and Environment*, 1978, *1*, 266–279.

Baum, A., Fisher, J. D., & Solomon, S. Type of information, familiarity, and the reduction of crowding stress. *Journal of Personality and Social Psychology*, 1981, *40*, 11–23.

Baum, A., Fleming, R., & Singer, J. E. Stress at Three Mile Island: Applying psychological impact analysis. In L. Bickman (Ed.), *Applied social psychology annual* (Vol. 3). Beverly Hills, Calif.: Sage, 1982.

Baum, A., & Greenberg, C. I. Waiting for a crowd: The behavioral and perceptual effects of anticipated crowding. *Journal of Personality and Social Psychology*, 1975, *32*, 671–679.

Baum, A., Harpin, R. E., & Valins, S. The role of group phenomena in the experience of crowding. *Environment and Behavior*, 1975, *7*, 185–198.

Baum, A., & Koman, S. Differential response to anticipated crowding: Psychological effects of social and spatial density. *Journal of Personality and Social Psychology*, 1976, *34*, 526–536.

Baum, A., Shapiro, A., Murray, D., & Wideman, M. Interpersonal mediation of perceived crowding and control in residential dyads and triads. *Journal of Applied Social Psychology*, 1979, *9*, 491–507.

Baum, A., Singer, J., & Baum, C. Stress and the environment. *Journal of Social Issues*, 1981, *37*(1), 4–35.

Baum, A., & Valins, S. *Architecture and social behavior: Psychological studies of social density.* Hillsdale, N.J.: Erlbaum, 1977.

Baum, A., & Valins, S. Architectural mediation of residential density and control: Crowding and the regulation of social contact. In L. Berkowitz (Ed.), *Advances in experimental social psychology* (Vol. 12). New York: Academic Press, 1979.

Baumann, D. J., Cialdini, R. B., & Kenrick, D. T. Altruism as hedonism: Helping and self-gratification as equivalent responses. *Journal of Personality and Social Psychology*, 1981, *40*, 1039–1046.

Baumeister, R. F. A self-presentational view of social phenomena. *Psychological Bulletin*, 1982, *91*, 3–26.

Baumeister, R. F., & Jones, E. E. When self-presentation is constrained by the target's knowledge: Consistency and compensation. *Journal of Personality and Social Psychology*, 1978, *36*, 608–618.

Baumrin, B. H. The immorality of irrelevance: The social role of science. In F. F. Korten, S. W. Cook, & J. I. Lacey (Eds.), *Psychology and the problems of society.* Washington, D.C.: American Psychological Association, 1970.

Baumrind, D. Some thoughts on the ethics of research after reading Milgram's "Behavioral study of obedience." *American Psychologist*, 1964, *19*, 421–423.

Beattie, C., & Spencer, B. G. Career attainment in Canadian bureaucracies: Unscrambling the effects of age, seniority, education, and ethnic linguistic factors in salary. *American Journal of Sociology*, 1971, *77*, 472–490.

Beattie, G. W., Agahi, C., & Spencer, C. Social stereotypes held by different occupational groups in post-revolutionary Iran. *European Journal of Social Psychology*, 1982, *12*, 75–87.

Beck, K. H., & Lund, A. K. The effects of health threat seriousness and personal efficacy upon intentions and behavior. *Journal of Applied Social Psychology*, 1981, *11*, 401–415.

Becker, F. D. Study of spatial markers. *Journal of Personality and Social Psychology*, 1973, *26*, 439–445.

Becker, F. D., & Mayo, C. Delineating personal distance and territoriality. *Environment and Behavior*, 1971, *3*, 375–381.

Becker, F. D., Sommer, R., Bee, J., & Oxley, B. College classroom ecology. *Sociometry*, 1973, *36*, 514–525.

Becker, L. J. Joint effect of feedback and goal setting on performance: A field study of residential energy conservation. *Journal of Applied Psychology*, 1978, *63*, 428–433.

Belk, R., Painter, J., & Semenik, R. Preferred solutions to the energy crisis as a function of causal attributions. *Journal of Consumer Research*, 1981, *8*, 306–312.

Bell, A. P., & Weinberg, M. S. *Homosexualities: A study of diversity among men and women.* New York: Simon and Schuster, 1978.

Bell, A. P., Weinberg, M. S., & Hammersmith, S. K. *Sexual preference: Its development in men and women.* Bloomington: Indiana University Press, 1981. (a)

Bell, A. P., Weinberg, M. S., & Hammersmith, S. K. *Sexual preference: Its development in men and women. Statistical appendix.* Bloomington: Indiana University Press, 1981. (b)

Bell, P. A., & Baron, R. A. Aggression and heat: The mediating role of negative affect. *Journal of Applied Social Psychology*, 1976, *6*, 18–30.

Bem, D. J. Self-perception: An alternative interpretation of cognitive dissonance phenomena. *Psychological Review*, 1967, *74*, 183–200.

Bem, D. J. Self-perception theory. In L. Berkowitz (Ed.), *Advances in experimental social psychology* (Vol. 6). New York: Academic Press, 1972.

Bem, D. J., & Allen, A. On predicting some of the people some of the time: The search for cross-situational consistencies in behavior. *Psychological Review*, 1974, *81*, 506–520.

Bem, S. L. The measurement of psychological androgyny. *Journal of Consulting and Clinical Psychology*, 1974, *42*, 155–162.

Bender, P. Definition of "obscene" under existing law. *Technical Reports of the Commission on Obscenity and Pornography* (Vol. 2). Washington, D.C.: U.S. Government Printing Office, 1971.

Benson, P. L., Karabenick, S. A., & Lerner, R. M. Pretty pleases: The effects of physical attractiveness, race, and sex on receiving help. *Journal of Experimental Social Psychology*, 1976, *12*, 409–415.

Bentler, P. M. Heterosexual behavior assessment: I. Males. *Behavior Research and Therapy*, 1968, *6*, 21–25. (a)

Bentler, P. M. Heterosexual behavior assessment: II. Females. *Behavior Research and Therapy*, 1968, *6*, 27–30. (b)

Bentler, P. M., & Abramson, P. R. The science of sex research: Some methodological considerations. *Archives of Sexual Behavior*, 1981, *10*, 225–251.

Berg, B. Helping behavior on the gridiron: It helps if you're winning. *Psychological Reports*, 1978, *42*, 531–534.

Berger, C. R., & Calabrese, R. J. Some explorations in initial interaction and beyond: Toward a developmental theory of interpersonal communication. *Human Communication Research*, 1975, *1*, 99–112.

Berglas, S., & Jones, E. E. Drug choice as an externalization strategy in response to noncontingent success. *Journal of Personality and Social Psychology*, 1978, *36*, 405–417.

Berkowitz, L. Some aspects of observed aggression. *Journal of Personality and Social Psychology*, 1965, *2*, 359–369. (a)

Berkowitz, L. The concept of aggressive drive: Some additional considerations. In L. Berkowitz (Ed.), *Advances in experimental social psychology* (Vol. 2). New York: Academic Press, 1965. (b)

Berkowitz, L. Impulse, aggression, and the gun. *Psychology Today*, 1968, *2*(4), 18–22.

Berkowitz, L. The frustration-aggression hypothesis revisited. In L. Berkowitz (Ed.), *Roots of aggression: A re-examination of the frustration-aggression hypothesis.* New York: Atherton, 1969.

Berkowitz, L. The contagion of violence: An S-R mediational analysis of some effects of observed aggression. In W. Arnold & M. Page (Eds.), *Nebraska Symposium on Motivation* (Vol. 18). Lincoln: University of Nebraska Press, 1971.

Berkowitz, L. Some determinants of impulsive aggression: Role of mediated associations with reinforcements for aggression. *Psychological Review*, 1974, *81*, 165–176.

Berkowitz, L. Decreased helpfulness with increased group size through lessening the effects of the needy individual's dependency. *Journal of Personality*, 1978, *46*, 299–310.

Berkowitz, L., & Alioto, J. T. The meaning of an observed event as a determinant of its aggressive consequences. *Journal of Personality and Social Psychology*, 1973, *28*, 206–217.

Berkowitz, L., & Daniels, L. R. Responsibility and dependency. *Journal of Abnormal and Social Psychology*, 1963, *66*, 664–669.

Berkowitz, L., & Daniels, L. R. Affecting the salience of the social responsibility norm: Effects of past help on the response to dependency relationships. *Journal of Abnormal and Social Psychology*, 1964, *68*, 275–281.

Berkowitz, L., & LePage, A. Weapons as aggression-eliciting stimuli. *Journal of Personality and Social Psychology*, 1967, *7*, 202–207.

Berkun, M. M. Performance decrement under psychological stress. *Human Factors*, 1964, *6*(1), 21–30.

Bernard, J. *Women, wives, mothers.* Chicago: Aldine, 1975.

Berry, J. W. Canadian psychology: Some social and applied emphases. *Canadian Psychologist*, 1974, *15*, 132–139.

Berry, J. W. Social psychology: Comparative, societal and universal. *Canadian Psychological Review*, 1978, *19*, 93–104.

Berscheid, E. Opinion change and communicator-communicatee similarity and dissimilarity. *Journal of Personality and Social Psychology*, 1966, *4*, 670–680.

Berscheid, E., Graziano, W., Monson, T., & Dermer, M. Outcome dependency: Attention, attribution and attraction. *Journal of Personality and Social Psychology*, 1976, *34*, 978–989.

Berscheid, E., & Walster, E. Physical attractiveness. In L. Berkowitz (Ed.), *Advances in experimental social psychology* (Vol. 7). New York: Academic Press, 1974.

Berscheid, E. & Walster, E. *Interpersonal attraction* (2nd ed.). Reading, Mass.: Addison-Wesley, 1978.

Berzins, J. I., Welling, M. A., & Wetter, R. E. *The PRF ANDRO scale user's manual.* Unpublished manual, University of Kentucky, 1975.

Beveridge, W. I. B. *The art of scientific investigation.* London: Mercury, 1964.

Bickman, L. Social influence and diffusion of responsibility in an emergency. *Journal of Experimental Social Psychology*, 1972, *8*, 438–445.

Bickman, L. Interpersonal influence and the reporting of a crime. *Personality and Social Psychology Bulletin*, 1979, *5*, 32–35.

Bickman, L. Introduction. In L. Bickman (Ed.), *Applied social psychology annual* (Vol. 1). Beverly Hills, Calif.: Sage, 1980.

Bickman, L. Some distinctions between basic and applied approaches. In L. Bickman (Ed.), *Applied social psychology annual* (Vol. 2). Beverly Hills, Calif.: Sage, 1981.

Bickman, L., & Kamzan, M. The effect of race and need on helping behavior. *Journal of Social Psychology*, 1973, *89*, 73–77.

Biddle, B. J., & Thomas, E. J. (Eds.). *Role theory: Concepts and research*. New York: Wiley, 1966.

Bird, C. *Social psychology*. New York: Appleton-Century-Crofts, 1940.

Birdwhistell, R. L. *Kinesics and context*. Philadelphia: University of Pennsylvania Press, 1970.

Block, J. H. Conceptions of sex roles: Some cross-cultural and longitudinal perspectives. *American Psychologist*, 1973, *28*, 512–526.

Blumstein, P. W., & Schwartz, P. Bisexuality: Some social psychological issues. *Journal of Social Issues*, 1977, *33*(2), 30–45.

Bond, C. F., Jr. Social facilitation: A self-presentational view. *Journal of Personality and Social Psychology*, 1982, *42*, 1042–1050.

Booth, A. Sex and social participation. *American Sociological Review*, 1972, 37, 183–192.

Booth, A., & Welch, S. The effects of crowding: A cross-national study. Unpublished manuscript, Ministry of State for Urban Affairs, Ottawa, Canada, 1973.

Booth, A., & Welch, S. Crowding and urban crime rates. Paper presented at the meeting of the Midwest Sociological Association, Omaha, Nebraska, 1974.

Borden, R. J. Witnessed aggression: Influence of an observer's sex and values on aggressive responding. *Journal of Personality and Social Psychology*, 1975, *31*, 567–573.

Borden, R. J. Audience influence. In P. B. Paulus (Ed.), *Psychology of group influence*. Hillsdale, N.J.: Erlbaum, 1980.

Borgatta, E. F., Couch, A. S., & Bales, R. F. Some findings relevant to the Great Man theory of leadership. *American Sociological Review*, 1954, *19*, 755–759.

Bouchard, T. J., Jr. Training, motivation, and personality as determinants of the effectiveness of brainstorming groups and individuals. *Journal of Applied Psychology*, 1972, *56*, 324–331.

Bouchard, T. J., Jr., Barsaloux, J., & Drauden, G. Brainstorming procedure, group size, and sex as determinants of the problem-solving effectiveness of groups and individuals. *Journal of Applied Psychology*, 1974, *59*, 135–138.

Bower, G. H. Emotional mood and memory. *American Psychologist*, 1981, *36*, 129–148.

Boykin, A. W., Franklin, A. J., & Yates, J. F. (Eds.). *Research directions of black psychologists*. New York: Russell Sage Foundation, 1979.

Bramson, L., & Goethals, G. W. (Eds.). *War* (Rev. ed.). New York: Basic Books, 1968.

Breed, G. The effect of intimacy: Reciprocity or retreat? *British Journal of Social and Clinical Psychology*, 1972, *11*, 135–142.

Brehm, J. W. *A theory of psychological reactance*. New York: Academic Press, 1966.

Brehm, J. W., & Cohen, A. R. *Explorations in cognitive dissonance*. New York: Wiley, 1962.

Brehm, J. W., Stires, L. K., Sensenig, J., & Shaban, J. The attractiveness of an eliminated choice alternative. *Journal of Experimental Social Psychology*, 1966, *2*, 301–313.

Brehm, S. S., & Aderman, D. On the relationship between empathy and the actor versus observer hypothesis. *Journal of Research in Personality*, 1977, *11*, 340–346.

Brehm, S. S., & Brehm, J. W. *Psychological reactance: A theory of freedom and control*. New York: Academic Press, 1981.

Brewer, M. B. Averaging versus summation in composite ratings of complex social stimuli. *Journal of Personality and Social Psychology*, 1968, *8*, 20–26.

Brewer, M. B. In-group bias in the minimal intergroup situation: A cognitive-motivational analysis. *Psychological Bulletin*, 1979, *86*, 307–324.(a)

Brewer, M. B. The role of ethnocentrism in intergroup conflict. In W. G. Austin & S. Worchel (Eds.), *The social psychology of intergroup relations*. Monterey, Calif.: Brooks/Cole, 1979.(b)

Brigham, J. C. Ethnic stereotypes. *Psychological Bulletin*, 1971, *76*, 15–38.

Brigham, J. C., Maass, A., Snyder, L. D., & Spaulding, K. Accuracy of eyewitness identifications in a field setting. *Journal of Personality and Social Psychology*, 1982, *42*, 673–681.

Brigham, J. C., Woodmansee, J. J., & Cook, S. W. Dimensions of verbal racial attitudes: Interracial marriage and approaches to racial equality. *Journal of Social Issues*, 1976, *32*(2), 9–21.

Brink, J. H. Effect of interpersonal communication on attraction. *Journal of Personality and Social Psychology*, 1977, *35*, 783–790.

Brislin, R. W. Introduction to social psychology. In H. C. Triandis & R. W. Brislin (Eds.), *Handbook of cross-cultural psychology: Social psychology* (Vol. 5). Boston: Allyn & Bacon, 1980.

Broll, L., Gross, A. E., & Piliavin, I. M. Effects of offered and requested help on help-seeking and reactions to being helped. *Journal of Applied Social Psychology*, 1974, *4*, 244–258.

Bronfenbrenner, U. *Two worlds of childhood: U.S. and U.S.S.R.* New York: Russell Sage Foundation, 1970.

Broude, G. J. Norms of premarital sexual behavior: A cross-cultural study. *Ethos*, 1975, *3*, 381–402.

Broverman, D. M., Klaiber, E. L., Kobayashi, Y., & Vogel, W. Roles of activation and inhibition in sex differences in cognitive abilities. *Psychological Review*, 1968, 75, 23–50.

Broverman, I. K., Broverman, D. M., Clarkson, F. E., Rosenkrantz, P. S., & Vogel, S. R. Sex-role stereotypes and clinical judgments of mental health. *Journal of Consulting and Clinical Psychology*, 1970, *34*, 1–7.

Broverman, I. K., Vogel, S. R., Broverman, D. M., Clarkson, F. E., & Rosenkrantz, P. S. Sex-role stereotypes: A current appraisal. *Journal of Social Issues*, 1972, *28*(2), 59–78.

Brown, B. R. Face-saving and face-restoration in negotiation. In D. Druckman (Ed.), *Negotiations: Social-psychological perspectives*. Beverly Hills, Calif.: Sage, 1977.

Brown, C. E. Shared space invasion and race. *Personality and Social Psychology Bulletin*, 1981, 7, 103–108.

Brown, P., & Elliott, R. Control of aggression in a nursery school class. *Journal of Experimental Child Psychology*, 1965, *2*, 103–107.

Brown, R. *Social psychology.* New York: Free Press, 1965.

Brown, S. M. Male versus female leaders: A comparison of empirical studies. *Sex Roles,* 1979, *5,* 595–611.

Bryan, J. H., & Walbek, N. The impact of words and deeds concerning altruism upon children. *Child Development,* 1970, *41,* 747–757. (a)

Bryan, J. H., & Walbek, N. Preaching and practicing self-sacrifice: Children's actions and reactions. *Child Development,* 1970, *41,* 329–353. (b)

Bryant, F. B., & Veroff, J. The structure of psychological well-being: A sociohistorical analysis. *Journal of Personality and Social Psychology,* 1982, *43,* 653–673.

Bryant, J., & Zillmann, D. The effect of the intensification of annoyance through residual excitation from unrelated prior stimulation on substantially delayed hostile behavior. *Journal of Experimental Social Psychology,* 1979, *15,* 470–480.

Buck, R. W., & Parke, R. D. Behavioral and physiological response to the presence of a friendly or neutral person in two types of stressful situations. *Journal of Personality and Social Psychology,* 1972, *24,* 143–153.

Buckhout, R. Nearly 2,000 witnesses can be wrong. *Bulletin of the Psychonomic Society,* 1980, *16,* 307–310.

Bugental, D. E., Kaswan, J. E., & Love, L. R. Perception of contradictory meanings conveyed by verbal and nonverbal channels. *Journal of Personality and Social Psychology,* 1970, *16,* 647–655.

Bugental, D. E., Love, L. R., & Gianetto, R. M. Perfidious feminine faces. *Journal of Personality and Social Psychology,* 1971, *17,* 314–318.

Bugental, J. F. T., & Zelen, S. L. Investigations into the self-concept. *Journal of Personality,* 1950, *18,* 483–498.

Bulman, R. J., & Wortman, C. B. Attribution of blame and coping in the "real world": Severe accident victims react to their lot. *Journal of Personality and Social Psychology,* 1977, *35,* 351–363.

Burgess, E. W., & Wallin, P. *Engagement and marriage.* Philadelphia: Lippincott, 1953.

Burstein, E., & Worchel, P. Arbitrariness of frustration and its consequences for aggression in a social situation. *Journal of Personality,* 1962, *30,* 528–540.

Buss, A. H. *The psychology of aggression.* New York: Wiley, 1961.

Buss, A. H. Physical aggression in relation to different frustrations. *Journal of Abnormal and Social Psychology,* 1963, *67,* 1–7.

Buss, A. H. Instrumentality of aggression, feedback, and frustration as determinants of physical aggression. *Journal of Personality and Social Psychology,* 1963, *3,* 153–162.

Buss, A. H. Aggression pays. In J. L. Singer (Ed.), *The control of aggression and violence.* New York: Academic Press, 1971.

Buss, A. H., Booker, A., & Buss, E. Firing a weapon and aggression. *Journal of Personality and Social Psychology,* 1972, *22,* 296–302.

Byrne, D. The influence of propinquity and opportunities for interaction on classroom relationships. *Human Relations,* 1961, *14,* 63–70.

Byrne, D. *The attraction paradigm.* New York: Academic Press, 1971.

Byrne, D. Social psychology and the study of sexual behavior. *Personality and Social Psychology Bulletin,* 1977, *3,* 3–30.

Byrne, D. Sex without contraception. In D. Byrne & W. A. Fisher (Eds.), *Adolescents, sex, and contraception.* Hillsdale, N.J.: Erlbaum, 1982.

Byrne, D., & Byrne, L. A. *Exploring human sexuality.* New York: Thomas Y. Crowell, 1977.

Byrne, D., & Clore, G. L. A reinforcement model of evaluative responses. *Personality: An International Journal,* 1970, *1,* 103–128.

Byrne, D., Ervin, C., & Lamberth, J. Continuity between the experimental study of attraction and real-life computer dating. *Journal of Personality and Social Psychology,* 1970, *16,* 157–165.

Byrne, D., Jazwinski, C., DeNinno, J. A., & Fisher, W. A. Negative sexual attitudes and contraception. In D. Byrne & L. A. Byrne (Eds.), *Exploring human sexuality.* New York: Thomas Y. Crowell, 1977.

Byrne, D., & Przybyla, D. P. J. Authoritarianism and political preferences in 1980. *Bulletin of the Psychonomic Society,* 1980, *16,* 471–472.

Byrne, D., & Wong, T. J. Racial prejudice, interpersonal attraction, and assumed dissimilarity of attitudes. *Journal of Abnormal and Social Psychology,* 1962, *65,* 246–253.

Caldwell, D. F., & O'Reilly, C. A., III. Boundary spanning and individual performance: The impact of self-monitoring. *Journal of Applied Psychology,* 1982, *67,* 124–127.

Calhoun, J. B. Population density and social pathology. *Scientific American,* 1962, *206*(2), 139–148.

Calvin, A. Social reinforcement. *Journal of Social Psychology,* 1962, *56,* 15–19.

Cameron, C. Sex-role attitudes. In S. Oskamp, *Attitudes and opinions.* Englewood Cliffs, N.J.: Prentice-Hall, 1977.

Campbell, A., Converse, P. E., & Rogers, W. L. *The quality of American life: Perceptions, evaluations, and satisfactions.* New York: Russell Sage Foundation, 1976.

Campbell, D. E. Interior office design and visitor response. Paper presented at annual convention of American Psychological Association, Toronto, Ontario, 1978.

Campbell, D. T. Reforms as experiments. *American Psychologist,* 1969, *24,* 409–429.

Campbell, D. T. On the genetics of altruism and the counter-hedonic components of human culture. In L. Wispé (Ed.), *Altruism, sympathy, and helping: Psychological and sociological principles.* New York: Academic Press, 1978.

Campbell, D. T. Comments on the sociobiology of ethics and moralizing. *Behavioral Science,* 1979, *24,* 37–45.

Campbell, D. T., & Stanley, J. C. *Experimental and quasi-experimental designs for research.* Chicago: Rand McNally, 1966.

Campbell, J. Homicide of women: An analysis of patterns of violence against women. Paper presented at the First Interdisciplinary Conference on Women, Haifa, Israel, December 1981.

Cannavale, F. J., Scarr, H. A., & Pepitone, A. Deindividuation in the small group: Further evidence. *Journal of Personality and Social Psychology,* 1970, *16,* 141–147.

Cantor, N., & Mischel, W. Prototypes in person perception. In L. Berkowitz (Ed.), *Advances in experimental social psychology* (Vol. 12). New York: Academic Press, 1979.

Cappella, J. N. Mutual influence in expressive behavior: Adult-adult and infant-adult dyadic interaction. *Psychological Bulletin*, 1981, *89*, 101–132.

Carlsmith, J. M., Ellsworth, P. C., & Aronson, E. *Methods of research in social psychology*. Reading, Mass.: Addison-Wesley, 1976.

Carlsmith, J. M., & Anderson, C. A. Ambient temperature and the occurrence of collective violence: A new analysis. *Journal of Personality and Social Psychology*, 1979, *37*, 337–344.

Carlson, E. R., & Coleman, C. E. H. Experiental and motivational determinants of the richness of an induced sexual fantasy. *Journal of Personality*, 1977, *45*, 528–542.

Carlson, H., Thayer, R. E., & Germann, A. C. Social attitudes and personality differences among members of two kinds of police departments (innovative vs. traditional) and students. *Journal of Criminal Law, Criminology and Police Science*, 1971, *62*, 564–567.

Carlson, R. Sex differences in ego functioning. *Journal of Consulting and Clinical Psychology*, 1971, *37*, 267–277.

Carnevale, P. J. D., Pruitt, D. G., & Britton, S. D. Looking tough: The negotiator under constituent surveillance. *Personality and Social Psychology Bulletin*, 1979, *5*, 118–121.

Carnevale, P. J. D., Pruitt, D. G., & Seilheimer, S. D. Looking and competing: Accountability and visual access in integrative bargaining. *Journal of Personality and Social Psychology*, 1981, *40*, 111–120.

Caron, A. H. First-time exposure to television: Effects on Inuit children's cultural images. *Communication Research*, 1979, *6*, 135–154.

Carpenter, C. F. Territoriality: A review of concepts and problems. In A. Roe & G. Simpson (Eds.), *Behavior and evolution*. New Haven, Conn.: Yale University Press, 1958.

Carr, S. J., & Dabbs, J. M., Jr. The effects of lighting, distance and intimacy of topic on verbal and visual behavior. *Sociometry*, 1974, *37*, 592–600.

Carter, J. H. Military leadership. *Military Review*, 1952, *32*, 14–18.

Cartwright, D. Risk taking by individuals and groups: An assessment of research employing choice dilemmas. *Journal of Personality and Social Psychology*, 1971, *20*, 361–378.

Cartwright, D. Theory and practice. *Journal of Social Issues*, 1978, *34*(4), 168–180.

Cartwright, D., & Zander, A. (Eds.). *Group dynamics: Research and theory* (3rd ed.). New York: Harper & Row, 1968.

Carver, C. S. A cybernetic model of self-attention processes. *Journal of Personality and Social Psychology*, 1979, *37*, 1251–1281.

Carver, C. S., & Scheier, M. F. A control-systems approach to behavioral self-regulation. In L. Wheeler (Ed.), *Review of personality and social psychology* (Vol. 2). Beverly Hills, Calif.: Sage, 1981.

Carver, C. S., & Scheier, M. F. Control theory: A useful conceptual framework for personality-social, clinical, and health psychology. *Psychological Bulletin*, 1982, *92*, 111–135.

Cary, M. S. The role of gaze in the initiation of conversation. *Social Psychology*, 1978, *41*, 269–271.

Cash, T. F., Begley, P. J., McCown, D., A., & Weise, B. C. When counselors are seen but not heard: Initial impact of physical attractiveness. *Journal of Counseling Psychology*, 1975, *22*, 273–279.

Cash, T. F., & Derlega, V. J. The matching hypothesis: Physical attractiveness among same-sexed friends. *Personality and Social Psychology Bulletin*, 1978, *4*, 240–243.

Cash, T. F., Kehr, J. A., Polyson, J., & Freeman, V. Role of physical attractiveness in peer attribution of psychological disturbance. *Journal of Consulting and Clinical Psychology*, 1977, *45*, 987–993.

Cashell, D. J. *Sex differences in linguistic style*. Unpublished doctoral dissertation, Purdue University, 1978.

Castore, C. H., & DeNinno, J. A. Investigations in the social comparison of attitudes. In J. M. Suls & R. L. Miller (Eds.), *Social comparison processes: Theoretical and empirical perspectives*. Washington, D.C.: Halsted, 1977.

Cattell, R. B., Kawash, G. F., & DeYoung, G. E. Validation of objective measures of ergic tension: Response of the sex erg to visual stimulation. *Journal of Experimental Research in Personality*, 1972, *6*, 76–83.

Cavan, S. Interaction in home territories. *Berkeley Journal of Sociology*, 1963, *8*, 17–32.

Chaiken, S. Communicator physical attractiveness and persuasion. *Journal of Personality and Social Psychology*, 1979, *37*, 1387–1397.

Chaiken, S. Heuristic versus systematic information processing and the use of source versus message cues in persuasion. *Journal of Personality and Social Psychology*, 1980, *39*, 752–766.

Chaiken, S., & Eagly, A. H. Communication modality as a determinant of message persuasiveness and message comprehensibility. *Journal of Personality and Social Psychology*, 1976, *34*, 605–614.

Chapanis, N. P., & Chapanis, A. C. Cognitive dissonance: Five years later. *Psychological Bulletin*, 1964, *61*, 1–22.

Chapman, L. J., & Chapman, J. P. Illusory correlations as an obstacle to the use of valid psychodiagnostic signs. *Journal of Abnormal Psychology*, 1969, *74*, 271–280.

Chemers, M. M., Rice, R. W., Sundstrom, E., & Butler, W. Leader esteem for the least preferred coworker score, training and effectiveness: An experimental examination. *Journal of Personality and Social Psychology*, 1975, *31*, 401–409.

Chemers, M. M., & Skrzypek, G. J. An experimental test of the Contingency Model of leadership effectiveness. *Journal of Personality and Social Psychology*, 1972, *24*, 172–177.

Cherry, F., & Byrne, D. Authoritarianism. In T. Blass (Ed.), *Personality variables in social behavior*. Hillsdale, N.J.: Erlbaum, 1977.

Chertkoff, J. M., & Esser, J. K. A review of experiments in explicit bargaining. *Journal of Experimental Social Psychology*, 1976, *12*, 464–486.

Cheyne, J. A., & Efran, M. G. The effect of spatial and interpersonal variables on the invasion of group controlled territories. *Sociometry*, 1972, *35*, 477–489.

Christian, J. J., Flyger, V., & Davis, D. E. Factors in the mass mortality of a herd of Sika deer, *Cervus nippon*. *Chesapeake Science*, 1960, *1*, 79–95.

Cialdini, R. B., Borden, R. J., Thorne, A., Walker, M. R., & Freeman, S. Basking in reflected glory: Three (football) field studies. *Journal of Personality and Social Psychology*, 1976, *34*, 366–375.

Cialdini, R. B., Cacioppo, J. T., Bassett, R., & Miller, J. A. Low-ball procedure for producing compliance: Commitment then cost. *Journal of Personality and Social Psychology*, 1978, *36*, 463–476.

Cialdini, R. B., Darby, B. L., & Vincent, J. E. Transgression and altruism: A case for hedonism. *Journal of Experimental Social Psychology*, 1973, *9*, 502–516.

Cialdini, R. B., & Kenrick, D. T. Altruism as hedonism: A social developmental perspective on the relationship of negative mood state and helping. *Journal of Personality and Social Psychology*, 1976, *34*, 907–914.

Cialdini, R. B., Levy, A., Herman, P., & Evenbeck, S. Attitudinal politics: The strategy of moderation. *Journal of Personality and Social Psychology*, 1973, *25*, 100–108.

Cialdini, R. B., Levy, A., Herman, P., Kozlowski, L., & Petty, R. E. Elastic shifts of opinion: Determinants of direction and durability. *Journal of Personality and Social Psychology*, 1976, *34*, 663–672.

Cialdini, R. B., Petty, R. E., & Cacioppo, J. T. Attitude and attitude change. In M. R. Rosenzweig & L. W. Porter (Eds.), *Annual review of psychology*, 1981, *32*, 357–404.

Cialdini, R. B., Vincent, J. E., Lewis, S. K., Catalan, J., Wheeler, D., & Darby, B. L. A reciprocal concessions procedure for inducing compliance: The door-in-the-face technique. *Journal of Personality and Social Psychology*, 1975, *21*, 206–215.

Clark, K. B., & Clark, M. P. Racial identification and preference in Negro children. In T. M. Newcomb & E. L. Hartley (Eds.), *Readings in social psychology*. New York: Holt, 1947.

Clark, M. S. Noncomparability of benefits given and received: A cue to the existence of friendship. *Social Psychology Quarterly*, 1981, *44*, 375–381.

Clark, M. S., & Mills, J. Interpersonal attraction in exchange and communal relationships. *Journal of Personality and Social Psychology*, 1979, *37*, 12–24.

Clark, R. D., III. Group-induced shift toward risk: A critical appraisal. *Psychological Bulletin*, 1971, *76*, 251–270.

Clark, R. D., III, & Word, L. E. Why don't bystanders help? Because of ambiguity? *Journal of Personality and Social Psychology*, 1972, *24*, 392–400.

Clark, R. D., III, & Word, L. E. Where is the apathetic bystander? Situational characteristics of the emergency. *Journal of Personality and Social Psychology*, 1974, *29*, 279–287.

Clee, M. A., & Wicklund, R. A. Consumer behavior and psychological reactance. *Journal of Consumer Research*, 1980, *6*, 389–405.

Clore, G. L., & Kerber, K. W. Toward an affective theory of attraction and trait attribution. Unpublished manuscript, University of Illinois, Champaign, 1978.

Clore, G. L., Wiggins, N. H., & Itkin, S. Gain and loss in attraction: Attributions from nonverbal behavior. *Journal of Personality and Social Psychology*, 1975, *31*, 706–712.

Cohen, C. E. Person categories and social perception: Testing some boundaries of the processing effects of prior knowledge. *Journal of Personality and Social Psychology*, 1981, *40*, 441–452.

Cohen, D., Whitmyre, J. W., & Funk, W. H. Effect of group cohesiveness and training upon creative thinking. *Journal of Applied Psychology*, 1960, *44*, 319–322.

Cohen, R. Altruism: Human, cultural, or what? In L. Wispé (Ed.), *Altruism, sympathy, and helping: Psychological and sociological principles*. New York: Academic Press, 1978.

Cohen, S. Environmental load and the allocation of attention. In A. Baum, J. E. Singer, & S. Valins (Eds.), *Advances in environmental psychology*. Hillsdale, N.J.: Erlbaum, 1978.

Cohen, S. The aftereffects of stress on human performance and social behavior: A review of research and theory. *Psychological Bulletin*, 1980, *88*, 82–108. (a)

Cohen, S. Cognitive processes as determinants of environmental stress. In I. Sarason & C. Spielberger (Eds.), *Stress and anxiety* (Vol. 7). Washington, D.C.: Hemisphere, 1980. (b)

Cohen, S., & Lezak, A. Noise and attentiveness to social cues. *Environment and Behavior*, 1979, *9*, 559–572.

Cohen, S., & Spacapan, S. The aftereffects of stress: An attentional interpretation. *Environmental Psychology and Nonverbal Behavior*, 1978, *3*(1), 43–57.

Coke, J. S., Batson, C. D., & McDavis, K. Empathic mediation of helping: A two-stage model. *Journal of Personality and Social Psychology*, 1978, *36*, 752–766.

Coleman, A. D. Territoriality in man: A comparison of behavior in home and hospital. *American Journal of Orthopsychiatry*, 1968, *38*, 464–468.

Collins, B. E. *Social psychology*. Reading, Mass.: Addison-Wesley, 1970.

Collins, B. E. Four components of the Rotter Internal-External scale: Belief in a difficult world, a just world, a predictable world, and a politically responsive world. *Journal of Personality and Social Psychology*, 1974, *29*, 381–391.

Conroy, J., & Sundstrom, E. Territorial dominance in a dyadic conversation as a function of similarity of opinion. *Journal of Personality and Social Psychology*, 1977, *35*, 570–576.

Constantinople, A. Masculinity-femininity: An exception to a famous dictum? *Psychological Bulletin*, 1973, *80*, 389–407.

Cook, S. W. Motives in a conceptual analysis of attitude-related behavior. In W. J. Arnold & D. Levine (Eds.), *Nebraska Symposium on Motivation, 1969*. Lincoln: University of Nebraska Press, 1970.

Cook, S. W. Ethical issues in the conduct of research in social relations. In C. Selltiz, L. S. Wrightsman, & S. W. Cook (Eds.), *Research methods in social relations* (3rd ed.). New York: Holt, Rinehart & Winston, 1976.

Cook, S. W., & Selltiz, C. A. Multiple-indicator approach to attitude measurement. *Psychological Bulletin*, 1964, *62*, 36–55.

Cook, T. D., & Campbell, D. T. (Eds.). *The design and analysis of quasi-experiments for field settings*. Chicago: Rand McNally, 1979.

Cooke, B. G. Nonverbal communication among Afro-Americans: An initial classification. In R. L. Jones (Ed.), *Black psychology* (2nd ed.). New York: Harper & Row, 1980.

Cooley, C. H. *Human nature and the social order* (Rev. ed.). New York: Scribner's, 1922. (Originally published, 1902.)

Cooper, J. Deception and role playing: In telling the good guys from the bad guys. *American Psychologist*, 1976, *31*, 605–610.

Cooper, J., Zanna, M. P., & Taves, P. A. Arousal as a necessary condition for attitude change following induced compliance. *Journal of Personality and Social Psychology*, 1978, *36*, 1101–1106.

Coopersmith, S. *The antecedents of self-esteem.* San Francisco: W. H. Freeman, 1967.

Costanzo, P. R. Conformity development as a function of self-blame. *Journal of Personality and Social Psychology,* 1970, *14,* 366–374.

Cottrell, N. B. Social facilitation. In C. G. McClintock (Ed.), *Experimental social psychology.* New York: Holt, 1972.

Cottrell, N. B., Wack, D. L., Sekerak, G. J., & Rittle, R. H. Social facilitation of dominant responses by the presence of an audience and the mere presence of others. *Journal of Personality and Social Psychology,* 1968, *9,* 245–250.

Cowan, C., Thompson, W., & Ellsworth, P. C. The effects of death qualification on jurors' predisposition to convict and on the quality of deliberation. *Law and Human Behavior,* in press.

Cox, D. F., & Bauer, R. A. Self-confidence and persuasibility in women. *Public Opinion Quarterly,* 1964, *28,* 453–466.

Cox, O. C. *Caste, class, and race.* New York: Doubleday, 1948.

Cozby, P. C. Self-disclosure: A literature review. *Psychological Bulletin,* 1973, *79,* 73–91.

Crandall, V. C., Katkovsky, W., & Crandall, V. J. Children's beliefs in their own control of reinforcement in intellectual-academic achievement situations. *Child Development,* 1965, *36,* 91–109.

Crawford, T. J. Sermons on racial tolerance and the parish neighborhood context. *Journal of Applied Social Psychology,* 1974, *4,* 1–23.

Cronbach, L. J. Processes affecting scores on "understanding others" and "assumed similarity." *Psychological Bulletin,* 1955, *52,* 177–193.

Crook, J. H. The nature and function of territorial aggression. In M. F. A. Montagu (Ed.), *Man and aggression* (2nd ed.). New York: Oxford University Press, 1973.

Crosby, F. A model of egoistical relative deprivation. *Psychological Review,* 1976, *83,* 85–113.

Cross, W. E., Jr. Models of psychological Nigrescence: A literature review. In R. L. Jones (Ed.), *Black psychology* (2nd ed.). New York: Harper & Row, 1980.

Crutchfield, R. S. Conformity and character. *American Psychologist,* 1955, *10,* 191–198.

Csikszentmihalyi, M., & Figurski, T. J. Self-awareness and aversive experience in everyday life. *Journal of Personality,* 1982, *50,* 15–28.

Cunningham, M. R. Weather, mood, and helping behavior: Quasi-experiments with the Sunshine Samaritan. *Journal of Personality and Social Psychology,* 1979, *37,* 1947–1956.

Cunningham, M. R. Sociobiology as a supplementary paradigm for social psychological research. In L. Wheeler (Ed.), *Review of personality and social psychology* (Vol. 2). Beverly Hills, Calif.: Sage, 1981.

Curran, J. P. Convergence toward a single sexual standard? *Social Behavior and Personality,* 1975, *3,* 189–195.

Curran, J. P., Neff, S., & Lippold, S. Correlates of sexual experience among university students. *Journal of Sex Research,* 1973, *9,* 124–131.

Cutrona, C. E. Transition to college: Loneliness and the process of social adjustment. In L. A. Peplau & D. Perlman (Eds.), *Loneliness: A sourcebook of current theory, research and therapy.* New York: Wiley, 1982.

Cvetkovich, G., Grote, B., Bjorseth, A., & Sarkissian, J. On the psychology of adolescents' use of contraceptives. *Journal of Sex Research,* 1975, *11,* 256–270.

Daly, M., & Wilson, M. *Sex, evolution and behavior.* North Scituate, Mass.: Duxbury Press, 1978.

Danheiser, P. R., & Graziano, W. G. Self-monitoring and cooperation as a self-presentational strategy. *Journal of Personality and Social Psychology,* 1982, *42,* 497–505.

Darley, J. M., & Berscheid, E. Increased liking as a result of the anticipation of personal contact. *Human Relations,* 1967, *20,* 29–39.

Darley, J. M., & Fazio, R. H. Expectancy confirmation processes arising in the social interaction sequence. *American Psychologist,* 1980, *35,* 867–881.

Darley, J. M., & Latané, B. Bystander intervention in emergencies: Diffusion of responsibility. *Journal of Personality and Social Psychology,* 1968, *8,* 377–383.

Darwin, C. *The expression of the emotions in man and animals.* London: John Murray, 1872.

Dashiell, J. F. An experimental analysis of some group effects. *Journal of Abnormal and Social Psychology,* 1930, *25,* 190–199.

Davidson, L. R., & Duberman, L. Friendship: Communication and interactional patterns in same-sex dyads. *Sex Roles,* 1982, *8,* 809–822.

Davies, J. C. Toward a theory of revolution. *American Sociological Review,* 1962, *27,* 5–19.

Davies, J. C. The J-curve of rising and declining satisfactions as a cause of great revolutions and a contained rebellion. In H. D. Graham & T. R. Gurr (Eds.), *Violence in America.* New York: New American Library, 1969.

Davis, J. D., & Skinner, A. E. G. Reciprocity of self-disclosure in interviews: Modeling or social exchange? *Journal of Personality and Social Psychology,* 1974, *29,* 779–784.

Davis, J. H. *Group performance.* Reading, Mass.: Addison-Wesley, 1969.

Davis, J. H. Group decision and social interaction: A theory of social decision schemes. *Psychological Review,* 1973, *80,* 97–125.

Davis, J. H., Bray, R. M., & Holt, R. W. The empirical study of social decision processes in juries. In J. L. Tapp & F. J. Levine (Eds.), *Law, justice and the individual in society.* New York: Holt, Rinehart & Winston, 1976.

Davis, J. H., Kerr, N. L., Atkin, R. S., Holt, R., & Meek, D. The decision processes of 6- and 12-person mock juries assigned unanimous and two-thirds majority rules. *Journal of Personality and Social Psychology,* 1975, *32,* 1–14.

Davis, J. H., Laughlin, P. R., & Komorita, S. S. The social psychology of small groups: Cooperative and mixed motive interaction. In M. R. Rosenzweig & L. W. Porter (Eds.), *Annual review of psychology,* 1976, *27,* 501–542.

Dawkins, R. *The selfish gene.* Oxford: Oxford University Press, 1976.

Day, H. R., & White, C. International prejudice as a factor in domestic versus foreign car ownership and preferences. Paper presented at the 20th International Congress of Psychology, Tokyo, August 1973.

Dean, L. M., Willis, F. N., & Hewitt, J. Initial interaction distance among individuals equal and unequal in military rank. *Journal of Personality and Social Psychology*, 1975, *32*, 294–299.

Deaux, K. Variations in warning, information preference, and anticipatory attitude change. *Journal of Personality and Social Psychology*, 1968, *9*, 157–161.

Deaux, K. To err is humanizing: But sex makes a difference. *Representative Research in Social Psychology*, 1972, *3*, 20–28.

Deaux, K. Sex: A perspective on the attribution process. In J. H. Harvey, W. J. Ickes, & R. F. Kidd (Eds.), *New directions in attribution research* (Vol. 1). Hillsdale, N.J.: Erlbaum, 1976.

Deaux, K. Sex differences. In T. Blass (Ed.), *Personality variables in social behavior*. Hillsdale, N.J.: Erlbaum, 1977.

Deaux, K. Sex-related patterns of social interaction. Paper presented at the meeting of the Midwestern Psychological Association, Chicago, May 1978.

Deaux, K. From individual differences to social categories: Analysis of a decade's research on gender. *American Psychologist*, in press.

Deaux, K., & Emswiller, T. Explanations of successful performance on sex-linked tasks: What is skill for the male is luck for the female. *Journal of Personality and Social Psychology*, 1974, *29*, 80–85.

Deaux, K., & Hanna, R. Courtship in the personals column: The influence of gender and sexual orientation. *Sex Roles*, in press.

Deaux, K., & Lewis, L. Components of gender stereotypes. *Psychological Documents*, in press.

Deaux, K., & Ullman, J. C. *Women of steel: Female blue-collar employment in the basic steel industry*. New York: Praeger, 1983.

DeJong, W. An examination of self-perception mediation of the foot-in-the-door effect. *Journal of Personality and Social Psychology*, 1979, *37*, 2221–2239.

DeLamater, J. A definition of "group." *Small Group Behavior*, 1974, *5*(1), 30–44.

Dembroski, T. M., Lasater, T. M., & Ramirez, A. Communicator similarity, fear arousing communications, and compliance with health care recommendations. *Journal of Applied Social Psychology*, 1978, *8*, 254–269.

DePaulo, B. M., Brown, P. L., Ishii, S., & Fisher, J. D. Help that works: The effects of aid on subsequent task performance. *Journal of Personality and Social Psychology*, 1981, *41*, 478–487.

DePaulo, B. M., Lassiter, G. D., & Stone, J. I. Attentional determinants of success at detecting deception and truth. *Personality and Social Psychology Bulletin*, 1982, *8*, 273–279.

DePaulo, B. M., Rosenthal, R., Eisenstat, R. A., Rogers, P. L., & Finkelstein, S. Decoding discrepant nonverbal cues. *Journal of Personality and Social Psychology*, 1978, *36*, 313–323.

DeRisi, D. T., & Aiello, J. R. Physiological, social and emotional responses to extended interaction distance. Paper presented at the meeting of the Eastern Psychological Association, Washington, D.C., April 1978.

Derlega, V. J., & Grzelak, J. (Eds.). *Cooperation and helping behavior: Theories and research*. New York: Academic Press, 1982.

Derlega, V. J., Wilson, M., & Chaikin, A. L. Friendship and disclosure reciprocity. *Journal of Personality and Social Psychology*, 1976, *34*, 578–582.

Deutsch, M. Field theory in social psychology. In G. Lindzey & E. Aronson (Eds.), *Handbook of social psychology* (Vol. 1) (2nd ed.). Reading, Mass.: Addison-Wesley, 1968.

Deutsch, M. *The resolution of conflict: Constructive and destructive processes*. New Haven, Conn.: Yale University Press, 1973.

Deutsch, M. Introduction. In M. Deutsch & H. A. Hornstein (Eds.), *Applying social psychology: Implications for research, practice, and training*. Hillsdale, N.J.: Erlbaum, 1975.

Deutsch, M., Canavan, D., & Rubin, J. The effects of size of conflict and sex of experimenter upon interpersonal bargaining. *Journal of Experimental Social Psychology*, 1971, *7*, 258–267.

DeVellis, B. M., Wallston, B. S., & Wallston, K. A. Stereotyping: A threat to individualized patient care. In M. Miller & B. Flynn (Eds.), *Current issues in nursing*, 1978, Vol. 2.

Diamond, I. Pornography and repression: A reconsideration of "who" and "what." *Signs*, 1980, *5*, 686–701.

Diamond, M. J., & Lobitz, W. C. When familiarity breeds respect: The effects of the experimental depolarization program on police and student attitudes toward each other. *Journal of Social Issues*, 1973, *29*(4), 95–109.

Di Giacomo, J.-P. Intergroup alliances and rejections within a protest movement (analysis of the social representations). *European Journal of Social Psychology*, 1980, *10*, 329–344.

Dillehay, R. C. On the irrelevance of the classical negative evidence concerning the effect of attitudes on behavior. *American Psychologist*, 1973, *28*, 887–891.

Dion, K. Physical attractiveness and evaluation of children's transgressions. *Journal of Personality and Social Psychology*, 1972, *24*, 207–213.

Dion, K. K. The incentive value of physical attractiveness for young children. *Personality and Social Psychology Bulletin*, 1977, *3*, 67–70.

Dion, K. K., Berscheid, E., & Walster, E. What is beautiful is good. *Journal of Personality and Social Psychology*, 1972, *24*, 285–290.

Dion, K. L. Intergroup conflict and intragroup cohesiveness. In W. G. Austin & S. Worchel (Eds.), *The social psychology of intergroup relations*. Monterey, Calif.: Brooks/Cole, 1979.

Dion, K. L., Baron, R. S., & Miller, N. Why do groups make riskier decisions than individuals? In L. Berkowitz (Ed.), *Advances in experimental social psychology* (Vol. 5). New York: Academic Press, 1970.

Dipboye, R. L., Arvey, R. D., & Terpstra, D. E. Sex and physical attractiveness of raters and applicants as determinants of resumé evaluations. *Journal of Applied Psychology*, 1977, *62*, 288–294.

Dipboye, R. L., Fromkin, H. L., & Wiback, K. Relative importance of applicant sex, attractiveness, and scholastic standing in evaluation of job applicant resumés. *Journal of Applied Psychology*, 1975, *60*, 39–45.

Dittman, A. T. *Kinesics and context* by R. L. Birdwhistell. *Psychiatry*, 1971, *34*, 334–342.

Dollard, J., Doob, L. W., Miller, N. E., Mowrer, O. H., & Sears, R. R. *Frustration and aggression*. New Haven, Conn.: Yale University Press, 1939.

Donnerstein, E. Erotica and human aggression. In R. G. Geen & E. Donnerstein (Eds.), *Aggression: Theoretical and empirical reviews.* New York: Academic Press, 1982.

Donnerstein, E., & Berkowitz, L. Victim reactions in aggressive erotic films as a factor in violence against women. *Journal of Personality and Social Psychology,* 1981, *41,* 710–724.

Donnerstein, E., Donnerstein, M., & Evans, R. Erotic stimuli and aggression: Facilitation or inhibition. *Journal of Personality and Social Psychology,* 1975, *32,* 237–244.

Donnerstein, E., & Wilson, D. W. The effects of noise and perceived control upon ongoing and subsequent aggressive behavior. *Journal of Personality and Social Psychology,* 1976, *34,* 774–781.

Donnerstein, M., & Donnerstein, E. Modeling in the control of interracial aggression: The problem of generality. *Journal of Personality,* 1977, *45,* 100–116.

Doob, A. N., Carlsmith, J. M., Freedman, J. L., Landauer, T. K., & Tom, S., Jr. Effect of initial selling price on subsequent sales. *Journal of Personality and Social Psychology,* 1969, *11,* 345–350.

Doob, A. N., & Gross, A. E. Status of frustrator as an inhibitor of horn-honking responses. *Journal of Social Psychology,* 1968, *76,* 213–218.

Doob, L. W. The behavior of attitudes. *Psychological Review,* 1947, *54,* 135–156.

Dreiser, T. *A gallery of women.* New York: Boni and Liveright, 1929.

Driscoll, J. M., Meyer, R. G., & Schanie, C. F. Training police in family crisis intervention. *Journal of Applied Behavioral Science,* 1973, *9,* 62–81.

Driscoll, R., Davis, K. E., & Lipetz, M. E. Parental influence and romantic love: The Romeo and Juliet effect. *Journal of Personality and Social Psychology,* 1972, *24,* 1–10.

Druckman, D. On concepts and methods in the study of international negotiation: Reflections on the "state of the art." Unpublished manuscript, 1978.

Druckman, D., & Mahoney, R. Processes and consequences of international negotiations. *Journal of Social Issues,* 1977, *33*(1), 60–87.

Dubos, R. *Man adapting.* New Haven, Conn.: Yale University Press, 1980.

Duck, S. W. (Ed.). *Personal relationships 4: Dissolving personal relationships.* New York: Academic Press, in press.

Duck, S. W., & Gilmour, R. (Eds.). *Personal relationships 1: Studying personal relationships.* New York: Academic Press, 1981. (a)

Duck, S. W., & Gilmour, R. (Eds.). *Personal relationships 2: Developing personal relationships.* New York: Academic Press, 1981. (b)

Duck, S. W., & Gilmour, R. (Eds.). *Personal relationships 3: Personal relationships in disorder.* New York: Academic Press, 1981. (c)

Duncan, S. Nonverbal communication. *Psychological Bulletin,* 1969, *72,* 118–137.

Duncan, S., Jr., & Fiske, D. W. *Face-to-face interaction.* Hillsdale, N.J.: Erlbaum, 1977.

Dunnette, M. D., Campbell, J., & Jaastad, K. The effect of group participation on brainstorming effectiveness for two industrial samples. *Journal of Applied Psychology,* 1963, *47,* 30–37.

Durkheim, E. Représentations individuelles et représentations collectives. *Revue de Métaphysique,* 1898, *6,* 274–302. (In D. F. Pocock [trans.], *Sociology and philosophy.* New York: Free Press, 1953.)

Dutton, D. G., & Aron, A. P. Some evidence for heightened sexual attraction under conditions of high anxiety. *Journal of Personality and Social Psychology,* 1974, *30,* 510–517.

Duval, S., Duval, V. H., & Neely, R. Self-focus, felt responsibility, and helping behavior. *Journal of Personality and Social Psychology,* 1979, *37,* 1769–1778.

Duval, S., & Wicklund, R. A. *A theory of objective self-awareness.* New York: Academic Press, 1972.

Dyck, R. J., & Rule, B. G. Effect of retaliation on causal attributions concerning attack. *Journal of Personality and Social Psychology,* 1978, *36,* 521–529.

Eagly, A. H. Sex differences in influenceability. *Psychological Bulletin,* 1978, *85,* 86–116.

Eagly, A. H., & Carli, L. L. Sex of researchers and sex-typed communications as determinants of sex differences in influenceability: A meta-analysis of social influence studies. *Psychological Bulletin,* 1981, *90,* 1–20.

Eagly, A. H., Chaiken, S., & Wood, W. An attribution analysis of persuasion. In J. Harvey, W. C. Ickes, & R. F. Kidd (Eds.), *New directions in attribution theory* (Vol. 3). Hillsdale, N.J.: Erlbaum, 1981.

Eagly, A. H., & Himmelfarb, S. Attitudes and opinions. In M. R. Rosenzweig & L. W. Porter (Eds.), *Annual review of psychology,* 1978, *29,* 517–554.

Eagly, A. H., & Telaak, K. Width of the latitude of acceptance as a determinant of attitude change. *Journal of Personality and Social Psychology,* 1972, *23,* 388–397.

Eagly, A. H., & Warren, R. Intelligence, comprehension and opinion change. *Journal of Personality,* 1976, *44,* 226–242.

Eagly, A. H., & Wood, W. Inferred sex differences in status as a determinant of gender stereotypes about social influence. *Journal of Personality and Social Psychology,* 1982, *43,* 915–928.

Ebbesen, E., Kjos, G., & Konečni, V. Spatial ecology: Its effects on the choice of friends and enemies. *Journal of Experimental Social Psychology,* 1976, *12,* 505–518.

Ebbesen, E. B., & Konečni, V. J. Decision making and information integration in the courts: The setting of bail. *Journal of Personality and Social Psychology,* 1975, *32,* 805–821.

Edney, J. J. Property, possession, and performance: A field study in human territoriality. *Journal of Applied Social Psychology,* 1972, *2,* 275–282.

Edney, J. J. Human territoriality. *Psychological Bulletin,* 1974, *81,* 959–975.

Edney, J. J., & Jordon-Edney, N. L. Territorial spacing on a beach. *Sociometry,* 1974, *37,* 92–104.

Efran, J., & Broughton, A. Effect of expectancies for social approval on visual behavior. *Journal of Personality and Social Psychology,* 1966, *4,* 103–107.

Efran, M. G., & Cheyne, J. A. The study of movement and affect in territorial behavior. *Man-Environment Systems,* 1972, *3,* 348–350.

Efran, M. G., & Cheyne, J. A. Shared space: The cooperative control of spatial areas by two interacting individuals. *Canadian Journal of Behavioural Science*, 1973, 5, 201–210.

Efran, M. G., & Cheyne, J. A. Affective concomitants of the invasion of shared space: Behavioral, physiological, and verbal indicators. *Journal of Personality and Social Psychology*, 1974, 29, 219–226.

Eibl-Eibesfeldt, I. *Ethology: The biology of behavior* (E. Klinghammer, trans.). New York: Holt, Rinehart & Winston, 1970.

Eisenberg, L. The *human* nature of human nature. *Science*, 1972, 176, 123–128.

Eisenberg, N. (Ed.). *Development of prosocial behavior*. New York: Academic Press, 1982.

Eisenberg-Berg, N. Relationship of prosocial moral reasoning to altruism, political liberalism, and intelligence. *Developmental Psychology*, 1979, 15, 87–89.

Ekman, P. A comparison of verbal and nonverbal behavior as reinforcing stimuli of opinion responses. Unpublished doctoral dissertation, Adelphi College, 1958.

Ekman, P. Universals and cultural differences in facial expressions of emotion. In J. K. Cole (Ed.), *Nebraska Symposium on Motivation* (Vol. 19). Lincoln: University of Nebraska Press, 1972.

Ekman, P., & Friesen, W. V. Hand movements. *Journal of Communication*, 1972, 22, 353–374.

Ekman, P., & Friesen, W. V. Detecting deception from body or face. *Journal of Personality and Social Psychology*, 1974, 29, 288–298.

Ekman, P., & Friesen, W. V. *Unmasking the face*. Englewood Cliffs, N.J.: Prentice-Hall, 1975.

Ekman, P., Friesen, W. V., & Ellsworth, P. C. *Emotion in the human face*. New York: Pergamon, 1972.

Ekman, P., Friesen, W. V., & Scherer, K. B. Body movement and voice pitch in deceptive interaction. *Semiotica*, 1976, 16, 23–27.

Ekstein, R. Psychoanalysis, sympathy, and altruism. In L. Wispé (Ed.), *Altruism, sympathy, and helping: Psychological and sociological principles*. New York: Academic Press, 1978.

Elkind, D. Praise and imitation. *Saturday Review*, January 16, 1971, pp. 51ff.

Ellis, H. *Studies in the psychology of sex*. New York: Random House, 1936. (Originally published, 1899.)

Ellsworth, P. C. From abstract ideas to concrete instances: Some guidelines for choosing natural research settings. *American Psychologist*, 1977, 32, 604–615.

Ellsworth, P. C., & Carlsmith, J. M. Effect of eye contact and verbal consent on affective response to a dyadic interaction. *Journal of Personality and Social Psychology*, 1968, 10, 15–20.

Ellsworth, P. C., Carlsmith, J. M., & Henson, A. The stare as a stimulus to flight in human subjects: A series of field experiments. *Journal of Personality and Social Psychology*, 1972, 21, 302–311.

Emswiller, T., Deaux, K., & Willits, J. E. Similarity, sex, and requests for small favors. *Journal of Applied Social Psychology*, 1971, 1, 284–291.

Endler, N. S., & Magnusson, D. Toward an interactional psychology of personality. *Psychological Bulletin*, 1976, 83, 956–974.

Eoyang, C. K. Effects of group size and privacy in residential crowding. *Journal of Personality and Social Psychology*, 1974, 30, 389–392.

Epley, S. W. Reduction of the behavioral effects of aversive stimulation by the presence of companions. *Psychological Bulletin*, 1974, 81, 271–283.

Epps, E. G. The impact of school desegregation on aspirations, self-concepts and other aspects of personality. In R. L. Jones (Ed.), *Black psychology* (2nd ed.). New York: Harper & Row, 1980.

Epstein, R. Aggression toward outgroups as a function of authoritarianism and imitation of aggressive models. *Journal of Personality and Social Psychology*, 1966, 3, 574–579.

Epstein, S. The stability of behavior: I. On predicting most of the people much of the time. *Journal of Personality and Social Psychology*, 1979, 37, 1097–1126.

Ericsson, K. A., & Simon, H. A. Verbal reports as data. *Psychological Review*, 1980, 87, 215–251.

Erkut, S., Jaquette, D. S., & Staub, E. Moral judgment-situation interaction as a basis for predicting prosocial behavior. *Journal of Personality*, 1981, 49, 1–14.

Eron, L. D. Relationship of TV viewing habits and aggressive behavior in children. *Journal of Abnormal and Social Psychology*, 1963, 67, 193–196.

Eron, L. D. Prescription for reduction of aggression. *American Psychologist*, 1980, 35, 244–252.

Eron, L. D. Parent-child interaction, television violence, and aggression of children. *American Psychologist*, 1982, 37, 197–211.

Eron, L. D., Huesmann, L. R., Lefkowitz, M. M., & Walder, L. O. Does television violence cause aggression? *American Psychologist*, 1972, 27, 253–263.

Esman, A. Toward an understanding of racism. *Psychiatry and Social Science Review*, 1970, 4, 7–9.

Esser, A. H., Chamberlain, A. S., Chapple, E., & Kline, N. S. Territoriality of patients on a research ward. In J. Wortis (Ed.), *Recent advances in biological psychiatry*. New York: Plenum Press, 1964.

Etzioni, A. Social science vs. government: Standoff at policy gap. *Psychology Today*, November 1978, pp. 24–26.

Evans, G. W. Human spatial behavior: The arousal model. In A. Baum & Y. Epstein (Eds.), *Human response to crowding*. Hillsdale, N.J.: Erlbaum, 1978.

Evans, G. W. Behavioral and physiological consequences of crowding in humans. *Journal of Applied Social Psychology*, 1979, 9, 27–46.

Evans, R. I. Behavioral medicine: A new applied challenge to social psychologists. In L. Bickman (Ed.), *Applied social psychology annual* (Vol. 1). Beverly Hills, Calif.: Sage, 1980.

Evans, R. I., Rozelle, R. M., Mittelmark, M. B., Hansen, W. B., Bane, A. L., & Havis, J. Deterring the onset of smoking in children: Knowledge of immediate physiological effects and coping with peer pressure, media pressure, and parent modeling. *Journal of Applied Social Psychology*, 1978, 8, 126–135.

Exline, R. V. Visual interaction: The glances of power and preference. In J. K. Cole (Ed.), *Nebraska Symposium on Motivation* (Vol. 19). Lincoln: University of Nebraska Press, 1971.

Exline, R. V., Ellyson, S. L., & Long, B. Visual behavior as an aspect of power role relationships. In P. Pliner, L. Krames, & T. Alloway (Eds.), *Nonverbal communication of aggression* (Vol. 2). New York: Plenum Press, 1975.

Exline, R., & Winters, L. Affective relations and mutual glances in dyads. In S. Tomkins & C. Izard (Eds.), *Affect, cognition, and personality.* New York: Springer, 1965.

Eysenck, H. J. *The biological basis of personality.* Springfield, Ill.: Charles C Thomas, 1967.

Fairweather, G. W. *Social change: The challenge to survival.* Morristown, N.J.: General Learning Press, 1972.

Fallon, B. J., & Hollander, E. P. Sex-role stereotyping in leadership: A study of undergraduate discussion groups. Paper presented at meeting of American Psychological Association, Washington, D.C., 1976.

Fawl, C. L. Disturbances experienced by children in their natural habitats. In R. G. Barker (Ed.), *The stream of behavior.* New York: Appleton-Century-Crofts, 1963.

Fazio, R. H., Effrein, E. A., & Falender, V. J. Self-perceptions following social interaction. *Journal of Personality and Social Psychology,* 1981, *41,* 232–242.

Fazio, R. H., Sherman, S. J., & Herr, P. M. The feature-positive effect in the self-perception process: Does not doing matter as much as doing? *Journal of Personality and Social Psychology,* 1982, *42,* 404–411.

Fazio, R. H., & Zanna, M. P. Attitudinal qualities relating to the strength of the attitude-behavior relationship. *Journal of Experimental Social Psychology,* 1978, *14,* 398–408.

Fazio, R. H., Zanna, M. P., & Cooper, J. Dissonance and self-perception: An integrative view of each theory's proper domain of application. *Journal of Experimental Social Psychology,* 1977, *13,* 464–479.

Feild, H. S. Attitudes toward rape: A comparative analysis of police, rapists, crisis counselors, and citizens. *Journal of Personality and Social Psychology,* 1978, *36,* 156–179.

Feldman, S. The presentation of shortness in everyday life— Height and heightism in American society: Toward a sociology of stature. Paper presented at meeting of American Sociological Association, Chicago, 1971.

Feldman-Summers, S. Implications of the buck-passing phenomenon for reactance theory. *Journal of Personality,* 1977, *45,* 543–553.

Fenigstein, A., Scheier, M., & Buss, A. Public and private self-consciousness: Assessment and theory. *Journal of Consulting and Clinical Psychology,* 1975, *43,* 522–527.

Ferguson, T. J., & Rule, B. G. An attributional perspective on anger and aggression. In E. Donnerstein & R. G. Geen (Eds.), *Aggression: Theoretical and empirical reviews.* New York: Academic Press, 1983.

Feshbach, S., & Singer, R. D. The effects of personal and shared threats upon social prejudice. *Journal of Abnormal and Social Psychology,* 1957, *54,* 411–416.

Feshbach, S., Stiles, W. B., & Bitter, E. The reinforcing effect of witnessing aggression. *Journal of Experimental Research in Personality,* 1967, *2,* 133–139.

Festinger, L. Informal social communication. *Psychological Review,* 1950, *57,* 271–282.

Festinger, L. A theory of social comparison processes. *Human Relations,* 1954, *7,* 117–140.

Festinger, L. *A theory of cognitive dissonance.* Stanford, Calif.: Stanford University Press, 1957.

Festinger, L., & Carlsmith, J. M. Cognitive consequences of forced compliance. *Journal of Abnormal and Social Psychology,* 1959, *58,* 203–210.

Festinger, L., Gerard, H., Hymovitch, B., Kelley, H. H., & Raven, B. The influence process in the presence of extreme deviates. *Human Relations,* 1952, *5,* 327–346.

Festinger, L., Pepitone, A., & Newcomb, T. Some consequences of deindividuation in a group. *Journal of Abnormal and Social Psychology,* 1952, *47,* 382–389.

Festinger, L., Riecken, H., & Schachter, S. *When prophecy fails.* Minneapolis: University of Minnesota Press, 1956.

Festinger, L., Schachter, S., & Back, K. *Social pressures in informal groups: A study of human factors in housing.* New York: Harper, 1950.

Fidell, L. S. Empirical verification of sex discrimination in hiring practices in psychology. *American Psychologist,* 1970, *25,* 1094–1098.

Fiedler, F. E. A contingency model of leadership effectiveness. In L. Berkowitz (Ed.), *Advances in experimental social psychology* (Vol. 1). New York: Academic Press, 1964.

Fiedler, F. E. *A theory of leadership effectiveness.* New York: McGraw-Hill, 1967.

Fiedler, F. E. Style or circumstance: The leadership enigma. *Psychology Today,* 1969, *2*(10), 38–43.

Fiedler, F. E. Personality, motivational systems, and behavior of High and Low LPC persons. *Human Relations,* 1972, *25,* 391–412.

Fiedler, F. E. Recent developments in research on the contingency model. In L. Berkowitz (Ed.), *Group processes.* New York: Academic Press, 1978.

Fiedler, F. E., Chemers, M. M., & Mahar, L. *Improving leadership effectiveness: The leader match concept.* New York: Wiley, 1976.

Filley, A. *Interpersonal conflict resolution.* Glenview, Ill.: Scott, Foresman, 1975.

Fink, H. C. Attitudes toward the Calley–My Lai case, authoritarianism and political beliefs. Paper presented at meeting of Eastern Psychological Association, Washington, D.C., May 1973.

Fishbein, M. Attitude and the prediction of behavior. In M. Fishbein (Ed.), *Readings in attitude theory and measurement.* New York: Wiley, 1967.

Fishbein, M., & Ajzen, I. Attitudes and opinions. *Annual review of psychology,* 1972, *23,* 487–544.

Fishbein, M., & Ajzen, I. Attitudes toward objects as predictors of single and multiple behavioral criteria. *Psychological Review,* 1974, *81,* 59–74.

Fishbein, M., & Ajzen, I. *Belief, attitude, intention, and behavior: An introduction to theory and research.* Reading, Mass.: Addison-Wesley, 1975.

Fisher, B. A. *Perspectives on human communication.* New York: Macmillan, 1978.

Fisher, J. D., & Nadler, A. The effect of similarity between donor and recipient on recipient's reactions to aid. *Journal of Applied Social Psychology,* 1974, *4,* 230–243.

Fisher, J. D., Nadler, A., & Whitcher-Alagna, S. Recipient reactions to aid. *Psychological Bulletin*, 1982, *91*, 27–54.

Fisher, J. D., Rytting, M., & Heslin, R. Hands touching hands: Affective and evaluative effects of an interpersonal touch. *Sociometry*, 1976, *39*, 416–421.

Fisher, W. A., & Byrne, D. Sex differences in response to erotica: Love versus lust? *Journal of Personality and Social Psychology*, 1978, *36*, 117–125.

Fisher, W. A., Byrne, D., Edmunds, M., Miller, C. T., Kelley, K., & White, L. A. Psychological and situation-specific correlates of contraceptive behavior among university women. *Journal of Sex Research*, 1979, *15*, 38–55.

Fiske, D. W. *Strategies for personality research: The observation versus interpretation of behaviors.* San Francisco: Jossey-Bass, 1978.

Fiske, S. T., & Taylor, S. E. *Social cognition.* Reading, Mass.: Addison-Wesley, 1983.

Fitz, D., & Gerstenzang, S. *Anger in everyday life: When, where, and with whom?* Paper presented at meeting of Midwestern Psychological Association, Chicago, May 1978.

Fitzgerald, R., & Ellsworth, P. C. Due process vs. crime control: Death qualification and jury attitudes. *Law and Human Behavior,* in press.

Flowers, M. L. A laboratory test of some implications of Janis's groupthink hypothesis. *Journal of Personality and Social Psychology*, 1977, *35*, 888–896.

Foa, E. B., & Foa, U. G. *Social structure of the mind.* Springfield, Ill.: Charles C Thomas, 1974.

Foa, U. G. Interpersonal and economic resources. *Science*, 1971, *171*, 345–351.

Fodor, E. M. Simulated work climate as an influence on choice of leadership style. *Personality and Social Psychology Bulletin*, 1978, *4*, 111–114.

Fong, G. T., & Markus, H. Self-schemas and judgments about others. *Social Cognition*, 1982, *1*, 191–204.

Ford, C., & Beach, F. A. *Patterns of sexual behavior.* New York: Paul Hoeber, 1951.

Form, W. H., & Nosow, S. *Community in disaster.* New York: Harper, 1958.

Forward, J., Canter, R., & Kirsch, N. Role-enactment and deception methodologies: Alternative paradigms? *American Psychologist*, 1976, *31*, 595–604.

Foti, R. J., Fraser, S. L., & Lord, R. G. Effects of leadership labels and prototypes on perceptions of political leaders. *Journal of Applied Psychology*, 1982, *67*, 326–333.

Fraczek, A., & Macaulay, J. R. Some personality factors in reaction to aggressive stimuli. *Journal of Personality*, 1971, *39*, 163–177.

Fraser, C. Group risk-taking and group polarization. *European Journal of Social Psychology*, 1971, *1*, 493–510.

Free, L. A., & Cantril, H. *The political beliefs of Americans: A study of public opinion.* New Brunswick, N.J.: Rutgers University Press, 1967.

Freedman, J. L. The effects of population density on humans. In J. T. Fawcett (Ed.), *Psychological perspectives on population.* New York: Basic Books, 1972.

Freedman, J. L., & Fraser, S. C. Compliance without pressure: The foot-in-the-door technique. *Journal of Personality and Social Psychology*, 1966, *4*, 195–202.

Freedman, J. L., Heshka, S., & Levy, A. Population density and pathology: Is there a relationship? *Journal of Experimental Social Psychology*, 1975, *11*, 539–552.

Freedman, J. L., Klevansky, S., & Ehrlich, P. R. The effect of crowding on human task performance. *Journal of Applied Social Psychology*, 1971, *1*, 7–25.

Freeman, S., Walker, M. R., Borden, R., & Latané, B. Diffusion of responsibility and restaurant tipping: Cheaper by the bunch. *Personality and Social Psychology Bulletin*, 1975, *1*, 584–587.

French, J. R. P., Jr., & Raven, B. H. The bases of social power. In D. Cartwright (Ed.), *Studies in social power.* Ann Arbor: University of Michigan Press, 1959.

Frenkel, O. J., & Doob, A. N. Post-decision dissonance at the polling booth. *Canadian Journal of Behavioural Science*, 1976, *8*, 347–350.

Freud, E. L. (Ed.) *Letters to Sigmund Freud.* New York: Basic Books, 1960.

Freud, S. *Civilization and its discontents.* London: Hogarth Press, 1930.

Freud, S. Three contributions to the theory of sex. In A. A. Brill (Ed.), *The basic writings of Sigmund Freud.* New York: Random House, 1938.

Freud, S. Fragment of an analysis of a case of hysteria. In *Collected papers* (Vol. 3). New York: Basic Books, 1959. (Originally published, 1905.)

Freud, S. Introductory lectures on psychoanalysis. In J. Strachey (Ed.), *The standard edition of the complete psychological works* (Vols. 15 & 16). London: Hogarth Press, 1963. (First German edition, 1917.)

Freund, K., Sedlacek, F., & Knob, K. A simple transducer for mechanical plethysmography of the male genital. *Journal of the Experimental Analysis of Behavior*, 1965, *8*, 169–170.

Friedman, H. S., & DiMatteo, M. R. Health care as an interpersonal process. *Journal of Social Issues*, 1979, *35*(1), 1–11.

Frieze, I. H. Causal attributions and information seeking to explain success and failure. *Journal of Research in Personality*, 1976, *10*, 293–305.

Frodi, A. The effect of exposure to weapons on aggressive behavior from a cross-cultural perspective. *International Journal of Psychology*, 1975, *10*, 283–292.

Frodi, A., Macaulay, J., & Thome, P. R. Are women always less aggressive than men? A review of the experimental literature. *Psychological Bulletin*, 1977, *84*, 634–660.

Gaebelein, J. W. Third party instigation of aggression: An experimental approach. *Journal of Personality and Social Psychology*, 1973, *27*, 389–395.

Gaebelein, J. W. The relationship between instigative aggression in females and sex of the target of instigation. *Personality and Social Psychology Bulletin*, 1977, *3*, 79–82. (a)

Gaebelein, J. W. Sex differences in instigative aggression. *Journal of Research in Personality*, 1977, *11*, 466–474. (b)

Gaebelein, J. W. Third party instigated aggression as a function of attack pattern and a nonaggressive response option. *Journal of Research in Personality*, 1978, *12*, 274–283.

Gaebelein, J. W., & Hay, W. M. Third party instigation of

aggression as a function of attack and vulnerability. *Journal of Research in Personality*, 1974, *7*, 324–333.

Gaebelein, J. W., & Taylor, S. P. The effects of competition and attack on physical aggression. *Psychonomic Science*, 1971, *24*, 65–67.

Gaertner, S. L., & Dovidio, J. F. The subtlety of white racism, arousal, and helping behavior. *Journal of Personality and Social Psychology*, 1977, *35*, 691–707.

Galle, O. R., Gove, W. R., & McPherson, J. M. Population density and pathology: What are the relations for man? *Science*, 1972, *176*, 23–30.

Gamson, W. A. Violence and political power: The meek don't make it. *Psychology Today*, 1974, *8*(2), 35–41.

Gamson, W. A. *The strategy of social protest.* Homewood, Ill.: Dorsey, 1975.

Gamson, W. A., & Scotch, N. A. Scapegoating in baseball. *American Journal of Sociology*, 1964, *70*, 69–72.

Gans, H. J. Planning and social life: Friendship and neighbor relations in suburban communities. In H. Proshansky, W. Ittelson, & L. Rivlin (Eds.), *Environmental psychology.* New York: Holt, Rinehart & Winston, 1970.

Garcia, L. T., & Griffitt, W. Evaluation and recall of evidence: Authoritarianism and the Patty Hearst case. *Journal of Research in Personality*, 1978, *12*, 57–67.

Gardner, R. C., Wonnacott, E. J., & Taylor, D. M. Ethnic stereotypes: A factor analytic investigation. *Canadian Journal of Psychology*, 1968, *22*, 35–44.

Geen, R. G. Effects of frustration, attack and prior training in aggressiveness upon aggressive behavior. *Journal of Personality and Social Psychology*, 1968, *9*, 316–321.

Geen, R. G. Effects of attack and uncontrollable noise on aggression. *Journal of Research in Personality*, 1978, *12*, 15–29.

Geen, R. G. The effect of being observed on performance. In P. B. Paulus (Ed.), *Psychology of group influence.* Hillsdale, N.J.: Erlbaum, 1980.

Geen, R. G., & Gange, J. J. Drive theory of social facilitation: Twelve years of theory and research. *Psychological Bulletin*, 1977, *84*, 1267–1288.

Geen, R. G., & O'Neal, E. C. Activation of cue-elicited aggression by general arousal. *Journal of Personality and Social Psychology*, 1969, *11*, 289–292.

Geen, R. G., & Stonner, D. Effects of aggressiveness habit strength on behavior in the presence of aggression-related stimuli. *Journal of Personality and Social Psychology*, 1971, *17*, 149–153.

Geen, R. G., & Stonner, D. Context effects in observed violence. *Journal of Personality and Social Psychology*, 1973, *25*, 145–150.

Geer, J. H. Cognitive factors in sexual arousal—toward an amalgam of research strategies. Paper presented at meeting of American Psychological Association, New Orleans, August 1974.

Geller, D. M. Involvement in role-playing simulations: A demonstration with studies on obedience. *Journal of Personality and Social Psychology*, 1978, *36*, 219–235.

Geller, E. S., Ferguson, J. F., & Brasted, W. S. Attempts to promote residential energy conservation: Attitudinal versus behavioral outcomes. Unpublished manuscript, Virginia Polytechnic Institute and State University, 1978.

Gentry, W. D. Effects of frustration, attack, and prior aggressive training on overt aggression and vascular processes. *Journal of Personality and Social Psychology*, 1970, *16*, 718–725.

Gerbasi, K. C., Zuckerman, M., & Reis, H. T. Justice needs a new blindfold: A review of mock jury research. *Psychological Bulletin*, 1977, *84*, 323–345.

Gergen, K. J. *The concept of self.* New York: Holt, 1971.

Gergen, K. J. The functions and foibles of negotiating self-conception. In M. D. Lynch, K. J. Gergen, & A. A. Norem-Hebeisen (Eds.), *Self-concept.* Cambridge, Mass.: Bollinger, 1981.

Gergen, K. J., Ellsworth, P., Maslach, C., & Seipel, M. Obligation, donor resources, and reactions to aid in three cultures. *Journal of Personality and Social Psychology*, 1975, *31*, 390–400.

Gergen, K. J., & Gergen, M. M. Understanding foreign assistance through public opinion. In *1974 yearbook of world affairs* (Vol. 27). London: Institute of World Affairs, 1974.

Gergen, K. J., Morse, S. J., & Gergen, M. M. Behavior exchange in cross-cultural perspective. In H. C. Triandis & W. W. Lambert (Eds.), *Handbook of cross-cultural psychology.* Vol. 5: *Social psychology.* Boston: Allyn & Bacon, 1980.

Gerrard, M. Sex, sex guilt, and contraceptive use. *Journal of Personality and Social Psychology*, 1982, *42*, 153–158.

Gibb, C. A. Leadership. In G. Lindzey & E. Aronson (Eds.), *Handbook of social psychology* (Vol. 4) (2nd ed.). Reading, Mass.: Addison-Wesley, 1969.

Glass, D. *Behavior patterns, stress, and coronary disease.* Hillsdale, N.J.: Erlbaum, 1977.

Glass, D. C., & Singer, J. E. *Urban stress.* New York: Academic Press, 1972.

Glassman, J. B., Burkhart, B. R., Grant, R. D., & Vallery, G. C. Density, expectation and extended task performance: An experiment in the natural environment. *Environment and Behavior*, 1978, *10*, 299–315.

Goethals, G. R., & Darley, J. M. Social comparison theory: An attributional approach. In J. M. Suls & R. L. Miller (Eds.), *Social comparison processes: Theoretical and empirical perspectives.* Washington, D.C.: Halsted-Wiley, 1977.

Goffman, E. On face-work: An analysis of ritual elements in social interaction. *Psychiatry*, 1955, *18*, 213–231.

Goffman, E. *The presentation of self in everyday life.* Garden City, N.Y.: Doubleday Anchor, 1959.

Goffman, E. *Interaction ritual: Essays on face-to-face behavior.* Garden City, N.Y.: Doubleday, 1967.

Goffman, E. *Relations in public.* New York: Basic Books, 1971.

Golden, J. Roundtable: Marital discord and sex. *Medical Aspects of Human Sexuality*, 1971, *1*, 160–190.

Gordon, C. Self-conceptions: Configurations of content. In C. Gordon & K. L. Gergen (Eds.), *The self in social interaction.* New York: Wiley, 1968.

Gorer, G. Man has no "killer" instinct. In M.F.A. Montagu (Ed.), *Man and aggression.* New York: Oxford University Press, 1968.

Gossett, T. F. *Race: The history of an idea in America.* Dallas: Southern Methodist University Press, 1963.

Gottlieb, J., & Carver, C. S. Anticipation of future interaction and the bystander effect. *Journal of Experimental Social Psychology*, 1980, *16*, 253–260.

Gouldner, A. W. The norm of reciprocity: A preliminary statement. *American Sociological Review*, 1960, *25*, 161–178.

Grabitz-Gneich, G. Some restrictive conditions for the occurrence of psychological reactance. *Journal of Personality and Social Psychology*, 1971, *19*, 188–196.

Graen, G., Alvares, K., Orris, J. B., & Martella, J. A. Contingency model of leadership effectiveness: Antecedent and evidential results. *Psychological Bulletin*, 1970, *74*, 284–296.

Graham, J. A., & Heywood, S. The effects of elimination of hand gestures and of verbal codability on speech performance. *European Journal of Social Psychology*, 1975, *5*, 189–195.

Gray-Little, B., & Appelbaum, M. I. Instrumentality effects in the assessment of racial differences in self-esteem. *Journal of Personality and Social Psychology*, 1979, 37, 1221–1229.

Greenberg, C., & Firestone, I. J. Compensatory responses to crowding: Effects of personal space intrusion and privacy reduction. *Journal of Personality and Social Psychology*, 1977, *35*, 637–644.

Greenberg, M. S. A theory of indebtedness. In K. J. Gergen, M. S. Greenberg, & R. H. Willis (Eds.), *Social exchange: Advances in theory and research.* New York: Plenum, 1980.

Greenberg, M. S., & Ruback, R. B. *Social psychology of the criminal justice system.* Monterey, Calif.: Brooks/Cole, 1982.

Greenfield, T. B., & Andrews, J. H. M. Teacher leader behavior. *Alberta Journal of Educational Research*, 1961, 7, 92–102.

Greenwald, A. G., & Ronis, D. L. Twenty years of cognitive dissonance: Case study of the evolution of a theory. *Psychological Review*, 1978, *85*, 53–57.

Greenwell, J., & Dengerink, H. A. The role of perceived versus actual attack in human physical aggression. *Journal of Personality and Social Psychology*, 1973, *26*, 66–71.

Gregory, W. L. Locus of control for positive and negative outcomes. *Journal of Personality and Social Psychology*, 1978, *36*, 840–849.

Griffith, C. R. A comment upon the psychology of the audience. *Psychological Monographs*, 1921, *30*(136), 36–47.

Griffitt, W. Environmental effects on interpersonal affective behavior: Ambient effective temperature and attraction. *Journal of Personality and Social Psychology*, 1970, *15*, 240–244.

Griffitt, W. Attitude similarity and attraction. In T. L. Huston (Ed.), *Foundations of interpersonal attraction.* New York: Academic Press, 1974.

Griffitt, W., May, J., & Veitch, R. Sexual stimulation and interpersonal behavior: Heterosexual evaluative responses, visual behavior, and physical proximity. *Journal of Personality and Social Psychology*, 1974, *30*, 367–377.

Griffitt, W., & Veitch, R. Hot and crowded: Influences of population density on interpersonal affective behavior. *Journal of Personality and Social Psychology*, 1971, *17*, 92–98.

Gross, A. E., & Crofton, C. What is good is beautiful. *Sociometry*, 1977, *40*, 85–90.

Gross, A. E., & Doob, A. N. Status of frustrator as an inhibitor of horn-honking responses: How we did it. In M. P. Golden (Ed.), *The research experience.* Itasca, Ill.: F. E. Peacock, 1976.

Gross, A. E., & Fleming, I. Twenty years of deception in social psychology. *Personality and Social Psychology Bulletin*, 1982, *8*, 402–408.

Gross, A. E., Wallston, B. S., & Piliavin, I. M. Beneficiary attractiveness and cost as determinants of responses to routine requests for help. *Sociometry*, 1975, *38*, 131–140.

Gross, A. E., Wallston, B. S., & Piliavin, I. M. Reactance, attribution, equity, and the help recipient. *Journal of Applied Social Psychology*, 1979, *9*, 297–313.

Gross, S. R. Social science and the law: Educating the judiciary and the limits of prescience. Paper presented at meeting of American Psychological Association, Montreal, September 1980.

Grujic, L., & Libby, W. L., Jr. *Nonverbal aspects of verbal behavior in French Canadian French-English bilinguals.* Paper presented at the meeting of the American Psychological Association, Toronto, September 1978.

Grusec, J. E., Saas-Korlsaak, P., & Simutis, Z. M. The role of example and moral exhortation in the training of altruism. *Child Development*, 1978, *49*, 920–923.

Grush, J. E., McKeough, K. L., & Ahlering, R. F. Extrapolating laboratory exposure research to actual political elections. *Journal of Personality and Social Psychology*, 1978, *36*, 257–270.

Grush, J. E., & Schersching, C. The impact of personal wealth on political elections: What has the Supreme Court wrought? Paper presented at meeting of Midwestern Psychological Association, Chicago, May 1978.

Gurin, P., Gurin, G., Lao, R. C., & Beattie, M. Internal-external control in the motivational dynamics of Negro youth. *Journal of Social Issues*, 1969, *25*(3), 29–53.

Guthrie, R. V. *Even the rat was white: A historical view of psychology.* New York: Harper & Row, 1976.

Guttentag, M., & Struening, E. L. (Eds.). *Handbook of evaluation research* (Vol. 2). Beverly Hills, Calif.: Sage, 1975.

Haber, G. M. Territorial invasion in the classroom. *Environment and Behavior*, 1980, *12*, 17–31.

Hagen, R., & Kahn, A. Discrimination against competent women. Paper presented at meeting of Midwestern Psychological Association, Chicago, 1975.

Hall, C. S., & Lindzey, G. The relevance of Freudian psychology and related viewpoints for the social sciences. In G. Lindzey & E. Aronson (Eds.), *Handbook of social psychology* (Vol. 1) (2nd ed.). Reading, Mass.: Addison-Wesley, 1968.

Hall, C. S., & Lindzey, G. *Theories of personality* (3rd ed.). New York: Wiley, 1978.

Hall, E. T. *The silent language.* New York: Doubleday, 1959.

Hall, E. T. A system for the notation of proxemic behavior. *American Anthropologist*, 1963, *65*, 1003–1026.

Hall, E. T. *The hidden dimension.* Garden City, N.Y.: Doubleday, 1966.

Hall, J. A. Gender effects in decoding nonverbal cues. *Psychological Bulletin*, 1978, *85*, 845–857.

Halpin, A. W. Studies in aircrew composition: III. In *The combat leader behavior of B-29 aircraft commanders.* Washington, D.C.: Human Factors Operations Research Laboratory, Bolling Air Force Base, September 1953.

Halpin, A. W. The leadership behavior and combat performances of airplane commanders. *Journal of Abnormal and Social Psychology*, 1954, *49*, 19–22.

Halpin, A. W. *Theory and research in administration.* New York: Macmillan, 1966.

Halpin, A. W., & Winer, B. J. *The leadership behavior of the airplane commander.* Columbus: Research Foundation, Ohio State University, 1952. (Mimeographed)

Hamilton, D. L. A cognitive-attributional analysis of stereotyping. In L. Berkowitz (Ed.), *Advances in experimental social psychology* (Vol. 12). New York: Academic Press, 1979.

Hamilton, D. L. (Ed.). *Cognitive processes in stereotyping and intergroup behavior.* Hillsdale, N.J.: Erlbaum, 1981.

Hamilton, W. D. The genetical evolution of social behavior, I & II. *Journal of Theoretical Biology,* 1964, *7,* 1–52.

Hammond, K. R. New directions in research on conflict resolution. *Journal of Social Issues,* 1965, *21*(3), 44–46.

Hamner, W. C. Effects of bargaining strategy and pressure to reach agreement in a stalemated negotiation. *Journal of Personality and Social Psychology,* 1974, *30,* 458–467.

Haney, C., Banks, C., & Zimbardo, P. Interpersonal dynamics in a simulated prison. *International Journal of Criminology and Penology,* 1973, *1,* 69–97.

Hansen, W. B., & Altman, I. Decorating personal places: A descriptive analysis. *Environment and Behavior,* 1976, *8,* 491–504.

Hanson, D. J. The influence of authoritarianism upon prejudice: A review. *Resources in Education,* 1975, *14,* 31.

Hardin, G. The tragedy of the commons. *Science,* 1968, *162,* 1243–1248.

Harding, J., Proshansky, H., Kutner, B., & Chein, I. Prejudice and ethnic relations. In G. Lindzey & E. Aronson (Eds.), *Handbook of social psychology* (Vol. 5) (2nd ed.). Reading, Mass.: Addison-Wesley, 1969.

Hare, A. P. *Handbook of small group research* (2nd ed.). New York: Free Press, 1976.

Harkins, S. G., & Petty, R. E. Effects of task difficulty and task uniqueness on social loafing. *Journal of Personality and Social Psychology,* 1982, *43,* 1214–1229.

Harlow, H. F. The nature of love. *American Psychologist,* 1958, *13,* 673–685.

Harris, A. S. The second sex in academe. *American Association of University Professors Bulletin,* 1970, *56,* 283–295.

Harris, M. B. Mediators between frustration and aggression in a field experiment. *Journal of Experimental Social Psychology,* 1974, *10,* 561–571.

Harrison, A. A. Exposure and popularity. *Journal of Personality,* 1969, *37,* 359–377.

Harrison, A. A., & Saeed, L. Let's make a deal: An analysis of revelations and stipulations in lonely hearts advertisements. *Journal of Personality and Social Psychology,* 1977, *35,* 257–264.

Hartmann, D. Influence of symbolically modeled instrumental aggression and pain cues on aggressive behavior. *Journal of Personality and Social Psychology,* 1969, *11,* 280–288.

Hartmann, H., Kris, E., & Loewenstein, R. M. Notes on a theory of aggression. *Psychoanalytic Study of the Child,* 1949, *3–4,* 9–36.

Harvey, J. H., Town, J. P., & Yarkin, K. L. How fundamental is "the fundamental attribution error"? *Journal of Personality and Social Psychology,* 1981, *80,* 346–349.

Hass, R. G. Persuasion or moderation? Two experiments on anticipatory belief change. *Journal of Personality and Social Psychology,* 1975, *31,* 1155–1162.

Hass, R. G., & Mann, R. W. Anticipatory belief change: Persuasion or impression management? *Journal of Personality and Social Psychology,* 1976, *34,* 105–111.

Hastie, R. Schematic principles in human memory. In E. T. Higgins, C. P. Herman, & M. P. Zanna (Eds.), *Social cognition: The Ontario symposium* (Vol. 1). Hillsdale, N.J.: Erlbaum, 1981.

Hastorf, A. H., Northcraft, G. B., & Picciotto, S. R. Helping the handicapped: How realistic is the performance feedback received by the physically handicapped? *Personality and Social Psychology Bulletin,* 1979, *5,* 373–376.

Hatfield, E., & Traupmann, J. Intimate relationships: A perspective from equity theory. In S. Duck & R. Gilmour (Eds.), *Personal relationships 1: Studying personal relationships.* New York: Academic Press, 1981.

Hazen, M. D., & Kiesler, S. B. Communication strategies affected by audience opposition, feedback, and persuasability. *Speech Monographs,* 1975, *42,* 56–68.

Heider, F. Social perception and phenomenal causality. *Psychological Review,* 1944, *51,* 358–374.

Heider, F. Attitudes and cognitive organization. *Journal of Psychology,* 1946, *21,* 107–112.

Heider, F. *The psychology of interpersonal relations.* New York: Wiley, 1958.

Heilbrun, A. B., Jr. Measurement of masculine and feminine sex role identities as independent dimensions. *Journal of Consulting and Clinical Psychology,* 1976, *44,* 183–190.

Heilman, M. E., & Guzzo, R. A. The perceived cause of work success as a mediator of sex discrimination in organizations. *Organizational Behavior and Human Performance,* 1978, *21,* 346–357.

Heiman, J. R. The physiology of erotica: Women's sexual arousal. *Psychology Today,* 1975, *8*(11), 90–94.

Heller, J., Groff, B. D., & Solomon, S. H. Toward an understanding of crowding: The role of physical interaction. *Journal of Personality and Social Psychology,* 1977, *35,* 183–190.

Hellmuth, J. (Ed.). *Disadvantaged child* (Vol. 3). *Compensatory education: A national debate.* New York: Brunner/Mazel, 1970.

Helmreich, R. Applied social psychology: The unfulfilled promise. *Personality and Social Psychology Bulletin,* 1975, *1,* 548–560.

Helson, H. *Adaptation-level theory: An experimental and systematic approach to behavior.* New York: Harper & Row, 1964.

Hemphill, J. K. Leadership behavior associated with the administrative reputation of college departments. *Journal of Educational Psychology,* 1955, *46,* 385–401.

Hemphill, J. K., & Coons, A. E. *Leader behavior description.* Personnel Research Board, Ohio State University, 1950.

Hendrick, C. Role-playing as a methodology for social research: A symposium. *Personality and Social Psychology Bulletin,* 1977, *3,* 454.

Hendrick, C., & Jones, R. A. *The nature of theory and research in social psychology.* New York: Academic Press, 1972.

Henley, N. M. *Body politics: Power, sex, and nonverbal communication.* Englewood Cliffs, N.J.: Prentice-Hall, 1977.

Hennigan, K. M., Del Rosario, M. L., Heath, L., Cook, T. D., Wharton, J. D., & Calder, B. J. Impact of the introduction of television on crime in the United States: Empirical findings and theoretical implications. *Journal of Personality and Social Psychology*, 1982, 42, 461–477.

Herrnstein, R. *IQ in the meritocracy.* Boston: Atlantic Monthly Press and Little, Brown, 1973.

Heslin, R., & Patterson, M. L. *Nonverbal behavior and social psychology.* New York: Plenum, 1982.

Hess, E. H. Ethology. In R. Brown, E. Galanter, E. H. Hess, & G. Mandler, *New directions in psychology.* New York: Holt, 1962.

Hewstone, M., & Jaspars, J. Explanations for racial discrimination: The effect of group discussion on intergroup attributions. *European Journal of Social Psychology*, 1982, 12, 1–16.

Hicks, D. Short- and long-term retention of affectively-varied modeled behavior. *Psychonomic Science*, 1968, 11, 369–370.

Higbee, K. L. Fifteen years of fear arousal: Research on threat appeals: 1953–1968. *Psychological Bulletin*, 1969, 72, 426–444.

Higgins, E. T., Rholes, C. R., & Jones, C. R. Category accessibility and impression formation. *Journal of Experimental Social Psychology*, 1977, 13, 141–154.

Hildum, D., & Brown, R. Verbal reinforcement and interview bias. *Journal of Abnormal and Social Psychology*, 1956, 53, 108–111.

Hill, C. T., Rubin, Z., & Peplau, L. A. Breakups before marriage: The end of 103 affairs. *Journal of Social Issues*, 1976, 32(1), 147–168.

Hill, C. T., & Stull, D. E. Sex differences in effects of social and value similarity in same-sex friendship. *Journal of Personality and Social Psychology*, 1981, 41, 488–502.

Hill, G. W. Group versus individual performance: Are N + 1 heads better than one? *Psychological Bulletin*, 1982, 91, 517–539.

Hills, L. R. The cruel rules of social life. *Newsweek*, October 1, 1973, p. 15.

Hiltrop, J. M., & Rubin, J. Z. Effects of intervention mode and conflict of interest on dispute resolution. *Journal of Personality and Social Psychology*, 1982, 42, 665–672.

Himmelfarb, S., & Eagly, A. H. (Eds.). *Readings in attitude change.* New York: Wiley, 1974. (a)

Himmelfarb, S., & Eagly, A. H. Orientations to the study of attitudes and their change. In S. Himmelfarb & A. H. Eagly (Eds.), *Readings in attitude change.* New York: Wiley, 1974. (b)

Hirota, K. Group problem solving and communication. *Japanese Journal of Psychology*, 1953, 24, 176–177.

Hirt, E., & Kimble, C. E. The home-field advantage in sports: Differences and correlates. Paper presented at meeting of Midwestern Psychological Association, Detroit, May 1981.

Hite, S. *The Hite report: A nationwide study of female sexuality.* New York: Macmillan, 1976.

Hochreich, D. J., & Rotter, J. B. Have college students become less trusting? *Journal of Personality and Social Psychology*, 1970, 15, 211–214.

Hockey, G. R. Effect of loud noise on attentional selectivity. *Quarterly Journal of Experimental Psychology*, 1970, 22(1), 28–36.

Hoffman, M. L. Altruistic behavior and the parent-child relationship. *Journal of Personality and Social Psychology*, 1975, 31, 937–943. (a)

Hoffman, M. L. Developmental synthesis of affect and cognition and its implications for altruistic motivation. *Developmental Psychology*, 1975, 11, 607–622. (b)

Hoffman, M. L. Is altruism part of human nature? *Journal of Personality and Social Psychology*, 1981, 40, 121–137.

Hofman, J. E., Beit-Hallahmi, B., & Hertz-Lazarowitz, R. Self-concept of Jewish and Arab adolescents in Israel. *Journal of Personality and Social Psychology*, 1982, 43, 786–792.

Hollander, E. P. Leadership and power. In G. Lindzey & E. Aronson (Eds.), *Handbook of social psychology* (3rd ed.). Reading, Mass.: Addison-Wesley, in press.

Hollander, E. P., Fallon, B. J., & Edwards, M. T. Some aspects of influence and acceptability for appointed and elected group leaders. *Journal of Psychology*, 1977, 95, 289–296.

Hollander, E. P., & Julian, J. W. Studies in leader legitimacy, influence, and innovation. In L. Berkowitz (Ed.), *Advances in experimental social psychology* (Vol. 5). New York: Academic Press, 1970.

Hollander, E. P., & Julian, J. W. A further look at leader legitimacy, influence, and innovation. In L. Berkowitz (Ed.), *Group processes.* New York: Academic Press, 1978.

Hollander, E. P., & Yoder, J. Some issues in comparing women and men as leaders. *Basic and Applied Social Psychology*, 1980, 1, 267–280.

Homans, G. C. Social behavior and exchange. *American Journal of Sociology*, 1958, 63, 597–606.

Homans, G. C. The relevance of psychology to the explanation of social phenomena. In R. Borger & F. Cioffi (Eds.), *Explanation in the behavioural sciences.* Cambridge, England: Cambridge University Press, 1970.

Homans, G. C. *Social behavior: Its elementary forms* (Rev. ed.). New York: Harcourt Brace Jovanovich, 1974.

Hook, S. *The hero in history.* Boston: Beacon Press, 1955.

Hopmann, P. T., & Walcott, C. The impact of external stresses and tensions on negotiations. In D. Druckman (Ed.), *Negotiations: Social-psychological perspectives.* Beverly Hills, Calif.: Sage, 1977.

Hoppe, R. A., Greene, M. S., & Kenny, J. W. Territorial markers: Additional findings. *Journal of Social Psychology*, 1972, 88, 305–306.

Horner, M. S. Toward an understanding of achievement-related conflicts in women. *Journal of Social Issues*, 1972, 28(2), 157–176.

Hornstein, H. A. Social psychology as social intervention. In M. Deutsch & H. A. Hornstein (Eds.), *Applying social psychology: Implications for research, practice, and training.* Hillsdale, N.J.: Erlbaum, 1975.

Hornstein, H. A. *Cruelty and kindness: A new look at aggression and altruism.* Englewood Cliffs, N.J.: Prentice-Hall, 1976.

Hornstein, H. A. Promotive tension: Theory and research. In V. J. Derlega & J. Grzelak (Eds.), *Cooperation and helping behavior: Theories and research.* New York: Academic Press, 1982.

Horton, R. W., & Santogrossi, D. A. The effect of adult commentary on reducing the influence of televised violence. *Personality and Social Psychology Bulletin,* 1978, *4,* 337–340.

House, J. S., & Wolf, S. Effects of urban residence on interpersonal trust and helping behavior. *Journal of Personality and Social Psychology,* 1978, *36,* 1029–1043.

Hovland, C., Harvey, O. J., & Sherif, M. Assimilation and contrast effects in reactions to communication and attitude change. *Journal of Abnormal and Social Psychology,* 1957, *55,* 244–252.

Hovland, C., Janis, I., & Kelley, H. H. *Communication and persuasion.* New Haven, Conn.: Yale University Press, 1953.

Hovland, C. I., & Weiss, W. The influence of source credibility on communication effectiveness. *Public Opinion Quarterly,* 1951, *15,* 635–650.

Howard, J. L., Liptzin, M. B., & Reifler, C. B. Is pornography a problem? *Journal of Social Issues,* 1973, *29*(3), 133–145.

Howard, J. L., Reifler, C. B., & Liptzin, M. B. Effects of exposure to pornography. In *Technical report of the Commission on Obscenity and Pornography* (Vol. 8). Washington, D.C.: U.S. Government Printing Office, 1971.

Hundert, A. J., & Greenfield, N. Physical space and organizational behavior: A study of an office landscape. *Proceedings, 77th annual convention, American Psychological Association,* 1969, pp. 601–602.

Hunt, M. *Sexual behavior in the 1970's.* Chicago: Playboy Press, 1974.

Huston, T. L., Ruggiero, M., Conner, R., & Geis, G. Bystander intervention into crime: A study based on naturally-occurring episodes. *Social Psychology Quarterly,* 1981, *44,* 14–23.

Hyde, J. S. Gender differences in aggression: A developmental meta-analysis. Unpublished manuscript, Denison University, 1982.

Ickes, W. Sex-role influences in dyadic interaction: A theoretical model. In C. Mayo & N. Henley (Eds.), *Gender and nonverbal behavior.* New York: Springer-Verlag, 1981.

Ickes, W. J., & Barnes, R. D. The role of sex and self-monitoring in unstructured dyadic interactions. *Journal of Personality and Social Psychology,* 1977, *35,* 315–330.

Ickes, W., & Barnes, R. D. Boys and girls together—and alienated: On enacting stereotyped sex roles in mixed-sex dyads. *Journal of Personality and Social Psychology,* 1978, *36,* 669–683.

Insko, C. A. Verbal reinforcement of attitude. *Journal of Personality and Social Psychology,* 1965, *2,* 621–623.

Insko, C. A. *Theories of attitude change.* New York: Appleton-Century-Crofts, 1967.

Insko, C. A., & Oakes, W. F. Awareness and the "conditioning" of attitudes. *Journal of Personality and Social Psychology,* 1966, *4,* 487–496.

Insko, C. A., & Schopler, J. Triadic consistency: A statement of affective-cognitive-conative consistency. *Psychological Review,* 1967, *74,* 361–376.

Insko, C. A., & Wilson, M. Interpersonal attraction as a function of social interaction. *Journal of Personality and Social Psychology,* 1977, *35,* 903–911.

Isen, A. M. Success, failure, attention and reactions to others: The warm glow of success. *Journal of Personality and Social Psychology,* 1970, *15,* 294–301.

Isen, A. M., & Levin, P. F. Effect of feeling good on helping: Cookies and kindness. *Journal of Personality and Social Psychology,* 1972, *21,* 384–388.

Isen, A. M., & Noonberg, A. The effect of photographs of the handicapped on donations to charity: When a thousand words may be too much. *Journal of Applied Social Psychology,* 1979, *9,* 426–431.

Isen, A. M., Shalker, T. E., Clark, M., & Karp, L. Affect, accessibility of material in memory, and behavior: A cognitive loop? *Journal of Personality and Social Psychology,* 1978, *36,* 1–12.

Isen, A. M., & Simmonds, S. F. The effect of feeling good on a helping task that is incompatible with good mood. *Social Psychology Quarterly,* 1978, *41,* 346–349.

Izard, C. E. The emotions and emotion constructs in personality and culture research. In R. B. Cattell (Ed.), *Handbook of modern personality theory.* Chicago: Aldine, 1969.

Izard, C. E. Cross-cultural perspectives on emotion and emotion communication. In H. C. Triandis & W. Lonner (Eds.), *Handbook of cross-cultural psychology.* Vol. 3: *Basic processes.* Boston: Allyn & Bacon, 1980.

Izzett, R. Authoritarianism and attitudes toward the Vietnam War as reflected in behavioral and self-report measures. *Journal of Personality and Social Psychology,* 1971, *17,* 145–148.

Jaccard, J. J. Predicting social behavior from personality traits. *Journal of Research in Personality,* 1974, *7,* 358–367.

Jaccard, J. Personality and behavioral prediction: An analysis of behavioral criterion measures. In L. Kahle & D. Fiske (Eds.), *Methods for studying person-situation interactions.* San Francisco: Jossey-Bass, 1977.

Jacobson, M. B., & Effertz, J. Sex roles and leadership: Perceptions of the leaders and the led. *Organizational Behavior and Human Performance,* 1974, *12,* 383–396.

Jacoby, J. *The handbook of questionnaire construction.* In preparation.

Jaffe, D. T., & Kanter, R. M. Couple strains in communal households: A four-factor model of the separation process. *Journal of Social Issues,* 1976, *32*(1), 169–191.

Jago, A. G., & Vroom, V. H. Sex differences in the incidence and evaluation of participative leader behavior. *Journal of Applied Psychology,* 1982, *67,* 776–783.

James, R. Status and competence of jurors. *American Journal of Sociology,* 1959, *64,* 563–570.

James, W. *The principles of psychology* (Vols. 1 and 2). New York: Henry Holt and Company, 1890.

Janis, I. L. *Victims of groupthink.* Boston: Houghton Mifflin, 1972.

Janis, I. L., & Feshbach, S. Effects of fear-arousing communications. *Journal of Abnormal and Social Psychology,* 1953, *48,* 78–92.

Janis, I. L., & Field, P. B. Sex differences and personality factors related to persuasibility. In I. L. Janis, C. I. Hovland, P. B. Field, H. Linton, E. Graham, A. R. Cohen, D. Rife, R. P. Abelson, G. S. Lesser, & B. T. King (Eds.), *Personality and persuasibility.* New Haven, Conn.: Yale University Press, 1959.

Janis, I. L., & Mann, L. *Decision making.* New York: Free Press, 1977.

Jellison, J. M., & Green, J. A self-presentation approach to the fundamental attribution error: The norm of internality. *Journal of Personality and Social Psychology,* 1981, *40,* 643–649.

Jellison, J. M., Jackson-White, R., Bruder, R. A., & Martyna, W. Achievement behavior: A situational interpretation. *Sex Roles,* 1975, *1,* 369–384.

Jenkins, W. O. A review of leadership studies with particular reference to military problems. *Psychological Bulletin,* 1947, *44,* 54–79.

Jensen, A. R. How much can we boost IQ and scholastic achievement? *Harvard Educational Review,* 1969, *39,* 1–123.

Jensen, A. R. *Educability and group differences.* New York: Basic Books, 1973.

Johnson, D. W., & Johnson, R. T. *Learning together and alone.* Englewood Cliffs, N.J.: Prentice-Hall, 1975.

Johnson, H. G., Ekman, P., & Friesen, W. V. Communicative body movements: American emblems. *Semiotica,* 1975, *15,* 335–353.

Johnston, A., DeLuca, D., Murtaugh, K., & Diener, E. Validation of a laboratory play measure of child aggression. *Child Development,* 1977, *48,* 324–327.

Jones, A. Women who kill their batterers. Paper presented at the First Interdisciplinary Conference on Women, Haifa, Israel, December 1981.

Jones, E. E. Major developments in social psychology since 1930. In G. Lindzey & E. Aronson (Eds.), *Handbook of social psychology* (3rd ed.). Reading, Mass.: Addison-Wesley, in press.

Jones, E. E., & Baumeister, R. The self-monitor looks at the ingratiator. *Journal of Personality,* 1976, *44,* 654–674.

Jones, E. E., & Berglas, S. Control of attributions about the self through self-handicapping strategies: The appeal of alcohol and the role of underachievement. *Personality and Social Psychology Bulletin,* 1978, *4,* 200–206.

Jones, E. E., & Davis, K. E. From acts to dispositions: The attribution process in person perception. In L. Berkowitz (Ed.), *Advances in experimental social psychology* (Vol. 2). New York: Academic Press, 1965.

Jones, E. E., Gergen, K. J., & Jones, R. G. Tactics of ingratiation among leaders and subordinates in a status hierarchy. *Psychological Monographs,* 1963, 77(Whole No. 566).

Jones, E. E., Kanouse, D. E., Kelley, H. H., Nisbett, R. E., Valins, S., & Weiner, B. *Attribution: Perceiving the causes of behavior.* Morristown, N.J.: General Learning Press, 1972.

Jones, E. E., & McGillis, D. Correspondent inferences and the attribution cube: A comparative reappraisal. In J. H. Harvey, W. J. Ickes, & R. F. Kidd (Eds.), *New directions in attribution research* (Vol. 1). Hillsdale, N.J.: Erlbaum, 1976.

Jones, E. E., & Nisbett, R. E. The actor and the observer: Divergent perceptions of the causes of behavior. In E. E. Jones, D. Kanouse, H. H. Kelley, R. E. Nisbett, S. Valins, & B. Weiner (Eds.), *Attribution: Perceiving the causes of behavior.* Morristown, N. J.: General Learning Press, 1972.

Jones, E. E., & Pittman, T. S. Toward a general theory of strategic self presentation. In J. Suls (Ed.), *Psychological perspectives on the self.* Hillsdale, N.J.: Erlbaum, 1982.

Jones, E. E., & Wortman, C. B. *Ingratiation: An attributional approach.* Morristown, N.J.: General Learning Press, 1973.

Jones, J. M. Conceptual and strategic issues in the relationship of Black psychology to American social science. In A. W. Boykin, A. J. Franklin, & J. F. Yates (Eds.), *Research directions of Black psychologists.* New York: Russell Sage Foundation, 1979.

Jones, J. M. The concept and usage of race in social psychology. *Review of Personality and Social Psychology,* in press.

Jones, M. B. Religious values and authoritarian tendency. *Journal of Social Psychology,* 1958, *45,* 83–89.

Jones, W. H., Freemon, J. E., & Goswick, R. A. The persistence of loneliness: Self and other determinants. *Journal of Personality,* 1981, *49,* 27–48.

Jourard, S. M. *Self-disclosure.* New York: Wiley, 1971.

Kaats, G. R., & Davis, K. E. The dynamics of sexual behavior of college students. *Journal of Marriage and the Family,* 1970, *32,* 390–399.

Kahneman, D., & Tversky, A. On the psychology of prediction. *Psychological Review,* 1973, *80,* 237–251.

Kalven, H., Jr., & Zeisel, H. *The American jury.* Boston: Little, Brown, 1966.

Kammann, R., Thomson, R., & Irwin, R. Unhelpful behavior in the streets: City size or immediate pedestrian density. *Environment and Behavior,* 1979, *11,* 245–250.

Kandel, D. B. Similarity in real-life adolescent friendship pairs. *Journal of Personality and Social Psychology,* 1978, *36,* 306–312.

Kanouse, D. E., & Hanson, L. R., Jr. Negativity in evaluations. In E. E. Jones, D. E. Kanouse, H. H. Kelley, R. E. Nisbett, S. Valins, & B. Weiner (Eds.), *Attribution: Perceiving the causes of behavior.* Morristown, N.J.: General Learning Press, 1972.

Kanter, R. M. *Men and women of the corporation.* New York: Basic Books, 1977.

Kaplan, J. A. A legal look at prosocial behavior: What can happen if one tries to help or fails to help another. In L. Wispé (Ed.), *Altruism, sympathy, and helping: Psychological and sociological principles.* New York: Academic Press, 1978.

Kaplan, M. F. Interpersonal attraction as a function of relatedness of similar and dissimilar attitudes. *Journal of Experimental Research in Personality,* 1972, *6,* 17–21.

Kaplan, M. F., & Anderson, N. H. Information integration theory and reinforcement theory as approaches to interpersonal attraction. *Journal of Personality and Social Psychology,* 1973, *28,* 301–312.

Karlin, R. A., Rosen, L. S., & Epstein, Y. M. Three into two doesn't go: A follow-up on the effects of overcrowded dormitory rooms. *Personality and Social Psychology Bulletin,* 1979, *5,* 391–395.

Karlins, M., & Abelson, H. I. *How opinions and attitudes are changed* (2nd ed.). New York: Springer, 1970.

Karlins, M., Coffman, T. L., & Walters, G. On the fading of social stereotypes: Studies in three generations of college students. *Journal of Personality and Social Psychology,* 1969, *13,* 1–16.

Karuza, J., Jr., & Brickman, P. Preference for similar and dissimilar others as a function of status. Paper presented at meeting of Midwestern Psychological Association, Chicago, May 1978.

Kassin, S. M. Consensus information, prediction, and causal attribution: A review of the literature and issues. *Journal of Personality and Social Psychology,* 1979, *37,* 1966–1981.

Kassin, S. M., & Wrightsman, L. S. Prior confessions and mock juror verdicts. *Journal of Applied Social Psychology,* 1980, *10,* 133–146.

Kassin, S. M., & Wrightsman, L. S. Coerced confessions, judicial instruction, and mock juror verdicts. *Journal of Applied Social Psychology,* 1981, *11,* 489–506.

Katz, D. The functional approach to the study of attitudes. *Public Opinion Quarterly,* 1960, *24,* 163–204.

Katz, D. Consistency for what? The functional approach. In R. P. Abelson, E. Aronson, W. J. McGuire, T. M. Newcomb, M. J. Rosenberg, & P. H. Tannenbaum (Eds.), *Theories of cognitive consistency: A sourcebook.* Chicago: Rand McNally, 1968.

Katz, D., & Braly, K. Racial stereotypes of one hundred college students. *Journal of Abnormal and Social Psychology,* 1933, *28,* 280–290.

Katz, D., & Kahn, R. L. *The social psychology of organizations* (2nd ed.). New York: Wiley, 1978.

Katz, D., Sarnoff, I., & McClintock, C. G. Ego-defense and attitude change. *Human Relations,* 1956, *9,* 27–45.

Katz, D., & Stotland, E. A preliminary statement to a theory of attitude structure and change. In S. Koch (Ed.), *Psychology: A study of a science* (Vol. 3). New York: McGraw-Hill, 1959.

Katz, I. *Stigma: A social psychological analysis.* Hillsdale, N.J.: Erlbaum, 1981.

Katz, I., Farber, J., Glass, D. C., Lucido, D., & Emswiller, T. When courtesy offends: Effects of positive and negative behavior by the physically disabled on altruism and anger in normals. *Journal of Personality,* 1978, *46,* 506–518.

Kauffman, D. R., & Steiner, I. D. Conformity as an ingratiation technique. *Journal of Experimental Social Psychology,* 1968, *4,* 400–414.

Kaufmann, H. *Social psychology: The study of human interaction.* New York: Holt, Rinehart & Winston, 1973.

Keeler, B. T., & Andrews, J. H. M. Leader behavior of principals, staff morale, and productivity. *Alberta Journal of Educational Research,* 1963, *9,* 179–191.

Keller, J. F., Elliott, S. S., & Gunberg, E. Premarital sexual intercourse among single college students: A discriminant analysis. *Sex Roles,* 1982, *8,* 21–32.

Kelley, H. H. The warm-cold variable in first impressions of persons. *Journal of Personality,* 1950, *18,* 431–439.

Kelley, H. H. Attribution theory in social psychology. In D. Levine (Ed.), *Nebraska Symposium on Motivation, 1967* (Vol. 15). Lincoln: University of Nebraska Press, 1967.

Kelley, H. H. Causal schemata and the attribution process. In E. E. Jones, D. Kanouse, H. H. Kelley, R. E. Nisbett, S. Valins, & B. Weiner (Eds.), *Attribution: Perceiving the causes of behavior.* Morristown, N.J.: General Learning Press, 1972.

Kelley, H. H. *Personal relationships: Their structures and processes.* Hillsdale, N.J.: Erlbaum, 1979.

Kelley, H. H., & Thibaut, J. W. *Interpersonal relations: A theory of interdependence.* New York: Wiley-Interscience, 1978.

Kelly, G. A. *A theory of personality: The psychology of personal constructs* (2 vols.). New York: Norton, 1955.

Kelman, H. C. *A time to speak: On human values and social research.* San Francisco: Jossey-Bass, 1968.

Kelman, H. C. Violence without moral restraint: Reflections on the dehumanization of victims and victimizers. *Journal of Social Issues,* 1973, *29*(4), 25–61.

Kendon, A. Some functions of gaze-direction in social interaction. *Acta Psychologica,* 1967, *26,* 22–63.

Kenrick, D. T., Baumann, D. J., & Cialdini, R. B. A step in the socialization of altruism as hedonism: Effects of negative mood on children's generosity under public and private conditions. *Journal of Personality and Social Psychology,* 1979, *37,* 747–755.

Kenrick, D. T., Cialdini, R. B., & Linder, D. E. Misattribution under fear-producing circumstances: Four failures to replicate. *Personality and Social Psychology Bulletin,* 1979, *5,* 329–334.

Kenrick, D. T., & Johnson, G. A. Interpersonal attraction in aversive environments: A problem for the classical conditioning paradigm? *Journal of Personality and Social Psychology,* 1979, *37,* 572–579.

Kenrick, D. T., & Springfield, D. O. Personality traits and the eye of the beholder: Crossing some traditional philosophical boundaries in the search for consistency in all of the people. *Psychological Review,* 1980, *87,* 88–104.

Kent, G. G., Davis, J. D., & Shapiro, D. A. Resources required in the construction and reconstruction of conversation. *Journal of Personality and Social Psychology,* 1978, *36,* 13–22.

Kerckhoff, A. C., & Davis, K. E. Value consensus and need complementarity in mate selection. *American Sociological Review,* 1962, *27,* 295–303.

Kerr, N., Atkin, R., Stasser, G., Meek, D., Holt, R., & Davis, J. Guilt beyond a reasonable doubt: Effects of concept definition and assigned rule on the judgments of mock jurors. *Journal of Personality and Social Psychology,* 1976, *34,* 282–294.

Kidd, R. F. Manipulation checks: Advantage or disadvantage? *Representative Research in Social Psychology,* 1976, *2,* 160–165.

Kiesler, C. A., Collins, B. E., & Miller, N. *Attitude change: A critical analysis of theoretical approaches.* New York: Wiley, 1969.

Kiesler, C. A., & Munson, P. A. Attitudes and opinions. *Annual Review of Psychology,* 1975, *26,* 415–456.

Kimble, C. E., & Forte, R. Simulated and real eye contact as a function of emotional intensity and message positivity. Paper presented at meeting of Midwestern Psychological Association, Chicago, May 1978.

Kimble, G. A. *Hilgard and Marquis's conditioning and learning.* New York: Appleton-Century-Crofts, 1961.

Kinder, D. R. Political person perception: The asymmetrical influence of sentiment and choice on perceptions of political candidates. *Journal of Personality and Social Psychology,* 1978, *36,* 859–871.

King, K., Balswick, J. O., & Robinson, I. E. The continuing premarital sexual revolution among college females. *Journal of Marriage and the Family,* 1977, *39,* 455–459.

Kinkead, E. *In every war but one.* New York: Norton, 1959.

Kinsey, A. C., Pomeroy, W. B., & Martin, C. E. *Sexual behavior in the human male.* Philadelphia: Saunders, 1948.

Kinsey, A. C., Pomeroy, W. B., Martin, C. E., & Gebhard, P. H. *Sexual behavior in the human female.* Philadelphia: Saunders, 1953.

Kipnis, D. M. Interaction between members of bomber crews as a determinant of sociometric choice. *Human Relations,* 1957, *10,* 263–270.

Kirkpatrick, C. *The family as process and institution* (2nd ed.). New York: Ronald Press, 1963.

Kirmeyer, S. I. Urban density and pathology: A review of research. *Environment and Behavior,* 1978, *10,* 247–269.

Kirscht, J. P., & Dillehay, R. C. *Dimensions of authoritarianism: A review of research and theory.* Lexington: University of Kentucky Press, 1967.

Klapper, J. T. The impact of viewing "aggression": Studies and problems of extrapolation. In O. N. Larsen (Ed.), *Violence and the mass media.* New York: Harper & Row, 1968.

Kleinke, C. L., Bustos, A. A., Meeker, F. B., & Staneski, R. A. Effects of self-attributed and other-attributed gaze on interpersonal evaluations between males and females. *Journal of Experimental Social Psychology,* 1973, *9,* 154–163.

Kluegel, J. R., & Smith, E. R. Whites' beliefs about blacks' opportunity. *American Sociological Review,* 1982, *47,* 518–532.

Kluegel, J. R., & Smith, E. R. Affirmative action attitudes: Effects of self-interest, racial affect and stratification beliefs on whites' views. *Social Forces,* 1983, *61,* 797–824.

Kluger, R. *Simple justice.* New York: Knopf, 1976.

Knapp, M. L. *Nonverbal communication in human interaction* (2nd ed.). New York: Holt, Rinehart & Winston, 1978.

Knapp, M. L., Hart, R. P., & Dennis, H. S. An exploration of deception as a communication construct. *Human Communication Research,* 1974, *1,* 15–29.

Knowles, E. S. Boundaries around social space: Dyadic responses to an invader. *Environment and Behavior,* 1972, *4,* 437–445.

Knowles, E. S. Boundaries around group interaction: The effect of group size and member status on boundary permeability. *Journal of Personality and Social Psychology,* 1973, *26,* 327–331.

Knowles, E. S. A comment on the study of classroom ecology: A lament for the good old days. *Personality and Social Psychology Bulletin,* 1982, *8,* 357–361.

Knowles, E. S., & Brickner, M. A. Social cohesion effects on spatial cohesion. *Personality and Social Psychology Bulletin,* 1981, *7,* 309–313.

Knox, R. E., & Inkster, J. A. Postdecision dissonance at post time. *Journal of Personality and Social Psychology,* 1968, *8,* 319–323.

Kogan, N., & Wallach, M. A. *Risk-taking: A study in cognition and personality.* New York: Holt, 1964.

Konar, E., Sundstrom, E., Brady, K., Mandel, D., & Rice, R. Status demarcation in the office. *Environment and Behavior,* 1982, *14,* 561–580.

Konečni, V. J. The mediation of aggressive behavior: Arousal level versus anger and cognitive labeling. *Journal of Personality and Social Psychology,* 1975, *32,* 706–712. (a)

Konečni, V. J. Annoyance, type and duration of postannoyance activity, and aggression: The "cathartic" effect. *Journal of Experimental Psychology: General,* 1975, *104,* 76–102. (b)

Koneya, M. Location and interaction in row-and-column seating arrangements. *Environment and Behavior,* 1976, *8,* 265–282.

Korda, M. *Power: How to get it, how to use it!* New York: Random House, 1975.

Korman, A. K. "Consideration," "initiating structure," and organizational criteria—A review. *Personnel Psychology,* 1966, *19,* 349–361.

Korman, A. K. The prediction of managerial performance: A review. *Personnel Psychology,* 1968, *21,* 295–322.

Korte, C., & Grant, R. Traffic noise, environmental awareness, and pedestrian behavior. *Environment and Behavior,* 1980, *12,* 408–420.

Korte, C., Ypma, I., & Toppen, A. Helpfulness in Dutch society as a function of urbanization and environmental input level. *Journal of Personality and Social Psychology,* 1975, *32,* 996–1003.

Kraut, R. E. Effects of social labeling on giving to charity. *Journal of Experimental Social Psychology,* 1973, *9,* 551–562.

Kraut, R. E., & Johnston, R. Social and emotional messages of smiling: An ethological approach. *Journal of Personality and Social Psychology,* 1979, *37,* 1539–1553.

Krebs, D. Empathy and altruism. *Journal of Personality and Social Psychology,* 1975, *32,* 1134–1146.

Krech, D., Crutchfield, R., & Ballachey, E. *Individual in society.* New York: McGraw-Hill, 1962.

Kronhausen, E., & Kronhausen, P. *Pornography and the law* (Rev. ed.). New York: Ballantine, 1964.

Kuhn, M. H., & McPartland, T. S. An empirical investigation of self-attitudes. *American Sociological Review,* 1954, *19,* 68–76.

Kuiper, N. A., & MacDonald, M. R. Self and other perception in mild depressives. *Social Cognition,* 1982, *1,* 223–239.

Kutchinsky, B. The effect of easy availability of pornography on the incidence of sex crimes: The Danish experience. *Journal of Social Issues,* 1973, *29*(3), 163–181.

Kutner, B., Wilkins, C., & Yarrow, P. R. Verbal attitudes and overt behavior involving racial prejudice. *Journal of Abnormal and Social Psychology,* 1952, *47,* 649–652.

LaFrance, M., & Mayo, C. Racial differences in gaze behavior during conversations: Two systematic observational studies. *Journal of Personality and Social Psychology,* 1976, *33,* 547–552.

LaFrance, M., & Mayo, C. *Moving bodies: Nonverbal communication in social relationships.* Monterey, Calif.: Brooks/Cole, 1978.

Lalljee, M., & Cook, M. Uncertainty in first encounters. *Journal of Personality and Social Psychology,* 1973, *26,* 137–141.

Lalljee, M., Watson, M., & White, P. Explanations, attributions, and the social context of unexpected behavior. *European Journal of Social Psychology,* 1982, *12,* 17–29.

Lamm, H., & Trommsdorff, G. Group versus individual performance on tasks requiring ideational proficiency (brainstorming): A review. *European Journal of Social Psychology,* 1973, *3,* 361–388.

Lando, H. A., & Donnerstein, E. The effects of a model's success or failure on subsequent aggressive behavior. *Journal of Research in Personality,* 1978, *12,* 225–234.

Landy, D., & Sigall, H. Beauty is talent: Task evaluation as a function of the performer's physical attractiveness. *Jour-*

nal of Personality and Social Psychology, 1974, *29,* 299–304.

Langer, E. J. The illusion of control. *Journal of Personality and Social Psychology,* 1975, *32,* 311–328.

Langer, E. J. The psychology of chance. *Journal for the Theory of Social Behaviour,* 1978, *7,* 185–207. (a)

Langer, E. J. The illusion of incompetence. In L. Perlmutter & R. Monty (Eds.), *Choice and perceived control.* Hillsdale, N.J.: Erlbaum, 1978. (b)

Langer, E. J. Rethinking the role of thought in social interaction. In J. H. Harvey, W. J. Ickes, & R. F. Kidd (Eds.), *New directions in attribution research* (Vol. 2). Hillsdale, N.J.: Erlbaum, 1978. (c)

Langer, E. J. Old age: An artifact? In *Biology, behavior and aging.* Washington, D.C.: National Research Council, 1979.

Langer, E. J., & Benevento, A. Self-induced dependence. *Journal of Personality and Social Psychology,* 1978, *36,* 886–893.

Langer, E., Blank, A., & Chanowitz, B. The mindlessness of ostensibly thoughtful action: The role of "placebic" information in interpersonal interaction. *Journal of Personality and Social Psychology,* 1978, *36,* 635–642.

Langer, E., Janis, I., & Wolfer, J. Reduction of psychological stress in surgical patients. *Journal of Experimental Social Psychology,* 1975, *11,* 155–165.

Langer, E. J., & Rodin, J. The effects of choice and enhanced personal responsibility for the aged: A field experiment in an institutional setting. *Journal of Personality and Social Psychology,* 1976, *34,* 191–198.

Langer, E. J., & Roth, J. Heads I win, tails it's chance: The illusion of control as a function of the sequence of outcomes in a purely chance task. *Journal of Personality and Social Psychology,* 1975, *32,* 951–955.

LaPiere, R. T. Attitude and actions. *Social Forces,* 1934, *13,* 230–237.

Latané, B. (Ed.). Studies in social comparison. *Journal of Experimental Social Psychology, Supplement,* 1966, No. 1.

Latané, B. The psychology of social impact. *American Psychologist,* 1981, *36,* 343–356.

Latané, B., & Bidwell, L. D. Sex and affiliation in college cafeterias. *Personality and Social Psychology Bulletin,* 1977, *3,* 571–574.

Latané, B., & Darley, J. M. Group inhibition of bystander intervention in emergencies. *Journal of Personality and Social Psychology,* 1968, *10,* 215–221.

Latané, B., & Darley, J. *The unresponsive bystander: Why doesn't he help?* New York: Appleton-Century-Crofts, 1970.

Latané, B., & Darley, J. M. *Help in a crisis: Bystander response to an emergency.* Morristown, N.J.: General Learning Press, 1976.

Latané, B., & Harkins, S. Cross-modality matches suggest anticipated stage fright as multiplicative function of audience size and status. *Perception and Psychophysics,* 1976, *20,* 482–488.

Latané, B., & Nida, S. A. Ten years of research on group size and helping. *Psychological Bulletin,* 1981, *89,* 308–324.

Latané, B., Nida, S. A., & Wilson, D. W. The effects of group size on helping behavior. In J. P. Rushton & R. M. Sorrentino (Eds.), *Altruism and helping behavior: Social, personality, and developmental perspectives.* Hillsdale, N.J.: Erlbaum, 1981.

Latané, B., Williams, K., & Harkins, S. Many hands make light the work: The causes and consequences of social loafing. *Journal of Personality and Social Psychology,* 1979, *37,* 822–832.

Latané, B., & Wolf, S. The social impact of majorities and minorities. *Psychological Review,* 1981, *88,* 438–453.

Lau, R. R. Origins of health locus of control beliefs. *Journal of Personality and Social Psychology,* 1982, *42,* 322–334.

Laughlin, P. R., & Jaccard, J. J. Social facilitation and observational learning of individuals and cooperative pairs. *Journal of Personality and Social Psychology,* 1975, *32,* 873–879.

Lawler, E. J., & Thompson, M. E. Impact of leader responsibility for inequity on subordinate revolts. *Social Psychology,* 1978, *41,* 264–268.

Lay, C. H., Burron, B. F., & Jackson, D. N. Base rates and informational value in impression formation. *Journal of Personality and Social Psychology,* 1973, *28,* 390–395.

Leach, C. The importance of instructions in assessing sequential effects in impression formation. *British Journal of Social and Clinical Psychology,* 1974, *13,* 151–156.

Leavitt, H. J. Some effects of certain communication patterns on group performance. *Journal of Abnormal and Social Psychology,* 1951, *46,* 38–50.

LeBon, G. *The crowd.* London: Ernest Benn, 1896.

Lefebvre, L. Encoding and decoding of ingratiation in modes of smiling and gaze. *British Journal of Social and Clinical Psychology,* 1975, *14,* 33–42.

Leone, C., Graziano, W., & Case, T. The effects of locus of control and utility on attributional processes. Paper presented at meeting of Midwestern Psychological Association, Chicago, May 1978.

Lerner, M. J. The unjust consequences of the need to believe in a just world. Paper presented at meeting of American Psychological Association, New York, September 1966.

Lerner, M. J. The justice motive in social behavior. *Journal of Social Issues,* 1975, *31*(3), 1–19.

Lerner, M. J. The justice motive: Some hypotheses as to its origins and forms. *Journal of Personality,* 1977, *45,* 1–52.

Lerner, M. J., Miller, D. T., & Holmes, J. G. Deserving and the emergence of forms of justice. In L. Berkowitz & E. Walster (Eds.), *Advances in experimental social psychology* (Vol. 9). New York: Academic Press, 1976.

Leventhal, H. Findings and theory in the study of fear communications. In L. Berkowitz (Ed.), *Advances in experimental social psychology* (Vol. 5). New York: Academic Press, 1970.

Levin, H. Psychologist to the powerless. In F. F. Korten, S. W. Cook, & J. I. Lacey (Eds.), *Psychology and the problems of society.* Washington, D.C.: American Psychological Association, 1970.

Levin, R. J., & Levin, A. Sexual pleasure: The surprising preferences of 100,000 women. *Redbook,* September 1975, pp. 51–58.

Levine, D. W., O'Neal, E., Garwood, S. G., & McDonald, P. J. Classroom ecology: The effects of seating position on grades and participation. *Personality and Social Psychology Bulletin,* 1980, *6,* 409–412.

Levinger, G. Little sand box and big quarry: Comment on Byrne's paradigmatic spade for research on interpersonal attraction. *Representative Research in Social Psychology*, 1972, *3*, 3–19.

Levinger, G. A three-level approach to attraction: Toward an understanding of pair relatedness. In T. L. Huston (Ed.), *Foundations of interpersonal attraction*. New York: Academic Press, 1974.

Levinger, G. A social psychological perspective on marital dissolution. In G. Levinger & O. C. Moles (Eds.), *Divorce and separation*. New York: Basic Books, 1979.

Levinger, G., & Moles, O. C. *Divorce and separation: Context, causes and consequences*. New York: Basic Books, 1979.

Levinger, G., Senn, D. J., & Jorgensen, B. W. Progress toward permanence in courtship: A test of the Kerckhoff-Davis hypotheses. *Sociometry*, 1970, *33*, 427–443.

Levinger, G., & Snoek, J. D. *Attraction in relationship: A new look at interpersonal attraction*. Morristown, N.J.: General Learning Press, 1972.

Levinson, D. J., & Huffman, P. E. Traditional family ideology and its relation to personality. *Journal of Personality*, 1955, *23*, 251–273.

Levitt, E., & Klassen, A. Public attitudes toward homosexuality: Part of the 1970 national survey by the Institute for Sex Research. *Journal of Homosexuality*, 1974, *1*, 29–43.

Levy, J. Autokinetic illusion: A systematic review of theories, measures and independent variables. *Psychological Bulletin*, 1972, *78*, 457–474.

Levy, S. G. A 150-year study of political violence in the United States. In H. D. Graham & T. R. Gurr (Eds.), *Violence in America*. New York: New American Library, 1969.

Levy, S. G. Authoritarianism and information processing. *Bulletin of the Psychonomic Society*, 1979, *13*, 240–242.

Lewin, A. Y., & Duchan, L. Women in academia. *Science*, 1971, *173*, 892–895.

Lewin, K. *A dynamic theory of personality*. New York: McGraw-Hill, 1935.

Lewin, K. *Principles of topological psychology*. New York: McGraw-Hill, 1936.

Lewin, K. The conceptual representation and measurement of psychological forces. *Contributions to Psychological Theory*, Vol. I, No. 4. Durham, N.C.: Duke University Press, 1938.

Lewin, K. *Resolving social conflicts*. New York: Harper, 1948.

Lewin, K. *Field theory in social science*. New York: Harper, 1951.

Leyens, J.-P., Camino, L., Parke, R. D., & Berkowitz, L. Effects of movie violence on aggression in a field setting as a function of group dominance and cohesion. *Journal of Personality and Social Psychology*, 1975, *32*, 346–360.

Leyens, J.-P., Herman, G., & Dunand, M. The influence of an audience upon the reactions to filmed violence. *European Journal of Social Psychology*, 1982, *12*, 131–142.

Leyens, J.-P., & Parke, R. D. Aggressive slides can induce a weapons effect. *European Journal of Social Psychology*, 1975, *5*, 229–236.

Leyhausen, P. The communal organization of solitary mammals. *Symposium of the Zoological Society of London*, 1965, *14*, 249–253.

Lieberman, M. A. Change induction in small groups. In M. R. Rosenzweig & L. W. Porter (Eds.), *Annual review of psychology*, 1976, *27*, 217–250.

Lieberman, S. The effects of changes of roles on the attitudes of role occupants. In H. Proshansky & B. Seidenberg (Eds.), *Basic studies in social psychology*. New York: Holt, Rinehart & Winston, 1965.

Liebert, R. M., & Schwartzberg, N. S. Effects of mass media. In M. R. Rosenzweig & L. W. Porter (Eds.), *Annual review of psychology* (Vol. 28). Palo Alto, Calif.: Annual Reviews, 1977.

Likert, R. A technique for the measurement of attitudes. *Archives of Psychology*, 1932, No. 140.

Lindskold, S. Managing conflict through announced conciliatory initiatives backed with retaliatory capability. In W. G. Austin & S. Worchel (Eds.), *The social psychology of intergroup relations*. Monterey, Calif.: Brooks/Cole, 1979.

Linville, P. W. The complexity-extremity effect and age-based stereotyping. *Journal of Personality and Social Psychology*, 1982, *42*, 193–211.

Lippa, R. Expressive control and the leakage of dispositional introversion-extraversion during role-played teaching. *Journal of Personality*, 1976, *44*, 541–559.

Lippa, R. The effect of expressive control on expressive consistency and on the relation between expressive behavior and personality. *Journal of Personality*, 1978, *46*, 438–461. (a)

Lippa, R. The naive perception of masculinity-femininity on the basis of expressive cues. *Journal of Research in Personality*, 1978, *12*, 1–14. (b)

Lippitt, R. *Training in community relations*. New York: Harper, 1949.

Lippmann, W. *Public opinion*. New York: Harcourt, Brace and World, 1922.

Litman-Adizes, T., Raven, B. H., & Fontaine, G. Consequences of social power and causal attribution for compliance as seen by powerholder and target. *Personality and Social Psychology Bulletin*, 1978, *4*, 260–264.

Loehlin, J., Lindzey, G., & Spuhler, J. N. *Race differences in intelligence*. San Francisco: W. H. Freeman, 1975.

Loftus, E. F. *Eyewitness testimony*. Cambridge, Mass.: Harvard University Press, 1979.

Logan, R. W. *The Negro in the United States*. Princeton, N.J.: Van Nostrand, 1957.

Loh, W. D. Perspectives on psychology and law. *Journal of Applied Social Psychology*, 1981, *11*, 314–355.

London, P. The rescuers: Motivational hypotheses about Christians who saved Jews from the Nazis. In J. Macaulay & L. Berkowitz (Eds.), *Altruism and helping behavior: Social psychological studies of some antecedents and consequences*. New York: Academic Press, 1970.

Longley, J., & Pruitt, D. G. Groupthink: A critique of Janis's theory. In L. Wheeler (Ed.), *Review of personality and social psychology* (Vol. 1). Beverly Hills, Calif.: Sage, 1980.

Lord, C. G. Predicting behavioral consistency from an individual's perception of situational similarities. *Journal of Personality and Social Psychology*, 1982, *42*, 1076–1088.

Lord, R. G., Binning, J. F., Rush, M. C., & Thomas, J. C. The effect of performance cues and leader behavior on questionnaire ratings of leadership behavior. *Organizational Behavior and Human Performance*, 1978, *21*, 27–39.

Lorenz, K. *On aggression*. New York: Harcourt, Brace and World, 1966.

Lott, A. J., & Lott, B. E. Group cohesiveness, communication level, and conformity. *Journal of Abnormal and Social Psychology*, 1961, 62, 408–412.

Lott, A. J., & Lott, B. E. The role of reward in the formation of positive interpersonal attitudes. In T. L. Huston (Ed.), *Foundations of interpersonal attraction*. New York: Academic Press, 1974.

Lott, D. F., & Sommer, R. Seating arrangements and status. *Journal of Personality and Social Psychology*, 1967, 7, 90–94.

Luchins, A. S. Experimental attempts to minimize the impact of first impressions. In C. I. Hovland (Ed.), *The order of presentation in persuasion*. New Haven: Yale University Press, 1957. (a)

Luchins, A. S. Primacy-recency in impression formation. In C. I. Hovland (Ed.), *The order of presentation in persuasion*. New Haven: Yale University Press, 1957. (b)

Luchins, A. S. Definitiveness of impression and primacy-recency in communications. *Journal of Social Psychology*, 1958, 48, 275–290.

Lucke, J. F., & Batson, C. D. Response suppression to a distressed conspecific: Are laboratory rats altruistic? *Journal of Experimental Social Psychology*, 1980, 16, 214–227.

Lumsdaine, A., & Janis, I. Resistance to counterpropaganda produced by a one-sided versus a two-sided propaganda presentation. *Public Opinion Quarterly*, 1953, 17, 311–318.

Lyman, S. M., & Scott, M. B. Territoriality: A neglected sociological dimension. *Social Problems*, 1967, 15(2), 236–249.

Maass, A., Clark, R. D., III, & Haberkorn, G. The effects of differential ascribed category membership and norms on minority influence. *European Journal of Social Psychology*, 1982, 12, 89–104.

Mabe, P. A., III, & West, S. G. Validity of self-evaluation of ability: A review and meta-analysis. *Journal of Applied Psychology*, 1982, 67, 280–296.

Maccoby, E. E., & Jacklin, C. N. *The psychology of sex differences*. Stanford, Calif.: Stanford University Press, 1974.

MacDonald, A. P., Jr. Anxiety, affiliation, and social isolation. *Developmental Psychology*, 1970, 3, 242–254.

Magnusson, D. (Ed.). *Toward a psychology of situations: An interactional perspective*. Hillsdale, N.J.: Erlbaum, 1981.

Magnusson, D., & Endler, N. S. (Eds.). *Personality at the crossroads: Current issues in interactional psychology*. Hillsdale, N.J.: Erlbaum, 1977.

Major, B. Information acquisition and attribution processes. *Journal of Personality and Social Psychology*, 1980, 39, 1010–1023.

Major, B. Gender patterns in touching behavior. In C. Mayo & N. M. Henley (Eds.), *Gender and nonverbal behavior*. New York: Springer-Verlag, 1981.

Major, B., & Heslin, R. Perceptions of same-sex and cross-sex touching: It's better to give than to receive. Paper presented at meeting of Midwestern Psychological Association, Chicago, May 1978.

Malamuth, N. M. Rape fantasies as a function of exposure to violent sexual stimuli. *Archives of Sexual Behavior*, 1981, 10, 33–47. (a)

Malamuth, N. M. Rape proclivity among males. *Journal of Social Issues*, 1981, 37(4), 138–157. (b)

Malamuth, N. M., & Donnerstein, E. The effects of aggressive-pornographic mass media stimuli. In L. Berkowitz (Ed.), *Advances in experimental social psychology* (Vol. 15). New York: Academic Press, 1982.

Mander, A. M., & Gaebelein, J. W. Third party instigation of aggression as a function of noncooperation and veto power. *Journal of Research in Personality*, 1977, 11, 475–486.

Mann, J., Sidman, J., & Starr, S. Effects of erotic films on sexual behavior of married couples. In *Technical report of the Commission on Obscenity and Pornography* (Vol. 8). Washington, D.C.: U.S. Government Printing Office, 1971.

Mann, J., Sidman, J., & Starr, S. Evaluating social consequences of erotic films: An experimental approach. *Journal of Social Issues*, 1973, 29(3), 113–131.

Mann, L. Cross-cultural studies of small groups. In H. C. Triandis & R. W. Brislin (Eds.), *Handbook of cross-cultural psychology*. Vol. 5: *Social psychology*. Boston: Allyn & Bacon, 1980.

Mann, L. The baiting crowd in episodes of threatened suicide. *Journal of Personality and Social Psychology*, 1981, 41, 703–709.

Mann, L., Newton, J. W., & Innes, J. M. A test between deindividuation and emergent norm theories of crowd aggression. *Journal of Personality and Social Psychology*, 1982, 42, 260–272.

Mann, R. D. A review of the relationship between personality and performance in small groups. *Psychological Bulletin*, 1959, 56, 241–270.

Margulis, S. T. Conceptions of privacy: Current status and next steps. *Journal of Social Issues*, 1977, 33(3), 5–21.

Markus, H. Self-schemata and processing information about the self. *Journal of Personality and Social Psychology*, 1977, 35, 63–78.

Markus, H., Crane, M., Bernstein, S., & Siladi, M. Self-schemas and gender. *Journal of Personality and Social Psychology*, 1982, 42, 38–50.

Marshall, G. D., & Zimbardo, P. G. Affective consequences of inadequately explained physiological arousal. *Journal of Personality and Social Psychology*, 1979, 37, 953–969.

Martin, G. B., & Clark, R. D., III. Distress crying in neonates: Species and peer specificity. *Developmental Psychology*, 1982, 18, 3–9.

Martin, J. Relative deprivation: A theory of distributive injustice for an era of shrinking resources. In *Research in organizational behavior* (Vol. 3). Greenwich, Conn.: JAI Press, 1980.

Martin, J., & Westie, F. The tolerant personality. *American Sociological Review*, 1959, 24, 521–528.

Martindale, D. A. Territorial dominance behavior in dyadic verbal interactions. *Proceedings, 79th Annual Convention, American Psychological Association*, 1971, 6, 305–306.

Marx, G. T. Civil disorder and agents of social control. *Journal of Social Issues*, 1970, 26(1), 19–57.

Maslow, A. H., & Mintz, N. L. Effects of esthetic surroundings: I. Initial effects of three esthetic conditions upon perceiving "energy" and "well-being" in faces. *Journal of Psychology*, 1956, 41, 247–254.

Massengill, D., & DiMarco, N. Sex-role stereotypes and requisite management characteristics: A current replication. *Sex Roles*, 1979, 5, 561–570.

Masters, W. H., & Johnson, V. E. *Human sexual response.* Boston: Little, Brown, 1966.

Masters, W. H., & Johnson, V. E. *Homosexuality in perspective.* Boston: Little, Brown, 1979.

Mathews, K. E., Jr., & Canon, L. K. Environmental noise level as a determinant of helping behavior. *Journal of Personality and Social Psychology,* 1975, *32,* 571–577.

Matlin, M. W. Response competition as a mediating factor in the frequency-affect relationship. *Journal of Personality and Social Psychology,* 1970, *16,* 536–552.

Matthews, K. A. Psychological perspectives on the Type A behavior pattern. *Psychological Bulletin,* 1982, *91,* 293–323.

Matthews, K. A., Batson, C. D., Horn, J., & Rosenman, R. H. "Principles in his nature which interest him in the fortune of others . . .": The heritability of empathic concern for others. *Journal of Personality,* 1981, *49,* 237–247.

Mayo, C. W., & Crockett, W. H. Cognitive complexity and primacy-recency effects in impression formation. *Journal of Abnormal and Social Psychology,* 1964, *68,* 335–338.

McArthur, L. A. The how and what of why: Some determinants of consequences of causal attribution. *Journal of Personality and Social Psychology,* 1972, *22,* 171–193.

McCallum, R. C., Rusbult, C., Hong, C., Walden, T., & Schopler, J. The effects of resource availability and importance of behavior upon the experience of crowding. *Journal of Personality and Social Psychology,* 1979, *37,* 1304–1313.

McCarrey, M., Edwards, H. P., & Rozario, W. Ego-relevant feedback, affect, and self-serving attributional bias. *Personality and Social Psychology Bulletin,* 1982, *8,* 189–194.

McCarty, D., Diamond, W., & Kaye, M. Alcohol, sexual arousal, and the transfer of excitation. *Journal of Personality and Social Psychology,* 1982, *42,* 977–988.

McCary, J. L. Teaching the topic of human sexuality. *Teaching of Psychology,* 1975, *2,* 16–21.

McCary, J. L. *Human sexuality: Physiological, psychological, and sociological factors* (3rd ed.). New York: Van Nostrand, 1978.

McCauley, C., Coleman, G., & DeFusco, P. Commuters' eye contact with strangers in city and suburban train stations: Evidence of short term adaptation in interpersonal overload in the city. *Environmental Psychology and Nonverbal Behavior,* 1978, *2*(4), 215–225.

McCauley, C., & Newman, J. Eye contact with strangers in city, suburb, and small town. *Environment and Behavior,* 1977, *9,* 547.

McCauley, C., & Stitt, C. L. An individual and quantitative measure of stereotypes. *Journal of Personality and Social Psychology,* 1978, *36,* 929–940.

McCauley, C., & Swann, C. P. Male-female differences in sexual fantasy. *Journal of Research in Personality,* 1978, *12,* 76–86.

McCauley, C., & Taylor, J. Is there overload of acquaintances in the city? *Environmental Psychology and Nonverbal Behavior,* 1976, *1*(1), 41–55.

McClelland, D. C., & Boyatzis, R. E. Leadership motive pattern and long-term success in management. *Journal of Applied Psychology,* 1982, *67,* 737–743.

McClelland, L., & Canter, R. J. Psychological research on energy conservation: Context, approaches, methods. In J. Singer, S. Valins, & A. Baum (Eds.), *Advances in environmental psychology.* Hillsdale, N.J.: Erlbaum, 1978.

McClelland, L., & Cook, S. W. Promoting energy conservation in master-metered apartments through group financial incentives. *Journal of Applied Social Psychology,* 1980, *10,* 19–31.

McClintock, C. G. Personality syndromes and attitude change. *Journal of Personality,* 1958, *26,* 479–493.

McClintock, C. G., & Hunt, R. C. Nonverbal indicators of affect and deception in an interview setting. *Journal of Applied Social Psychology,* 1975, *5,* 54–67.

McCorkle, L. W., & Korn, R. R. Resocialization within walls. *Annals of the American Academy of Political and Social Science,* 1954, *293,* 88–98.

McGhee, P. E., & Teevan, R. C. Conformity behavior and need for affiliation. *Journal of Social Psychology,* 1967, *72,* 117–121.

McGinniss, J. *The selling of the President, 1968.* New York: Pocket Books, 1970.

McGrath, J. E. (Ed.). *Social and psychological factors in stress.* New York: Holt, Rinehart & Winston, 1970.

McGuire, W. J. Inducing resistance to persuasion. In L. Berkowitz (Ed.), *Advances in experimental social psychology* (Vol. 1). New York: Academic Press, 1964.

McGuire, W. J. Theory-oriented research in natural settings: The best of both worlds for social psychology. Symposium paper presented at Pennsylvania State University, May 1967.

McGuire, W. J. Personality and attitude change: A theoretical housing. In A. G. Greenwald, T. C. Brock, & T. M. Ostrom (Eds.), *Psychological foundations of attitudes.* New York: Academic Press, 1968. (a)

McGuire, W. J. Personality and susceptibility to social influence. In E. F. Borgatta & W. W. Lambert (Eds.), *Handbook of personality theory and research.* Chicago: Rand McNally, 1968. (b)

McGuire, W. J. The nature of attitudes and attitude change. In G. Lindzey & E. Aronson (Eds.), *Handbook of social psychology* (Vol. 3) (2nd ed.). Reading, Mass.: Addison-Wesley, 1969.

McGuire, W. J. The yin and yang of progress in social psychology: Seven koan. *Journal of Personality and Social Psychology,* 1973, *26,* 446–456.

McGuire, W. J., & McGuire, C. V. The spontaneous self-concept as affected by personal distinctiveness. In M. D. Lynch, A. A. Norem-Hebeisen, & K. J. Gergen (Eds.), *Self-concept: Advances in theory and research.* Cambridge, Mass.: Ballinger, 1981.

McGuire, W. J., & Millman, S. Anticipatory belief lowering following forewarning of a persuasive attack. *Journal of Personality and Social Psychology,* 1965, *2,* 471–479.

McGuire, W. J., & Padawer-Singer, A. Trait salience in the spontaneous self-concept. *Journal of Personality and Social Psychology,* 1976, *33,* 743–754.

McGuire, W. J., & Papageorgis, D. Effectiveness of forewarning in developing resistance to persuasion. *Public Opinion Quarterly,* 1962, *26,* 24–34.

McMillen, D. L., Sanders, D. Y., & Solomon, G. S. Self-esteem, attentiveness, and helping behavior. *Personality and Social Psychology Bulletin,* 1977, *3,* 257–261.

McNemar, Q. *The revision of the Stanford-Binet scale: An analysis of the standardization data.* Boston: Houghton Mifflin, 1942.

Mead, G. H. *Mind, self, and society.* (C. W. Morris, Ed.) Chicago: University of Chicago Press, 1934.

Mehrabian, A. Some referents and measures of nonverbal behavior. *Behavioral Research Methods and Instrumentation,* 1969, *1,* 203–207. (a)

Mehrabian, A. Significance of posture and position in the communication of attitude and status relationships. *Psychological Bulletin,* 1969, *71,* 359–372. (b)

Mehrabian, A. Nonverbal betrayal of feeling. *Journal of Experimental Research in Personality,* 1971, *5,* 64–73.

Mehrabian, A. *Nonverbal communication.* Chicago: Aldine-Atherton, 1972.

Mehrabian, A., & Diamond, S. Effects of furniture arrangement, props, and personality on social interaction. *Journal of Personality and Social Psychology,* 1971, *20,* 18–30. (a)

Mehrabian, A., & Diamond, S. Seating arrangement and conversation. *Sociometry,* 1971, *34,* 281–289. (b)

Mehrabian, A., & Ferris, S. R. Inference of attitudes from nonverbal communication in two channels. *Journal of Consulting Psychology,* 1967, *31,* 248–252.

Mehrabian, A., & Weiner, M. Decoding of inconsistent communications. *Journal of Personality and Social Psychology,* 1967, *6,* 109–114.

Mellon, P. M., Crano, W. D., & Schmitt, N. An analysis of the role and trait components of sex-biased occupational beliefs. *Sex Roles,* 1982, *8,* 533–541.

Mercer, G. W., Bunting, B., & Snook, S. The effects of location, experiences with the civil disturbances, and religion on death anxiety and manifest anxiety in a sample of Northern Ireland university students. *British Journal of Social and Clinical Psychology,* 1979, *18,* 151–158.

Mercer, G. W., Bunting, B., & Snook, S. Some psychological and social attitude correlates of Northern Ireland university students' contact with the civil disturbances. *Journal of Applied Social Psychology,* 1980, *10,* 272–282.

Meyer, W.-U., & Starke, E. Own ability in relation to self-concept of ability: A field study of information-seeking. *Personality and Social Psychology Bulletin,* 1982, *8,* 501–507.

Michaels, J. W., Blommel, J. M., Brocato, R. M., Linkous, R. A., & Rowe, J. S. Social facilitation and inhibition in a natural setting. *Replications in Social Psychology,* 1982, *2,* 21–24.

Michelson, W. *Man and his urban environment: A sociological approach.* Reading, Mass.: Addison-Wesley, 1970.

Michener, H. A., & Lawler, E. J. The endorsement of formal leaders: An integrative model. *Journal of Personality and Social Psychology,* 1975, *31,* 216–223.

Milgram, S. Behavioral study of obedience. *Journal of Abnormal and Social Psychology,* 1963, *67,* 371–378.

Milgram, S. Group pressure and action against a person. *Journal of Abnormal and Social Psychology,* 1964, *69,* 137–143. (a)

Milgram, S. Issues in the study of obedience: A reply to Baumrind. *American Psychologist,* 1964, *19,* 848–852. (b)

Milgram, S. Some conditions of obedience and disobedience to authority. *Human Relations,* 1965, *18,* 57–76.

Milgram, S. Reply to the critics. *International Journal of Psychiatry,* 1968, *6,* 294–295.

Milgram, S. The experience of living in cities. *Science,* 1970, *167,* 1461–1468.

Milgram, S. *Obedience to authority.* New York: Harper & Row, 1974.

Miller, A. G. Role playing: An alternative to deception? A review of the evidence. *American Psychologist,* 1972, *27,* 623–636.

Miller, A. G. Actor and observer perceptions of the learning of a task. *Journal of Experimental Social Psychology,* 1977, *11,* 95–111.

Miller, C., & Crandall, R. Bargaining and negotiation. In P. B. Paulus (Ed.), *Psychology of group influence.* Hillsdale, N. J.: Erlbaum, 1980.

Miller, D. T., Norman, S. A., & Wright, E. Distortion in person perception as a consequence of the need for effective control. *Journal of Personality and Social Psychology,* 1978, *36,* 598–607.

Miller, D. T., & Porter, C. A. Effects of temporal perspective on the attribution process. *Journal of Personality and Social Psychology,* 1980, *39,* 532–541.

Miller, D. T., & Ross, M. Self-serving biases in the attribution of causality: Fact or fiction? *Psychological Bulletin,* 1975, *82,* 213–255.

Miller, F. E., & Rogers, L. E. A relational approach to interpersonal communication. In G. R. Miller (Ed.), *Explorations in interpersonal communication.* Beverly Hills, Calif.: Sage, 1976.

Miller, G. A. Psychology as a means of promoting human welfare. *American Psychologist,* 1969, *24,* 1063–1075. (Reprinted in F. F. Korten, S. W. Cook, & J. I. Lacey [Eds.], *Psychology and the problems of society.* Washington, D.C.: American Psychological Association, 1970.)

Miller, G. R. The current status of theory and research in interpersonal communication. *Human Communication Research,* 1978, *4,* 164–178.

Miller, J. G. Adjusting to overloads of information. In R. Waggoner & D. Carek (Eds.), *Disorders of Communication,* 1964, *42,* 87–100.

Miller, N. Involvement and dogmatism as inhibitors of attitude change. *Journal of Experimental Social Psychology,* 1965, *1,* 121–132.

Miller, N., & Campbell, D. T. Recency and primacy in persuasion as a function of the timing of speeches and measurements. *Journal of Abnormal and Social Psychology,* 1959, *59,* 1–9.

Miller, N. E. The frustration-aggression hypothesis. *Psychological Review,* 1941, *48,* 337–342.

Miller, N. E. Some implications of modern behavior theory for personality change and psychotherapy. In P. Worchel & D. Byrne (Eds.), *Personality change.* New York: Wiley, 1964.

Miller, N. E., & Dollard, J. *Social learning and imitation.* New Haven: Yale University Press, 1941.

Mills, J., & Clark, M. S. Exchange and communal relationships. In L. Wheeler (Ed.), *Review of personality and social psychology* (Vol. 3). Beverly Hills, Calif.: Sage, 1982.

Mills, R. T., & Krantz, D. S. Information, choice, and reactions to stress: A field experiment in a blood bank with laboratory analogue. *Journal of Personality and Social Psychology,* 1979, *37,* 608–620.

Mintz, N. L. Effects of esthetic surroundings: II. Prolonged and repeated experience in a "beautiful" and an "ugly" room. *Journal of Psychology*, 1956, *41*, 459–466.

Mirels, H. L. Dimensions of internal versus external control. *Journal of Consulting and Clinical Psychology*, 1970, *34*, 226–228.

Mischel, W. *Personality and assessment*. New York: Wiley, 1968.

Mischel, W. On the future of personality measurement. *American Psychologist*, 1977, *32*, 246–254.

Mischel, W., & Peake, P. K. Beyond déjà vu in the search for cross-situational consistency. *Psychological Review*, 1982, *89*, 730–755.

Mita, T. H., Dermer, M., & Knight, J. Reversed facial images and the mere-exposure hypothesis. *Journal of Personality and Social Psychology*, 1977, *35*, 597–601.

Mitnick, L., & McGinnies, E. Influencing ethnocentrism in small discussion groups through a film communication. *Journal of Abnormal and Social Psychology*, 1958, *56*, 82–90.

Moe, J. L., Nacoste, R. W., & Insko, C. A. Belief versus race as determinants of discrimination: A study of Southern adolescents in 1966 and 1979. *Journal of Personality and Social Psychology*, 1981, *41*, 1031–1050.

Monahan, J., & Loftus, E. F. The psychology of law. In M. R. Rosenzweig & L. W. Porter (Eds.), *Annual review of psychology* (Vol. 33). Palo Alto, Calif.: Annual Reviews, 1982.

Money, J., & Athanasiou, R. Pornography: Review and bibliographic annotations. *American Journal of Obstetrics and Gynecology*, 1973, *115*, 130–146.

Money, J., & Ehrhardt, A. A. *Man and woman; boy and girl*. Baltimore: Johns Hopkins Press, 1972.

Money, J., & Tucker, P. *Sexual signatures: On being a man or a woman*. Boston: Little, Brown, 1975.

Monson, T. C., Hesley, J. W., & Chernick, L. Specifying when personality traits can and cannot predict behavior: An alternative to abandoning the attempt to predict single act criteria. *Journal of Personality and Social Psychology*, 1982, *43*, 385–399.

Monson, T. C., Keel, R., Stephens, D., & Genung, V. Trait attributions: Relative validity, covariation with behavior, and prospect of future interaction. *Journal of Personality and Social Psychology*, 1982, *42*, 1014–1024.

Monson, T. C., & Snyder, M. Actors, observers, and the attribution process: Toward a reconceptualization. *Journal of Experimental Social Psychology*, 1977, *13*, 89–111.

Montagu, A. *The nature of human aggression*. New York: Oxford University Press, 1976.

Moore, B., & Underwood, B. The development of prosocial behavior. In S. S. Brehm, S. M. Kassin, & F. X. Gibbons (Eds.), *Developmental social psychology: Theory and research*. New York: Oxford University Press, 1981.

Moreland, R. L., & Levine, J. M. Socialization in small groups: Temporal changes in individual-group relations. In L. Berkowitz (Ed.), *Advances in experimental social psychology* (Vol. 15). New York: Academic Press, 1982.

Morgan, M. Television and adolescents' sex role stereotypes: A longitudinal study. *Journal of Personality and Social Psychology*, 1982, *43*, 947–955.

Moriarty, T. Crime, commitment and the responsive bystander: Two field experiments. *Journal of Personality and Social Psychology*, 1975, *31*, 370–376.

Morris, J. *Conundrum*. New York: Harcourt Brace Jovanovich, 1974.

Morton, T. L. Intimacy and reciprocity of exchange: A comparison of spouses and strangers. *Journal of Personality and Social Psychology*, 1978, *36*, 72–81.

Moscovici, S. Society and theory in social psychology. In J. Israel & H. Tajfel (Eds.), *The context of social psychology: A critical assessment*. New York: Academic Press, 1972.

Moscovici, S. *Social influence and social change*. New York: Academic Press, 1976.

Moscovici, S., & Doise, W. Decision making in groups. In C. Nemeth (Ed.), *Social psychology: Classic and contemporary integrations*. Chicago: Rand McNally, 1974.

Moscovici, S., & Zavalloni, M. The group as a polarizer of attitudes. *Journal of Personality and Social Psychology*, 1969, *12*, 125–135.

Mosher, D. L. Sex differences, sex experience, sex guilt, and explicitly sexual films. *Journal of Social Issues*, 1973, *29*(3), 95–112.

Moss, M. K., & Andrasik, F. Belief similarity and interracial attraction. *Journal of Personality*, 1973, *41*, 192–205.

Moss, M. K., & Page, R. A. Reinforcement and helping behavior. *Journal of Applied Social Psychology*, 1972, *2*, 360–371.

Mowen, J. C., & Cialdini, R. B. On implementing the door-in-the-face compliance technique in a business context. *Journal of Marketing Research*, 1980, *17*, 253–258.

Mower-White, C. J. Factors affecting balance, agreement, and positivity biases in POQ and POX triads. *European Journal of Social Psychology*, 1979, *9*, 129–148.

Mueller, C. W., & Donnerstein, E. Film-facilitated arousal and prosocial behavior. *Journal of Experimental Social Psychology*, 1981, *17*, 31–41.

Mueller, J. H. Self-awareness and access to material rated as self-descriptive or nondescriptive. *Bulletin of the Psychonomic Society*, 1982, *19*, 323–326.

Mugny, G. Negotiations, image of the other and the process of minority influence. *European Journal of Social Psychology*, 1975, *5*, 209–229.

Mullen, B., & Suls, J. "Know thyself": Stressful life changes and the ameliorative effect of private self-consciousness. *Journal of Experimental Social Psychology*, 1982, *18*, 43–55.

Mulvihill, D. J., & Tumin, M. M. *Crimes of violence. Staff report to the National Commission on the Causes and Prevention of Violence* (Vol. 11). Washington, D.C.: U.S. Government Printing Office, 1969.

Murray, H. A. *Explorations in personality*. New York: Oxford University Press, 1938.

Murray, J., & Feshbach, S. Let's not throw the baby out with the bathwater: The catharsis hypothesis revisited. *Journal of Personality*, 1978, *46*, 462–473.

Murstein, B. I. Physical attractiveness and marital choice. *Journal of Personality and Social Psychology*, 1972, *22*, 8–12.

Murstein, B. I., & Christy, P. Physical attractiveness and marriage adjustment in middle-aged couples. *Journal of Personality and Social Psychology*, 1976, *34*, 537–542.

Myers, D. G., & Bishop, G. D. Discussion effects on racial attitudes. *Science*, 1970, *169*, 778–789.

Myers, D. G., & Bishop, G. D. Enhancement of dominant attitudes in group discussion. *Journal of Personality and Social Psychology*, 1971, *20*, 386–391.

Myers, D. G., & Kaplan, M. F. Group-induced polarization in simulated juries. *Personality and Social Psychology Bulletin*, 1976, 2, 63–66.

Myers, D. G., & Lamm, H. The group polarization phenomenon. *Psychological Bulletin*, 1976, 83, 602–627.

Nadler, A., Altman, A., & Fisher, J. D. Helping is not enough: Recipient's reactions to aid as a function of positive and negative information about self. *Journal of Personality*, 1979, 47, 615–628.

Nadler, A., Fisher, J. D., & Streufert, S. The donor's dilemma: Recipient's reactions to aid from friend or foe. *Journal of Applied Social Psychology*, 1974, 4, 275–285.

Natale, M., & Hantas, M. Effect of temporary mood states on selective memory about the self. *Journal of Personality and Social Psychology*, 1982, 42, 927–934.

Nemeth, C. The role of an active minority in intergroup relations. In W. G. Austin & S. Worchel (Eds.), *The social psychology of intergroup relations*. Monterey, Calif.: Brooks/Cole, 1979.

Newcomb, M. D., & Bentler, P. M. Marital breakdown. In S. Duck & R. Gilmour (Eds.), *Personal relationships 3: Personal relationships in disorder*. New York: Academic Press, 1981.

Newcomb, T. M. *The acquaintance process*. New York: Holt, Rinehart & Winston, 1961.

Newman, O. *Defensible space*. New York: Macmillan, 1973.

Newton, J. W., & Mann, L. Crowd size as a factor in the persuasion process: A study of religious crusade meetings. *Journal of Personality and Social Psychology*, 1980, 39, 874–883.

Newtson, D. Dispositional inference from effects of actions: Effects chosen and effects foregone. *Journal of Experimental Social Psychology*, 1974, 10, 489–496.

Newtson, D., & Czerlinsky, T. Adjustment of attitude communications for contrasts by extreme audiences. *Journal of Personality and Social Psychology*, 1974, 30, 829–837.

Nguyen, T., Heslin, R., & Nguyen, M. L. The meanings of touch: Sex differences. *Journal of Communication*, 1975, 25, 92–103.

Nisbett, R. E., & Borgida, E. Attribution and the psychology of prediction. *Journal of Personality and Social Psychology*, 1975, 32, 932–943.

Nisbett, R. E., Caputo, C., Legant, P., & Marecek, J. Behavior as seen by the actor and as seen by the observer. *Journal of Personality and Social Psychology*, 1973, 27, 154–165.

Nisbett, R. E., & Wilson, T. D. Telling more than we can know: Verbal reports on mental processes. *Psychological Review*, 1977, 84, 231–259.

Nizer, L. *The implosion conspiracy*. New York: Doubleday, 1973.

Noller, P. Misunderstandings in marital communication: A study of couples' nonverbal communication. *Journal of Personality and Social Psychology*, 1980, 39, 1135–1148.

Noller, P. Gender and marital adjustment level differences in decoding messages from spouses and strangers. *Journal of Personality and Social Psychology*, 1981, 41, 272–278.

Norvell, N., & Worchel, S. A reexamination of the relation between equal status contact and intergroup attraction. *Journal of Personality and Social Psychology*, 1981, 41, 902–908.

Novak, D., & Lerner, M. J. Rejection as a consequence of perceived similarity. *Journal of Personality and Social Psychology*, 1968, 9, 147–152.

Nutt, R. L., & Sedlacek, W. E. Freshman sexual attitudes and behavior. *Journal of College Student Personnel*, 1974, 15, 346–351.

Orne, M. T. Demand characteristics and the concept of quasi-controls. In R. Rosenthal & R. Rosnow (Eds.), *Artifact in behavior research*. New York: Academic Press, 1969.

Orne, M. T., & Holland, C. C. On the ecological validity of laboratory deceptions. *International Journal of Psychiatry*, 1968, 6, 282–293.

Orvis, B. R., Cunningham, J. D., & Kelley, H. H. A closer examination of causal inference: The role of consensus, distinctiveness, and consistency information. *Journal of Personality and Social Psychology*, 1975, 29, 426–434.

Osborn, A. F. *Applied imagination*. New York: Scribner, 1957.

Osgood, C. E. *Perspective in foreign policy*. Palo Alto, Calif.: Pacific Books, 1966.

Osgood, C. E. GRIT for MBFR: A proposal for unfreezing force-level postures in Europe. Unpublished manuscript, University of Illinois, 1974.

Osgood, C. E., Suci, G. J., & Tannenbaum, P. H. *The measurement of meaning*. Urbana: University of Illinois Press, 1957.

Oskamp, S. *Attitudes and opinions*. Englewood Cliffs, N.J.: Prentice-Hall, 1977.

Osmond, H. Function as the basis of psychiatric ward design. *Mental Hospitals*, 1957, 8, 23–30.

Ovcharchyn-Devitt, C., Calby, P., Carswell, L., Perkowitz, W., Scruggs, B., Turpin, R., & Bickman, L. Approaches towards social problems: A conceptual model. *Basic and Applied Social Psychology*, 1981, 2, 275–287.

Owens, D. J., & Straus, M. A. The social structure of violence in childhood and approval of violence as an adult. *Aggressive Behavior*, 1975, 1, 193–211.

Pagano, M., & Kirschner, N. M. Sex guilt, sexual arousal, and urinary acid phosphatase output. *Journal of Research in Personality*, 1978, 12, 68–75.

Page, M. M. Social psychology of a classical conditioning of attitudes experiment. *Journal of Personality and Social Psychology*, 1969, 11, 177–186.

Page, M. M. Postexperimental assessment of awareness in attitude conditioning. *Educational and Psychological Measurement*, 1971, 31, 891–906.

Page, M. M. Demand characteristics and the classical conditioning of attitudes experiment. *Journal of Personality and Social Psychology*, 1974, 30, 468–476.

Page, M., & Scheidt, R. The elusive weapons effect: Demand awareness, evaluation and slightly sophisticated subjects. *Journal of Personality and Social Psychology*, 1971, 20, 304–318.

Page, R. Noise and helping behavior. *Environment and Behavior*, 1977, 9, 311–334.

Palamarek, D. L., & Rule, B. G. The effects of ambient temperature and insult on the motivation to retaliate or escape. *Motivation and Emotion*, 1979, 3, 83–92.

Pallak, M. S., & Cummings, W. Commitment and voluntary energy conservation. *Personality and Social Psychology Bulletin*, 1976, 2, 27–30.

Park, B., & Rothbart, M. Perception of out-group homogeneity and levels of social categorization: Memory for the subordinate attributes of in-group and out-group members. *Journal of Personality and Social Psychology*, 1982, *42*, 1051–1068.

Parke, R. D., Berkowitz, L., Leyens, J.-P., West, S. G., & Sebastian, R. J. Some effects of violent and nonviolent movies on the behavior of juvenile delinquents. In L. Berkowitz (Ed.), *Advances in experimental social psychology* (Vol. 10). New York: Academic Press, 1977.

Parks, M. R. Relational communication: Theory and research. *Human Communications Research*, 1977, *3*, 372–381.

Parlee, M. B. The friendship bond: PT's survey report on friendship in America. *Psychology Today*, October 1979, 43–54, 113.

Parnes, S. J., & Meadow, A. Effects of "brainstorming" instructions on creative problem solving by trained and untrained subjects. *Journal of Educational Psychology*, 1959, *50*, 171–176.

Patterson, A. H. Territorial behavior and fear of crime in the elderly. *Environmental Psychology and Nonverbal Behavior*, 1978, *2*, 131–144.

Patterson, M. L. An arousal model of interpersonal intimacy. *Psychological Review*, 1976, *83*, 235–245.

Patterson, M. L. A sequential function model of verbal exchange. *Psychological Review*, 1982, *89*, 231–249.

Patterson, M. L., Mullens, S., & Romano, J. Compensatory reactions to spatial intrusion. *Sociometry*, 1971, *34*, 114–121.

Patterson, M. L., Roth, C. P., & Schenk, C. Seating arrangement, activity and sex differences in small group crowding. *Personality and Social Psychology Bulletin*, 1979, *5*, 100–103.

Paulhus, D. L., Shaffer, D. R., & Downing, L. L. Effects of making blood donor motives salient upon donor retention: A field experiment. *Personality and Social Psychology Bulletin*, 1977, *3*, 99–102.

Paulus, P. B., Annis, A. B., Seta, J., Schkade, J., & Matthews, R. B. Density does affect task performance. *Journal of Personality and Social Psychology*, 1976, *34*, 248–253.

Paulus, P. B., Cox, V., McCain, G., & Chandler, J. Some effects of crowding in a prison environment. *Journal of Applied Social Psychology*, 1975, *5*, 86–91.

Paulus, P. B., & Matthews, R. W. When density affects task performance. *Personality and Social Psychology Bulletin*, 1980, *6*, 119–124.

Paulus, P., McCain, G., & Cox, V. Death rates, psychiatric commitments, blood pressure, and perceived crowding as a function of institutional crowding. *Environmental Psychology and Nonverbal Behavior*, 1978, *3*, 107–116.

Pearce, P. L. Strangers, travelers, and Greyhound terminals: A study of small-scale helping behaviors. *Journal of Personality and Social Psychology*, 1980, *38*, 935–940.

Pellegrini, R. J., & Empey, J. Interpersonal spatial orientation in dyads. *Journal of Psychology*, 1970, *76*, 67–70.

Pennebaker, J. W. *The psychology of physical symptoms.* New York: Springer-Verlag, 1982.

Peplau, L. A., Miceli, M., & Morasch, B. Loneliness and self-evaluation. In L. A. Peplau & D. Perlman (Eds.), *Loneliness: A sourcebook of current theory, research and therapy.* New York: Wiley, 1982.

Peplau, L. A., & Perlman, D. (Eds.). *Loneliness: A sourcebook of current theory, research and therapy.* New York: Wiley, 1982.

Peplau, L. A., Rubin, Z., & Hill, C. T. Sexual intimacy in dating relationships. *Journal of Social Issues*, 1977, *33*(2), 86–109.

Perlman, D. The sexual standards of Canadian university students. In D. Koulack & D. Perlman (Eds.), *Readings in social psychology: Focus on Canada.* Toronto: Wiley, 1973.

Perlman, S. D., & Abramson, P. R. Sexual satisfaction among married and cohabiting individuals. *Journal of Consulting and Clinical Psychology*, in press.

Peterson, P. D., & Koulack, D. Attitude change as a function of latitudes of acceptance and rejection. *Journal of Personality and Social Psychology*, 1969, *11*, 309–311.

Pettigrew, T. F. Social psychology and desegregation research. *American Psychologist*, 1961, *16*, 105–112.

Pettigrew, T. F. *A profile of the Negro American.* Princeton, N.J.: Van Nostrand, 1964.

Petty, R. E., & Brock, T. C. Effects of responding or not responding to hecklers on audience agreement with a speaker. *Journal of Applied Social Psychology*, 1976, *6*, 1–17.

Petty, R. E., & Cacioppo, J. T. Forewarning, cognitive responding, and resistance to persuasion. *Journal of Personality and Social Psychology*, 1977, *35*, 645–655.

Petty, R. E., & Cacioppo, J. T. *Attitudes and persuasion: Classic and contemporary approaches.* Dubuque, Iowa: William C. Brown, 1981.

Petty, R. E., Wells, G. L., & Brock, T. C. Distraction can enhance or reduce yielding to propaganda: Thought disruption versus effort justification. *Journal of Personality and Social Psychology*, 1976, *34*, 874–884.

Pfeffer, J. The ambiguity of leadership. In M. W. McCall, Jr., & M. M. Lombardo (Eds.), *Leadership: Where else can we go?* Durham, N.C.: Duke University Press, 1978.

Phares, E. J. *Locus of control in personality.* Morristown, N.J.: General Learning Press, 1976.

Phillips, D. P. Dying as a form of social behavior (Doctoral dissertation, Princeton University). Ann Arbor, Mich.: University Microfilms, 1970. No. 70-19, 799.

Phillips, D. P. Deathday and birthday: An unexpected connection. In J. M. Tanur (Ed.), *Statistics: A guide to the unknown.* San Francisco: Holden-Day, 1972.

Phillips, D. P. The deterrent effect of capital punishment: New evidence on an old controversy. *American Journal of Sociology*, 1980, *86*, 139–148.

Phillis, D. E., & Allgeier, E. R. Morality, responsibility, and contraceptive initiation in adolescent couples. Paper presented at Eastern regional meeting of Society for the Scientific Study of Sex, Philadelphia, April 1982.

Pile, J. *Open office planning: A handbook for interior designers and architects.* New York: Whitney Library of Design, 1978.

Piliavin, I. M., & Gross, A. E. The effects of separation of services and income maintenance on AFDC recipients' perceptions and use of social services: Results of a field experiment. *Social Service Review*, 1977, *9*, 389–406.

Piliavin, I. M., Piliavin, J. A., & Rodin, J. Costs, diffusion, and the stigmatized victim. *Journal of Personality and Social Psychology*, 1975, *32*, 429–438.

Piliavin, I. M., Rodin, J., & Piliavin, J. A. Good Samaritanism: An underground phenomenon? *Journal of Personality and Social Psychology,* 1969, *13,* 289–299.

Piliavin, J. A., Dovidio, J. F., Gaertner, S. L., & Clark, R. D., III. *Emergency intervention.* New York: Academic Press, 1981.

Piliavin, J. A., & Piliavin, I. M. Effect of blood on reaction to a victim. *Journal of Personality and Social Psychology,* 1972, *23,* 353–361.

Platt, J. Social traps. *American Psychologist,* 1973, *28,* 641–651.

Pocs, O., & Godow, A. G. Can students view parents as sexual beings? In D. Byrne & L. Byrne (Eds.), *Exploring human sexuality.* New York: Crowell, 1977.

Poor, D. The social psychology of questionnaires. Unpublished bachelor's thesis, Harvard University, 1967. (Cited in R. Rosenthal & R. L. Rosnow [Eds.], *Artifact in behavioral research.* New York: Academic Press, 1969.)

Potter, D. A. Personalism and interpersonal attraction. *Journal of Personality and Social Psychology,* 1973, *28,* 192–198.

Prentice-Dunn, S., & Rogers, R. W. Effects of public and private self-awareness on deindividuation and aggression. *Journal of Personality and Social Psychology,* 1982, *43,* 505–513.

Price, R. A., & Vandenberg, S. G. Matching for physical attractiveness in married couples. *Personality and Social Psychology Bulletin,* 1979, *5,* 398–400.

Price, R. A., Vandenberg, S. G., Iyer, H., & Williams, J. S. Components of variation in normal personality. *Journal of Personality and Social Psychology,* 1982, *43,* 328–340.

Proshansky, H., & Newton, P. The nature and meaning of Negro self-identity. In M. Deutsch, I. Katz, & A. R. Jensen (Eds.), *Social class, race, and psychological development.* New York: Holt, Rinehart & Winston, 1968.

Pruitt, D. G. Choice shifts in group discussion: An introductory review. *Journal of Personality and Social Psychology,* 1971, *20,* 339–360. (a)

Pruitt, D. G. Conclusions: Toward an understanding of choice shifts in group discussion. *Journal of Personality and Social Psychology,* 1971, *20,* 495–510. (b)

Pruitt, D. G. *Negotiation behavior.* New York: Academic Press, 1981.

Pruitt, D. G. Integrative agreements: Nature and antecedents. Unpublished manuscript, 1982.

Putnam, L. L., & Jones, T. S. The role of communication in bargaining. *Human Communication Research,* 1982, *8,* 262–280.

Pyszczynski, T., Greenberg, J., Mack, D., & Wrightsman, L. S. Opening statements in a jury trial: The effect of promising more than the evidence can show. *Journal of Applied Social Psychology,* 1981, *11,* 434–444.

Pyszczynski, T. A., & Wrightsman, L. S. The effects of opening statements on mock jurors' verdicts in a simulated criminal trial. *Journal of Applied Social Psychology,* 1981, *11,* 301–313.

Rada, J. B., & Rogers, R. W. Obedience to authority: Presence of authority and command strength. Paper presented at meeting of Southeastern Psychological Association, New Orleans, April 1973.

Radloff, R. Opinion evaluation and affiliation. *Journal of Abnormal and Social Psychology,* 1961, *62,* 578–585.

Radloff, R., & Helmreich, R. *Groups under stress: Psychological research in SEALAB II.* New York: Irvington, 1968.

Ramirez, A. Chicano power and interracial group relations. In J. L. Martinez (Ed.), *Chicano psychology.* New York: Academic Press, 1977.

Ramirez, J., Bryant, J., & Zillmann, D. Effects of erotica on retaliatory behavior as a function of level of prior provocation. *Journal of Personality and Social Psychology,* 1982, *43,* 971–978.

Rands, M., & Levinger, G. Implicit theories of relationship: An intergenerational study. *Journal of Personality and Social Psychology,* 1979, *37,* 645–661.

Ransford, H. E. Isolation, powerlessness, and violence: A study of attitudes and participation in the Watts riot. *American Journal of Sociology,* 1968, *73,* 581–591.

Raps, C. S., Peterson, C., Jonas, M., & Seligman, M. E. P. Patient behavior in hospitals: Helplessness, reactance, or both? *Journal of Personality and Social Psychology,* 1982, *42,* 1036–1041.

Reddy, D. M., Baum, A., Fleming, R., & Aiello, J. R. Mediation of social density by coalition formation. *Journal of Applied Social Psychology,* 1981, *11,* 529–537.

Reeder, G. D. Let's give the fundamental attribution error another chance. *Journal of Personality and Social Psychology,* 1982, *43,* 341–344.

Regan, D. T., & Fazio, R. H. On the consistency between attitudes and behavior: Look to the method of attitude formation. *Journal of Experimental Social Psychology,* 1977, *13,* 28–45.

Reich, J. W. An historical analysis of the field. In L. Bickman (Ed.), *Applied social psychology annual* (Vol. 2). Beverly Hills, Calif.: Sage, 1981.

Reichner, R. F. Differential responses to being ignored: The effects of architectural design and social density on interpersonal behavior. *Journal of Applied Social Psychology,* 1979, *9,* 13–26.

Reingen, P. H. Test of a list procedure for inducing compliance with a request to donate money. *Journal of Applied Psychology,* 1982, *67,* 110–118.

Reis, H. T., Nezlek, J., & Wheeler, L. Physical attractiveness in social interaction. *Journal of Personality and Social Psychology,* 1980, *38,* 604–617.

Reis, H. T., Wheeler, L., Kernis, M. H., Spiegel, N., & Nezlek, J. On specificity in the impact of social participation on physical and psychological health. Unpublished manuscript, University of Rochester, 1982.

Reis, H. T., Wheeler, L., Spiegel, N., Kernis, M., Nezlek, J., & Perri, M. Physical attractiveness in social interaction, II: Why does appearance affect social experience? *Journal of Personality and Social Psychology,* in press.

Reiss, I. *Premarital sexual standards in America.* New York: Free Press, 1960.

Reiss, I. *The social context of premarital sexual permissiveness.* New York: Holt, Rinehart & Winston, 1967.

Rheingold, H. L. Little children's participation in the work of adults, a nascent prosocial behavior. *Child Development,* 1982, *53,* 114–125.

Rhodewalt, F., Saltzman, A. T., & Wittmer, J. Self-handicapping among competitive athletes: The role of practice in self-esteem protection. Unpublished manuscript, University of Utah, 1982.

Rice, R. W. Construct validity of the least preferred coworker score. *Psychological Bulletin*, 1978, *85*, 1199–1237.

Richer, S., & Laporte, P. Culture, cognition, and English-French competition. In D. Koulack & D. Perlman (Eds.), *Readings in social psychology: Focus on Canada*. Toronto: Wiley, 1973.

Riesman, D. (in association with N. Glazer and R. Denney). *The lonely crowd: A study of the changing American character*. New Haven: Yale University Press, 1950.

Ring, K. Experimental social psychology: Some sober questions about frivolous values. *Journal of Experimental Social Psychology*, 1967, *3*, 113–123.

Roberts, A. H., & Jessor, R. Authoritarianism, punitiveness, and perceived social status. *Journal of Abnormal and Social Psychology*, 1958, *56*, 311–314.

Roberts, D. F., & Bachen, C. M. Mass communication effects. In M. R. Rosenzweig & L. W. Porter (Eds.), *Annual review of psychology* (Vol. 32). Palo Alto, Calif.: Annual Reviews, 1981.

Rochester, S. R. The significance of pauses in spontaneous speech. *Journal of Psycholinguistic Research*, 1973, *2*, 51–81.

Rodin, J. Density, perceived choice, and response to controllable and uncontrollable outcomes. *Journal of Experimental Social Psychology*, 1976, *12*, 564–578.

Rodin, J. Somatopsychics and attribution. *Personality and Social Psychology Bulletin*, 1978, *4*, 531–540.

Rodin, J., & Baum, A. Crowding and helplessness: Potential consequences of density and loss of control. In A. Baum & Y. Epstein (Eds.), *Human response to crowding*. Hillsdale, N.J.: Erlbaum, 1978.

Rodin, J., & Langer, E. J. Long-term effects of a control-relevant intervention with the institutionalized aged. *Journal of Personality and Social Psychology*, 1977, *35*, 897–902.

Rodin, J., Solomon, S. K., & Metcalf, J. Role of control in mediating perceptions of density. *Journal of Personality and Social Psychology*, 1978, *36*, 988–999.

Rogers, C. R. A note on the "nature of man." *Journal of Counseling Psychology*, 1957, *4*, 199–203.

Rogers, L. E., & Farace, R. V. Analysis of relational communication in dyads: New measurement procedures. *Human Communication Research*, 1975, *1*(3), 222–239.

Rogers, R. W. A protection motivation theory of fear appeals and attitude change. *Journal of Psychology*, 1975, *91*, 93–114.

Rohner, R. P. A worldwide study of sex differences in aggression: A universalist perspective. Paper presented at meeting of Eastern Psychological Association, New York, April 1976.

Rokeach, M. *The open and closed mind*. New York: Basic Books, 1960.

Rokeach, M. *Beliefs, attitudes, and values*. San Francisco: Jossey-Bass, 1968.

Rokeach, M. Faith, hope, bigotry. *Psychology Today*, 1970, *3*(11), 33–37ff.

Rokeach, M. *The nature of human values*. New York: Free Press, 1973.

Rokeach, M., & Mezei, L. Race and shared belief as factors in social choice. *Science*, 1966, *151*, 167–172.

Rokeach, M., Smith, P. W., & Evans, R. I. Two kinds of prejudice or one? In M. Rokeach, *The open and closed mind*. New York: Basic Books, 1960.

Rook, K. S., & Hammen, C. L. A cognitive perspective on the experience of sexual arousal. *Journal of Social Issues*, 1977, *33*(2), 7–29.

Rose, A. M. Anti-Semitism's root in city-hatred. *Commentary*, 1948, *6*, 374–378.

Rosen, E. Differences between volunteers and nonvolunteers for psychological studies. *Journal of Applied Psychology*, 1951, *35*, 185–193.

Rosenberg, M. J. When dissonance fails: On eliminating evaluation apprehension from attitude measurement. *Journal of Personality and Social Psychology*, 1965, *1*, 28–42.

Rosenberg, S., & Jones, R. A. A method for investigating and representing a person's implicit theory of personality: Theodore Dreiser's view of people. *Journal of Personality and Social Psychology*, 1972, *22*, 372–386.

Rosenberg, S., & Sedlak, A. Structural representations of implicit personality theory. In L. Berkowitz (Ed.), *Advances in experimental social psychology* (Vol. 6). New York: Academic Press, 1972.

Rosenfeld, H. M. Effect of an approval-seeking induction on interpersonal proximity. *Psychological Reports*, 1965, *17*, 120–122.

Rosenhan, D. L. The natural socialization of altruistic autonomy. In J. Macaulay & L. Berkowitz (Eds.), *Altruism and helping behavior: Social psychological studies of some antecedents and consequences*. New York: Academic Press, 1970.

Rosenhan, D. L. Toward resolving the altruism paradox: Affect, self-reinforcement, and cognition. In L. Wispé (Ed.), *Altruism, sympathy, and helping: Psychological and sociological principles*. New York: Academic Press, 1978.

Rosenhan, D. L., Karylowski, J., Salovey, P., & Hargis, K. Emotion and altruism. In J. P. Rushton & R. M. Sorrentino (Eds.), *Altruism and helping behavior: Social, personality, and developmental perspectives*. Hillsdale, N.J.: Erlbaum, 1981.

Rosenhan, D. L., Salovey, P., & Hargis, K. The joys of helping: Focus of attention mediates the impact of positive affect on altruism. *Journal of Personality and Social Psychology*, 1981, *40*, 899–905.

Rosenkrantz, P. S., & Crockett, W. H. Some factors influencing the assimilation of disparate information in impression formation. *Journal of Personality and Social Psychology*, 1965, *2*, 397–402.

Rosenthal, R. *Experimenter effects in behavioral research*. New York: Appleton-Century-Crofts, 1966.

Rosenthal, R., & DePaulo, B. M. Sex differences in eavesdropping on nonverbal cues. *Journal of Personality and Social Psychology*, 1979, *37*, 273–285.

Rosenthal, R., & Rosnow, R. L. *The volunteer subject*. New York: Wiley, 1975.

Rosnow, R. L., & Arms, R. L. Adding versus averaging as a stimulus-combination rule in forming impressions of groups. *Journal of Personality and Social Psychology*, 1968, *10*, 363–369.

Rosow, I. The social effects of the physical environment. *Journal of the American Institute of Planners*, 1961, *27*, 127–133.

Ross, L. The intuitive psychologist and his shortcomings: Distortions in the attribution process. In L. Berkowitz (Ed.), *Advances in experimental social psychology* (Vol. 10). New York: Academic Press, 1977.

Ross, L. D., Amabile, T. M., & Steinmetz, J. L. Social roles, social control, and biases in social-perception processes. *Journal of Personality and Social Psychology*, 1977, *35*, 485–494.

Rossi, P. H., & Williams, W. (Eds.). *Evaluating social programs: Theory, practice, and politics.* New York: Seminar Press, 1972.

Rothbart, M., Fulero, S., Jensen, C., Howard, J., & Birrell, B. From individual to group impressions: Availability heuristics in stereotype formation. *Journal of Experimental Social Psychology*, 1978, *14*, 237–255.

Rotter, J. B. *Social learning and clinical psychology.* Englewood Cliffs, N.J.: Prentice-Hall, 1954.

Rotter, J. B. Generalized expectancies for internal versus external control of reinforcement. *Psychological Monographs*, 1966, *80*(1, Whole No. 609).

Rotter, J. B., Chance, J., & Phares, E. J. (Eds.). *Applications of a social learning theory of personality.* New York: Holt, Rinehart & Winston, 1972.

Rowland, K. F. Environmental events predicting death for the elderly. *Psychological Bulletin*, 1977, *84*, 349–372.

Rubenstein, C., & Shaver, P. The experience of loneliness. In L. A. Peplau & D. Perlman (Eds.), *Loneliness: A sourcebook of current theory, research, and therapy.* New York: Wiley, 1982.

Rubin, J. Z., & Brown, B. R. *The social psychology of bargaining and negotiation.* New York: Academic Press, 1975.

Rubin, Z., Peplau, L. A., & Hill, C. T. Loving and leaving: Sex differences in romantic attachments. Unpublished manuscript. Brandeis University, 1978.

Rubin, Z. Measurement of romantic love. *Journal of Personality and Social Psychology*, 1970, *16*, 265–273.

Rubin, Z. *Liking and loving: An invitation to social psychology.* New York: Holt, Rinehart & Winston, 1973.

Rugg, E. A. Social research practices opinion survey: Summary of results. Unpublished paper, George Peabody College, May 1975.

Rule, B. G., & Hewitt, L. S. Effects of thwarting on cardiac response and physical aggression. *Journal of Personality and Social Psychology*, 1971, *19*, 181–187.

Rule, B. G., & Leger, G. J. Pain cues and differing functions of aggression. *Canadian Journal of Behavioural Science*, 1976, *8*, 213–222.

Rule, B. G., & Nesdale, A. R. Cognition, arousal and aggression. In W. W. Waid (Ed.), *Sociophysiology.* New York: Springer-Verlag, 1983.

Rule, B. G., & Percival, E. The effects of frustration and attack on physical aggression. *Journal of Experimental Research in Personality*, 1971, *5*, 111–118.

Runkel, P. J., & McGrath, J. E. *Research on human behavior: A systematic guide to method.* New York: Holt, Rinehart & Winston, 1972.

Rush, M. C., Thomas, J. C., & Lord, R. G. Implicit leadership theory: A potential threat to the internal validity of leader behavior questionnaires. *Organizational Behavior and Human Performance*, 1977, *20*, 93–110.

Rushton, J. P. Effects of prosocial television and film material on the behavior of viewers. In L. Berkowitz (Ed.), *Advances in experimental social psychology* (Vol. 12). New York: Academic Press, 1979.

Rushton, J. P. *Altruism, socialization, and society.* Englewood Cliffs, N.J.: Prentice-Hall, 1980.

Rushton, J. P., & Sorrentino, R. M. (Eds.). *Altruism and helping behavior: Social, personality, and developmental perspectives.* Hillsdale, N.J.: Erlbaum, 1981.

Rushton, J. P., & Teachman, G. The effects of positive reinforcement, attributions, and punishment on model-induced altruism in children. *Personality and Social Psychology Bulletin*, 1978, *4*, 322–325.

Russell, J. A., & Mehrabian, A. Approach-avoidance and affiliation as functions of the emotion-eliciting quality of an environment. *Environment and Behavior*, 1978, *10*, 355–387.

Russo, N. F. Eye contact, interpersonal distance, and the equilibrium theory. *Journal of Personality and Social Psychology*, 1975, *31*, 497–502.

Ryan, W. *Blaming the victim.* New York: Pantheon, 1971.

Rychlak, J. F. *Introduction to personality and psychotherapy: A theory-construction approach.* Boston: Houghton Mifflin, 1973.

Rychlak, J. F. Psychological science as a humanist views it. In W. J. Arnold & J. K. Cole (Eds.), *Nebraska Symposium on Motivation* (Vol. 22). Lincoln: University of Nebraska Press, 1975.

Ryder, R. Husband-wife dyads versus married strangers. *Family Process*, 1968, *7*, 233–238.

Sadava, S. W. Teaching social psychology: A Canadian dilemma. *Canadian Psychological Review*, 1978, *19*, 145–151.

Saegert, S. C. Effects of spatial and social density on arousal, mood, and social orientation. Unpublished doctoral dissertation, University of Michigan, 1974.

Saegert, S. C., MacIntosh, B., & West, S. Two studies of crowding in urban spaces. *Environment and Behavior*, 1974, *7*, 159–184.

Saegert, S. C., Swap, W., & Zajonc, R. B. Exposure, context, and interpersonal attraction. *Journal of Personality and Social Psychology*, 1973, *25*, 234–242.

Saks, M. J. *Jury verdicts: The role of group size and social decision rule.* Lexington, Mass.: Lexington Books/Heath, 1977.

Saks, M. J., & Baron, C. H. (Eds.). *The use/nonuse/misuse of applied social research in the courts.* Cambridge, Mass.: Abt Books, 1980.

Saks, M. J., & Hastie, R. *Social psychology in the court.* New York: Van Nostrand Reinhold, 1978.

Saks, M. J., & Ostrom, T. M. Jury size and consensus requirements: The laws of probability versus the laws of the land. *Journal of Contemporary Law*, 1975, *1*, 163–173.

Salancik, G. R., & Pfeffer, J. Constraints on administrator discretion: The limited influence of mayors on city budgets. *Urban Affairs Quarterly*, 1977, *12*, 475–496.

Salinger, J. D. *The catcher in the rye.* New York: Signet, 1953.

Saltzer, E. B. Social determinants of successful weight loss: An analysis of behavioral intentions and actual behavior. *Basic and Applied Social Psychology*, 1980, *1*, 329–341.

Samerotte, G. C., & Harris, M. B. Some factors influencing helping: The effects of a handicap, responsibility, and requesting help. *Journal of Social Psychology*, 1976, *98*, 39–45.

Sampson, E. E. Psychology and the American ideal. *Journal of Personality and Social Psychology*, 1977, *35*, 767–782.

Sanday, P. R. The socio-cultural context of rape: A cross-cultural study. *Journal of Social Issues*, 1981, *37*(4), 5–27.

Sanders, G. S. Driven by distraction: An integrative review of social facilitation theory and research. *Journal of Experimental Social Psychology*, 1981, *17*, 227–251.

Sanford, F. H. *Authoritarianism and leadership*. Philadelphia: Institute for Research in Human Relations, 1950.

Sanford, N. The approach of the authoritarian personality. In J. L. McCary (Ed.), *Psychology of personality*. New York: Grove Press, 1956.

Sanford, N. Whatever happened to action research? *Journal of Social Issues*, 1970, *26*(4), 3–23.

Sasfy, J., & Okun, M. Form of evaluation and audience expertness as joint determinants of audience effects. *Journal of Experimental Social Psychology*, 1974, *10*, 461–467.

Saxe, L., & Fine, M. *Social experiments: Methods for design and evaluation*. Beverly Hills, Calif.: Sage, 1981.

Scarr, S., & Weinberg, R. A. IQ test performance of black children adopted by white families. *American Psychologist*, 1976, *31*, 726–739.

Schachter, S. Deviation, rejection, and communication. *Journal of Abnormal and Social Psychology*, 1951, *46*, 190–207.

Schachter, S. *The psychology of affiliation*. Stanford, Calif.: Stanford University Press, 1959.

Schachter, S. The interaction of cognitive and physiological determinants of emotional state. In L. Berkowitz (Ed.), *Advances in experimental social psychology* (Vol. 1). New York: Academic Press, 1964.

Schachter, S., Ellertson, N., McBride, D., & Gregory, D. An experimental study of cohesiveness and productivity. *Human Relations*, 1951, *4*, 229–238.

Schachter, S., & Singer, J. Cognitive, social, and physiological determinants of emotional state. *Psychological Review*, 1962, *69*, 379–399.

Schaeffer, G. H., & Patterson, M. L. Intimacy, arousal, and small group crowding. *Journal of Personality and Social Psychology*, 1980, *38*, 283–290.

Schaps, E. Cost, dependency, and helping. *Journal of Personality and Social Psychology*, 1972, *21*, 74–78.

Scheflen, A. *Body language and the social order*. Englewood Cliffs, N.J.: Prentice-Hall, 1972.

Scheier, M. F., & Carver, C. S. Individual differences in self-concept and self-process. In D. M. Wegner & R. R. Vallacher (Eds.), *The self in social psychology*. New York: Oxford University Press, 1980.

Scheier, M. F., & Carver, S. C. Private and public aspects of self. In L. Wheeler (Ed.), *Review of personality and social psychology* (Vol. 2). Beverly Hills, Calif.: Sage, 1981.

Scheier, M. F., Carver, C. S., & Gibbons, F. X. Self-directed attention, awareness of bodily states and suggestibility. *Journal of Personality and Social Psychology*, 1979, *37*, 1576–1588.

Schein, E. H. Reaction patterns to severe chronic stress in American army prisoners of war of the Chinese. *Journal of Social Issues*, 1957, *13*(3), 21–30.

Schill, T., & Chapin, J. Sex guilt and males' preference for reading erotic literature. *Journal of Consulting and Clinical Psychology*, 1972, *39*, 516.

Schlenker, B. R. Social psychology and science. *Journal of Personality and Social Psychology*, 1974, *29*, 1–15.

Schlenker, B. R. *Impression management: The self-concept, social identity, and interpersonal relations*. Monterey, Calif.: Brooks/Cole, 1980.

Schlenker, B. R., & Forsyth, D. R. On the ethics of psychological research. *Journal of Experimental Social Psychology*, 1977, *13*, 369–396.

Schlosberg, H. Three dimensions of emotion. *Psychological Review*, 1954, *61*, 81–88.

Schmidt, G., & Sigusch, V. Sex differences in responses to psychosexual stimulation by film and slides. *Journal of Sex Research*, 1970, *6*, 268–283.

Schmidt, G., Sigusch, V., & Meyberg, V. Psychosexual stimulation in men: Emotional reactions, changes of sex behavior, and measures of conservative attitudes. *Journal of Sex Research*, 1969, *5*, 199–217.

Schneider, D. J. Implicit personality theory: A review. *Psychological Bulletin*, 1973, *79*, 294–309.

Schneider, D. J., Hastorf, A. H., & Ellsworth, P. C. *Person perception* (2nd ed.). Reading, Mass.: Addison-Wesley, 1979.

Schneier, C. E. The contingency model of leadership: An extension of emergent leadership and leader's sex. *Organizational Behavior and Human Performance*, 1978, *21*, 220–239.

Schopler, J., & Stockdale, J. An interference analysis of crowding. *Environmental Psychology and Nonverbal Behavior*, 1977, *4*, 171–186.

Schopler, J., & Thompson, V. D. Role of attribution processes in mediating amount of reciprocity for a favor. *Journal of Personality and Social Psychology*, 1968, *10*, 243–250.

Schriesheim, C., & Kerr, S. Psychometric properties of the Ohio State leadership scales. *Psychological Bulletin*, 1974, *81*, 756–765.

Schulz, R., & Barefoot, J. Nonverbal responses and affiliative conflict theory. *British Journal of Social and Clinical Psychology*, 1974, *13*, 237–243.

Schwartz, G. E., Fair, P. L., Salt, P., Mandel, M. R., & Klerman, G. L. Facial muscle patterning to affective imagery in depressed and nondepressed subjects. *Science*, 1976, *192*, 489–491.

Schwartz, S. Effects of sex guilt and arousal on the retention of birth control information. *Journal of Consulting and Clinical Psychology*, 1973, *41*, 61–64.

Schwartz, S. H. Normative explanations of helping behavior: A critique, proposal, and empirical test. *Journal of Experimental Social Psychology*, 1973, *9*, 349–364.

Schwartz, S. H. Normative influences on altruism. In L. Berkowitz (Ed.), *Advances in experimental social psychology* (Vol. 10). New York: Academic Press, 1977.

Schwartz, S. H., & Clausen, G. T. Responsibility, norms, and helping in an emergency. *Journal of Personality and Social Psychology*, 1970, *16*, 299–310.

Schwartz, S. H., & Gottlieb, A. Bystander reactions to a violent theft: Crime in Jerusalem. *Journal of Personality and Social Psychology*, 1976, *34*, 1188–1199.

Schwartz, S. H., & Gottlieb, A. Bystander anonymity and reactions to emergencies. *Journal of Personality and Social Psychology*, 1980, *39*, 418–430.

Schwartz, S. H., & Gottlieb, A. Participants' postexperimental reactions and the ethics of bystander research. *Journal of Experimental Social Psychology*, 1981, *17*, 396–407.

Schwartz, S. H., & Howard, J. A. A normative decision-making model of altruism. In J. P. Rushton & R. M. Sorrentino (Eds.), *Altruism and helping behavior: Social, personality, and developmental perspectives*. Hillsdale, N.J.: Erlbaum, 1981.

Scott, J. P. *Aggression*. Chicago: University of Chicago Press, 1958.

Scott, R. L. Communication as an intentional, social system. *Human Communication Research*, 1977, *3*, 258–267.

Selby, J. W., Calhoun, L. G., & Brock, T. A. Sex differences in the social perception of rape victims. *Personality and Social Psychology Bulletin*, 1977, *3*, 412–415.

Seligman, C., & Darley, J. M. Feedback as a means of decreasing residential energy consumption. *Journal of Applied Psychology*, 1977, *62*, 363–368.

Seligman, C., Kriss, M., Darley, J. M., Fazio, R. H., Becker, L. J., & Pryor, J. B. Predicting summer energy consumption from homeowners' attitudes. *Journal of Applied Social Psychology*, 1979, *9*, 70–90.

Seligman, M. E. P. *Helplessness: On depression, development, and death*. San Francisco: W. H. Freeman, 1975.

Selltiz, C., Wrightsman, L. S., & Cook, S. W. *Research methods in social relations* (3rd ed.). New York: Holt, Rinehart & Winston, 1976.

Selye, H. The evolution of the stress concept. In L. Levi (Ed.), *Society, stress, and disease* (Vol. I). London: Oxford University Press, 1971.

Seta, J. J. The impact of comparison processes on coactor's task performance. *Journal of Personality and Social Psychology*, 1982, *42*, 281–291.

Seyfried, B. A., & Hendrick, C. When do opposites attract? When they are opposite in sex and sex-role attitudes. *Journal of Personality and Social Psychology*, 1973, *25*, 15–20.

Shannon, C., & Weaver, W. *The mathematical theory of communication*. Urbana: University of Illinois Press, 1949.

Shanteau, J., & Nagy, G. F. Probability of acceptance in dating choice. *Journal of Personality and Social Psychology*, 1979, *37*, 522–533.

Sharp, G. *Exploring nonviolent alternatives*. Boston: Porter Sargent, 1970.

Sharp, G. *The politics of nonviolent action*. Philadelphia: Pilgrim Press, 1971.

Shaver, P. State and trait loneliness during the transition into college. Paper presented at Nags Head Conference on Social Interaction, North Carolina, 1982.

Shaver, P., & Klinnert, M. Schachter's theories of affiliation and emotion: Implications of developmental research. In L. Wheeler (Ed.), *Review of personality and social psychology* (Vol. 3). Beverly Hills, Calif.: Sage, 1982.

Shaw, M. E. A comparison of individuals and small groups in the rational solution of complex problems. *American Journal of Psychology*, 1932, *44*, 491–504.

Shaw, M. E. Some effects of unequal distribution of information upon group performance in various communication nets. *Journal of Abnormal and Social Psychology*, 1954, *49*, 547–553.

Shaw, M. E. Communication networks. In L. Berkowitz (Ed.), *Advances in experimental social psychology* (Vol. 1). New York: Academic Press, 1964.

Shaw, M. E. Communication networks fourteen years later. In L. Berkowitz (Ed.), *Group processes*. New York: Academic Press, 1978.

Shaw, M. E. *Group dynamics: The psychology of small group behavior* (3rd ed.). New York: McGraw-Hill, 1981.

Shaw, M. E., & Costanzo, P. R. *Theories of social psychology* (2nd ed.). New York: McGraw-Hill, 1982.

Shaw, M. E., & Rothschild, G. H. Some effects of prolonged experience in communication nets. *Journal of Applied Psychology*, 1956, *40*, 281–286.

Shein, V. E. The relationship between sex-role stereotypes and requisite management characteristics. *Journal of Applied Psychology*, 1973, *57*, 95–100.

Shein, V. E. Relationships between sex-role stereotypes and requisite management characteristics among female managers. *Journal of Applied Psychology*, 1975, *60*, 340–344.

Sherif, C. W., Sherif, M., & Nebergall, R. E. *Attitude and attitude change: The social judgment approach*. Philadelphia: Saunders, 1965.

Sherif, M. A study of some social factors in perception. *Archives of Psychology*, 1935, *27*, No. 187, 1–60.

Sherif, M. *In common predicament: Social psychology of intergroup conflict and cooperation*. Boston: Houghton Mifflin, 1966.

Sherif, M., Harvey, O. J., White, B. J., Hood, W. E., & Sherif, C. W. *Intergroup conflict and cooperation: The Robber's Cave experiment*. Norman: University of Oklahoma Book Exchange, 1961.

Sherif, M., & Hovland, C. *Social judgment*. New Haven, Conn.: Yale University Press, 1961.

Sherif, M., & Sherif, C. W. Research on intergroup relations. In W. G. Austin & S. Worchel (Eds.), *The social psychology of intergroup relations*. Monterey, Calif.: Brooks/Cole, 1979.

Sherif, M., Taub, D., & Hovland, C. I. Assimilation and contrast effects of anchoring stimuli on judgments. *Journal of Experimental Psychology*, 1958, *55*, 150–155.

Sherrod, D. R. Crowding, perceived control, and behavioral aftereffects. *Journal of Applied Social Psychology*, 1974, *4*, 171–186.

Sherrod, D. R., Armstrong, D., Hewitt, J., Madonia, B., Speno, S., & Teruya, D. Environmental attention, affect and altruism. *Journal of Applied Social Psychology*, 1977, *7*, 359–371.

Sherrod, D. R., & Downs, R. Environmental determinants of altruism: The effects of stimulus overload and perceived control on helping. *Journal of Experimental Social Psychology*, 1974, *10*, 468–479.

Shettel-Neuber, J., Bryson, J. B., & Young, L. E. Physical attractiveness of the "other person" and jealousy. *Personality and Social Psychology Bulletin*, 1978, *4*, 612–615.

Shields, S. A. Functionalism, Darwinism, and the psychology of women. *American Psychologist*, 1975, *30*, 739–754.

Shirom, A. Strike characteristics as determinants of strike settlements: A chief negotiator's viewpoint. *Journal of Applied Psychology*, 1982, *67*, 45–52.

Shotland, R. L., & Stebbins, C. A. Bystander response to rape: Can a victim attract help? *Journal of Applied Social Psychology*, 1980, *10*, 510–527.

Shuntich, R. J., & Taylor, S. P. The effects of alcohol on human physical aggression. *Journal of Experimental Research in Personality*, 1972, *6*, 34–38.

Siegman, A. W. A cross-cultural investigation of the relationship between ethnic prejudice, authoritarian ideology, and personality. *Journal of Abnormal and Social Psychology*, 1961, *63*, 654–655.

Sigall, H. E., Aronson, E., & Van Hoose, T. The cooperative subject: Myth or reality? *Journal of Experimental Social Psychology*, 1970, *6*, 1–10.

Sigall, H., & Landy, D. Radiating beauty: The effects of having a physically attractive partner on person perception. *Journal of Personality and Social Psychology*, 1973, *28*, 218–224.

Silverman, I. Why social psychology fails. *Canadian Psychological Review*, 1977, *18*, 353–358.

Silverthorne, C. P., & Mazmanian, L. The effects of heckling and media of presentation on the impact of a persuasive communication. *Journal of Social Psychology*, 1975, *96*, 229–236.

Simonton, D. K. Multiple discovery and invention: *Zeitgeist*, genius, or chance? *Journal of Personality and Social Psychology*, 1979, *37*, 1603–1616.

Singer, J. E., & Shockley, V. L. Ability and evaluation. *Journal of Personality and Social Psychology*, 1965, *1*, 95–100.

Singer, J. L., & Singer, D. G. *Television, imagination, and aggression: A study of preschoolers' play.* Hillsdale, N.J.: Erlbaum, 1981.

Sivacek, J., & Crano, W. D. Vested interest as a moderator of attitude-behavior consistency. *Journal of Personality and Social Psychology*, 1982, *43*, 210–221.

Skinner, B. F. *Beyond freedom and dignity.* New York: Knopf, 1971.

Slater, P. E. Contrasting correlates of group size. *Sociometry*, 1958, *25*, 129–139.

Sloan, L. R., Love, R. E., & Ostrom, T. M. Political heckling: Who really loses? *Journal of Personality and Social Psychology*, 1974, *30*, 518–525.

Smedley, J. W., & Bayton, J. A. Evaluative race-class stereotypes by race and perceived class of subjects. *Journal of Personality and Social Psychology*, 1978, *36*, 530–535.

Smigel, E. O., & Seiden, R. The decline and fall of the double standard. *Annals of the American Academy of Political and Social Sciences*, 1968, *376*, 1–14.

Smith, D. E., Gier, J. A., & Willis, F. N. Interpersonal touch and compliance with a marketing request. *Basic and Applied Social Psychology*, 1982, *3*, 35–38.

Smith, E. R., & Kluegel, J. R. Cognitive and social bases of emotional experience: Outcome, attribution, and affect. *Journal of Personality and Social Psychology*, 1982, *43*, 1129–1141.

Smith, M. B., Bruner, J. S., & White, R. W. *Opinions and personality.* New York: Wiley, 1956.

Smith, P. W., & Brigham, J. C. The functional approach to attitude change: An attempt at operationalization. *Representative Research in Social Psychology*, 1972, *3*, 73–80.

Smith, R. E., Keating, J. P., Hester, R. K., & Mitchell, H. E. Role and justice considerations in the attribution of responsibility to a rape victim. *Journal of Research in Personality*, 1976, *10*, 346–357.

Smith, E. R., & Miller, F. D. Limits on perception of cognitive processes: A reply to Nisbett and Wilson. *Psychological Review*, 1978, *85*, 355–362.

Smitherman, G., & McGinnis, J. Black language and Black liberation. In R. L. Jones (Ed.), *Black psychology* (2nd ed.). New York: Harper & Row, 1980.

Snyder, C. R., Ingram, R. E., Handelsman, M. M., Wells, D. S., & Huwieler, R. Desire for personal feedback: Who wants it and what does it mean for psychotherapy? *Journal of Personality*, 1982, *50*, 316–330.

Snyder, M. The self-monitoring of expressive behavior. *Journal of Personality and Social Psychology*, 1974, *30*, 526–537.

Snyder, M. Self-monitoring processes. In L. Berkowitz (Ed.), *Advances in experimental social psychology* (Vol. 12). New York: Academic Press, 1979.

Snyder, M. On the influence of individuals on situations. In N. Cantor & J. F. Kohlstrom (Eds.), *Personality, cognition, and social interaction*. Hillsdale, N.J.: Erlbaum, 1981.

Snyder, M., & Ickes, W. Personality and social behavior. In G. Lindzey & E. Aronson (Eds.), *Handbook of social psychology* (3rd ed.). Reading, Mass.: Addison-Wesley, in press.

Snyder, M., & Monson, T. C. Persons, situations, and the control of social behavior. *Journal of Personality and Social Psychology*, 1975, *32*, 637–644.

Snyder, M., & Swann, W. B., Jr. Behavioral confirmation in social interaction: From social perception to social reality. *Journal of Experimental Social Psychology*, 1978, *14*, 148–162.

Snyder, M., Tanke, E. D., & Berscheid, E. Social perception and interpersonal behavior: On the self-fulfilling nature of social stereotypes. *Journal of Personality and Social Psychology*, 1977, *35*, 656–666.

Snyder, M., & White, P. Moods and memories: Elation, depression, and the remembering of the events of one's life. *Journal of Personality*, 1982, *50*, 149–167.

Snyder, M. L., & Mentzer, S. Social psychological perspectives on the physician's feelings and behavior. *Personality and Social Psychology Bulletin*, 1978, *4*, 541–547.

Solano, C. H., Batten, P. G., & Parish, E. A. Loneliness and patterns of self-disclosure. *Journal of Personality and Social Psychology*, 1982, *43*, 524–531.

Sole, K., Marton, J., & Hornstein, H. A. Opinion similarity and helping: Three field experiments investigating the bases of promotive tension. *Journal of Experimental Social Psychology*, 1975, *11*, 1–13.

Solly, C. M. Effects of stress on perceptual attention. In B. P. Rourke (Ed.), *Explorations in the psychology of stress and anxiety*. Ontario: Longmans Canada Ltd., 1969.

Solomon, L. Z., Solomon, H., & Stone, R. Helping as a function of number of bystanders and ambiguity of emergency. *Personality and Social Psychology Bulletin*, 1978, *4*, 318–321.

Solomon, S., & Saxe, L. What is intelligent, as well as attractive, is good. *Personality and Social Psychology Bulletin*, 1977, *3*, 670–673.

Sommer, R. The ecology of privacy. *Library Quarterly*, 1966, *36*, 234–248.

Sommer, R. Classroom ecology. *Journal of Applied Behavioral Science*, 1967, *3*, 489–503.

Sommer, R. *Personal space: The behavioral basis of design.* Englewood Cliffs, N.J.: Prentice-Hall, 1969.

Sommer, R. *Tight spaces.* Englewood Cliffs, N.J.: Prentice-Hall, 1974.

Sommer, R., & Becker, F. D. Territorial defense and the good neighbor. *Journal of Personality and Social Psychology*, 1969, *11*, 85–92.

Sommer, R., & Olsen, H. The soft classroom. *Environment and Behavior*, 1980, *12*, 3–16.

Sommer, R., & Ross, H. Social interaction on a geriatrics ward. *International Journal of Social Psychiatry*, 1958, *4*, 128–133.

Sorenson, R. C. *Adolescent sexuality in contemporary America.* New York: World Publishing, 1973.

Sorrentino, R. M., & Boutilier, R. G. Evaluation of a victim as a function of fate similarity/dissimilarity. *Journal of Experimental Social Psychology*, 1974, *10*, 84–93.

Spence, J. T., Deaux, K., & Helmreich, R. L. Sex roles in contemporary American society. In G. Lindzey & E. Aronson (Eds.), *Handbook of social psychology* (3rd ed.). Reading, Mass.: Addison-Wesley, in press.

Spence, J. T., & Helmreich, R. L. Who likes competent women? Competence, sex-role congruence of interests, and subjects' attitudes toward women as determinants of interpersonal attraction. *Journal of Applied Social Psychology*, 1972, *3*, 197–213.

Spence, J. T., & Helmreich, R. L. *Masculinity and femininity: Their psychological dimensions, correlates, and antecedents.* Austin: University of Texas Press, 1978.

Spence, J. T., & Helmreich, R. L. Masculine instrumentality and feminine expressiveness: Their relationships with sex role attitudes and behaviors. *Psychology of Women Quarterly*, 1980, *5*, 147–163.

Spence, J. T., Helmreich, R., & Stapp, J. The Personal Attributes Questionnaire: A measure of sex-role stereotypes and masculinity-femininity. *JSAS Catalog of Selected Documents in Psychology*, 1974, *4*, 127.

Staats, A. W. An outline of an integrated learning theory of attitude formation and function. In M. Fishbein (Ed.), *Readings in attitude theory and measurement.* New York: Wiley, 1967.

Staats, A. W., & Staats, C. K. Attitudes established by classical conditioning. *Journal of Abnormal and Social Psychology*, 1958, *57*, 37–40.

Stagner, R., & Eflal, B. Internal union dynamics during a strike: A quasi-experimental study. *Journal of Applied Psychology*, 1982, *67*, 37–44.

Stang, D. J. Conformity, ability, and self-esteem. *Representative Research in Social Psychology*, 1972, *3*, 97–103.

Stang, D. J. Group size effects on conformity. *Journal of Social Psychology*, 1976, *98*, 175–181.

Staub, E. Helping a distressed person: Social, personality, and stimulus determinants. In L. Berkowitz (Ed.), *Advances in experimental social psychology* (Vol. 7). New York: Academic Press, 1974.

Staub, E. (Ed.). *Positive social behavior and morality* (Vol. 1). *Social and personal influences.* New York: Academic Press, 1978.

Staub, E. (Ed.). *Positive social behavior and morality* (Vol. 2). *Socialization and development.* New York: Academic Press, 1979.

Steck, L., Levitan, D., McLane, D., & Kelley, H. H. Care, need, and conceptions of love. *Journal of Personality and Social Psychology*, 1982, *43*, 481–491.

Steele, C. M., Southwick, L. L., & Critchlow, B. Dissonance and alcohol: Drinking your troubles away. *Journal of Personality and Social Psychology*, 1981, *41*, 831–846.

Stein, D. D., Hardyck, J. A., & Smith, M. B. Race and belief: An open and shut case. *Journal of Personality and Social Psychology*, 1965, *1*, 281–289.

Steiner, I. D. *Group process and productivity.* New York: Academic Press, 1972.

Steiner, I. D., & Johnson, H. Authoritarianism and "tolerance of trait inconsistency." *Journal of Abnormal and Social Psychology*, 1963, *67*, 388–391. (a)

Steiner, I. D., & Johnson, H. H. Authoritarianism and conformity. *Sociometry*, 1963, *26*, 21–34. (b)

Steinmetz, S. K., & Straus, M. A. The family as cradle of violence. *Society* (formerly *Trans/Action*), 1973, *10*, 50–56.

Steinmetz, S. K., & Straus, M. A. (Eds.). *Violence in the family.* New York: Dodd, Mead, 1974.

Steinzor, B. The spatial factor in face-to-face discussion groups. *Journal of Abnormal and Social Psychology*, 1950, *45*, 522–555.

Stephan, W. G. School desegregation: An evaluation of predictions made in *Brown v. The Board of Education. Psychological Bulletin*, 1978, *85*, 217–238.

Stephan, W., Berscheid, E., & Walster, E. Sexual arousal and heterosexual perception. *Journal of Personality and Social Psychology*, 1971, *20*, 93–101.

Stern, P. C., & Gardner, G. T. Psychological research and energy policy. *American Psychologist*, 1981, *36*, 329–342.

Stewart, A. J., & Rubin, Z. The power motive in dating couples. *Journal of Personality and Social Psychology*, 1976, *34*, 305–309.

Stires, L. K. Classroom seating location, student grades, and attitudes: Environment or self selection? *Environment and Behavior*, 1980, *12*, 241–254.

Stogdill, R. M. Personal factors associated with leadership. *Journal of Psychology*, 1948, *23*, 36–71.

Stogdill, R. M. *Manual for the Leader Behavior Description Questionnaire—Form XII.* Bureau of Business Research, Ohio State University, 1963.

Stogdill, R. M. Validity of leader behavior descriptions. *Personnel Psychology*, 1969, *22*, 153–158.

Stogdill, R. M. *Handbook of leadership: A survey of theory and research.* New York: Free Press, 1974.

Stokols, D. The experience of crowding in primary and secondary environments. *Environment and Behavior*, 1976, *8*, 49–86.

Stokols, D. A typology of crowding experiences. In A. Baum & Y. Epstein (Eds.), *Human response to crowding.* Hillsdale, N.J.: Erlbaum, 1978.

Stokols, D., Rall, M., Pinner, B., & Schopler, J. Physical, social, and personal determinants of the perception of crowding. *Environment and Behavior*, 1973, *5*, 87–115.

Stoller, R. J. Sexual excitement. *Archives of General Psychiatry*, 1976, *33*, 899–909.

Stoner, J. A. F. A comparison of individual and group decisions involving risk. Unpublished master's thesis, School of Industrial Management, M.I.T., 1961.

Storms, M. D. Videotape and the attribution process: Reversing actors' and observers' points of view. *Journal of Personality and Social Psychology*, 1973, 27, 165–175.

Storms, M. D. A theory of erotic orientation development. *Psychological Review*, 1981, *88*, 340–353.

Stotland, E., Katz, D., & Patchen, M. The reduction of prejudice through the arousal of self-insight. *Journal of Personality*, 1959, *27*, 507–531.

Straus, M. Some social antecedents of physical punishment: A linkage theory interpretation. *Journal of Marriage and the Family*, 1971, *33*, 658–663.

Straus, M. A. A general systems theory approach to a theory of violence between family members. *Social Science Information*, 1973, *12*, 105–125.

Straus, M. A. The marriage license as a hitting license: Social instigation of physical aggression in the family. Paper presented at meeting of American Psychological Association, Chicago, September 1975.

Straus, M. A., Gelles, R. J., & Steinmetz, S. K. *Behind closed doors: Violence in the American family.* New York: Doubleday, 1980.

Streufert, S., Castore, C. H., & Kliger, S. C. *A tactical and negotiations game: Rationale, method, and analysis.* Technical Report No. 1, 1967, Purdue University, Office of Naval Research.

Strickland, B. R. Internal-external control of reinforcement. In T. Blass (Ed.), *Personality variables in social behaviors.* Hillsdale, N.J.: Erlbaum, 1977.

Strodtbeck, F. L. Husband-wife interaction over revealed differences. *American Sociological Review*, 1951, *16*, 468–473.

Strodtbeck, F. L. Family interaction, values and achievement. In D. McClelland (Ed.), *Talent and society.* Princeton, N.J.: Van Nostrand, 1958.

Strodtbeck, F., & Hook, H. The social dimensions of a 12-man jury table. *Sociometry*, 1961, *24*, 397–415.

Strodtbeck, F., James, R., & Hawkins, C. Social status in jury deliberations. *American Sociological Review*, 1957, 22, 713–718.

Strodtbeck, F., & Mann, R. Sex role differentiation in jury deliberations. *Sociometry*, 1956, *19*, 3–11.

Strube, M. J. & Garcia, J. E. A meta-analytic investigation of Fiedler's contingency model of leadership effectiveness. *Psychological Bulletin*, 1981, *90*, 307–321.

Struening, E. L., & Guttentag, M. (Eds.). *Handbook of evaluation research* (Vol. 1). Beverly Hills, Calif.: Sage, 1975.

Suedfeld, P. Aloneness as a healing experience. In L. A. Peplau & D. Perlman (Eds.), *Loneliness: A sourcebook of current theory, research and therapy.* New York: Wiley, 1982.

Suedfeld, P., & Rank, A. D. Revolutionary leaders: Long-term success as a function of changes in conceptual complexity. *Journal of Personality and Social Psychology*, 1976, *34*, 169–178.

Sullivan, H. S. *The interpersonal theory of psychiatry.* New York: Norton, 1953.

Suls, J., Gaes, G., & Gastorf, J. Evaluating a sex-related ability: Comparison with same-, opposite-, and combined-sex norms. *Journal of Research in Personality*, 1979, *13*, 294–304.

Suls, J., Gastorf, J., & Lawhon, J. Social comparison choices for evaluating a sex- and age-related ability. *Personality and Social Psychology Bulletin*, 1978, 4, 102–105.

Suls, J. M., & Miller, R. L. (Eds.). *Social comparison processes: Theoretical and empirical perspectives.* Washington, D.C.: Halsted-Wiley, 1977.

Suls, J., & Mullen, B. Life change and psychological distress: The role of perceived control and desirability. *Journal of Applied Social Psychology*, 1981, *11*, 379–389.

Summers, D. A., Ashworth, C. D., & Feldman-Summers, S. Judgment processes and interpersonal conflict related to societal problem solutions. *Journal of Applied Social Psychology*, 1977, 7, 163–174.

Sundstrom, E. An experimental study of crowding: Effects of room-size, intrusion, and goal-blocking on nonverbal behavior, self-disclosure, and self-reported stress. *Journal of Personality and Social Psychology*, 1975, 32, 645–654. (a)

Sundstrom, E. Toward an interpersonal model of crowding. *Sociological Symposium*, 1975, *No. 14*, 124–144. (b)

Sundstrom, E. Crowding as a sequential process: Review of research on the effects of population density on humans. In A. Baum & Y. Epstein (Eds.), *Human response to crowding.* Hillsdale, N.J.: Erlbaum, 1978.

Sundstrom, E., & Altman, I. Field study of territorial behavior and dominance. *Journal of Personality and Social Psychology*, 1974, *30*, 115–124.

Sundstrom, E., & Altman, I. Personal space and interpersonal relationships: Research review and theoretical model. *Human Ecology*, 1976, *4*(1), 47–67.

Sundstrom, E., Herbert, R. K., & Brown, D. Privacy and communication in an open plan office: A case study. *Environment and Behavior*, 1982, *14*, 379–392.

Sundstrom, E., Town, J., Brown, D., Forman, A., & McGee, C. Physical enclosure, type of job, and privacy in the office. *Environment and Behavior*, 1982, *14*, 543–559.

Swann, W. B., Jr., & Miller, L. C. Why never forgetting a face matters: Visual imagery and social memory. *Journal of Personality and Social Psychology*, 1982, *43*, 475–480.

Swift, J. *Gulliver's travels.* New York: New American Library, 1960. (Originally published, 1726.)

Symonds, M. Victims of violence: Psychological effects and aftereffects. *American Journal of Psychoanalysis*, 1975, *35*, 19–26.

Szent-Györgyi, A. Looking back. *Perspectives in Biology and Medicine*, 1971, *15*, 1–6.

Szybillo, G. J., & Heslin, R. Resistance to persuasion: Inoculation theory in a marketing context. *Journal of Marketing Research*, 1973, *10*, 396–403.

Tajfel, H. Social psychology of intergroup relations. In M. R. Rosenzweig & L. W. Porter (Eds.), *Annual review of psychology* (Vol. 33). Palo Alto, Calif.: Annual Reviews, 1982.

Taylor, D. W., Berry, P. C., & Block, C. H. Does group participation when using brainstorming facilitate or inhibit creative thinking? *Administrative Science Quarterly*, 1958, *3*, 23–47.

Taylor, M. C., & Hall, J. A. Psychological androgyny: Theories, methods, and conclusions. *Psychological Bulletin*, 1982, *92*, 347–366.

Taylor, R. B. Human territoriality: A review and discussion of research needs. Unpublished manuscript, Virginia Polytechnic Institute and State University, 1978.

Taylor, R. B., & Lanni, J. C. Territorial dominance: The influence of the resident advantage in triadic decision making. *Journal of Personality and Social Psychology*, 1981, *41*, 909–915.

Taylor, S. E. A developing role for social psychology in medicine and medical practice. *Personality and Social Psychology Bulletin*, 1978, *4*, 515–523.

Taylor, S. E. Social cognition and health. *Personality and Social Psychology Bulletin*, 1982, *8*, 549–562.

Taylor, S. E., & Crocker, J. Schematic bases of information processing. In E. T. Higgins, C. P. Herman, & M. P. Zanna (Eds.), *Social cognition: The Ontario Symposium* (Vol. 1). Hillsdale, N. J.: Erlbaum, 1981.

Taylor, S. E., Fiske, S. T., Etcoff, N. L., & Ruderman, A. J. Categorical and contextual bases of person memory and stereotyping. *Journal of Personality and Social Psychology*, 1978, *36*, 778–793.

Taylor, S. E., & Levin, S. *The psychological impact of breast cancer: Theory and research*. San Francisco: West Coast Cancer Foundation, 1976.

Taylor, S. E., & Thompson, S. C. Stalking the elusive "vividness" effect. *Psychological Review*, 1982, *89*, 155–181.

Taylor, S. P. Aggressive behavior and physiological arousal as a function of provocation and the tendency to inhibit aggression. *Journal of Personality*, 1967, *35*, 297–310.

Taylor, S. P., & Epstein, S. Aggression as a function of the interaction of sex of the aggressor and the sex of the victim. *Journal of Personality*, 1967, *35*, 474–486.

Taylor, S. P., & Gammon, C. B. Effects of type and dose of alcohol on human physical aggression. *Journal of Personality and Social Psychology*, 1975, *32*, 169–175.

Taylor, S. P., & Gammon, C. B. Aggressive behavior of intoxicated subjects: The effect of third-party intervention. *Journal of Studies on Alcohol*, 1976, *37*, 917–930.

Taylor, S. P., Gammon, C. B., & Capasso, D. R. Aggression as a function of the interaction of alcohol and threat. *Journal of Personality and Social Psychology*, 1976, *34*, 938–941.

Taylor, S. P., & Pisano, R. Physical aggression as a function of frustration and physical attack. *Journal of Social Psychology*, 1971, *84*, 261–267.

Taylor, S. P., Schmutte, G. T., & Leonard, K. E., Jr. Physical aggression as a function of alcohol and frustration. *Bulletin of the Psychonomic Society*, 1977, *9*, 217–218.

Taylor, S. P., Vardaris, R. M., Rawtich, A. B., Gammon, C. B., Cranston, J. W., & Lubetkin, A. I. The effects of alcohol and delta-9-tetrahydrocannabinol on human physical aggression. *Aggressive Behavior*, 1976, *2*(2), 153–161.

Taynor, J., & Deaux, K. When women are more deserving than men: Equity, attribution, and perceived sex differences. *Journal of Personality and Social Psychology*, 1973, *28*, 360–367.

Terborg, J. R., & Ilgen, D. R. A theoretical approach to sex discrimination in traditionally masculine occupations. *Organizational Behavior and Human Performance*, 1975, *13*, 352–376.

Tesser, A., Gatewood, R., & Driver, M. Some determinants of gratitude. *Journal of Personality and Social Psychology*, 1968, *9*, 233–236.

Tessler, R. C., & Schwartz, S. H. Help-seeking, self-esteem, and achievement motivation: An attributional analysis. *Journal of Personality and Social Psychology*, 1972, *21*, 318–326.

Tetlock, P. E. Identifying victims of groupthink from public statements of decision makers. *Journal of Personality and Social Psychology*, 1979, *37*, 1314–1324.

Tetlock, P. E. Pre- to post-election shifts in Presidential rhetoric: Impression management or cognitive adjustment? *Journal of Personality and Social Psychology*, 1981, *41*, 207–212.

Thibaut, J. W., & Kelley, H. H. *The social psychology of groups*. New York: Wiley, 1959.

Thompson, W. C., Cowan, C. L., & Rosenhan, D. L. Focus of attention mediates the impact of negative affect on altruism. *Journal of Personality and Social Psychology*, 1980, *38*, 291–300.

Thorngate, W. The analysis of variability in social psychology. Unpublished manuscript, University of Alberta, 1974.

Thornton, B. Toward a linear prediction model of marital happiness. *Personality and Social Psychology Bulletin*, 1977, *3*, 674–676.

Thurstone, L. L. Attitudes can be measured. *American Journal of Sociology*, 1928, *33*, 529–554.

Tiger, L. *Men in groups*. New York: Random House, 1969.

Tillack, W. S., Tyler, C. W., Paquette, R., & Jones, P. H. A study of premarital pregnancies. *American Journal of Public Health*, 1972, *62*, 676–679.

Trager, G. L. Paralanguage: A first approximation. *Studies in Linguistics*, 1958, *13*, 1–12.

Traupmann, J., Petersen, R., Utne, M., & Hatfield, E. Measuring equity in intimate relations. *Applied Psychological Measurement*, 1981, *5*, 467–480.

Triandis, H. C. A note on Rokeach's theory of prejudice. *Journal of Abnormal and Social Psychology*, 1961, *62*, 184–186.

Triandis, H. C. *Interpersonal behavior*. Monterey, Calif.: Brooks/Cole, 1977. (a)

Triandis, H. C. Some universals of social behavior. Address presented at meeting of American Psychological Association, San Francisco, August 1977. (b)

Triandis, H. C. Introduction. In H. C. Triandis & W. W. Lambert (Eds.), *Handbook of cross-cultural psychology*. Vol. 1: *Perspectives*. Boston: Allyn & Bacon, 1980.

Triandis, H. C., Davis, E. E., & Takezawa, S. I. Some determinants of social distance among American, German, and Japanese students. *Journal of Personality and Social Psychology*, 1965, *2*, 540–551.

Triandis, H. C., & Lambert, W. W. (Eds.). *Handbook of cross-cultural psychology*. Vol. 1: *Perspectives*. Boston: Allyn & Bacon, 1980.

Triandis, H. C., & Lonner, W. (Eds.). *Handbook of cross-cul-*

tural psychology. Vol. 3: *Basic processes.* Boston: Allyn & Bacon, 1980.

Triandis, H. C., & Vassiliou, V. Frequency of contact and stereotyping. *Journal of Personality and Social Psychology,* 1967, *7,* 316–328.

Triplett, N. The dynamogenic factors in pacemaking and competition. *American Journal of Psychology,* 1897, *9,* 507–533.

Trivers, R. L. The evolution of reciprocal altruism. *Quarterly Review of Biology,* 1971, *46,* 35–57.

Trivers, R. L., & Hare, H. Haplodiploidy and the evolution of the social insects. *Science,* 1976, *191,* 249–263.

Trope, Y., & Ben-Yair, E. Task construction and persistence as means for self-assessment of abilities. *Journal of Personality and Social Psychology,* 1982, *42,* 637–645.

Tunnell, G. B. Three dimensions of naturalness: An expanded definition of field research. *Psychological Bulletin,* 1977, *84,* 426–437.

Turner, C. W., & Berkowitz, L. Identification with film aggressor (covert role taking) and reactions to film violence. *Journal of Personality and Social Psychology,* 1972, *21,* 256–264.

Turner, C. W., Layton, J. F., & Simons, L. S. Naturalistic studies of aggressive behavior: Aggressive stimuli, victim visibility, and horn honking. *Journal of Personality and Social Psychology,* 1975, *31,* 1098–1107.

Turner, C. W., & Simons, L. S. Effects of subject sophistication and evaluation apprehension on aggressive responses to weapons. *Journal of Personality and Social Psychology,* 1974, *30,* 341–348.

Tversky, A., & Kahneman, D. Availability: A heuristic for judging frequency and probability. *Cognitive Psychology,* 1973, *5,* 207–232.

Tyler, L. *Individuality: Human possibilities and personal choice in the psychological development of men and women.* San Francisco: Jossey-Bass, 1978.

Tyler, T. R., & Caine, A. The influence of outcomes and procedures on satisfaction with formal leaders. *Journal of Personality and Social Psychology,* 1981, *41,* 642–655.

Tyler, T. R., & Sears, D. O. Coming to like obnoxious people when we must live with them. *Journal of Personality and Social Psychology,* 1977, *35,* 200–211.

Underwood, B., & Moore, B. Perspective-taking and altruism. *Psychological Bulletin,* 1982, *91,* 143–173.

U.S. Commission on Civil Rights. *Racism in America and how to combat it.* Washington, D.C.: U.S. Government Printing Office, 1969.

U.S. President's Commission on Obscenity and Pornography. *Report.* Washington, D.C.: U.S. Government Printing Office, 1971.

U.S. Riot Commission. *Report of the National Advisory Commission on Civil Disorders.* New York: Bantam Books, 1968.

Valle, V. A., & Frieze, I. H. Stability of causal attributions in changing expectations for success. *Journal of Personality and Social Psychology,* 1976, *33,* 579–587.

Varela, J. A. Aplicación de hallazgos provenientes de las ciencias sociales. *Revista Interamericana de Psicología,* 1969, *3,* 45–52.

Varela, J. A. *Psychological solutions to social problems: An introduction to social technology.* New York: Academic Press, 1971.

Varela, J. A. Social technology. *American Psychologist,* 1977, *32,* 914–923.

Varela, J. A. Solving human problems with human science. *Human Nature,* October 1978, pp. 84–90.

Vinsel, A., Brown, B. B., Altman, I., & Foss, C. Privacy regulation, territorial displays, and effectiveness of individual functioning. *Journal of Personality and Social Psychology,* 1980, *39,* 1104–1115.

Vinokur, A. A review and theoretical analysis of the effects of group processes upon individual and group decisions involving risk. *Psychological Bulletin,* 1971, *76,* 231–250.

Vollmer, H. M. Basic rules for applying social science to urban and social problems. *Urban and Social Change Review,* 1970, *3*(2), 32–33.

von Baeyer, C. L., Sherk, D. L., & Zanna, M. P. Impression management in the job interview: When the female applicant meets the male (chauvinist) interviewer. *Personality and Social Psychology Bulletin,* 1981, *7,* 45–51.

von Cranach, M., & Ellgring, J. H. Problems in the recognition of gaze direction. In M. von Cranach and I. Vine (Eds.), *Social communication and movement.* New York: Academic Press, 1973.

Vraa, C. W. Emotional climate as a function of group composition. *Small Group Behavior,* 1974, *5,* 105–120.

Waller, W. W. The rating and dating complex. *American Sociological Review,* 1937, *2,* 727–737.

Wallston, B. S., & Wallston, K. A. Locus of control and health: A review of the literature. *Health Education Monographs,* 1978, *6,* 107–117.

Walster, E., Aronson, E., & Abrahams, D. On increasing the persuasiveness of a low prestige communicator. *Journal of Experimental Social Psychology,* 1966, *2,* 325–342.

Walster, E., Aronson, V., Abrahams, D., & Rottman, L. Importance of physical attractiveness in dating behavior. *Journal of Personality and Social Psychology,* 1966, *4,* 508–516.

Walster, E., & Berscheid, E. A little bit about love: A minor essay on a major topic. In T. L. Huston (Ed.), *Foundations of interpersonal attraction.* New York: Academic Press, 1974.

Walster, E., & Piliavin, J. A. Equity and the innocent bystander. *Journal of Social Issues,* 1972, *28*(3), 165–189.

Walster, E., & Walster, G. W. *Love.* Reading, Mass.: Addison-Wesley, 1978.

Walster, E., Walster, G. W., & Berscheid, E. *Equity: Theory and research.* Boston: Allyn & Bacon, 1978.

Walster, E., Walster, G. W., & Traupmann, J. Equity and premarital sex. *Journal of Personality and Social Psychology,* 1978, *36,* 82–92.

Walters, R. H., & Brown, M. Studies of reinforcement of aggression. III. Transfer of responses to an interpersonal situation. *Child Development,* 1963, *34,* 536–571.

Walters, R., & Thomas, E. Enhancement of punitiveness by visual and audiovisual displays. *Canadian Journal of Psychology,* 1963, *17,* 244–255.

Warriner, C. H. Groups are real: A reaffirmation. *American Sociological Review,* 1956, *21,* 549–554.

Watson, G. *Action for unity.* New York: Harper, 1947.

Watson, R. I., Jr. Investigation into deindividuation using a cross-cultural survey technique. *Journal of Personality and Social Psychology*, 1973, *25*, 342–345.

Waxler, N. E., & Mishler, E. G. Experimental studies of families. In L. Berkowitz (Ed.), *Group processes*. New York: Academic Press, 1978.

Weary, G., Harvey, J. H., Schwieger, P., Olson, C. T., Perloff, R., & Pritchard, S. Self-presentation and the moderation of self-serving attributional biases. *Social Cognition*, 1982, *1*, 140–159.

Webb, E. J., Campbell, D. T., Schwartz, R. D., & Sechrest, L. *Unobtrusive measures: Nonreactive research in the social sciences*. Chicago: Rand McNally, 1966.

Wegner, D. M., & Vallacher, R. R. *Implicit psychology: An introduction to social cognition*. New York: Oxford University Press, 1977.

Weick, K. The spines of leaders. In M. W. McCall, Jr., & M. M. Lombardo (Eds.), *Leadership: Where else can we go?* Durham, N.C.: Duke University Press, 1978.

Weigel, R. H., Vernon, D. T. A., & Tognacci, L. N. Specificity of the attitude as a determinant of attitude-behavior congruence. *Journal of Personality and Social Psychology*, 1974, *30*, 724–728.

Weinberger, A. Responses to old people who ask for help: Field experiments. *Research on Aging*, 1981, *3*, 345–368.

Weiner, B. (Ed.). *Achievement motivation and attribution theory*. Morristown, N.J.: General Learning Press, 1974.

Weiner, B. A cognitive (attribution)-emotion-action model of motivated behavior: An analysis of judgments of help-giving. *Journal of Personality and Social Psychology*, 1980, *39*, 186–200.

Weiner, B., Frieze, I., Kukla, A., Reed, L., Rest, S., & Rosenbaum, R. M. Perceiving the causes of success and failure. In E. E. Jones, D. E. Kanouse, H. H. Kelley, R. E. Nisbett, S. Valins, & B. Weiner, *Attribution: Perceiving the causes of behavior*. Morristown, N.J.: General Learning Press, 1972.

Weiss, C. H. *Evaluation research: Methods for assessing program effectiveness*. Englewood Cliffs, N. J.: Prentice-Hall, 1972.

Weiss, R. F., Buchanan, W., Altstatt, L., & Lombardo, J. P. Altruism is rewarding. *Science*, 1971, *171*, 1262–1263.

Weiss, R. S. *Loneliness: The experience of emotional and social isolation*. Cambridge, Mass.: M.I.T. Press, 1973.

Weiss, R. S. The emotional impact of marital separation. *Journal of Social Issues*, 1976, *32*(1), 135–145.

Weiss, R. S. Issues in the study of loneliness. In L. A. Peplau & D. Perlman (Eds.), *Loneliness: A sourcebook of current theory, research and therapy*. New York: Wiley, 1982.

Weissbach, T. Racism and prejudice. In S. Oskamp, *Attitudes and opinions*. Englewood Cliffs, N.J.: Prentice-Hall, 1977.

Weitz, S. Sex differences in nonverbal communication. *Sex Roles*, 1976, *2*, 175–184.

Wellman, D. T. *Portraits of White racism*. New York: Cambridge University Press, 1977.

Werner, C. M., Brown, B. B., & Damron, G. Territorial marking in a game arcade. *Journal of Personality and Social Psychology*, 1981, *41*, 1094–1104.

Werner, C. M., Kagehiro, D. K., & Strube, M. J. Conviction proneness and the authoritarian juror: Inability to disregard information or attitudinal bias? *Journal of Applied Psychology*, 1982, *67*, 629–636.

Werner, C., & Latané, B. Responsiveness and communication medium in dyadic interactions. *Bulletin of the Psychonomic Society*, 1976, *8*, 569–571.

West, S. G., & Gunn, S. P. Some issues of ethics and social psychology. *American Psychologist*, 1978, *33*, 30–38.

Westie, F. R. A technique for the measurement of race attitudes. *American Sociological Review*, 1953, *18*, 73–78.

Westin, A. *Privacy and freedom*. New York: Atheneum, 1970.

Wexler, M. The behavioral sciences in medical education: A view from psychology. *American Psychologist*, 1976, *31*, 275–283.

Weyant, J. M. Effects of mood states, costs, and benefits on helping. *Journal of Personality and Social Psychology*, 1978, *36*, 1169–1176.

Wheeler, L., Koestner, R., & Driver, R. E. Related attributes in the choice of comparison others: It's there, but it isn't all there is. *Journal of Experimental Social Psychology*, 1982, *18*, 489–500.

Wheeler, L., & Nezlek, J. Sex differences in social participation. *Journal of Personality and Social Psychology*, 1977, *35*, 742–754.

Wheeler, L., Reis, H., & Nezlek, J. Loneliness, social interaction, and sex roles. *Journal of Personality and Social Psychology*, in press.

Whitcher, S. J., & Fisher, J. D. Multidimensional reaction to therapeutic touch in a hospital setting. *Journal of Personality and Social Psychology*, 1979, *37*, 87–96.

White, G. L. Some correlates of romantic jealousy. *Journal of Personality*, 1981, *49*, 129–147.

White, J. W., & Gruber, K. J. Instigative aggression as a function of past experience and target characteristics. *Journal of Personality and Social Psychology*, 1982, *42*, 1069–1075.

Whitehead, G. I., III, Smith, S. H., & Eichhorn, J. A. The effect of subject's race and other's race on judgments of causality for success and failure. *Journal of Personality*, 1982, *50*, 193–202.

Whiting, B., & Edwards, C. P. A cross-cultural analysis of sex differences in the behavior of children aged three through eleven. *Journal of Social Psychology*, 1973, *91*, 171–188.

Whyte, W. H., Jr. *The organization man*. New York: Simon & Schuster, 1956.

Wicker, A. W. Attitudes versus actions: The relationship of verbal and overt behavioral responses to attitude objects. *Journal of Social Issues*, 1969, *25*(4), 41–78.

Wicker, A. W. *An introduction to ecological psychology*. Monterey, Calif.: Brooks/Cole, 1979.

Wicklund, R. A. Objective self-awareness. In L. Berkowitz (Ed.), *Advances in experimental social psychology* (Vol. 8). New York: Academic Press, 1975.

Wicklund, R. A., & Frey, D. Self-awareness theory: When the self makes a difference. In D. M. Wegner & R. R. Vallacher (Eds.), *The self in social psychology*. New York: Oxford University Press, 1980.

Wiemann, J. M., & Knapp, M. L. Turn-taking in conversations. *Journal of Communication*, 1975, *25*, 75–92.

Wiener, F. Altruism, ambience and action: The effects of rural and urban rearing on helping behavior. *Journal of Personality and Social Psychology*, 1976, *34*, 112–124.

Wilder, D. A. A theory of social entities: Effects of group membership on social perception and social influence. Unpublished doctoral dissertation, University of Wisconsin, Madison, 1975.

Williams, W., & Evans, J. W. The politics of evaluation: The case of Head Start. In P. H. Rossi & W. Williams (Eds.), *Evaluating social programs: Theory, practice, and politics.* New York: Seminar Press, 1972.

Willie, C. V. (Ed.). *Black/Brown/White relations: Race relations in the 1970's.* New Brunswick, N.J.: Transaction Books, 1977.

Wilson, E. O. *Sociobiology: The new synthesis.* Cambridge, Mass.: Belknap Press of Harvard University Press, 1975.

Wilson, E. O. *On human nature.* Cambridge, Mass.: Harvard University Press, 1978.

Wilson, J. P. Motivation, modeling, and altruism: A person × situation analysis. *Journal of Personality and Social Psychology,* 1976, *34,* 1078–1086.

Wilson, P. R. Perceptual distortion of height as a function of ascribed academic status. *Journal of Social Psychology,* 1968, *74,* 97–102.

Wilson, W. C. Pornography: The emergence of a social issue and the beginning of psychological study. *Journal of Social Issues,* 1973, *29*(3), 7–17.

Winch, R. F., Ktsanes, I., & Ktsanes, V. The theory of complementary needs in mate selection: An analytic and descriptive study. *American Sociological Review,* 1954, *19,* 241–249.

Winsborough, H. The social consequences of high population density. *Law and Contemporary Problems,* 1965, *30,* 120–126.

Wishner, J. Reanalysis of "impressions of personality." *Psychological Review,* 1960, *67,* 96–112.

Wispé, L. G. Positive forms of social behavior: An overview. *Journal of Social Issues,* 1972, *28*(3), 1–19.

Wispé, L. G. (Ed.). *Altruism, sympathy, and helping: Psychological and sociological principles.* New York: Academic Press, 1978.

Wispé, L. G. Research on positive and negative social behavior. *Social Behavior and Personality,* 1981, *9,* 203–209.

Wohlwill, J. F. Human adaptation to levels of environmental stimulation. *Human Ecology,* 1974, *2*(2), 127–147.

Wohlwill, H., & Kohn, I. The environment as experienced by the migrant: An adaptation-level view. *Representative Research in Social Psychology,* 1973, *4,* 135–164.

Wolf, S. Behavioural style and group cohesiveness as sources of minority influence. *European Journal of Social Psychology,* 1979, *9,* 381–395.

Wollin, D. D., & Montagne, M. College classroom environment. *Environment and Behavior,* 1981, *13,* 707–716.

Wood, F. A. *The influence of monarchs.* New York: Macmillan, 1913.

Woodmansee, J., & Cook, S. W. Dimensions of verbal racial attitudes. *Journal of Personality and Social Psychology,* 1967, *7,* 240–250.

Worchel, S. The effect of three types of arbitrary thwarting on the instigation to aggression. *Journal of Personality,* 1974, *42,* 301–318.

Worchel, S. Cooperation and the reduction of intergroup conflict: Some determining factors. In W. G. Austin & S. Worchel (Eds.), *The social psychology of intergroup relations.* Monterey, Calif.: Brooks/Cole, 1979.

Worchel, S., Andreoli, V. S., & Folger, R. Intergroup cooperation and intergroup attraction: The effect of previous interaction and outcome of combined effort. *Journal of Experimental Social Psychology,* 1977, *13,* 131–140.

Worchel, S., Arnold, S., & Baker, M. The effects of censorship on attitude change: The influence of censor and communication characteristics. *Journal of Applied Social Psychology,* 1975, *5,* 227–239.

Worchel, S., & Esterson, C. The effects of misattribution on the experience of crowding. Paper presented at meeting of American Psychological Association, Washington, D.C., 1978.

Worthy, M., Gary, A. L., & Kahn, G. Self-disclosure as an exchange process. *Journal of Personality and Social Psychology,* 1969, *13,* 59–63.

Wortman, C. B., & Brehm, J. W. Responses to uncontrollable outcomes: An integration of reactance theory and the learned helplessness model. In L. Berkowitz (Ed.), *Advances in experimental social psychology* (Vol. 8). New York: Academic Press, 1975.

Wright, P. H., & Crawford, A. C. Agreement and friendship: A close look and some second thoughts. *Representative Research in Social Psychology,* 1971, *2,* 52–69.

Wrightsman, L. S. Effects of waiting with others on changes in level of felt anxiety. *Journal of Abnormal and Social Psychology,* 1960, *61,* 216–222.

Wrightsman, L. S. Measurement of philosophies of human nature. *Psychological Reports,* 1964, *14,* 743–751.

Wrightsman, L. S. The presence of others does make a difference—sometimes. *Psychological Bulletin,* 1975, *82,* 884–885.

Wrightsman, L. S. The American trial jury on trial: Empirical evidence and procedural modifications. *Journal of Social Issues,* 1978, *34*(4), 137–164.

Wrightsman, L. S. *The social psychology of U.S. presidential effectiveness.* Invited address to fifth annual meeting of Society of Southeastern Social Psychologists, New Orleans, March 1982.

Wyer, R. S., Jr., & Srull, T. K. Category accessibility: Some theoretical and empirical issues concerning the processing of social stimulus information. In E. T. Higgins, C. P. Herman, & M. P. Zanna (Eds.), *Social cognition: The Ontario symposium* (Vol. 1). Hillsdale, N.J.: Erlbaum, 1981.

Wynne-Edwards, V. *Animal dispersion in relation to social behavior.* New York: Hafner, 1962.

Yarkin, K. L., Town, J. P., & Wallston, B. S. Blacks and women must try harder: Stimulus person's race and sex attributions of causality. *Personality and Social Psychology Bulletin,* 1982, *8,* 21–24.

Yarmey, A. D., & Johnson, J. Evidence for the self as an imaginal prototype. *Journal of Research in Personality,* 1982, *16,* 238–243.

Yinon, Y., & Bizman, A. Noise, success, and failure as determinants of helping behavior. *Personality and Social Psychology Bulletin,* 1980, *6,* 125–130.

Zacker, J. Authoritarian avoidance of ambiguity. *Psychological Reports,* 1973, *33,* 901–902.

Zahn-Waxler, C., Radke-Yarrow, M., & King, R. A. Child rearing and children's prosocial initiations toward victims of distress. *Child Development*, 1979, *50*, 319–330.

Zajonc, R. B. Social facilitation. *Science*, 1965, *149*, 269–274.

Zajonc, R. B. Attitudinal effects of mere exposure. *Journal of Personality and Social Psychology Monograph Supplement*, 1968, *9*(2, Part 2), 2–27.

Zajonc, R. B. Feeling and thinking: Preferences need no inferences. *American Psychologist*, 1980, *35*, 151–175.

Zajonc, R. B., & Sales, S. Social facilitation of dominant subordinate responses. *Journal of Experimental Social Psychology*, 1966, *2*, 160–168.

Zanna, M., Goethals, G., & Hill, J. Evaluating a sex-related ability: Social comparison with similar others and standard setters. *Journal of Experimental Social Psychology*, 1975, *11*, 86–93.

Zillmann, D. Attribution and misattribution of excitatory reactions. In J. H. Harvey, W. J. Ickes, & R. F. Kidd (Eds.), *New directions in attribution research* (Vol. 2). Hillsdale, N. J.: Erlbaum, 1978.

Zillmann, D. *Hostility and aggression*. Hillsdale, N. J.: Erlbaum, 1979.

Zillmann, D., & Bryant, J. Pornography, sexual callousness, and the trivialization of rape. *Journal of Communication*, in press.

Zillmann, D., Bryant, J., Cantor, J. R., & Day, K. D. Irrelevance of mitigating circumstances in retaliatory behavior at high levels of excitation. *Journal of Research in Personality*, 1975, *9*, 282–293.

Zillmann, D., & Cantor, J. R. Effect of timing of information about mitigating circumstances on emotional responses to provocation and retaliatory behavior. *Journal of Experimental Social Psychology*, 1976, *12*, 38–55.

Zillmann, D., Katcher, A., & Milavsky, B. Excitation transfer from physical exercise to subsequent aggressive behavior. *Journal of Experimental Social Psychology*, 1972, *8*, 247–259.

Zimbardo, P. G. The human choice: Individuation, reason, and order versus deindividuation, impulse, and chaos. In W. J. Arnold & D. Levine (Eds.), *Nebraska Symposium on Motivation, 1969*. Lincoln: University of Nebraska Press, 1970.

Zlutnick, S., & Altman, I. Crowding and human behavior. In J. F. Wohlwill & D. Carson (Eds.), *Environment and the social sciences*. Washington, D.C.: American Psychological Association, 1972.

Zuckerman, M. Physiological measures of sexual arousal in the human. *Psychological Bulletin*, 1971, *75*, 297–329.

Zuckerman, M. Attribution of success and failure revisited, or: The motivational bias is alive and well in attribution theory. *Journal of Personality*, 1979, *47*, 245–287.

Zuckerman, M., Amidon, M. D., Bishop, S. E., & Pomerantz, S. D. Face and tone of voice in the communication of deception. *Journal of Personality and Social Psychology*, 1982, *43*, 347–357.

Zuckerman, M., DePaulo, B. M., & Rosenthal, R. Verbal and nonverbal communication of deception. In L. Berkowitz (Ed.), *Advances in experimental social psychology* (Vol. 14). New York: Academic Press, 1981.

Zuckerman, M., Lazzaro, M. M., & Waldgeir, D. Undermining effects of the foot-in-the-door technique with extrinsic rewards. *Journal of Applied Social Psychology*, 1979, *9*, 292–296.

Author Index

Subject Index

CREDITS

This page constitutes an extension of the copyright page.

by the Washington Post Co. Reprinted by permission. **147,** *Peanuts* Cartoon ©1978 by United Feature Syndicate, Inc. Reprinted by permission. **148,** Painting "Lincoln at Gettysburg III" by William H. Johnston. Courtesy of the National Collection of Fine Arts, Smithsonian Institution. **151,** Photos courtesy of Bonnie Hawthorne. **153,** Photo courtesy of United Press International, ©1974. **154,** Figure 6-2 from "Measurement of Romantic Love," by Z. Rubin, *Journal of Personality and Social Psychology*, 1970, *16*, 267. Copyright 1970 by the American Psychological Association. Reprinted by permission. **155,** Figure 6-3 adapted from "Measurement of Romantic Love," by Z. Rubin, *Journal of Personality and Social Psychology*, 1970, *16*, 267–268. Copyright 1970 by the American Psychological Association. Reprinted by permission. **156,** Figure 6-4 adapted from "Attraction in Relationship: A New Look at Interpersonal Attraction," by G. Levinger and J. S. Snoek. Copyright transferred to authors in 1978. (Morristown, N.J.: General Learning Press, 1972). Reprinted by permission of the authors. Illustration by Nigel Holmes. **159,** Table 6-1 adapted from "Breakups before Marriage: The End of 103 Affairs," by C. T. Hill, L. Rubin, and L. A. Peplau, *Journal of Social Issues, 32*, 147–168. Copyright 1976 by the Society for the Psychological Study of Social Issues. Reprinted by permission. **160,** Figure 6-8 by Evard Munch, *Man and Woman*, 1899. Oslo Kommunes Kunstsamlinger, Munch-Museet.

CHAPTER 7. 164, Photo by Frank Siteman, ©1978 by Stock, Boston, Inc. All rights reserved. **167,** (left), Photo courtesy of Culver Pictures, New York. **167,** (right), Photo ©Jay Dorin, 1980. Courtesy of Omni-Photo Communications Inc., New York. **171,** Table 7-1 from "Convergence toward a Single Sexual Standard," by J. P. Curran, *Social Behavior and Personality*, 1975, *3*, 189–195. Reprinted by permission. **173,** Figure 7-2 from *The Sexual System: A Theory of Human Sexual Behavior*, by P. R. Abramson. Copyright 1981, by Academic Press. Reprinted by permission. **174,** Photo courtesy of Culver Pictures, New York. **176,** Photo by Ellis Herwig, ©1981 by Stock, Boston, Inc. All rights reserved. **178,** Table 7-2 from "Sexual Intimacy in Dating Relationships," by L. A. Peplau, Z. Rubin, and C. T. Hill, *Journal of Social Issues*, 1977, *33*(2), 86–109. Reprinted by permission. **180,** Photo by Arthur Grace, © 1978 by Stock, Boston, Inc. All rights reserved. **181,** Photo ©Phiz Mezey. Courtesy of Design Photographers International, Inc., New York. **183,** Photo by Peter Menzel, ©1977 by Stock, Boston, Inc. All rights reserved. **186,** Photo ©Joel Gordon, 1980. Courtesy of Design Photographers International, New York. **188,** Figure 7-3 from "Victim Reactions in Aggressive Erotic Films as a Factor in Violence against Women," by E. Donnerstein and L. Berkowitz, *Journal of Personality and Social Psychology*, 1981, *41*, 710–724. Copyright 1981 by the American Psychological Association. Reprinted by permission.

CHAPTER 8. 190, Photo ©James T. Coit. Courtesy of Jeroboam, Inc., San Francisco. **192,** Photo by J. Berndt, ©1977 by Stock, Boston, Inc. All rights reserved. **193,** Photo by T. M. Huffman. Printed with permission of Wolf Park, Battle Ground, Indiana. **197,** Photos courtesy of Bonnie Hawthorne. **198,** Table 8-1 from "Film Violence and Cue Properties of Available Targets," by L. Berkowitz and R. G. Geen. In *Journal of Personality and Social Psychology*, 1966, *3*, 525–530. Copyright 1966 by the American Psychological Association. Reprinted by permission. **199,** Photos by Mark Antman, ©1977 by Stock, Boston, Inc. All rights reserved. **201,** Photo from "Imitation of Film-Mediated Aggressive Models," by A. Bandura, D. Ross and S. A. Ross. In *Journal of Abnormal and Social Psychology*, 1963, *66*, 3–11. Copyright 1963 by the American Psychological Association. Reprinted by permission. **206,** Figure 8-1 from "The Effects of Alcohol and Delta-9-Tetrahydrocannabinol on Human Physical Aggression," by S. P. Taylor, R. M. Vardaris, A. B. Rawtich, C. B. Gammon, J. W. Cranston, and A. I. Lubetkin. In *Aggressive Behavior*, Vol. 2, No. 2. Copyright 1976 by Alan R. Liss, Inc. Reprinted by permission. **207,** Box 8-2 from "Ambient Temperature and the Occurrence of Collective Violence: The 'Long Hot Summer' Revisited," by R. A. Baron and V. M. Ransberger. In *Journal of Personality and Social Psychology*, 1978, *36*, 351–360. Copyright 1978 by the American Psychological Association. Reprinted

by permission. **208,** Photo ©David Strickler, Monkmeyer Press Photo Service, New York. **210,** Photo by Jean-Claude Lejeune, ©1978 by Stock, Boston, Inc. All rights reserved. **213,** Photo courtesy of Wide World Photos. **215,** Figure 8-2 adapted from "Model's Behavior and Attraction toward the Model as Determinants of Adult Aggressive Behavior," by R. A. Baron and C. R. Kepner. In *Journal of Personality and Social Psychology*, 1970, *14*, 335–344. Copyright 1970 by the American Psychological Association. Reprinted by permission. **216,** Box 8-3 from "The Deterrent Effect of Capital Punishment: New Evidence on an Old Controversy," by D. P. Phillips. In the *American Journal of Sociology*, 1980, *86*, 139–148. Copyright 1980 by The University of Chicago Press. Reprinted by permission. **217,** Photo ©Frank Siteman MCMLXXX. Courtesy of Jeroboam, Inc., San Francisco.

CHAPTER 9. 220, Photo by Ellis Herwig, ©1980 by Stock, Boston, Inc. All rights reserved. **222,** Photo ©Jan Dorn. Courtesy of Omni-Photo Communications Inc., New York. **231,** Photos courtesy of Frank Keillor. **233,** Photo by Ellis Herwig, ©1981 by Stock, Boston, Inc. All rights reserved. **235,** Photo by Elizabeth Hamlin, ©1976 by Stock, Boston, Inc. All rights reserved. **236,** Photo by Irene Bayer, Monkmeyer Press Photo Service, New York. **241,** Photo ©Alan Reininger. Courtesy of Design Photographers International, Inc., New York. **244,** Figure 9-5 from "The Joys of Helping: Focus of Attention Mediates the Impact of Positive Affect on Altruism," by D. L. Rosenhan, P. Salovey, and K. Hargis. In *Journal of Personality and Social Psychology*, 1981, *40*, 899–905. Copyright 1981 by the American Psychological Association. Reprinted by permission. **247,** Photo by Elizabeth Hamlin, ©1976 by Stock, Boston, Inc. All rights reserved. **249,** Photo ©1978, the American Red Cross.

CHAPTER 10. 252, Photo ©1983, *The Chicago Tribune*. **255,** Photo courtesy of Wide World Photos. **256,** Photo courtesy of Monkmeyer Press Photo Service, New York. **258,** Table 10-1 adapted from "Sex-Role Stereotypes: A Current Appraisal," by I. K. Broverman, S. R. Vogel, D. M. Broverman, F. E. Clarkson, and P. S. Rosenkrantz, *Journal of Social Issues*, 1972, *28*(2), 59–78. Copyright 1972 by Plenum Publishing Corporation. Reprinted by permission. **259,** *Doonesbury* Cartoon, Copyright 1974 by G. B. Trudeau. Reprinted with permission of Universal Press Syndicate. All rights reserved. **259,** Photo ©United States Steel Co., Braddick, Pa. Courtesy of Omni-Photo Communications Inc., New York. **261,** Figure 10-1 adapted from "Prejudice: A Problem in Psychological and Social Causation," by G. W. Allport. In *Journal of Social Issues*, Supplement Series No. 4, 1950. Copyright 1950 by Society for the Psychological Study of Social Issues. Reprinted by permission. **261,** Photo courtesy of The Granger Collection, New York. **263,** Figure 10-2 from *How Nations See Each Other*, by W. Buchanan and H. Cantril. Copyright ©1953, 1981 by the University of Illinois Press. Reprinted by permission. Illustration by Nigel Holmes. **264,** Photo courtesy of United Press International. **273,** Photo ©Ilka Hartman. Courtesy of Jeroboam, Inc., San Francisco. **274,** Photo courtesy of Stock, Boston, Inc. All rights reserved.

CHAPTER 11. 278, Photo ©Bruck Kliewe. Courtesy of Jeroboam, Inc., San Francisco. **282,** Photo by Hugh Rogers, Monkmeyer Photo Press Service, New York. **284,** Photos courtesy of the American Cancer Society. **286,** Photo by Frank Owen, ©1978 by Stock, Boston, Inc. All rights reserved. **287,** Photo by Donald Dietz, ©1976 by Stock, Boston, Inc. All rights reserved. **289,** Figure 11-3 adapted from "Assimilation and Contrast Effects of Anchoring Stimuli on Judgments," by M. Sherif, D. Taub, and C. I. Hovland, *Journal of Experimental Psychology*, 1958, *55*, 150–155. **290,** Figure 11-4 from "Width of the Latitude of Acceptance as a Determinant of Attitude Change," by A. Eagly and K. Telaak, *Journal of Personality and Social Psychology*, 1972, *23*, 388–397. Copyright 1972 by the American Psychological Association. Reprinted by permission. **291,** Photo courtesy of Wide World Photos. **292,** Figure 11-5 from *The Political Beliefs of Americans: A Study of Public Opinion*, by Lloyd A. Free and Hadley Cantril. Copyright ©1967 by Rutgers, The State University. Reprinted by per-

sible Space, by O. Newman. Copyright ©1972, 1973 by Oscar Newman. Reprinted by permission of Macmillan Publishing Co., Inc. and The Architectural Press Ltd. **440,** Figure 17-5 by Nigel Holmes. **441,** Photos courtesy of Frank Keillor. **443,** Figure 17-6 from "The Environment as Experienced by the Migrant: An Adaptation-Level View," by J. Wohlwill and I. Kohn. In *Representative Research in Social Psychology,* 1973. Reprinted by permission. **443,** Photo by Peter Menzel, ©1981 by Stock, Boston, Inc. All rights reserved. **448,** Photo ©Donald L. Miller, Monkmeyer Press Photo Service, New York. **452,** Photo ©Henry Monroe. Courtesy of Design Photographers International, Inc., New York. **453,** Photo ©1981 by Stock, Boston, Inc. All rights reserved. **453,** Figure 17-9 reproduced by special permission from *The Journal of Applied Behavioral Science,* "Classroom Ecology," by Robert Sommer, Volume 3, Number 4, pp. 489–503. Copyright 1967, NTL Institute. **455,** Figure 17-10 from "Reducing the Stress of High-Density Living: An Architectural Intervention," by A. Baum and G. E. Davis. In *Journal of Personality and Social Psychology,* 1980, *38,* 471–478. Copyright 1980 by the American Psychological Association. Reprinted by permission.

CHAPTER 18. 458, Photo courtesy of NASA. **463,** Photo by Paul Conklin, Monkmeyer Press Photo Service, New York. **464,** Photo by Lionel J-M Delevigne, ©1981 by Stock, Boston, Inc. All rights reserved. **464,** Figure 18-1 from "Stress at Three Mile Island: Applying Psychological Impact Analysis," by A. Baum, R. Fleming, and J. E. Singer. In L. Bickman (Ed.), *Applied Social Psychology Annual,* Vol. 3. Copyright 1982 by Sage Publications, Inc. Reprinted by permission. **465,** Photo by David Powers, ©1978 by Stock, Boston, Inc. All rights reserved. **466,** Photo ©1977 by Stock, Boston, Inc. All rights reserved. **467,** Photos courtesy of Frank Keillor. **468,** Figure 18-2 from "Behavioral Medicine: A New Applied Challenge to Social Psychologists," by R. I. Evans. In L. Bickman (Ed.), *Applied Social Psychology Annual,* Vol. 1. Copyright 1980 by Sage Publications, Inc. Reprinted by permission. **469,** and **471,** Photos by Irene Bayer, Monkmeyer Press Photo Service, New York. **475,** Figure 18-3 from "The Effects of Opening Statements on Mock Jurors' Verdicts in a Simulated Criminal Trial," by T. A. Pyszczynski and L. S. Wrightsman. In *Journal of Applied Social Psychology,* 1981, *11,* 301–313. Copyright 1981 by Sage Publications, Inc. Reprinted by permission. **477,** Figure 18-4 from "Approaches towards Social Problems: A Conceptual Model," by C. Ovcharchyn-Devitt, P. Colby, L. Carswell, W. Perkowitz, B. Scruggs, R. Turpin, and L. Bickman. In *Basic and Applied Social Psychology,* 1981, *2,* 275–287. Copyright 1981 by Sage Publications, Inc. Reprinted by permission. **480,** Figure 18-5 adapted from "Reforms as Experiments," by D. T. Campbell. In *American Psychologist,* 1969, *24*(4), 409–429. Copyright 1969 by the American Psychological Association. Reprinted by permission. **483,** Photo by Christopher Brown, ©1978 by Stock, Boston, Inc. All rights reserved. **484,** Box 18-4, Photo courtesy of Wide World Photos.